Motown: The Golden Years

The Stars and Music That Shaped a Generation

BY Bill Dahl

PHOTOS BY Weldon A. McDougal III

Published by:

Krause Publications
700 E. State Street
Iola, WI 54990-0001
Telephone: 715/445-2214
Web: www.krause.com

Please, call or write us for our free catalog of antiques, collectibles, sports and music publications. To place an order or receive our free catalog, call 800-258-0929.

Library of Congress Catalog Number: 2001090717
ISBN: 0-87349-286-2

Printed in the United States of America

DEDICATION

To Margie Dahl,

who instilled a love of swinging, soulful music in me at a very young age that refuses to fade (just like my love for her).

CREDITS

The author and editors extend a special thank you to the following people and companies for their photo contributions to this book:

David Alston's Mahogany Archives: Photos, picture sleeves, records
Hank Thompson: Motown concert posters
John Rothenberg: Supremes albums covers
Orpheus: Sheet music covers
BMI Archives Photo Collection: Photos
Robert Pruter: Record album covers
George Livingston: Photos
Allan Slutsky: Photos

◆ CONTENTS

PART 1

PART 2

PART 3

It's a daunting prospect to write a book about Motown. After all, millions of words have already been committed to paper about the greatest rhythm and blues label of the 1960s, the company that obliterated the chasm between soul and pop and launched the careers of a dozen superstars. There have been beautifully illustrated coffee table examinations of the label, honest and revealing autobiographies of its stars, and a few sleazy tell-all tomes that deserve permanent enshrinement in the nearest trash barrel. In researching this volume I've read most of them, and credit their combined insights accordingly in the bibliography.

Instead of focusing on the sociological implications of the Motown story (and they're gargantuan), this book examines the music that Berry Gordy and his associates marketed during the label's golden years and the myriad artists, writers, and producers that worked so diligently to conceive it. The Motown story officially began in early 1959, when Marv Johnson's "Come To Me" was the first 45 to proudly bear the Tamla label (though in reality it harks back a couple of years before that, when Berry Gordy began writing and producing hits for other labels), and we end in 1972, when the company pulled up stakes and headed west to Los Angeles. In any event, it's a convenient stopping point for a logo that thrives to this day under corporate ownership. The book is divided into three parts—a basic overview of the golden years, in-depth examinations of the superstars most inexorably associated with Motown (and the band that backed them), and shorter bios on the rest of the greats that comprised the label's talent roster in the last section.

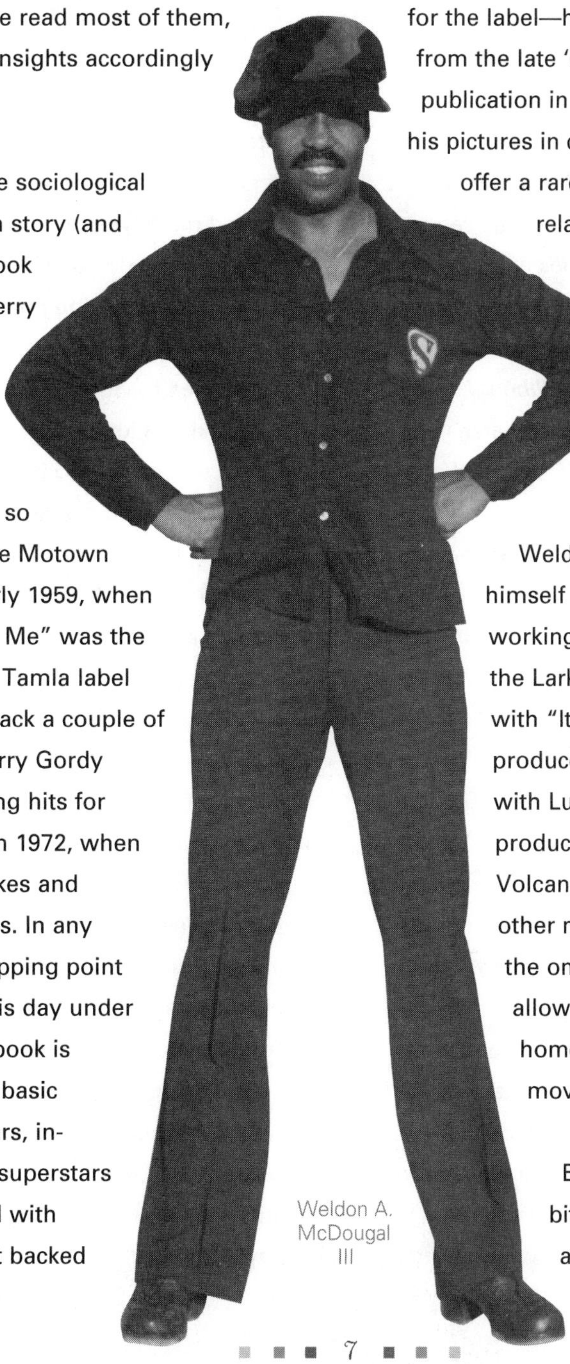

Weldon A. McDougal III

The genesis for the project was the revelation that Weldon A. McDougal III—former Motown promotion guru (he traveled extensively with Motown's top artists on the road, introducing them to the important deejays who could make or break their next release while making sure that everything ran smoothly for his acts at their shows) and one-time director of special projects for the label—had a treasure trove of candid photos from the late '60s and early '70s that deserved publication in book form. Weldon snapped most of his pictures in color, and the ones gracing this book offer a rare glimpse of Motown royalty in more relaxed settings than circumstances generally allowed—letting their hair down after concerts, during the creative process, or playfully posing for the camera (there are a few striking performance shots as well).

Weldon had already made a name for himself in the music industry before he began working for Motown. He was one-quarter of the Larks, a doo-wop group that hit in 1961 with "It's Unbelievable," and a successful producer (he formed Harthon Productions with Luther Randolph and Johnny Stiles and produced releases by Eddie Holman, the Volcanos, Barbara Mason, and a wealth of other mid-'60s notables). Weldon was surely the only full-time Motown employee allowed to retain his residence in his hometown of Philadelphia rather than moving to the Motor City.

Born October 28, 1936, McDougal was bitten by the doo-wop bug while attending West Philadelphia High

School. "It was a group called the Dreams, and another group called the Castelles, and both of the lead singers were my friends," said Weldon, who adds his first-person insights on the stars he knew as friends throughout the book. "George Grant was in the Castelles, and George Tindley was in the Dreams. They used to get so much notoriety when we'd go to school—everybody was talking to them—that I wanted to sing with them. And they wouldn't let me sing with them. They said, 'Why don't you get your own group, man?' So that's what I did."

American Bandstand was airing live every day after school a few blocks from Weldon's house, and the tall lad snagged a gig as a doorman at the TV studio prior to enlisting in the Marines. When he got out of the service in 1959, he reassembled the Larks. "It took a year before I finally found the guys that were the Larks, that we finally recorded," he said. Jerry Ross produced their "It's Unbelievable," which rose to No. 69 on *Billboard's* pop charts in early '61 on the strength of Jackie Marshall's strong lead tenor and the harmonies of Calvin Nichols, Earl Oxendine, and the deep-voiced McDougal. Talk about full circle: the Larks guested on Dick Clark's legendary TV program one day, sharing the spotlight with future Motown star Chuck Jackson.

Philly was loaded with R&B talent. "Screamin' Jay Hawkins used to live in my neighborhood. There was a hoagie store across the street from where he lived. So it was a running joke: You ever see his casket out there, you know he's home," said Weldon. "If you ever messed with his casket, he would go off. And the thing that was so ironic about it, it was sitting outside of his door!"

Though Harthon thrived for a time, Weldon grew disenchanted with the business end of the operation and branched into promotion during the mid-'60s for locally based Chips Record Distributors. "They handled Motown Records. So I just started promoting Motown. When I say I started promoting, nobody ever told you what record was a hit or wasn't a hit. I would listen to 'em, and I'd promote what I thought the disc jockeys would play. I started doing that, then I started talking to some of the guys at Motown. Because, at this time, I didn't know anybody at Motown. Then I started talking to Irv Biegel, who was the director of promotion. And Irv used to say, 'Hey, man, promote this record,' or 'Promote that,' or do this and that. I was doing pretty good, meaning he would tell people at Motown what I was doing. Because I was just a local guy; I hadn't met Berry at this time.

"I worked like that for around eight months. Then Irv Biegel left Motown. I don't know why. When he left, I used to talk to Phil Jones and another guy from Texas, his name was Al Klein. I did such a great job in Philly, they asked me to work from Boston to Miami doing the same thing I was doing in Philly. That would have made me a regional promotion man. I said okay.

"So I started to work for Motown regionally, and I started making a lot of noise, started getting a lot of records on. I'd be able to promote records in New Orleans where the average guy couldn't even get in there to talk to the music director," he said. "After that, they hired me to do the Midwest also. I worked like that for a couple years. Then they hired me to do the whole country. I was the national promotion director. And I did that for a couple of years.

"Working for Motown, I worked with all the acts in different capacities. Most of the time, I would meet 'em in a different city, and I would introduce 'em to the disc jockeys," he said. "I used to take all of the artists to record hops, when they used to have record hops. Here in Philadelphia, the Temptations, I would take 'em to Hy Lit's record hop. 'Heavy' Harvey Miller, Jerry Blavat, Georgie Woods, and all of these guys. I would take 'em to their record hops, and have 'em sign autographs.

"One day, the director of sales and promotion, Barney Ales, said, 'You're doing a pretty good job.

What do you want to do?' I said, 'Why don't I have a department called special projects?' He said, "Let's try it.' So one of the things I thought I should do was, when an artist would go to a city, I hooked them up with the disc jockeys. Not by just going over to the station. Like I would invite 'em to lunch. That was the main thing, invite 'em to lunch. When I was with the Jackson 5, I used to have them bring their kids over to lunch with the Jackson 5. And that worked out really well."

Being a Motown promo guru sometimes meant making the impossible possible. When there were no limousines left in all of Nashville to chauffeur Smokey Robinson to the Grammys, he knew a woman to contact at a local radio station for last-second advice. "She told me to call an undertaker," said Weldon. "He was dressed so impressive. I mean, he had on a red mohair suit, and a red hat. When the limousine drove up to the Grammys, people were just saying, 'Oh, man, Smokey—I knew he would have the best.' I really felt proud that I worked that out."

Weldon remained at Motown into the mid-1970s, when he was unceremoniously let go by then-president Ewart Abner. Knowing how to pick a winner, he then hooked up with Kenny Gamble and Leon Huff's Philadelphia International empire in a promotional capacity. Weldon remains a player in the industry as a record producer. He's been in the studio lately with his protege, singer Shirley Slaughter. He steadfastly prefers not to live in the past, looking instead towards the next potential hit.

Along with Weldon, whose Herculean efforts towards lining up interviewees from Motown's golden years have been invaluable, I'd like to thank Goldmine R&B editor Robert Pruter, as always an indefatigable source of research material and sage advice. And of course, thanks are due to Paul Kennedy, Brian Earnest, Kevin Sauter, and Greg Loescher of Krause Publications.

Thanks are also due the many Motown luminaries who took time to share their memories specifically for the book (several are preparing autobiographies, promising more insight into the Hitsville creative experience): Katherine Anderson Schaffner, Jack Ashford, Bertha Barbee-McNeal, Norma Barbee-Fairhurst, Janie Bradford, Johnny Bristol, G.C. Cameron, Hank Cosby, Carl Cutler, Louvain Demps, Freddie Gorman, Cornelius Grant, Jackie Hicks, Brenda Holloway, Joe Hunter, Mable John, Jeannie Long, Pete Moore, Frances Nero, Nate Newsome, Gino Parks, Sylvester Potts, Johnny Powers, Martha Reeves, Jimmy Ruffin, Edwin Starr, Barrett Strong, Kim Weston, Sondra "Blinky" Williams, Frank Wilson, Mary Wilson, and Timothy Wilson. I conducted the interviews with Arthur Adams, the late Luther Allison, Tommy Chong, Dennis Edwards, Abdul "Duke" Fakir, King Floyd, William Guest, Chuck Jackson, Earl King, Merald "Bubba" Knight, Jay Proctor, Smokey Robinson, Claudette Rogers Robinson, Bobby Rogers, the late Jr. Walker, the late Ronnie White, Andre Williams, and Otis Williams for various feature articles over the last two decades, and thanks are due all of them as well.

Thanks, too, to Kingsley Abbott, Bill Baker, Cary Baker, Bruce Bramoweth, John Broven, Bill Brown, Dave Christiansen, Gina Cutro, Margie Dahl, Peter Gibbon, Rob Gillis, Julie Henderson, Lori Jernberg, Dave Juricic, Dave Leoschke, Jim Letrich, Miriam Linna, Brenda Mabra, Gabrielle Metz, Billy Miller, Stephen Nicholas, Yvonne Odell, Liz Rodgers, Liese Rugo, Barbara Shelley, Val Shively, Mark Sodetz, R.J. Spangler, Dave Specter, Harry Weinger, and Robert Jr. and Shirley Mae Whitall, all of whom contributed in one way or another (and in some cases, several).

This book can best be enjoyed when accompanied by a non-stop soundtrack from Motown's golden years. If it inspires you to stock up on more, whether on exquisitely packaged boxed sets of shiny CDs or scratchy, beat-to-hell original vinyl, so much the better!

Hitsville U.S.A. at 2648 W. Grand Blvd.–Motown's Detroit headquarters.

MOTOWN 1959-1972 DEFINING THE SOUND OF YOUNG AMERICA

$800 and a dream.

That was the sum total of Berry Gordy, Jr.'s assets when he launched Tamla Records in 1959. Over the course of the next 13 years, his enterprise grew so successful on such a massive scale that its name would become an eternal synonym for its original Detroit home base. Motown.

(Photo courtesy of George Livingston)

Gordy borrowed those eight bills on January 12, 1959 from his extraordinarily tight-knit family, and they were none too thrilled about forking it over to fund the formation of something so frivolous as a rhythm and blues record label. After all, his track record wasn't the greatest. His jazz record shop had been a flop, and writing R&B songs could hardly be construed as a reliable source of income, even if he'd built a fairly enviable track record as a supplier of hit material to Jackie Wilson. But Berry possessed a few intangibles that set him apart from the other feisty music entrepreneurs sprouting up around Detroit as the city developed a reputation as a hotbed of hard-nosed, church-imbued rhythm and blues.

First of all, he had a razor-sharp eye for talent, surrounding himself with young standouts like Smokey Robinson & the Miracles, Mable John, and Marv Johnson. Second, he understood the importance of telling a self-contained story in his songs, intrinsically grasped the value of a catchy hook and a memorable chorus, and wasn't shy about offering songwriting advice to others. Most importantly, Gordy possessed a steely determination—an unquenchable will to win, no matter the obstacles before him—and the icy nerve of a riverboat gambler. Nothing would deter him from making Motown the most successful black-owned record firm in the country.

Gordy would market his label's output as "The Sound of Young America" during the mid-1960s. Though the slogan may seem presumptuous, it was no idle boast. Black or white, rich or poor, teenagers loaded their record collections with the latest hits by the Supremes, Temptations, Miracles, Marvelettes, Martha & the Vandellas, Four Tops, Stevie Wonder, and Marvin Gaye. Pop deejays might have sometimes hesitated to spin new platters from well-established R&B diskeries such as Stax or Chess, assuming their appeal might be limited largely to African-American listeners, but they harbored no such qualms about airing Motown's product.

This was happy, immaculately produced soul with a tightly crafted pop edge and an uplifting tinge of gospel at its core, and its appeal was universal.

As the decade progressed, Motown led the charge to eliminate the gap between pop and rhythm and blues. Not only did Berry retain his bedrock demographic (labels from coast to coast as well as in his own backyard were copying the Motown sound shamelessly), his scrupulously groomed acts were versatile enough to croon Broadway ditties on Ed Sullivan's Sunday evening CBS-TV variety hour and perform song-and-dance routines on the stages of mainstream nightclubs that would never have considered booking other soul-rooted acts. The instruction those artists received from Motown's Artist Development Department during the mid-'60s encompassed everything from choreography to advanced vocal harmonies to etiquette.

With all that explosive success came wholesale expansion as the decade climaxed, leading to a gradual dissolution of the all-for-one, one-for-all family atmosphere that had defined and nurtured the creative experience at Hitsville, U.S.A. (as the sign above the door of Motown's humble headquarters—a rehabbed two-story home at 2648 West Grand Boulevard—proudly proclaimed). Some of the label's artists began to question the firm's handling of their careers and finances (Motown managed and booked its artists through the in-house International Talent Management, Inc., acting as their financial adviser as well), and the acrimonious 1968 exit of red-hot songwriting/production team Holland-Dozier-Holland caused an avalanche of high-profile litigation that tarnished the company's carefully cultivated image of familial harmony. Florence Ballard was ousted from the Supremes and David Ruffin left the Temptations,

survived the upheaval. ver blunted Motown's millions flowing into the

adily shifting his base of les during the late '60s. r in 1972, leaving a great oducers, and staff igh some recording for a while, the move own's golden era, though —the Jackson 5, Diana nder, Smokey Robinson, nue to prosper for the me.

...ding triumphs

Berry Gordy, Jr. entered 29 at Detroit's Harper child born to Berry Sr. d all later at Motown as had emigrated from hree of their children in ould number eight: Fuller, later change the), George, Gwen, Berry

business allowed the building on the corner an intersection located a Hastings Street, and the st about that whole block belonged to the Gordys," noted Mable John. After studying business in college, Mrs. Gordy co-founded the Friendship Mutual Life Insurance Company. Berry eagerly embraced the finer points of jazz, gambling, and boxing during his formative years, fighting on the same 1948 card as the legendary Brown Bomber, Joe Louis, at Detroit's Olympia Stadium. He voluntarily closed out a respectable career as a featherweight fighter in 1950, determining that songwriting was more conducive to his long-term health and well being.

After a 1951-1953 Army stint in Korea, Gordy returned to civilian life, opening his own 3-D Record Mart–House of Jazz. Though it promised "Everything in Music" on its business card, the store ended up being a resounding dud because a jazz-obsessed Berry was too stubborn to stock 78s by down-home bluesmen John Lee Hooker and Muddy Waters that neighborhood folks craved. By the time he relented, it was too late to bail out the business.

Opting for domestic bliss, Berry married Thelma Coleman and quickly sired three children, settling into an assembly line job at the Lincoln-Mercury plant (its mechanical efficiency would inspire a similarly strict work ethic at Motown). But by 1957, Gordy had quit his steady job at the auto manufacturer to pursue a career as a professional songwriter.

The Motor City's massive concentration of auto manufacturing plants brought thousands of southern blacks to town during the 1940s and '50s in search of work, and they packed their love for gospel and blues for the long trip north. The blues strip was jumping with John Lee Hooker, Eddie Kirkland, Eddie Burns, and Bobo Jenkins among its resident headliners, and a healthy local jazz scene was happening thanks to gents like Barry Harris and Yusef Lateef. Rev. C.L. Franklin was building a gospel dynasty from within at his New Bethel Baptist Church, where his three startlingly talented young daughters—Erma, Carolyn, and Aretha—starred on Sundays.

The Flame Show Bar, located at the corner of John R and Canfield, opened in 1949 and was the showplace for top African-American entertainment in Detroit during the '50s. Billie Holiday, T-Bone Walker, Wynonie Harris, and Dinah Washington all starred at the 250-seat

"...we had Berry Gordy, and that was what gave us the outlet."

Flame at one time or another, and its house band, the Wolverines, was led by future Motown Artists Development Department mainstay Maurice King. The Gordys were already entrenched in the luxurious nightspot by the time Berry began hanging out there. Glamorous older sister Gwen was in charge of snapping souvenir photos of the club's patrons, vivacious Anna ably assisted her, and brothers George and Robert developed the film. Flame co-owner Al Green invited Berry to write songs for the artists he managed, including a young knockout named Jackie Wilson. Teaming with Roquel "Billy" Davis at Green's office, he cut his teeth as a songsmith even as his marriage disintegrated.

Wilson tore into "Reet Petite (The Finest Girl You Ever Want To Meet)," a brassy, swinging collaboration by Berry and Billy (under his exotic Tyran Carlo alias), as his first dynamic single for Brunswick, and it became a pop hit in late 1957. Bringing Gwen into the creative equation, the trio penned several huge sellers for Wilson over the next couple of years—the majestic "To Be Loved," a stirring "Lonely Teardrops," the rocking "That's Why (I Love You So)" and "I'll Be Satisfied"—solidly establishing themselves as purveyors of hits. Berry was getting his feet wet behind the studio glass, too. His first official production in 1957, "Ooh, Shucks," was sung by the Five Stars and pressed on the Mark-X label. The vocal quintet included future Originals C.P. Spencer, Walter Gaines, and Hank Dixon.

When Raynoma Liles and her sister, Alice, nervously auditioned for Berry one auspicious day, not only did Gordy meet his next wife, he came across a dynamic lady who could help him make hit records. Miss Ray, as she came to be known around the fledgling company, had perfect pitch and could write lead sheets. The romantic duo soon formed the Rayber Music Writing Company. For $100, they would do whatever was necessary to help a young singer make a record, be it writing, arranging, rehearsing, or recording a demo at local deejay Bristol Bryant's basement recording studio.

This was a fine way to uncover fresh talent as undiscovered singers flocked to the facility. One of those walk-ins, Wade Jones, had the only known release on the Rayber label: "Insane." Another, Eugene Remus, cut a 1960 45 for Motown. The diminutive Raynoma put together the Rayber Voices, a studio vocal group that backed most of Motown's first acts on their early recordings. Named for Raynoma and Berry—Gordy had an ongoing thing for contractions—their initial ranks also included bass Robert Bateman, Brian Holland, and William "Sonny" Sanders.

But the aggregation that would change Gordy's life forever (and vice versa) first crossed his path during an unsuccessful audition for Wilson's manager, Nat Tarnopol (Green had since passed away), and Alonzo Tucker. Though that pair of misguided talent scouts gave the Matadors the thumbs-down, Berry dug their unusual blend and chased them down after the audition to enthusiastically tell them so. It was the beginning of a close friendship between Gordy and the Matadors' lead singer, Smokey Robinson—and the start of something big for the group. They soon changed their handle to the Miracles.

Berry produced the quintet's 1958 debut single, a sly answer to the Philadelphia-based Silhouettes' smash "Get A Job" logically titled "Got A Job," and licensed it to George Goldner's End Records in New York. There was an End follow-up for the quintet as well, but when the postman finally delivered the long-awaited royalty check to Berry's door, its ridiculously tiny sum total and a similar lack of tangible return on the hits he'd co-written for Wilson prompted Gordy to form his own label, Tamla Records (he tried to name it Tammy after Debbie Reynolds' sugary hit ballad, but the moniker was already in circulation).

"That was the turning point in all of our lives, no question about it," said Smokey in a 1993 interview. "That's what made Detroit different, as far as I'm concerned, because there are talented people everywhere in the world, in every small township. Every big city has talented people. But we had Berry Gordy, and that was what gave us the outlet."

Gordy made what may have been his best move of all by founding his own Jobete Publishing Company (named after his three children with Thelma: Hazel Joy, Berry, and Terry). If you wrote for Motown, you were published by Jobete—simple as that. During the '60s and '70s, the Jobete catalog's holdings would multiply exponentially as it grew to be one of the most powerful publishing houses in the industry. However, the first Jobete-published song didn't appear on a Gordy-owned label. Herman Griffin's '58 waxing of "I Need You" for Carmen Murphy's House of Beauty logo was a Gordy production, however.

The $800 loan from the Gordy family's Ber-Berry Co-Op savings fund was enough to get Tamla up and running on a local basis, but Berry didn't have sufficient national distribution set up for his new enterprise. "He was going to record this song on Marv Johnson, which was the very first Motown song ever," said Robinson. "It was a song called 'Come To Me.' He decided he was going to do it on his own label, but it was going to be a local label. So he did that, and the record broke so big locally until he had to go to New York and make a deal for Marv Johnson with United Artists Records."

Johnson's enviable run of 1959-1961 national hits—notably "Come To Me" (the first locally issued Tamla release in January of '59) and his Top Ten pop sellers "You Got What It Takes" and "I Love The Way You Love"–were placed with United Artists, while the Miracles' "Bad Girl," Motown's debut single in the fall of '59, was leased to Chicago's Chess Records, although they all emanated from Berry's domain. Perhaps because his top sellers came out on UA instead of Motown (a contraction of Motor Town), Johnson's role in the launch of Hitsville has too often been overlooked.

"He was in there, too," said Barrett Strong, whose "Money (That's What I Want)" put Tamla on the map in 1960. "Nobody mentions Marv, but Marv had a bunch of hits there in the beginning."

In what amounted to regional prototypes for the national Motown tours to follow, Berry set up revues that spotlighted several of his young artists. Two February 21, 1959 shows at the Melody Theatre in nearby Inkster, Michigan, for example, were headlined by Marv Johnson, with the Miracles, Mable John, Eddie Holland (whose first Tamla 45, "Merry Go Round," was handed to United Artists for national release just as Johnson's had been), and the Rayber Voices sharing the evening's bill.

"In the early days, whenever there was a release on two or three artists, Berry would arrange for theaters to have a show in theaters, so that we could be seen and be heard. Because you have to have a place even to be bad, so you can get good with an audience. He always arranged to showcase the artists," said Mable. "When he recorded us, even if we were on another label at first, his

Mabel John's "Who Wouldn't Love a Man Like That" was the first Motown release by a female (courtesy of David P. Alston's Mahogany Archives).

"He had a way of making us all feel very wanted, very much a part of a family."

whole thing was to promote us and do as managers do. Showcase us, see to it that the public knows who we are, and break the record. 'Cause that's what he was trying to do—first of all, in our hometown. That's one of the first things that put Detroit on the map."

Gordy was generally cautious about signing vocal groups, settling for only the tightest harmonic blends. He landed the Satintones very early in his empire's rise. They debuted on Tamla in late '59 with the jumping "Motor City" and inaugurated Motown's 1000 series in 1960 with a creamy "My Beloved." Despite the presence of Sonny Sanders, later a prolific soul arranger, and Robert Bateman, who doubled as the Rayber Voices' bass singer and one of Motown's early recording engineers, the group never got going and was history by late '61.

Even when Motown was operating out of the couple's tiny apartment at 1719 Gladstone Street, before Ray happened upon the Grand Boulevard site that would be designated as Hitsville U.S.A, Gordy fostered a nurturing family atmosphere much like the one he had known to encourage his talented young proteges and offer them a home away from home where they could indulge their passion to make music.

Mrs. Bertha Gordy, the matriarch of the mighty Gordy clan, sits at her Hitsville desk while signing Weldon's monthly expense check (Weldon A. McDougal III photo).

"It was a part of my life," said Smokey. "In the beginning of Motown, when he very first started Motown, there were only five people there. And we did everything, man. We packaged records. We called disc jockeys. We took records to record stores, to radio stations. We did everything."

Mable John, whose 1960 single "Who Wouldn't Love A Man Like That" was the first Motown single by a female singer, had been patiently coached by Gordy and was there from day one. "We were a family, and we were trying to make it work, build a company, see that everybody had a hit, so everybody contributed to whatever was needed. I did, actually, the first promotion on the first release that was on the Tamla label. I got on a bus in Detroit and went to Chicago," she said. "I talked to United Record Distributors that was in Chicago there on South Michigan Avenue. Ernie Leaner was the man that owned it. Because he was a black guy and he had a big line, we thought that he would be sensitive to our needs. And I went on a bus and did that—just carried it to him in my hand and made the first contact."

"He had a way of making us all feel very wanted, very much a part of a family," said Bertha Barbee-McNeal of the Velvelettes, who would join the company in 1963. "Berry had that sense about him, because he was raised that way. We are the way we're raised, and I think all of us that came under his auspices are lucky for him to have been a role model, a father role model that some of us didn't have. He got it from his father and mother, who were together until the day they died."

"Berry's parents were there. They shared their parents with us," said Martha Reeves.

A deal was struck for the building at 2648 West Grand Boulevard in August of 1959. Utilizing Pops' construction expertise, the place was quickly whipped into shape as Motown's new home. Studio A, where so many immortal classics were painstakingly laid down, was located just a short stroll past saucy receptionist Janie Bradford's desk. There was an apartment upstairs for Berry, Ray, and their infant son, Kerry.

"I remember when they first got the building on the boulevard. It was an old artist's studio. I think it was an artist, a painter, who had that place. I go back to when there was nothing in that room that we used to record in but a ping-pong table and an upright piano," said the Originals' Freddie Gorman, then an aspiring songwriter and singer and a full-time mailman. "It started from there. Then they started getting the equipment. Berry Gordy's father was a carpenter, and he started working with that control room to make that what it was. He changed things around several times."

Gordy was admittedly a perfectionist in the studio who wasn't averse to tinkering with his early releases even after they had been pressed up and shipped off, resulting in several intriguing variations on certain singles. One version might have strings and another not, or one pressing may sport a different 'B' side from the next, despite bearing the same release number.

Tamla and Motown had some local competition. Though its recording scene was relatively primitive during the '50s, Detroit hosted a few small indie labels: Hastings Street record store owner Joe Von Battle's JVB (original purveyors of Aretha's earliest gospel efforts and a load of rough-timbred blues wax), Wes Higgins and Robert West's Flick, Contour, and LuPine imprints (the Falcons' West-produced 1959 hit "You're So Fine," initially on Flick before sharp-eared United Artists picked it up nationally, is often cited as one of the first true soul recordings), and the most successful outfit of the lot up to that point, Jack and Devora Brown's Fortune Records, which boasted a fine talent roster stocked with the influential doo-woppers Nolan Strong & the Diablos, the Five Dollars, the Royal Jokers, and Andre Williams.

What's more, Berry's sister had beaten him into the record business. In 1958, Gwen and Billy Davis set up Anna Records (named after Anna Gordy) in the family building, with Berry sometimes producing masters for the label. Anna's first two releases were polished outings by the Voice Masters. Later releases included sides by veteran New Orleans pianist Paul Gayten, the Falcons, and young unknown Joe Tex (his '61 outing "Ain't I A Mess" rocked like crazy and finished the label off in style). Gwen was as busy a budding music entrepreneur as Berry in the early days. Splitting with Davis, she formed another partnership with ex-Moonglows lead singer Harvey Fuqua in 1961, with the pair inaugurating the Tri-Phi and Harvey logos. Over the next couple of years, their labels would introduce the Spinners, Shorty Long, Jr. Walker & the All Stars, and Johnny (Bristol) & Jackey (Beavers) before Berry absorbed both labels in '63 and welcomed Fuqua—by then his brother-in-law—into the extended Motown family.

Davis, in turn, hooked up with Chicago-based Chess Records to open the short-lived Check-Mate imprint, which issued singles by David Ruffin, Ty Hunter, and Allen "Bo" Story—all later associated with Motown—during its brief early '60s run. More than in any other urban metropolis, Detroit's R&B labels were primarily the province of feisty African-American entrepreneurs during the '60s. Even rarer, the scene was by no means a male enclave. Even Berry's ex-wife Thelma got in on the act: her mother Hazel Coleman and session guitarist/producer Don Davis formed Thelma Records and put out fine platters by Emanuel Lasky and Ohio Untouchables guitarist Robert Ward during the early-to-mid-'60s. Davis would operate other notable Detroit diskeries, including Groove City, before hooking up with Stax and producing Johnnie Taylor's '68 million seller "Who's Making Love" in Memphis.

The first national hit Gordy produced for his own company emanated from

We had dreams, and we believed in our dream."

an impromptu writing session with Bradford. Eighteen-year-old pianist Barrett Strong was on the premises when the pounding rocker "Money (That's What I Want)" was being brainstormed on the fly, pounding the 88s and cutting loose with a raucous vocal that translated into stardom when the song vaulted to No. 2 on *Billboard's* R&B charts and a highly impressive No. 23 pop in early 1960. Tamla still wasn't equipped to break a national hit on its own, so Gwen stepped up to help out her little brother, pressing Barrett's incendiary rocker on her bigger Anna label once it got hot locally.

"We were just a bunch of kids getting together after school, and just hanging out and making music and having a good time," said Strong. "I think until this day we really don't understand it. But it all worked out. We had dreams, and we believed in our dream."

Every general needs a loyal, trustworthy lieutenant, and Berry unexpectedly had his stroll through the front door of Hitsville, looking for work. William "Mickey" Stevenson was hoping to interest Gordy in his singing skills. Mickey was second-generation show biz (his mother Kitty was a respected Detroit R&B singer), having sung professionally, written songs, and dabbled in record production. Gordy wasn't all that impressed with the newcomer's pipes, but envisioned the streetwise Stevenson in the heretofore unfilled role of A&R (artist and repertoire) man. The job description turned out to be a great deal more complicated at Motown than most companies. Mickey wrote songs, produced sessions, procured musicians from the local clubs, and took care of sundry day-to-day problems that sprang up around the facility, with Berry fearlessly delegating authority to his assistants.

"Mickey took over something that was brand new, even to the company: A&R. He did that very well. A lot of the artists were under his direction," said Janie, who kept a close watch from her bird's-eye perch at the receptionist's desk during the early years. "We had a big A&R department, and he was over it, so he must have been doing whatever he was doing right." Stevenson's corner of Hitsville became a beehive of musical activity.

"I had 14 people in that office," said Reeves, who went to work as his secretary in the fall of 1961 and immediately encountered creative folks requesting, 'Hey Martha, sing that song!' 'What do you think of this?' 'What word goes with that?' 'We need a third voice down here,' or 'Can you do the handclaps with these two people?' Or 'How about some handclaps? How about some finger snaps? Stomp on this board!'"

Santa Claus was good to Berry and Motown during the Yuletide season of 1960. As the snow flew and bells jingled, the Miracles' "Shop Around" was rocketing to the top of the R&B charts, where it remained for eight long weeks from mid-January to mid-March of '61, and made a thrilling No. 2 showing on *Billboard's* pop hit parade. "Shop Around" was perhaps the ultimate example of Gordy's perfectionist tendencies as a producer: He roused Smokey out of a sound sleep in the wee small hours of the morning and commanded him to immediately convene his group at the studio to recut it—after it had already been pressed, shipped, and at least locally, aired on the radio. At the same time, Berry's new discovery, 17-year-old Mary Wells, was well on her way to scoring a Top Ten R&B seller with her debut Motown release, the bluesy, hoarse-voiced "Bye Bye Baby."

If all those glad tidings weren't enough to make Berry's holidays merry, Gwen introduced him to an introspective young man noodling at the Studio A piano during Motown's Christmas party. In short order, Marvin Gaye, who had migrated to the Motor City from Washington, D.C., as Fuqua's protege, was signed to a Tamla contract. It took a little time before

Marvin could be convinced that his jazz leanings wouldn't propel him to stardom, but after his mellow first album stiffed, he got with the program.

Motown execs Phil Jones and Barney Ales (Weldon A. McDougal III photo).

As important as it was to produce potential hit records, it didn't mean much if they weren't flying off the shelves. That was Barney Ales's responsibility. Hired near the end of 1960 to head the sales department after impressing Berry as a local distributor for Tamla and Motown, the Italian-American Ales would accrue massive power over the course of the decade—so much that perhaps only Gordy himself had more power within the halls of Hitsville. Ales and his crack sales staff—Phil Jones, Irv Biegel, Al Klein, and others—would tirelessly ensure that Motown's pop profile was stronger than any other R&B company's in existence, helping to obliterate the barriers that had artificially separated the two genres in years past.

Not content to simply sell records, Gordy launched International Talent Management, Inc. Choosing his sister, Esther Gordy Edwards, to head the venture, Berry thus kept every facet of his budding stars' careers positioned securely under one corporate umbrella. ITMI managed Motown's artists, helped get them bookings, acted as their accountant and financial adviser, and provided career guidance.

Practically the entire Gordy clan was heavily involved in Motown's day-to-day operations. Sister Loucye, who married saxist Ron Wakefield (he took the solo on "Shop Around"), headed the sales and manufacturing departments as well as Jobete Music. "She's the one who would call us in when we were struggling with our impatience, waiting on a record to actually hit, to make the charts," said Martha. "She would call us over and she'd show us the progress, which was a kindly gesture. She didn't have to do that. She kept our minds settled when other records were soaring, that ours were coming up in the ranks." Tragically, Loucye died in 1965 of a cerebral hemorrhage.

Berry's younger brother Robert Gordy, one-time recording artist (as Bob Kayli) and longtime head of Jobete Publishing Company, in his office on Woodward Avenue (Weldon A. McDougal III photo).

Berry's younger brother Robert then assumed the Jobete reins, his resume listing a brief stint as a recording artist under the alias of Bob Kayli (his rocking novelty "Everyone Was There" was one of Berry's first hits as a producer in 1958 on the Carlton imprint). George Gordy often went under the nickname of "Horgay" Gordy when he wrote songs, and he also worked as a producer. Oldest brother Fuller Gordy was in charge of administration, dealing with personnel and company policy. Even Berry's mom had her own desk at Hitsville. "His mother used to have to sign all of the expense checks," said Weldon. "When you'd go in there for her to sign the checks, she would ask you what you do, and how's things goin', you know?" Berry brought his blue-collar business experience to the enterprise: His employees punched a time clock every morning, just like at the Lincoln-Mercury plant.

When five young ladies from Inkster, calling themselves the Casinyets, dropped by for an audition in April of '61 after placing fourth in their high school talent contest, there was no outward indication that they would be the act to hand Motown its first pop chart-topper—especially coming as it did on their Tamla debut single. Informed by young producers Brian Holland and Robert Bateman (billed collectively as Brianbert, another of Berry's contracted handles) that an original piece of material was required if they wanted to make a record, they went home and cooked up "Please Mr. Postman." After a quick name change to the Marvelettes, their rocking concoction blasted off and landed at the top of the pop charts that December, with Gladys Horton shining bright as their lead vocalist.

The Marvelettes scored their very first time out and kept on making smashes, but some other acts took longer to break. Such was the case with the teenaged girls who introduced themselves to Berry as the Primettes. They would hang out endlessly in the Hitsville lobby, soaking up the atmosphere and volunteering to sing backgrounds. They were officially signed to the label in 1961 and renamed the Supremes, but their first singles—"I Want A Guy" and the dance workout "Buttered Popcorn"—sold in such minuscule quantities that they were known in some quarters as "the no-hit Supremes." Still, there was something about that lead singer with the big eyes and dazzling smile that one couldn't help but notice.

"They were young girls, but they had class. And they hadn't been taught anything. They just carried themselves that way," said Gorman, who co-wrote "I Want A Guy." "Diana, she would always dress differently. I remember where she used to live, down in the Brewster Projects. I don't know if she would wear her mother's clothes or what, but the way she would dress, she just was different. She always carried herself that way. It was obvious that she was destined to be someone of notoriety."

Singing Sammy Ward and Gino Parks were also on the primordial roster. Both were the proud owners of prodigious pipes, Ward specializing in gut-grabbing blues. But by the time Motown began to make its move toward the top in 1963 and '64, both of these standout vocalists were gone, as was Mable John, who thought the bluesier environs of Stax Records in Memphis more conducive to her vocal strengths.

Some acts contributed a grand total of one or two memorable singles to the early Motown legacy. The Equadors, whose "Someone To Call My Own" was a fine slice of flowing mid-tempo doo-wop (ditto the Creations' "This Is Our Night"), LaBrenda Ben (her strutting "The Chaperone" was written by gospel A&R man George Fowler), Pete Hartfield, Don McKenzie, Mickey McCullers, and anonymous instrumental outfits like the Swinging Tigers and Nick & the Jaguars didn't tarry for long as Berry momentarily tried different acts and discarded them just as quickly. Gordy had a thing for answer records: The Satintones responded to the Shirelles' 1960 mega-hit "Will You Love Me Tomorrow" with an affirmative "Tomorrow And Always," and someone named Little Otis had the temerity to taunt Gene "Duke Of Earl" Chandler with his '62 sequel "I Out-Duked The Duke."

Not all of Berry's new imprints were major successes. Miracle Records debuted in January of 1961 and was gone by the end of the year, having introduced both Jimmy Ruffin and the Temptations during its truncated lifespan.

"They discontinued that, because when the distributors would be calling in ordering the Miracles' records, they would get it confused with the Miracle label," explained the Tempts' Otis Williams in a 1981 interview. "So Berry changed that, because it was a conflict with the Miracles group. He changed it to Gordy." Its purple label featured the inarguable if grammatically debatable slogan "It's what's in the grooves that count." Gordy was inaugurated by the Tempts in March of '62 and both thrived over the long haul, though of the quintet's first half dozen releases, only "Dream Come True" made any national impact.

Another less-than-prolific imprint, Mel-O-Dy, was inaugurated as an R&B outlet in mid-1962 for a few 45s, then reborn as a pop-country imprint as 1963 ended, attracting Dorsey Burnette, Bruce Channel, ex-Dot Records rockabilly Howard Crockett, and Oklahoma-born Gene Henslee (he made some fine country boogie sides for Imperial a decade earlier) to its limited stable until it closed up shop in '65. Divinity Records, Motown's short-lived foray into gospel, opened shop in '62 and lasted approximately a year. The Wright Specials, with a pre-secular Kim Weston in their ranks, had two of its few releases.

Workshop Jazz was likely the most ambitious undertaking of the bunch. Launched in 1962 with a series of singles that preceded a dozen LPs or so in 1963-64, the logo afforded a cadre of Studio A regulars with jazz proclivities a welcome chance to stretch out for the length of an album. Among them was pianist Johnny Griffith with and without vocalist Paula Greer, guitarist/vibist Dave Hamilton, trombonist George Bohanon, saxist Lefty Edwards, and trumpeter Herbie Williams. Chicago pianist Earl Washington, a longtime member of drummer Red Saunders' band and the brother of saxman Leon Washington, cut a pair of Workshop Jazz LPs (he'd enjoyed a regional hit for Checker in '58 with "Misirlou"), and the Four Tops almost had their jazz-rooted debut album, *Breaking Through*, appear on the imprint (it was canceled at the last moment).

Though the Supremes and Tempts were slow out of the gate, **1962 was a terrific year for Motown overall.** Under Smokey Robinson's patient tutelage, Wells softened her vocal persona and embarked on a string of airy, Caribbean-tinged delights. Her "The One Who Really Loves You," "You Beat Me To The Punch," and the sly "Two Lovers" all cracked the pop Top Ten, and the latter pair were R&B chart-toppers. Smokey's Miracles ended the year with what would prove their second record to pace the R&B hit parade, "You've Really Got A Hold On Me."

With several hits under their collective belt, the Miracles were in demand for out-of-town gigs, but the endless road jaunts were less than luxurious. "They were hectic, man," said Robinson. "Hectic and grinding. Fifty one-nighters, that kind of stuff. Driving, you know. Very seldom did we have a bus. We had a bus sometimes, but most of the time it was a car caravan."

The Marvelettes rocked their way onto the airwaves again with "Playboy" and "Beechwood 4-5789." Gaye finally found the right formula with a gritty "Stubborn Kind Of Fellow" that fall. And the Contours—a wild local crew with an acrobatic stage act—popped the eternal question "Do You Love Me (Now That I Can Dance)" on the Gordy logo, its hard-charging rhythm and Billy Gordon's sandpaper-raw lead translating into another No. 1 R&B smash that sold massively on the pop front as well during the autumn of '62.

Young artists kept finding their way to the Hitsville front door—few of them younger than sightless 11-year-old Steveland Judkins. Adjudged a "wonder" by Berry's sister Esther shortly after he arrived in 1962, the rambunctious child prodigy was fluent on bongos, drums, and, most importantly at that stage of his career, harmonica. It took a while for Motown's brain

"...that segregated audience became integrated. I was there to see that."

trust to figure out precisely how to harness Little Stevie Wonder's kinetic energy into something commercial, but in the meantime the crowds gobbled up his antics wherever he performed. Martha Reeves and her Vandellas also made their debut on the Gordy logo that year. She had bided her time as Mickey's secretary until the proper moment came along to begin recording. She and the Vandellas also backed Gaye on his first three smashes.

It was time to introduce Hitsville's artists to the rest of the country, up close and personal. So in the autumn of 1962, practically the entire Motown roster—from Singing Sammy to the Supremes—and a cadre of road-tested Detroit musicians piled into an overloaded bus and embarked on a historic tour that would extend nearly two months. The jaunt began at the Howard Theater in Washington, D.C., and climaxed with 10 days at the world-famous Apollo in Harlem— chitlin' circuit stops of legendary repute. In between, the young singers would experience serious culture shock as the itinerary took them through the still-segregated South.

"Being out there performing for people, for us at that point, being so young, that was pretty much all (that was) on our mind," said Mary Wilson of the Supremes, then a primarily unknown quantity that sang backgrounds for Mary Wells in addition to her group's own featured spot. "Looking back, yeah, I guess we were breaking down barriers."

"You had to go in a black-only bathroom," remembered the Marvelettes' Katherine Anderson Schaffner. "You had to eat in bus stops in the South. You had to go to the back in order to get something to eat, or somebody would have to get whatever you wanted at the back door. But you couldn't necessarily come in, and going in to sit down was just totally out of the question, unless you were going into a black restaurant in the black area of the city."

A threat of danger always hung menacingly in the air, and sometimes turned into reality. "We got ran out of Mississippi," said the Contours' Sylvester Potts. "Bobby Rogers of the Miracles, he went into this gas station. I guess he kind of forgot where he was. The proprietor reminded him of where he was with a gun. Bobby come running back to the bus: 'He got a gun! He got a gun!' So we had to have state troopers escort us out of there."

Yet there was hope for the future every time the troupe's soulful sounds brought the races a little closer together. "That'll make somebody sick, hating that bad," Martha said. "We knew that couldn't last, because we saw Smokey calm the crowd down and talk to the security guards. He said, 'Listen—our music is music to make you fall in love by. There ain't nobody gonna fight and have no riots in here. If y'all just stand back and don't hit the kids with those sticks anymore, you'll see there'll be peace in here.' Because people wanted to dance. But when they started dancing, they forgot where they were sitting. And that segregated audience became integrated. I was there to see that."

Tragedy struck just before Thanksgiving when road manager Thomas "Beans" Bowles, who played flute on several of Marv Johnson's and Marvin Gaye's early hits, was seriously hurt in an auto wreck while driving from Greenville, South Carolina, to Tampa, Florida ahead of the artists and band. His driver, Eddie McFarland, died of his injuries. Despite the calamities, the tour and other less-celebrated southern junkets played a part in closing the racial divide.

"We had a lot of white teenagers that really loved us," said the Miracles' Pete Moore. "We traveled through the South, down through South Carolina, North Carolina, Mississippi, all the southern states there. White kids used to come by the dressing room, and we talked to them a lot. They said, 'We really like you guys' music. If we would buy it and bring it home'—they said a lot of times their parents would slash the music up. And they had to go underground and listen to black radio stations.

"We knocked down a lot of barriers. I think we brought people together. And that's what music does." Gordy did his part by marketing many of Motown's early albums with innocuous cover drawings so they would move in the segregated south. As late as 1966, the Isley Brothers' first Tamla LP, *This Old Heart Of Mine*, bore a color photo of a sunbathing Caucasian couple at the beach on its front. The Isleys were relegated to the black-and-white back of the jacket.

Toledo played host to a star-studded lineup in 1963 (Photo courtesy of Hank Thompson).

Little Stevie finally broke through in 1963. All the way through, in fact, scoring a No. 1 pop hit that summer with "Fingertips–Part 2." After all the studio experimentation, it was an impromptu live outing that caught the public's fancy, and the youth was an overnight star. Stevie's in-concert album—likewise a pop chart topper—wasn't the only one unleashed by the company that year. Gaye, Wells, the Miracles, and the Marvelettes were each gifted with their own full-length live sets, all of them retaining a rough edge or two as the young acts learned how to command a crowd. Motown would continue to issue live albums throughout the decade. Other than James Brown, who seemed to cut a new set on location every other month or so, such remote recordings were otherwise scarce on the soul front.

No longer presenting himself as a moody crooner, Gaye was racking up one hit after another with the chunky dance outing "Hitch Hike" and the impeccable groover "Pride And Joy." The Miracles were gleefully doing "Mickey's Monkey," and Mary Wells continued her reign as Motown's first queen with "Laughing Boy" and "You Lost The Sweetest Boy."

But 1963 might be most notable for the ascendancy of a three-headed compositional juggernaut. Brian and Eddie Holland and Lamont Dozier had all started out as singers, with only Eddie enjoying success via his '62 Motown hit "Jamie." Brian and Lamont were already successful Hitsville composers, but when Eddie joined them as their lyricist, hits poured down like rain. Martha & the Vandellas were one of the triumvirate's chief beneficiaries that year: "Come And Get These Memories," "Heat Wave," and "Quicksand"—H-D-H copyrights all—were major hits, with "Heat Wave" topping the R&B lists and flying sky-high on the pop side.

The Motown sound was in full bloom by 1963, thanks in no small part to the impeccable house band known, at least to themselves, as the Funk Brothers. Where drummer Benny Benjamin had once used brushes and kept the backbeat relatively light, his sound was steadily becoming more aggressive as he drove the rhythmic thrust like a steam engine. Incomparable bassist James Jamerson asserted himself with lines of startling suppleness and imagination. Together they formed a world-class rhythm section. Keyboardist Earl Van Dyke masterfully meshed with guitarists Robert White, Joe Messina, and Eddie Willis to weave musical tapestries that grew richer and more ambitious every time out.

Percussionists Jack Ashford, Jack Brokensha, and Eddie "Bongo" Brown provided the spice, and a full complement of horn players and violinists—the latter on loan from the Detroit Symphony—added the sweetening that factored into Motown's phenomenal pop crossover success.

Not only was the musical approach becoming more complex, so was the way that soulful sound was captured for posterity. In the early days, Berry and Robert Bateman, who left in 1962 to produce elsewhere, made do with a two-track tape recorder and the most basic of sonic extras. "At one time, they were using the men's room for the echo chamber," said producer Hank Cosby. A sizable hole was cut into the second-floor ceiling next door at 2644-46 W. Grand so that the music could be pumped up into the attic to create a more practical echo facility.

In Motown's earliest days, the engineers were forced to improvise if something malfunctioned in the control room. "I remember when Robert Bateman was at the controls," said Louvain Demps of the Andantes, whose sumptuous, gospel-streaked vocal backgrounds were heard on countless Motown hits. "Something happened and they couldn't get the thing to work. And he came running out, and he told Berry, 'I patched it! I got it together!' (Berry) said, 'Man, how'd you do it?' And he said, 'With bubble gum!'"

Once Mike McLean came aboard, things tightened up technically. "I think Mike might have been the first real engineer. Robert Bateman used to do a lot of engineering," said Gorman. "Robert went by ear, which was great. It paid off in the early days. Robert, he was an excellent engineer. When he left, that's when Mike came into being over there." McLean was a trained technical whiz. "He was really something," said Cosby. "He was very creative." In mid-1964, McLean supervised the design and construction of an eight-track recorder, then a rare luxury that offered vastly improved sound quality and expanded overdubbing possibilities.[2] All the studio equipment had to be impeccably maintained.

"They would repair 'em every day, the repair guys," said Cosby. "We had our own engineering staff. They were very good. You've gotta give them credit too. They were very inventive. The guys would be out there testing microphones in the ground. They were young—very, very creative. Some of the sounds that we developed were developed by the engineers."

As the technical end of the operation became more advanced, so did overdubbing techniques. Instrumental tracks would be laid, then the backing vocals, then lead vocals (or vice versa on the last two).

"In the early days, we recorded everything right there together. But as technology advanced, then they could record the vocals and everything separately, and put the voices down later. It all depended on the availability of the artists," said the Supremes' Mary Wilson. "There was a point when we had to actually record whenever we could, because we were pretty much on the road. And in order to get a record out, they would have to put the band tracks down."

That meant singers crossed paths with the Studio A band more sparingly as the decade progressed and renders the compilation of sessionographies a nightmare. Some songs were reworked, overdubbed, and modified four or five times over a period of months or even years, with different titles and different lyrics that would be altered or jettisoned altogether during the drawn-out, but ultimately rewarding, creative process.

"They'd cut a lot of stuff and didn't have no name for it," said Cosby. "Probably the biggest producers that did more of that than anyone was Holland-Dozier-Holland. 'Cause I used to write all of their arrangements in the beginning. And they would write four or five sessions a week with no titles. They would call it anything. And it'd be recorded that way, and it'd go to the union that way."

"If I Could Build My Whole World Around You" was the third in a series of Marvin Gaye-Tammi Terrell duet hits in the 1960s (Photo courtesy of David Alston's Mahogany Archives).

you do a master, you play it on the small speakers. And that's what you'll hear coming through those old AM radios."

Billie Jean Brown started out full-time at Hitsville in 1961 as a tape librarian before being named head of the Quality Control Department. A disc-cutting machine was acquired in 1963 and kept in virtually constant rotation as Robert Dennis cranked out contrasting copies of various mixes that could be compared to one another. It was Brown's responsibility to listen to the countless mixes and offer her notoriously frank opinions of each.[3]

"She chose the records," said Martha. "She was the one that would get with Berry and listen to them and decide with the council, as they called it, what record would go out. Most of the successes and failures were blamed on Billie Jean. She had a lot of responsibility."

"If somebody was out of key, that record wouldn't have went out. Somebody hit a bad note—anything that was wrong, that was Quality Control. If it didn't get out of Quality Control, that was it," said McDougal. "She would say, 'So-and-so sang too loud in this spot. The mix isn't good.' Anything that was wrong with the record, that was her department."

A car radio was rigged up inside Hitsville so Billie Jean could experience a simulation of the tinny, high-end reproduction that a great many fans would ultimately enjoy their Motown music over. "See, the tiny speakers give you what you hear on the radio," said Cosby. "So that's why we were using those. After

Berry acquired the rights to sister Gwen and Harvey Fuqua's Tri-Phi and Harvey labels in 1963, absorbing several of their top acts: Jr. Walker & the All Stars, Shorty Long, the Spinners, and Johnny Bristol. With substantial cash flowing into the burgeoning operation, Berry bought Detroit's Graystone Ballroom, once a mecca for big bands that had more recently hosted boxing matches and rock-and-roll record hops, in June of '63. In addition to being a grandiose facility to stage his annual employee Christmas parties, the five-story Graystone, located at 4237 Woodward, hosted a series of "Battle of the Stars" concerts pitting Motown artists against one another in good-natured musical competitions.

Gordy was also steadily acquiring real estate closer to home, acquiring most of a row of lookalike structures situated on either side of Hitsville. After he purchased 2644-46 W. Grand in April of 1961 and placed Jobete and the sales, shipping, and public relations departments therein, 2650-52 was landed in January of '62 to house offices for Berry and his sister Esther, as well as ITMI (the building burned down in October of 1971). The 2656 building hosted the finance department from 1965 on; 2662/64, acquired the next year, was home to sales and marketing. Ditto 2666-68, secured at the same time. ITMI moved into 2670-72 after it was obtained in late 1966. Across the expansive roadway routinely lined with shiny new Cadillacs once Hitsville was in full gear, another building at 2657 was converted into Artist Development Department headquarters in

"I think it was healthy, because it made us work,"

early 1966.[4] "It was like going from house to house," said Weldon. "It was unique."

Gordy loved competition, whether it was between his artists on the stage of the Graystone, or his creative staff hotly debating the merits of one another's productions. Each Friday morning at 9 a.m. sharp (five minutes late and you were locked out), chairman Gordy and his loyal employees—producers, songwriters, department heads, sales personnel—met to evaluate product. They listened, they argued, and they ultimately decided what would be presented to the public with a coveted Motown, Tamla, or Gordy label on it. Billie Jean brought the choices to the meetings, and sometimes the stack ran 40 songs high.

Berry Gordy (far left) was the toast of Detroit in 1965. Here the Motown chief is raising a glass with (from left) Lamont Dozier, Brian Holland, The Four Tops and Eddie Holland (Photo courtesy of David Alston's Mahogany Archives).

"We would pick out the singles that we thought were viable, should be out on the market. And Berry would have everybody vote. He would watch how you voted. He felt like if you missed too many of the records, and you were voting negatively, he would put it down. He'd make a note of it. Next thing you know, these people were not in the meeting!" said Cosby. "You had to be careful how you voted, 'cause he was watching." Ultimately, Gordy could overrule the majority, but used his veto power sparingly.

"I think it was healthy, because it made us work," said producer/writer Johnny Bristol, whose triumphs included Diana Ross & the Supremes' "Someday We'll Be Together" and who, with Harvey Fuqua, produced Marvin Gaye & Tammi Terrell's "Ain't No Mountain High Enough." "We were young, and we could have gotten lazy in our efforts, and just relaxed after our first record was cut: 'Hey, I'm a big writer!' We were fortunate that there was a stable of people there that, they had pride in writing. It meant something to each individual. Many of those guys were inspirational in encouraging what they could do. Like a Norman Whitfield and Holland-Dozier-Holland—you could hear them and say, 'Well, I can do that! I can make hit records! It can be done!' There was an image there to follow. I didn't necessarily try to produce like them, or do what they did. I just felt that as a producer, I could produce, too.

"The votes were honest. I think all the producers and the writers and the secretaries and people that they used to vote on the product, I think they were fair with what their comments were," he said. "I think they were healthy meetings. I think they were good, and made the producers want to get their product accepted as one of the tunes selected in the meeting to be played. Because everyone's tune didn't make the meeting."

"It was competition, but it was friendly competition," said Temptations guitarist Cornelius Grant, who co-wrote their '66 hit "(I Know) I'm Losing You." "Everybody kind of enjoyed the competition, really, because it really made you. If you went to create something, you knew you had to come back with the goods. Otherwise, you got guys like Holland-Dozier-Holland writing together, you got Smokey, you got Whitfield. These guys, the veins were popping out of their necks to try to come up with the best song. You really had to have it together."

The staff's views weren't necessarily the final word on a song's potential either, as far as Gordy was concerned. "A lot of times, he would even go get teenagers off the street, or from some school, because that's who was buying the records at that time, and get their opinions on certain records," said Janie. "He was definitely a leader. He always had these leader-type ideas."

Their marriage in ruins, Miss Ray relocated to New York in 1963 to establish a Motown outpost in the Brill Building. A few intriguing talents were discovered. The Serenaders, whose "If Your Heart Says Yes" was the inaugural release on the newly established V.I.P. subsidiary in early '64, contained Sidney Barnes and George Kerr, who would write for Jobete. George Clinton was also pacted, though nothing he cut was issued. Clinton's Parliaments would hit in 1967 for Detroit deejay LeBaron Taylor's Revilot label with "(I Wanna) Testify." Revilot also scored the year before with Darrell Banks' "Open The Door To Your Heart."

Motown's New York venture was fatally underfunded from the outset. A desperate Raynoma bootlegged 5,000 copies of Wells' red-hot "My Guy" to raise some operating capital, but the foolish scheme was quickly busted and the Big Apple outpost shut down for good. Miss Ray's first tenure at Motown had come to an ignominious end, though she would return to the fold later in the decade.[5]

Speaking of "My Guy," the irresistible Smokey-penned charmer was the No. 1 pop record in the country for a couple of weeks in May of 1964—quite a way for Wells to celebrate her 21st birthday. That milestone was important in more ways than one: Once she passed it, Wells announced her intentions to disaffirm her Motown contract on the grounds she signed it when she was a minor. After protracted negotiations, Wells departed to record for 20th Century Fox. Though she made some nice records that sold reasonably well, she'd never hit the same rarified heights again.

As soon as H-D-H took an interest in the Supremes, that maddening "no-hit" tag was erased forever. "Where Did Our Love Go," complete with marching footsteps that drove it along like a rampaging army, was a relentless vehicle for Diana Ross's kittenish allure, and it rocketed to the peak of the pop hit parade during the summer of '64. From there, Ross, Mary Wilson, and Florence Ballard embarked on a meteoric rise that truly reads like a fairy tale. Their next four Motown 45s also blasted off to the No. 1 slot: "Baby Love" that fall, "Come See About Me" in the winter, "Stop! In The Name Of Love" during the spring of '65, and "Back In My Arms Again" that summer. From no hits to nothing but, the Supremes were suddenly the label's biggest stars.

The prolific H-D-H found time to supply Gaye with a string of winners: "Can I Get A Witness," "You're A Wonderful One," "Baby Don't You Do It," and in late '64, the utterly in-the-pocket "How Sweet It Is (To Be Loved By You)." And they latched onto a recently signed quartet comprised of anything but starry-eyed newcomers. The Four Tops had generally been regarded as Detroit's most advanced vocal harmonizers since the mid-'50s. Their musical preferences generally ran towards jazz and pop, but H-D-H tailored a perfect piece of material to render them R&B stars. "Baby I Need Your Loving" properly introduced stirring lead singer Levi Stubbs to the soul field.

"Those were beautiful days, back in the days at Motown when we were all starting out together," said the Tops' Abdul "Duke" Fakir in a 1980 interview. "We all had no money. When I say all of us, I mean people like the Supremes, Temptations, Marvin, Stevie—he was just a little kid then—the Marvelettes, Martha & the Vandellas. Everybody was just hangin' around. Then all of a sudden, things just started happening. It was just like living in fantasyland. It was great. Nobody really wanted to leave town to go to work, we was having so much fun just recording and hanging out with each other."

Hanging out often led to love around the halls of Hitsville. A daunting number of Motown artists and front office personnel were romantically entwined over the years: Marvin Gaye married Berry's older sister Anna, while Berry's sister Gwen got hitched to Harvey Fuqua and later on, singer G.C. Cameron. Berry's niece Iris married Johnny Bristol, and the Miracles' Bobby Rogers took the Marvelettes' Wanda Young as his bride. Contours lead singer Billy Gordon wed Georgeanna Tillman of the Marvelettes, whose Katherine Anderson married road manager Joe Schaffner. Tammi Terrell was involved with the Temptations' David Ruffin, and Velvelettes lead singer Caldin Gill married the Monitors' Richard Street. The Supremes' Florence Ballard wed Berry's chauffeur Thomas Chapman, while Mary Wells went for singer Herman Griffin, who unwisely convinced her to exit the label. A&R kingpin Mickey Stevenson captured the heart of Kim Weston, Stevie Wonder was briefly betrothed to Syreeta Wright, and Berry was involved from the mid-'60s on with Diana Ross. The tab for wedding gifts must have eaten up sizable chunks of Motown employees' paychecks.

Simultaneous with the Supremes' launch, the Temptations took off for the moon in 1964. Boasting the slickest choreography in the R&B lexicon and no less than three outstanding lead singers in falsetto-blessed Eddie Kendricks, rough-edged Paul Williams, and dynamic newcomer David Ruffin, the group was primed for action. Smokey handed them the right piece of material: "The Way You Do The Things You Do" was bountifully enriched by clever metaphors irresistibly delivered by Kendricks, and they were at last on their way.

Berry launched two more imprints in 1964, both of them successful over the long haul. Soul Records debuted early in the year with the original version of "Devil With The Blue Dress" by diminutive belter Shorty Long (Mitch Ryder & the Detroit Wheels would grab the spins with a rocked-out cover a couple of years later), while V.I.P. sported the most eclectic roster of any long-term Motown imprint of the '60s, initially dominated by L.A. acts and newcomers.

Motown's new West Coast office fared somewhat better than its New York counterpart. Headed by Hal Davis, it didn't operate for all that long either, but it did unearth one legitimate star—the statuesque Brenda Holloway. Her stately "Every Little Bit Hurts," produced by Davis and his partner Marc Gordon, was set to a waltz time meter and veritably oozed uptown soul majesty as it became a major hit during the spring of '64. Back in Detroit, the Velvelettes, whose members hailed from Flint and Kalamazoo rather than the Motor City, made their mark with the V.I.P. girl group gem "Needle In A Haystack," courtesy of young producer Norman Whitfield.

Not all of Berry's strategies paid off so handsomely. Perhaps to accrue more viability as a full-service entity, he went out and signed well-past-their-prime pop crooners Tony Martin, Bobby Breen, and Connie Haines, none of whom experienced even a glimmer of Motown success. The eternally suave Billy Eckstine arrived in 1965 and was a more sensible acquisition. Gorgeous actress/vocalist Barbara McNair came closest to achieving an effective marriage of the Motown sound and middle-of-the-road leanings. Some of her mid-'60s singles crossed over into the R&B realm altogether, though none charted.

1965 was *the* year for the Motown empire from an artistic standpoint, and sales figures shot through the roof. The Motown Sound—instantly discernible from all the other seminal soul being produced elsewhere at the time—was America's primary antidote to the all-encompassing British Invasion. The label scored five No. 1 pop hits, three of them by the Supremes ("Stop! In The Name Of Love," "Back In My Arms Again," and "I Hear A Symphony") and one apiece by the Four Tops (the H-D-H classic "I Can't Help Myself") and the Temptations (Smokey's immortal "My Girl," a landmark that established lead singer David Ruffin overnight as a primary force within the quintet). Ruffin encored with "It's Growing," "Since I Lost My Baby," and "My Baby," temporarily elbowing Kendricks out of his front man role.

Smokey had plenty of material salted away in his portfolio to keep his own group satisfied. The Miracles enjoyed three major hits with the spine-chilling "Ooo Baby Baby," "The Tracks Of My Tears," and "My Girl Has Gone." Gaye paced the R&B lists twice with "I'll Be Doggone" and "Ain't That Peculiar," also from Smokey's corner. Brenda Holloway's pipes proved as captivating as ever under Robinson's astute supervision on "When I'm Gone" and "Operator," both originally waxed by Wells, whose absence was scarcely noticeable.

Kim Weston, who had married A&R boss Mickey Stevenson the previous year, broke through in a big way with the romping H-D-H groover "Take Me In Your Arms (Rock Me A Little While)" after two years of wonderful singles often overlooked by the public. The Velvelettes were sassy and classy on another girl group goodie, "He Was Really Sayin' Somethin'." And Motown was scorched by a heady blast of honking roadhouse funk when rollicking tenor saxman Jr. Walker & the All Stars' "Shotgun"—as sweaty and straightahead a dance workout as ever graced the Soul records catalog, and the antithesis of the meticulously polished Motown sound—catapulted to the top of the R&B hit parade. Walker's encores "Do The Boomerang" and "Shake And Fingerpop" were also hot sellers.

"It was a big thing, man, when you walked into Motown then at that time. Oh man, it was just like heaven! You walk in there, everybody was makin' hits!" said Walker in 1994. "You had to go in the studio and go to work. You didn't go in there and sit down. You didn't have people goin' there sayin', 'Oh, I'm a big star,' you know, and have a chip on their shoulder. Because when they walked in the door, somebody was kickin' a record. They was kickin' you in the hips! And when that guy would open the studio doors, you'd go in there and go to work. Nobody would have to tell you to go to work. You'd just go in there and go to work."

The international market was quickly succumbing to a case of **Motown fever,** just as Americans were going absolutely ga-ga over English rock bands. Gaye had journeyed to the U.K. in 1964 for some TV and radio guest shots, and he wasn't the only early Hitsville visitor to the mother country. "The first time we went over, we went over with Kim Weston," recalled percussionist Jack Ashford, who was part of a skin-tight Funk Brothers backing aggregation comprised of drummer Uriel Jones, keyboardist Earl Van Dyke, and guitarist Robert White. "We went over and did that thing as a feel-out thing, trying to feel that market out. So when the report came back so good, that's when Berry and a whole slew of everybody went."

In late March of '65, nearly everybody embarked on the first overseas edition of the Motortown Revue. The Supremes, Temptations, Miracles, Martha & the Vandellas, Stevie, and the Earl Van Dyke Sextet (along with Berry, his mom and dad, additional family members, and a coterie of chaperones and assistants) barnstormed Europe for two weeks. The jaunt tied in with the inauguration of the British Tamla-Motown label, which would issue quite a bit of the company's voluminous stateside output. Dusty Springfield hosted a TV special, *The Sound of Motown*, while the troupe was visiting Great Britain that showcased all of the tour's acts.

"We pretty much toured all over Europe," said Mary Wilson. "I don't know if there was a place I liked best. It was a pretty phenomenal tour. Every place was very, very exciting—Paris, Italy, Sweden, the Scandinavian countries, and obviously Great Britain. The entire tour was pretty fantastic."

The troupe encountered cultural differences of an entirely different nature than what they'd endured in Alabama and Mississippi. "We played a place called the Olympia in Paris," said the Miracles' Pete Moore. "We were the closers, the headliners on the show. When the Supremes came on, and then they left, and Stevie came on, and the Tempts came on—there wasn't any applause. The place was packed. We didn't have a problem drawing people there, but we wasn't getting any response. We were all backstage, we were nervous. It was time for us to go on, and we went on, and we went through our whole show. In those days, we closed our show with 'Going To A Go-Go.' We had everyone come onstage, like a finale, a big finale. And then the curtains closed, and all of a sudden we heard this thunderous applause, after the whole show was done. The curtains opened back up, and everybody was standing. It was a standing ovation. It was incredible. The curtains closed again, they opened back up, we took another bow. And we learned afterwards that was the custom of France—that they didn't clap for you until the whole show was done. They didn't clap after every song like Americans did. We didn't know that."

The tour also brought a temporary revolt among the musicians. "We went on a strike over there one time. We did some Dusty Springfield stuff. We did a session with her over there. Esther Edwards came to us and said, 'You guys are not gonna be paid for the session.' We went off!" said percussionist Ashford. "We said, 'What do you mean we're not gonna be paid?' So we said, 'We're not goin' on then!' Earl said, 'Let's not go on. We're gonna strike!' So we're standing back there in the wings, man, and the people out there are raising hell like they was getting ready to riot, 'cause we wasn't goin' on. So Berry came and said, 'What's wrong? What's wrong? What's the problem? What's the problem?' We told him what happened—'Esther don't want to pay us, she's not gonna pay us on the session.' He said, 'You'll be paid for the session. Don't even worry about that. Just go on out there and work!'"

Along with the occasional fiscal dispute, there were plenty of good times as the young stars became accustomed to their new surroundings. "We traveled along a lot of back roads. Obviously, England doesn't have the highway system that the United States has, and getting from city to city, we traveled a lot of back roads that went through a lot of farm areas," said Moore. "We were all in the bus, and all of a sudden Jack Ashford says, 'Stop the bus! Stop the bus!' So we thought something was wrong, right? So the driver pulls over to the side of the road. We said, 'Jack, what's up? Why do you want to stop?' He said, 'Pete, look at that cow!' There's a cow out there that has this big cowbell. He said, **'I have to have that cowbell!'** So he got off the bus, went to the pasture, took the damn cowbell off of the cow, came back to the bus, and we drove off!"

The international appeal of the Motown catalog was so strong that Gordy had several of his artists record foreign language versions of their hits—a virtually unheard-of ploy in the R&B field, though pop stars Gene Pitney, Connie Francis, and The Beatles routinely engaged in similar continental pursuits for the overseas market. Over the same backing tracks that powered their hits, the Tempts phonetically navigated "The Way You Do The Things You Do" in Italian ("Bluebird," sung half in German, half in English, had no stateside equivalent); the Supremes did an Italian rendition of "You Can't Hurry Love," and Gaye tried "How Sweet It Is" in German, inserting a soulful "Oh, baby" or two requiring no translation. Naturally, the background vocals on the latter had to be reworked too.

"We wrote it out how we could say it, and then we just did it," said Louvain Demps, who was cautioned by her fellow Andantes to tone down her natural exuberance. "When it was time to do this in German, they were trying to tell me, 'Don't sing so loud!'" she giggled. Velvelettes lead Caldin Gill's fluency in French was put to good use when she and the group cut a track or two for foreign consumption (the group started out with the apropos name of Les Jolie Femmes).

Gordy considered his proteges more than just recording artists. His ultimate goal was to prepare them for presentation at the finest mainstream venues, where the bookings tended to be far more lucrative than the venerable chitlin' circuit stops most R&B acts were customarily consigned to. To that end, sisters Gwen and Anna established the Artist Development Department under Fuqua's stewardship in the building across the street at 2657 W. Grand. There his acts were groomed on all the prerequisites for prolonged stardom besides the making of hits. Maxine Powell, who had headed her own finishing school in Detroit for many years, was hired to instruct Motown's resident girl groups on the finer points of etiquette.

"We loved her dearly, though she could get very stern. She'd keep you in line and in check. I'll never forget, she had these stools. She would have us practice on how to sit like a lady on them. Being young and stuff, we were like giggling a lot on all that stuff," said Bertha Barbee-McNeal of the Velvelettes. "She would teach you how to walk up to that stool and put your tush at a certain place, and you slid that tush on that stool. You didn't just clump down on it. You put that one foot behind the other, always. And you'd always point your toe. If you were going to cross your legs as you were sitting, as a female, you'd have to cross your leg at the same time you were sitting. That was a feminine kind of thing that you did. You don't sit down, and then cross your legs.

"There were so many things. The way you held your hands, you point that index finger out if you wanted to be feminine and look more like a lady. You didn't talk too much as a female. If we were interviewed, you just said what you had to say. They didn't want a talkative female. All those kind of things—the way you carried your purse, the way you did your steps. You always had one leg in back of the other."

"Everything was beneficial to our image," said Mary Wilson. "We were like the movie artists who went to finishing school."

Veteran hoofer Cholly Atkins, formerly half of a fabled dance duo with Honi Coles who had already worked wonders with the Cadillacs and Gladys Knight & the Pips prior to arriving at Hitsville, was in charge of sharpening each act's choreography to a razor's edge. "He was just phenomenal to work with. The rhythm that that man had," said Barbee-McNeal. "He always taught us to count. That was his big thing. 'You gotta count to get those steps. I want you to feel 'em, but you gotta count 'em.' And you had to look the part too. You had to show it in your face, and you'd throw those shoulders and point that toe. And he'd go over and over and over and over. You wanted to work for him."

Robinson endured Cholly's good-natured ribbing over his lack of dancing acumen. "When we went to Artist Development, he used to always say, 'Smoke, I am so glad you're the lead singer!'" said Robinson. "Because I couldn't dance at all. So he'd say, 'I'm so glad you're the lead singer, so I don't have to be bothered by you! I don't have to show you these steps!'"

"...We ate, slept, and played together."

The imposing Maurice King, who led the house band at the Flame Show Bar back when Gordy was there hustling songs, worked on the musical aspects of each group's live presentation, polishing their harmonies and coming up with arrangements and special material with the help of Johnny Allen. The ambitious program got rapid results. The Supremes opened July 29, 1965 at Jules Podell's prestigious Copacabana in Manhattan, a landmark engagement for the group, Gordy, and Motown itself. The versatile group usually performed a song-and-dance routine or a refined Broadway number along with its latest hit whenever it visited Ed Sullivan's Sunday evening CBS-TV extravaganza, which was often.

"Prior to then, any performance or routines that anyone saw basically were put together by the artists within the group," said the Marvelettes' Katherine Anderson Schaffner. "They did not have a Cholly Atkins. They did not have a Maxine Powell. They did not have a Maurice King or a Johnny Allen that was teaching you the different entities of the business in regards to performing. When you take 15- and 16-year-old kids, and they have a million-seller record and they don't really have anyone to guide and direct them in order to how to be a professional, then they can only come up the best they can with what they can come up with as far as performing."

Some of Motown's best-selling LP's were displayed on the back side of a Mary Wells 45 sleeve in 1962 (Photo courtesy of David Alston's Mahogany Archives).

All that attention to his artists earned Gordy some major loyalty.

"The Christmas parties—he didn't have to do that. He sent us lavish money, and he gave gifts. I still have the pure crystal necklace and earrings that he gave the Velvelettes. He gave you monetarily what you sold," she continued. "Some of the groups would sing at the Christmas parties. We ate well. The man paid for it. And then in the summer, the baseball games, the picnics—you brought your brothers and sisters, your cousins. He never acted once like he was better than anybody. He was just as down-to-earth and talked to everybody, took time to say hello. That to me is why Motown lasted, and it's still lasting.

"I would have went out and dug a hole for Motown. You just felt like, 'I'm a part of something. I'm proud to be here, and I want to be here.' It was a good feeling."

"When we'd go on the road, different things would happen, and we'd have to end up helping each other," said Kim Weston. "That's how it was. We worked together, we helped each other. We ate, slept, and played together."

Holland-Dozier-Holland extended their reign as Motown's premier writing and production team in 1966. The Supremes posted another pair of No. 1 pop smashes with their "You Can't Hurry Love" and "You Keep Me Hangin' On." Their "My World Is Empty Without You" and "Love Is Like An Itching In My

Heart" cracked the Top Ten. The Four Tops paced the pop list with the dramatic "Reach Out, I'll Be There," and their "Standing In The Shadows Of Love" was another huge seller. Jr. Walker blasted off with "(I'm A) Road Runner" and a remake of "How Sweet It Is (To Be Loved By You)," and the Isley Brothers—a recent acquisition already renowned for their gospel-fired raveups "Shout" and "Twist And Shout" prior to arriving at Hitsville—benefitted from H-D-H's largesse with "This Old Heart Of Mine."

Robinson was firing on all cylinders. His Miracles scored with "Going To A Go-Go," and he helmed "Don't Mess With Bill" for the Marvelettes and "Get Ready" for the Tempts. Though it paced the R&B hit parade, the latter didn't post a lofty enough pop chart position to suit Gordy, so responsibility for the group was turned over to Norman Whitfield, who produced "Ain't Too Proud To Beg" and "Beauty Is Only Skin Deep." Wonder's voice had changed from a little boy's into that of a young man, and he asserted himself as a mature hitmaker that year with "Uptight (Everything's Alright)" and "Blowin' In The Wind," the latter a soulful recasting of the Bob Dylan ode with an uncredited duet appearance by Wonder's producer and mentor, Clarence Paul.

After running through a raft of talent during the label's early days in a continual weeding-out process that paid mighty dividends, Motown's roster solidified during the mid-1960s, with only a handful of new recruits brought into the equation. Jimmy Ruffin might have been mistaken for a newcomer when his anguished "What Become Of The Brokenhearted" soared high on the charts in 1966, but he'd been around Hitsville for half a decade, searching for the right piece of material. His encore hit "I've Passed This Way Before" at year's end guaranteed he'd be around for some time to come.

The West Coast office was closed in 1966, with Frank Wilson moving to Hitsville and another of its principals going on to bigger things of his own. "Marc Gordon, of course, was Hal's partner," said Wilson. "Hal and Marc were both asked to open up the office, and when Berry Gordy was convinced that he was wasting money and shut it down, Marc took a group that Hal had called the Versatiles, took them over to Johnny Rivers and changed their name to the 5th Dimension."

Hitsville's A&R department wielded some serious clout, even occasionally deciding who would join what group. "Hank Cosby one night came into the 20 Grand with Mickey Stevenson and said, 'Hey, man, we just left B.G.'s house. And we decided that you should be in the Contours,'" said Jimmy Ruffin. "I didn't understand the power of the A&R director. To me, he was just Mickey. He had a job to do. And I was the artist. And as far as I was concerned, I was as important as he was.

"I said, 'No way, man, I can't do that.' He said, 'But, man, we already had the meeting. We've already decided.' I said, 'Hey, come on, man, I didn't join the Temptations!'" Ruffin continued. "He just stormed out angry. I was supposed to go, 'Yeah, sure, Mickey, whatever you say.'" Ruffin stuck to his guns and became a solo star.

Any operation the size of Hitsville is bound to have a few inequities. Allocation of writers' credits appears to have been fairly loose. It was often claimed during interviews for this book that producers and various other bigwigs affixed their names to compositions brought in by artists or staff writers without substantially changing the songs—sometimes acing out the original composer altogether—or a newcomer's contributions to a collaboration went uncredited. Granted, these practices were standard operating procedure in the R&B industry back then, and what the producers brought to the songs may have indeed merited their addition in some instances. Few of the victims seem to hold grudges. It was simply the price of doing business in a creative environment where your work was likely to attract the widest possible audience.

It's time that one persistent rumor about Motown's rapid rise to dominance is buried once and for all. Without citing specific instances (that's another book altogether), evidence is overwhelming that the mob had its hooks sunk into several R&B labels from the same era, but there's absolutely no substantiation that Hitsville was ever invaded at any time by da boys.[6]

As the label grew more prosperous, accusations of underpayment of royalties to the artists would crop up from time to time—a charge Gordy denies in his autobiography, stating that he painstakingly patterned his standard contracts after the ones United Artists laid on him back in the days when his Marv Johnson and Eddie Holland masters were farmed out to the major imprint for national distribution.[7]

As was standard practice in those days, all costs related to the recording sessions were subtracted against royalty payments, and the sheer volume of material recorded by the label's stars—the vaults overflow with unreleased masters to this day—guaranteed that this would not be an insignificant amount of cash. Spread what was left in the way of royalties over three to five members of a group after sundry other manufacturing and promotional expenses were deducted, and fair or not, complaints were bound to surface from stars whose catalogs abounded with hits.[8]

Access to the company's ledgers for artists, their legal representatives, or anyone else outside the immediate family was extremely limited. Gordy's staunch refusal to allow the Recording Industry Association of America to examine his sales figures meant that Motown and its artists never officially received gold records commemorating their million sellers.[9] Instead, the company manufactured its own, eventually lining a wall in the hulking Motown office building on Woodward Avenue with plaques bearing unofficial gold records that paid tribute to the artists and their massive hits.

Competition for top-flight material was fierce. "There were two or three people standing in the doorway when you were recording," said Martha, whose1966 hit "My Baby Loves Me" was originally designated by co-writer Stevenson for his wife, Kim Weston. "There was always an artist on the prowl, and if there was a song that you couldn't sing, they would get it. Then they'd say, 'I can sing that!'"

"When I would go fly into Detroit to record, they would call me on the phone. 'Hey, Bren, we've got a lot of things for you to do when you get here!'" said Brenda Holloway. "When I'd get there, they'd say, 'Oh, excuse me—Gladys came in and she recorded your tune. She had to go back out of town.' I'm like, 'Oh, she did? Oh, joy!'"

If any single local competitor came close to stealing a little of Motown's thunder, it was Golden World Records and its Ric-Tic subsidiary. Golden World was formed in 1963 by Joanne Jackson and Ed Wingate—reputedly a powerful Detroit numbers man with plenty of money to throw in the direction of the Funk Brothers to acquire their moonlighting services.[10] Golden World notched a major pop hit in 1964 with the Reflections' "(Just Like) Romeo & Juliet" and scored in '66 with the Holidays' "I'll Love You Forever," a Don Davis production featuring an uncredited Edwin Starr as lead singer. Starr enjoyed a series of 1965-66 hits on Ric-Tic with his "Agent Double-O Soul," "Back Street," and "Stop Her On Sight (S.O.S.)" before Gordy bought out the operation in September of 1966, acquiring Starr and J.J. Barnes (who never had a Motown release, perhaps due to his uncanny vocal similarity to Gaye, but appeared on at least one Motortown Revue at

Detroit's Fox Theater).

Starr was in England when the deal went down and learned he had become a Motown artist from one of the Tempts when both played the Apollo. "They bought the company, bought the artists, but they didn't know what to do with me, because for the most part, I was too hardcore for what they did," said Starr. "Everything they did was basically pop-orientated." A couple of years down the road, artist and label would connect in spectacular fashion. Ric-Tic remained in business well into 1968, scoring several hits with the Fantastic Four (who would move over to soul in mid-run when their "I Love You Madly" was high on the R&B charts in the fall of '68) and issuing memorable 45s by the Detroit Emeralds, Andre Williams, Al Kent, and the Flaming Embers, a white soul outfit that would have much success on H-D-H's Hot Wax imprint during the early '70s as the Flaming Ember. Golden World's recording facility at 3246 Davison West was also acquired by Motown and renamed Studio B.

Songwriting talent turned up in unexpected places. Stevenson first met Ron Miller when the aspiring composer delivered a pizza to Mickey's hotel room. The white Chicagoan haughtily informed Gordy early in his Motown tenure that he wasn't interested in supplying boilerplate R&B. Miller had an uncanny knack for writing new songs that sounded like old standards—so much so that Gordy inaugurated a separate publishing company, Stein and Van Stock, for Miller in an attempt to disguise his fresh compositions as ancient copyrights.[11]

Working with several collaborators, Miller gave a number of his compositions to Stevie Wonder. "Give Your Heart A Chance" appears to have been the earliest, from Wonder's late '63 LP *With a Song In My Heart*, and he also provided Wonder with his 1966 hit "A Place In The Sun" and the '67 follow-up "Travlin' Man." Miller wrote his masterwork "For Once In My Life" with Orlando Murden, and it turned up on the *Four Tops on Broadway* album in early '67 and the Tempts' *In a Mellow Mood* set a few months later. But it was Stevie Wonder's 1968 smash that made it a standard (Tony Bennett actually beat Stevie onto the charts with it in late '67).

"The song was the biggest copyright Motown owned at one time. Ron Miller was very talented. We were very good friends. I used to love some of his stuff. Very good writer. But he would try to sing his own material, and that would kill it," laughed Cosby. "He could not sing a lick!"

Gordy lost his invaluable right-hand man in early 1967. Mickey Stevenson received a lucrative offer from MGM Records to head their West Coast division. He would soon settle in at their Venture subsidiary, purveying soul wax that frequently sounded very Motownish by the Ballads, Vernon Garrett, Madlyn Quebec, and Calvin Arnold with production as often as not performed by his old pal Clarence Paul, who exited Motown in 1968. Stevenson's wife, Kim Weston, dutifully made the move to MGM, too, but not before teaming with Gaye for one of the most dynamic duets in Motown history: "It Takes Two" was a solid hit for the pair in early '67. Before year's end, Gaye paired off with another lovely duet partner, Tammi Terrell, and embarked on an amazing run of smashes. Their "Ain't No Mountain High Enough," "Your Precious Love," and "If I Could Build My Whole World Around You" all hit big before the end of the year.

Eddie Holland replaced Stevenson as A&R boss, and his brother Brian supplanted a vacationing Billie Jean Brown as Quality Control head. Along with their partner Lamont Dozier, they kept cranking out smashes for much of 1967: "Love Is Here And Now You're Gone," "The Happening," and "Reflections" for Diana Ross and her girls, the baroque-sounding

"Bernadette" and "7 Rooms Of Gloom" for the Tops, and "Jimmy Mack" for Martha & the Vandellas (a number that had inexplicably languished in the vaults for a couple of years).

The Tempts remained red-hot in '67 with "All I Need" and "You're My Everything," and Wonder proved the previous year was no fluke as he rode the crest of "I Was Made To Love Her" and "I'm Wondering." Smokey gave the Marvelettes a major seller ("The Hunter Gets Captured By The Game") and kept his Miracles sky-high on the charts with "The Love I Saw In You Is Just A Mirage" and "I Second That Emotion." Producer Norman Whitfield rebounded from having his ominous "I Heard It Through The Grapevine" by Marvin Gaye rejected for release by Gordy himself, revamping it into a rousing gospel-fired rocker by the recently acquired Gladys Knight & the Pips that paced the R&B hit parade and very nearly accomplished the same feat on the pop side. Like the Isleys, Knight and her Pips had established themselves as R&B luminaries before they arrived at Hitsville with "Every Beat Of My Heart" and "Letter Full Of Tears."

Still, dark days were nigh. Convinced they deserved a bigger piece of the pie, Holland-Dozier-Holland engaged in a work slowdown that escalated into a strike. Suddenly the Supremes, Martha & the Vandellas, and Four Tops were minus their principal source of top-flight material. Gordy sued his dream team for $4 million, citing breach of contract; H-D-H fired back a few months later for $22 million in damages, and when the legal smoke cleared, they were gone for good. They formed their own labels, Invictus and Hot Wax, in 1969, and went head-to-head with Motown, racking up hits by the Honey Cone, 100 Proof Aged in Soul, Freda Payne, Laura Lee, Chairmen of the Board, and the Glass House.[12] Their posts were quickly filled: Billie Jean returned to her Quality Control command center, while new A&R head Ralph Seltzer's Motown specialties had previously been in the legal and administrative arenas.

Some of the company's stars may have been bummed over the loss of H-D-H, but their departure allowed the rest of the writers and producers access to the Supremes and other artists who had been serviced exclusively by the trio—in the long run making the company stronger. "They no longer had their particular artists exclusively," said Bristol. Noted McDougal, "Norman Whitfield and Ivy Jo Hunter and a lot of the other writers, they weren't upset that they left."

Their defection was by no means the only chink in the familial armor. Florence Ballard was ousted from the Supremes that spring after tensions mounted between her and Ross, who was by then romantically entwined with Gordy and well on her way toward fulfilling his dream of becoming a mainstream superstar. Cindy Birdsong left Patti LaBelle & the Blue Belles to replace her. Birdsong inadvertently played a huge role in the label's future by introducing Gordy to her pal Suzanne de Passe, who would serve as his creative assistant and later head of the company's Creative Division.

A suitable hit vehicle was required pronto for the Supremes to prove that Motown wouldn't collapse into ruins without H-D-H. A consortium of up-and-coming composers—Frank Wilson, British lyricist Pam Sawyer, R. Dean Taylor, and Deke Richards—was convened at Detroit's Pontchartrain Hotel for a weekend of concentrated brainstorming, and the end result was the lyrically daring and socially conscious "Love Child," a much-needed No. 1 pop hit for Ross and her group near the end of '68.

Norman Whitfield was poised to take over as the most influential and innovative producer at Motown. His streak of hits with the Tempts seemed infinite. The majestic "I Wish It Would Rain" began 1968 for the group on a traditional note, but by year's end, the group's entire attack had been overhauled with an infusion of Sly Stone/George Clinton-influenced funk and a dollop of rock guitar from house band newcomer Dennis Coffey. The abstract lyrics on "Cloud Nine"—like nearly all his productions at the time, a collaboration between Norman and Barrett Strong—were misinterpreted in conservative quarters as being pro-drug.

"It was during that time when it was psychedelic," said Strong. "Most people misconstrued what you were saying during those times. That was that era that everybody was flyin' high, you know?" Those controversial lyrics were fierily roared by a new member of the quintet, Dennis Edwards, who replaced an unhappy David Ruffin. "'Cloud Nine' was like a natural high," agreed Edwards in 1984. "It's like just getting out of the dumps, man, getting your life together. It didn't mean anything about dope." The controversy didn't stop Grammy voters from making "Cloud Nine" Motown's first award winner. The honor was long overdue.

David Ruffin was still cranking out hits after leaving the Temptations for a solo career. "Everything's Coming Up Love" appeared on the charts in 1976.

Norman also co-wrote and produced another rip-roaring hybrid of secular and sanctified influences for Knight and her guys. "The End Of Our Road" gave them a huge follow-up to "Grapevine," which just happened to be the label's biggest seller that year once Gaye's pre-Gladys rendition finally emerged as an album track. So many deejays picked up on it that his version was belatedly issued as a single, catapulting straight to the top of the pop charts in December of '68 for seven weeks. Marvin and Tammi remained a hot-selling entity too, scoring with Ashford & Simpson's uplifting "Ain't Nothing Like The Real Thing" and "You're All I Need To Get By." Terrell was suffering the ravages of a brain tumor, though she fought valiantly through a series of operations. Her health steadily worsened and she passed away in 1970.

The Four Tops were scrambling in the wake of H-D-H's defection, enjoying success with two leftovers from their *Reach Out* album of the year before (covers of the Left Banke's "Walk Away Renee" and Tim Hardin's "If I Were A Carpenter"). Fortunately, Robinson was still lethal with a pen, coming up with the Miracles' "If You Can Want." Wonder stayed on his roll with "Shoo-Be-Doo-Be-Doo-Da-Day" and "For Once In My Life," and Shorty Long came up with the feel-good novelty "Here Comes The Judge," a takeoff on the zany Sammy Davis, Jr. skit from *Rowan & Martin's Laugh-In* that proved to be the Alabama native's only trip to the pop Top Ten. Long died in a 1970 boating accident on the Detroit River.

As the tumultuous year came to a close, Motown's two supergroups—the Supremes and Temptations—teamed for a top-rated TV special, *TCB*, and an uplifting revival of the Philly soul classic "I'm Gonna Make You Love Me," with Eddie Kendricks' gossamer falsetto outsoaring Diana's gutsy co-lead. During the last week of the year, Motown could boast of having no less than five records on *Billboard's* pop Top Ten—

"...I've got to call him Mr. Gordy!"

proof positive that Gordy's goal of total pop domination had been achieved and then some.

Gordy had come a long way indeed, and he had a lot further to go. He was intrigued by the film and television industries in Hollywood, and the possibilities for some of his stars therein (especially a certain Miss Ross). To help make that happen, Gordy moved his family to L.A. in the fall of '68, and the seat of power began to shift west. Massive expansion back in Detroit precipitated the purchase of a 10-story office building at 2457 Woodward Avenue. Though Hitsville remained in constant use, many of the label's principals now had offices over on Woodward, eroding the all-for-one atmosphere that once defined the label's will to win.

"He kept the buildings we were in," said Cosby. "He just moved the administration down there. But it was so big. They never fixed it up, never like it was supposed to be. They were trying to discuss whether to tear it down or build a new building. It was never finalized. They had all kinds of drawn plans and this and that, a real Motown building. But it never materialized."

"It took the intimacy out, because it was like a big 10-story building," said Bradford. "We weren't all over each other. It became phased, and everybody had their own office. It became big business. It just wasn't the same. Then very shortly after that, slowly the move began to California. I don't know if it was the move downtown, or it was just the timing. Maybe that era had ran its course."

"It got so big. I mean, so big," continued Cosby. "It was making so much money—$30, $40 million a year. And we started out making nothing. You can imagine. He was serving hot dogs for lunch free, and then next thing I know, God almighty. Millions and millions of dollars. Everybody was making money. So the good feeling really left.

"Before that time, I could say, 'How you doing, Berry?' He'd say, 'Hi!' But after that, you've got to call him 'Mr. Gordy.' I knew things had changed. We were informed no longer will we call him Berry. Call him 'Mr. Gordy.' God almighty! Ridiculous. I've been knowing the man for 15 years. I've got to call him Mr. Gordy! That's what happened."

"By it being so much business, you kind of lose that kind of thing that you started out with," said the Temptations' Otis Williams. "Because at the beginning, it was a whole big melting pot of talent. And things started falling into place. I guess when hits started coming in the succession that they did, that started Berry to really make it more of a business. Which it was that at the beginning, but it really started taking on a business kind of a shake."

Though Bobby Taylor actually brought the Jackson 5 to Motown, the singer didn't receive credit for it at the time. Taylor and his Vancouvers, then touring on the strength of "Does Your Mama Know About Me," their brave '68 debut hit for Gordy, were headlining a Chicago card with the pint-sized pubescents from Gary, Indiana (McDougal first brought them to Taylor's attention). A knocked-out Taylor escorted the Jacksons to Hitsville and began producing them in a traditional R&B mode, but when Berry finally had a chance to listen to little Michael and his sibs, he immediately recognized an act that had no idiomatic limitations and dispatched them to the coast to work with a crew he dubbed the Corporation: Deke Richards, Fonce Mizell, Freddie Perren, and Gordy himself. Released in October of 1969, "I Want You Back" was the J5's first Motown platter and first pop chart topper, closely followed by the equally seismic "ABC," "The Love You Save," and "I'll Be There." Motown had another superstar act on its hands, and Diana was officially anointed as their discoverer instead of Taylor.

Whitfield's reign as resident production genius continued apace in '69, with smashes from the Tempts ("Run Away Child, Running Wild" and "I Can't

Get Next To You"), Gaye ("Too Busy Thinking About My Baby" and "That's The Way Love Is"), and Gladys ("The Nitty Gritty," "Friendship Train"). Jr. Walker proved he could sing more than roadhouse R&B with the comparatively tender "What Does It Take (To Win Your Love)," supervised by the team of Harvey Fuqua and Johnny Bristol. The same pair was behind Edwin Starr's stomping "25 Miles." Wonder was smooth and sensuous on "My Cherie Amour" and Ron Miller's "Yester-Me, Yester-You, Yesterday," and Gaye summoned up ghosts of doo-wop past in a contemporary framework on "Baby, I'm For Real," his spine-chilling production on the Originals.

David Ruffin proved there was life after the Tempts as his first solo offering for Motown when the anguished "My Whole World Ended (The Moment You Left Me)" registered impressive sales. The Supremes were about to undergo similar upheaval with the impending exit of Ross. "Someday We'll Be Together," their Bristol-penned swan song with Diana in the lead, was likely her most soulful performance ever, holding down the top pop slot at the close of the year.

Creativity was in session around the clock. "Berry had two studios," said Cosby. "He told me he wanted both of the studios running 24 hours a day. That's when we started sounding more like a production line. More like Ford's plant. It was one of the things I had to see about doing was to make sure that both studios ran 24 hours a day. Something would be going on activity-wise. He didn't want 'em standing still for no minutes."

Having conquered the R&B and pop fields, Motown was ready to take the plunge into other musical arenas. In the fall of '69, the label began distributing Chisa Records, a jazz imprint headed by South Africa-born trumpeter Hugh Masekela and his business partner, Stewart Levine. The deal only lasted a couple of years, with L.A.-based Chisa issuing product on the Jazz Crusaders, soul-blues guitarist Arthur Adams, and Masekela with his band, the Union of South Africa.

More ambitious was Motown's plunge into rock (or "underground music," as a Hitsville press release dubbed it) with Rare Earth Records. Perhaps recognizing their lack of acumen in the field, Barney Ales, recently named executive vice president and general manager of Motown, announced a separate management team for the Rare Earth logo consisting of Joe Summers as label head (he'd been sales manager for Motown LP and tape sales) and Al DiNoble, formerly assistant director of national promotion for the parent label, as his assistant. Harry Balk, producer of Del Shannon's '61 smash "Runaway," became the Rare Earth product coordinator.

The logo was inaugurated with a gala affair held August 18, 1969 at the Roostertail in Detroit, but apart from the homegrown rock band of the same name whose marathon treatment of Smokey's "Get Ready" in 1970 and the anthemic "I Just Want To Celebrate" the next year made them a genuine rock force and longtime Motown songsmith R. Dean Taylor's easy-going '70 hit "Indiana Wants Me," little of Rare Earth's output made a dent in the rock consciousness.

Rochester, New York-based Rustix's debut album *Bedlam* squeaked onto the bottom rung of the pop LP charts for a couple of weeks in late '69 and the Messengers—a Milwaukee rock band that had recorded for Soul four years prior—managed a decent-selling single in late '71. But licensed-in sets by British blues-rockers the Pretty Things (whose *S.F. Sorrow* is now cited as a rock opera precedent) and the Dave Edmunds-fronted Love Sculpture did nothing sales-wise. Had the male half of Stoney &

Meatloaf stuck around longer, perhaps the label would have realized more of a payoff than one minor seller, "What You See Is What You Get," in the spring of '71. British chanteuse Kiki Dee became a star after leaving, the Easybeats had already had their day in the sun, and the Virgil Brothers, an Australian act, sank without trace.

Producers Nick Ashford and Valerie Simpson, whose uplifting collaborations had given Gaye and Terrell numerous hits prior to her tragic passing on March 16, 1970, were entrusted with providing Diana Ross with the right vehicles to properly launch her solo career. And they succeeded, coming up with "Reach Out And Touch (Somebody's Hand)" and a revival of "Ain't No Mountain High Enough" that topped the pop and R&B lists. The Supremes weren't doing badly at all without Ross. With Jean Terrell installed as their new lead singer, they scored in 1970 with "Up The Ladder To The Roof" and "Stoned Love."

Not only did Frank Wilson produce the Supremes' Diana-less triumphs, he created the placid "Still Water (Love)" with Smokey Robinson for the Four Tops and brought the veteran quartet out of their post-H-D-H doldrums in the process. The Miracles scored the biggest pop hit of their long and distinguished career with "The Tears Of A Clown," a three-year-old album track that began building momentum in England and then captured the top pop slot stateside in December of 1970.

Stevie Wonder was one of the song's co-writers, and he was growing up fast. He produced the Spinners' "It's A Shame" and his own "Signed, Sealed, Delivered I'm Yours," and he took label mate Syreeta Wright for his bride (the marriage would be a brief one). Autonomy became a major issue for Wonder in 1971, when he hit 21 and his contract expired. He took a sabbatical to investigate the brand-new Moog synthesizer and allow his lawyers to negotiate total artistic freedom for him at Motown. The deal worked out well for both sides, with Stevie ascending to an exalted place as one of the leading musical lights of the 1970s and beyond.

The Tempts continued to benefit from Whitfield's ongoing funk fascination, visiting a "Psychedelic Shack" and insisting the world was a "Ball Of Confusion" over roiling, rock-infused backing tracks. Norman gave musical voice to an entire generation within the deeply divided populace with "War." Co-written by Whitfield and Strong, the angry protest was first out by the Tempts as an album track, but once Edwin Starr wrapped his fiery pipes around it, the song was his. Along the same socially conscious lines, Gordy inaugurated a new spoken word subsidiary, Black Forum, in the autumn of 1970 with a posthumous speech by Dr. Martin Luther King on *Why I Oppose the War in Vietnam*. He won a Grammy for it a few months later.

Norman assembled his own one-man, two-woman group, the Undisputed Truth, to disseminate more of his funk-drenched treatises, and in 1971 they made the grade and then some with the darkly paranoid "Smiling Faces Sometimes," another standout he'd already cut on the Temptations. Ironically, the Tempts' top seller that year was a welcome return to their immaculately polished ballad approach, "Just My Imagination (Running Away With Me)." It paced both charts and provided Kendricks with an indelible sendoff as he left to launch a solo career that peaked in '73 with the disco-friendly "Keep On Truckin'" and "Boogie Down."

Haunted by deep-seated emotional and artistic turmoil, Gaye took matters into his own hands as the new decade dawned, eschewing the Motown production approach and cloistering himself away to create a self-contained and deeply personal masterpiece that Gordy initially deemed uncommercial and refused to release. Stubborn as ever, Gaye wouldn't even consider any alternate studio activity, and his instincts were on the money. *What's Going On* was a monster seller, housing three No. 1 R&B hits that elevated him to an entirely new strata.

Since there was so much Motown activity in L.A., it was only natural to open up a subsidiary out there. Mowest Records was established with an early roster that included ex-Spinners lead G.C. Cameron (pursuing a solo career because his Motown contract didn't expire at the same time as his groupmates' did), Bobby Taylor, Frankie Valli & the Four Seasons (whose brief stay was as hitless as their earlier output for Vee-Jay and Philips was hit-filled), the Devastating Affair (who would serve as Diana's backing vocal group and opening act), L.A. deejay Tom Clay (his spoken word piece "What The World Needs Now Is Love/Abraham, Martin And John" gave Mowest its first trip to the pop Top Ten in the summer of '71), and Leland, Mississippi-born Thelma Houston, whose first Mowest offering that fall was Berry's "I Want To Go Back There Again." Houston, who had previously recorded the Jimmy Webb-helmed *Sunshower* LP for Dunhill, would finally perch at the top of the charts for Tamla in '76 with her disco anthem "Don't Leave Me This Way."

Marvin Gaye: Motown's most enigmatic star (Photo courtesy of David Alston's Mahogany Archives).

The Commodores—a young self-contained unit formed at Alabama's Tuskegee Institute—made their initial appearances on Mowest before moving over to the parent label with "Machine Gun."

The cherubic appeal of the Jacksons endured as they proved they could credibly tackle more serious fare with "Never Can Say Goodbye" as well as the effervescent "Mama's Pearl," and Michael spun off a simultaneous solo streak with "Got To Be There." Knight and her Pips thrived, working with Whitfield protege Clay McMurray on "If I Were Your Woman" and Bristol on "I Don't Want To Do Wrong" and enjoying major sellers in both cases.

In June of 1972, the ominous rumors that had been swirling around Hitsville and the comparatively sterile edifice on Woodward Avenue for some time came true. **The label was abandoning Detroit for glitzier L.A.,** and a great many musicians, producers, and writers would be left behind in the transition. Much of the action had actually been transpiring there, anyway.

"I was still going to Detroit, but there was nothing happening," said McDougal. "I had to go to Los Angeles to talk to everybody or deal with anything." The little studio on Grand Boulevard that had spawned so many worldwide smashes would remain operational for a while—that's where the Tempts, who resisted moving to L.A. until 1974, cut the Grammy-winning "Papa Was A Rollin' Stone" under Whitfield's astute direction. The city's economy suffered upon Motown's withdrawal and so did the front-office personnel, staff musicians and singers, and other creative mainstays who weren't invited to make the trip west. There were plenty of them.

"I didn't have a job, so I didn't know what to do," said Louvain Demps of the Andantes, who were unceremoniously jettisoned after contributing sweet harmonies to thousands of classic Motown recordings. "I know when I first came there, Berry gave everybody this talk. And I was in on that talk. And I listened. And I didn't forget what he was talking about. He was always gonna be there for us. And I really felt really bad. I really felt bad. Because when I really did try to get to him, **he was unreachable.**

"Maybe it wasn't intentional. Maybe it was just like survival, or whatever. But a lot of people were really depending on him, and depending on his word."

Some of the Funk Brothers reluctantly migrated west, but their signature sound didn't weather the trip intact. "The thing is, when you mix Joe Sample on a date with Jack Ashford and James Jamerson, and then bring in Paulinho Da Costa to play congas and not Eddie 'Bongo,' then you're not getting the Motown sound," said Ashford. "So our sound was neutralized, because David T. Walker was there instead of Robert White. Everything got neutralized, and we started sounding like an L.A. group."

Unsuspecting record buyers probably never noticed the difference as the hits kept right on coming throughout the '70s, thanks to Marvin, Stevie, Diana, the Tempts, and the Commodores. Motown was entrenched as the world's largest independent record company, and a black-owned one at that. Gordy realized his dream of entering the film business as executive producer of *Lady Sings the Blues*, the acclaimed 1972 Billie Holiday bio that made Ross a bankable movie star. But many of the artists that had thrived at Motown during the 1960s moved on to other labels or simply faded away.

Since 1985, Esther Gordy Edwards has operated the Motown Historical Museum inside the meticulously restored Hitsville building and its next-door neighbor, offering tours of the legendary edifice that produced so many seminal performances. Though there have been rumors that the hulking downtown office building on Woodward would soon be utilized as a larger museum facility, it remained abandoned, boarded up and forlorn as 2000 came to a close, its menacing, wind-swept doorways serving as shelter for the homeless instead of a proud salute to its former occupant's vast corporate might.

British producer Ian Levine unsuccessfully tried to cast himself as the reincarnation of Berry Gordy by forming Nightmare Records in 1986 and snapping up nearly every available artist associated with Motown's golden years, from Mary Wilson, Mary Wells, and Marv Johnson to Carolyn Crawford, the Velvelettes, and Sammy Ward. Although Levine's marathon Detroit sessions brought a welcome blast of local publicity to singers who had been all but forgotten by then, a lack of stateside distribution undermined Levine's Motor City label and turned more than a few comeback dreams into real nightmares. Levine-helmed singles by Johnny Bristol and Frances Nero did manage to nick the British charts.

With the move to L.A., Motown's golden years effectively ended. Over the past three decades, the label's 1960s rise has become ingrained as part of our nation's folklore, hailed as an example of African-American empowerment at its most inspiring. Most of the label's top acts have been enshrined in the Rock and Roll Hall of Fame, and movies have been made reenacting the careers of the Temptations and Jackson 5. Also filmed was the considerably less inspiring saga of ex-Motown recording engineer Lawrence T. Horn, who co-produced Jr. Walker & the All Stars' "Shotgun." In 1996, long after leaving Motown, Horn was convicted of hiring a hit man three years earlier to murder his ex-wife, their severely retarded quadriplegic son, and the son's nurse for insurance money from the 8-year-old boy's estate.[13]

When all was said and done, Berry Gordy's once-humble enterprise, founded on 800 bucks and a unifying vision, accomplished something no other record label had ever done, or likely will again. Motown had become a musical genre unto itself.

■ ■ ■ ◆ ■ ■ ■

[1] Much of the information on Berry Gordy's early years and the beginnings of Rayber and Motown was culled from two essential autobiographies: Berry Gordy, *To Be Loved* (New York: Warner Books, Inc., 1994), and Raynoma Gordy Singleton with Bryan Brown and Mim Eichler, *Berry, Me, and Motown* (Chicago, Contemporary Books, Inc., 1990).

[2] Robert Dennis, "Our Motown Recording Heritage (Part 2)," <www.recordingeq.com/motown2.html>.

[3] Don Waller, *The Motown Story* (New York: Charles Scribner's Sons, 1985), p. 59-64.

[4] Dates obtained from a display at the Motown Museum.

[5] Raynoma Gordy Singleton with Bryan Brown and Mim Eichler, *Berry, Me, and Motown* (Chicago, Contemporary Books, Inc., 1990), p. 153-155.

[6] Berry Gordy, *To Be Loved* (New York: Warner Books Inc., 1994), p. 269-270.

[7] Ibid, p. 270-271.

[8] Mary Wilson with Patricia Romanowski and Ahrgus Juilliard, *Dreamgirl: My Life as a Supreme* (New York: St. Martin's Press, 1986), p. 86-87.

[9] Nelson George, *Where Did Our Love Go? The Rise & Fall of the Motown Sound* (New York: St. Martin's Press, 1985), p. 29.

[10] David Mills, Larry Alexander, Thomas Stanley and Aris Wilson, *George Clinton and P-Funk–An Oral History* (New York: Avon Books, 1998), p. 12-13.

[11] Berry Gordy, *To Be Loved* (New York: Warner Books Inc., 1994), p. 226-227.

[12] Ibid, p. 261-263.

[13] Karl Vick, "Horn Convicted for Three Murders," *Washington Post*, May 4, 1996.

(Clockwise from top left) Lawrence Payton, Renaldo Benson, Abdul Fakir and Levi Stubbs—The Four Tops—remained intact as a hit-making group for more than four decades before Payton's death in 1997 (Photo courtesty of David Alston's Mahogany Archives).

A DOZEN MOTOWN SUPER STARS AND ONE TERRIFIC HOUSE BAND

THE FOUR TOPS

(Photo courtesy of David Alston's Mahogany Archives).

Forty-three years is a staggering span for any marriage to endure, let alone a musical institution involving twice that many members forced to navigate a stormy sea of shifting trends. But that's how long the Four Tops remained a bonded quartet, undergoing not a single personnel change. If not for the June 20, 1997 passing of Lawrence Payton, that would still be the case now.

"...He could always wow the audience..."

The Tops were products of Detroit's North End. Lead Levi Stubbs (born June 6, 1936) and first tenor Abdul "Duke" Fakir (born December 26, 1935) sang together in a group while attending Pershing High School. Tenor Payton (born March 2, 1938), who would double as the Tops' harmony arranger, and baritone Renaldo "Obie" Benson (born June 14, 1936) attended Northern High. A graduation soiree brought the two factions together in their teens.

"We were just getting ready to finish high school," said Fakir in a 1980 interview. "In that time of our lives in Detroit, singing in groups, that was the thing to do, as well as playing sports. So everybody was singing in different groups at that particular time. We were at a party, and the four of us were just kind of like together. And they wanted to hear some singing. So knowing everybody, we didn't feel like it was a big thing. We just got together and sang a tune or two. I think it was 'Money Honey,' or something like that. It sounded pretty good the way we did it.

"So we got the idea, we said, 'Look—why don't we tomorrow call a rehearsal, and see if we can sing a couple of other tunes?' We rehearsed, and we found out we had a kind of a unique sound, we thought. We said, 'Hey, let's form this group, and let's do our own thing. Let's go around and try to get some of this amateur money'—which was $25, and things like that. And of course, you can always pick up a girl like that!

"During these dances, an agent had come around. He had heard that we were really good singers, and he'd seen us at an amateur show. He said he could book us as soon as we got out of school. He started booking us right around Detroit. And that's how we got started."

Dubbing themselves the Four Aims, the young group developed an advanced sense of jazz-steeped harmony. Payton's cousin, Roquel "Billy" Davis, who sometimes sang with the group as a fifth Aim and would soon team with Berry Gordy as his writing partner on a series of Jackie Wilson hits, shipped a demo tape of the group to Chess Records. A reply came in the form of a bus ticket to Chicago. It turned out the label was more interested in Davis' compositional skills than acquiring the Aims' services, but his persistence paid off. Not only did he win a Chess contract for his pals, he wrote hits that year for Chess' two top vocal groups. "See Saw" cracked the R&B Top Ten for the Moonglows, while "A Kiss From Your Lips" just missed the same lofty status for the Flamingos.

Something had to be done about the group's name, however. "We started out as the Four Aims, and we kept that name for a couple of years," said Fakir. "When we came to Chicago to record for Chess, we had to change that name because of the Ames Brothers, who were quite popular at that particular time. Since our theme was aiming for the top—that's why we picked the name the Aims—we just switched it around and used the Tops."

The Chess commitment to the newly christened Tops tallied up to one swinging 1956 single, "Could It Be You" and its flip "Kiss Me Baby." That didn't stop the Tops from working. During a 1959 Las Vegas lounge stint at the Thunderbird, veteran crooner Billy Eckstine caught their act and found their harmonies so enticing that he hired them for his show. The debonair Mr. B was one of Stubbs' favorite entertainers, along with Jackie Wilson and Frank Sinatra. Even then, Levi's voice possessed scintillating power.

"He's definitely always been the main lead," said Fakir. "Even as a kid at 10, 11, and 12, he was singing around at a place in Detroit called the Paradise Theater, where the big bands would come around. People like Dizzy Gillespie's big band, Lucky Millinder. He'd always come in as the little young singer. He could always wow the audience. I think he was one of those guys just born with that type of voice and that type of thing. He's always had that lead voice and that lead atmosphere."

The Tops received scattered studio opportunities. In 1960, Columbia issued the rocking Stubbs original "Ain't That Love" and wasted no time reissuing it five years later during the Tops' Motown ascendancy, notching a tiny hit. The group twisted its Tin Pan Alley tendencies into a tasty rock-and-roll version of "Pennies From Heaven" for Riverside in 1962.

Gordy signed the Tops in '63. "We'd known him for quite a few years prior to us coming to Motown," said Fakir. "Berry Gordy used to write tunes for Jackie Wilson with Roquel Davis, who is Lawrence's cousin. So we were in close contact with him during the time that they were writing. And when he started this company, he told us he was starting it, and he said anytime we wanted to come to the company, he'd love to have us. In fact, he wanted us premierly. We were interested in other companies like Columbia and Riverside and stuff, but it never worked. So after we tried all these different companies and nothing happened, we took him up on his word and went back to Detroit. We talked to him, and he was more than glad to have us."

Instead of plugging them into the label's hit-making machinery, Gordy and A&R boss Mickey Stevenson acquiesced to the Tops' wishes to cut a jazz album. Throughout 1963, under the supervision of Stevenson and saxist Hank Cosby, the quartet ladled four-part harmonies over Rodgers & Hart's "This Can't Be Love," George & Ira Gershwin's "Fascinating Rhythm," and even a Count Basie medley of "Every Day I Have The Blues" and "Goin' To Chicago Blues" in front of a storming big band. Motown assigned the results a catalog number on its new Workshop Jazz logo, but *Breaking Through* was scrapped at the 11th hour.

The Four Tops would instead break through as soul singers, benefiting from the inestimable creativity of songwriters Brian and Eddie Holland and Lamont Dozier. The first Tops/H-D-H collaboration for Motown, a profoundly stirring "Baby I Need Your Loving" produced by Brian and Lamont, established the group as it just missed the pop Top Ten during the late summer of 1964.

FILLMORE AUDITORIUM
1805 Geary St. San Francisco
ONE NITE ONLY
Tuesday, Sept. 27th
STARTS AT 9:00 P.M.
THE FOUR TOPS
"Reach Out I'll Be There"
"Baby I Need Your Loving"
"Ask The Lonely"
WITH
Johnny Tabot and De Thangs
DANCE CONCERT SHOW

The Four Tops headlined at the Fillmore in the fall of 1966 (Photo courtesy of Hank Thompson).

"Really what happened, Holland-Dozier-Holland teamed themselves with us," said Fakir. "When we first signed, they started leaning toward us. We kind of hung out for a year, and they got to know us, and we got to be really close. They more or less studied us. They said, 'Man, when we write a tune for you, it's gonna be a monster!' And we got to be very, very close. They started writing, and that was the first tune they wrote. It seemed like the closer we got, the more they wrote. The more they wrote, the more we sold."

As if strings, horns, and the Tops' harmonies weren't a lush enough backdrop for Stubbs to roar over like a hungry lion, H-D-H added the pristine voices of the Andantes, Motown's resident female backing group (Marlene Barrow, Jackie Hicks, and Louvain Demps). Their lovely, high-end contributions would distinguish the group's subsequent H-D-H-generated hits, blending with the Tops to form something of a heavenly choir.

"They were the ones that were the easiest to sing with, 'cause they were musicians," said Hicks. "They were readers. They could read music, and they could write music and all." Levi's piercing tenor sported strong overtones of longing even on carefree lyrics; on sad laments, it was practically overwhelming in its unabridged anguish. Considering that younger brother Joe Stubbs provided a plaintive lead vocal on "You're So Fine," the Falcons' '59 landmark for the local Flick logo, it's a safe bet that soul was never in short supply around the Stubbs household.

H-D-H was also responsible for the Tops' followup hit, the moving "Without The One You Love (Life's Not Worth While)," before year's end. Stevenson stepped up in to supervise the quartet's first smash of 1965, co-writing a breath-taking "Ask The Lonely" with Ivy Jo Hunter. The Tops' eponymous debut LP, released in late '64, contained their first three hits as well as Mickey's "Sad Souvenirs," Marv Johnson's "Left With A Broken Heart," and the H-D-H gems "Your Love Is Amazing," "Where Did You Go," "Love Has Gone," and "Call On Me"—the latter sporting Payton's pleasing tenor. After that first album, H-D-H pretty much assumed responsibility altogether for the Four Tops' output. One of their most celebrated collaborations was conceived during an evening of revelry.

The Four Tops took the smooth Frank Wilson-Smokey Robinson penned "Still Water (Love)" release to the charts in 1970.

"We were out one night," said Duke. "We were celebrating, me and Lamont Dozier and a couple of guys. We were kind of loaded, drinking some beers or what have you. And this tune came to his head, and he said, 'Come on, Duke, let's go home.' I took him home. He started bangin' on the piano. He come up with this tune. And the next day, the Holland brothers went in and cut the track, and called us that evening and said, 'Man, we got another smash!' We went in there and did it, and it shot right off. It came out two weeks later. Over the weekend, it was a national smash."

That classic was "I Can't Help Myself," customarily subtitled "Sugar Pie, Honey Bunch." Powered by a relentless James Jamerson bass line, the anthem vaulted to the top of the pop and R&B charts during the spring and summer of 1965. Less than three months later, the group came right back with another H-D-H piledriver, "It's The Same Old Song," nearly equaling their monumental previous hit in the process. The tune's title was apropos: Set in the same key as "I Can't Help Myself," its chord changes and tempo were nearly identical.

"That was another quickie," said Fakir. "That came right after 'I Can't Help Myself.' 'I Can't Help Myself' moved up the charts so well, they just turned that song around musically a little bit and added a little lyrics to it. It went right off the bat."

With Motown's hit-making machinery in high gear, the Tops nailed yet another H-D-H-generated smash before 1965 was through. "Something About You" rode a crackling shuffle rhythm, Levi emoting over punchy horns and low-end guitar. Four huge sellers in one year brought the group plenty of national TV exposure: *Shindig!*, *Hullabaloo*, *Where the Action Is*, and in January of 1966, Ed Sullivan invited them on his Sunday evening extravaganza. Though they weren't the synchronized equal of the Temptations in the choreography department (who was?), the Tops' signature move—swaying from the waist, arms upstretched and palms raised— was no less distinctive in its own way than the Temptation Walk.

Along with their last three hits of '65, the functionally titled *Four Tops Second Album*, released that November, contained a slew of H-D-H-penned standouts: The hard-charging "Helpless" (label mate Kim Weston hit the following spring with a very similar rendition) and "Since You've Been Gone," a cheery "I Like Everything About You," the heart-melting "Stay In My Lonely Arms," a revival of Martha & the Vandellas' '63 'B' side "Darling, I Hum Our Song," and the Payton-led "Love Feels Like Fire."

The Four Tops had a No. 1 hit with "Reach Out and I'll be There" in 1966. The song was included on the "Reach Out" LP a year later. The album also featured several cover tunes, including two by The Monkees.

1966 was just as successful for the Tops. First out of the box as winter began to fade was the H-D-H-penned smash "Shake Me, Wake Me (When It's Over)," followed three months later by "Loving You Is Sweeter Than Ever." Produced by the usual team of Dozier and Brian Holland, the latter joyous ode was the work of Hunter and a fast-maturing Stevie Wonder. Before summer was over, Motown unleashed another Four Tops masterpiece, the H-D-H pop chart-topper "Reach Out, I'll Be There."

"It was the biggest, no doubt about it," said Fakir. "It was a big, big world hit. At first when we heard it, we wasn't sure, 'cause it had such a different little tune to it. Nobody was predicting then it was gonna be No. 1. In fact, right after we cut it, Berry called us into the office and said, 'Well, it looks like we really got you all more than on your way now. With this record, I can see you going to No. 1 everywhere. We're gonna really start promoting you,' and doing all the big things and so forth and so on.

"And I was looking at him like, 'Yeah, okay, sure. Right. Great. I understand.' You know, that type of feeling? But it jumped right out of the chute all across the world." Levi delivered the song's reassuring message of eternal support as though his hair was on fire over an extremely ambitious arrangement incorporating Far Eastern musical influences. Similarly advanced were their next follow-ups: The spectacular "Standing In The Shadows Of Love" (spanning late '66 and early '67 at the uppermost reaches of the pop and R&B lists) and the chilling "Bernadette," its title inspired by a female friend of Dozier's.

"Something about 'Bernadette,' it makes me think of the church," said the Andantes' Demps, whose soprano peals forth just before the song's dramatic break. "I grew up in the Catholic church, and we had Gregorian chants. It kind of reminds me of that. That's why I love that one so much." Louvain is glad to testify to the quartet's class. "The people that were really the nicest to us were the Four Tops," she said. "Every time they had a hit, we got a little bonus."

The Tops' album catalog grew exponentially as 1966 progressed. That August, *Four Tops On Top* hit the streets: Its 'A' side consisted of two recent hits, three more H-D-H efforts in the same vein ("Until You Love Someone," "There's No Love Left," and the upbeat "I Got A Feeling"), and Eddie Holland's "Brenda," which its writer cut himself in '63. The other side must have shocked new fans. The quartet brought a sophisticated harmonic approach to a breakneck arrangement of Cole Porter's "In The Still Of The Night," got jazzy on "Bluesette," and caressed The Beatles' "Michelle." Smokey's "Then" sounded out of place in such highbrow company.

The Four Tops scored a Top 10 hit in 1967 with "Bernadette."

Only three months later, *Four Tops Live!*—with Funk Brothers keyboardist Earl Van Dyke leading their band at one of Detroit's top nightspots, the Upper Deck of the Roostertail—spotlighted the quartet performing in front of an appreciative crowd that included Marvin Gaye, the Supremes, and the Everly Brothers. Gordy always sought mainstream acceptance for his headliners by channeling them into albums of standards aimed primarily at an older generation. The Tops leaned strongly in that direction, anyway, so *Four Tops On Broadway*—bearing a cover photo of the red-jacketed quartet marveling at the bright lights of Times Square—was a breeze. Cut in Los Angeles by producer Frank Wilson, it was packed with Great White Way fare, with Payton sketching out the complex vocal arrangements. "Nice 'N' Easy," nearly 4 years old, was rescued from *Breaking Through* oblivion.

"That was their forte, so I was basically taking them back home," said Wilson. "Hello Broadway," the set's lead track, was co-written by Ron Miller. Another of his contributions to the album, "For Once In My Life," would prove a massive hit for Stevie Wonder in 1968.

The Tops didn't confine their studio activities to Broadway ditties during '67. Throbbing with dread over a racing minor key-dominated arrangement, "7 Rooms Of

"They were the ones that bridged the gap."

Gloom" was a hit that summer. Its flip, the less frantic but still up-tempo "I'll Turn To Stone," also cracked the charts. Both were H-D-H works—the latter brought on board Canadian R. Dean Taylor, then recording for Motown's V.I.P. subsidiary—though the Tops' *Reach Out* album that year was a bit light in that regard despite the "Produced by Holland & Dozier" tag on its cover.

Nevertheless, *Reach Out* ranks as one of the Tops' hottest-selling Motown LPs, dominated by their renditions of material from outside the Hitsville fraternity along with a healthy sampling of hits. The Monkees' "I'm A Believer" elicited a particularly intense performance from Stubbs (more than another Pre-Fab Four cover, "Last Train To Clarksville"), and their treatments of the Left Banke's pop hit "Walk Away Renee" and Tim Hardin's haunting "If I Were A Carpenter" packed enough of a punch that Motown issued them as hit singles in '68. Motown's writers weren't entirely shut out: Smokey contributed a galloping "Wonderful Baby," and Stevie, Clarence Paul, and Morris Broadnax combined to pen an enchanting "What Else Is There To Do (But Think About You)."

The Four Tops released more than 40 albums, including this British compilation.

"You Keep Running Away," another H-D-H pleader, ended 1967 on a high-selling note, but turbulence loomed dead ahead. Eddie Holland, by then Gordy's head of A&R, his brother Brian, in charge of Quality Control, and Dozier basically went on strike in search of a more lucrative agreement covering their writing and producing skills. They left in 1968 when they couldn't renegotiate a mutually satisfying agreement with Gordy, the litigational repercussions resonating for years.

"We certainly missed 'em when they left Motown. Because they were like 90 percent of what was going on for the Four Tops. They just knew where we were musically, record-wise, for the general public," said Duke. "They were the ones that bridged the gap. They wrote the kind of music that reached everybody. It was happy music. It reached everybody. It was kind of like on the ence of that good R&B feeling lead-wise, but it had that good pop flavor running all through the music. So they really did a marvelous thing in bridging that gap."

A committee of Hunter, Pam Sawyer, and two others came up with "Yesterday's Dreams," a relatively minor hit by Tops standards in the summer of '68, while a leftover H-D-H track, "I'm In A Different World," did marginally better before year's close. Johnny Bristol's "What Is A Man" and the Norman Whitfield/Barrett Strong collaboration "Don't Let Him Take Your Love From Me" were the Tops' only minor pop chart entries in 1969.

British audiences had been into the Tops ever since "I Can't Help Myself" became the quartet's first 45 to chart overseas. During a Brian Epstein-promoted 1967 tour, the Tops sold out the 7,000-seat Royal Albert Hall, forcing the Beatles' mastermind to slate a second concert to accommodate the overflow. They were loyal, endorsing the four-part harmonies at the heart of "What Is A Man" and propelling it to hitdom when it couldn't crack the pop Top 40 stateside in the spring of '69. "That should have been a hit record, if they had pushed it," said Bristol.

Without H-D-H providing their usual sheaf of stellar material, the Tops' albums were less consistent. Issued in the fall of '68, *Yesterday's Dreams* contrasted the impressive "Remember When," "We've Got A Strong Love (On Our Side)," and the Nickolas Ashford/Valerie Simpson-penned "Can't Seem To Get You Out Of My Mind" with MOR-ish covers of the Association's "Never My Love," the Monkees' "Daydream Believer," and Bobby Hebb's "Sunny" (benefitting from a James Bond-ish guitar riff). Stubbs' fiery reading of Stevie Wonder's '66 hit "A Place In The Sun" was a highlight.

Four Tops Now!, the first of their two LPs in 1969, was also heavy on remakes. Ornate productions were becoming the norm in the pop field, and the Tops' renditions of the Beatles' "Eleanor Rigby" and Jimmy Webb's "MacArthur Park" mirrored the trend (the latter was a solid-selling 1971 single). But the hard-hitting Jobete copyrights "The Key" (the work of sightless ex-Chess house scribe Raynard Miner), "My Past Just Crossed My Future" (a collaboration between Miner and Motown mainstay Janie Bradford), "Don't Bring Back Memories" (written by Gordy's ex-wife Raynoma), and "Wish I Didn't Love You So" offset the familiar stuff.

Enter Frank Wilson, who returned to re-ignite their recording fortunes. It didn't happen overnight. Wilson produced *Soul Spin*, the other '69 Tops LP, and nothing from it saw light of day as a 45, though the brass might have missed the boat on "Look Out Your Window," the Smokey Robinson/Al Cleveland composition "Nothing," and a passionate "Stop The World."

The tide turned in the spring of 1970. Latching onto a melody written by U.S. Vice President Charles Dawes in 1912 (though it was crooner Tommy Edwards' mellow 1958 reading for MGM that caught Wilson's ear), the quartet's mellow revival of "It's All In The Game" restored it to the R&B Top Ten and proved an impressive pop seller.

"It was one of my favorite songs growing up as a kid. I loved that song!" said Wilson. "Our desire was to capture that melody, and maybe add just a little bit more flavor to it." Four months later, the flowing "Still Water (Love)," a collaboration by Frank and Smokey, was even bigger. Wilson was inspired by an unlikely source. "I liked a lot of the rock bands. One of my favorites was Iron Butterfly," he said. "And I got an idea regarding doing a concept album from Iron Butterfly's 'In-A-Gadda-Da-Vida.' So as I began to work on the idea of a concept album, I came up with that melody, which is really a bass piano kind of a melody. It just kind of clicked.

"I had cut the track, and I had cut some of the background with the Four Tops. And Smokey came through. He had been out on the road. He came by the house, and he said, 'What are you working on?' So I played it, I sang it to him, and he loved it. Said, 'Man, I love it! Let me do the lyrics on that!' I hadn't done any lyrics, except for the chorus. So I said, 'Great!' So I made him a copy, he took it home. About two days later, he came back by the house and sang it."

With Wilson's help, the Tops were successfully staying abreast of the trends, slipping a taste of psychedelic guitar into a remake of the Supremes' "Reflections" on the *Still Waters Run Deep* LP. However, it was a mite unsettling to hear these stalwart sons of the Motor City crooning "L.A. (My Town)," complete with overdubbed traffic noises, on the same album. Nilsson's "Everybody's Talkin'" also received the cover treatment. "One of my favorite movies was *Midnight Cowboy*. That song used to just play in my mind all the time," said Wilson.

Wilson incorporated recurring sound effects into *Changing Times*, the Tops' next LP six months later. A ticking timepiece tied one track to the next, and a lengthy soundscape montage preceded the musical portion of the title item. David Van de Pitte and Jimmy Roach supplied dense arrangements for Burt Bacharach and Hal David's "Raindrops Keep Fallin' On My Head," as well as the in-house material. A chunk of "In These Changing Times" even turned up in the midst of a revival of the Beatles' "The Long And Winding Road."

Diana Ross had exited the Supremes by the time producers Nick Ashford and Valerie Simpson teamed them with the Four Tops in the studio to successfully revive Ike & Tina Turner's Phil Spector-helmed masterpiece "River Deep-Mountain High" in late 1970 (Levi and Jean Terrell were an electrifying duo), but the combination otherwise operated in much the same fashion as the earlier Supremes/Temptations combo had with Ross. Three albums by "The Magnificent Seven," as Motown dubbed the supergroup, produced only one more chart entry, the uplifting Clay McMurray production "You Gotta Have Love In Your Heart," in '71.

Wilson's hot hand brought the Tops two more hits that year—the Top Ten R&B smash "Just Seven Numbers (Can Straighten Out My Life)" and "In These Changing Times"—and in '72, "(It's The Way) Nature Planned It," writing the latter pair with Pam Sawyer. The back cover of the 1972 album *Nature Planned It* contained complete musicians' credits, singling out Jamerson on "bass (personified)."

Wilson wasn't the only gent overseeing the Tops' output. Though it seems an odd pairing, they teamed with Moody Blues producer Tony Clarke to wax "A Simple Game," a British hit in '71 written by the Blues' keyboardist, Mike Pinder, that barely made a stateside blip.

Frustrated by what they perceived as a lack of attention from their bosses, the Four Tops split with Motown before 1972 was through. Landing at ABC-Dunhill with writers Dennis Lambert and Brian Potter, they immediately struck paydirt with "Keeper Of The Castle" and went gold with the luxurious "Ain't No Woman (Like The One I've Got)" the next year. "Are You Man Enough," their contribution to the soundtrack of *Shaft in Africa*, likewise bolted up the charts. The hits kept coming for the rest of the decade, the Tops descending into disco via the insipid "Catfish" in 1976. In 1981, they triumphantly ascended to the peak of the R&B charts once more with the resplendent "When She Was My Girl," a major pop hit on the Casablanca logo that was at once contemporary and nostalgic. A dazzling hits medley with the Tempts on the TV special *Motown 25* anticipated their return home in 1983, the Tops scoring fresh Motown hits with "I Just Can't Walk Away" and "Sexy Ways" two years later.

Somehow the Four Tops have always avoided being stereotyped as an oldies act. "Maybe it's because we're always looking for something 'now' to happen," said Fakir. "I think we always kind of gear ourselves to be somewhat 'now.' Because we always mix our hits with things that are fairly current that we enjoy doing, that we try to put a little twist to it that would have the audience, say, **'Hey, those guys, they're pretty good!** They can sing this, they can sing that, but they still don't get away from what they are.' So I think it might add just another little flavor. Instead of being just straight oldies, they say, 'You know, these guys entertain!'"

The late James Jamerson, the virtuoso bass player that drove the Motown sound (Photo courtesy of Allan Slutsky).

THE FUNK BROTHERS AND THE MOTOWN HOUSE BAND

The Chit Chat Lounge in Detroit was rocking when the Funk Brothers were in the house. From left: Robert White, Dan Turner, Earl Van Dyke, Uriel Jones, James Jamerson and local DJ Martha Jean Steinberg (Photo courtesy of Allan Slutsky).

Defining the "Motown sound" in a few pat phrases can be a frustrating proposition. Gordy disingenuously referred to it as "a combination of rats, roaches, talent, guts and love."[1] Perhaps the most essential ingredient was its house band, whose members referred to themselves inside Hitsville's walls as the Funk Brothers.

Though not everything released on Motown during its golden years featured their grooves—Hal Davis, Marc Gordon, and Frank Wilson produced many mid-'60s sessions in L.A., and dates were held in New York and Chicago—they laid down the backing for the lion's share of the label's seminal smashes. Only those in the local know realized this at the time, since Gordy steadfastly kept the Funk Brothers' names under wraps until the early 1970s. Worldwide renown caught up with these Studio A stalwarts anyway, and now their names are spoken with the same reverence as Booker T. & the MG's, their Memphis counterparts at Stax.

Bassist extraordinaire James Jamerson was born January 29, 1936 in Charleston, South Carolina, and arrived in Detroit in 1954. He began playing the upright bass at Northwestern High School and was by all accounts a fast study. Jazz and R&B were his passions, and Jamerson began gigging locally with blues percussionist Washboard Willie during the late '50s. "He was playing the upright when he was playing with Washboard Willie & his Supersuds of Rhythm," said singer Gino Parks. "He had a Volkswagen. He used to tie that bass on top." Jamerson also worked with harpist Aaron "Little Sonny" Willis and singer J.J. Barnes.[2]

James Jamerson specialized in the upright bass during his early years as a musician. (Photo courtesy of Allen Slutsky).

His first Motown session of note produced the Miracles' "Way Over There," the upright still his axe of choice despite its cumbersome aspects when taking public transportation. "I used to ride the bus, and I rode the bus with one of the Funk Brothers when I first met him, Jamerson," said the Andantes' Louvain Demps. "He was with the upright bass." By 1961 he'd largely switched to the electric Fender with which he would revolutionize R&B bass.

Drummer William "Benny" Benjamin was Jamerson's esteemed partner in the Funk Brothers rhythm section and predated the bassist's ascent as Gordy's first-call sessioneer. Less is known about the flawless timekeeper whose self-professed nickname was "Papa Zita." He apparently hailed from Louisiana and played 1951-52 sessions behind leather-lunged blues shouter Wynonie Harris for King in Cincinnati that produced the uproariously raunchy "Lovin' Machine." Benny was part of Gordy's fledgling operation from the get-go.

"Berry already knew him. In fact, he was the first one. At the first rehearsal that I made, he was there," said pianist Joe Hunter, who had just left Hank Ballard & the Midnighters in the fall of '58 when Gordy invited him to join his studio band. "Berry came through there and told me what he was about and what he was looking for." That late '58 date produced Marv Johnson's first hit "Come To Me." Until he departed Hitsville in 1963, Hunter played piano on many early Motown classics—Marvin Gaye's "Pride And Joy," the Miracles' "You've Really Got A Hold On Me," the Temptations' "I Want A Love I Can See." Richard "Popcorn" Wylie was another Motown 88s ace prior to Earl Van Dyke's arrival.

Hunter credits Benjamin with coining the band's nickname. "Our drummer really named us that, Benny. He used to call us the Funk Brothers," he said. "We were the two that remained, and the rest of the group was formed behind us. Jamerson came a little later." Benny wasn't the only Motown timekeeper, but he was its primary one; Uriel Jones and Richard "Pistol" Allen also did time behind the kit.

Guitarist Robert White joined the ranks at the end of a tour with Harvey Fuqua's new Moonglows (who included a then-unknown Marvin Gaye). Born November 19, 1936, White would constitute one-third of the Funk Brothers' interlocking guitar triumvirate along with Eddie Willis, who got started as Marv Johnson's axeman while still in his teens, and Italian-American Joe Messina, who had been part of the house band for comic Soupy Sales' zany TV program. Famous for taking thousands of cream pies in the kisser and a '65 novelty hit, "The Mouse," Sales would briefly be a Motown artist in 1969, parodizing Jimmy Webb's "Muck-Arty Park."

Keyboardist Earl Van Dyke came into the Funk Brothers in 1962, following road stints with Lloyd Price and Aretha Franklin. Born July 8, 1930, the native Detroiter was fluent on piano by the age of 14 and, like several fellow Funk Brothers, considered jazz his first love. After a stint in New York—he played organ behind ex-Chuck Willis saxist Fred Jackson on a '62 Blue Note jazz album, *Hootin' 'N Tootin'*—he returned home to gradually assume the Studio A ivories load.

"Earl Van Dyke was very businesslike," said McDougal. "Most of the time when I saw Earl Van Dyke, he was either in the session, going to the session, or coming out of the session. They played on the road a lot, too. But he was always preparing the music, getting things ready to go on." Van Dyke usually played piano at Hitsville, leaving the Hammond organ in Johnny Griffith's hands (Griffith cut two '63 albums for the short-lived Workshop Jazz subsidiary, one co-starring singer Paula Greer). Again, nothing was etched in stone. The two would trade off when the urge arose. James Gittens also played keys until his 1965 death in an auto wreck.

Percussionist Jack Ashford's impeccable tambourine accents were integral to the impact of Motown's trademark beat. "I got to Motown through Marvin Gaye," said the Philadelphia native, who became a Funk Brother in 1962. "He saw me playing in Boston and offered me a job, or an interview, more or less, to join his band. I'd never heard of him before. Because all I was playing at that particular time was jazz. I played vibes with a group out of New York with Johnny 'Hammond' Smith. So that's how I got to Detroit.

"They had other percussionists there. They had a guy named Dave Hamilton that played vibes before I got there. Then I played vibes, and I would play an unusual instrument called 'jazz tambourine.' They had never heard anybody play tambourine in jazz before. After I got there, because of the fact that I was more or less multi-faceted, they didn't have anyone to play tambourine like me, so I was getting a lot of tambourine work. Then by me being able to play vibes also, it afforded me the opportunity to double. So it kind of moved Dave to the side a little bit, because I was able to do both."

Hamilton, born January 15, 1925 in Savannah, Georgia, moved to Detroit as a child and was well versed on guitar as well as vibes. His combo, the Noc-Tunes, cut "I Fell For You" and its flip "Lazy Daisy" for locally based Sensation Records in 1949. By 1954 he was working with a vocal group, the Peppers, with whom he cut the jumping "Rocking Chair Baby" for Checker. In addition to playing on a slew of Motown hits, Hamilton stretched out on his own '63 LP, *Blue Vibrations*, for Workshop Jazz and gave Gordy a little competition from 1964 on as owner of a succession of little labels: Temple, Topper, TCB, and Demoristic. He died in the mid-1990s.

Percussionist Jack Brokensha had the most exotic background, having been with the Australian Jazz

"The Funk Brothers were the band of life."

Quintet, and slightly predated Ashford's arrival. Vibes was one of his specialties. "They said, 'Look, bring Jack in, 'cause we can't get Brokensha to play tambourine," said Ashford. "So let Jack play the tambourine, and let the other Jack play the vibes and other percussion. And that way we'll be able to get the best of both worlds.' So that's how he was able to come in. 'Cause sometimes they would use a guy named Bob Pangborn, who played with the Detroit Symphony." To keep them straight, Brokensha was nicknamed "White Jack," while Ashford answered to "Black Jack." "I think it was Earl that did that," said Ashford.

Eddie "Bongo" Brown plugged his chosen instrument every time his handle was uttered. Born in 1932 in Clarksdale, Mississippi, Brown grew up in Memphis before moving to Detroit. He joined the Funk Brothers in 1962. "Eddie started out as Marvin's valet. He would pull his bongos out when Marvin hit the stage, and his sound was so effective—he was doubling when I first came to Detroit," said Ashford. "Then he just segued right on into the rhythm section. He was just that good. Eddie was just a phenomenal cat. He practiced all the time."

Gordy demanded assembly-line efficiency inside Studio A. "The sessions started at 10 o'clock, and we were over in the afternoon. Three-hour sessions most of the time. But they could call a session seven days a week," said Ashford. "We were on call. A lot of times, we did cut at night. Various times we would go in on somebody's whim, which we didn't mind. It was a gig. 'Cause we were only getting, most of the time, $10 a song, until everything got right. It was the only game in town.

"We did what we had to do. Sometimes in that three-hour date, we may have two or three producers, if they had one song or two songs. You could cut no more than four songs in a date. Sometimes we would cut three or four or five. 'Cause it was an in-house thing. I don't ever remember seeing a person from the union come in there. So we were just cutting whatever they needed done.

"We lived as one. By us playing in the clubs at night, and then playing in the day at the sessions, we would do things in the sessions on some of them charts that weren't written. Most of the stuff we did wasn't written. It's stuff that we tried that night before. Earl would say, 'Hey, do that song that we did, so-and-so.' Okay—bam! And it would fit so well into the songs. Motown wasn't a blues company. We didn't play blues. That's why the things that we did were so hip. The changes and the moves that we would make rhythmically **were so hip** simply because we'd tried 'em the night before." As Motown came to dominate the pop airwaves as well, the musicians' salaries climbed commensurately. Their name recognition did not.

"We knew we were hot. But the general consensus was that they would downplay our importance, so that we wouldn't get a representative to go in there and cut a deal," said Ashford. "Had we done that, it would be a different story now."

When the Funk Brothers weren't hard at work in Studio A, they were letting their collective hair down jamming at Millie's Chit Chat Lounge on 12th Street. "We all played jazz. And on our gigs at night, that's what we would play, was jazz," said Ashford. "The Chit Chat was an incredible place. It was the place to be. In fact, after the riots, it was one of the places that was left standing, because the proprietor was accepted by the people in the community."

Before he assumed a Motown managerial post, Hank Cosby gigged on tenor sax with Hunter and Willis. Sometimes the spirit grabbed hold of their eminent rhythm section and wouldn't let go. "We had a little four-piece band that played at Phelps', man, we'd take a break," said Cosby. "The band would take a break, and leave Jamerson and Benny on the stand. They wouldn't come down. They would be playing a song. They'd say, 'We're gonna play.' Man, we'd go outside for 15 minutes and come back, they would have tore the house down! People would be hollering and screaming and standing on the tables! Those guys, they were really something."

There were a few scattered singles under Van Dyke's name on Soul. "Soul Stomp," paired with "Hot 'N' Tot" came first during the fall of '64. And in 1965—the same year Earl, Robert, and Jack went overseas to anchor the band for Motown's first full-scale invasion—the Funk Brothers made their own instrumental album. Well, sort of. *That Motown Sound* featured Earl playing organ over what sounds like the same tracks that powered the hit versions of the Tempts' "My Girl" and "The Way You Do The Things You Do," Marvin Gaye's "Can I Get A Witness," "Try It Baby," and "You're A Wonderful One," the Marvelettes' "Too Many Fish In The Sea," and Martha & the Vandellas' "Nowhere To Run." Barrett Strong's "Money (That's What I Want)" was recut, and "All For You," a swinger penned by producers Cosby and Mickey Stevenson and Ivy Jo Hunter, seems to have been newly recorded, since it was slated as a 45 but canceled.

Released on Motown, the album was credited to Earl Van Dyke and the Soul Brothers, not the Funk Brothers. "I know that Berry didn't like the name. He thought it was an offensive thing to say the Funk Brothers," said Ashford. "We thought that was offensive. Soul Brothers? What does that mean?" Superfluous renditions of the Four Tops' "I Can't Help Myself" (not on the LP) and Gaye's "How Sweet It Is (To Be Loved By You)" did gain release as a single on Soul. In late '65, still as Van Dyke and the Soul Brothers, the two-part "The Flick" hit the streets. Written by Van Dyke, Jamerson, and White, it showcased the Brothers at their funkiest; everyone took a ride, the rhythm section steaming and Van Dyke's fatback organ rampaging like it was last call at the Chit Chat. A year later, Earl Van Dyke & the Motown Brass cooked up "6 By 6" with "There Is No Greater Love."

Fraternization between the road-toughened studio musicians and the youthful singers was discouraged by Motown's hierarchy. "We didn't see the singers much when we did our sessions. Very rarely," said Ashford. "They were instructed to stay away from us. So they really didn't associate with us." Since the backing tracks were usually laid down prior to the singers' arrival at the studio from the mid-'60s on, interaction between the two factions was effectively minimized.

Even if the public couldn't identify the Funk Brothers by name or face, their efforts were heartily appreciated by the stars whose fortunes largely rested on their musicianship.

"The Funk Brothers were the band of life," said Smokey Robinson.

"Musically, they were what was going on for Motown," noted the Four Tops' Duke Fakir in 1980.

"We had some hellified musicians," said the Marvelettes' Katherine Anderson Schaffner.

"They were really responsible for the Motown sound. They kept us all going and alive, record-wise," said Martha Reeves in a 1982 interview.

"Those guys were fabulous," said Barrett Strong. "They were so innovative that you could give 'em an idea, and they'd say, 'Okay, fine—let me show you something!'"

The Joe Hunter Band featured several of the famed Funk Brothers: (top row) Joe Hunter, (middle row, from left) James Jamerson, Hank Cosby, (bottom, from left) Benny Benjamin, Larry Veeder and Mike Terry (Photo courtesy of Allen Slutsky).

Though Van Dyke is credited as the bandleader, his role wasn't so clearly defined. "The Funk Brothers really didn't have a leader," said Ashford. "Let's say Earl was the leader of the gig that we worked at night—that transcended right on into the studio, where he would suggest a lot of things. And something else—remember, when a producer comes to the studio, he's going to the piano to show what he wants. So therefore, he's sitting right there with Earl. So he can be getting Earl together on, this is the way he wants it to go. So Earl cops what he wants. 'Okay, this is what you want?' 'Yeah.' So Earl says, 'Okay, well, Jack, I'm voicing this chord this way,' or 'Robert, I'm voicing this way.' So Earl would be the one (that was) more vocal. So it would appear for all intents and purposes for somebody looking at it that Earl was the leader. But there was no leader."

So essential to the '60s Motown sound was Jamerson—after he was through working out his improvisations, songs took on entirely new directions—that he had no backup for years. If he was indisposed or on the road with the Miracles in the early years, sessions had to wait. Bob Babbitt came over from Golden World in the late '60s to pick up some of the bass slack. James could find inspiration even from an unsuspecting passerby.

"Sometimes, Jamerson would do this thing where he'd see somebody walk by, and he'd pick up their shakes or whatever, and he would do some rhythm off of that. It is crazy, but he'd do it," noted Demps. He was also one of the band's cut-ups. "A lot of people were scared of Jamerson," said Cosby. "But he was really a clown. He just liked to make fun of things." The bassist dubbed the cramped Studio A "the Snakepit." "Every time he'd see Berry, he called Berry 'the Fuhrer!'" laughed Cosby, who wrote and produced what may be the best-recorded instance of Jamerson stretching out: "Mutiny" was a jazzy tour de force on Jr. Walker's '66 *Road Runner* LP where the two wailed like crazy and Jamerson cut loose on a bopping solo.

Though imbibing while laying down tracks was officially frowned upon, Jamerson caught a nip or two now and then. "Sure, we drank in the studio," said Ashford. "Jamerson used to drink Metaxa. It's like a liqueur, Greek or Russian. Comes in a long, thin bottle. He used to drink that. He didn't chain-drink it, but once in a while he'd come up with a bottle of it, and he'd put it back in his case."

Once in a while, Jamerson slipped over the line of decorum. "He used to hang out with me," said McDougal. "We was in Chicago, and Jamerson used to kind of go off. He knew karate, and he'd be playing, and he'd just go off. He'd break something, or chop something. He checked into the hotel—I was at an airport hotel, and he was down the Dan Ryan a little ways, maybe a mile-and-a-half, at a hotel on the left-hand side. So he called me one day and said, 'Hey, man, can you come over here? Because the guy won't let me get my axe, and I gotta get ready to go down to the show.' So I go down, and when I walk in, he's being all right. Just then the guy says, 'Man, I can't give him nothin' until he pays me more money, or somebody takes care of this bill.' He just went berserk, and jumped over the counter and started beating the guy up! I used my credit card, and I got him out of that hotel."

The carefree Benny's demons eventually got the better of him, but not before his backbeat thundered at the heart of countless smashes. "Benny was a character. He was a Navy vet. We were all drinkin' buddies," said Parks. "They didn't allow 'em to drink at Hitsville, so they went next door. When we drank, we drank." Benny was omniscient on occasion. "He told me one time, he said, 'Mamacita, I'm gonna tell you this: One day they're gonna be trying to duplicate your sound all over the world!'" said

"He had rolls you wouldn't believe."

Louvain. "I loved the guy. I think everybody loved Benny. He was a case, but everybody loved him. He would show up sometimes, he'd have blood on his face, and he'd say that he just fell and cut his face. But he was something else.

"When they first started out on that old (mixing) board, on that old-fashioned board, they marked a place for his foot," she continued. "He was the greatest drummer. I don't think they had anybody—I mean, they had some good drummers—but I don't think anybody was like Benny."

"He had rolls you wouldn't believe," raved Cosby. "He was such a nice guy, too. He never had a bad word to say about no one. He was one of those kind of guys. He'd come by my house at 4 o'clock in the morning: 'Hey, Hank! I need a buck! Give me a slat!' He called a dollar a slat. 'I need a slat!' He was goin' to get his fix."

"It was a joke, in a way, how they used to save up Benny. They would say, 'Benny, play,' and then he would drink, and the next thing you know, he'd fall right off the stand," said McDougal. "He'd be playing, and I mean, the thing is going good, and he'd just fall right off the drums. Pistol would jump in."

The combination of Benjamin's drums and Ashford's tambourine was formidable. "I didn't have a microphone," said Jack. "When I was recording, I would have to sit close to the sock cymbal mic, which was played by Benny Benjamin. So I was on the sock mic, so they couldn't turn me up and down, otherwise they would turn the drums up and down. They only had four tracks. So whatever volume they had, they'd say, 'Move a little closer.' And then when it was acceptable by the engineer, they'd say, 'Okay, let's go.'" Jack still marvels at Benny's technique. "The way he did his pickups. The way he kept his rhythm. He had unusual rhythm," he noted. "He'd do that pickup like a press roll with his left hand. He would do that little press roll, with the left hand on the snare. It was just unique, man. It was unique. He had an incredible sense of rhythm. That set that tone for that Motown thing."

Benjamin died in 1969, a victim of the physical damage his substance abuse inflicted. His loss shook Motown to its core. "Especially to the musicians, 'cause they didn't know what to do," said Cosby. "When he passed, we had to use two drummers to emulate what he was doing. That's how we come to use two drummers." Jones and Allen stepped up to keep the beat strong.

Ashford established Pied Piper Productions with Shelley Haims and saxist Mike Terry during the mid-'60s, producing soul sides by the Metros, Sharon Scott, and Lorraine Chandler for RCA Victor and the Hesitations for Kapp. He also launched his own self-named label. If his productions sounded like what was going down at Hitsville, they should have. A session log from one of his 1966 RCA dates by singer Willie Kendrick lists pianist Joe Hunter, bassist Bob Babbitt, saxist Norris Patterson, guitarist Dave Hamilton, Eddie "Bongo" Brown, and Ashford himself on percussion.

The two-part 1969 single "Do The Choo Choo," credited to Jack Ashford and the Sound of New Detroit, turned out to be the only Motown-distributed release on the Blaze logo. "When Barney Ales went back to Motown, I was running his label's A&R department before he went back. And I had a label called Blaze Records. I released that single on Blaze Records, and it was acquired by Motown, so that officially made me a Motown artist," said the percussionist.

Though he tried, Gordy never could stop various permutations of the Funk Brothers from

The Funk Brothers convene for a birthday bash for guitarist Robert White (holding sign). Pictured are (top, from left), Danny Turner, James Jamerson, friend Freddy Mann, (bottom, from left) Hank Cosby, White, Earl Van Dyke and Uriel Jones (Photo courtesy of Allan Slutsky).

moonlighting. Most of the stuff cut for Ed Wingate's Golden World and Ric-Tic labels, a load of H-D-H-produced smashes after they got their Invictus/Hot Wax operation up and running, the Capitols' "Cool Jerk," the Volcanos' "Storm Warning" (produced by McDougal for Philly-based Arctic)—the list goes on and on. Jackie Wilson's Chicago-cut '67 smash "(Your Love Keeps Lifting Me) Higher And Higher," Dave Crawford-produced dates by Wilson Pickett, a Candi Staton date in Muscle Shoals, and Don Davis-helmed Stax sessions by Carla Thomas, Johnnie Taylor, and the Soul Children all benefited from various Funk Brothers' largesse.

"...without the Funk Brothers, there would have been no Motown."

Whenever word trickled down that his musicians were working for another label, Gordy would dispatch someone from management to investigate. "They had already devised a way to stop us from moonlighting, because they had a Gestapo-type thing where they would bust in a session late at night, 2, 3, 4 in the morning, sometimes in their robes, just to come in there and take names of the guys that worked at Motown that were doing outside dates," said Ashford. "We had to go out and forage on our own, and almost feel like thieves out there plying our trade, because we may have been busted and fined for doing these dates. And you were punished when you were caught." Those ugly incidents caused deep rifts between former friends and musical cohorts that remain unresolved to this day.

Now that we're acquainted with the mighty rhythm section, let's meet the horn players.

Hank Cosby was the most frequently used tenor sax soloist during Motown's early years, though Ron Wakefield took the ride on the Miracles' "Shop Around." Baritone saxist Andrew "Mike" Terry made his presence known with a load of high-profile jabbing solos during the mid-'60s on smashes by the Supremes and the Four Tops (no small innovation—the low-end horn—had seldom been used as an R&B solo instrument before). "They liked what Mike was doing," noted Cosby. "Mike is from Detroit. Him and Jamerson were the same age. They went to school together."

Norris "Kasuku Mafia" Patterson came in as another primary tenor sax soloist during the mid-'60s. Thomas "Beans" Bowles was the flute specialist early on and doubled on baritone sax. Teddy Buckner, Wild Bill Moore, Dan Turner, Lefty Edwards (another Workshop Jazz alumnus with 1964's *The Right Side of Lefty Edwards*), and Eli Fontaine distinguished the reed section.

Marcus Belgrave, formerly of Ray Charles' orchestra and a Chester, Pennsylvania, native who played at Philly's Uptown Theater before joining Motown, was a standby of the trumpet platoon, along with Johnny Trudell, Herbie Williams, John "Little John" Wilson, and Russell Conway. Trombone duties were taken care of by George Bohanon ("The day he left and went to California, I really felt bad. We were never able to replace George," said Cosby), Bob Cousar, Jimmy Wilkins, Patrick Lanier, and Paul Riser, who ended up a top Motown arranger.

"I pulled him out of high school. Just had graduated, and somebody was telling me how talented he was, and I met him. He played trombone," said Cosby. "So I said, 'Well, I'll give you a chance.' I gave him a chance. The guy could blow! And then on top of that, he could write. Out of high school, 18 years old. And he just got books, and started studying, and started writing. See, that was one good thing about Motown—it was like a school. Everybody had a chance to grow, to learn and grow. And by playing with musicians every day—he worked with the symphony two, three times a week. He got so he would write strings you wouldn't believe."

Music came first for young Riser, even over a rumbling stomach. "He just came out of school, and he was struggling, and he was saving for a car. He wouldn't eat lunch because he was saving for car. And I told him, 'We're going down to Cunningham's Drug Store, and we're going to have lunch,'" said Louvain. "He was a genius. He was just an incredible arranger," said Ashford. "I was on a plane one time, going from one coast to the other. And Paul was doing an arrangement without a keyboard, just sitting up there doing all the parts in his head. Writing 'em out, 'cause he had to give 'em to the copyist when we landed. He was doing his charts, man."

Motown attracted talented arrangers in droves. "They should get their dues," said producer Johnny Bristol. "They worked hard, just as hard as we did. Sometimes we left them at the studio doing arrangements, trying to get them ready for the next morning." Along with Riser, there was keyboardist Willie Shorter (who handled much of the Miracles' early output), Wade Marcus, and David Van de Pitte. And there were the violinists that sweetened the final product. "We used the Detroit Symphony from '62 to '69," said Hank. "Just about everything that came out on Motown had strings on it, and it was the Detroit Symphony."

During the late '60s, former Golden World bassist Bob Babbitt (real name Robert Kleinar) came over to augment Jamerson. Guitarist Dennis Coffey's reliance on rock-rooted distortion brought a new psychedelic dimension to the Motown sound. Melvin "Wah Wah Watson" Ragin (guess what his favorite effect was) made his first significant Motown bow at age 20 on Edwin Starr's "Stop The War Now," and he injected the Tempts' "Papa Was A Rollin' Stone" with snaky guitar riffage. Ragin was one of the few Detroit sessioneers to make a full transition to the L.A. studio scene. He went west for what he assumed was a four-day contribution to Rare Earth's Norman Whitfield-produced *Ma* album and never came back to the Motor City.

Van Dyke cut his second and final Soul LP, *The Earl of Funk*, for issue in 1970. Once again, he was victimized by questionable production techniques, though he seems to have been a willing participant. A phony live audience was overdubbed between tracks, marring the intro and close of each selection, yet Earl verbally introduced the sleek "Fuschia Moods" concert style, saying saxist George Benson (no, not *that* George Benson) wrote it while in Hawaii. Van Dyke's own "The Stingray," "The Whip A Rang" (co-written with Hank and Stevie Wonder), and a reprise of "The Flick" (likely the original version) were wonderfully funky originals, their impact compounded by a fine reprise of the Meters' "Cissy Strut" and Ben E. King's "Stand By Me."

When Motown shifted its base of operations to L.A., Van Dyke, Jamerson, Brown, Ragin, and Ashford migrated west, while most of the rest stayed put. "When they officially moved and padlocked the door in Detroit, I was the last one to leave Detroit of the Funk Brothers," said Ashford. "'Cause Uriel wouldn't leave, and Pistol wouldn't go."

The move was particularly deleterious to Jamerson, who hit L.A. in 1973 and at first picked up where he left off. But booze got the better of him; he grew unreliable and opportunities got scarcer. When he died on August 2, 1983, it was his son, James Jr., whose bass skills were locally in demand. Van Dyke lasted a few years on the coast before returning home to teach at Osborn High School. He died September 20, 1992. Bongo Brown stuck it out until his December 28, 1985 death at age 52. Robert White died October 27, 1994. The surviving Funk Brothers recently reunited to film a documentary by Jamerson biographer Allan "Dr. Licks" Slutsky.

"These guys died brokenhearted," said Ashford. "They felt as though their lives were unfulfilled. But I'm here to testify that that's not true, because our legacy will live on. Our legacy will always be there. We set a precedent in the annals of music that will always exist. We brought about a change in music, and a change in society.

"If God blessed Berry Gordy for making it happen, then the angels kissed the Funk Brothers for furthering his dream. Because without the Funk Brothers, there would have been no Motown."

(Photo courtesy of David Alston's Mahogany Archives).

MARVIN GAYE

There were plenty of Marvin Gaye duets to go around in the 1960s. In his 1969 release *Marvin Gaye and His Girls*, Gaye sings four songs apiece with duet partners Tammi Terrell, Mary Wells and Kim Weston.

Marvin Gaye was much, much more than just another pretty voice, though there's no denying his was among the most beautiful and haunting to stroll through the Hitsville portals. A restless spirit perpetually seeking new musical horizons, a reluctant sex symbol who made women salivate, Marvin was a tortured figure never content to follow one musical path for long. If he'd had his way, Gaye would have concentrated on crooning pop standards like Frank Sinatra or Nat King Cole. Fortunately for the future of soul, his forays along those lines didn't sell.

The psychological conflicts that ultimately manifested themselves in his downfall were in evidence from the very beginning. Marvin Pentz Gay, Jr. (the 'e' was added later) was born April 2, 1939, in Washington, D.C. His father was a preacher with an obscure sect, the House of God, and the two clashed often.[3] Nothing could stop Marvin from singing—first in church, then in emulation of the doo-wop groups proliferating at the time. The Orioles, Capris, Clovers, and Five Keys enchanted him, as did Ray Charles, Little Willie John, and Clyde McPhatter. Marvin's 'hood housed Don Covay, Billy Stewart, and Herb Fame (of Peaches & Herb). He joined his first group, the D.C. Tones (they included Stacy Lattisaw's mother Sondra), in high school. Instead of graduating, he enlisted in the Air Force, but his hitch was a disaster. He returned to D.C. in 1957.

Music was Marvin's salvation. That summer, he joined the Marquees, a doo-wop outfit comprised of ex-D.C. Tone Reese Palmer, James Nolan, and Chester Simmons. Bo Diddley produced their debut 45 "Wyatt Earp" paired with "Hey, Little School Girl" for Columbia's OKeh subsidiary (Palmer sang lead on both). The single stiffed, but Harvey Fuqua hired the group to be his new Moonglows in late 1958. They hit the road for Chicago in early '59, adding the Dells' Chuck Barksdale to expand the ranks to six. Harvey's tutelage was invaluable, and Gaye received his first chance to sing lead on record that year on the Moonglows' rocking "Mama Loocie" for Chess. But Fuqua soon broke up the group and moved to Detroit to form Tri-Phi Records with new girlfriend Gwen Gordy, bringing Marvin along.

Gwen introduced Gaye to her brother Berry at Motown's 1960 Christmas party. Seated at the piano, Marvin crooned a moody version of the Chordettes' "Mr. Sandman." Gordy brought the introspective newcomer aboard, producing a Tamla debut that came out in May of '61 and officially changed the spelling of his surname to Gaye (in part because Sam Cooke—nee Cook—had done the same). "Let Your Conscience Be Your Guide" was a gospel-tinged ballad by Berry showcasing Marvin's lilting tenor, while its flip "Never Let You Go," penned by Harvey and Gordy's sister Anna, was a brisk rocker.

Anna Gordy Gaye (Marvin's wife) and Diana Ross (Weldon A. McDougal III photo).

But few record buyers picked up on it, and just as few bought the young singer's first album, *The Soulful Moods of Marvin Gaye*, that June. Other than both sides of his R&B-slanted debut 45, the LP spotlighted Marvin in his preferred guise as a debonair jazz singer. "He wanted to sing standards," said saxist Hank Cosby. "He wanted to be another Nat King Cole. That was his ambition—just stand still, and sit down, and sing ballads." Gaye brought a fetching appeal to "Witchcraft," "How High The Moon," and Cole Porter's "Love For Sale," but this clearly wasn't the path to stardom. Gaye also played drums on the Marvelettes' "Please Mr. Postman." "Marvin had always been creative," said Cosby. "He wanted to be a drummer. He was there trying to play the piano. He played the piano on a lot of his later sessions, and drums also."

Though every eligible female at Hitsville swooned in his shy, soft-spoken yet sensuous presence, it was Anna Gordy—17 years Marvin's senior—who swept Gaye off his feet. "Oh, Mr. Wonderful!" exclaimed Janie Bradford, then Motown's receptionist. "All the girls just fell down on their knees and said, 'Who is this clean-cut, All-American, good-looking guy?' And Anna just walked in and broke all our hearts!" Marvin and glamorous Anna would marry in 1963, though by the late '60s the union was disintegrating. Following their bitter 1977 divorce, Marvin chronicled their breakup on his two-LP package *Here, My Dear.*

For his second Tamla 45 in January of '62, Marvin resurrected "Sandman." His wistful delivery, floating over vibes, brushed drums, and female vocal backing, was gorgeous and owed little to the Chordettes' perky '54 hit. Berry and A&R boss Mickey Stevenson co-wrote its 'B' side, "I'm Yours, You're Mine," in an R&B bag, built around lively call-and-response banter between Marvin and a male vocal group. That May, Tamla tried a third time with the mournful "Soldier's Plea." Set to a military drum-roll cadence, the Stevenson/George Gordy/Fay Hale copyright was oppressive and must have felt weird considering Marvin's failed Air Force stint. "Taking My Time," the Gordy/Stevenson charmer on the flip, gracefully glided over a mid-tempo rhythm.

Writing from personal experience gave Gaye his first hit. Admittedly stubborn to his core, he was jamming with Mickey one day when Gordy happened along and showed him a few strategic piano chords that sparked the completion of "Stubborn Kind Of Fellow." From its boisterous opening salvo, this Stevenson production was a surefire bet to propel Marvin to stardom. Coarsening his voice to summon a gospel-fired grittiness, he belted the pounder over uplifting harmonies from Martha Reeves' pre-Vandellas vocal group, the Del-Phis.

"That Stubborn Kinda' Fellow" was the title track to one of Gaye's two 1963 LPs.

"We stood there with Mickey and Marvin, and he sang his line. Gloria (Jean Williamson) was very good at making up backgrounds, and we went, 'Doo-doo-doo-oww!' Marvin was very thrilled. He even sang, 'Yeah!' to our backgrounds," said Martha. "We complemented each other very well vocally." Gaye let it all hang out, even allowing his voice to crack near the end, and the upsurge in intensity was startling. End result: A No. 8 R&B hit in *Billboard* during the fall of '62 that made sizable pop inroads. "Mickey Stevenson is really responsible for having him sing more of the bluesy kind of songs, the R&B songs," noted guitarist Cornelius Grant, who played behind Gaye prior to casting his lot with the Temptations. "It Hurt Me Too," the Gaye/Stevenson-penned 'B' side, was an attractive up-tempo outing.

Dancing onstage was one activity Marvin could have lived without. "He hated it," said Cosby. "His wife Anna, oh, man. She had a fit with him, made him—'You gotta move! You can't just stand up there! You gotta do something!' She had him dancing." That reluctance to move with the groove (he was actually a natural hoofer, as he proved in the 1964 film *The T.A.M.I. Show*) didn't stop him from co-writing an encore with Stevenson and Clarence Paul that forced him onto the floor. "Hitch Hike" hit just as hard as "Stubborn Kind Of Fellow," Gaye doubling on piano and drums while Martha & the Vandellas answered in kind and Beans Bowles returned with another flute solo. The sweaty workout rose to No. 12 R&B and No. 30 pop in early '63. "Hello There Angel," by Berry and Mickey, offered lilting contrast on the flip.

Jamerson's cool walking bass led off "Pride And Joy," an exultant celebration of Anna's charms that made it three hits in a row for Marvin. It was easily the biggest yet, topping out at No. 2 R&B and piercing the pop Top Ten that summer. Marvin sounded wonderfully relaxed delivering the suave swinger, which the singer had penned along with producer Stevenson and a young Norman Whitfield. A blues-stained approach distinguished its flip, "One Of These Days"; poured over a chunky groove, Gaye displayed compelling phrasing on the Stevenson copyright.

That Stubborn Kinda Fellow, Gaye's second LP, was a far cry from its predecessor, boasting three major hits and exclusively R&B in its content. There were only a couple of songs on the LP that weren't available as singles: Whitfield earned an early production credit on the surging "Wherever I Lay My Hat (That's My Home)," which he wrote with Marvin and Barrett Strong, and the spine-chilling "Get My Hands On Some Lovin'," an up-tempo Gaye/Stevenson collaboration. So integral were Reeves and her Vandellas' harmonies that their photo appeared prominently on its back cover. "We were very good friends with Marvin," noted Martha. "We never got compensated for singing backup for him. We never received record royalties for that."

Holland-Dozier-Holland dropped into Marvin's professional life in a resounding manner during the summer of 1963, handing him "Can I Get A Witness." Gaye's sanctified roots ran close to the surface on this storming rocker, a No. 15 R&B hit near year's end and a sizable pop seller constructed atop a modified version of the low-end guitar lick powering Lonnie Mack's '63 hit instrumental "Memphis." Stevenson mined some of the same walking rhythm on its 'B' side "I'm Crazy 'Bout My Baby" that he'd so skillfully employed for "Pride And Joy."

Much as they would do with the Four Tops when "I Can't Help Myself" begat "It's The Same Old Song," the prolific H-D-H quickly cooked up a canny variation on "Can I Get A Witness" entitled "You're A Wonderful One," and Marvin had himself another smash during the spring of '64 that climbed to No.15 pop (this time, the Supremes supplied the backing vocals). Berry Gordy took time out from his administrative duties to dream up Marvin's next solo hit. "Try It Baby" was a blues-tinged strutter with a tasty trumpet solo and sturdy backing vocals by the Temptations that equaled the pop showing of its predecessor that summer.

Issued in September of '63, *Recorded Live/Marvin Gaye On Stage* was the first of the singer's in-concert LPs. Cut with a large, horn-leavened outfit, the set found Gaye zipping through his hits and sported two tunes that were otherwise unavailable: A dynamic cover of Henry Lumpkin's rocker "Mo Jo Hanna" and a Ray Charles-inspired "You Are My Sunshine." Sound quality noticeably degenerates on the latter, perhaps explaining its positioning as the final track.

That unquenchable desire to caress Tin Pan Alley standards explained *When I'm Alone I Cry* in April of '64. Clarence Paul commissioned jazz arrangers Ernie Wilkins, Melba Liston, and Jerome Richardson to paint lavish big-band arrangements that were laid down in New York and Chicago. The title item and "If My Heart Could Sing" were Jobete copyrights but fit the wee-small-hours-of-the-morning concept seamlessly, as did Gaye's yearning revival of pianist Cecil Gant's 1944 blues ballad "I Wonder." Before the year was through, Marvin would further appeal to the sensibilities of the MOR crowd with another adult-themed album, *Hello Broadway*.

On the verge of her exit from the firm for less green pastures, Mary Wells was teamed with Gaye for a two-sided pop hit that May. "Once Upon A Time," the combined work of Paul, Stevenson, sales head Barney Ales, and vibes ace Dave Hamilton, was the more refined and pop-slanted of the pair, but the duo sounded as if they had a better time on the playful "What's The Matter With You Baby" by the same crew, minus Hamilton. Gaye and Wells endured as a tandem long enough to make an album, *Together*. With Wells out, Motown wasted no time in teaming Marvin up with another sultry duet partner. Gospel-trained Detroiter Kim Weston, whose own Tamla discography already included the '63 hit "Love Me All The Way," was Mickey's wife, but she and Gaye sounded sufficiently devoted to one another on the driving "What Good Am I Without You" to notch a late '64 mid-level pop hit.

It was the solo Marvin that racked up the gargantuan sellers for Tamla. H-D-H came up with the crackling "Baby Don't You Do It," a hit in the fall of '64, and the irresistible "How Sweet It Is (To Be Loved By You)"—its relaxed mid-tempo drive a prime example of the maturing Motown sound. "How Sweet It Is" was Gaye's biggest pop hit yet, rocketing to No. 6, and achieved a No. 4 R&B showing in early '65. It was also his first British hit following a November '64 visit (a lip-synched rendition on *Ready, Steady, Go!* didn't hurt its prospects), and had such universal appeal that a version was cut in German."

A subsequent LP named after the smash was loaded with gems, notably Marvin's tender reading of the Marvelettes' "Forever," Smokey's "Now That You've Won Me," the Whitfield/Strong collaboration "Me And My Lonely Room," and the Stevenson-generated "No Good Without You" and "Need Somebody" (the latter co-written with Ivy Jo Hunter). Marvin and Harvey co-wrote and co-produced "Stepping Closer To Your Heart," while Gaye penned the chunky "Need Your Lovin' (Want You Back)" with Paul.

The unbeatable team of Smokey Robinson and Marvin Gaye soared on the charts in 1965. The Robinson-penned "Ain't That Peculiar" gave Gaye a winner on both the pop and R&B play lists.

Smokey Robinson assumed the reins for producing his pal Gaye in early 1965 and helmed his first R&B chart-topper that spring. "I'll Be Doggone," the work of Robinson, fellow Miracle Pete Moore, and their guitarist Marv Tarplin, rode a jaunty rhythm and blasted up to No. 8 pop. "The music was primarily done by Marv Tarplin," said Pete. "He was the one that came up with the original riff. Once we heard it, then Smokey and I put the lyrics to it." H-D-H supplied the lovely flip, "You've Been A Long Time Coming." Along with Paul and Hamilton, Gaye wrote "Pretty Little Baby"; an ornate piano figure and prominent female vocal backing dominated the exquisite Paul production, which sported an Eastern feel perhaps too exotic to be quite as big a hit that summer.

Robinson returned with another surefire winner in the buoyant "Ain't That Peculiar," hung on a descending bass figure and filled with typically sly lyrics (Robinson co-wrote it with Tarplin, Moore, and Bobby Rogers). "We had an arranger that we worked with back in those days. His name was Willie Shorter," said Pete. "Willie used to do the rhythm charts for us. He put the arrangement to 'Ain't That Peculiar,' and he came up with that bass riff." The parallels between "Ain't That Peculiar" and "I'll Be Doggone" don't stop with its creators. They nailed identical chart peaks in *Billboard* ("Ain't That Peculiar" sat atop the R&B listings in the last week of November). "She's Got To Be Real" on the other side was an engaging up-tempo ditty from Smokey and fellow Miracle Ronnie White.

That November, Tamla issued Gaye's *A Tribute To The Great Nat King Cole* (the legendary crooner had passed away in February). Its production split between Fuqua and the L.A.-based team of Hal Davis and Marc Gordon, it was a tasteful tribute awash in violins that seldom caught fire. "Straighten Up And Fly Right," harking back to Cole's jazz beginnings, and "Send For Me" benefited from swinging Basie-styled big-band arrangements.

Weldon A. McDougal III talks to a happy Marvin Gaye after the singer won an award on Hy Lit's popular Philadelphia TV program (Weldon A. McDougal III photo).

The Marvin/Smokey tandem continued to thrive in 1966. "One More Heartache," the compositional work of all five male Miracles, had an open, bluesy feel and unusual chord changes, Tarplin's ringing guitar woven within its midst. "That's all he used to do, was sit down and be playing that guitar," said Moore. "He'd play it 24 hours a day. He'd come up with these real fantastic riffs." It was a No. 4 R&B seller in early '66, but somehow the relentless Robinson/Moore/Tarplin-penned "Take This Heart Of Mine"—easily one of the most compelling Gaye waxings of Motown's golden era with its joyous drive, and Jamerson's elastic bass line—didn't sell on the same lofty level that summer.

"As songwriters, we always wanted to be as realistic as we possibly could. We would look at people around us, and a lot of our lyrics was based on actual life experiences that we seen people go through," said its co-producer Moore. "As far as Marvin is concerned, a lot of those lyrics are based on the relationship we saw with him and his wife."

Both sides of Marvin's next single deserved hitdom, but it was the H-D-H-helmed "Little Darling, I Need You" that made the grade to Top Ten R&B status late that summer. Its upbeat groove was rock solid, a baritone sax solo spicing the proceedings. On the 'B' side was the playful "Hey Diddle Diddle," produced by Fuqua and Johnny Bristol (they wrote it with Gaye).

"We were just sitting around clowning one day and wrote that," said Bristol. "At the time, it took other producers to come up with what it took to get Marvin Gaye a hit record, and make him a sound that became unique to himself. 'Cause he had an incredible voice. Marvin could sing pretty, like Johnny Mathis-type material, or he could sing Wilson Pickett. The boy was just incredible."

Coming on the heels of "Take This Heart Of Mine," *Moods Of Marvin Gaye* was a very consistent R&B-slanted affair, sporting a half-dozen hits along with the Stevie Wonder/Paul/Morris Broadnax ballad "You're The One For Me," a surprising cover of Willie Nelson's late-night country-blues hybrid "Night Life" produced by jazzman Bobby Scott, and a pair of Fuqua-helmed forays into Tin Pan Alley territory, notably a moving reprise of the gin-soaked Sinatra standard "One For My Baby (And One More For The Road)."

After a lengthy hiatus between collaborations, Marvin reunited with Weston and waxed one of his greatest duets. "It Takes Two" radiated unabridged joy, the pair's chemistry as explosive as its rhythm. Written by Kim's husband Stevenson and Sylvia Moy, and produced by Mickey and Cosby, the supercharged duet proved a No. 4 R&B smash that barely missed Top Ten pop status in early '67. The violin-enriched "It's Got To Be A Miracle (This Thing Called Love)" was its inspiring flip. *Take Two*, the pair's lone LP together, actually predated the single issue of "It Takes Two" by more than three months and was scarcely less invigorating, thanks to "Baby Say Yes" (written by Mickey and Kim), "Heaven Sent You I Know," and a sweet "Secret Love."

Along with her spouse, Kim exited the company in early '67, leaving Marvin once again in search of a duet partner. This time the label teamed him with vivacious Philly native Tammi Terrell, whose solo Motown career encompassed two '66 hits, "I Can't Believe You Love Me" and "Come On And See Me." From the outset, it was a match made in heaven. "That was Mr. Gordy's idea, as far as I know," said Bristol, who produced their first duets with partner Harvey Fuqua. The pair also benefitted mightily from the writing talents of another exuberant duo who had just arrived at Hitsville, Nickolas Ashford and Valerie Simpson.

"When Nick and Valerie had come to Motown as writers, their product was distributed to various producers," said Bristol. "So Harvey and I were given 'Ain't No Mountain High Enough,' 'Your Precious Love,' and I think a couple more. But I think those two were the ones we just jumped up and down about. Mr. Gordy assigned us these particular songs, the material, to do Marvin and Tammi." A molten romantic fire raged between Marvin and Tammi throughout "Ain't No Mountain High Enough," a No. 3 R&B smash (No. 19 pop) in mid-1967 that escalated to dizzying emotional heights. "Most of that was there when Nick and Valerie brought it to us, and we just added some of our own flavor and touch to it," said Johnny. "It actually could have been produced the way they brought it in, if you want to know the truth." Fuqua and Bristol supplied the mellow flip, "Give A Little Love."

The laidback finger-snapper "Your Precious Love" was even bigger, going Top Five pop and No. 2 R&B for Gaye and Terrell that fall. "On 'Your Precious Love,' we had the opportunity to do the background—Marvin and Harvey and myself and Tammi," noted Bristol. "We called ourselves 'the Riff Brothers Plus One.' Tammi was the 'Plus One.' But we had fun in the studio doing those things. There was a lot of laughter, a lot of clowning around. And I think the joy from the personalities and the energy—it was a very relaxed arrangement." Harvey handed them the chunky flip, "Hold Me, Oh My Darling" (also cut by Terrell as a solo vehicle).

United, the duo's first album, was uncommonly strong, distinguished by the pounding "Two Can Have A Party," a heartbroken "Sad Wedding," and the bouncy "Little Ole Boy, Little Ole Girl" (the last written by the intriguing triumvirate of Fuqua, Etta James, and Brook Benton). Marv Johnson's "You Got What It Takes" received a welcome rebirth, while "Oh How I Miss You" was done in L.A. by Hal Davis.

Along with Vernon Bullock, producers Fuqua and Bristol co-wrote the duo's third smash, the inspiring "If I Could Build My Whole World Around You." Vaulting to No. 2 R&B and the pop Top Ten at the close of '67, its massive success underscored the public's hunger for more Marvin and Tammi. Its flip, Gaye's own spine-chilling "If This World Were Mine," registered its own sizable chart presence.

Simultaneous with his duets with Terrell, Gaye was notching solo smashes. "Your Unchanging Love," another H-D-H standout with a mid-tempo drive, was a Top Ten R&B hit during the summer of '67. Proving how far ahead of their time the trio was, the song was cut two-and-a-half years earlier. Ivy Jo Hunter, who had collaborated with Marvin and Mickey on the creation of Martha & the Vandellas' "Dancing In The Street," was dominant behind "You," a minor-key pounder that equaled the R&B chart position of "Your Unchanging Love" in early '68. That fall, Marvin's riveting "Chained"—introduced by ex-teen sitcom star Paul Petersen during a brief Motown dalliance the year before—made it three Top Ten trysts in a row.

"He grabbed that song and just laid it out," said Frank Wilson, the writer/producer of "Chained." "Marvin was an extraordinary talent. There are very few words to describe Marvin, other than the fact that he understood songs. You could show Marvin the song, and Marvin would interpret the song far better than you could have shown it to be sung. He brought stuff

Marvin Gaye's handsome looks and heavenly voice were a winning combination.

out of songs. You knew that it had potential, but you didn't know it had that much potential until he did it." Gaye did a bang-up job on the equally insistent flip "At Last (I Found A Love)," one of his hottest non-hits with prominent Jamerson bass and Marvin's uncommonly hard-edged vocal.

Ashford and Simpson inherited the dual duties of writing for and producing Marvin and Tammi in 1968, and the prolific pair devised back-to-back No. 1 R&B smashes with "Ain't Nothing Like The Real Thing" that June and "You're All I Need To Get By" in August. Both of them cracked the pop Top Ten. Two more Ashford & Simpson concoctions—"Keep On Lovin' Me Honey" in late '68 and "Good Lovin' Ain't Easy To Come By" in early '69—fell one slot shy of the R&B Top Ten.

At the risk of busting the romantic bubble, Marvin and Tammi apparently recorded some of their later duets separately. "Oh yeah, that's true, but that was very seldom true with us," said Bristol. "Because we all enjoyed being there together. I think it was more when Nick and Valerie were producing them. I think it started more around that time."

One of Marvin Gaye's most heartfelt efforts was undoubtedly his classic "What's Going On," a 1971 blockbuster that took a hard look at the Vietnam War.

Tammi's faltering health—she had collapsed onstage in Marvin's arms during the summer of '67 at Virginia's Hampden-Sydney College, suffering from a brain tumor and enduring a series of operations that ultimately fell short of curing her—isn't evident on their exuberant *You're All I Need* LP. Ashford and Simpson provided "You Ain't Livin' Till You're Lovin'," but Fuqua and Bristol supervised "Give In, You Just Can't Win," "When Love Comes Knocking At My Heart," "That's How It Is (Since You've Been Gone)," and "I'll Never Stop Loving You Baby," all illustrating the synergy between the two singers. "Baby Don't Cha Worry" and "Come On And See Me" had previously been tackled by a solo Tammi.

Terrell's labelmates, Barbara Randolph and Brenda Holloway, occasionally filled in for her on the road as Gaye's duet partners. "I went to the Latin Casino in Ohio with Marvin," said Brenda. "I liken him to a big thoroughbred stallion of a horse. He was just so fabulous! When you fell in his arms, you just wanted to stay there."

Gaye had achieved the sort of mainstream acceptance that he had seemingly sought since he arrived at Hitsville, but he found it less than fulfilling.

"He was at the Copa, and we were standing in the wings. They were playing the overture. And Marvin told me, **'Man, I feel like a damn monkey on a string!'** I said, 'Why, man?' He said, 'Man, I don't want to wear this high hat.' He had to sing show tunes, which he wasn't all that hopped on," said McDougal. "When I saw him perform, he did a good job, but I could feel what he was feeling, because he told me that."

Whitfield went through hell to give Marvin his biggest seller and one of the greatest successes in Motown history. Strong had dreamed up "I Heard It Through The Grapevine" while living in Chicago, before he returned to Berry's employ in 1966. "I was walking down Michigan Avenue, and the idea just popped in my mind," Strong said. "I heard people say it all the time: 'I heard it through the grapevine.' Nobody wrote a song about it, so I sat at a piano and came up with the bass line. And the melody came back. Norman said, 'What do you have, man?' I showed it to him. He said, 'I'll cut that!'" It was the beginning of a prolific and very lucrative writing partnership between the two longtime friends.

Though Marvin set "I Heard It Through The Grapevine" afire, the ominous Whitfield production had lost out during a heated Quality Control meeting to "Your Unchanging Love" as Gaye's next 45 release (for once, Gordy overrode the vote of his lieutenants). So the resourceful producer recast the paranoid pounder as a gospel-soaked rocker and handed it to Gladys Knight & the Pips, who enjoyed a smash with it. The headstrong Norman wasn't satisfied; he campaigned to insert Marvin's anguished early '67 rendition on his *In The Groove* album, and Gordy finally relented. "A disc jockey in Chicago heard Marvin's version, and decided that was the one he wanted to play," said Barrett. "That was how it took off." Gauging the groundswell of support, Tamla was forced to pull "Grapevine" as a single. It charged up to the top of the pop and R&B lists for seven weeks in late '68/early '69, only a year after Gladys and the Pips' smash.

Whitfield constantly recycled and reworked backing tracks. "That track that Marvin Gaye came out with, 'I Heard It Through The Grapevine'—that was supposed to be our next track," said the Pips' William Guest in 1996. "That song was called 'Restless.' Next thing we know, he had given that track to Marvin Gaye, and Marvin had sang 'I Heard It Through The Grapevine' on that track! They put it out the next year." "It was over then," fellow Pip Bubba Knight chimed in.

In The Groove carried more than its share of treasures even before "Grapevine's" addition. "Change What You Can" (the offspring of Marvin, Harvey, and Elgie Stover), "It's Love I Need," "Every Now And Then," "You're What's Happening (In The World Today)," and Ashford and Simpson's "Tear It On Down" could have all been hits given the chance. *Two Drifters* covers, "There Goes My Baby" and "Some Kind Of Wonderful," stuck close to the sweeping uptown soul originals.

Whitfield retained just enough of "Grapevine's" flavor on "Too Busy Thinking About My Baby" to ensure it would be Gaye's next R&B chart-topper during the spring of '69 (it stopped at No. 4 pop). In its '66 incarnation on the Temptations' *Gettin' Ready* LP, the Whitfield/Strong/Janie Bradford composition was bouncy and happy, an approach Marvin retained during a tour de force performance filled with falsetto excursions and unexpected melodic liberties. Which version did Bradford favor? "I have a preference for anything Marvin," she said.

"That's The Way Love Is" throbbed to the same bottom end-heavy, minor-key pulse as "Grapevine," anchored by the same conspicuous tinkling electric piano, and Marvin had himself another Whitfield-helmed smash (No. 2 R&B, No. 7 pop) during the fall of '69. The song was first cut by the Isleys in 1967, and Norman had recycled it earlier for Gladys and the Pips' *Feelin' Bluesy* LP. *M.P.G.*, Gaye's only solo LP during 1969, was another rock-solid set surrounding three smashes with two gems from Smokey Robinson ("More Than A Heart Can Stand," co-penned with Hunter, and "It's A Bitter Pill To Swallow" with Moore), the Hunter-generated "I Got To Get To California," "Only A Lonely Man Would Know," and "Seek And You Shall Find" (the latter with Mickey Stevenson), and H-D-H's "It Don't Take Much To Keep Me."

Distressed over Terrell's illness, his failing marriage, and various artistic dilemmas, Gaye made it difficult for Motown to entice him into the studio—disrupting its stringent production schedule. "We used to have sales meetings, and they would always complain," said McDougal. "They'd say, 'Man, where's Marvin Gaye's album?' They'd say, 'Well, he won't get in the studio.' Or, 'We're trying to get him.' And somebody like Phil Jones would say, 'I called, but he doesn't answer the phone.' They just could never get Marvin to do albums on schedule. Like they would schedule Marvin to come out in June, and this would be maybe in October of the year before. And it never came out like that. It was just that he had to get himself situated to go and do it. That's what he wouldn't do."

Terrell was suffering so from the brain cancer that tragically killed her on March 16, 1970 that their last "duet" hits, "What You Gave Me" and "The Onion Song," anonymously featured co-writer/co-producer Valerie Simpson vocally substituting for her. Most of Gaye and Terrell's last album together, *Easy*, was similarly bereft of legit Terrell participation.[4] "He told me that he was really terribly afraid that she wasn't gonna make it," said Demps. "And he was right. Then after that, it just kind of fell apart for him." Convinced he was bad luck to his partners (Wells and Weston had left Motown shortly after their collaborations with him), Marvin would avoid duets until teaming with Diana Ross in 1973 for the Hal Davis-produced *Diana & Marvin*. "That's because he was a sensitive guy," said Weldon. "He used to feel like he had some kind of hex on himself, 'cause everybody who sang with him, something happened to 'em."

Gaye's solo outing "How Can I Forget" and its flip, "Gonna Give Her All The Love I've Got," both by Whitfield and Strong, received split airplay in early 1970 to the detriment of both (Jimmy Ruffin had enjoyed a bigger hit with the latter in '67). But the coursing "The End Of Our Road" restored him to the R&B Top Ten that summer. Whitfield's remake habit remained in high gear—Gladys and her guys had nailed a huge hit with it in early 1968, employing an incendiary gospel groove on the rousing order of their "Grapevine."

"I dreamed about that song in my sleep, and I woke up and wrote the lyrics out," said co-writer Strong. "Took it down there—it was supposed to be like a followup to Gladys's version of 'Grapevine.'" Gaye revered Gladys's pipes. "I said, 'Oh, Marvin, if I could sing like you,'" said the Andantes' Louvain Demps. "He said, 'Oh, and if I could sing like Gladys Knight!' I said, 'What?' So I guess everybody's got somebody that they wish they could sound like."

That's The Way Love Is, Gaye's last album under the traditional Motown production regime, was issued in January of '70 and betrayed a deficiency of fresh ideas. Remakes of The Beatles' "Yesterday," the Young Rascals' "Groovin'," and "Abraham, Martin And John" wouldn't do for singles; the Tempts' "I Wish It Would Rain" (ignited by crunchy rock-drenched guitar) and "Cloud Nine," the Marvelettes' "No Time For Tears," the oft-covered "Gonna Keep On Tryin' Till I Win Your Love," and the Jimmy Ruffin remake "Don't You Miss Me A Little Bit Baby" were unlikely candidates as well. However, the Motown brass missed a good bet with the infectious "So Long," penned by Whitfield, Eddie Holland, and R. Dean Taylor.

An emotionally devastated Gaye sequestered himself away to create the acclaimed 1971 masterpiece *What's Going On.* Crying out at the injustice of an indefensible war in Vietnam, Gaye crafted a profoundly personal statement that flew in the face of the assembly-line creativity at the heart of the Motown empire. "I think the hardest thing we ever did was *What's Going On,*" said the Andantes' Louvain Demps. "Marvin heard what he heard, and he heard it in the heavenlys. And we couldn't get it together. He would hear something, and we just couldn't hear what he was hearing. It was really strange." Berry Gordy heard little commercial potential in the self-produced project, but Gaye brashly informed his boss that this would be the only album he would be submitting.

Even after Gordy acquiesced, there were more hurdles to leap before *What's Going On* spawned three R&B chart toppers—"Mercy Mercy Me (The Ecology)," "Inner City Blues (Make Me Wanna Holler)," and the title track—that were arranged by Van de Pitte with airy jazz overtones. "Berry wasn't thrilled, but I was promoting it, and the disc jockeys weren't thrilled. They heard the record and said that they didn't like it because he didn't have any breaks in it. They gave a lot of excuses," McDougal said. "And they would all say that Marvin Gaye had his day. He was finished. What I did to get it played was, I went to the record stores. And I just kept giving it out to all the deejays that I could. Next thing I knew, everybody was playing it. The public loved it, that's how that really made it."

Free of the restraints of working within the regimented Motown structure, Gaye took his own sweet time creating *Trouble Man* (1972), *Let's Get It On* (while recording the 1973 set, he became involved with teenager Janis Hunter, eventually his second wife), and *I Want You* (1976). The '70s weren't kind to him emotionally. The high-profile divorce from Anna, a growing dependence on drugs, and his own instability made life difficult. Leaving Motown for Columbia Records, he went gold in 1982 with the reggae-based "Sexual Healing." But the strained relationship he'd had all his life with his father finally boiled over on April 1, 1984. While involved in a heated physical dispute at their L.A. home, the elder Gay fatally shot his son.

May his soul rest in peace.

Marvin Gaye had it all as a performer: Talent, style, grace and desire. Ultimately, however, his troubling and tumultuous personal life caught up with him one day short of his 45th birthday.

Michael Jackson and his four brothers, shown here at the Los Angeles Forum in 1970, brought a new style and energy to Motown and its fans in the late 1960s and early 70s (Paul Roberson photo courtesy of George Livingston).

THE JACKSON 5

This 1970 Ebony magazine cover proclaimed the Jackson 5 "the hottest young group in history" (Photo courtesy of David Alston's Mahogany Archives).

Pubescent rhythm and blues singers were by no means an unknown entity prior to the Jackson 5's phenomenal rise to superstardom at Motown. Frankie Lymon, the ill-fated lead singer of the Teenagers, had rocketed to the top in 1956 with his immortal "Why Do Fools Fall In Love" before drugs and a fickle public snuffed the New Yorker's promising career. Closer to home, Little Stevie Wonder lived up to his name from the moment he set foot inside Hitsville.

None made the impact of the five lads from Gary, Indiana. Their spellbinding act had been polished to a glistening sheen by authoritarian papa Joe Jackson, and little Michael—11 years of age when the quintet's first Motown 45, "I Want You Back," topped the charts in 1969— was a born showman whose pint-sized flying feet could challenge the likes of James Brown. Those obvious attributes render it surprising that Michael and his precocious siblings were at first put on hold by the label's powers that be.

The Jackson 5 hit the charts for the first time with "I Want You Back" in 1969, when lead singer Michael was just 11 years old.

Jackie (born May 4, 1951), Tito (born October 15, 1953), Jermaine (born December 11, 1954), Marlon (born March 12, 1957), and Michael (born August 29, 1958) had undergone grooming as a unit since 1964, when Joe relegated his own aspirations (he played guitar with a Gary group called the Falcons, no relation to the Motor City crew of the same name) to the back burner to develop the budding talent of his five oldest sons, who were the Ripples & Waves Plus Michael early on. Honing their stage moves by mimicking Brown, Joe Tex, and Jackie Wilson, Michael and the J5 made their debut single in 1968 for Gary-based Steeltown, nationally distributed by Atco. The chipper "You've Changed" displayed a Motown feel structurally, though its rudimentary guitar-bass-drums instrumentation retained a down-home quality. The sweet ballad "Big Boy" lyrically traded on Michael's youth.

The J5 were branching further afield, trying to crack the Chicago market by entering the weekly amateur contest at the High Chaparral nightclub on the South Side. One week, the headliners happened to be Motown's Bobby Taylor & the Vancouvers. "The way the High Chaparral did it, on Wednesday, they would have a talent show," said McDougal. "Whoever won the talent show on Wednesday opened up for the headliner on Friday, Saturday, and Sunday, and got paid. I go in on Wednesday (because they were closed on Thursday) to pick out the table that I wanted for the disc jockeys on Friday, so everything will be set up. When I was there, they had the talent show. And that's when I saw the Jackson 5.

"(High Chaparral boss) Clarence introduced me to Joe Jackson, and (Joe) said, 'Listen, man, I want to be with Motown.' And I said, 'Hey, man, I'm just a promotion man. Ain't nothing I could do.' He said, 'Oh, man, I'm gonna show you something.' So he showed me the label they were on, which was Steeltown. And he also had a contract for Atlantic Records. I mean, all he had to do was sign it, and he would have been on Atlantic.

"What I saw on stage, they impressed me. Only reason they impressed me because I had a group when I was in Philly called the Twilights who were 9 years old. They used to do a James Brown routine, where they would throw the cape off and all that kind of stuff. And Michael did the same thing, and everybody seemed to really enjoy that. So the next day, which was Thursday, I saw Bobby Taylor. And I said, 'Listen man, I saw some young guys last night. They're going to be on the show with you guys, because they won.'

"When they got there that Friday night, the first thing, Michael, he was just a nice guy. A little boy, he was so inquisitive. He'd walk up to Bobby Taylor, 'Man, I hear you was good. You're a good guy.' Just jumping up in Bobby Taylor's face, talkin' all kinds of stuff. So I said, 'Hey man, this is the guy, this is the lead singer.' Bobby said, 'No kidding! I gotta hear this guy!' So when he heard him, he was so impressed that he told Joe that he could sign 'em up to him. He didn't have to worry about being with Motown, because he had a production deal with Motown, and Motown would accept any of his acts. So Bobby Taylor signed 'em up to him as a manager and producer. And that's how they really got with Motown."

Taylor and Vancouvers guitarist Tommy Chong cite a memorable J5 amateur show victory at another Windy City landmark during the summer of '68 as a deciding factor in Taylor championing the group. "The Regal Theater," said Chong. "They opened for us. They had won a contest. They'd won an amateur night contest at the Regal, and the prize was that they got to open for Bobby Taylor & the Vancouvers. And we were so impressed that we took 'em to Detroit with us. And it took 'em months before Motown would see 'em. They finally got wise."

"After they got there, I would see 'em all the time," continued McDougal. "But they could never get in the studio, because they would be sittin' on

The Jackson 5 from left to right: Jackie, Jermaine, Tito, Marlon, and Michael.

the benches, waiting. Just like a football team. They were waitin', because everybody else had studio time for important records. One thing about Motown: if you had a hit, then you had to come up with another record in the next three to six months. So the studio was pretty busy, and it was serious business. It wasn't about one guy trying to outdo another guy by staying in the studio all the time. They had to actually do records, so we could sell 'em. So they wouldn't let the Jackson 5 in for a while."

An impatient Taylor shot a demonstration videotape in a spartan rehearsal room that captured Michael doing the Popcorn as he blazed through a vintage James Brown number. It should have been enough to convince anyone of his infinite potential, grainy black-and-white reproduction or not. As their first producer at Motown, Taylor weaned his charges on a non-stop diet of classic soul, typified by their spine-chilling David Van de Pitte-arranged rendition of the Miracles' "Who's Loving You" that comprised half of the J5's debut Motown single (challenging Smokey Robinson on his home turf took supreme confidence). Taylor hunkered his proteges down in Studio A with the Funk Brothers, investigating Sly & the Family Stone's "Stand!" (issued on the J5's debut LP), the Isley Brothers ("It's Your Thing"), even Ray Charles ("A Fool For You") in his quest to make them the next worldwide soul sensation.[5]

Live exposure was just as integral to their successful launch. "After the Jackson 5 got signed, Bobby Taylor got 'em on a couple of gigs with him. Like, if you booked Bobby, you had to book the Jacksons. But one of the shows where Bobby wasn't on was at the Apollo. So when the Jacksons were at the Apollo, I drove up," said McDougal. "I go to the Apollo, and the headliners at the time were the Five Stairsteps. That's the reason the Jacksons were on, because there was already one kid act, and the people felt like that would be kind of nice, to have two kid acts. When I went in, there was a big stir in the back.

The Jackson 5 getting down during the filming of *Save the Children* for Rev. Jesse Jackson's Operation PUSH (Weldon A. McDougal III photo).

"Everybody was mad because the Jackson 5 had just came off, and they got such a great hand. But when I went out in the wings, I heard people talking about, 'Jackson 5!' They'd just keep on hollering. And the emcee tried to say, 'They'll be back in just a minute, folks. Now, ladies and gentlemen, we've got so-and-so...' They wouldn't let him bring 'em on! So then he finally brought the other act on,'" Weldon said. "Clarence (Burke) of the Five Stairsteps, he was their manager. He was pretty disturbed. He didn't want them on the show. So I used a pay phone at the Apollo to call Georgie Woods at the Uptown (in Philadelphia). Georgie Woods said, 'Yeah, I'll take 'em, man. You say they're good?' I said, 'They're fabulous.' So they went to the Uptown, and they got the same response. The people just loved 'em."

J5 stock was rising at Hitsville too. "Finally, Bobby Taylor got Berry Gordy to hear them at the pool house," said McDougal. "Berry Gordy used to have a house that had a swimming pool. On the hill was the house, and you come down, there's like a guesthouse and a swimming pool. A very nice place. This was in Detroit. And you could perform in there. So the Jackson 5 performed, and Berry Gordy heard 'em."

"Hallelujah Day" was one of the Jackson 5's 17 non-seasonal Motown singles to appear on the charts.

Recognizing a pop act of the highest potential magnitude, he teamed the J5 with guitarist Deke Richards and keyboardists Freddie Perren and Fonce Mizell to brainstorm a suitable debut vehicle, dubbing his new crew of collaborators the Corporation. Gordy brought the boys out to L.A., where he was now ensconced as the seat of Motown's power moved west (the J5 would record the great majority of their Motown output in the City of Angels). Taylor was relieved of his post as their producer, and the Corporation handed Michael and his brothers the torrid "I Want You Back." Released in October of '69, it defined the concept of bubblegum soul.

"When I went out to get it played, it was very difficult," said McDougal. "Everybody said, 'Man, who wants those little young guys? What are they? They don't know nothin' about love, and I can't do nothin' with these guys.' The sales department was dedicated now to do something with the Jackson 5. Everything that we used to do, we used to do it on the back of another artist. The Supremes were No. 1, so Berry told Diana, 'Let's make the Jackson 5 your proteges.' And then we wrote it up, 'Diana Ross's proteges, the Jackson 5.' And ABC-TV had a show called *Hollywood Palace*. Diana Ross was co-starring with Sammy Davis, Jr. That gave them the opportunity. The first time they ever went on national TV was on *Hollywood Palace*. After that, we had the opportunity to go on Ed Sullivan."

Anyone who missed the J5's *Hollywood Palace* debut was surely floored by their appearance on Ed Sullivan's December 14, 1969 CBS-TV program. "I went to *The Ed Sullivan Show* with 'em," said McDougal. "Everybody was so excited. I mean, they were really excited. They did *The Ed Sullivan Show*, and the next day, I was home. And people were calling me like mad, talking about, 'Hey, man—you still got them records on them little guys?' They never called them the Jackson 5. They would say 'them little guys,' or 'them boys you got,' or something like that. And 'I Want You Back' started climbing up the charts and hit No. 1."

By early January of 1970, "I Want You Back" sat at the top of the R&B charts. Before the month was over, the insidious rocker followed suit on the pop side. J5 pandemonium was spreading like wildfire, the supreme Supreme's name glittering as their official benefactor. In theory, Ross even wrote the liner notes to their first LP, *Diana Ross Presents the Jackson 5*, which began with a treatise on the value of honesty and proceeded to offer a highly fanciful account of how she became involved with their career. Taylor received mention as the "first professional to work with the guys"–not true either, unless Steeltown's bosses were deemed rank amateurs.

"They gave Diana Ross the credit," noted Chong. "It looked much neater for the press if she found 'em than the Vancouvers."

Jobete copyrights were the order of the day: The Tops' "Standing In The Shadows Of Love," Marvin's "Chained," Stevie's "My Cherie Amour," and the Tempts' "(I Know) I'm Losing You" were all summarily Jacksonized, little Michael's voice so high-pitched that unsuspecting album buyers may have double-checked the speed of their stereos. Outside covers ranged from Bob B. Soxx & the Blue Jeans' Phil Spector-devised treatment of "Zip-A-Dee Doo-Dah" to the Delfonics' Philly soul ballad "Can You Remember" and the J5's own Steeltown-era "You've Changed"—its title altered to "You've Changed Me" and its arrangement beefed up with horns. The Corporation wasn't about to waste fresh material. "Nobody" was the LP's only original besides "I Want You Back."

The formula thus established, the Corporation fashioned a barely perceptible variation entitled "ABC" and watched it soar to the same No. 1 position on both charts in the spring of 1970 (Michael ordered everyone to make a path for "The Young Folks"on the flip). That summer, "The Love You Save"—another Corporation-penned up-tempo raveup in the "I Want You Back"/"ABC" vein—made it three unanimous chart toppers in a row. So suddenly consequential were young Michael and his brothers that "The Love You Save's" lovely Corporation-penned ballad flip, "I Found A Girl," charted in tandem with "The Love You Save," just as the sumptuous "Who's Loving You" had on the 'B' side of "I Want You Back."

The Corporation and Motown's L.A. mainstay, Hal Davis, co-produced *ABC*, the group's encore LP in the spring of '70, which surrounded its title cut and "The Love You Save" with Wonder's "Never Had A Dream Come True" and "Don't Know Why I Love You," the Parliaments' throbbing "I'll Bet You," and the Delfonics' silky "La-La Means I Love You." The Corporation anted up "One More Chance," while Pam Sawyer and Gloria Jones' "2-4-6-8" cashed in on another classroom motif.

The J5 had become Motown superstars on an unprecedented level in an incredibly short time span, seducing kids of every creed and color. Still, it was time to try something new, and producer Hal Davis, along with Willie Hutch, Bob West, and Gordy, brainstormed a beautiful ballad, "I'll Be There," that proved the quintet's talents did not lie exclusively with schoolyard soul. This time, Michael wasn't the sole focus. He handed off to Jermaine for the uplifting bridge. "I'll Be There" was the J5's fourth pop/R&B chart-topper in a row during the fall of 1970. "Mama's Pearl," on the other hand, was basically a delightful by-the-numbers Corporation vehicle, Michael sailing over a churning guitar-and-bass line and propulsive drumming. Relatively speaking, it proved a commercial disappointment, "only" making it to No. 2 on *Billboard's* pop and R&B lists in early '71.

The songs were culled from the quintet's functionally titled *Third Album*, a September 1970 release that saw them growing artistically (physically too, for that matter) by leaps and bounds. No longer was Michael the sole focus of the group, though obviously he remained its main little man. Another trio of Jobete classics—the Miracles' "The Love I Saw In You Was Just A Mirage" and "Darling Dear," and Edwin Starr's ecstatic "Oh How Happy"—was joined by the Delfonics' "Ready Or Not (Here I Come)" and a treatment of Simon & Garfunkel's "Bridge Over Troubled Water" bloated by overblown orchestration.

On the other hand, "Goin' Back To Indiana" was as close as the J5 ever dared venture to a straight-ahead blues shuffle, Tito stepping up for a two-chorus guitar solo bathed in wah-wah (the lads indulged in a high school cheerleading chant near the cold ending of the rocker, never issued as a single but useful as a title theme to their '71 network TV special). "Can I See You In The Morning," the work of Corporation conspirator Deke Richards, bore a touch of psychedelia, and "How Funky Is Your Chicken" deposited the Jacksons in one-chord groove land. A month later, the J5's *Christmas Album* hit the shelves in time for the holidays. Its single, "Santa Claus Is Coming To Town," was redolent of Spector's Wall of Sound production by the Crystals.

The spring of '71 brought another all-time Jackson 5 classic showcasing their more mature side to great advantage. Hal Davis produced "Never Can Say Goodbye," its flute-enriched arrangement flowing gently and easily over a vaguely funky rhythmic bed and Michael sounding a tad more grown up than before. Written by actor Clifton Davis, the number restored the group to the peak of the R&B charts that May, though it fell one slot short on the pop side. That fall, they starred in their very own ABC-TV cartoon series, much as the Beatles had a few years earlier.

Motown developed many young stars, but few could approach the talent and charisma of the adolescent Michael Jackson.

The title track of their fifth LP, *Maybe Tomorrow,* provided the J5's next smash that summer, again in a more adult vein though permeated in teen appeal. The album was a departure in its comparative lack of retread material. Martha & the Vandellas' "Honey Chile" and the Crests' '59 doo-wop smash "16 Candles" were dwarfed by a half dozen Corporation-penned numbers, notably "She's Good" (led by Jermaine), "My Little Baby," and "I Will Find A Way."

When Diana Ross and Smokey Robinson decided it was time to embark on solo careers, it marked the end of their lengthy tenure leading their respective groups. No such dilemma faced the J5: Michael spun off his first solo smash in late '71 with the distinctive ballad "Got To Be There" and continued to score the next year with a frothy revival of Bobby Day's '58 smash "Rockin' Robin," the catchy "I Wanna Be Where You Are" (from the team of Leon Ware and Diana Ross's brother T-Boy) and Michael's infamous love ode to a rodent, the pop chart-topper "Ben," without missing a step beside his brothers. Jermaine followed suit, hitting with a solo "That's How Love Goes" and a revival of Shep & the Limelites' '61 classic "Daddy's Home" during 1972—meaning three releases by various Jackson permutations were sometimes climbing the charts concurrently.

This glut of product doesn't seem to have hurt their prospects in the slightest. All 17 of the J5's non-seasonal Motown singles placed in the R&B Top Ten, though their pop precedence lagged toward the end of their astonishing run. Throw in a half dozen Top Ten R&B hits by a solo Michael and another by Jermaine and you're looking at gargantuan sales. The Jacksons' unblemished track record extended through the rest of 1971 ("Sugar Daddy"), '72 (a faithful remake of Bobby Day's 1957 rocker "Little Bitty Pretty One," "Lookin' Through The Windows," and from the Gordy-financed Broadway musical *Pippin*, "Corner Of The Sky"), '73 ("Hallelujah Day" and "Get It Together"), '74 (the disco-friendly Hal Davis production "Dancing Machine" and "Whatever You Got, I Want") and 1975's two-part "I Am Love" and "Forever Came Today."

England wasn't immune from J5 fever. "We had just arrived in London," said Jeannie Long, whose vocal group, the Sisters Love, opened for the Jacksons. "I can't remember the place where we were, but the Jacksons were in this limousine, this Rolls Royce limousine. They had phoned ahead, and there were so many people there expecting the Jacksons that they took us off the coach and put us in the limousine.

"And when we got to the venue, the kids were climbing up on the fence. The fence was so very, very high, and the kids were climbing up on the fence, and they were about to break the fence down! Then after we got to where we were going to be staying, we went to have something to eat. And the kids—the wall of the restaurant was all glass. And it scared me so badly, because it seemed like they were going to break the wall down.

"It was like pandemonium."

An increasing yen to helm their own musical ship without outside interference and father Joe's unyielding influence convinced the Jacksons to exit Motown for the major label security of Columbia's Epic subsidiary. Their Epic debut, "Enjoy Yourself," was produced by Philly soul architects Kenny Gamble and Leon Huff and went gold in late '76. Jermaine wasn't part of the act, electing to remain at Motown. He had married Berry Gordy's daughter, Hazel, three years earlier. Little brother Randy took his place in the newly renamed Jacksons.

Try to ignore the tabloid sleaze, the endless plastic surgeries, and the eccentric behavior that has characterized his reign as an incessantly unfathomable solo superstar (difficult though it may be). When wee Michael Jackson and his brothers came storming out of steel country with their game down tight, there was no questioning his credentials as the littlest soul giant of all.

Since the early 1960s Gladys Knight and the Pips have performed as a quartet: (from left) William Guest, Bubba Knight, Edward Patten and Gladys (Photo courtesy of David Alston's Mahogany Archives).

GLADYS KNIGHT & THE PIPS

Nitty Gritty, a 1969 release by the Pips, contained material from a handful of big-name composers, but was largely a collection of remakes.

Stars when they arrived at Motown in 1966 and superstars after they left, Gladys Knight & the Pips enjoyed a longevity few of their contemporaries could dream of. Knight's dynamic leads were sweet as honey one moment and erupted volcanically the next as her perpetually in-motion Pips dished up flawless harmonies behind her.

Child prodigies don't come any more prodigious than Gladys. Born May 28, 1944 in Atlanta, Georgia, she was rattling the rafters of the Mount Moriah Baptist Church at age 4. A 7-year-old Gladys picked up a cool $2,000 first prize on *Ted Mack's Original Amateur Hour* by crooning Nat King Cole's "Too Young." In 1952, at a bash for her older brother Merald "Bubba" Knight (born September 4, 1942), her career path became crystal clear.

"Gladys gave a surprise birthday party for me at our house in Atlanta," said Bubba in 1996. "There was a kid that brought his record player to play music at the party. And he decided to take his record player, to make a long story short, because we weren't playing the kind of music that he wanted to hear. So we were left without any music. So we decided that everybody at the party would do something to entertain the guests. We would entertain each other. So we decided to sing. And we sounded pretty good. Everybody was applauding and everything. And then after the party was over, my mom came to us and asked us if we wanted to pursue this, being performers, you know? So we said, 'Yeah, this is fun!' And that's how it really got started, at my birthday party."

Their cousin William Guest (born June 2, 1941) was another amateur harmonizer at the same soiree. "The original group then, there was three girls and two boys. There was Gladys and Bubba's other sister Brenda, and my sister Eleanor Guest," he said in 1996. Another cousin, James Woods, stepped up to manage the freshly minted vocal quintet. "After we decided we was gonna sing together, he took up a lot of time, he would take us around to different places that let us rehearse so people could hear us," said Guest. "He took us to different things, like we found that a lot of church organizations would have teas on Sundays. And we would go over there and we would sing. And he would take us from there to other places for people to hear us.

"So after we started rehearsing, one time we said, 'Well, we're gonna find us a name.' So everybody went home and brought back a list of names. Had all kinds of birds and flowers and stuff like that. We couldn't decide on the names that everybody brought in, so we decided that we'd name it after him. His nickname was Pip. And so he said, 'Oh, no, you don't want to name yourself that!' We said, 'Yeah! We're gonna name ourselves the Pips, and we'll never change.'"

In the beginning, the Pips' repertoire was eclectic. "We didn't focus in on just R&B. We just was doing songs that we liked to do. And they was all type of songs," said Guest. "Spiritual songs, gospel songs, popular songs," agreed Knight. "'Canadian Sunset,' 'How High The Moon,' songs of that nature. We did 'Bless This House' and 'The Glory Of Love.'"

The Pips continually polished their act, coached by a future Motown mainstay. "There was a guy by the name of Maurice King. Musical director at the Flame Show Bar. We used to go to Detroit every summer, when we would get out of school. Our parents would take us up," said Bubba. "Mr. King would train us vocally during the summer. He liked us so well, and he saw the potential in us being a successful group, that he went out and got us a record deal with Brunswick Records. And he brought to us the songs 'Whistle My Love' and 'Ching Chong.' And that was our first experience in recording. We recorded it in Detroit on Brunswick. They released the record. Came out, didn't make a whole lot of noise, but it did introduce us to the recording industry." King assembled a larger orchestra than customary, the Pips' high-pitched voices providing chirpy counterpoint on the swinging "Whistle My Love" and a choppy "Ching Chong," one of a slew of Oriental-themed novelties flooding the 1958 market.

Eleanor and Brenda dropped out of the Pips in '59. Instead of hiring two more females, Gladys would now front an all-male cast: Cousin Edward Patten (born August 2, 1939) and Langston George were the new Pips. "Eleanor and Brenda went on to college," said Guest. "Later on, they got married. So it was just Bubba, William Guest, and Gladys—the three of us—left. And Pip said we needed two more people to replace Eleanor and Brenda. And he went out and brought people back every once in a while to rehearse with us, and we never were satisfied with any of those people. Then when Langston and Edward came in, they was part of a group in Atlanta that was real popular. We decided to keep them.

"We just did a lot of work in Atlanta, because I think that was the only place they really played the record," said Guest. "And we were already the No. 1 group in Atlanta," continued Bubba. "That was just like a little bit of icing on the cake, because people could say, 'Yeah, they're recording artists! They're not just a local group. They record also.'"

The group found the means for their breakthrough on the road. "We was on a tour with Hank Ballard & the Midnighters, the people that made 'The Twist,'" said Guest. "So at night on the bus, there was a guy in the group, his name was Sonny Woods. And he said, 'I've got a song, kids, I'd like to teach you that we recorded.' They recorded 'Every Beat Of My Heart,' and he taught it to us. Little did we know that later on, we would have an opportunity to record it.

"We worked at a place called the Builders Club in Atlanta. And they bought some equipment, and they asked us, could we come after church to come over and test the equipment out. So they asked us what we was gonna sing. So we decided we would sing the song that Sonny Woods taught us. We rehearsed it with the band, Cleveland Lyons' trio. And we sang that song. Little did we know that Clifford Hunter would be putting the song out without our permission."

Surreptitiously issued by Hunter and partner Tommy Brown on their tiny Huntom logo, the breathtaking ballad "Every Beat Of My Heart" took about six weeks to start happening regionally. "He had put the record out all in Florida and South Carolina and North Carolina, which we wasn't aware of," said Guest. "And then the record got to Atlanta. I never will forget, I went to get my clothes from the cleaners. And I heard this song, 'Every Beat Of My Heart,' and I passed by the record store, and they had it on the outside speakers. And I just started singing right along with the song. But then I said, 'Hey!! That's us!!' And I ran off and called Bubba. I said, 'Bubba! Guess what I heard! I heard our song!' And Bubba said, 'Yeah, I've been hearing it on the radio all day.' And that's how we found out we had a record out."

Hunter peddled the master to Chicago's Vee-Jay Records. "Once we found that this guy had put this record out without our permission, then all of the record companies from New York and everyplace was calling, wanting to know who we were signed up (with)," said Guest. "So we finally decided to go to New York and sign with Bobby Robinson, who owned Fire and Fury Records. When we got there, Bobby said, 'Let's go into the studio and record the same record again,' because we wasn't under contract with anyone.

"So we was in the studio that night and recorded the same song again. A telegram came in that night saying that Huntom Records out of Atlanta had sold his master tape to Vee-Jay Records in Chicago. Therefore, our record was out on three labels at the same time, and they was trying to outdo each other. As a result of that, it exposed our name to the world. People started knowing who the Pips were at the time. But we had to make a distinction between the labels.

"Huntom, when they sold their masters to Vee-Jay, we was known as the Pips. Just the Pips. Then we had to make a distinction between Vee-Jay and Fury, and that's when Gladys Knight & the Pips came along, 'cause Gladys was our lead singer," said Guest. "Bobby Robinson asked if we'd mind naming his record *Gladys Knight & the Pips*, so we would know the difference." The hubbub left the Pips in the enviable position of having two versions of the same song simultaneously climbing the charts in late May of 1961. Their original Vee-Jay cut topped Billboard's R&B charts and went to No. 6 pop, while the Fury remake peaked at No. 15 R&B.

After the Pips' revival of Jesse Belvin's "Guess Who" sank without trace that summer, they called Don Covay, then acquiring quite a reputation as a performer and songwriter. Covay gave them the bluesy ballad "Letter Full Of Tears." "Don Covay wrote it specifically for us, and then Bobby Robinson had Horace Ott to do the arrangement. And that was the first time we had ever used a string section," said Bubba. "There was a guy that had just jumped on Bobby Robinson's promotional team by the name of Marshall Sehorn. Bobby didn't really want to record strings, and Marshall Sehorn begged him to put strings on this song for us. Because during that time, when you used strings, it kind of made yourself a little bit more sophisticated than the regular R&B thing." "Letter Full Of Tears" was a smash on Fury at the end of '61.

Gladys Knight & the Pips in an Apollo Theatre dressing room. Left to right: William Guest, Bubba Knight, Edward Patten and Gladys (Weldon A. McDougal III photo).

"We thought we was on our way then," said Bubba. Little did they know. Gladys and her guys waxed "Operator," but it barely squeaked onto the pop charts in the spring of '62. Their other follow-ups, including Covay's "Come See About Me," did even less. George left after "Operator," cementing a lineup of tenors Patten and Guest and baritone Bubba. Even Gladys briefly split. "Gladys went home to start a family. She got married, and she started a family," said Bubba. "She wanted to raise her child. She didn't want to drag a child up and down the road, and she wanted to start a family. So she decided that she was gonna come off the road for a while. So William, Edward and myself decided to keep the name of the Pips going, 'cause we felt like we still had enough talent to keep rolling. Langston went solo. We called Bobby Robinson and told him we wanted to record some music. And he said, 'What kind are you gonna record? Y'all background singers!'

"That's when we started writing. That's when we wrote 'Darling' and 'Linda.' Bobby Robinson didn't have no idea we could sing by ourselves. So when we sang that in front of him in person, his eyes lit up like a light. He saw another group inside the group." The hip three-part harmonies displayed by the Pips on their Gladys-less Fury singles didn't translate into hits. Fortunately, Gladys soon grew restless and rejoined the group.

Two more future Motown stalwarts gave the reconstituted Pips' fortunes a boost. Larry Maxwell, later an ace promo man at Hitsville, signed the group to his fledgling Maxx label. And Cholly Atkins—the veteran hoofer who would devise the Temptations' untouchable stage moves—met the Pips through baseball star Willie Mays' ex-wife Marguerite.

"She asked him, 'Would you start working with us on choreography?'" said Guest. "And he was more than happy to, 'cause he had heard about us. Because we were doing a lot of high steppin', and our own unique type dancing, even before we met him. That's what made us so popular, because we took the dances that we knew in Atlanta along with the creative minds in the group, and created our own style. The people loved us because of our performances. So Cholly Atkins came along and enhanced that a thousand percent.

Gladys Knight at the Latin Casino in Cherry Hill, N.J. (Weldon A. McDougal III photo).

"Larry Maxwell, he was about to start his own label called Maxx Records. So he asked Marguerite, could he record us? So he did, and people still thought we was broken up. The first record we recorded was 'Giving Up.'" A substantial hit in the spring of '64, "Giving Up" was the work of Van McCoy, who would allow his singing career to lapse to focus on producing and composing. "Van McCoy was a *writer*, boy," said Bubba. "I loved doing Van McCoy's songs."

After scoring a minor follow-up hit that summer for Maxx with "Lovers Always Forgive" and a few more 45s for the label the next year, Gladys and the Pips moved to Motown in 1966. "Berry Gordy had tried to get us before then. We were interested. Gladys wasn't interested," said Bubba. "We felt that if we had the recognition from records like we had had recognition from our live performances—if we combined the two—that spelled success all the way across the board. So when the vote came up to go to Motown, we had three for and one against. We had three yeas and one nay. Because Gladys didn't want to go to Motown. For a good reason—she didn't want to be put in that line of Motown artists that she felt that we would have to come behind. Which was legitimate, and we understood that.

"But we decided that we didn't have that much to lose. Because if we hit it big at Motown, that meant we would hit it *big*. But if we didn't at least we could get over there and get the experience, work with the best writers and producers, and all of that. We could learn ourselves how to become better writers and better producers. So here was a win-win situation for us, by going over there, even if we did not get a hit record."

Of course, it didn't hurt that several friends who had played previous roles in the Pips' success had joined the label's Artist Development Department. "During that time, Motown did start hiring people like Cholly Atkins, Maurice King, people that we used to have to pay," noted Guest. "Motown was the first company that started opening up a lot of doors for black acts. They was getting radio play from all jocks. Not just R&B jocks, the pop jocks, too. So me and Bubba and Edward, we had a legitimate reason for going there, too."

"After we signed with Motown, Berry Gordy had a meeting with us. He said, 'You know, every time an artist would come back after working with you guys, there'd be something about them damn Pips! They're saying the Pips do this, they're saying the Pips do that! So I figured I'd go hire everybody that you work with!'" laughed Bubba.

"So we went to Motown, and we were very well accepted. I have to say we were accepted with open arms, although we didn't get the top-of-the-line material at first. Because most of the top producers like Holland-Dozier-Holland and producers like that, and Smokey and the guys, were working with the Temptations, the Supremes, the regular top-of-the-line acts. Which we knew that that was gonna happen. But eventually they started giving us material, and allowing us to put our own creativity to it. And when we did that, then we started getting some recognition from some of the producers and some of the better writers. Because they were saying, 'Whoa! Take my song and fool around with it like you guys do!'"

Gladys and the Pips take center stage at the Valley Forge Theater in Valley Forge, Pennsylvania (Weldon A. McDougal photo).

Johnny Bristol and Harvey Fuqua were the first producers to inherit Gladys and the Pips, supervising their thumping "Just Walk In My Shoes." Written by the Lewis Sisters (Helen and Kay), it became the group's first single on Motown's Soul imprint in mid-'66. Norman Whitfield entered to produce their next Soul offering, "Take Me In Your Arms And Love Me," an upbeat collaboration by Barrett Strong, Roger Penzabene, and Tempts guitarist Cornelius Grant. "I think that was Barrett Strong's idea," noted Grant, "between him and Roger Penzabene. I was kind of on the outer edges of it, 'cause I was in and out of town. Roger and I were friends, so if I did any work on a song, I didn't have to worry about getting my credits as far as having worked on 'em." Though it did marginal business stateside in early '67, "Take Me In Your Arms" was a British smash.

The group's third time out on Soul proved the charm. Spiced by finger snapping and the Pips' retorts, Gladys cooed "Everybody Needs Love" with captivating subtlety. Whitfield, who co-wrote the number with Eddie Holland, had previously produced it for the '65 LP The *Temptin' Temptations* with Eddie Kendricks as lead. "We came along and put our little touch on it," said Guest, and that apparently made all the difference. "Everybody Needs Love" established Gladys and her Pips at Motown, blasting to No. 3 on *Billboard's* R&B listings in the summer of '67.

When Norman handed them "I Heard It Through The Grapevine," it was a marriage made in heaven.

"Norman gave us the track, and we took the track home, man, we would rehearse that thing night and day, in the morning and at night!" said Bubba. "Took it on the road with us and the whole shot, until we molded 'I Heard It Through The Grapevine' the way we wanted to with our own creativity. And we took it back to Norman Whitfield one day. He said, 'How ya'll comin' with that song I gave you, "Grapevine"?' And we went over to the studio one day at Motown and we sung it for him. We put the tape recorder on and we sung what we had on there. And he said, 'Good God! Get me a studio right now!'

"Smokey was in the studio at the time. And he called up there and asked Smokey, could we use some of his studio time, 'cause he wanted to record this song 'I Heard It Through The Grapevine' on us right then. And Smokey let us use the studio, man, and we went in there, and Norman Whitfield cut 'I Heard It Through The Grapevine,' boy, like the way we had it. They did a few moderations to it, changed it around a little bit, but basically took our whole background like the way we had done it, and took the lead like the way that 'G' had done it, and cut it like that. Together, we molded 'I Heard It Through The Grapevine' like the way that you heard it."

By opening with a drum salvo so intricate that its execution required two great trapsmen (Benny Benjamin and Uriel Jones) and sporting a storming Hank Cosby sax solo, Gladys and the Pips transformed "Grapevine" into a rave-up revival-meeting rocker destined for the top of the R&B charts in December of '67. It just missed the same happy fate on the pop side and garnered the group its first Grammy nomination. Gladys and her guys traded spirited call-and-response patterns over ominous piano riffs and a killer James Jamerson bass line. Not that the Pips were actually present when the groove was going down, mind you.

"What they did was, they had recorded the track that we actually sung on before it had gotten to us," said Bubba. "See, Norman just gave us the track with the drums and everything all on it, and we made up the rest of it. He just gave us how the melody went. Norman couldn't sing. Then Gladys picked up on that, and then we made up the background."

Those enduring gospel leanings once landed the group in hot water. "It's a funny thing," recalled William. "During that time, I think the A&R person was a girl by the name of Billie Jean (Brown). She came down once to the studio and said, 'Who is this down here singing all this gospel stuff? We're looking for a hit!'" Nor was their precious name immune from theoretical tinkering.

"One time Berry Gordy was having a meeting with us," recalled Guest. "During that time, we was going through a little slump with our records. He said, 'Well, guys, maybe it's that name you guys have. Maybe you should change that name!' And we told him we would never change our name. It's not the name that makes the group, it's the group that makes the name."

The group's first Soul LP, *Everybody Needs Love*, released in the late summer of '67, conclusively showed the veteran outfit sparkling within Motown's hit-making machinery. Along with their first four singles, the set included another Tempts cover ("Ain't No Sun Since You've Been Gone"), Whitfield's "Since I've Lost You," Nickolas Ashford and Valerie Simpson's stately "I'll Be Standing By," and Smokey's bluesy "My Bed Of Thorns."

Whitfield retained much of the same sanctified rhythmic drive for the quartet's next Soul smash in early '68. "The End Of Our Road," penned by Whitfield, Strong, and Penzabene, was almost as potent a seller as "Grapevine," with Gladys again summoning up a heavenly fury as the Pips whooped it up in response. Its rousing Whitfield/Strong-penned

"It's not the name that makes the group, it's the group that makes the name."

flip, "Don't Let Her Take Your Love From Me," was a house favorite: Jimmy Ruffin cut it as a '68 single, Whitfield recycled it as a Tempts album track, and the Four Tops charted with it in '69.

"Triangle" songs had done well for Etta James over the years, and Gladys tried her hand at a similar girl-left-at-the-altar weeper in mid-'68. "It Should Have Been Me," written by Whitfield and Mickey Stevenson and introduced by Kim Weston on Tamla five years earlier, cast Gladys as a jilted lover forced to watch her ex stroll down the aisle with someone new. The public gobbled up the musical soap opera, making it four Top Ten R&B hits in a row.

Feelin' Bluesy, their first LP of '68, was another strong collection featuring "I Know Better," Smokey's "Ain't You Glad You Chose Love," the stirring "Don't Turn Me Away," and a swaying "It's Time To Go Now." Gladys tore into Mary Wells' "Your Old Standby" and laid down a driving "That's The Way Love Is" by Whitfield and Strong that predated Marvin Gaye's hit version by a year. Gaye enjoyed smashes with "I Heard It Through The Grapevine," "That's The Way Love Is," and "The End Of Our Road," all done previously by Gladys and the Pips.

The Pips' 1967 LP *Everybody Needs Love* featured the title track and "I Heard it Through the Grapevine."

This musically incestuous situation didn't go unnoticed by the Pips. "They did that a lot, man," said Bubba. "That was one of the things that Gladys was talking about (as to why) she didn't want to go over there. We weren't used to cover songs." But when Gladys and the Pips revived "I Wish It Would Rain" in late summer of 1968, less than a year after the Temptations issued their R&B chart-topping original on Gordy, the remake was a Top 15 R&B hit itself. *Silk n' Soul*, their other LP that year, maxed out the trend by consisting of nothing but covers.

As successful as their partnership with Whitfield was proving, Gladys and the Pips momentarily switched to the stewardship of Nickolas Ashford and Valerie Simpson for a powerhouse "Didn't You Know (You'd Have To Cry Sometime)," which just missed the R&B Top Ten during the spring of '69. "We knew them before we ever moved to Detroit for Motown," said William. "Because we used to work in New York a lot together. They wasn't the Ashford & Simpson team during that time. They used to sing in a different group, they sang together as a group."

Whitfield reached outside the Jobete catalog for Gladys' next hit, a treatment of "The Nitty Gritty" that rode a far funkier edge than Shirley Ellis's 1963 Top Ten original. "That was supposed to be Diana Ross &

the Supremes' song," said Bubba. "They let us hear it in the studio one day. We heard Diana and them's version of it. And they let us kinda do our thing again, and ours came out a lot stronger. So it came out on us." Gladys and the Pips' funky "The Nitty Gritty" went to just shy of the top slot on the R&B hit parade in mid-'69. On the *Nitty Gritty* album, Gladys challenged Etta on her triangle turf with a treatment of her 1960 hit "All I Could Do Was Cry" (penned by Berry Gordy, his sister Gwen, and Roquel "Billy" Davis) in addition to covering more Tempts classics and ripping into Whitfield and Strong's "Got Myself A Good Man." Gladys, Bubba, and William teamed with producers Bristol and Fuqua to brainstorm "I Want Him To Say It Again."

Whitfield and Strong went back to the funk well for Gladys and the Pips' last smash of the turbulent decade, the wah-wah-guitar-driven brotherhood plea "Friendship Train," which fell just short of topping the R&B lists. "It was a good song to put into our act, 'cause it brought a lot of action," said William. "We would let the audience participate and stuff. They would shake hands and make a friend in the audience. That was a good tune for us." The Pips even got a rare chance to deliver a few lines unto themselves for a change.

Feelin' Bluesy, the Pips' first LP of 1968, was one of several albums that featured songs that were performed by other Motown artists. Sometimes the Pips got new material first, other times they wound up recycling songs.

Gladys & the Pips could do no wrong as the decade turned, immediately hitting paydirt in the spring of '70 with the funk-soaked Whitfield/Strong collaboration, "You Need Love Like I Do (Don't You)." Norman handed the production reins to Clay McMurray, who promptly helped the group score a No. 1 R&B smash and Top Ten pop hit with the magnificent "If I Were Your Woman" in January of '71. "That was Clay McMurray's song," said Bubba (Pam Sawyer and Gloria Jones, writing as Laverne Ware, were its co-writers). "He was a protege of Norman Whitfield's. Norman was teaching Clay how to be a producer and a writer." "His background was in publicity," said Hank Cosby. "He had worked as a promotion man for a while. And when he came to Motown, he hooked up with Norman Whitfield and became a co-producer."

"They wrote this song for Gladys Knight & the Pips called 'If I Were Your Woman.' And we were going like, 'Hey, how are we gonna sing "If I Were Your Woman" when we're men?' So we decided to do the background in a way where we sung, 'If you were my woman.' That's how the background lyrics became 'If you were my woman.' We changed it around so we could be a part of the song." The exciting call-and-response scenario was an essential ingredient in the song's tremendous charm, Gladys simmering as she pines for an unrequited love over a churning Paul Riser arrangement.

Riser remained in the arranger's chair for the quartet's next No. 2 R&B hit that summer, though Bristol replaced McMurray as producer. Gladys turned in another bravura outing on "I Don't Want To Do Wrong," soaring over swirling strings as the Pips echoed her exhortations. This was a homegrown composition, Gladys, Bubba, William, and Bristol writing with the Marvelettes' Katherine Anderson Schaffner. "I started that back in 10th grade. I got hung up on lyrics, and then Gladys and Johnny Bristol came in and helped me with the lyrics, and we finished it up," said Guest. "I remember when they wrote it on the back porch of our house in Detroit," said Bubba. "They finished it up there."

Gladys and the Pips were on a roll in the early 70s with hits like the title track to the LP *If I Were Your Woman* in 1971.

In Gladys's hands, even Traffic's "Feelin' Alright" and the Beatles' "Let It Be" inherited a dollop of unadulterated getdown on the group's '71 set *If I Were Your Woman* (production split between Bristol, McMurray, and Cosby protege Joe Hinton, who contributed "One Step Away," a gliding "How Can You Say That Ain't Love," and with longtime staffer Janie Bradford as his partner, "Your Love's Been Good For Me"). McMurray brought "Here I Am Again," a mellow "Is There A Place (In His Heart For Me)," and "Signed Gladys."

Clay was responsible for the quartet's last smash that year, "Make Me The Woman That You Go Home To," as both writer and producer. Riser and Funk Brothers guitarist Robert White came up with a lush arrangement that kicked Gladys' pipes into overdrive. The group's only 1972 hit didn't emanate from in-house channels. Kris Kristofferson's "Help Me Make It Through The Night" had surfaced as a 1971 crossover country smash by Sammi Smith, then entered the R&B lexicon via O.C. Smith and Joe Simon. Gladys invested its lyrics with a steely reserve buttressed by L.A.-based H.B. Barnum's arrangement. A growing reliance on hits of the day defined the '71 LP *Standing Ovation*; half its selections were pop and rock-derived.

Thanks to their latest producer, Gladys and her Pips crossed paths with the songwriter who would propel them to a new level of superstardom—mostly after they exited Motown. "The latter part of our contract with Motown, we met Joe Porter, who was raving over this new writer that he had ran across," said Bubba. "His name was Jim Weatherly. And Joe Porter was a good string man. To me, he wasn't a great producer, but he could make strings sound so lush. And so they decided to pair us up with Joe Porter on one of our albums.

"Joe Porter gave us creative freedom. Joe Porter didn't do anything but let us do whatever we wanted to do in the studio," he said. "We actually produced the songs. He would bring 'em to us, and we'd take the lead sheet and the demo and mold it, like the rest of the songs we used to do. We molded it to Gladys Knight & the Pips' way, and man, Joe would just sit in there in the studio and just tell 'em to turn the tape on."

Such was the case with Weatherly's shattering "Neither One Of Us (Wants To Be The First To Say Goodbye)," cut in L.A. "The night that we recorded it, we were supposed to fly back to Detroit," said Bubba. "We was in Los Angeles, and we had a flight back to Detroit. And we got the lead vocal down on it, and we had done a part of the background. And we were singing the song on the way to the airport in the car. I said, 'God, that song sure is stickin' with us a lot.' We got to the airport, man, we were getting ready to get on the plane. And it just struck us: 'Go back to the studio. We've got a vibe, man, the spirit moved on us!' We got back in the car, called the studio and told 'em we were coming back to the studio. And they held the studio open 'til we got back, man. We went back there and laid down the background to 'Neither One Of Us,' and man, when we played that thing back, we knew we had something great." It proved their last Motown No. 1 R&B hit in March of '73, nearly equaling that lofty standing on the pop charts, and Grammy voters named it the year's Best Pop Vocal Performance by a Duo, Group or Chorus (one of two statues they took home that year).

Naturally, an LP was released in early '73 to capitalize on *Neither One of Us.* But all was not hearts and flowers between group and label. "Once we finished *Neither One Of Us*, our contract ran out with Motown," said Bubba. "Our seven years was up. And we tried to negotiate with them to re-sign with the company, but they didn't want to negotiate in good faith, as far as paying us what we felt like that we deserved. They wouldn't give us the kind of perks that we wanted in the contract. So we decided that that was not a good deal for us. After that point, we said okay, we started talking to Buddah Records. That's when the real success started coming."

Though Motown enjoyed one more huge hit by the group in the spring of '73 with the clever "Daddy Could Swear, I Declare," another self-generated piece of material from Gladys, Bubba, and Bristol that Gordy allegedly didn't care for and buried until the group left for greener pastures. "I don't know if he didn't like it so much as just didn't think it was a hit," said Bristol. The label kept on issuing its backlog of material with diminishing returns for another year-and-a-half as the group rocketed to new heights at Buddah. The Weatherly composition "Midnight Train To Georgia" topped both charts for the group and went gold in the fall of '73, picking up that aforementioned Grammy as Best Rhythm & Blues Vocal Performance by a Duo, Group or Chorus and kicking off a string of smashes that extended to "I've Got To Use My Imagination," Weatherly's "Best Thing That Ever Happened To Me," and Curtis Mayfield's "On And On."

Before decade's end, Gladys Knight & the Pips hosted their own network TV variety show. In 1976, Gladys starred on the silver screen in *Pipe Dreams.* It wasn't all smooth sailing—she was legally enjoined from recording with the Pips for a time because of contract disputes—but as late as 1987, the reunited group nailed an R&B chart-topper with "Love Overboard." A year later, they separated for good, with Gladys embarking on a solo career and the group retiring to the good life.

Betty Kelley (middle) performed with Rosalind Ashford (left) and Martha Reeves from 1964-68 (Photo courtesy of David Alston's Mahogany Archives).

MARTHA & THE VANDELLAS

Recorded by MARTHA and THE VANDELLAS on Gordy Records
DANCING IN THE STREET
By WILLIAM STEVENSON and MARVIN GAYE
75¢

Martha and the Vandellas broke through in 1964 with "Dancing in the Street," with a little writing help from Marvin Gaye.

Just before Diana Ross and her Supremes permanently laid claim to the throne as **glamor queens** *of Motown's golden years, Martha & the Vandellas proudly held the same regal position. Thanks to the 1-2-3 punch of the Holland-Dozier-Holland-helmed hits "Come And Get These Memories," "Heat Wave," and "Quicksand," Martha Reeves and her lovely associates Rosalind Ashford and Annette Sterling (Beard) catapulted to the peak of Hitsville's pecking order in 1963.*

Born in Eufaula, Alabama on July 18, 1941, Martha Reeves moved with her folks to the Motor City before she was a year old. Gospel music was an abiding influence within her large family. "My grandfather was a Methodist minister. We went to church every Wednesday for rehearsals, and we went to Bible study on Sunday mornings," said Reeves. "We didn't listen to secular music until I was about 11, 12. My mom idolized Billie Holiday. She would sing to us at night. We didn't have TV." Once she did pick up on jazz and R&B, her list of influences boomed. "I listened to Dinah Washington," she said, "along with Nancy Wilson, and Sarah Vaughan and Ella Fitzgerald, Yma Sumac, Morgana King, Jaye P. Morgan. I listened to Carmen McRae and Gloria Lynne. I listened to Lena Horne, who was my first influence, and Della Reese.

"I just knew I could sing, and if I could hold on to my dream, I could one day make people feel the same way that Lena Horne made me feel that first time I saw her when I was 3 years old."

Martha Reeves was one of Motown's greatest female singers (Weldon A. McDougal III photo).

Reeves got serious about singing after graduating from high school in 1959, when she teamed up with a girl group called the Fascinations. Detroit was filled to bursting with young talent, and Reeves was anxious to get a toehold. In late summer of 1960, she met Rosalind Ashford and was invited to join the Del-Phis, whose other members were alto Annette Sterling and lead Gloria Jean Williamson. After making the rounds of talent shows and local gigs, the Del-Phis cut "I'll Let You Know" for Billy Davis' Chess-affiliated Check-Mate Records, an answer to J.J. Barnes' "Won't You Let Me Know."[6] "Our manager, Fred Brown, managed both of us," noted Reeves.

Martha wasn't confining her exploits to the Del-Phis. In October of '61, she landed a three-evening solo engagement at the 20 Grand. "I had won an amateur contest, and had been awarded a Happy Hour debut," she said. "I was singing 'Fly Me To The Moon,' 'Gin House Blues,' and 'Canadian Sunset,' because those were songs I could tell the band to play, because I had no musical director, and I had no music charts. I had to just wing it." She was billed as Martha LaVaille for the gig. "My Aunt Bernice gave me that name as she pierced my ears. She said, 'You're going to be famous, and when you get famous, call yourself Martha LaVaille!'"

Opportunity strolled through the door in the suave form of Motown A&R boss Mickey Stevenson. "Someone with a card approached me, a good-looking man who I thought might be my knight in shining armor," said Martha. "He invited me to Hitsville, U.S.A." Clearly, this would be her big break. "I quit my job that night. My job was at the cleaners, 9 to 5, and I went at 9 o'clock, secretary time, to Hitsville, U.S.A. And I got there a little early, 'cause there was this man who I had seen the night before. He was still dressed, but he had his jacket off, his tie loose, and he had his sleeves rolled up.

"When I approached him, he said, 'What are you doing here?' after being buzzed in. And I said, 'What do you mean, what am I doing here? Don't you remember giving me your card last night? You asked me to come here.' He said, 'Yeah, you're supposed to take that card and call for an audition. We have auditions the third Thursday of every month.' And I'm going, 'Oh God, what am I gonna do?'

"And then he said, 'Answer the phone. I'll be right back.' And he left me there. Three hours. These people started coming in. I didn't know none of those guys. Hummin' and mumblin' and bangin' on the piano, asking me who I am. So I assumed that I was the A&R secretary. And when the phone rang, I said, 'A&R Department.' He said, 'Who is this?' I said, 'It's Martha Reeves, A&R secretary.' 'There's no A&R secretary!' I said, 'There is one now!'"

Her secretary post was initially an unpaid one. "I didn't know Berry Gordy until three weeks after I was working there, and the only reason I got to meet him was because my dad said if I didn't get money from him, I couldn't go back to his company," said Reeves. "I was making $5 when I hand clapped or sang, but it wasn't sufficient."

While awaiting her chance to shine solo, Martha did plenty of vocal work on other artists' sessions. "I was asked to sing every day," she noted. She also booked background singers. When the Andantes proved unavailable for a Marvin Gaye date in July of '62, she called her old group. "The Del-Phis had kind of dissolved after graduation," she noted. But they rose to the occasion for Marvin. The song cut that day, "Stubborn Kind Of Fellow," turned out to be his breakthrough, and Martha and the Del-Phis' harmonies were by no means the least of its charms.

A couple of months later, Martha found herself in the right place at the right time again. Stevenson summoned her to the studio, where a union rep was on the prowl to ensure the label followed a rule stipulating a singer had to be on mic when tracks were laid. In Mary Wells' absence, Reeves cut loose on "I'll Have To Let Him Go," impressing Stevenson enough for him to invite the Del-Phis in to cut their own Williamson-fronted sides. "You'll Never Cherish A Love So True ('Til You Lose It)" was written and produced by Berry, while Brian Holland and Lamont Dozier took over behind the glass for the flip, "There He Is (At My Door)," penned by Eddie Holland and Freddie Gorman. The session was deemed a success, but Gloria Jean wanted out. "She decided she didn't want to be in show business. She didn't want to leave her city job," said Reeves. Williamson left, but Gordy issued the 45 anyway on Mel-O-Dy as by the Vells.

Martha, Rosalind, and Annette assured Gordy that they would stick together as a trio. But before Gordy released "I'll Have To Let Him Go" on his Gordy imprint (Reeves co-wrote "My Baby Won't Come Back" for its flip with producer Stevenson), he implored the girls to come up with a new moniker. So Reeves cleverly combined the names of one of her favorite singers, her former group, and a thoroughfare close to her home.

"I was at church one day when I attended New Liberty Baptist. I might have been 19 years old," she said. "The pastor, Rev. Rundless, before he got into his actual sermon, had looked into the audience and seen someone named Della. He said, 'Della's here! Della, come on and give us your favorite song.' And she stood up, and this woman's voice was so heavenly, so contralto, so many positive tones and so rich that the rafters shook and the church came all undone with her amazing grace.

"So the next day, I was watching TV, and I'm seeing her sing 'Don't You Know.' And my Lord, it was the same Della! But she's Della Reese. She's Della at church, but she's Della Reese on television. And that's so close to Reeves. And when Berry pressured us and said, 'We're gonna name you the Tillies or the Pansies if you don't come up with a name in 10 minutes,' well, I thought—Del-Phis we couldn't use, because of legal reasons. Van Dyke Street signifies the East Side. There's always an East Side/West Side thing," said Martha. "I lived very near Van Dyke, on the East Side." Presto—Martha & the Vandellas were born.

"Come And Get These Memories" was one of the first hits to bear the official Holland-Dozier-Holland compositional seal in the spring of '63, and it made Reeves and her group stars as it cracked the R&B Top Ten and did serious pop business. "I saw them write that. I was with them when they became a team. I was the secretary, sitting there taking the notes. I knew it was my song!" said Reeves. "That was a special moment. That was the first song that they wrote together. And it was ours. They wrote it for us, not the Supremes."

The contents of the group's '63 debut album *Come and Get These Memories* were more attractive than the LP's nondescript cover. H-D-H maintained their presence with "This Is When I Need You Most" and "Old Love (Let's Try It Again)," Smokey Robinson checked in with "Give Him Up," Brian Holland teamed with Berry's brother Robert to write "To Think You Would Hurt Me," and there were a smattering of covers that included Jennell Hawkins' "Moments (To Remember)" and a soulful redo of Andy Williams' then-fresh "Can't Get Used To Losing You."

As if summer in the Motor City wasn't sweltering enough, Martha & the Vandellas raised the thermometer to the boiling point with "Heat Wave," which copped the top slot on *Billboard's* R&B board that September and zipped all the way up to No. 4 pop. H-D-H devised a relentless groove matched by Martha's energy; suddenly she and the Vandellas were a hit-making force to be reckoned with. The only problem was that "Heat Wave's" tremendously appealing mid-tempo 'B' side, "A Love Like Yours (Don't Come Knocking Everyday)"—another H-D-H classic—slipped through the cracks. "That's Brian singing in the background," Reeves noted. Mostly cut in one evening, the trio's *Heat Wave* LP consisted of 10 covers and the title hit.

H-D-H came right back that November with the storming "Quicksand," another rocking Top Ten pop smash for Martha and her girls. It was backed with the plaintive "Darling, I Hum Our Song," where her Vandellas were augmented, if not replaced altogether, by the Andantes—not an uncommon practice on the group's later hits (or on sides by the Supremes and Marvelettes, for that matter). Even more torrid was the trio's first '64 release, another H-

D-H hit titled "Live Wire" that lived up to its name with a tempo so fevered it might have flown apart at the seams had the Funk Brothers not been so impossibly tight.

The first of several departures within the ranks came in December of '63, when newly married Sterling left to ensure the health of her unborn baby. Martha found a worthy replacement in Betty Kelley from the Velvelettes, though the Andantes again appeared anonymously on Martha's next H-D-H-generated hit that spring, "In My Lonely Room."

But the group's biggest smash of 1964 came instead from her old friend Marvin Gaye. "When I first heard 'Dancing In The Street,' I started to get annoyed, because I didn't know the intent of it," said Martha. "The words were saying something about, 'Every guy, grab a girl, around the world'—and the only place I could identify with that would be Rio de Janeiro at Carnival Time, or Mardi Gras.

"Marvin had another melody, and I asked him if I could sing it once the way I felt it, the way I felt the melody with the words. And they said, 'Go ahead.' And the miracle in that session was when I finished, the engineer told them that the machinery wasn't turned on. And I had to sing it again. I sang it straight through without overdubs, without a stop or a punch-in, punch-out. That's why it has that live sound. So I knew after I did that, if that performance wasn't good, then I might as well just stop doing this. And it was fabulous."

The Vandellas released more than 25 singles under the Motown umbrella in the 60s, including "Nowhere to Run" in 1965.

Gaye's co-writers played crucial roles in the pounding anthem's gargantuan success (No. 2 pop in late summer of '64). Stevenson assumed the production reins, while Hunter dragged tire chains into Studio A and beat them on a piece of lumber as extra percussive muscle. "His hands were bleeding when he finished with the song," said Reeves. "That's what I call creative energy to get the sound that you want."

"I'm supposed to be a true artist."

Mickey and Ivy Jo weren't through providing hits for Reeves, laying another rocker, "Wild One," on them before year's end. But H-D-H resumed responsibility for the Vandellas, emerging with the relentless "Nowhere To Run," a Top Ten hit on both the R&B and pop listings in early '65. "I was very ill that day. I could barely walk," noted Reeves, whose vigorous lead betrayed no weakness. "I knew it was a hit, though. James Jamerson had come up with this beautiful bass line for it, and the drums fit the bass line so good." That spring, they joined the Miracles, Supremes, Tempts, and Stevie Wonder on a gala European tour that included the BBC-TV special The *Sound of Motown* (Martha duetted on "Wishin' And Hopin'" with her friend, hostess Dusty Springfield).

In the tradition of the incendiary "Dancing In The Street," "Nowhere To Run," and "Wild One," the group's Dance Party album was a blazing up-tempo affair. Stevenson and Hunter were behind "Dancing Slow," "Motoring," "Mobile Lil The Dancing Witch," "The Jerk," the title cut, and "Nobody'll Care," which brought Stevie Wonder into the writing process.

Both sides of the trio's next 45 were so strong that they split airplay down the middle during the fall of '65. Clarence Paul, Stevenson, and Hunter were behind the insistent 'A' side "You've Been In Love Too Long," while H-D-H were responsible for the aching "Love (Makes Me Do Foolish Things)." "That was my first ballad," Reeves said of the latter. "I had to ask (H-D-H) to leave. They're good-looking

Martha and her Vandellas were big hit makers on the Gordy label in the 1960s.

men, and I knew I couldn't sing and have them feel anything, because they were so handsome, and they had wives and stuff. I had to come from my heart, so I said, 'Y'all gotta go. Go down and get y'all something out of the candy machine'—they had a nickel candy machine in the lobby at the time—'go get some candy and come back, and by the time you come back, I'll have sung the song.' And they let me do it that way."

No such confusion surrounded the Stevenson/Hunter production "My Baby Loves Me." Adopting a relaxed, jazzy swing, the superb outing showcased Reeves in front of both the Andantes and Four Tops and proved a monster seller in early 1966. Oddly, the group's captivating "What Am I Going To Do Without You" missed the R&B charts entirely that spring and barely slipped onto the pop hit parade despite first-class Stevenson/Hunter production. H-D-H reversed that trend by giving Reeves the pulsing rocker "I'm Ready For Love," a No. 2 R&B seller that pierced the pop Top Ten near year's end.

Martha and her girls were laying down so much great material that one of their classics almost got lost in the shuffle. Fortunately, the infectious "Jimmy Mack," which languished in the can for two years before it was belatedly released in early '67, vaulted to the top of the R&B listings that May (their second No. 1 hit on that front). Its issue apparently came as a surprise to Reeves, who was on her way to a record hop in Philly when she learned about it.

"We were in the car, and 'Jimmy Mack' came on," remembered McDougal. "And she said, 'Hey, man! What is that record? When did that come out?' I said, 'It's been out, and it's No. 1 in Philly!' She said, 'Boy, I didn't know that!' She was so shocked. She had cut that record so long ago. When we got to the record hop, the people wanted to hear 'Jimmy Mack.' She couldn't even pantomime it good, because they had never rehearsed to the record."

"Jimmy Mack" would be their last H-D-H-penned smash. Like the Four Tops and Supremes, Martha & the Vandellas would feel the negative effect of the prolific triumvirate's rancorous departure from Motown the following year. But they did contribute the charging "One Way Out" to the group's late '66 album *Watchout!,* a solid set incorporating fine material from Smokey Robinson, Johnny Bristol and Harvey Fuqua, and Stevenson and Hunter.

Other writers at Motown picked up the slack. "Love Bug Leave My Heart Alone," the work of producer Richard Morris and Sylvia Moy, was a brisk seller during the autumn of '67, and it touched Reeves deeply. "I'd be lying if I told you I didn't cry every time I try to sing 'Love Bug,'" she said. "They knew me well enough to write a tear in my song." It was the newest tune on the set list when the trio cut their only full-length live album at the 20 Grand.

Richard Morris, who had returned to Motown from Golden World after Gordy bought out his chief local competitor, remained at the helm to produce and co-write with Moy the group's next untypically downhome hit, "Honey Chile." The stirring number was the first of their singles to bill them as Martha *Reeves &* the Vandellas. That wasn't the only change in the wind. That June, Martha fired Betty Kelley. Replacements were in short supply, so Reeves simply looked homeward and recruited her 19-year-old sister for the position. Born April 12, 1948 in Detroit, Sandra Delores "Lois" Reeves proved a loyal complement to her big sister.

"She traveled with me a year-and-a-half before she decided that she would let me have a break," said Martha. "Because the people were being very mean to me. She thought that they should at least give me a little more credit, and respect me and embrace me a little more. I was being viciously assaulted—not physically, but gestures and things that were just entirely uncalled for." Personal upheaval was no stranger to Reeves' existence during this era. "A lot of the time, everything was so hectic around her. Either Martha was mad with somebody at the company, or things weren't right at the gig, the musicians weren't right, or she didn't get paid right. There was always something wrong," said McDougal.

"I Promise To Wait My Love," a solid seller in the spring of '68, boasted a torrid groove with pronounced gospel overtones veering closer to down-home soul than anything Martha had undertaken. It was credited to four composers, including Berry's brother George and Quality Control queen Billie Jean Brown (she co-produced it with Hank Cosby and sang on it to boot).

"She wrote that song, and Berry wanted me, as a favor to him, to sing a song with his secretary, and let her sing background. She did the production. It was her first time to produce," said Martha. "There wasn't a Vandella on there. It was hand tailored—a song written especially for me. It was like a gift, and I felt very blessed to have it." Its flip, "Forget Me Not," was a touching farewell to a departing soldier written by Moy, whose brother Melvin was Navy bound.

1968's *Ridin' High* was another consistent long-player, even though pop covers—"Always Something To Remind Me" and "I Say A Little Prayer" from Bacharach and David, Lulu's "To Sir With Love"—had begun to creep into the equation. Morris and Moy were responsible for the lighthearted "(We've Got) Honey Love," pulled as a hit single in the spring of '69, and along with Jimmy Barnes, "Show Me The Way"; Cosby, Stevie, and James Dean chimed in with "I'm In Love (And I Know It)," and Dean joined with H-D-H to pen "Leave It In The Hands Of Love."

Problems surrounded the trio's next 45, "I Can't Dance To That Music You're Playin'." Producer Deke Richards (who co-wrote it with Debbie Dean) refused to alter his lyric detailing a love affair with a philandering musician, so Martha declined to finish the song. "I didn't like the lyrics," she said. "I'm supposed to be a true artist. Anything I ever sang, I had to live up to it." Richards overdubbed Syreeta Wright on the chorus in her place, and the finished product was shipped against Reeves' wishes.[7] Truthfully, its chunky Morris-produced flip "I Tried" was more appealing. "I Can't Dance" proved a sizable hit—bigger than "Sweet Darlin'," the superior Morris-helmed offering that followed—and Martha's unhappiness did not bode well for her long-term future at Motown. Nor did confronting Gordy on the subject of royalties she believed due her the following year.[8] Another notable moment in 1969 saw Reeves dismissing her last original Vandella, Rosalind Ashford. Her replacement was Sandra Tilley, a recent member of the Velvelettes who had worked part-time with the Orlons.

Only one single, the elegant "Taking My Love (And Leaving Me)," produced by George Gordy, who co-wrote it with Allen Story, was featured on the group's 69 album *Sugar n' Spice*, and it was a relatively minor R&B hit at that. Additional highlights included leftovers from H-D-H and Reeves' first crack at material by Nickolas Ashford and Valerie Simpson ("I'm A Winner," "It Ain't Like That"). The Andantes were a virtual fixture on the Vandellas' records by now. They were on hand for "I Should Be Proud," its brave anti-war sentiment (written by Pam Sawyer, Joe Hinton, and producer Hank Cosby) just enough ahead of its time in early 1970 to prevent it from charting. Clarence Paul produced and co-wrote the 'B' side, "Love, Guess Who," blessed with a swirling arrangement by guitarist Robert White and trombonist Paul Riser.

The group's 1970 LP *Natural Resources* was an inconsistent mixture of tasty homegrown material ("Easily Persuaded," "The Hurt Is Over [Since I've Found You]," and "Won't It Be So Wonderful") and an array of covers. The stark isolation at the heart of Nilsson's hit "Everybody's Talkin'" clashed with its incongruous full-speed-ahead dance arrangement, though Jackie DeShannon's "Put A Little Love In Your Heart" and the Rascals' million-seller "People Got To Be Free" benefited from similar treatments. Tackling Jimmy Webb's schmaltzy "Didn't We" with neither the Vandellas nor the Andantes at her side, Martha relied instead on pianist Earl Van Dyke for her primary accompaniment.

"I Gotta Let You Go," the trio's only hit that year, was a Norman Whitfield concoction that came out of the gate like wild horses, with a rampaging sax solo. Gordy was spacing the group's releases further apart; "Bless You," a storming collaboration by the Corporation (Freddie Perren, Fonce Mizell, Richards, and Berry), emanated some of the same energy associated with their primary beneficiaries, the Jackson 5, and did fairly well for the trio in late '71.

Reeves prepares for another show (Weldon A. McDougal III photo).

Black Magic, the group's last album, contained the group's final two hits: A mid-tempo "In And Out Of My Life" was given an inspiring arrangement by Riser and David Van De Pitte and was a sizable R&B seller in early 1972, and the gospel-fired Ashford & Simpson creation "Tear It On Down." This was a stirring swan song that should have registered huge but made a minor chart impression that summer. The Corporation supplied one of *Black Magic's* best items, "Your Love Makes It All Worthwhile," and Reeves took a spirited shot at the J5's "I Want You Back."

Martha & the Vandellas disbanded after a December 21, 1972 show at Detroit's Cobo Hall. A solo single, "I Won't Be The Fool I've Been Again" paired with "Baby (Don't You Leave Me)" was slated for release in early '73, but was canceled—officially ending her Motown tenure. Lois Reeves ended up in another female vocal group, Quiet Elegance, alongside ex-Glories Frankie Gearing and Mildred Vaney. They scored a hit in 1973 for Hi Records, "You've Got My Message," produced by Willie Mitchell in Memphis. Sandra Tilley died of a brain aneurysm in 1985, and Del-Phis lead singer Gloria Jean Williamson passed away in 1999. Reeves soldiered on, inaugurating a solo career with albums for MCA (1974), Arista (1976), and Fantasy (1978 and 1980). After appearing on the acclaimed *Motown 25* TV special in 1983, she reformed the group with her sisters Lois and Delphine. Today, she has several options for live appearances.

"I will first call the original Vandellas," she said. "Rosalind just retired from Ameritech. And Annette still works as a phlebotomist for St. John's Hospital, and she's been working there 40 years. If their jobs don't allow them to go, then I'll call my sisters."

Martha Reeves' Hitsville legacy is never far from her heart. "I feel good about any accomplishments and all accomplishments that Motown allowed me to achieve," she said. "Berry wanted his music to make you feel young, and I feel young every time I sing it. Even when I'm at the end of a song, my heart is racing so fast—and it's beating with joy, knowing I'm part of the Motown sound."

THE MARVELETTES

The Marvelettes' *Please Mr. Postman* LP from 1961 had one of Motown's most unique album covers.

Few Motown moments are as historically significant as when the firm nailed its ***first No. 1 pop hit.*** *The Marvelettes scored that landmark when their rocking Tamla debut "Please Mr. Postman" vaulted to the peak of the pop hit parade in December of 1961.*

The Marvelettes began as a quintet in the early 60s and ended as a trio in the 70s. They were a quartet, however, from 1963-65: (from left) Gladys, Wanda, Georgeanna and Katherine.

Not bad for five high school lasses from suburban Inkster, Michigan, who hadn't even harmonized together for long. "We all sang in the school choir. At our school during that time, they had the chorus and the glee club. So we all sang in one or the other," said Katherine Anderson (Schaffner). "We came together in preparation for a school talent show. We all had heard about the talent show, but Gladys is the one that asked different ones, what do they think about having a group and participating in the talent show." First prize was a Motown audition.

Deciding on a group name was an early order of business, and what they came up with—the Casinyets—was more of a pun than something practical. "We were just joshing around, and trying to find a name, and needless to say, couldn't really come up with a whole lot of anything. So then we all just broke out laughing and said, 'Well, we can't sing yet!' And we just fell out laughing and said, 'Okay, then that'll be our name!'" said Anderson, born January 16, 1944.

"Georgia Dobbins, who was in the group prior to Wanda Young (Rogers), she sang soprano. And I sang soprano. Georgeanna Tillman (Gordon), (born February 5, 1944) sang alto. Juanita Cowart (Motley), she sang alto. And Gladys sang alto. But Gladys was like a first alto, which she could fluctuate between second soprano and alto. She could get that middle spot in there."

The quintet built their contest repertoire around girl group hits of the day. "I know it was one by the Chantels and one by the Shirelles," said Anderson. "Because they were the female groups that were out at that time. 'Maybe' was one of 'em." The Casinyets finished fourth. "There were three other people that were a part of the talent show, and those were the people that were chosen as the winners of the talent show. But then we had a teacher at that time, and her name was Mrs. Shirley Sharpley. Really, she and Mrs. Anita Cox, they thought that our presentation and performance was really good." Mrs. Sharpley prevailed upon Motown rep John O'Den (Berry Gordy's driver and bodyguard) to listen to the Casinyets. The girls passed their April 1961 audition for Brian Holland and Robert Bateman with flying colors. But the producers told them that they had to bring back an original piece of material to record. So Dobbins got in touch with a songwriter friend and instructed him to meet the quintet at Georgeanna's place.

"William Garrett was a gentleman that lived here in Inkster that had a lot of different songs. But a lot of his things were more on a blues format. With her God-given talent of being able to sing and play instrumentation, (Georgia) was able to find that particular song 'Please Mr. Postman' and change it from a blues kind of thing into what 'Please Mr. Postman' became," Anderson recalled. "He had quite a bit in there. And by the time she got through changing it around, bringing it into a more upbeat kind of song current for that time period, then it became the song that it did."

Before the group returned to Hitsville, however, they had to locate a last-second replacement for Dobbins. "Georgia stepped out because of family commitments, and things that were going on with her personally," said Katherine. "She stepped out prior to then because of the fact of other things that she had in mind that she wanted to do." Horton found Wanda Young, a recent grad of the same Inkster High that the rest of the group attended, to replace Dobbins. The five young ladies came back to Motown, Georgia having taught Gladys the lead parts.

"I sang the lead for the talent show," noted Anderson. "However, having a soprano voice—and maybe I can go from second into first—it didn't have, in some cases, enough bottom. So Motown, being one that had what is considered a lot of funk, Gladys had the more versatile voice, because she was in the alto-contralto area. She had the commercial sound.

"Gladys and Wanda—it was dual leadership. That was one of the unique things about the Marvelettes, was that it was dual leadership in regards to the vocals, as to who was going to sing lead." With fellow newcomer Marvin Gaye on drums, the girls tore into "Please Mr. Postman," its structure altered enough at Hitsville to add the names of producers Holland and Bateman (under the compact alias Brianbert) and Freddie Gorman as co-composers.

"I didn't hear it when Georgia Dobbins brought that song in. Brian Holland, he was the keyboardist, and he started to work on it. I was over there that day in my uniform, as usual," said Gorman. "'Freddie, come on over here! We need some help! You're a postman, you can help us with this!' We started working on it, and I started lending lyrics that I had experienced—'Check one more time for me,' and all of that. When I first started carrying mail, someone would catch me outside of the apartment building to say, 'Wait a minute! There's got to be something! I know I was supposed to

Long Baby" on the flip. One more task remained for Berry—dreaming up a new name for the teen quintet.

"I guess when they had a meeting of the producers and himself and a couple of other people that were going to be a part of it, some way or another through the years I've heard that they thought that we were really good, that we were marvelous," said Katherine. "I think from that point on, Berry said, 'Well, then we'll just name 'em the Marvelettes.'"

Tamla wasted no time in assembling the Marvelettes' first album, logically titled after their No. 1 smash and released before year's end. The girls stayed in the same vein on their encore "Twistin' Postman," Horton again stomping over a brisk beat on a fun sequel penned by Bateman, Holland, and Mickey Stevenson. Young returned to the front spot for the fetching flip, "I Want A Guy" (the brainchild of Gordy, Gorman, and Holland, introduced by the Supremes).

Most of the Marvelettes were still attending Inkster High when "Please Mr. Postman" hit. Nevertheless, they squeezed in live appearances whenever they could. "At that

(From left) Wanda Rogers, Gladys Horton, Georgeanna Tillman and Katherine Anderson (Schaffner), shown here in 1964, enjoyed a productive run as the Marvelettes with a string of hits on the Tamla label in the mid-60s.

were record hops, where the deejays had little teenage parties at different venues and halls. And black kids as well as white kids were able to go to these little dance parties and dance to their favorite artists. So you got some rehearsal in besides the regular rehearsal that you had to do. In doing that, Motown had set up one of their first Motown tours. They were doing more or less theaters. Smokey Robinson, Mary Wells, the Miracles, Marv Johnson, and someone else had gone to the Howard Theater. They were calling it, in part, the Motown tour.

"During that time, our record had been released. The chants for the Marvelettes were so overpowering that Berry called back from Washington, D.C., and told his sister that the Marvelettes needed to get there to Washington, D.C., as soon as they possibly could. Because the chants were so loud and so overpowering that the other artists were having a problem to a point performing. Because the people wanted to see the Marvelettes. And if we, the Marvelettes, the five of us originals, could not attend, then (they would) find five girls that could, because the audience had never seen them anyway.

"Hell was gonna freeze over before that happened! At that point, we made a decision that we would go ahead and leave school. But it was also under the auspices that we were going to have tutors. We had our schoolwork from Inkster High, and our teachers, and all like that. But we did not have tutors." Since they were still minors and Gloria was an orphaned ward of the court, Berry's sister Esther became their legal guardian. She accompanied the Marvelettes on their first Eastern swing, consisting of stints at the Apollo, the Howard, and in Philly.

The Marvelettes recorded 10 LPs for Tamla, including *The Marvellous Marvelettes* in 1963 (seen here in its British incarnation).

1962 was a terrific year for the Marvelettes. The boisterous hand claps sparking "Please Mr. Postman" returned for "Playboy," a splendid confection that Dobbins had a hand in writing along with Holland, Bateman, and Stevenson. Gladys was powerful up front, the churning rhythm pushed as insistently, and "Playboy" was a No. 7 pop and No. 4 R&B hit during the summer of '62. Both sides of their next Tamla platter—the ebullient "Beechwood 4-5789" (producer Stevenson wrote it with Gaye and Berry's brother George) and the softer Brian Holland production "Someday, Someway," co-written by Brian, Freddie, and Lamont Dozier, cracked the R&B Top Ten later that year (Gladys handled the leads on each). Tamla rolled out two LPs, *The Marvelettes Sing* and *Playboy*, over a five-month period.

The Marvelettes closed 1962 with another Holland-produced Top Ten R&B hit featuring Gladys up front, the heartfelt ballad "Strange I Know" (he wrote it with Gorman and Dozier). "Locking Up My Heart," their initial hit of '63, was one of the first Motown platters to officially carry the Holland-Dozier-Holland compositional seal (Brian and Lamont, as always, combined on production). Instead of exclusively featuring one lead, Gladys traded off with higher-voiced Wanda on the bouncy entry, creating an exciting tandem. Wanda took over for the heart-melting ballad "Forever" on the 'B' side; it became a sizable hit in its own right.

"After 'Postman,' then naturally everybody wanted to write on them, because the record was so big. During that time was when Brian Holland and myself, we had brought Lamont Dozier in. Lamont Dozier had this other feel," said Gorman. "'Forever' is really his feeling. Brian and I contributed on the lyrics, and Brian was in the studio at that time producing. That's how that came about, and 'Strange I Know.'" Berry took over for the Marvelettes' next outing, "My Daddy Knows Best"—but despite a convincing Horton vocal and a tough mid-tempo beat, the tune barely cracked the pop charts and missed the R&B hit parade entirely.

The Marvelettes were reduced to a quartet when Cowart quit in 1963. "Juanita was the first one to leave the group. During that time, the accommodations were not the same as they are now. You can't even begin to compare what the accommodations were like. You had to stay in guesthouses, because a black artist, you were not allowed to stay in part in some of the bigger name hotels. So therefore you ended up staying in guest houses, where black people could stay," said Katherine. "If primarily a lot of their time has been spent at home with their family and with their friends in their own area, and you're out and about, and you're traveling in a crowded bus or a crowded station wagon, you're sleeping curled up in your own little spot but not able to stretch out anywhere, that becomes very, very taxing."

The realigned quartet was attractively pictured on the front of their fourth album, *The Marvelous Marvelettes*, in the spring of '63. Working primarily with combinations of Holland, Dozier, Stevenson, and Norman Whitfield, the girls kept the energy levels pumping on "Which Way Did He Go," "I Forgot About You," a clever "Smart Aleck," "Too Strong To Be Strung Along," and "Silly Boy," and even when the lyrics got serious on "It's Gonna Take A Lot Of Doing (To Undo All The Damage That You've Done)," there was still a chunky beat underneath.

Smokey Robinson instantly brought the Marvelettes' mini-slump to an end, penning and producing the inexorably catchy "As Long As I Know He's Mine" in late '63, a romping "He's A Good Guy (Yes He Is)" early the next year, and the infectious "You're My Remedy" in the summer of '64. The last featured Wanda's lead instead of Gladys—a trend that became more pronounced under Smokey's watch. There was also a curious experiment in late '63: H-D-H paired Gladys with the Andantes for "Too Hurt To Cry, Too Much In Love To Say Goodbye," an unabashed attempt to muscle in on Phil Spector's Wall of Sound turf under the moniker of the Darnells. "Berry named us that himself," said the Andantes' Louvain Demps. Horton's vocal power certainly rivaled that of Ronnie Spector and Darlene Love.

Smokey wasn't the only in-house heavyweight working closely with the Marvelettes. Their first hit of 1965, the percussion-laden stormer "Too Many Fish In The Sea," was the work of Eddie Holland and its producer, Norman Whitfield. Despite her captivating vocal charm, it was the last Marvelettes hit to feature Horton's dynamic lead vocal. H-D-H had originally intended "Where Did Our Love Go" for her and the Marvelettes, even cutting a backing track in a sympathetic key, but they turned it down—opening a window of opportunity for the Supremes.

The Marvelettes were growing up rapidly, reflected by their more sophisticated sound. "Our ages were moving on up," noted Katherine. "Just like we were maturing as young adults, we had to begin to start moving our music in the same vein. We couldn't very

well still be doing 'Please Mr. Postman'-type music when we were maturing into young adults." Romance was always in the air at Hitsville, and the lovely Marvelettes were hardly immune to Cupid's arrows. Wanda married Bobby Rogers of the Miracles, Katherine tied the knot with Joe Schaffner, road manager for the Supremes, and in 1965, Georgeanna wed the Contours' Billy Gordon and retired.

"You worked a lot with those same people. Those people became your peers. Therefore, you worked a lot with them, and you partied a lot with them. You just had a good time with those people, because you spent a lot of time with those people. And when you spend a lot of time with people, then there is an affection that grows that can turn into a love affair," said Katherine.

"Georgeanna left for medical reasons, because Georgeanna had leukemia and lupus. And with that being the case, under the doctors' advisement, and because the lifestyle was so hard during that time, she was advised for her medical health that it would be inadvisable for her to continue. So then we broke down to a trio." She died of lupus on January 6, 1980.

"I'll Keep Holding On," produced in New York by co-writers Stevenson and Ivy Jo Hunter, was the first Marvelettes hit reflecting the new three-woman lineup. That and a pounding "Danger Heartbreak Dead Ahead" kept the Marvelettes floating around the upper reaches of the charts in 1965. Smokey returned to helm one of the Marvelettes' biggest hits, "Don't Mess With Bill," Wanda's seductive lead and an elastic mid-tempo glide steering the group in a smoother direction contrasted by the Horton-led flip, "Anything You Wanna Do" (the handiwork of Stevie Wonder, Ron Miller, and producer Clarence Paul). Robinson wrote "Don't Mess With Bill," a No. 7 pop/No. 3 R&B seller in early '66, specifically for Young's "sexy country voice,"[9] and she glowed

(From left) Schaffner, Horton, and Rogers didn't miss a beat as a trio in the Marvellettes' later years after two members left the group.

under his savvy supervision on the Marvelettes' next hit that spring, "You're The One."

"The Hunter Gets Captured By The Game" was special, even for the indefatigable Smokey. Its melody introduced by a unison line of low-end guitar and plaintive harmonica (the harpist later took a brief solo), the mid-tempo charmer was pitched in a minor key, Young barely raising her voice above a whisper while singing Smokey's vivid metaphors (another anomaly: It ended cold, instead of fading as the great majority of Motown classics do). The number proved the Marvelettes' second biggest R&B seller, climbing to No. 2 on *Billboard's* lists in early '67. Robinson temporarily relinquished the reins to producers James Dean and William Weatherspoon for the group's next R&B Top Ten hit that spring. "When You're Young And In Love" had been written by Van McCoy for Ruby & the Romantics, who scored with it in late '64.

Strangely, the group was seldom showcased on album during Motown's mid-'60s heyday. Apart from a 1966 greatest hits collection, they went nearly three-and-a-half years between their live LP and 1967's *The Marvelettes*, which boasted Smokey's "The Day You Take One (You Have To Take The Other)," Frank Wilson's "I Can't Turn Around," the R. Dean Taylor/Whitfield collaboration "I Know Better," another street sign takeoff in Johnny Bristol's "Keep Off, No Trespassing," a cover of the Velvelettes' "He Was Really Sayin' Somethin'," and a Motor City treatment of New Orleanian Robert Parker's "Barefootin'."

Longtime fans may be surprised to learn that quite a bit of the Marvelettes' later output didn't feature their actual background voices. "Motown had begun to start using studio vocals. And so therefore, the recordings and things like that, a lot of them were done with the vocals of the Andantes, who were the young ladies that would do the background singing for any number of the different female groups, as well as singing backup on even some of the male stuff," said Katherine. "Fortunately enough, the tones that they had, our vocals could fit right into them. It would not be that much of notice. The young lady that pretty much sang in the vocal range where I sang, our tones were very, very close.

"I think as Motown was growing, and they were becoming larger and larger, producers wanted to record certain things," she said. "We were traveling an awful lot. And because of fans all across the country, they kept us quite busy in performing. When you came home, you only had limited amount of time. You may have a new record that was released, so therefore you would have to rehearse and practice so you would be able to perform that new release when you got back out there on the road. So for the time factor—because they were releasing songs a lot quicker than they are now—they would use the studio backup singers, and just take and do primarily the lead singer."

Whoever supplied the bewitching backing vocals on Smokey's "My Baby Is A Magician," there's no denying their magnetism. Young was more forceful behind the mic, the ascending guitar slide at the end of each chorus—the musical equivalent of "Alakazam!"–a small stroke of genius. So was recruiting the Tempts' Melvin Franklin to supply the rumbling spoken intro in his rich bass tones. "My Baby Must Be A Magician" proved the group's final Top Ten R&B smash in early '68, though the sensuous "Here I Am Baby"—another Smokey standout introduced the year before by labelmate Barbara McNair—came close that summer.

Nickolas Ashford and Valerie Simpson wrote and supervised the Marvelettes' final R&B chart appearance. "Destination: Anywhere" pulsated with an urgency and unusual lyrics that suited Wanda as she strategically broke into a falsetto to drive her point home. The flip, a revved-up revival of Smokey's "What's Easy For Two Is So Hard For One"—a 1963 Mary Wells hit—with Wanda in the driver's seat and Robinson behind the glass, bubbled under the Hot 100.

Jumping from one producer to another wasn't a problem. "Each one had their own personality," said Katherine. "And with that being the case, you would conform to the person who was in front of you. Because you know as a producer what they expected of you as an artist, and what they were looking for. So then you would conform to that particular producer's wishes."

What proved tough was replacing Horton, who left the Marvelettes after wedding Joe Tex's ex-trumpeter. "When Gladys got married, and was expecting her first child—and we had gone down to a trio, which was Gladys, Wanda, and myself—we were hoping beyond hopes that we would be able to stay that way," said Katherine. "However, she fell in love, got married, and was expecting. Unlike today, you were not able to perform and keep that clean-cut kind of image that you had to keep and be expecting and performing. So then at that point, she had to leave the group. I don't think that it was necessarily anything that she thought about or contemplated, that it would be an issue about. But it was a big issue about her expecting and performing. So then with that being the case, we had to find someone else, which it took us some time to find a replacement person. We had been together for so long, we didn't necessarily have the total and full support of Motown in trying to locate or find another person to do that."

They found a worthy replacement in Anne Bogan. "Harvey Fuqua knew of Anne and her singing ability, and he brought her in," said Katherine. "We auditioned her, and I liked her right away because I knew that we would be able to do what we needed to do in order to continue to perform." Bogan didn't have to wait long for the spotlight. Her incendiary lead sparked the Marvelettes' next single, "I'm Gonna Hold On As Long As I Can"; the Frank Wilson production blazed with sanctified passion and made some pop chart noise in early '69.

"I remember writing that song," said Wilson, then a recent arrival in Detroit. "I was staying in the hotel. The only piano they could let me have was an old Wurlitzer 73. That's why the record even sort of has that sound to it, because that's the piano they let me use at the hotel to work with until they got me another place to stay."

The Marvelettes' extraordinarily solid 1968 album *Sophisticated Soul* sported no less than five hits alongside solid material: Smokey's "You're The One For Me Bobby," Ashford and Simpson's "Your Love Can Save Me," and Ivy Jo Hunter's "The Stranger." Young returned to the fore for their final pop chart entry, a faithful remake of Baby Washington's '63 hit ballad "That's How Heartaches Are Made." That one and its flip "Rainy Mourning" were featured on the album *In Full Bloom* along with a remake of the Crystals' "Uptown," but time was clearly running out for the venerable group. Somewhere around the turn of the decade, the Marvelettes were no more.

"It wasn't a decision that we necessarily made," said Katherine. "The decision was pretty much made for us. We did have some internal problems, but we were not receiving the assistance of Motown in trying to correct some of those internal problems. Because the only original two that were still there was Wanda and myself. And we had internal problems within the group with Wanda. And they were making no effort whatsoever to help to try to resolve some of those problems. Motown, of course, was really beginning to catch on fire then.

"The Marvelettes became obsolete. With that being the case, the decision more or less was made for us," she said. "When I began to start seeing the handwriting on the wall of the way things were beginning to develop, I went into a spiritual meditation for almost two years. In doing that, it allowed for me to accept what is occurring. Because there wasn't anything that I could do to change it."

Still, the name was worth enough to Motown to give it a last try—even if only one Marvelette was actually involved (the Andantes again deputized). "They did try to have an album that was released after things had been down for quite some time. It was called *The Return of the Marvelettes*. Wanda is primarily the only one that you can tell who it really is. They used more or less like stand-in people, in order to take and do that. They did call and ask me if I would attend the photo session for doing that album. And I told them, 'Since I'm not good enough to sing on it, or to be a part of it, then I'm not good enough to be on the album.'"

The cover photo clearly showed Wanda but obscured the identities of the other women. "They don't necessarily want you to see who those people are, because they are indeed not Marvelettes," said Katherine. Nevertheless, Wanda gave it her all on the Stevenson/Smokey copyright "Marionette" and a bouncy revival of the Robinson-penned "A Breath Taking Guy" that had been introduced by the Supremes back in 1963.

Though Katherine never sang professionally again, Bogan later fronted the Fuqua-backed New Birth on RCA, and a revitalized Gladys Horton still works the oldies circuit. Unfortunately, she has to compete with fake Marvelettes aggregations whose ages are often half those of the original members. "If they're not Gladys Horton, none of them are original Marvelettes. So then it's fraud," said Katherine, aware of the unique qualities she and her high school pals brought to fledgling Motown.

"The Marvelettes were a high-energy group," she said. "We were different, more or less, from any other female group that was out there at the time."

Smokey's wife Claudette Rogers Robinson was an original member of the Miracles, joining (from left), Pete Moore, Smokey, Bobby Rogers and Ronnie White.

SMOKEY ROBINSON & THE MIRACLES

Hi, We're the Miracles was the group's first album and featured the 1961 hit single, "Shop Around."

If not for Smokey Robinson and his Miracles, the Motown empire might have never taken flight at all. Discouraged by the meager fiscal returns on the young group's first singles for End, Berry adopted a different strategy for their next offering.

"He was saying, 'I don't know who I'm going to put this with nationally,'" said Smokey in a 1993 interview. "And I said, 'Hey, man, why don't you just do it nationally yourself? Because nobody's paying us anyway, so you might as well just go national with the record and do it yourself.' So he said, 'Well, man, if you've got that much faith in me, that's exactly what I'm gonna do.'" The gambit represented a watershed moment for both Gordy and the Miracles.

Along with Smokey (born in Detroit on February 19, 1940), the group consisted of his wife, Claudette Rogers Robinson (born in New Orleans, her family moved to Detroit when she was 8), tenor Bobby Rogers (born the same day in the same hospital as Smokey), baritone Ronnie White (born April 5, 1939), bass Warren "Pete" Moore (born November 19, 1939), and Smokey's invaluable writing partner, guitarist Marv Tarplin.

William Robinson loved cowboy movies as a child. His uncle Claude bestowed him with his enduring nickname—initially Smokey Joe—after they watched a celluloid shoot-'em-up. The lad cherished his new gunslinger handle, later realizing that his uncle was subtly reminding him of his strikingly fair complexion as well.[10] He grew up in a household awash with jazz. "My mom and my two sisters played a lot of Sarah Vaughan," said Robinson. "I heard all kinds of music in my house. Mostly Sarah Vaughan, Billy Eckstine, Ella Fitzgerald, Count Basie, people like that. Sarah Vaughan, I think, was probably my favorite vocalist out of all of them. She used to cry her songs. She was like an instrument to me. She just did things with her voice that only she and Ella could do."

But his allegiance to jazz was not absolute. "When I got to be about 11 or 12, I became interested more in what they termed then as the R&B music and the rock 'n' roll kind of sound," said Smokey. "Billy Ward was the leader of a group called the Dominoes, in which Clyde McPhatter sang the lead vocals. The first record I ever heard by them was a record called 'Have Mercy Baby.' I mean, I thought it was a woman singing the song! And I had one of these real high voices when I used to sing.

"Then I went to this theater in Detroit called the Broadway Capitol, and they were playing there. And I saw that it was Clyde McPhatter singing, man, and that really was inspirational to me, because I had a high voice, and the girls were going crazy over him. So Clyde McPhatter was probably like my first male idol as a singer. Then, of course, Nolan Strong in Detroit with a group, the Diablos. So he was a Detroiter, and he had that same voice, and when we'd go to see them in person, he'd sing a lot of Clyde McPhatter songs.

"Then along came Frankie Lymon and the Teenagers. I had five idols. They were Clyde McPhatter, Nolan Strong, Frankie Lymon, Sam Cooke and Jackie Wilson. Jackie Wilson turned out to be probably my greatest idol that I ever had, as far as an entertainer. Because to me, he had everything. Jackie was just a complete package. The other guys could sing, but Jackie could sing and dance and entertain. He was really just great. So I think I probably admired him more so than all the other guys."

Robinson assembled his own vocal group, the Five Chimes, while attending Northern High School in 1955. "Ronnie White and Pete Moore and I had been singing since we were about 11," said Smokey. "I met those guys when I was just about to graduate from elementary school. In fact, I knew Ron before then, because Ron used to be our paperboy.

Rogers, White, Robinson and Moore became a quartet, at least on the road, when Claudette Robinson stopped performing in 1964 (Photo courtesy of David Alston's Mahogany Archives).

"Then we had a neighborhood group. There were so many groups in our neighborhood. Every other person was in a group. When we got to be about 14 or so, we met Emerson Rogers, who was Claudette's brother. And we had some other guys singing with us—James Grice, a guy named Clarence Dawson. It was Ron, Pete, Clarence, James and me. We called ourselves the Chimes. Clarence Dawson quit, and Emerson Rogers took his place, and we changed our name to the Matadors. And then James had gotten his girlfriend pregnant when we were about 16, so he quit the group. He got married, and Bobby Rogers, who was Claudette's cousin, took his place."

"We were singing at high school affairs and house parties in the neighborhood," said Moore. "Singing on street corners." One last crucial personnel addition remained. "After we graduated from high school, Emerson wanted to go into the Army, so that's what he did," said Robinson. "He had his parents sign for him to go to the Army. And then shortly after he had left to go to the Army, we got a chance to go for this audition. So we were used to singing with five voices, and Claudette was in a sister group to our group called the Matadorettes. So we asked her if she would go down with us to this audition, and she did. And that was how it all started."

A trio of industry professionals sat in stoic judgment of the nervous young group. Alonzo Tucker, who would co-write several Jackie Wilson hits (notably "Baby Workout"); Jackie's manager Nat Tarnopol, and a quiet young guy who kept his mouth shut during the audition. Tucker was unimpressed. "When he saw us, he didn't like us because of the fact that Claudette was with us," said Bobby Rogers in 1993. "He said we were a similar group to the Platters, and (there) can't be two groups in America like that with a woman in the group."

"He really wanted more of a Mickey & Sylvia-type duo, with the three guys singing in the background

and Smokey and I singing dual leads," said Claudette in '93. "I wanted to sing, but I didn't really want to do the lead. I wanted to do the background." After Tucker and Tarnopol rejected the group, the other gent caught up to them in the hall. "It just so happened that Berry Gordy was writing songs for Jackie at the time we went for that first audition. And he just happened to be there that day that we were to audition for Jackie's managers," said Smokey.

Gordy was especially taken by Robinson's notebook full of originals. "That was what made him interested in us, because he heard a couple of songs that he liked," continued Smokey. "He met us outside, and we started talking about where we had gotten the songs from. He introduced himself as Berry Gordy. I had all of Jackie Wilson's records. I couldn't believe he was Berry Gordy, because he looked so young. He looked like he was about our age at the time.

"He introduced himself, and we struck up a conversation about where the songs had come from, and I had written them and so forth. So he said to me, 'Well, do you sing anybody else's songs?' I said, 'Yeah.' So he said, 'What's a current song that you know right now that you can sing for me?' I said, 'Well, how about "I'm Not A Know It All"?' Frankie Lymon had a song out at the time called 'I'm Not A Know It All.' And so I said, 'I'll sing that for you.' So he played the piano, and I sang it. And he told me, 'Man, I really, really like your voice. You've got a different sound. Nobody sounds like you, or you don't sound like anybody. I really, really like your voice. I want to work with you guys.'"

In January of '58, Robinson barged in on Berry with a tune he was sure his mentor would like—an answer to the Silhouettes' "Get A Job" entitled "Got A Job."

(From left) Smokey Robinson, Pete Moore, Ronnie White (bottom) and Bobby Rogers were at the peak of their superstardom in the mid-60s.

"I heard their record all day long, every day," said Smokey of the Silhouettes' smash. "It was the international anthem." Gordy liked the number but was short on cash. "He borrowed some money from Gwen and Loucye, his older sisters, in order for him to take us in the studio," said Moore. Backed by pianist Joe Hunter's band, the group cut "Got A Job" and its Latin-tinged flip "My Mama Done Told Me" under Gordy's supervision at United Sound. Berry struck a deal with George Goldner's New York-based End label, and the single hit the streets under their new moniker: the Miracles.

"We needed a name that would suit us," said Smokey. "We couldn't very well be the Matadors, because there was a girl in the group now. So we needed a name that would suit a group of guys that had a girl with the group. So we all picked a name and put them in a hat. And it just so happened that the name I picked, which was the Miracles, was the one we pulled out of there." Said Rogers, "I think the name that came out was 'Miracletones' or something, but we took the 'Tones' off."

End picked up the group's encore, coupling the rhumba-rocking "Money" with the delicious doo-wop ballad "I Cry." The grand total of Gordy's producer's royalty check from Goldner? A whopping $3.19![11] That indignity spurred Gordy to make the Miracles' next single the first ever to proudly sport his Motown logo. The dreamy "Bad Girl," replete with a trilling flute that became an early Gordy production staple, was picked up for national consumption by Chicago's Chess Records and became the group's first national hit in October of '59. It might have done even better had it not carried a touch of controversy with it.

"'Bad girl' at that time meant a girl who had gone out and gotten pregnant out of wedlock," said White in 1993. "But that absolutely had nothing to do with the song." Chess also released the Miracles' next 45, the atmospheric "I Need A Change," as well as a one-time-only duet with White credited to Ron & Bill. The duo's "It" was a lighter-than-air novelty about a rambunctious homesick space alien that was right in step with Sheb Wooley's "The Purple People Eater" and other extraterrestrial fare. It first saw light of day on the fledgling Tamla imprint before being licensed to Chess' Argo subsidiary.

Hitting the road, the Miracles played the Apollo Theatre in Harlem and bombed, even though headliner Ray Charles took the time to sketch out horn charts for them. "I don't know how we got there, but Berry coerced Bobby Schiffman into signing us, booking us for the week," said White. "It was horrible. We were ridiculous." Not long after the Apollo debacle, Smokey found the guitarist of his dreams accompanying some future labelmates. "Marv Tarplin was actually playing for Diana Ross and the Primettes," he explained. "I had them come and sing for us one night, and Marv Tarplin was their guitar player. So we were getting ready to go out and do some dates, and I said, 'Hey, baby, I want to use your guitar player to go out and do some dates.' So she said, 'Fine.' And I never gave him back!"

Things were looking up in 1959. The group was coming together nicely, and on the home front, Smokey and Claudette tied the knot. "We had gone together for a while, and he kept saying that he thought we should get married," said Claudette. "Of course, with us being so young and my mother having extremely high aspirations of her daughter getting her college degree before doing anything, I wasn't sure if this was gonna go over too well.

"My recollection of it is that he came over to my house, and he got down on his knee and proposed. I didn't dare tell her that he only was making, at that point from Motown, $5 a week—which was increased to $8 a week when we got married."

Released in April of 1960, "Way Over There" was a quantum leap into the soul era for the Miracles. "The first time we appeared in Chicago, we appeared at a place called the Regal Theater," said Moore. "The Isley Brothers appeared on the show. It was the Isley Brothers, the Drifters, Jerry Butler, and a couple other people. We were so impressed with those guys. Those guys were terrific. The song 'Shout' kind of gave Smokey the idea of doing 'Way Over There.' It's what we called in those days a major-minor type thing."

Free of the Chess connection, Tamla would reap the reward. "It broke really, really, really, really big locally," said Smokey, seldom one to skimp on adverbs. But Gordy wasn't satisfied with the production and decided to recut it for national airing. "Berry took us to Chicago and re-recorded it. Because the Drifters had come out then, and they were using violins on all their records. Everybody started jumping on the violin bandwagon. So Berry took us to Chicago and recorded this song with violins." Tucked on the 'B' was a fragile "(You Can) Depend On Me."

Smokey summoned his late mother's wisdom in writing his group's first national R&B chart-topper for Tamla in late 1960, though he originally intended to give "Shop Around" to Barrett Strong, whose "Money (That's What I Want)" had provided the company with a crucial smash earlier that year. Gordy convinced Robinson to instead cut it with the Miracles, and "Shop Around" paced the R&B hit parade in January of '61 and fell just one slot short of doing the same on *Billboard's* pop charts. Berry second-guessed himself again, retooling the platter after it had already been pressed up.

"There were two different versions of 'Shop Around,'" said Smokey. "The first one was slower and bluesy. I had recorded it myself. Berry called me at 3 o'clock in the morning one morning. He said,

'Hey, man, what's happening?' I said, 'What's happening?!? Are you kidding? I'm sleeping!' So he said, 'I want you to call everybody in the group and come over to the studio, because I'm going to re-record "Shop Around." I can't sleep.' I said, 'I can see that you can't sleep, man!' But he had us come over to the studio about 3 o'clock in the morning, and he had called all of the musicians. And everybody showed up except the piano player, so Berry played the piano himself. And we re-recorded 'Shop Around.' That was the one that went to No. 1." "Who's Lovin' You," its flip, was a breath-taking ballad with an exquisite ending centering on Claudette's sweet pipes. "On the end of the song when I just do my 'who's lovin' you' part,' in a live performance, people would just wait for that part," she said. Coming off "Shop Around," "Ain't It Baby," the Miracles' first follow-up that spring, was a relative commercial disappointment despite a No. 15 R&B showing.

The Miracles were definitely on their way up when they scored with "I'll Try Something New" in 1962 (photo courtesy of David Alston's Mahogany Archives).

Hi...We're the Miracles, the group's debut LP, hit the streets in June of '61 and included the bluesy "Your Love," covers of Strong's "Money (That's What I Want)" and Marv Johnson's "Don't Leave Me," the piano-led "Won't You Take Me Back," and Claudette's lead debut on a doo-woppish "After All" that had also been recorded by the Supremes. She would seldom step out in similar fashion. "I was quite shy even with the group when it came to leads," she said. "What I would do was I'd ask them to turn the lights really low, and sort of turn my back to them so I wouldn't have to see their faces peering down at me. 'Cause I thought being outnumbered as the lone female, I was feeling that they were expecting more out of than I could give. However, Smokey kept saying, 'You can do it. You can do it.'"

"Mighty Good Lovin'," another muscular up-tempo effort, was a solid if not spectacular seller that summer. Its flip, the strings-enriched "Broken Hearted," snuck onto the pop list for a week in its own right. "Everybody's Gotta Pay Some Dues" just avoided the R&B Top Ten that fall, its galloping rhythm abetted by a swirling strings arrangement from Riley Hampton.

The Miracles survived some rough patches during the early '60s that might have scuttled lesser aggregations, exacerbated by Moore's overseas Army hitch and Smokey falling sick during a stand at the Howard Theater in D.C. "Smokey came down with what we know as the first case of the Hong Kong flu," said Claudette. "He was really, really ill. His temperature was up to about 106. I flew him back to Detroit, where he stayed for a month while we went on tour."

Robinson's writing skills were progressing exponentially as he dreamed up metaphors and hooks worthy of a true bard. "I always tried to do that, 'cause there are no new words," he said. "There are no new notes, or any of that. So I always try to say things differently than how they've been said. Because they're all the same ideas that have been around for eons. So you just have to try to say it that it's going to be ear-catching to the people."

Its stirring arrangement built around Duane Eddy-derived twangy guitar and rousing violin figures that would have fit the theme from TV's *Bonanza*, "What's So Good About Good-bye" was a prime example of Smokey's gift for inspired lyrical twists—and a No.16 R&B hit in early '62. "I was looking at TV one night, and this woman and this man were talking," said Smokey, who was rewarded for his loyalty the same year by being named a Motown vice president. "They were saying goodbye. They were lovers, you know, and she was asking him, 'What's good about that?' That was where it came from." Its recriminatory 'B' side "I've Been Good To You" was a downbeat lament, Smokey quavering over doo-wop-flavored chords.

Cookin' with the Miracles, the group's encore LP, hosted the otherwise unavailable gems "That's The Way I Feel," "Determination," and the incendiary rocker "Mama" along with the 'B' sides "You Never Miss A Good Thing," "I Can't Believe," and "The Only One I Love" and a few hits. The album cover was eye-catching: The six Miracles were viewed from above, all but Tarplin hoisting cooking gear and Smokey modeling a chef's chapeau.

I'll Try Something New was the Miracles' second LP of 1962 and one of seven the group recorded over a three-year period.

Hampton's plush arrangement for "I'll Try Something New" was a sheer delight, layering violins and a rippling harp behind Smokey's breathy declaration of eternal devotion. The sugary ballad was the Miracles' first hit to credit Robinson as co-producer with Gordy and came to him at Tiger Stadium while he and his dad were watching a Tigers/Indians game. It just missed the R&B Top Ten during the spring of '62 and served as a title cut for the group's third album. Leads were split democratically, White stepping up for "A Love That Can Never Be" and Claudette spotlighted on "He Don't Care About Me." The LP found the Miracles courting the adult market with the pop warhorses "On The Street Where You Live" and Cole Porter's "I've Got You Under My Skin," sporting big band backing that was a far cry from the stripped-down "Shop Around."

The Miracles returned to the pinnacle of the R&B hit parade for the second time at year's end with a passionate "You've Really Got A Hold On Me" that cracked the pop Top Ten. Smokey, who wrote and produced this one all by his lonesome, found his muse in Sam Cooke's then-current hit "Bring It On Home To Me." "Sam had that record out at the time," he said. "I was in New York taking care of some business for Berry for the company with another publisher. And I wanted to write something like 'Bring It On Home To Me.' I was in my hotel room with nothing to do, so that's what I did, 'You've Really Got A Hold On Me.'" Cooke's platter was an uncredited duet with Lou Rawls, and Bobby Rogers pulled similar duty on "You've Really Got A Hold On Me." "We had like a double lead vocal there," said Robinson. "He was singing the other lead part." Tarplin and Eddie Willis expertly split the song's guitar parts.

If ever a Miracles track was unjustly overlooked, the scorcher "Happy Landing"—the Robinson/White-penned flip of "You've Really Got A Hold On Me"—is surely the one. Smokey's vocal is scarred with jagged edges as he revels in the concept of romantic revenge over a sanctified groove. He emits a satisfied-sounding little grunt coming off the wailing tenor sax break that mirrors the supreme confidence of his pal Wilson.[12]

"A Love She Can Count On," the Miracles' first chart single of '63, rode a relaxed rhythm and was once again written and produced by the head Miracle. Before the year was half over, Tamla had brought out *The Fabulous Miracles*, containing plenty of hits along with the flute-softened "Such Is Love, Such Is Life" and a spirited "I Can Take A Hint."

The group's hottest selling slab of wax that year emanated from a prolific source: Brian and Eddie Holland and Lamont Dozier. Smokey overheard Dozier mapping out its Bo Diddley-derived rhythm on a rehearsal hall piano and staked his claim to "Mickey's Monkey," a relentless raveup that broke into the pop Top Ten that summer. It elicited one of the Miracles' hottest dance routines, Rogers ferociously beating his chest like the baddest gorilla in the jungle. Choreographed by the group itself, it was filmed for posterity for the

Smokey borrowed guitarist Marv Tarplin in 1960 and "never gave him back."

1964 concert extravaganza *The T.A.M.I. Show*. "Bobby was a great dancer. In the early days, he made up a great deal of our routines," noted Smokey. But the Miracles eventually benefited from some expert coaching.

"A guy named Honi Coles, who used to work with Cholly Atkins as a tap dance duo, came to us and said, 'Look, why don't you go and see this guy? He can help you out with the choreography,'" said White. "We followed his advice and we went to Cholly. And Cholly groomed us, and created the choreographed act for us. Because of the work he did with us, and because of the improvement that the people at the company could see in us, they hired Cholly to come in and work with other acts."

H-D-H came back with another gem for the Miracles before year's end, but "I Gotta Dance To Keep From Crying," upbeat despite its heartbroken lyric, couldn't touch "Mickey's Monkey" in the sales department. The group celebrated the Yuletide with Motown's first holiday album, the Ronnie White-produced *Christmas With the Miracles*, decorated with Robinson's "Christmas Everyday." The same month, Tamla issued *The Miracles Doin' Mickey's Monkey*, a Holland/Dozier-helmed compendium of dance covers. Smokey wrote and produced "The Groovey Thing," but his contributions were otherwise limited to vocals.

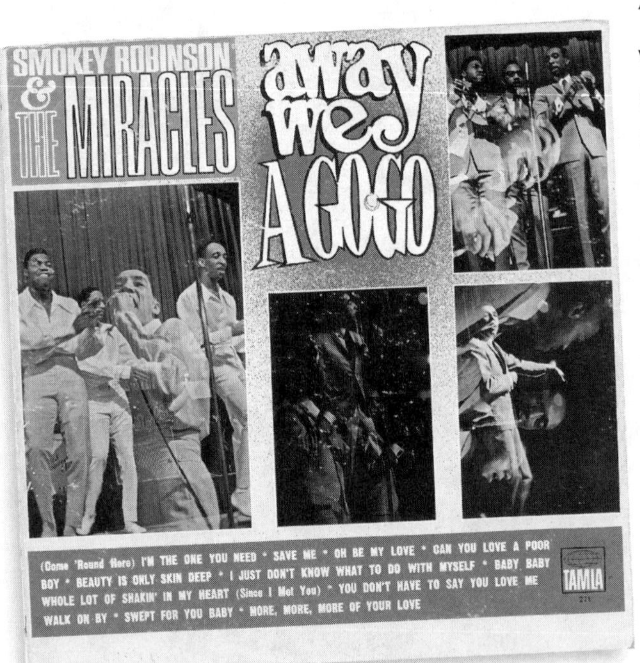

The Miracles' 1965 release *Away We A Go-Go* featured the group's hit title track and "The Tracks of My Tears."

The Miracles rolled on in 1964, though Smokey's sage slice of advice "(You Can't Let The Boy Overpower) The Man In You" was only a minor hit (Chuck Jackson revived it four years later as his first Motown single). The Miracles' next two sublime outings, "I Like It Like That" and "That's What Love Is Made Of," made far more of an impact, each strutting with mid-tempo fluidity as the Motown sound began to noticeably mature.

Though she would continue to provide her captivating vocals to their recordings until Smokey departed in '72, Claudette retired from the road in 1964 after suffering a series of miscarriages. "Becoming a mother was very, very important in my life. I had gotten to the point after so many miscarriages that I didn't think I would ever have children of my own," she said. "Smokey and Berry Gordy were the ones who really felt first and foremost that my health was suffering, and that I should come off the road."

The Jerk was a universally happening dance step in '64, and the Miracles hopped aboard the train with "Come On Do The Jerk." "Some of the ladies like Brenda Holloway was singing in the background on that song with us," said Rogers. "We were in Los Angeles." Robinson was convinced that the continuing popularity of "Mickey's Monkey" hurt the record's sales. "At the time 'Come On Do The Jerk' came out, it was the follow-up record to 'Mickey's Monkey,'" he said. "'Mickey's Monkey' was one of those records that just would not die."

With the emergence of the silky "Ooh Baby Baby" in March of '65, the Miracles cranked their pace a few notches higher. Co-written with Moore, the resplendent ballad—a No. 4 R&B hit—combusted spontaneously onstage. "We used to sing a medley of love songs," said Robinson, whose ethereal tenor ached with vulnerability. "It was some of the songs that we had done, some songs that other artists had done. There was a song called 'Please Say You Want Me Too,' which was by a group called the Schoolboys. That was like the last song in the medley. We had that there, and right after we sang 'Please Say You Want Me Too,' we were on stage, and spontaneously we started to sing, 'Ooh, baby baby.' So we left that in, and everywhere we went, when we would sing that thing, when we got to 'Ooh, baby baby,' even though people had never heard that, they loved it. So we said, 'Hey, we're going to write a song like that!'"

Three months later, the No. 2 R&B smash "The Tracks Of My Tears" sent the group right back to the winner's circle. The mid-tempo epic opened with a liquid lick from co-writer Tarplin, whose distinctive chording sparked its birth. "I had it for about two weeks, and the first thing that I was thinking about on it was the music, which is the chorus," said Smokey. "Finally, I came up with this thing one day, 'Take a good look at my face, if you look closer it's easy to trace,' and then I didn't know what 'trace' was! It took me about two more days to think about somebody crying enough so that their tears had left tracks in their face—if you look close enough to them, you can see these little ridges, these little tracks that have been left by these tears." "My Girl Has Gone" hit three months after that, making it three releases in a row to crack the top four slots in *Billboard's* R&B listings and the pop Top 20.

Near the close of 1965, the group cut loose with the pummeling "Going To A Go-Go," another No. 2 R&B smash tailor-made for the discotheques springing up across America. "We did a lot of go-gos," said Rogers. "That's how we wrote that song." "Choosey Beggar," a first-rate piece of Robinson wordplay, graced the flip and charted as well. The resultant *Going to a Go-Go* album boasted the buoyant "From Head To Toe" and "Let Me Have Some," a metaphor-loaded "In Case You Need Love," the slinky "All That's Good," and "A Fork In The Road."

Frank Wilson stepped in to write and produce "Whole Lot Of Shakin' In My Heart (Since I Met You)." Riding a forceful horn arrangement and pumping rhythm track, the number made Top 20 R&B status in mid-'66. H-D-H took over behind the glass for the Miracles' next 45, the Brian Holland/Dozier production "(Come 'Round Here) I'm The One You Need." Reminiscent of the Four Tops' classically informed output, it restored the group to the rarified chart heights they were accustomed to late in the year. Its flip, the bubbly "Save Me," marked Bobby Rogers' maiden voyage as a co-producer.

"Smokey has just been a great person in saying, 'Hey man, come on, let's do this,'" said Rogers. "That's how I was able to co-produce. I think it was because I had written the background for 'Save Me' for the group. I sat in the control room and directed the guys, directed him on what to sing." *Away We A Go-Go*, the Miracles' only album of 1966, was a mixed bag that augmented Smokey-generated material ("Swept For You Baby," the danceable "More, More, More Of Your Love," a gentle "Oh Be My Love") with the Ivy Jo Hunter/Stevie Wonder copyright "Can You Love A Poor Boy" and a cover of the Tempts' "Beauty Is Only Skin Deep."

A big change was in the offing as 1967 dawned: The group would now be billed as Smokey Robinson & the Miracles. First out of the box under the new appellation was the Top Ten R&B hit "The Love I Saw

In You Was Just A Mirage," Smokey's stunning lyrics weaving a poetic tale of heartbreak over Tarplin's acoustic guitar. "His music has always inspired me to write," said Smokey. "He always used to give me tapes of his music, and I would fool around with 'em 'til I got an idea on 'em. So that just was the idea that came on that song."

"More Love," a Top Five R&B entry that summer cut in L.A. rather than the Motor City, was a message of devotion from Smokey to Claudette. "We had many miscarriages. Every time I went to the hospital after a miscarriage, Claudette was in there, and she was apologizing to me: 'Oh, I'm so sorry, baby. I let you down.' And all that stuff like that," said Robinson. "And I'd always tell her, 'You didn't let me down, because even though I wanted those babies, and it would have been a great thing, I know you. I didn't know those babies, but I know you. You're the person who's been in my life since I was 14 years old. I love you. You're okay; I'm fine! We'll try again on another baby.' After one of those times, I went home and I said, 'I'm going to write a song to her.' And I wrote 'More Love,' because I wanted her to know that was how I felt. Like I said, it would have been great to have the babies, but we didn't. But we had each other, so that was what was important to me."

The '67 LP *Smokey Robinson and the Miracles Make It Happen* contrasted the non-stop workout "The Soulful Shack," an H-D-H-generated "It's A Good Feeling," and the pounding singalong "Dancing's Alright" (the latter bearing all five Miracles' writing imprimaturs) with the dramatic uptown soul ballad "Don't Think It's Me" and a richly textured "You Must Be Love" ("Smokey and I were into doing a lot of love songs back then," said co-writer Moore). Stevie had a hand in writing "My Love Is Your Love (Forever)," "After You Put Back The Pieces (I'll Still Have A Broken Heart)," and what turned out to be the LP's greatest hit of all, even if it did have to wait three years for release as a single. Once unearthed from its humble spot as the closer on *Make It Happen*, "The Tears Of A Clown," by Stevie, Smokey, and Hank Cosby, belatedly earned the group its only simultaneous trip to the top of the pop and R&B charts.

"'Tears Of A Clown' was a track that Stevie had," said Robinson. "We were having a Christmas party at Motown. And he came to me, because at that time we were doing a lot of collaboration. Guys who did great music who didn't necessarily write songs would give their music to someone who did. Guys who wrote lyrics who didn't do music would give their lyrics to guys who did music. So he came to me, and he said he had this track he wanted me to hear. And he wanted me to write a song to it. So he gave it to me, and I listened to it. And the (opening riff), that's a circus thing. So I just wanted to write something that would be profound about the circus and touch people's hearts, I guess. And the only thing I could think of was Pagliacci, who was the clown who made everybody else happy while he was sad because he had nobody to love him.

"In 1970, a young lady who worked for Motown in England was listening to the album. And she said, 'Hey, we should release this song over here.' And they did, and it was No. 1. So Berry said, 'Hey, it's No. 1 over there. It's the first No. 1 record we've ever had over there. It's starting to be a No. 1 everywhere over in Europe.' So we released it over here."

But that victory was a long way down the road in late '67, when Smokey and his cohorts paced the R&B lists and vaulted to No. 4 pop with the clever "I Second That Emotion." "'I Second That Emotion' was written because of the fact the guy who wrote it with me, Al Cleveland, and I were very good friends, and we were Christmas shopping one day in a department store," said Robinson. "You know, there's an old saying, 'I second the motion.' So we were talking to this girl behind the counter about something, and Al says, 'Yeah, I second that emotion!' And we started laughing, because he had made that grammatical error."

The following year, 1968, was another banner year for the group, each of the group's Tamla singles breaking into the R&B Top Ten and the Robinson-penned "If You Can Want" bubbling beneath the pop Top Ten as well. "Yester Love" and "Special Occasion" were percolating collaborations by Smokey and Cleveland. The same month "If You Can Want" debuted on the charts, the group was booked on CBS-TV's Sunday evening variety spectacular, *The Ed Sullivan Show*.

"The only show that stood apart from all the other shows was Ed Sullivan," said Smokey. "It was the class show of shows." The notoriously stiff Sullivan botched their introduction. Before millions of viewers, Old Stoneface solemnly solicited a round of applause for "Smokey and the Little Smokeys!" What ran through Robinson's mind? "'This guy is really ridiculous!'" chuckled Smokey. "It was embarrassing to me, because that's not who the guys were. They were the Miracles." A spine-tingling staging of the Beatles' "Yesterday" on the same show came off free of hitches, opening with the camera focused tight on Tarplin as he provided accompaniment. "The Beatles wrote some wonderful songs," noted Smokey. "That rendition of the song was vocally put together by Maurice King, who was our vocal director at Artist Development."

"Yesterday" was one of the highlights of *Special Occasion*, their only fresh album during 1968. Smokey contributed "You Only Build Me Up To Tear Me Down" and "Give Her Up." Consumers didn't realize that the Miracles' "I Heard It Through The Grapevine" actually predated the hit versions by Gladys & the Pips and Marvin Gaye. Cut in August of '66 (a second lead vocal was later added), it throbbed with the same minor-key dread that producer Norman Whitfield cooked up for Marvin's smash.

Robinson's vulnerable side resurfaced for the Miracles' first Top Ten hit of '69, the sumptuous "Baby, Baby Don't Cry." Both sides of their May release ended up charting impressively, the carefree "Doggone Right" followed by its flip, "Here I Go Again." Everyone from Dion to Moms Mabley took their best shot at Dick Holler's sentimental tribute to fallen heroes "Abraham, Martin And John," the Miracles being no exception. Taken at a sprightlier pace than most renditions, their unusual treatment barely bested old Moms on the R&B charts.

Along with their second live album, 1969 brought *Time Out for Smokey Robinson and the Miracles*, which saw the group reclaiming "My Girl." Perhaps because Diana Ross & the Supremes were enjoying some chart action with it, the set contained Smokey's "The Composer"—though this version had actually been cut a couple of years earlier. The doo-woppish "You Neglect Me," an ebullient "I'll Take You Any Way That You Come," and "Once I Got To Know You (Couldn't Help But Love You)" rated with the LP's memorable Robinson compositions.

As the new decade commenced, Smokey and the Miracles were riding high with the infectious No. 4 R&B smash "Point It Out," constructed by Robinson, Cleveland, and Tarplin. Its flip "Darling Dear" also squeaked onto the pop lists). Nick Ashford and Valerie Simpson wrote and produced the group's spring hit, "Who's Gonna Take The Blame." Significant as those platters were, they truly paled in comparison to "The Tears Of A Clown" that fall.

Maybe it was a case of too much product piling up and not enough space on the release schedule, but a couple of potential hits never transcended album-only status on *Four in Blue*, issued in late '69. The engaging "You Send Me (With Your Good Lovin')" and "Dreams, Dreams" deserved a higher profile. *What Love Has Joined Together*, the Miracles' first LP of the new decade, was their mellowest—nothing but plush ballads—and shortest—six songs barely spanning 27 minutes. In 1970, *A Pocket Full of Miracles* boasted the untypically aggressive "Flower Girl" and the Johnny Bristol-produced "Backfire," an insistent "Wishful Thinking," and Smokey's reclaiming of another Tempts hit that he wrote: "Get Ready."

Few Robinson compositions bore a sturdier hook than "I Don't Blame You At All," the Miracles' biggest seller of 1971. Over a surging bass line and the group's jaunty harmonies, Smokey's stratospheric tenor bobbed and weaved like a champion prizefighter. He also penned their next two hits, the teasing "Crazy About The La La La" and a "Satisfaction" that had nothing to do with the Rolling Stones. All three were aboard *One Dozen Roses*, the group's sole album that year, along with a funkier "The Hunter Gets Captured By The Game," the Marvelettes' Robinson-penned classic.

Though the title of their last Top Ten R&B smash in mid-1972, the Johnny Bristol-produced "We've Come Too Far To End It Now," suggests otherwise, Robinson decided after much soul searching that it was time to exit the group. The blessed arrival of the healthy babies that Smokey and Claudette had prayed for ended up playing a crucial role in his decision. "What really started those wheels to turning was Berry's birth," Robinson explained. "He was born in 1968, and I was so in love with him. I was so attached to him, I would put him in a baby seat and sit him on the table while I ate. Watch him, and just look at him, everything he did. When he moved his hand, I'd say, 'Oh baby, he just moved his hand!' And then when he started to grow up, I just hated leaving him. I got to the point where I hated leaving him more and more.

"Then Tamla was born, and there were some things that were going on with the group. We were always gone, man. We were gone 90 percent of the time. In fact, we were gone so much at one point, by me being the vice president—see, I never really had a rest, 'cause I was always working with some other artists. When I came home, I had to go to the office. And then I was on the road 90 percent of the time.

"So I had gotten them some jobs at Motown. But of course, they didn't like that, 'cause they made as much money in one night as they'd make for two weeks at Motown," he continued. "Then at that time, Berry was starting to move Motown out to Los Angeles. There was just a lot of things going on that made me know I had to leave, because I wasn't contributing 100 percent anymore. It was better for them and for me if I left."

The news didn't altogether come as a shock to the other Miracles. "We talked about it two years before," said Rogers. "It gave us an opportunity to go out and explore and see what we could do on our own," said White. That didn't make the actual parting of the ways any less traumatic. The end of Smokey's reign as lead singer of the Miracles transpired at the Carter Barron Amphitheatre in Washington, D.C., on July 16, 1972 (the show was issued as the two-LP package *1957-1972*).

"It was just a sad event, because I had been with those guys all my life," said Robinson. "It wasn't that I regretted leaving. I've never regretted leaving." Gordy convinced Smokey it was time to conquer his fear of earthquakes, and two months after that final concert, the singer and Claudette relocated to the coast. Though he declined concert bookings for three years, Smokey inaugurated a solo recording career the next year with "Sweet Harmony" and his first solo Top Ten R&B hit, "Baby Come Close." The latter was inspired—like so many Miracles hits—by the guitar of Tarplin, reunited with Robinson after a last fling with the post-Smokey Miracles.

"He stayed there for about a year after I left," said Robinson. "And then he called me and said, 'Hey, man, I'm coming to be with you.' 'Cause I wasn't doing any road work, or even recording at the time. He said, 'I'm coming to be with you, man. We can just write some songs, 'cause I don't like it with you not being here.' He came out to Los Angeles."

After a final Smokey-led hit with "I Can't Stand To See You Cry" and a last LP, *Flying High Together*, the Miracles regrouped around new lead Billy Griffin. "Billy found us," said Moore. "When we got back to Detroit, we made an announcement that we were looking for a replacement for Smokey. Then we got a lot of calls, we did a lot of interviews and auditions. Billy was living in Baltimore at the time. He came to Detroit from Baltimore, and he was about the fifth or sixth person that we listened to and auditioned. When we heard him and saw him, we knew that he was the person. He was a nice-looking kid, he was a good songwriter, he was very enthusiastic, and he knew a lot about the group because as a kid, he studied what we did."

Baby Come Close

Words and Music by WILLIAM ROBINSON, PAMELA MOFFETT, MARVIN TARPLIN
As Recorded by SMOKEY ROBINSON on TAMLA RECORDS

JOBETE MUSIC CO., INC.

Smokey Robinson left the Miracles in 1972 and kicked off his solo career a year later with "Baby Come Close."

For most of the '70s, both the solo Smokey and the Griffin-fronted Miracles provided Tamla with hits. After making their presence felt in 1973 with "Don't Let It End ('Til You Let It Begin)" and "Give Me Just Another Day," the Miracles blasted up to the R&B Top Five the following year on the strength of "Do It Baby" and "Don't Cha Love It," leaping to the peak of the pop charts in '75 with "Love Machine." "It was one of the records that was responsible for breaking disco," noted Moore. "There was some gratification, no doubt about it," said White. Robinson scored with "I Am I Am" in '74, "Baby That's Backatcha," "The Agony And The Ecstasy," and "Quiet Storm" in '75, "Cruisin'" in '79, and the gold "Being With You" in 1981.

In 1977, the Miracles ended two decades at Motown by signing with Columbia. Two minor hits preceded their retirement at the turn of the decade. "I think everybody was tired. I know I was," said White, who died August 26, 1995. "After so much traveling, it just really wears you down." Sadly, the marriage of Smokey and Claudette came to a close as well.

More than four decades after the Miracles flunked their big audition but met the man who guided them to stardom, their success story still reads like a fairy tale. "We never thought it would be what it ultimately became. How could five kids back in Detroit at that time envision what would happen to us? It was just a joyride," said Moore. "We started rehearsing in Claudette's basement, and we went from Claudette's basement to sitting in Ed Sullivan's dressing room, talking to Bob Hope and Charlton Heston. It was a dream come true."

DIANA ROSS
& THE SUPREMES

Love Child, a 1968 release from Diana Ross and the Supremes, was named after one of the group's many hit singles. It's shown here in its British incarnation.

Hundreds of girl groups traversed the R&B landscape during the 1950s, '60s, and '70s. Yet the Supremes will forever define the term, both visually (their sexy, sophisticated image was simultaneously glamorous yet reassuringly wholesome) and vocally via the kittenish leads of Diana Ross and the lovely backing voices of Mary Wilson and Florence Ballard. Their astonishing run of **five consecutive No. 1 pop hits** in 1964-65 under the supervision of Holland-Dozier-Holland, followed closely by four more by the same team in 1966-67, made them global superstars for the rest of the decade.

Mary Wilson (left), Cindy Birdson and Diana Ross: The undisputed queens of Motown in the late 1960s.

It didn't happen overnight for the three girls from the Brewster Projects on Detroit's East Side. Ross was born March 26, 1944, in Detroit, her close-knit family having come north from Alabama before she was born. Born March 6, 1944, in Greenville, Mississippi, Wilson came to Detroit when she was three. Ballard was born June 30, 1943, into a large Motor City family that also had southern roots on her father's side.[13]

Flo and Mary were already friends when they joined their first singing group in early '59. Milton Jenkins managed the Primes, a local trio of transplanted Alabamians comprised of Paul Williams, Eddie Kendricks, and Kel Osborne, and he proposed the formation of a "sister group" called the Primettes (Smokey Robinson's Matadors had a similar sister outfit, the Matadorettes). Williams' girlfriend, alto Betty McGlown, and a luminescent waif with impossibly large eyes and a sparkling smile named Diane Ross (her name was changed to Diana after the group signed with Motown) were the other recruits.

Mary Wilson (left), Florence Ballard and Diana Ross first rose to the top of the charts in 1964 with "Where Did Our Love Go."

The Primettes were thus born while their three principals were in eighth grade. Flo was the primary lead, her booming rendition of the Nappy Brown/Ray Charles flagwaver "(Night Time Is) The Right Time" serving as their showstopper. The girls spied Marv Tarplin strolling down the street one day and impetuously invited him to show them what he could do on his guitar; he was hired immediately. Smokey would snatch him away for the Miracles in mid-1960 during a living room audition that at least introduced Robinson to the young group.

"I've known her since she was about 8," said Smokey of Ross. "She grew up down the street from me. And when I started making records and stuff like that, she used to always tell me, 'Smokey, I want to make some records,' and all that."

Sock hops and deejay-sponsored dances would be the Primettes' training ground. Though the girls went to different high schools—Flo and Mary attended Northeastern, Diane Cass Tech—the Primettes persevered. Jenkins dropped out of the picture, but an amateur contest victory in nearby Windsor, Ontario, in July of 1960 led to an inquiry from young Motown writer/engineer Richard Morris. The girls ventured to Hitsville for an a cappella audition later that summer. Gordy took a pass, citing their ages as a primary consideration.

Betty exited to get married (not to Williams), so the Primettes were down to three official members when they cut their first single that fall in a basement studio for the tiny LuPine label. "In terms of being young girls and not ever recording before, and having that happen to you at that age, it was very exciting," said Wilson. Morris wrote and co-produced both songs: The rhumba-rocking "Tears Of Sorrow" featured Ross up front, while its equally up-tempo flip "Pretty Baby" showcased Wilson as lead. The record never made it, leaving the Supremes free to return to Motown with Barbara Martin making them a quartet once more.

"After we had recorded, we just kind of felt that more was happening at Motown than we saw going on at LuPine—and just made that decision that we'd rather be at Motown," Wilson said. "Since they really were not interested in signing us, we just decided to more or less wait for that opportunity where we could get in. And that's kind of what happened. We figured if we stayed around there long enough, they would eventually see how dedicated we were to it."

The strategy paid off. On January 15, 1961, the Supremes—with Flo, Mary, and Diane still in high school, contrary to legend—signed with the company after spending untold hours parked on the bench in front of Janie Bradford's desk in the Hitsville lobby and eagerly singing backgrounds whenever asked. Freddie Gorman, then a songwriting mailman, later bass singer for the Originals, handed Diana and the Supremes a dreamy mid-tempo ditty called "I Want A Guy" that Berry and Brian Holland also contributed to before it was perfected.

"That's the song that got them their recording contract. Because Berry Gordy had asked them to leave. He wasn't going to sign another group," said Gorman. "They were there in the studio, just hanging around. So we had them come over and start singing it. Brian Holland and myself were working it out. And Berry came in. He said, 'Are you girls still here? Didn't I tell you to go home? I don't want another girls group!' And we said, 'Berry, you should hear this song that we're doing!' He heard it, he came down and he listened to it. Diana was singing the lead, they were doing the backgrounds we showed 'em. And he liked it. Then he got involved, actually wrote some lyrics to it." Ross also fronted Berry's ballad "Never Again," and the two numbers comprised their Tamla debut in March of '61.

"I Want A Guy" was released under their new name, selected on the Hitsville premises. "We each had gone out and asked for people to give us suggestions," said Mary. "Pretty much everywhere we'd go, we'd just ask someone to suggest a name. We each had our own suggestions, and we ended up choosing a name from Florence's list, because I think actually she was the only one who brought her list to the rehearsal that day. So she chose the name from her list." The Supremes it was.

Ballard exhibited her powerful lead delivery on the Supremes' second Tamla release that summer, the dance workout "Buttered Popcorn" (a collaboration by Berry and sales head Barney Ales). Diana compellingly led a flute-spiced remake of the Miracles' "Who's Loving You" on the 'B.' That fall, Barbara announced she was pregnant; she married in December and was gone in the spring. The Supremes would be a trio from here on, though Barbara bowed out by leading the chirpy flip of their third single—and first on Motown proper—"He's Seventeen." But it was the Diana-fronted "Your Heart Belongs To Me" on the opposite side, penned and produced by Smokey, that gave the group its first modest ride on *Billboard's* pop charts that August.

"We liked everything we did," laughed Wilson of the group's earliest efforts. "A lot of them were produced by Smokey Robinson. We felt we did some pretty good harmony on them. It was a pretty good representation of what the group could do, in terms of the harmonies." Gordy's upbeat "Let Me Go The Right Way" was another minor hit at year's end that marked their first appearance on the R&B hit parade. Brian Holland, Janie Bradford, and Lamont Dozier combined to supply the flip, "Time Changes Things." Perhaps unfairly, considering they had a couple of low-end chart entries, the group was tagged by some Hitsville wags as the

"no-hit Supremes."

"You just recorded, and sometimes people would get one right off," mused Wilson of the search for their first hit. "And sometimes it would be like us. It would take a while." That didn't stop Motown from issuing the trio's first LP, *Meet the Supremes*, at year's end. Largely compiled of recent singles, the set also featured Gordy's "Baby Don't Go" and "Play A Sad Song" and Smokey's "You Bring Back Memories," all solid additions to their catalog.

Clarence Paul wrote the Supremes' first single of 1963, the country-based "My Heart Can't Take It No More," which featured unorthodox pedal steel guitar accompaniment. The perky flip "(The Man With The) Rock And Roll Banjo Band" came complete with a bluegrass-derived solo on the you-know-what. The original title of the trio's more alluring follow-up rated with the longest of all time. Smokey's "A Breath Taking, First Sight Soul Shaking, One Night Love Making, Next Day Heart Breaking Guy" was how the first pressing read in June of '63, though it was sensibly shortened to "A Breath Taking Guy" by the time the tune became a minor hit.

It was time for a change in musical direction. Enter Brian and Eddie Holland and Lamont Dozier, then just establishing themselves as a writing/production triumvirate. "When The Lovelight Starts Shining Through His Eyes," penned by H-D-H and produced by Brian and Lamont, came out of the chute like a hurricane, echoing Phil Spector's hefty Wall of Sound brawn without sounding overly derivative. With H-D-H and the Four Tops beefing up the cheery chorus, it flew up to No. 23 pop in late '63.

"It was a wonderful song, and it was a wonderful song to record," said Wilson. "Some of them were more fun than others to sing, and that had a little more fun going with it." A mellower flavor defined the flip, "Standing At The Crossroads Of Love." "Run, Run, Run," actually cut by H-D-H prior to "Lovelight," captured some of the same aggressive up-tempo attack, yet it barely registered a blip in early '64. Gordy reiterated his faith in Ross by pronouncing her the group's sole lead, brooking no discussion on the matter from Wilson or Ballard.

The early version of the Supremes featured the quartet of (clockwise from left) Barbara Martin, Diana Ross, Florence Ballard and Mary Wilson.

A blast of mainstream exposure was essential if the Supremes were going to achieve real stardom. Gordy engineered that by shoehorning them onto *Dick Clark's Caravan of Stars* that summer at a rock-bottom price as a requisite for snaring Brenda Holloway as a headliner for the cross-country bus tour. "He said, 'If you take Brenda, you've got to take the Supremes,'" said Holloway. The Supremes worked their way up the card week by week as their new single "Where Did Our Love Go" sailed to No. 1 pop status that August.

"Each time we would go out, it got better and better," Wilson said. "Obviously, when we first went out there, they hadn't heard the song. As the time went by, and the more it was played on the radio, the more people recognized it. We did get more applause. Pretty soon it was a hit, and then we started getting the screams."

H-D-H apparently offered "Where Did Our Love Go" to the Marvelettes prior to laying it on the Supremes. In truth, the Supremes didn't have much faith in its chances of becoming a hit either. "That was one that for us didn't sound like one, didn't feel like one that we thought it should feel like," said Wilson. "But like I say, we didn't know." Set in a lower key than normal for Diana, its simple set of repeating chord changes was hammered home by the marching foot stomps of Hitsville stalwarts Johnny Powers and Mike Valvano.

"There was a time there that we had foot stomps on a lot of records," noted Powers. "You put the plywood on the floor, and you had hard-soled shoes, and you started stomping." Mike Terry's booting baritone sax solo—a staple on mid-'60s H-D-H productions—was straight to the point, and Flo and Mary offered simple yet effective responses to Ross's seductive lead. Instead of placing another of their songs on the opposite side, Motown attached Norman Whitfield's "He Means The World To Me" to what proved the Supremes' breakthrough.

"He made more money than Holland-Dozier-Holland. He had the 'B' side of 'Where Did Our Love Go,'" said Janie Bradford. "Now he had it 100 percent, and they had to split it three ways." It was the beginning of Norman's ascendancy as a Motown force. "They couldn't run him away," said Janie. "He was in!"

"Baby Love" boasted some of the same insistent stomping as "Where Did Our Love Go," and another baritone sax ride midway through. H-D-H wasn't about to let loose of a winning formula. It shot straight to the top of the pop hit parade during the fall of '64 (H-D-H learned a lesson about giving away 'B' sides, inserting their own elegant "Ask Any Girl"). It was a happy season that saw the Supremes make their first trip to England and then co-star in the tumultuous rock-and-roll concert film *The T.A.M.I. Show* alongside labelmates Marvin Gaye and the Miracles as well as James Brown, the Beach Boys, and the Rolling Stones.

The Supremes' streak of H-D-H-generated No. 1 hits continued in early 1965 with the chunky "Come See About Me." The sturdy song had first surfaced on *Where Did Our Love Go*, the Supremes' encore LP in August of '64. It quickly garnered a cover version by 14-year-old Havre de Grace, Maryland-born singer Nella Dodds on Wand that actually beat the Supremes' original onto the charts by a couple of months. Whose idea was it? Weldon McDougal's, during his pre-Motown days as a Philly producer.

"Nella Dodds came in one day, and she had the Supremes' album," he said. "And she played it, and was singing along with the record, and said that she could do the same thing Diana Ross did. And she sounded pretty close. So I said to my partners, 'Listen to this, man, she sounds just like Diana Ross!' So they said, 'Why don't we cut that?'" said McDougal, who sang in the background with the Tiffanys. "We used the VU meters and tried to find out where the bass was, and the drums and everything so we'd have the same sound that they had. That was basically what we were trying to do, was to capture the Motown sound."

Only two tracks on *Where Did Our Love Go* didn't see light of day as seven-inchers: Smokey's hand-clapper "Long Gone Lover" and Harvey Fuqua and Robert Gordy's "Your Kiss Of Fire." The exhilarating year ended with a Yuletide appearance on Ed Sullivan's Sunday evening TV variety program. The group would make 20 appearances in all with old Stoneface over the next half-decade, usually performing its latest hit as well as a show tune.

The Supremes went from "no-hit" status to being the label's biggest stars in a minuscule span of time. In response to the British Invasion, Motown issued their *A Bit of Liverpool* in October of '64, its production split between Berry and West Coasters Hal Davis and Marc Gordon. The girls did a nice job on "You've Really Got A Hold On Me," and Diana sparkled on The Beatles' "You Can't Do That," which was blessed with a savage guitar solo. *The Supremes Sing Country Western & Pop* galloped in the next March. These three daughters of the Motor City ghetto found something to savor even in "Lazy Bones" and "Tumbling Tumbleweeds."

"We enjoyed singing, so for us, pretty much anything we would sing, if it had harmonies and if the song was interesting, we enjoyed it," said Wilson. "In fact, a lot of times it was our suggestion to record certain things, because we enjoyed singing *songs*, not just Motown songs."

H-D-H maintained a prolific writing pace that matched the Supremes' own hectic touring schedule, the triumvirate giving the girls another pair of back-to-back pop No. 1s during the first half of 1965. The insistent "Stop! In The Name Of Love," which paced the competition in late March, rode a more advanced mid-tempo chord progression, though its percussive thrust was still fattened by foot stomps. The jubilant "Back In My Arms Again" followed it in June.

"That was pretty much a great feeling. It's like the hits kept on coming," said Wilson. Their producers left little to chance in the studio, right down to the vocal backgrounds. "Pretty much Holland-Dozier-Holland worked with us on every aspect of the songs. We would always do our input, but that particular area was pretty much designated to Lamont Dozier. So Florence and I would work with Lamont."

love is like an itching in my heart

By EDDIE HOLLAND · LAMONT DOZIER · BRIAN HOLLAND

As Recorded by THE SUPREMES on MOTOWN Record M-1094

JOBETE MUSIC CO., INC.

Holland-Dozier-Holland continued its string of hits with the Supremes in 1966 with "Love is Like An Itching in My Heart."

The Supremes stormed Europe with the Miracles, Martha & the Vandellas, the Tempts, Marvin Gaye, and Little Stevie in March and April. Diana stumbled a bit vocally while leading their cover of Sam Cooke's "Shake" on the British TV special *The Sound Of Motown*. The number was a highlight of *We Remember Sam Cooke*, a well-timed tribute album to the fallen soul star with production split between Harvey Fuqua and the L.A. team of Davis and Gordon. The gentle lilt of Cooke's "You Send Me" and "Wonderful World" suited Diana, and a rocking "Havin' A Party" found the lyrics updated to request "Twine Time" and "Shotgun." Flo received a rare chance to step out front on a rousing "(Ain't That) Good News."

H-D-H's thumping "Nothing But Heartaches" broke the Supremes' consecutive chart-topping streak in the summer of '65, though other groups would have killed for its No. 11 pop showing. The girls were cranking out albums like crazy, and *More Hits By the Supremes* was a great one. Entirely penned by H-D-H and produced by Brian and Lamont, the set illustrated the synergy between the two trios on "Mother Dear" and "Honey Boy." That same year, the Supremes lip-synched "Surfer Boy" and the title song in the teen film musical *Beach Ball*, providing a welcome respite from its insipid plot.

After some coaching from the Artist Development

Department, the group made its long-awaited Copacabana debut in July of 1965, cutting a live album. By the time *The Supremes at the Copa* emerged in November (along with a Christmas LP), the trio were back atop the pop charts with the majestic H-D-H concoction "I Hear A Symphony." "That's one of my favorites," said Mary. "Who Could Ever Doubt My Love," its engaging 'B' side, did identical duty for the Isleys the following year. The symphonic concept defined their *I Hear a Symphony* album, which was loaded with sumptuous pop oldies like "Unchained Melody" and "Without A Song" alongside a homegrown "Everything Is Good About You" and "He's All I Got" and a cover of the Toys' Supremes sound-alike "A Lover's Concerto."

With H-D-H still at the helm, 1966 was another banner year for the Supremes. It began with the pulsating Top Five pop smash "My World Is Empty Without You," and the relentless "Love Is Like An Itching In My Heart" crashed the pop and R&B Top Ten in the spring. Ross and Gordy were a hot offstage item by this time, and rumors that she would be seeking solo stardom began circulating. Tensions between Ross and Ballard—long the group's onstage comic relief—were growing as a Svengali-like Gordy focused his energies on making Ross a superstar.

In September, the Supremes commenced another streak of four consecutive No. 1 pop sellers with the driving "You Can't Hurry Love," James Jamerson's elastic bass driving the number with immaculate precision (the Elgins had introduced the 'B' side, "Put Yourself In My Place," the year before on V.I.P.). "You Can't Hurry Love" anchored the chart-topping LP *The Supremes A' Go-Go*, which may as well have been titled *The Jobete Songbook*. Ross and company tackled "Get Ready," "Baby I Need Your Loving," "This Old Heart Of Mine," "I Can't Help Myself," and "Money (That's What I Want)," detouring to cover Nancy Sinatra's defiant "These Boots Are Made For Walking." Wilson made the most of a chance to front a revival of "Come And Get These Memories."

An emergency song-writing session produced the hit "Love Child" in 1968 and ended a brief sales slump for the Supremes. The Andantes provided background vocals on the track.

Late that autumn, the trio's electrifying "You Keep Me Hangin' On" topped the pop hit parade, its laser-beam guitar an attention grabber before the galloping rhythm and Diana's forceful vocal came into play. Brian and Lamont temporarily moved their base of operations to L.A. to cut the backing tracks for "Love Is Here And Now You're Gone," the Supremes' third consecutive No. 1 pop seller in March of '67 (Gene Page arranged the opulent strings). Both songs graced *The Supremes Sing Holland/Dozier/Holland*, a smorgasbord of new gems (the lovely "Mother You, Smother You," "There's No Stopping Us Now," a roaring "Going Down For The Third Time") and recent triumphs for others ("Love Is Like A Heat Wave," "It's The Same Old Song," "I'll Turn To Stone").

"The Happening," a zesty romp with razzmatazz, was their fourth pop chart-topper in May of '67—it was the theme of a silly film with Faye Dunaway and Anthony Quinn. That same month, the trio exhibited an allegiance to Broadway when Motown issued *The Supremes Sing Rodgers & Hart*. Hits were flowing nonstop, but things weren't running as smoothly behind the scenes. The wheels were greased for Ballard's painful dismissal in April of '67, and McDougal inadvertently played a role in the drama.

"Larry Maxwell called me and said, 'Hey, do you know Cindy Birdsong?' I said, 'Yeah!' He said, 'Listen, I need to talk to her immediately tonight. It's really urgent.' So I said, 'What is it about?' He said, 'That's all right, man. Do you know her number?' So I got her number, and that's when Cindy took Flo's place. I felt like I betrayed Flo, in a sense," he said. "I had no idea that they were planning on getting rid of Florence."

Born December 15, 1939, Cindy had been a charter member of Philadelphia's Patti LaBelle & the Blue Belles, who hit with "Down The Aisle (Wedding Song)" in 1963 and "You'll Never Walk Alone" and "Danny Boy" the next year.

Cindy made her debut as a Supreme on April 29 at the Hollywood Bowl. Flo returned for a few shows while Birdsong fulfilled her Blue Belles commitments, but she was gone by July—the same month the H-D-H-helmed "Reflections" hit the streets. Dotted with futuristic electronic blips, "Reflections" climbed to No. 2 pop, the group's first single released under the new moniker of Diana Ross & the Supremes. Ballard married Gordy's chauffeur, Thomas Chapman, and he became her manager as she unsuccessfully tried to mount a solo career. In July of 1968, Ballard signed with ABC Records, but neither "It Doesn't Matter How I Say It" nor its follow-up "Love Ain't Love" did anything (her Motown settlement stipulated she couldn't mention her tenure in the Supremes in any promotional material).

The personnel upheaval didn't impede the Supremes' hit streak. The catchy "In And Out Of Love" pierced the pop Top Ten in late '67, and "Forever Came Today" was a moderate seller in the spring of '68. Both were aboard the *Reflections* album, along with the H-D-H-generated "I Can't Make It Alone." A variety of composers were utilized for the set—Smokey and Pete Moore came up with "Misery Makes Its Home In My Heart," Brenda and Patrice Holloway were responsible for "Bah-Bah-Bah," and Bobbie Gentry's "Ode To Billie Joe" and Jimmy Webb's "Up, Up And Away" were brought in from outside. There was a simple explanation: H-D-H had gone on strike in search of a bigger piece of the pie. When the legal ramifications stopped reverberating, they were gone, leaving the Supremes in the breach.

"Not only for us, because they produced for a lot of different groups," noted Wilson. "It was not a good time anyway, because the company was moving to L.A. So it was really a time when certain things were falling apart." Something had to be done, especially when Nick Ashford and Valerie Simpson's "Some Things You Never Get Used To" proved the lowest charting non-seasonal Supremes single in mid-'68 since "Run, Run, Run" more than four years earlier. The track didn't feature Mary and Cindy's backing vocals. The Andantes replaced the Supremes in the studio.

Gordy knew he had to do something pronto. "He called me up in the middle of the night, 2 o'clock in the morning, saying, 'Hank, Holland-Dozier have left Motown. They just left. What are we gonna do? We need a record for the Supremes,'" said Hank Cosby. "So I told him, 'We do the same way they do. We get the best writers, the best producers, take 'em down to a hotel, lock 'em up. See what they come up with.'" British lyricist Pam Sawyer, guitarist Deke Richards, R. Dean Taylor, and Frank Wilson were summoned to the Pontchartrain Hotel and instructed to write the Supremes a No. 1 smash. "We checked in on Friday, and Monday morning we were ready to go into the studio and record," said Wilson. The ad hoc committee, provocatively dubbed "the Clan" by Gordy, brainstormed "Love Child."

"Every idea was thrown out until we came up with that one," said Frank. "We probably came up with that one sometime on Saturday, so we'd already spent Friday up. Sometime on Saturday we came up with the idea. Berry came by, loved the idea. Pam, between she and R. Dean Taylor, they were knocking out the lyrics, and R. Dean and I, for the most part, were doing the chord structure and the melody." Sawyer, a British wordsmith who first scored as co-writer of the Young Rascals' '65 breakthrough "I Ain't Gonna Eat My Heart Out Anymore," bravely introduced the taboo concept of an out-of-wedlock baby into the narrative. "Pam, she did a lot on that song," said Hank. "She had such an intense feeling for what she wrote. Everything she wrote, she felt so deeply. That's what kind of person she was."

The Supremes themselves had no qualms about the daring lyrics. "Pretty much when songs were brought to us, we didn't have much to say about it, unless it was something that we were totally against," said Mary. "It was probably very good, because we wanted to be more socially conscious."

With the Andantes again providing background harmonies, "Love Child" was the elixir that nursed the Supremes back to robust chart health, topping the pop lists in November. The Jobete family turned

Wilson (left), Birdsong and Jean Terrell, shown here in 1971, capably carried on after Ross's departure.

out in force to make the *Love Child* LP one of the Supremes' strongest. Ashford and Simpson came up with "You Ain't Livin' Till You're Lovin'," Sawyer and Wilson wrote "How Long Has That Evening Train Been Gone," Smokey coughed up a lighthearted "He's My Sunny Boy," Richards, Debbie Dean, and Janie collaborated on "Honey Bee (Keep On Stinging Me)," and Ross wrested "Does Your Mama Know About Me" away from Bobby Taylor & the Vancouvers. Sidney Barnes and George Clinton helped create the insistent "Can't Shake It Loose," first cut by Pat Lewis for Golden World.

Lynda Laurence (left) eventually joined Wilson and Terrell during Birdsong's hiatus from 1972-74.

Wilson and Ashford were entrusted with combining Motown's two hottest entities into one supergroup in 1968. The Supremes and Temptations teamed for the highly rated NBC-TV special *TCB* that December, just about the same time their thrilling remake of "I'm Gonna Make You Love Me" was zipping up to No. 2 on the pop listings on the strength of its inspiring leads by Diana and Eddie Kendricks.

"The contrast between him and Diana just worked splendidly," said Wilson. "I guess the reason it was not a challenge was because I had the Supremes in the studio first. They finished, and then I had the Temptations come in later. I gave everybody the lines I wanted them to sing. It really didn't take much of anything at all. I guess the greatest challenge would have been getting the background done." "I'm Gonna Make You Love Me"—a Philly soul sender by Kenny Gamble, Leon Huff, and Jerry Ross that first hit for Dee Dee Warwick in 1966 on Mercury—was a great cover choice. "It was an idea given to me by Suzanne de Passe," noted Frank.

The first two joint albums were massive successes, the *TCB* soundtrack topping the pop list for a week and *Diana Ross & the Supremes Join the Temptations* falling one slot short despite being devoid of fresh material. The Tempts' leads were doled out democratically on the latter LP—bass Melvin Franklin carried a remake of Marvin Gaye's "Try It Baby," and Kendricks, Dennis Edwards, and Paul Williams made their individual presences felt as the large aggregation covered the Miracles' "I Second That Emotion," Stevie's "A Place In The Sun," and the Sweet Inspirations' "Sweet Inspiration." But there was no mistaking who was in charge of their female counterparts: Diana handled every lead. The hybrid group's follow-up single, a revival of the Miracles'

"I'll Try Something New," was a solid if unspectacular seller in early '69.

Much the same crew that spawned "Love Child"—Wilson, Sawyer, Cosby, Taylor, and Gordy—reconvened to dream up the Supremes' next smash. Once again, they pushed the envelope with another slice of soapy social commentary, "I'm Livin' In Shame," which went Top Ten pop in early '69. "That was Pam's idea," said Wilson. "It was intended to be a follow-up, but the idea may have just been too radical. 'Love Child' had redeeming values. It was uplifting. 'I'm Living In Shame' was not uplifting. But we didn't think about that at the time. We wanted to capture the flavor of the first record, and we never even thought about the fact that the second one, lyrically, was a downer."

"They were talking about the times," said Mary. "So I guess the statements were getting more socially relevant." *Let the Sunshine In*, the album the song graced, was an enjoyable one. Diana restored the expurgated introductory monolog to a remake of Jimmy Ruffin's "What Becomes of The Brokenhearted" for producer William Weatherspoon, cut fine outings for George Gordy ("I'm So Glad I Got Somebody [Like You Around]"), Johnny Bristol ("Discover Me [And You'll Discover Love]"), and Smokey Robinson and Pete Moore ("Will This Be The Day"), and covered Jerry Butler's "Hey Western Union Man." Two other singles from the LP—Smokey's "The Composer" and the Gordy/Cosby-helmed "No Matter What Sign You Are"—were modest hits. "The Young Folks," the latter's 'B' side, was later picked up by the Jackson 5.

The ceaseless rumors finally became reality. In November of 1969, it was officially announced that Diana was leaving the Supremes. Gordy skillfully masterminded the superstar-launching machinery every step of the way. A month earlier, the group had hosted the *Hollywood Palace* on ABC-TV, introducing the J5 to America's heartland and in effect passing the torch. It wouldn't do for Ross to exit the Supremes without a smash swan song. Bristol had cut the original "Someday We'll Be Together" with then-singing partner Jackey Beavers as Johnny & Jackey in 1961, and he wanted to revive it—though not initially as a Ross star vehicle.

"That was Berry Gordy's idea," said Bristol. "I cut the song with the intent of doing one of two things: Singing it myself as a solo artist, or getting Jackey and I to do it again as a duet. So I presented the idea to B.G. He really loved the track of the song, and the first thing that popped out of his mouth was, 'How would you like to do it on the Supremes?' And I said, 'When?' I forgot all about Jackey and myself at that point. You don't turn down a good offer like that, especially coming directly from the boss. If he likes it, then you've won all the battle."

With Robert White's fluid guitar winding around a church-derived groove by Wade Marcus, and Maxine and Julia Waters standing in for Mary and Cindy, "Someday" coaxed what may well be Diana's most soulful recorded performance—with a little unbilled help from Bristol. "That was also an accident," he said. "We weren't getting the feel out of Diana on the microphone that we were looking for, 'cause Berry and I were both in the control room.

"There were two booths. And I asked him what he thought about me getting in the other booth, and just kind of singing along with her: 'From listening to me, she may get the feeling that I'm after.' So he said, 'Oh, okay, great. Go ahead.' So as we started running it down maybe a minute into the song, he stopped the track and said, 'Okay, I'm going to start it back over from the top.' Then we did it from the top and did it all the way down, and I did my thing and she did hers. The end result is what was released. But what I didn't know was, when I got back in the control room and he played it back, he had recorded me. I didn't know he was recording me. So evidently he liked what he was hearing when we first started, when he stopped and started over again. And he said, 'I'm gonna leave that on the record.' I said, 'You're kidding!' He said, 'No, I love that. That's great!'"

"Someday We'll Be Together" roared to the top of the R&B hit parade in December of '69 and followed suit on the pop side in the last week of the year. *Cream of the Crop*, the last Supremes studio album with Ross, was another attractive smorgasbord involving producers Smokey Robinson ("Till Johnny Comes," "Loving You Is Better Than Ever"), Bristol and Harvey Fuqua ("You Gave Me Love"), Ivy Jo Hunter ("Can't You See It's Me"), James Dean and Weatherspoon ("When It's To The Top [Still I Won't Stop Giving You Love]"), even Marv Johnson, who supervised a bluesy "The Beginning Of The End" (flip of "The Composer").

On January 14, 1970, the Supremes played their last concert with Ross out front at the Frontier Hotel in Las Vegas. While it marked the kickoff of Diana's solo star trip, it also marked a new beginning for the group. Her replacement, Jean Terrell, had been singing with the Heavyweights, a group led by her brother, boxer Ernie Terrell. "Berry Gordy, I guess, had signed her to the company as a solo artist, and recommended her," said Wilson. With Terrell installed as the Supremes' new lead, the group was stockpiling material by late fall for a smooth transition.

Both acts thrived. The Supremes were a full-fledged group again, not merely Ross's backing vocalists. Meanwhile, Ashford and Valerie Simpson were given the responsibility of properly launching Diana's solo recording career. They responded with "Reach Out And Touch (Somebody's Hand)," a very respectable hit in the spring of 1970. Diana's remake of "Ain't No Mountain High Enough" came next and propelled her to the peak of both charts that autumn, Paul Riser's bombastic arrangement framing Ross's divaesque delivery. "Remember Me," another Ashford/Simpson copyright that Valerie originally intended to record herself, made it three Top Ten R&B smashes in a row for Berry's favorite chanteuse in early '71. A year later, he made Diana a movie star by casting her as Billie Holiday in the Gordy-produced *Lady Sings the Blues*, and she scored triumphs for Motown for another decade.

Meanwhile, the reorganized Supremes weren't doing too shabbily, either. With guitarist Vincent DiMirco (who waxed "I Can Make It Alone" as his own Rare Earth single in '72), Wilson wrote the effervescent "Up The Ladder To The Roof," a Top Ten pop seller in the spring of 1970. "(DiMirco) played guitar, which was kind of different. Because most of the stuff I had done prior to that was with piano," Frank Wilson said. "That one was done around the guitar. That's why it has a decidedly different flavor about it." Terrell made it easy by acquitting herself dynamically out front. "There was no pressure at all," said Wilson. "I guess that's why it was so easy for me. Because I hadn't been at the company that long, so I wouldn't have had first dibs. So it was wide open. Every producer was recording them, but Berry just liked the stuff I did better."

Right On, their first LP without Ross, was a team effort: Bristol and Sawyer's "Bill, When Are You Coming Back," Jimmy Roach's "Then I Met You," Helen and Kay Lewis's "Baby Baby." "All that first album, I think may have had two songs. One would have been 'Up The Ladder To The Roof,' and there was one other one, 'Everyone's Got The Right To Love,'" said Wilson, who also co-penned "But I Love You More." "All of the other songs were other folks' songs, but because I had the record and it was a big record, it gave me the first position in terms of the next project."

The captivating "Stoned Love" was the crown jewel within that next LP, *New Ways But Love Stays*; it was the last R&B chart-topper of 1970 and rose to No. 7 pop. "Because I had just done *Still Waters Run Deep*, I decided to do another concept album—which was the one with 'Stoned Love' in it," said Wilson. His concept blended "Bridge Over Troubled Water," "Come Together," and Steam's anthem "Na Na Hey Hey Kiss Him Goodbye" with his own "Shine On Me" and with Sawyer, "I Wish I Were Your Mirror."

As they had done in Diana's day, the Supremes were paired off in 1970 with a male group, only this time it was the Four Tops. Again the concept clicked when their remake of "River Deep-Mountain High." The Phil Spector-produced Tina Turner Wall of Sound masterpiece from 1966 broke into the R&B Top Ten at the end of the year, but the follow-up, "You Gotta Have Love In Your Heart," was only a mild seller in mid-'71 (two joint albums were issued, *The Magnificent Seven* and *Return of the Magnificent Seven*).

Wilson remained at the helm for "Nathan Jones," the Supremes' brassy Leonard Caston, Jr.-Kathy Wakefield-penned hit in the spring of '71. "There was a guy that we brought from L.A., Cal Harris," said Wilson. "Cal had built this huge Moog synthesizer. It took up a whole wall. And so because I was not under pressure to duplicate anything that was already going on at Motown, I had unbelievable freedom. And then coming from the West Coast, too, my mind was just outside of just about everything that was going on musically. So with Cal with that huge Moog synthesizer, I experimented. He and I spent days in that room, just checking out all the things we could do. If you remember the record 'Nathan Jones,' we had that sound—that came from out of that huge Moog synthesizer."

The title track from the Supremes' *Touch* album, written by Wilson and Sawyer, was a disappointment commercially that autumn, so Smokey was elected to oversee the trio's next set, *Floy Joy* (he wrote or co-wrote all nine of its tracks). He'd be supervising a different lineup: Birdsong was out in April of '72 and Lynda Laurence came in for a year-and-a-half. The album was done back in Detroit with a full complement of Funk Brothers, arranger Paul Riser, and all three Andantes individually credited on the back cover. Smokey still knew how to write a carefree R&B confection: "Floy Joy" hopped up to No. 5 R&B in early '72.

Two more sizable sellers, "Automatically Sunshine" and "Your Wonderful Sweet, Sweet Love," were culled from *Floy Joy*, but after that the Supremes found hits scarcer. Only 1976's "I'm Gonna Let My Heart Do The Walking" broke into the pop Top 40. Maybe it was partially due to all the personnel changes: Jean and Lynda exited in October of '73 as Cindy came back and Scherrie Payne, formerly of the Glass House, was the new lead singer. Birdsong split again at the beginning of 1976 and Susaye Greene, formerly a background singer for Ray Charles and Stevie Wonder, took her spot. Tragically, on February 22, 1976, Florence Ballard, whose health had declined drastically, died of a heart attack. The Supremes officially disbanded the next year.

After the 2000 "reunion tour" debacle orchestrated by Ross that left Mary Wilson fuming and Diana wiping egg from her still-lovely face, it's highly unlikely that we'll see a legit Supremes reunion anytime soon. Better to revere the Supremes the way they were, all dolled up in flowing wigs and sparkling gowns—the absolute epitome of Motown glamour and style.

THE SUPREMES
bring it on home to me
shake

YOU CAN'T HURRY LOVE
THE SUPREMES
PUT YOURSELF IN MY PLACE

THE SUPREMES
sing
HOLLAND·DOZIER·HOLLAND
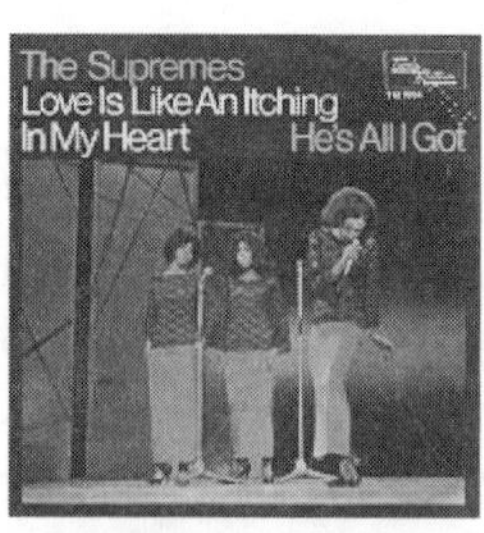
The Supremes
Love Is Like An Itching In My Heart
He's All I Got

the supremes
Everybody's got the right to love

NOTHING BUT HEARTACHES
HE HOLDS HIS OWN
THE SUPREMES

MY WORLD IS EMPTY WITHOUT YOU
EVERYTHING IS GOOD ABOUT YOU
THE SUPREMES

Diana Ross and the Supremes

THE WEIGHT

Diana Ross & the Supremes & the Temptations

STOP! IN THE NAME OF LOVE
I'M IN LOVE AGAIN

SUPREMES

MORE HITS BY THE SUPREMES

THE SUPREMES
WHERE DO I GO FROM HERE
early morning love

THE SUPREMES
HE'S MY MAN

THE SUPREMES
ALWAYS IN MY HEART
COME SEE ABOUT ME

CHILDREN'S CHRISTMAS SONG
TWINKLE TWINKLE LITTLE ME

THE SUPREMES
A BREATHTAKING GUY
RUN, RUN, RUN

TOUCH
THE SUPREMES

Nathan Jones
Happy (is a bumpy road)
The Supremes

YOU KEEP ME HANGIN' ON
REMOVE THIS DOUBT
THE SUPREMES

supremes
ERSTMALIG IN DEUTSCH
MOONLIGHT AND KISSES
BABY, BABY, WO IST UNSERE LIEBE

WHERE DID OUR LOVE GO
HE MEANS THE WORLD TO ME
THE SUPREMES

Diana Ross & the Supremes
The Composer
The Beginning of the End

LOVE IS HERE AND NOW YOU'RE GONE
THE SUPREMES
THERE'S NO STOPPING US NOW

The Supremes
THANK YOU DARLING
Jonny and Joe

BABY LOVE
ASK ANY GIRL
THE SUPREMES

COME SEE ABOUT ME
LONG GONE LOVER
THE SUPREMES

THE SUPREMES
TUMBLING TUMBLE WEEDS
tears in vain

The Supremes inspect a WFIL promotional album. Left to right: Cindy Birdsong, Jean Terrell, and Mary Wilson (Weldon A. McDougal III photo).

(Clockwise from top) Eddie Kendricks, Melvin Franklin, David Ruffin, Paul Williams and Otis Williams had plenty of reason to smile during their Motown heyday in the 1960s (Photo courtesy of David Alston's Mahogany Archives).

THE TEMPTATIONS

The Tempts' 1966 LP *Gettin' Ready* was loaded with Grade A material from the top writers at Motown, including Smokey Robinson and Norman Whitfield.

Along with their distaff counterparts the Supremes, the Temptations were the **glamor and glory group** *of Motown's golden years. Their choreography was rehearsed to razor-sharp precision, 10 feet moving as two. They even introduced their own often-imitated dance, the Temptation Walk. Their harmonic blend was sinfully sumptuous. Whoever fronted the quintet at any given instant was riveting in his passion. This was the ultimate in ultra-polished Motor City soul, bursting with infinite pop crossover potential entirely realized as the decade wore on.*

Though he's taken precious few lead vocals on record over the years, second tenor Otis Williams has been the leader of the Temptations since day one. Born October 30, 1941, in Texarkana, Texas, Williams moved to Detroit to live with his mother and stepdad when he was 10 or 11. He was already singing while attending junior high, inspired by nationally known doo-wop quintets as well as local harmonizers such as the Diablos.[14]

"They were one of the many groups that we were listening to when we started out," said Williams in a 1981 interview. "A group called the Five Dollars that was on the same label that Nolan Strong & the Diablos were on (Fortune). The El Dorados, the Spaniels, there was a lot of groups that we would listen at." Otis also dug the Moonglows and Flamingos, and was enthralled with the Cadillacs, a Harlem aggregation famous for their dazzling Cholly Atkins-devised choreography. Williams assembled some of his buddies to follow in their footsteps.

Local singer/producer Johnnie Mae Matthews took the promising crew under her wing. They had coalesced into Otis Williams & the Distants by 1959, when she cut their "Come On" for her fledgling Northern label. By then the personnel lineup was beginning to resemble that of the Tempts: Mobile, Alabama, emigre Melvin Franklin (real name David English; born October 12, 1942) possessed a subterranean bass range; tenor Richard Street, who sang lead on "Come On," would eventually be a Tempt after fronting another Motown group, the Monitors; Elbridge "Al" Bryant stuck around long enough to be on the Tempts' first half-dozen 45s; James "Pee Wee" Crawford rounded out the group. "Come On" made enough noise to be picked up nationally by Warwick Records, but their Warwick encore "Alright" was less successful.

The Temptations: (from left) Ruffin, Franklin, Paul Williams, Otis Williams, and Kendricks (photo courtesy of David Alston's Mahogany Archives).

In the autumn of 1960, the wheels began turning to propel Williams and his mates to stardom. "We were at a disc jockey record hop, St. Stephen's Community Center," Williams said. "At the same time, the Miracles were hot with their first million seller, 'Shop Around.' We were doing the record hop together, and Berry was coming in with the Miracles. He saw us onstage and how the crowd was reacting to us. I guess he was very glad to see that. So we had to go to the men's room. That's where he approached me: 'Say, I'm starting my own company, and if you guys should ever leave where you are, come see me.' We were disenchanted with the people that we were with at the time, and a few weeks or months after that, we went to see him."

Though their ranks were thinned down to Williams, Franklin, and Bryant, Otis scheduled an audition with Gordy anyway. His personnel dilemma was solved when falsetto-blessed tenor Eddie Kendricks (born December 17, 1939, in Union Springs, Alabama) got in touch and offered to bring in his pal, baritone Paul Williams (born July 2, 1939). Both had recently been members of the Primes, a respected local group of transplanted Alabamians rounded out by Kel Osborne. They even had a "sister group," the Primettes, who would find their own way to Motown stardom.

"Paul and Eddie were from a place called Tuxedo Junction, in a subdivision called Ensley," explained labelmate and fellow Birmingham native Gino Parks. "Paul's father sang with one of the leading groups around Birmingham called the Ensley Jubilees." Back up to fuller strength than ever, the group passed its audition for Gordy and Mickey Stevenson with flying colors. One piece of business remained: Deciding on a name for the freshly minted quintet.

"We were the Elgins for two weeks, and there was another group called the Elgins," Otis said. "We were standing outside with this fellow named Bill Mitchell, and we were kidding around with a name. Jumped up, somebody said, 'The Temptations.' I said, 'That's the one!'"

The Tempts' debut 45 in the summer of '61, "Oh, Mother Of Mine" (written by Otis and Mickey) paired with "Romance Without Finance" (by Stevenson and Kendricks), was produced by Mickey and Andre Williams (as Dre-Mic) and released on Miracle. A few months later, Miracle tried again with "Check Yourself," carrying writer's credits to Otis, Melvin, Bryant, and producer Gordy. Its 'B' side, "Your Wonderful Love," was a solo Gordy theme in the time-honored doo-wop mode. "Check Yourself" was a large leap forward, constructed around quirky chords, tempo shifts, and Paul Williams' vulnerable lead. These would be their only singles on short-lived Miracle, which didn't survive to year's end.

Ex-Primes Paul and Eddie split the lead duties for the Tempts' first four releases on Berry's new Gordy imprint, beginning with the imprint's inaugural issue, "Dream Come True" and its 'B' side, "Isn't She Pretty," in March of '62. Kendricks' sky-high falsetto oozed over the former like melting butter, and there was a solo by Berry's then-wife Raynoma on a keyboard contraption called an Ondioline that simulated strings but could be construed as a primitive synthesizer. The outing gave the Tempts their first taste of national R&B chart action. "Isn't She Pretty," the combined work of Gordy, Williams, and Kendricks, was a rowdy "Shout" variation, Eddie's falsetto careening all over the place and Melvin stepping up for the bridge.

Gordy decided to switch the group over to another lesser logo, Mel-O-Dy, in late September to cover Nolan Strong & the Diablos' infectious "Mind Over Matter," disguising them as the Pirates. Staff producer Clarence

The Temptations and Supremes gave Motown two of the biggest acts in the business in the 1960s. Clockwise from top left: Paul Williams, Melvin Franklin, Eddie Kendricks, Otis Williams, Dennis Edwards, Cindy Birdsong, Diana Ross and Mary Wilson (Photo courtesy of David Alston's Mahogany Archives).

Paul built its flip "I'll Love You 'Til I Die" in the blues-soaked style of the "5" Royales (his older brother Lowman Pauling was the Royales' guitarist). Virtually simultaneously the Tempts returned to Gordy with a doo-wop-enriched "Paradise" penned and produced by the label's namesake; its mid-tempo rhythm was anchored by Melvin's burbling bass and Eddie's fluttering lead. For the first time in the Tempts' Motown tenure, Smokey Robinson assumed the reins for the 'B': "Slow Down Heart" found Paul's grainy baritone hovering over the group's harmonies.

The two producers who would keep the Tempts on top split the Tempts' first single of '63 right down the middle. Smokey helmed the 'A' side, Joe Hunter's rippling ivories setting an atmospheric groove for Paul to deliver "I Want A Love I Can See"; Norman Whitfield, who had rapidly advanced from tambourine duty on the Distants' "Come On," supervised and co-wrote with Robinson the attractive "The Further You Look, The Less You See," Franklin and bassist James Jamerson weaving a complex bottom end. The summer of '63 brought a gem few folks picked up on at the time. "Farewell My Love" was a doo-wop throwback from B.G.'s pen featuring Paul and Eddie suavely trading leads (Kendricks seals it with a flourish that's pure street corner). Norman and Motown staffer Janie Bradford were responsible for "May I Have The Dance" on the other side, Eddie's lower-than-usual lead recalling the Drifters' Rudy Lewis.

Seven singles on three labels under two different names, and all the Tempts had to show was three weeks on the R&B hit parade with "Dream Come True." "It was rough and lean," said Williams. "When you love something, you hang with it, especially if you believe in it, and it's not breaking the law and carryin' on! So we loved singing, and being guys from the ghetto, we felt as though it would be a way out." But they were having difficulty with Bryant, who was axed after a Christmas show at Detroit's Fox Theater. David Ruffin, born January 18, 1941, in Whynot, Mississippi, came in after older brother Jimmy turned down an invitation to join the group.

"I used to travel with them on the Motown Revues. We used to travel together in a station wagon. They wanted me to join the group, because they knew me," said Jimmy. "I told 'em I didn't think I would fit into the group. They kept after me. They gave me all kinds of propositions. I had a job. I was working at Ford Motor Company, and they were just guys unemployed, just hustling and struggling.

"David didn't want to join that group, and they didn't want him in the group," Jimmy asserted. "I was like David's manager by proxy, him being the younger brother. I suggested that they should have David join the group, because I had been trying to get David signed with Motown, and they didn't want to sign him." Once they joined forces, the classic Tempts lineup was fully in place. "There was more than two lead singers, 'cause Paul did some leads, Melvin, and on occasions I did," said Williams. "We've always tried to spread the lead around. That kind of helped from putting all the weight on one guy." Bryant took the news hard. "I guess the brother did feel kind of left out," said Otis. "But sometimes you have to make a change."

Bryant's timing was abysmal, because Smokey was handing the Tempts their breakthrough. Guitarist Eddie Willis' chunky intro chords and some of Smokey's most inventive metaphors (who else would rhyme "cool crook" with "school book"?) rendered the enchanting "The Way You Do The Things You Do" a star-making vehicle for the Tempts, the Kendricks-led confection barely missing the pop Top Ten in early '64.

"Smokey, just being the good songwriter and producer that he is—it was one of those good songs at the right time. We just made magic happen that particular time," said Williams. "It was about time that we struck gold somewhere along the way." The celebration continued when Gordy issued their debut LP, *Meet the Temptations*, that March. It gathered most of their pre-hit singles along with "Way You Do" and its delicious flip "Just Let Me Know."

Now that momentum was on their side, the Tempts came back that spring with another carefree Kendricks showcase, "I'll Be In Trouble." Though the Smokey-penned-and-produced romp wasn't a smash on the level of "The Way You Do," it sold well. Its upbeat flip, "The Girl's Alright With Me" (a collaboration by Whitfield, Eddie Holland, and lead Kendricks) nearly broke through in its own right. Whitfield jumped in to oversee the Tempts' next hit in the fall, "Girl (Why You Wanna Make Me Blue)," which he'd written with Holland. But Robinson was about to interrupt Eddie's reign as primary front man.

"Smokey saw us at the 20 Grand, and he liked the way David sounded. He said, 'I've got a song for you,'" said Otis. Mind you, we're not talking about just any ditty: this one was titled "My Girl." "Smokey Robinson didn't just give him 'My Girl,'" said Jimmy Ruffin. "David kept bugging Smokey to give him a song."

"Smokey would come to us with various ideas, because he didn't want to get locked into a pattern of writing," said co-writer Ronnie White. "He said, 'Okay, Ron, look, I want you to help me with this song. I've got this idea I've got for the Temptations.' He came to me, and he bugged me for about a month or so. He said, 'Look, we gotta do this song.' So we sat down one day and we started writing it, and eventually finished it."

"I always loved being involved in something positive in the other artists' careers," said Smokey. "I had recorded them, and the first hit they had was 'The Way You Do The Things You Do,' and that was with Eddie Kendricks' voice. So all the producers and writers at Motown jumped on the Eddie Kendricks bandwagon. And whenever we recorded the Tempts, everybody was using Eddie Kendricks' voice because he had had the first hit with them.

The Temptations Sing Smokey included the group's breakthrough hit "The Way You Do The Things You Do," a 1964 Smokey Robinson gem.

"But I knew that David was in there, man. He was like a sleeping giant. So if I could get a hit on him, man, they would be multi-faceted. I had also used Paul Williams' voice on a few things. In fact, the first record I ever recorded on them was a thing called 'I Want A Love I Can See,' and I used Paul Williams' voice. But 'My Girl' was written specifically with David Ruffin in mind."

Over the course of nearly two months during the fall of '64, one of the seminal songs in Motown history was committed to posterity with Robert White winding the immortal guitar filigree around Jamerson's bass line and trombonist Paul Riser concocting an enchanting string arrangement. Ruffin made the most of his first chance to front the group on record: "My Girl" rocketed to the top of both the R&B and pop charts in early '65.

Not only were the Temptations untouchable in the studio, they were elevating their choreography to unmatched standards. The man responsible, Cholly Atkins, had dreamed up the Cadillacs' routines a decade earlier. After coaching the Miracles and Pips, Atkins had joined Motown's Artist Development Department to teach its groups how to properly execute their footwork onstage. No aggregation embraced his instructions with the flair of the Tempts.

Smokey enlisted "sleeping giant" Ruffin to once again front the Tempts' next smash in the spring of '65. "It's Growing" was chock-full of inventive Robinson metaphors (he co-wrote it with fellow Miracle Pete Moore) and boasted a key change midway through for good measure, the tune zipping up *Billboard's* R&B charts to the No. 3 slot. "We relished the fact of giving our material to them, because we knew they would do it so well. We knew that they would get the most that could be gotten out of a song, because they were such great artists," said Moore. "It's Growing" expertly melded the Tempts' harmonies with those of the Andantes, though Melvin's little joke at a pregnant Louvain Demps' expense caused a bout of temporary discord that day.

"That's when I was carrying my baby boy. And he put this basketball under his shirt at the session. I was so mad at him!" she said. Unlike their ongoing collaboration with the Four Tops, the combination of the Andantes and Tempts didn't last for too long. "After a while, they said they couldn't duplicate that particular thing (onstage), and they didn't want us to do that anymore," said Demps.

Temptin' Temptations (1965) was another hit-packed album that included "Everybody Needs Love," which was also a winner two years later for Gladys Knight and the Pips.

For their encore album in early '65, the group paid homage to their favorite producer with *The Temptations Sing Smokey*—the first of eight consecutive R&B chart-topping LPs for the group. Predictably, Kendricks' falsetto mirrored Smokey's high-pitched exploits as the Tempts took on the Miracles' "You've Really Got A Hold On Me" and "Way Over There," while "You'll Lose A Precious Love" would return as the flip of "Ain't Too Proud To Beg." Smokey and his partners provided the Tempts with two more R&B smashes that year that made major pop inroads. The summer hit "Since I Lost My Baby" and "My Baby" in the fall were opposite sides of the relationship coin, each spotlighting David atop the group's impeccable vocal cushion (Hank Cosby handled the sax solo on "My Baby" as he had on "I'll Be In Trouble").

The prolific Robinson was on a roll, churning out so much exceptional material that even the Tempts' 'B' sides were charting. "Don't Look Back," an all-too-rare opportunity for Paul Williams to seize the spotlight, accompanied "My Baby," while "You've Got To Earn It"—a treasure trove of tongue-in-cheek Smokey metaphors delivered by Eddie—was co-written by Tempts guitarist Cornelius Grant and tucked on the other side of "Since I Lost My Baby." Grant couldn't play on it because the Tempts were touring when Robinson cut the backing tracks.

"Cornelius used to be like a resident guitar player for Motown," said Williams. "He was traveling with Mary Wells and Marvin Gaye. Then he went out a couple of times with us, and things just started clicking once we started getting hits and consistency of work, where we could afford to pay a guitarist."

With no less than seven hits aboard, *Temptin' Temptations*, issued in late '65, was a two-fisted powerhouse. Smokey helmed a bouncy "You're The One I Need," but Whitfield and Eddie Holland collaborated on "I Gotta Know Now" and the sleek "Everybody Needs Love," the latter revived by Gladys Knight & the Pips as their first Motown success in mid-'67. Mickey Stevenson and Ivy Jo Hunter stepped in to co-write and produce the other pair of numbers, "Just Another Lonely Night" and a driving, Kendricks-led "Born To Love You."

Smokey's hot streak as a producer continued with the Tempts' first offering of 1966. "Get Ready," a straightforward anthem with a savage hook, cast Kendricks as lead and vaulted to the top of the R&B charts that spring. That wasn't sufficient for Gordy. Since "Get Ready" didn't score as high on the pop side as the group's last few releases, he decided to press up Whitfield's "Ain't Too Proud To Beg" as their next single three months later. Norman and lyricist Eddie Holland brainstormed a benchmark for Ruffin, set in a higher key than normal to intensify the soul quotient all the more. The result was another R&B chart-topper and a massive pop seller, giving Whitfield the honor of taking over as the Tempts' primary producer.

Nearly all the big Motown writers had material on the 1967 LP *With A Lot O' Soul.*

"You really can't compare Norman and Smokey, because they're two innovative people in their own right. We had a lot of hits with Smokey, then we had a lot of hits with Norman. It's just two good, talented, creative people that we had the good fortune of working with," said Williams. Norman and Eddie Holland came right back with "Beauty Is Only Skin Deep," placing Ruffin in charge of a captivating tribute to plain-looking women that again captured the top slot on the R&B lists and actually outscored "Ain't Too Proud To Beg" on the pop charts that fall. It was paired with "You're Not An Ordinary Girl," a Smokey-produced collaboration.

Norman gave the Tempts their fourth R&B chart-topper in a row before year's end with "(I Know) I'm Losing You," a Ruffin-led firebrand penned by Whitfield, Holland, and Grant, who cooked up its laser-beam intro. "Our original bass player (touring bandsman Bill Upchurch) and myself were sitting in one of the songwriter rooms. He was doing those fifths—he was playing those fifths on the bass. And I liked that sound. I said, 'What is that?' He said, 'These are fifths,'" said Grant. "He said, 'We call these double stops.' I said, 'Hmmm, double stops. I like that.' So I just started messin' around with it. As I was doing it, the guitar rang louder than the bass. So I was playing those double stops as Norman Whitfield happened to walk by the door. And he heard me playing it. He said, 'Hey!' He walked in, he said, 'What's that you're playing?' I said, 'Oh, just some fifths.' He said, 'Play that again! Put some chords with it!'" Grant had been digging George Clinton and the Parliaments' funky "(I Wanna) Testify," and he plugged a bit of its structure into "(I Know) I'm Losing You." "As I played those changes, Norman Whitfield said, 'That's it! I want to cut this!'" said Grant.

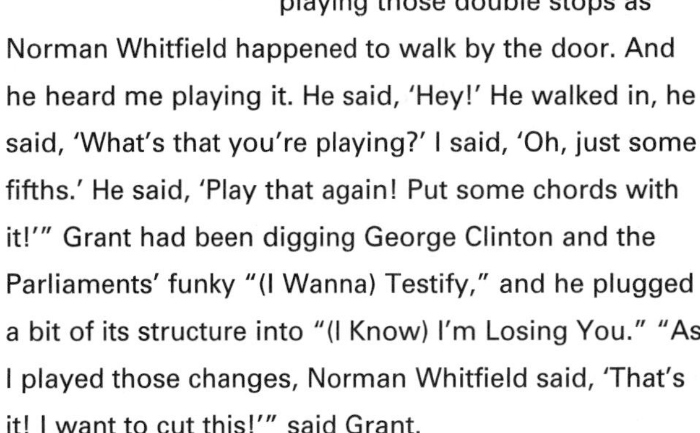

"Eddie was brought into the studio, and we were listening to the track. As he was listening to the track, he played it a few times, and he said, 'I got it!' He just started putting together those lyrics. At the very beginning, the song was called 'I Don't Wanna Lose You,' but there was another song called 'I Don't Wanna Lose You,' so they changed the title to '(I Know) I'm Losing You.'"

Gettin' Ready, the quintet's only 1966 album of fresh material (there was a top-selling greatest hits compilation near year's end), rates with their best, benefiting from productions by Smokey, Norman, Mickey Stevenson and Ivy Jo Hunter ("It's A Lonely World Without Your Love"), and Robert Staunton and Robert Walker. It's tough to fathom how Whitfield's "Too Busy Thinking About My Baby" (penned by Norman, Barrett Strong, and Janie Bradford; Jimmy Ruffin cut an unissued version over the same track) and "Lonely, Lonely Man Am I" (the work of Kendricks, Whitfield, and Eddie Holland) avoided 45 release. Smokey's metaphorically bountiful "Fading Away" served as 'B' side to "Get Ready." Robinson also contributed "Little Miss Sweetness" and "Who You Gonna Run To." Particularly intriguing was the '63 relic "Not Now, I'll Tell You Later," written by Smokey and Otis, where the Supremes are quite audible.

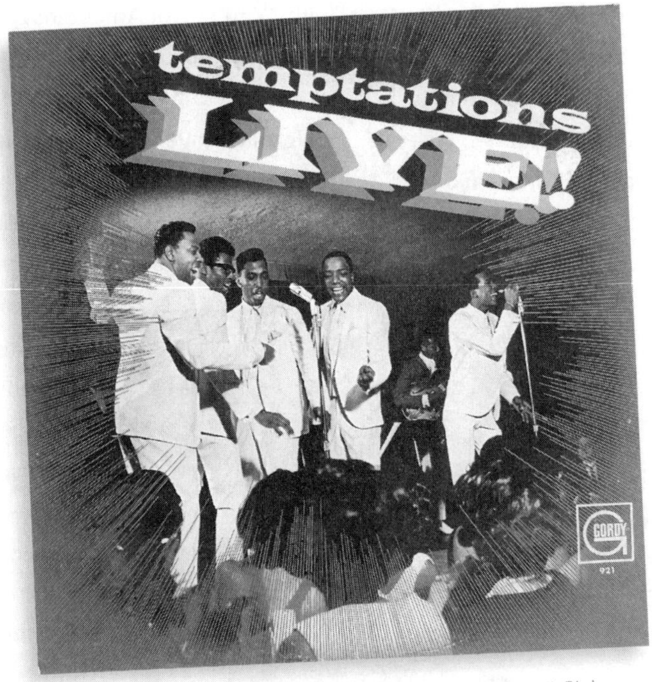

Temptations Live! was recorded in Detroit's Roostertail Club in 1966.

"All I Need," the Tempts' first '67 offering, barely broke their string of No. 1 R&B hits and leaped into the pop Top Ten. Ruffin tore it up on a pounder produced by Frank Wilson, who wrote it with lyricist Holland and R. Dean Taylor. "It was just a song, a melody that I had playing in my head," said Wilson. "I don't even know why it has that kind of flavor, that kind of feel, because that was not the principal feel that was happening at the time. But I just felt it. Then when I let Eddie Holland hear it, and Eddie fell in love with it, we just went on and knocked it out in a couple of days. I went in and I cut the track. And David—boy, did he just do it! I mean, it would have been hard to turn that record down. I don't care what else they had. I mean, a little skinny guy with a voice that big."

Kendricks finally regained the spotlight on the devotional "You're My Everything," written by Whitfield, Holland, and the ill-fated Roger Penzabene, who lived down the street from Grant and sometimes collaborated with him. "I had come home off of a little tour, and I was telling Roger that I wanted to do a song for Eddie," said Cornelius. "We needed to do a song so when he walked forward to the stage, he could sing a song that would be directed to a young lady. So Roger came up with stuff like, 'You're the girl I sing about in every love song I sing.'" The romantic angle was a natural: "You're My Everything" went No. 6 pop and No. 3 R&B that summer. Ruffin regained the spotlight on the group's last hit of '67, "(Loneliness Made Me Realize) It's You That I Need," another Whitfield/Holland partnership.

Team effort was always a Hitsville byword, the Tempts' '67 album *With A Lot O' Soul* being a prime example. Along with four smashes, the set included productions by Norman ("Save My Love For A Rainy Day," the ominous Whitfield/Grant/Sylvia Moy collaboration "Ain't No Sun Since You've Been Gone"), Smokey (the uncommonly hard-edged "No More Water In The Well" fronted by Paul, and a luscious "Now That You've Won Me"), Ivy Jo Hunter ("Sorry Is A Sorry Word"), and a rare turn with H-D-H, "Just One Last Look."

Temptations Live! chronicled an October 3, 1966, show at the Upper Deck of the swanky Roostertail overlooking the Detroit River, while the breathtaking '67 studio set *The Temptations In a Mellow Mood* seductively courted the supper club crowd. "That was so much fun," said *Mellow Mood* co-producer Wilson, who partnered with Jeffrey Bowen. "I got a chance to pick great songs, and match up these great songs with five unbelievable voices. Eddie doing something like 'With These Hands,' and having David do 'What Now My Love,' and having Paul do 'For Once In My Life'—it was just phenomenal. Just the wonderful range of stuff we were able to do with some of the most accomplished arrangers in the country." Breezy five-part harmonies flew through "Hello Young Lovers," and Melvin invested "Ol' Man River" with a dramatic fervor that tabbed him as a worthy successor to Ravens' front man Jimmy Ricks.

"That's one of the main reasons that album was recorded—to show the diversification that we could do, other than regular R&B, or ballads and things—which we always will do, 'cause it's our bread and butter," said Otis. "But we wanted to let 'em know that can get on the other serious side and sing some legit songs." One exception to the MOR concept: A swinging cover of "I'm Ready For Love," Martha & the Vandellas' un-mellow hit of a year before.

A major measure of heartbreak inevitably informed Ruffin's rough-edged vocals, but seldom more achingly than on the Tempts' "I Wish It Would Rain," which paced the soul charts in 1968 and went to No. 4 pop. Producer Whitfield, Strong, and Penzabene crafted a spine-chiller that floated free and easy over the Tempts' rich vocal blend, majestic strings, and subtly placed seagull and thunderstorm sound effects. Its flip, "I Truly, Truly Believe," was a delectable chance for Melvin to step out front on a piece of material tailor-made for his low-end rumble.

Surrounded by intricate harmonies from his groupmates, David came right back with another bravura R&B chart-topper, "I Could Never Love Another (After Loving You)," that spring. The same trio that gave them their previous smash supplied this one too, Penzabene writing from the depths of his lovesick soul. When he shot himself in the head over an untrue love at the end of 1967, the Motown family was devastated.

Eddie took over for the lovely "Please Return Your Love To Me," another major seller later that summer. It was one of a dozen highlights aboard *The Temptations Wish It Would Rain*, issued in April of '68. Kendricks took part in writing the buoyant "No Man Can Love Her Like I Do" with Whitfield and Holland. Smokey contributed "Cindy," and Nick Ashford and Valerie Simpson were behind "This Is My Beloved." Jimmy Ruffin's recent hits got a going-over with covers of "I've Passed This Way Before" and "Gonna Give Her All The Love I Got," while "He Who Picks A Rose" would be revived by labelmate Edwin Starr on his '69 LP *25 Miles*.

Though it wasn't apparent from their flawless five-piece harmonies, trouble was brewing behind the scenes. Former tee-totaler Paul Williams—still fantastic leading "How Can I Forget," the 'B' side of "Please Return Your Love To Me"—was drinking more. And

Ruffin wanted star billing similar to Robinson with the Miracles or Ross with the Supremes. "He didn't want to travel with them. He wanted to have his own limousine," remembered McDougal. "Then it got to the point where he would show up sometimes, and sometimes he wouldn't show up."

"He was never comfortable in the Temptations. Even the thing about being David Ruffin & the Temptations," said Jimmy Ruffin. "All he wanted to do was do what Diana Ross was doing—be in the group, and sing. 'Cause he always wanted to be a single artist. He never considered himself a member of the group, except that he had to be, 'cause that was his group. But in his heart of hearts, he was a single artist." After Ruffin missed a gig in Cleveland, the other four Tempts voted him out in June of 1968. The bespectacled, rail-thin vocalist took the news hard, showing up at subsequent shows to try to join his ex-cohorts uninvited onstage.

"David, he was so distraught," said McDougal. "At first, he wanted to leave the Temptations. Then when he saw the Temptations still thriving and doing good, I think he must have wanted to get back. Because he used to give 'em a lot of trouble by appearing at their gigs and wanting to sing." Ruffin finally settled into a solo career at Motown, debuting in early '69 with the smash "My Whole World Ended (The Moment You Left Me)."

Fortunately, the group had a suitable replacement in mind even before Ruffin's painful dismissal: Dennis Edwards, an ex-member of the Contours who boasted the physique of a middle linebacker and the rafter-rattling pipes of a country preacher. "Dennis was very convenient in the sense that he was with the Contours," said Williams. "It was an easy transition, 'cause he was right there at Motown. We had seen Dennis perform with the Contours while we were at the Howard Theater in D.C. We were very impressed with the way he sang. So we just kept our eye on him." The minister's son, born February 3, 1943, in Birmingham (by design or coincidence, the Tempts' Birmingham connection endured) and mostly raised in the Motor City, had recently been fronting his own Firebirds after leaving the Contours. Edwards had been sparingly recording on his own for Motown. His "Which Way To My Baby," produced by James Dean and William Weatherspoon, was a four-alarm blazer that failed to win release.[15]

The Temptations' talented original lineup: (from left) Eddie Kendricks, David Ruffin, Melvin Franklin, Otis Williams, Paul Williams.

"I was kind of despondent with Motown at the time," Edwards said in 1984. "I was trying to get a release. And I went up to see Mr. Ralph Seltzer at the time. I thought they were going to release me. What they were trying to tell me was that the Temptations would like me to be a member of their group! It was really amazing. I'm up there for one thing, and naturally that floored me, man. I was like, 'Wow, the Temptations!' I never even thought about it. That was my wildest dream."

Not only was the look of the group changing, so was its sound. Sly & the Family Stone were briskly expanding the outer boundaries of soul with their free-form, rock-soaked excursions, and Whitfield wholeheartedly embraced the funk movement by writing "Cloud Nine" for the Tempts with Strong. This represented a 180-degree stylistic shift. Though Dennis was principal lead, everyone else chimed in on the challenging anthem as recently added staff guitarist Dennis Coffey cut loose with laser-like rock riffage. Though its lyrics were interpreted in some quarters to glorify the use of illegal substances, the controversy didn't impede the track's commercial potential in the slightest as it flew up to No. 2 R&B and No. 6 pop in late '68.

"We understood where we were coming from lyrically," said Otis. "I guess the country had to try and digest it, because they were used to us singing 'Please Return Your Love To Me,' 'My Girl,' 'Since I Lost My Baby,' and 'The Girl's Alright With Me.' And here we were talking about—to them, it sounded like we were talking about drugs. But we were talking about just a state of mind, 'cause the word 'Cloud Nine' has been used a lot of years before we started recording. But they thought we were just talking about drugs, and we weren't. But all in all, we sold over a million copies and won a Grammy for it, so it served more than its purpose." That Grammy, for Best R&B Performance by a Duo or Group, Vocal or Instrumental, was the first for the group and for Motown itself.

Barrett Strong and Norman Whitfield gave the Temptations one of their biggest hits with "Just My Imagination" in 1971.

"I think Norman Whitfield, at that time, had great foresight," said Edwards. "Sly Stone was coming up. He had a record called 'Dance To The Music' which was just tearing the charts all apart. We decided to go into more of a psychedelic funk thing, because Norman could do it with my voice." They hadn't abandoned their old sound entirely: Whitfield and Strong devised a smooth "Why Did She Have To Leave (Why Did She Have To Go)" for Dennis to torch on the flip.

Edwards presided over the harrowing psychedelic soul maelstrom "Run Away Child, Running Wild," another funk-driven Whitfield/Strong opus that topped the R&B charts in March of '69 and vaulted high on the pop side. Its 'B' side was the less ambitious mid-tempo piece "I Need Your Lovin'." The Motown sound was whimsically applied to their version of the Yuletide perennial "Rudolph The Red-Nosed Reindeer" at year's end.

Apart from its title track and "Runaway Child," the *Cloud Nine* LP, released in early '69, was largely business as usual. "Don't Take Your Love From Me" and "Gonna Keep On Tryin' Till I Win Your Love" had been singles the previous year for Jimmy Ruffin; "Hey Girl" and "Love Is A Hurtin' Thing" had been hits for crooners Freddie Scott and Lou Rawls. "I Heard It Through The Grapevine," done Gladys Knight & the Pips-style, benefited from a rhythm section-only arrangement showcasing spiffy harmonies. Only the tasty "I Gotta Find A Way (To Get You Back)" was a previously unknown entity.

In addition to extending their own endless string of hits, the Tempts joined forces with Motown's other supergroup in 1968. Any doubts that the Temptations and Supremes could musically co-exist were erased when their inspiring "I'm Gonna Make You Love Me" (a Kenny Gamble/Jerry Ross composition that first hit for Dee Dee Warwick on Mercury in 1966), a Wilson/Nickolas Ashford production, proved a No. 2 smash on both the R&B and pop charts in late '68/early

'69. Kendricks' gossamer falsetto ignited the song, outpointing even Diana's kittenish allure as James Jamerson's bass rippled beneath the groups' combined strength.

The Tempts/Supremes experiment endured long enough to produce four albums and the acclaimed TV special *TCB*. But after scoring a respectable encore hit on a revival of Smokey's "I'll Try Something New" in the spring of '69, their treatment of the Band's "The Weight" was a comparative failure, and a revival of Marvin Gaye's "Stubborn Kind Of Fellow" flopped.

No such speed bumps marred the Tempts' own hit-making streak. Whitfield and his songwriting partner Strong poured on the funk as the end of the decade drew near. Edwards' leonine roar fueled "Don't Let The Joneses Get You Down," a No. 2 R&B smash during the spring of '69 before "I Can't Get Next To You"—a sophisticated variation on the funk formula with Dennis again in prime form and plenty of exciting interplay from the entire group—bolted to No. 1 status on both charts that fall.

"We were trying to do what they called then the psychedelic music," said Strong. "This was going on then—George Clinton and the Funkadelic and all that. So we were trying to go with that same type of flow, but with a little different twist—give it a more of a gospel-type R&B sound."

The Whitfield-produced *Puzzle People* featured a demand for African-American empowerment ("Message From A Black Man") and a funk treatment of the Beatles' "Hey Jude." More traditional were the Whitfield/Strong/Penzabene-penned "You Don't Love Me No More," an increasingly rare Kendricks lead vehicle; the impassioned "Since I've Lost You" (introduced by Jimmy Ruffin back in '64), and a "That's The Way Love Is" owing nothing to versions by Marvin Gaye or Gladys Knight & the Pips. Cranking out product at this prolific pace was no problem. "We were with Norman for seven years, so Norman—a lot of times when we would come in, he would have the tracks recorded," said Williams. "It would be pretty much laid out. And we would rehearse it with him, make up the background and decide on who was leading."

The Tempts gave themselves over to the almighty funk entirely in 1970. "Psychedelic Shack," "Ball Of Confusion (That's What The World Is Today)," and the Swahili-titled "Ungena Za Ulimwengu (Unite The World)" chased one another up the R&B Top Ten, the first two climbing as high as No. 2. Predictably, the latter had less appeal in the pop marketplace. *The Psychedelic Shack* album, entirely written by Strong and producer Whitfield, continued the trend, featuring the original "War"—a rallying cry for Edwin Starr a few months later.

Gladys Knight & the Pips shared Whitfield's production largesse with the Tempts; the quartet came out with "You Need Love Like I Do (Don't You)" as a single at just about the same time the Tempts' LP version hit the shelves (it also contained an extended cover of Gladys and the Pips' recent smash "Friendship Train"). The spacy "Take A Stroll Thru Your Mind" detoured into a cool walking groove over bass and bongos, offering stark contrast to the uncompromising "Hum Along And Dance" and "You Make Your Own Heaven And Hell Right Here On Earth."

Kendricks' last hurrah with the Temptations spectacularly propelled the group back to its ballad-singing roots in early 1971. The pristine across-the-board No. 1 hit "Just My Imagination (Running Away With Me)"—written by the tireless Whitfield and Strong—was breathtaking in its pure innocence, arranger Jerry Long providing the perfect shimmering backdrop for Eddie to ethereally float atop (Paul Williams muscles in magnificently on the bridge). But after Eddie and Otis clashed once too often, Eddie left the group. Like Ruffin, he landed on his feet as a Motown solo artist, notching his first hit with the ironically titled "It's So Hard For Me To Say Good-Bye" in the spring of '71.

After briefly trying to fill Kendricks' spot with the Vibrations' Ricky Owens, the group hired 21-year-old Damon Harris as his replacement. Born in July of 1950 in Baltimore, Harris was the right man for the job. He had grown up idolizing Kendricks and the Tempts, forming a high school group called the Tempos. In 1970 he fronted a minor hit for the Isley Brothers' T-Neck label with his Young Vandals coupling covers of the Tempts' "Too Busy Thinking About My Baby" and the Miracles' "I've Been Good To You."

The contents of *Sky's the Limit* were already in the can prior to Kendricks' departure. The smash changed Whitfield's direction in crafting material for the Tempts; ballads ("Man," "Throw A Farewell Kiss," and the enchanting "I'm The Exception To The Rule," the latter pair first cut by the Velvelettes) were back, Kendricks' falsetto looming larger than it had in ages. The group tackled "Gonna Keep On Tryin' Till I Win Your Love" again, this time slower. When the Tempts did delve into funk, the results ran long. "Love Can Be Anything (Can't Nothing Be Love But Love)" went on for 9:20, and "Smiling Faces Sometimes," predating the Undisputed Truth's smash version by a month or so, timed out at 12:35.

The first time the Tempts crooned "It's Summer" on *Psychedelic Shack*, Melvin handled the lead. For the Whitfield/Strong collaboration's second incarnation in mid-1971, Dennis was installed to provide a rougher edge, and Paul Riser's arrangement upped the energy level—yet it proved the group's poorest-selling single in ages. So it was back to stone-cold funk for "Superstar (Remember How You Got Where You Are)." Franklin anchored the bottom as Damon made his presence known for the first time on the Top Ten R&B smash near year's end. Harris wasn't the only fresh face: Paul Williams was ailing to the point where he had to give up the road, and ex-Distant Richard Street, who had been with the Monitors on their '66 V.I.P. hits "Say You" and "Greetings (This Is Uncle Sam)" before signing on as Paul's understudy, was his replacement.

No matter how potentially devastating the loss of an individual member, the Temptations persevered. "It's no easy task, but you just work at it and go through the procedure of checking out different guys. It's just one of those things that you have to go through," said Williams. "Talent is not enough. It's a thing of if you click spiritually, as well as professionally.

"You have to live together out here on the road, so it's trying to see if someone is compatible aside from the talent aspect, but from the human side. We go through the weeding-out process, and settle on whomever we think is the one, and still take a chance because you never know how someone might be."

"Superstar" and the remade "It's Summer" hailed from the 1972 album *Solid Rock*, which also contained the Tempts' next hit, the message song "Take A Look Around." Harris sounded uncannily like Kendricks on "Smooth Sailing," its happy mid-'60s throwback groove a hybrid of "Too Busy Thinking About My Baby" and "Girl (Why You Wanna Make Me Blue)." The LP was one of the first on Motown to list musicians' credits, and it showed the Funk Brothers still largely intact for all 12:20 of "Stop The War Now," the funk-permeated "What That Is?" and a rip-roaring "The End Of Our Road" that veered closer to Gladys than Gaye.

The Tempts' next 45 that summer, "Funky Music Sho Nuff Turns Me On" split its airplay with its flip "Mother Nature." For a guy who seldom seized the opportunity to front the group, Otis acquitted himself beautifully on the doo-wop-soaked "I Ain't Got Nothin'" (the group's shoo-bops recalled the Flamingos' "I Only Have Eyes For You") that was a highlight of its second LP of 1972, *All Directions*. Most of Motown's luminaries had abandoned Hitsville, but the Tempts remained loyal, utilizing a cast of Funk Brothers augmented by guitarist Robert Ward, founder of the Ohio Untouchables, the band that backed the Falcons on their gospel-soaked '62 smash "I Found A Love" for LuPine. Ward also made some marvelous '60s singles of his own for producer Don Davis.

The most memorable item on the set was an epic Whitfield/Strong composition that the group initially tried to avoid recording. Fortunately, its persuasive producer prevailed. Despite having recently been cut by the Undisputed Truth (Whitfield was never one to abandon a good song), "Papa Was A Rollin' Stone" was a universal sensation, a team effort that topped the pop charts in December of '72.

"You hear these stories—you hear people tell stories about different things," said Strong of its genesis. "These things never happened to me in my life, but you're around, you hear kids tell stories, you have people tell stories about their lives or about someone else's life. You say, 'Oh, wow, that's an interesting situation.'" "Papa" picked up three Grammys. Its Best Rhythm & Blues Song and Best Rhythm & Blues Vocal Performance By a Duo, Group or Chorus honors are inarguable, but its victory as Best Rhythm & Blues Instrumental Performance for its flip side remains an eternal head-scratcher. "Papa" was a mighty tough hit to follow, but the Tempts roared right back in April of 1973 when "Masterpiece" rocketed to the top of the R&B charts. It marked the end of the group's reign as pop hit makers on a massive scale.

On August 17, 1973, 34-year-old Paul Williams, for so long the unsung hero of the Tempts, was found lying dead on a Detroit street, the result of a self-inflicted gunshot to the head. He'd recently cut a couple of solo sides for Motown in an attempt to jumpstart his career, the ironically titled "Feel Like Givin' Up" produced and co-written by Kendricks, but the label didn't issue them. The incident cast a pall over the group but didn't impede its non-stop string of hits. The Tempts followed the rest of their labelmates' lead by relocating to L.A. in '74. There have been numerous personnel changes since then; David and Eddie returned to the fold in 1982 for the acclaimed *Reunion* album and resultant tour before breaking away again as a duo.

After bringing his thunder to the '75 R&B chart-topper "Shakey Ground" and a heart-melting "A Song For You," Edwards eventually went on his own and scored a solo hit in 1984 with "Don't Look No Further" for Gordy. He currently fronts a Tempts tribute act. Street stuck with the group until 1993 before retiring. Ruffin and Kendricks have passed on, as did Franklin on February 23, 1995. Otis carries the torch, flanked by a new generation of Tempts. They had a huge hit in 1998 with "Stay" and garnered a 2000 Grammy nomination for their album *Ear-Resistible*—both on Motown.

"I think a man is strongest when he knows his limitations. I know I'm a group man. I like working with groups of people, in a singing group or a team in writing songs or whatever. So I know my thing is to be with a group," Otis said. "It's just good music, and anything good is always gonna be around. It might fade, but it really is not goin' anywhere. It's just making its round, and it'll come back around again. That's just the way it is with anything of good quality, and Motown has made very good quality music over the years. And that stands up. That stands the test of time."

(From left) One-of-a-kind saxman Jr. Walker and bandmates Victor Thomas, Willie Woods and James Graves.

JR. WALKER
& THE ALL STARS

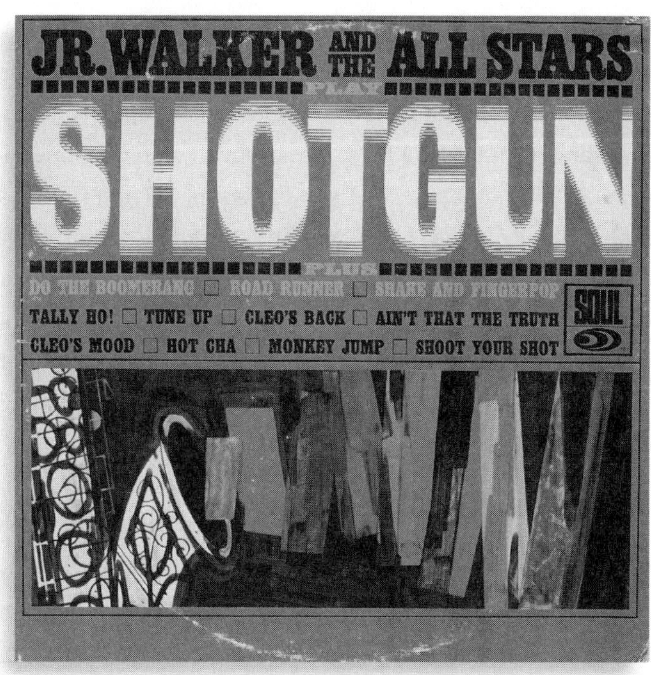

Jr. Walker and the All Stars hit the proverbial bulls-eye with *Shotgun* in 1964. Thanks to some no-shows during the recording session, the title track was Walker's singing debut, and it eventually rose to No. 4 on the pop charts.

The muscular, in-your-face tenor saxophone squeal of Jr. Walker and the **funky**, *sweat-stained rhythms dished up by his self-contained unit, the All Stars, never quite jibed with the impeccably crafted Motown sound—and that was just fine with Berry Gordy.*

"I was just different from everybody else," said Walker in 1994. "We just had our own thing goin'. Berry Gordy, he kept it that way. He just said, 'I'd rather for him to record the way he's doin'.' And he'd tell everybody else to leave me alone!" Walker also wrote quite a bit of his own material, further distancing him from many of his labelmates. Gordy acquired the dynamic services of the ebullient horn man long after his blues-laced bar-walking talents had been put to the supreme dance floor test on bandstands from South Bend, Indiana to Battle Creek, Michigan.

Born with the unwieldy handle of Autry DeWalt Mixon (or Mixom) in Blythesville, Arkansas on June 14, 1931 (early Motown press material cited 1942 as the saxman's birth year; since he was actually in the neighborhood of 34 years old at the time of his 1965 breakthrough, shaving 11 years off was a prescient move), his stage handle was devised in his early teens.

"They gave me that, walkin' to school," he said. "I just walked, and they just gave me that name. And my stepfather was Walker.'" Inspired by the jumping jive of alto ace Louis Jordan, Junior fell in love with the roar of the horn. South Bend saxist George Mason gave him his first chance to play one. "That was the guy that started me out, messin' around with George. I used to go over and blow horn with him, and mess around with his horn. He snatched it one day. A guy told me, 'You blowin', boy!' I said, 'Yeah?' He said, 'Man, you're tearin' it up!' So (Mason) took it away from me. I said, 'Well, okay then. That's the way that goes.'"

An uncommonly diverse array of horn men impressed Walker. "There's quite a few guys that were blowin' saxophone when I picked up. Boots Randolph, Stan Getz, and there was Charlie Parker. I used to listen to him a lot," said Walker in 1980, citing jazz luminaries Lester Young and Gene Ammons and R&B wailer Rusty Bryant as well. "I used to practice after all those different guys. I used to sit and listen to 'em, practice by 'em. That's how I got it down."

Pretty soon Junior went professional. "I came out of high school like any other kid, and we started trying to put a little band together," he said. "At first we called ourselves the Jumping Jacks, and then we played little clubs for two or three dollars, five dollars, whatever we could pick up. We played for little school proms and stuff like that."

The screaming high note at the heart of Walker's full-bore attack came from digging Illinois Jacquet, whose extended solo on Lionel Hampton's 1943 Decca flagwaver "Flying Home" fueled the imagination of countless tenor men. "I was blowin' like him, tryin' to do some things like him, and that's where I got it from," said Walker. "I started blowin' that high note, and I just went on up a little higher than what he was doin', and just went on and blowed. I don't know how I struck it—I said, 'Well, dog!'

"I was playing at a little club, and I was screamin' like that with the horn. So a guy that was playing the guitar told me, 'Oh, man, you shouldn't be doin' that. And another guy was standing behind me, he said, 'You keep doin' what you're doin'! Don't pay that man no attention. You blow that note, 'cause there ain't nobody else blowin' it!'"

Junior accumulated plenty of hard-fought experience around South Bend, recruiting guitarist Willie Woods, organist Victor Thomas (he ably provided the band's bottom with his foot pedals—no bassist necessary), and drummer Tony Washington, who lined up an open-ended gig for the quartet at a Battle Creek juke joint, the El Grotto.

"We was playing jazz and R&B. We was doin' it all," said Junior. "When I got off into the R&B, I started makin' a little money then!" So entrenched was Walker at the El Grotto that he came to epitomize the concept of cool to young singer Al Green, then fronting a Grand Rapids vocal group known as the Creations that also performed there. Green adopted Junior as an early role model in the all-important demeanor department.[16]

Harvey Records, owned by Harvey Fuqua and Gwen Gordy, snapped up Walker's combo on the advice of singer Johnny Bristol, then half of the singing duo Johnny & Jackey (on Harvey's sister Tri-Phi logo) and later to play a crucial role in Walker's musical development. "Johnny Bristol came and got me out of the club and took me to Detroit," said Walker. "He said, 'You wanna cut records?' I said, 'If there's some money in it, yeah!'" "Twist Lackawanna," Junior's 1962 Harvey debut, was a house-rocking instrumental in the great honking tradition, as were his sledgehammer followups "Brain Washer" and 1963's "Good Rockin'" (something of a sideways "Night Train"). But it was the flip of "Brain Washer," the sultry blues instrumental "Cleo's Mood," that indicated bigger things to come.

Junior and the All Stars revived Marvin Gaye's smash "How Sweet It Is (To Be Loved By You)" and scored their own hit with it in 1966 (Photo courtesy of David Alston's Mahogany Archives).

"Willie Woods was writing that tune one night. We was at a club, and we was playin' it. This was before we was famous. And we was fiddlin' around with it, and he looked at me and said, 'What about this tune?'" recalled Walker. "I said, 'Boy, that's a bad tune!' And this chick walked across, and I said, 'Mmmmm! Ol' Cleo's back!' Just like that. I don't know if the girl was named Cleo, but we always called her Cleo."

Tri-Phi and Harvey folded not too long thereafter, with Junior and roster mates Shorty Long and the Spinners following Fuqua over to Motown. "I walked over to Motown and talked with Mr. Gordy," said Walker. "He said, 'Well, you want to cut records, huh?' I said, 'Yeah! I wanna blow a little bit!' So he signed me up, and the first thing I did was 'Monkey Jump.'" Produced by Gordy himself, the chunky workout was issued on the Soul imprint during the summer of '64.

Walker found inspiration for his first national smash on the jam-packed dance floor of the El Grotto. "I was watching 'em when they came out with this new dance," he said. "They was doing the Karate too, but this dance kind of got to me. They was goin' across the floor like they was shootin'. So I called a couple of 'em. I said, 'What are you doin' *now*? What kind of junk is this?' The girl looked at me and said, 'Man, that's the Shotgun!' I said, 'The Shotgun?!?' They said, 'You better write a tune to that! That's what's happenin'!'

"So I said okay, and went on and wrote the thing. I called Mr. Gordy up—at that point you could call him and talk to him. So I called him up. And he said, 'Yeah, what's happening?' I said, 'Well, I've got a tune called "Shotgun!"' And he fell out and went to laughing, and said, 'Come on in and record it.' And we went on in and did it, and it come to be a great tune."

Talk about snatching victory from the jaws of defeat: Not only was Walker forced to overcome the flailings of a short-tenured All Star drummer that couldn't locate the proper groove (Benny Benjamin was duly summoned and filled in magnificently), Walker's invited vocalist, ex-Jumping Jacks pianist Fred Paton, failed to show up for the auspicious date altogether, prompting Junior's reluctant singing debut (with a little harmony aid from Woods on the chorus).

"That was the first song I *ever* sung!" he said. "We had a guy gonna come in to sing it, and man, that guy didn't show up. We went on, and Berry Gordy said, 'You guys come here and set this thing up!' I said, 'Yeah.' He said, 'I can't waste no time with you. Go in there and record it.' I said, 'Well, we need a singer!' He said, '*You* sing it then!' Everybody else said, 'You sing it! Get up there and do something!' So we went in there, and I got up there and sung it. I just hollered it, you know. Just went on through it like it should be. And I told the guy when we got through, 'We'll get somebody else, we'll bring somebody in.' He said, 'Man, I got what I want!'"

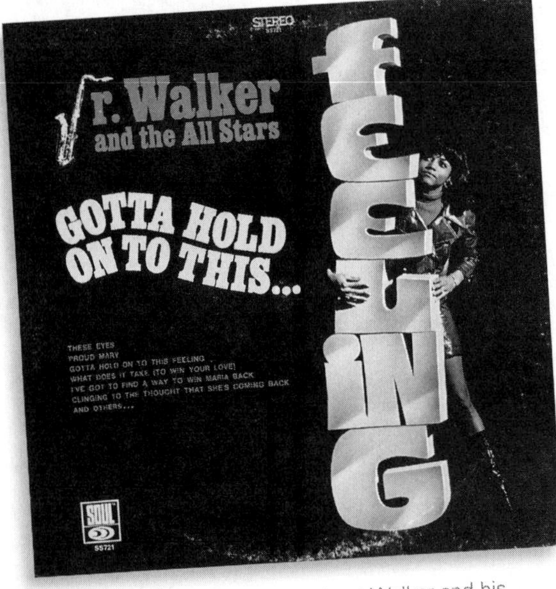

Gotta Hold On To This Feeling kept Walker and his All Stars on the charts in 1970.

Once it was cocked and fired, "Shotgun" blasted up to the top of the R&B charts and to No. 4 on *Billboard's* pop listings in early '65, earning Walker and the All Stars a barrage of national TV exposure on *Shindig!*, *Hullabaloo*, and *American Bandstand*. By then, Cleveland-based drummer James Graves was officially an All Star. Four months later, Junior cracked the R&B Top Ten with the similarly sweaty "Do The Boomerang." "I was playing in Cleveland, and I started putting 'The Boomerang' together," said Walker. "When we come back, we cut it." "Shake And Fingerpop" made it three in a row later that summer, flipped with the atmospheric sequel and hit in its own right "Cleo's Back" (its predecessor did better its second time around, "Cleo's Mood" charting high when Soul unleashed it anew). *Shotgun*, Junior's debut LP, came out mid-year and was a non-stop dancer's delight, surrounding the hits with the incendiary instrumentals "Tune Up" and "Tally Ho," a raw-edged "Ain't It The Truth," and "Shotgun's" atmospheric Latin-tempoed flip, "Hot Cha" (a Woods composition).

Walker deviated from his basic formula for one of his biggest sellers of 1966, the relentless "(I'm A) Road Runner," written specifically for him by Holland-Dozier-Holland (Dozier and Brian Holland doubled as producers). "I always run in and out of the studio, so Brian Holland and Dozier—they was kind of the ones that wrote the tune—they called me when I was comin' in," said Walker. "He says, 'Hey man, where's your horn?' "I said, 'Well, I left it in the car. I left it at home, I think.' He said, 'From now on, when you come to the studio, always bring your horn!' I said, 'All right, sir.' And then he told me, 'Look, I got a tune for you.' I said, 'What's the name of it?' He said, 'The same thing you're doing—"Road Runner."' So I said, 'The next time I come in, I'll record it.' So we went on a road trip, and when we came back in, I came in the door, runnin' again. And he said, 'You ready?' I said, 'Yeah, I'm ready.' And we went right in the studio and cut it."

Nineteen sixty-six brought two more fiery Walker LPs. *Soul Session* gathered up a dozen torrid Fuqua-produced instrumentals, most likely dating from the Harvey label days and virtually all written by various band members. "Us," "Shake Everything," "Everybody

Gets Together," and "Decidedly" showcased Junior's rocking side; "Eight Hour Drag," "Hewbie Steps Out," "Marc Anthony (Speaks)," and "Satan's Blues" conjured up a late-night ambiance, and "Moonlight In Vermont" recalled Walker's days as a jazz enthusiast. No album better captures just how fine a roadhouse outfit the All Stars were. Woods and Thomas were self-effacing accompanists of the first order, always giving Junior precisely what he needed to aim straight for the ionosphere.

Road Runner followed hot on its heels, combining more instrumental stunners (the hair-raising "Last Call," a churning "Ame' Cherie [Soul Darling]," and a nasty adaptation of Chicago blues guitarist Freddy King's "San-Ho-Zay") with the raucous vocals "Anyway You Wanna" and "Baby You Know You Ain't Right." The LP also featured a magical cross-pollination that occurred when bassist James Jamerson dropped by to jam on the Hank Cosby-penned "Mutiny."

Jr. and the All Stars were in their element with up-tempo hits like "Pucker Up Buttercup."

"We was doin' the tune, and the Motown band came in," explained Walker. "Jamerson picked it up and started playing the bass to it. (Co-producer) Lawrence Horn said, 'Why don't y'all cut it like that?' We was doin' it a different way, and he said, 'Why don't you cut it the way he's startin' the tune? That sounds good!' I said, 'Well, don't make me no difference. Cut it!'" Inspired by Jamerson's free-roaming bass lines, "Mutiny" was as close as Walker would ever come to straight jazz on wax.

Two of Walker's 1966 smashes, hot-wired revivals of the Motown classics "How Sweet It Is (To Be Loved By You)" (a major hit a year-and-a-half earlier for Marvin Gaye) and "Money (That's What I Want)" (Barrett Strong's 1960 breakthrough), benefited from a pseudo-live ambiance added after the fact. "When I heard it, then I heard all them people on it. It was like a party thing," said Walker. "They wasn't there when I recorded it." Soul did eventually issue two legit in-concert LPs with nearly identical titles: 1967's *Jr. Walker & the All Stars "Live!"* and *Jr. Walker & the All Stars Live* three years later—the latter containing his only documented stabs at the Tempts' "[I Know] I'm Losing You" and Chris Kenner's "Something You Got".

Torrid hits abounded for Junior throughout 1967. The rock-solid dance effort "Pucker Up Buttercup," a derivative but delightful "Shoot Your Shot" from the *Shotgun* LP, and a revved-up revival of the Supremes' "Come See About Me." The following year, 1968, saw another smash in the form of the funky two-sided travelog "Hip City," which required a little last-second lyrical assistance from staffer Janie Bradford.

"My phone rang on Mother's Day to come and finish up this song on Jr. Walker in the studio. I was so mad and so angry. So I said, 'Okay, that's alright. I'll write this song,'" said Bradford, who got down to business seated behind the mixing board in the control room. "You had this board, but then it went straight down, and there was a couch down in front of it. And I

couldn't see the couch. And I said, 'I'll get his nose wide open and take all his money, so I don't have to worry about coming down here and writing no songs for him.' And his wife stood up! I didn't know she was there! She got so mad, she didn't say a word to me. She went and snatched Junior out of the studio!"

Junior served up a succulent hit in early '69, "Home Cookin'," that was the combined handiwork of staff guitarist Eddie Willis, Melvin Moy, and producer Hank Cosby. But his top mover by far that year almost failed to see light of day as a Soul single at all. "What Does It Take (To Win Your Love)" was a major departure from Walker's gutbucket sound; the Funk Brothers supplied smoother, more melodic backing than anything the saxman had attempted up to that point. The Johnny Bristol/Fuqua production initially hit the streets on Junior's *Home Cookin' album*, only to emerge belatedly as a single.

Gotta Hold On To This Feeling

Joe Hinton - Pam Sawyer - Johnny Bristol

Recorded by JR. WALKER & THE ALL STARS on SOUL 35070

95¢

JOBETE MUSIC COMPANY, INC.

exclusive distributor Belwin Mills Publishing Corp.

Johnny Bristol fed Jr. and the All Stars a non-stop diet of hits, including "Gotta Hold On To This Feeling" in 1970.

"(Gordy) didn't think that that was the record that should have been released, so they released 'Home Cookin.' It was between 'Home Cookin' and 'What Does It Take.' Those were the choices. So they released 'Home Cookin'," said Bristol. "Yet the disc jockeys, about 38 or 40 disc jockeys across the country, picked it out of the album over 'Home Cookin'."

(Weldon A. McDougal III photo)

The boss's trepidation was understandable, and initially shared by Junior. "Johnny Bristol was trying to get me to do the tune, and I turned it down," said Walker. "I said, 'Oh man, I don't want to cut that tune.' So he said okay. He didn't say nothin'. So I didn't cut the tune. And it was a year later, I came back in at the time we was cuttin' 'Hip City.' So I came in the door, and he was standing up there lookin' at me just as funny, silly, you know.

"I said, 'What's happenin', "Brits"?' He said, 'Nothin' to it. What's goin' on?' I said, 'Oh, everything's mellow. What're you doin' here?' He said, 'I'm waitin' on you to cut this tune!' I said, '*What* tune?' He said, '"What Does It Take (To Win Your Love)." If you turn me down, I'll be here next year!' I said, 'Come on, man.' So we went on in and cut that tune. And that was a big one. I said, 'I'm glad that I cut it.' I didn't think I could do it. I really didn't. But he pushed it on me, so I did it."

"He was unfortunately like several other people at the company that didn't like it after it was finished—including Mr. Gordy," said Bristol, who sang harmony with Walker on the number. "They just felt it was too pretty: 'Junior doesn't sing with strings and girls. Junior Walker is meat and potatoes. He can't sing about love.' I just felt a transition when I was producing him. I knew he was not a great singer, but I knew he could carry a melody. And I knew he had a unique sound already, in the manner of the way he sang from his other stuff, even though he didn't necessarily sing. He yelled 'Shotgun,' so to speak. But I wanted him to do something a little more melodic. And that was hard to sell. Junior didn't think he could sing." Eventually, everyone dug "What Does It Take" as it paced the R&B charts in July of '69, peaking at No. 4 pop.

That wasn't the only highlight gracing *Home Cookin'*. Along with the expected hits came the hard-charging "Baby Ain't You Shame" and "The Things I Do For You" (both produced by Motown engineer Horn, who shared in the writing), a snazzy reprise of blues harpist Buster Brown's 1959 hit "Fannie Mae," a comically down-home "Sweet Daddy Deacon," and an edgy mid-tempo instrumental "Sweet Soul" rife with sky-high squeals.

Rainbow Funk definitely had a funky album cover, but the 1971 release was light in the hit department.

"What Does It Take (To Win Your Love)" proved that Walker could surround himself with the slicker musical trappings that defined the Motown sound and cope handily—indicating the services of the All Stars would no longer be required in the studio (guitarist Woods died in Kalamazoo on May 27, 1997 at the age of 60). Truth be told, the Funk Brothers had actually been present on selected Walker waxings well before that. "Most of the stuff that you see Junior's name on that he wrote, he pretty much rehearsed and had very tight when he got to the studio. So they used his band," said Bristol. "But when they assigned him to other producers—guys like myself—I used the Funk Brothers and various other people."

Junior got used to the change in recording philosophy. "After I got into it, I just went on and went to doin' 'em," he explained. "I stopped sayin' what I couldn't do. I said I couldn't do those slow songs. I really didn't want to do 'em. Johnny said, 'This is all I got.' So we did it, and it was a big hit. I turned down 'Someday We'll Be Together.' I should have cut that record!"

"I think he got his confidence and accepted this new style when he really got out there in public and saw people going crazy over 'What Does It Take,' and accepted him singing that way," agreed Bristol. Covering a rock hit such as the Guess Who's "These Eyes" might have been dismissed in the past by Walker, but eventually the prospect no longer intimidated him. In fact, his rendition of "These Eyes" actually challenged the original for pop chart supremacy before 1969 ended, though its flip, the irresistible "I've Got To Find A Way To Win Maria Back," better indicated his growth as a vocalist, his stratospheric sax winding through lush instrumentation provided by writer/producer Bristol. "It was amazing to sit there and see what he would do next. If you'd just give him a direction, he just went crazy," said Bristol.

The Bristol-produced "Gotta Hold On To This Feeling" and "Do You See My Love (For You Growing)" provided two more monster hits for Junior in 1970, the ebullient saxman maintaining his rootsy appeal in a polished soul setting. The latter was first cut in 1962 by

Bristol and his ex-duet partner Jackey Beavers as Johnny & Jackey for Tri-Phi. "I tried to pick the ones I felt he could do, that would fit his voice, and the limit of his vocal ability," noted Bristol. "Carry Your Own Load" was another Johnny & Jackey remake that should have extended Walker's Top Ten R&B status in early '71 but fell short; airplay was split with a cover of Neil Diamond's recent million-seller "Holly Holy" as its 'A' side. *A Gasssssssss*, Walker's second 1970 LP, had a few nice things on it—"Riding High On Love," "At A Saturday Matinee," "Groove And Move"—but covers dominated, with versions of Jimmy Webb's maudlin "Honey Come Back," Blood, Sweat & Tears' "And When I Die," the Beatles' "Hey Jude," and Stevie Wonder's "I Was Made To Love Her."

Junior's biggest hit of '71, "Take Me Girl, I'm Ready," stayed in the same attractive upbeat soul vein under Bristol's reign, while his vocal rendition of Crusaders reedman Wilton Felder's nostalgic "Way Back Home" scored sizably, too. *Rainbow Funk*, the LP that both hailed from, was a bit disappointing, Junior doing his best with George Harrison's "Something" and Dave Mason's "Feeling Alright." The closer, a revival of the Velvelettes' '66 outing for V.I.P., "These Things Will Keep Me Loving You," was a substantial improvement.

"Walk In The Night," the saxman's final Top Ten R&B entry in the spring of 1972, resembled a blaxploitation flick theme, Willie Shorter's jazz-funk arrangement framing Walker's echo-laden sax in what was a serious departure from the Motown sound. "In working with Junior, I just saw a man who could play the saxophone like I had never heard before," Bristol said. "And to me, if I could hear him doing anything that was unique, that would give him his versatile sound, I tried to do that. In working with Marilyn McLeod, she and I were just sitting, and she'd play a little bit of something she had, and then we extended it together. And I just heard Junior Walker doing it. I didn't hear it as a song with lyrics. I just heard it as an instrumental. I said, 'Junior could kill this!'" "Groove Thang," the other hit (albeit a relatively minor one) from the Bristol-produced *Moody Jr.* LP, navigated similar jazz-tinged territory.

The non-charting '73 Bo Diddley-beat rocker "Peace And Understanding (Is Hard To Find)" proved that in possession of the right slab of meaty material, Walker could return to his roadhouse roots. Junior helmed this one himself (ditto the only mild hit from the set, the two-sided "Gimme That Beat"). Much of the *Peace & Understanding Is Hard To Find* album bore a harder edge, with Walker reverting to his old fire-breathing self for "Country Boy," "Soul Clappin'," "I Ain't Goin' Nowhere," and an instrumental take on Johnny Nash's "I Can See Clearly Now."

Don Cornelius must have loved the sentiment behind Junior's '74 offering "Dancin' Like They Do On Soul Train," but the public didn't pick up on it. Apart from a middling '76 hit with "I'm So Glad," that was basically the end of Walker's scorching Motown run. The label kept releasing product on him into 1978, but disco attire really didn't suit the no-holds-barred honker. After migrating briefly to Norman Whitfield's self-named label in 1979, he returned to the Motown fold for a last long-player, *Blow the House Down*, in '83.

Junior kept right on running the road non-stop until cancer claimed him on November 23, 1995. For quite a while during the '80s, his son, drummer Autry DeWalt III, deftly anchored his road band. Try as they might, his legion of devoted disciples never came close to duplicating that trademark wallpaper-peeling high note that the exuberant, compactly constructed horn man from Battle Creek wailed inside countless gin joints night after night, year after year until the very end.

"It's just like Satchmo," he reasoned. "You hear Satchmo, and you know him. And you hear Junior Walker, and I guess you just know him. And that's good. I'm glad everybody knows me."

Wells' LP *Bye Bye Baby I don't Want to Take a Chance* combined the titles of two of her first successful singles in 1961.

MARY WELLS

Mary Wells packed up and left Motown shortly after turning 21, but not before the company assembled *"Mary Wells Sings My Guy,"* capitalizing on the young star's hit single.

Motown's first major star was a shy, winsome teen when she unexpectedly dropped into Berry Gordy's life. As soon as she hit the age of 21, she was gone—a dubious career decision she reportedly regretted later. Mary Wells was an untutored vocalist who benefited greatly from the Hitsville staff's collective efforts. Smokey Robinson, in particular, crafted brilliant songs that brought out the best in her delivery. From the tail end of 1960 to mid-1964, she reigned as ***Motown's first queen.***

Born May 13, 1943, in the Motor City, the Northwestern High School grad had been on the outskirts of the local R&B scene before she hooked up with Motown. "I knew her since she was about 9 or 10 years old. Her brother was my next door neighbor in Detroit," said labelmate Gino Parks. "She was affiliated with (producer/singer/manager/Northern Records owner) Johnnie Mae Matthews prior to Berry. She didn't live too far from Fortune Records. She used to walk to Fortune." Matthews never got around to releasing a Wells single.

Mary wouldn't let anything stop her from auditioning "Bye Bye Baby"—a ditty she meant for Jackie Wilson. Spotting Berry one evening at the 20 Grand, Mary pounced, beseeching him for a moment of his time. Gordy convinced her to sing the tune a cappella for him in the middle of the jam-packed club. But instead of channeling it to Wilson or one of his young Motown performers, Gordy declared Wells' gritty delivery would suit the number perfectly and invited her to drop by Hitsville the next day.[17]

WHAT'S EASY FOR TWO IS SO HARD FOR ONE
by WILLIAM ROBINSON
Recorded by MARY WELLS on Motown Records
75¢
04107 nr
JOBETE MUSIC COMPANY, INC.

Wells put her sweet voice to good use on Smokey Robinson's "What's Easy For Two Is So Hard For One" in 1963 (Photo courtesy of David Alston's Mahogany Archives).

"Her mother brought her there, I remember," said Janie Bradford. "Came by for an audition." Gordy eventually subjected young Wells to 22 takes of "Bye Bye Baby" in dogged search of the ultimate performance for her Motown debut single, leaving her with a compelling hoarseness. Supported by a tough, bluesy groove, Mary's voice cracks several times—especially on the fade, where she unleashes a series of banshee wails that would later be banished from her repertoire (she sounded wise beyond her years on the bluesy 'B' side ballad, "Please Forgive Me"). "Bye Bye Baby" was a huge success during the winter of 1960-61, cracking the R&B Top Ten.

"A happy little kid that just wanted to sing, and had a unique sound," said Mable John of her labelmate, who incited the adoration of her audiences from the outset. "Everybody was running after her and pulling after her, and they'd have to pick her up and run out of the building with her to keep the kids from tearing her clothes off of her."

Gordy remained at the helm for Mary's follow-up. "I Don't Want To Take A Chance" was an up-tempo collaboration between the producer and Mickey Stevenson that made it two Top Ten R&B sellers in a row for her during the summer of '61 and actually

Mary Wells shares the bill with The Contours and The Temptations in a 1964 "Battle of The Stars" (photo courtesy of Hank Thompson).

fared slightly better than its predecessor on the pop side, the addition of jabbing strings not interfering with its Motor City ambiance. Oddly, Mickey's violin-enriched "Strange Love," issued that fall, dodged the charts.

By year's end, Wells had her first Motown album—in fact, the imprint's first long-playing release. The 10 tracks on *Bye Bye Baby* were something of a microcosm of the Motown story up to that point, with Mary tackling the Miracles' "Bad Girl" (gender-switched to "Bad Boy") and "Shop Around," Marv Johnson's "Come To Me" and "I Love The Way You Love," and a passionate "Let Your Conscience Be Your Guide" that outdid Marvin Gaye's debut version of a few months prior. Gordy's "I'm Gonna Stay" was a fine soul ballad.

As soon as Smokey entered her life in a supervisory capacity, a whole new Mary emerged. Instead of straining her vocal cords to the breaking point, Wells cooled out with Robinson as her patient producer, emphasizing a captivating maturity. The first of Smokey's productions on Wells, "The One Who Really Loves You," was a wafting delight, Mary's enchanting lead buttressed by a male vocal group billed as the Love-Tones and a sophisticated Carribbean-based rhythm. Robinson's inspiration arose from an unexpected source.

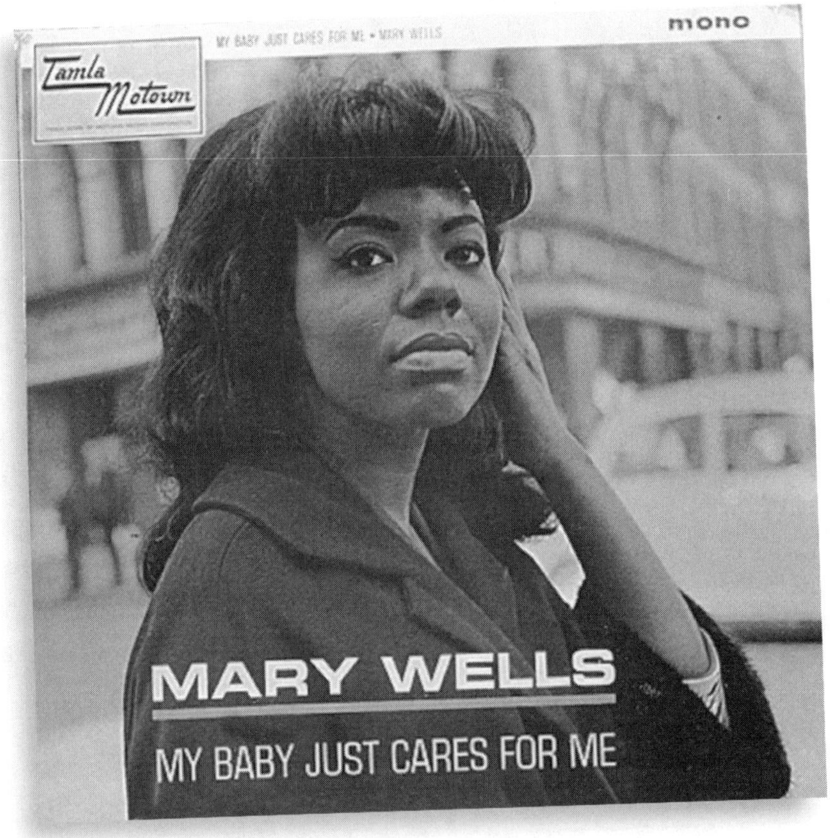

"Harry Belafonte was very big at the time, but nobody in our end of music was doing his feel on records. So that's why I went sort of for a Latin island-y kind of feeling on her 'The One Who Really Loves You,'" he explained. "I always had people in mind, and I tried to tailor the songs to what I thought they would sound like and feel like. I used to even pick words that they would sing well." "The One Who Really Loves You" was a No. 2 R&B smash that broke into the pop Top Ten during the spring of '62, propelling Wells to a new level of mainstream stardom.

"My Baby Just Cares for Me" was one Wells's last projects at Motown before she moved on to 20th Century Fox.

The same Belafonte-influenced approach held tight for Mary's first R&B chart-topper that autumn, "You Beat Me To The Punch." Smokey and fellow Miracle Ronnie White were its co-writers, with Wells summoning up the same seductive delivery over enchanting backing layering the Love-Tones, bongos, and vibes on what proved her second Top Ten pop smash in a row.

"If you listen to Mary Wells' recording, the group behind Mary Wells on 'You Beat Me To The Punch,' that's me and those same fellows that are called the Love-Tones," noted Parks. "They didn't actually perform with me, but we recorded together. Mickey Stevenson's brother was one of them." Its flip, "Old Love (Let's Try It Again)," is notable as one of H-D-H's earliest collaborations (Brian Holland produced it). All those major hits brought Wells prestige. When the Motortown Revue took off from Detroit that October to barnstorm the South, 19-year-old Mary and the Miracles were headliners.

Mary Wells chalked up her 10th LP in 1965 with a tribute to The Beatles after leaving Motown for 20th Century Fox. The title to this early release eventually became *Mary Wells Sings Love Songs To The Beatles.*

The Latin motif spiced "I'll Still Be Around," a Janie Bradford/Richard "Popcorn" Wylie composition produced by Smokey for Wells' encore LP, *The One Who Really Loves You*. It wasn't Bradford's only contribution to the set; she also penned the Brian Holland/Robert Bateman-produced "The Day Will Come" with Raynoma Liles Gordy's older brother, staffer Stanley "Mike" Ossman. "Mike didn't write that much," noted Bradford. "He was mostly administrative, in finance/payroll." Gordy's rocking "She Don't Love You" and "I've Got A Notion" were splendid throwbacks to Wells' old sound, as was her own aggressive ballad "Drifting Love." Most surprising of all was "Two Wrongs Don't Make A Right," an unadorned slow blues number from Smokey and Berry that Mary torched.

Seldom was Smokey more clever than on Wells' second consecutive R&B chart-topper (in January of '63) and third Top Ten pop smash, "Two Lovers." For most of the enticing record—another mid-tempo gem abetted by bongos and an uncredited male vocal group—Mary appears to be a two-timer, but the payoff line reveals that she's describing both sides of the same schizoid guy. Though its flip made no waves for Wells, "Operator" was a sizable seller for Motown chanteuse Brenda Holloway in 1965.

"Laughing Boy," yet another of Smokey's Latin-tinged triumphs, opened with a dramatic flourish before Mary enticingly entered, a male vocal group strategically inserting "ha-ha-ha-ha-ha" choruses and flowery piano. Sizable R&B and pop sales resulted in the spring of '63, and it led off side two of her LP *Two Lovers*, which boasted the aggressive rocker "Stop

Right Here" (written by Mary and Tempts bass Melvin Franklin), the Clarence Paul/Marvin Gaye/Stevenson collaboration "My 2 Arms - You = Tears," and a faithful rendition of "(I Guess There's) No Love," a plaintive Gordy-penned blues ballad first introduced by Mable John.

Janie joined Smokey to write Mary's next hit during the summer of '63. "Your Old Stand By" was more forceful than Wells' previous hits, Mary pushing a little harder without sacrificing an ounce of appeal. Testifying to her hit-making prowess, and the song crafting going on inside the walls of Hitsville, both sides of her last single of 1963 cracked the R&B Top Ten. "What's Easy For Two Is So Hard For One" was another gentle Smokey confection, as smooth and assuring as a sweet summer breeze, while "You Lost The Sweetest Boy" was unremittingly upbeat, sporting a churchy choir and a stomping beat. It was another early H-D-H triumph, reminiscent of the material they'd been handing the Marvelettes and Martha & The Vandellas.

Thanks to the indefatigable Smokey, Mary made herself at home in the No. 1 slot of the pop charts in May of 1964. "My Guy" would be hailed as her crowning achievement, the cats in Studio A soaking it in musical sophistication. Its intro was freely adapted from Eddie Heywood's "Canadian Sunset," and Smokey's buoyant chord changes floated under Mary like a fluffy cloud, the whole thing driven by James Jamerson's supple bass line (his finger-busting turnarounds on the vamp during the fadeout are mind-blowing as the Andantes sigh "What you say?" in response to Wells' declarations of undying love).

"We were there when she did most of the stuff. She was right there in the studio with us. It was just really cute," said the Andantes' Louvain Demps. "Smokey gave us a bonus for that. They called us in, and we didn't know what we were being called in the office for. Berry was there, and a photographer. I've never seen the pictures, but we took the pictures with Mary Wells, and he gave us a bonus of $500. That was the first bonus we ever got." The flip of "My Guy" was a total contrast: Producer Andre Williams brought out Mary's pleading side on the impassioned soul ballad "Oh Little Boy (What Did You Do To Me)," a Stevenson/Eddie Holland opus.

Released in May of 1964, the subsequent *My Guy* LP also showcased her previously untapped versatility. Side one spotlighted the hit and five more originals: H-D-H's ornate "He Holds His Own" and a "Whisper You Love Me Boy" that predates the better-known Supremes version; Smokey's "He's The One I Love" and "How? When My Heart Belongs To You;" and the Robinson/Ivy Jo Hunter collaboration "Does He Love Me." But side two found Mary delving into Tin Pan Alley fare. Fortunately, the arrangements sported a decided Motown feel.

As if her solo career wasn't progressing by leaps and bounds, Paul and Stevenson teamed Mary up with Marvin Gaye for a duet single released that April. Both sides charted strong. The stately, Latin-tinged "Once Upon A Time" and a more playful "What's The Matter With You Baby" both broke into the pop Top 20. The pair also cut an LP's worth of duets, *Together.*

Then the bubble abruptly burst. Apparently at the urging of her husband, ex-Motown singer Herman Griffin, Wells hired a lawyer and sued her label, seeking the disaffirmation of her contract upon reaching her 21st birthday on the grounds that she signed it when she was underage. Her wish was granted, but never again would Wells scale the lofty heights she had at Motown.

"I didn't quite understand her move, what she was doing, 'cause there was a lot of stuff going on. She mismanaged herself all the time," said Brenda Holloway, who had auditioned for Berry by singing one of Wells' songs and inherited several more when Mary left. "I think that was the worst mistake that Mary ever made in her life. Because Motown was her family, and Motown would cover her and keep her and love her."

Swayed by a huge signing bonus and the promise of movie roles that never materialized by 20th Century Fox Records boss Morty Craft,[18] Wells' reign as Motown's first queen came to an ignominious end. Contrary to some accounts, Wells continued to make quality records after bidding adieu to Hitsville, but fewer folks bought them. Fox surrounded her with a first-rate support cast, several of them former Motown staffers. Robert Bateman produced her first single for the logo, "Ain't It The Truth," a competent Motown knockoff that charted respectably in late '64. The breezy "Use Your Head" did even better, just missing R&B Top Ten status in early '65. Producer and ex-Motown mainstay Andre Williams obviously knew the territory (as did Windy City writers Chuck Barksdale, Wade Flemons, and Barrett Strong, who was then in the midst of a temporary relocation). The uptown soul ballad "Never, Never Leave Me" almost equaled its chart showing a couple of months later. Not everything Fox foisted upon her clicked, though — the 1965 LP *Mary Wells Sings Love Songs to the Beatles*, for example.

Atco Records was Mary's next stop. Once again, she was lucky to hook up with a gifted producer, Chicagoan Carl Davis. "Dear Lover," her first Atco platter, came as close to matching the charm of her Motown catalog as anything she did (ex-Satintone Sonny Sanders pitched in with a graceful arrangement) and broke into the R&B Top Ten in early 1966. Motown countered by assembling a fine LP from its leftovers. *Vintage Stock* contained Smokey's finger-snapper "When I'm Gone" (Brenda Holloway had hit with a very similar rendition) and a metaphorically enriched "I'll Be Available" (also inherited by Holloway), H-D-H's "Honey Boy" and the pounder "One Block From Heaven," and an early rendition of "Everybody Needs Love" that Gladys Knight & the Pips embraced after her exit.

By the time she landed at Jubilee Records at 1968, Mary had a new collaborator. Hubby Cecil Womack had been a charter member of the Valentinos (originators of the early '60s gospel-soaked hits "Lookin' For A Love" and "It's All Over Now" for Sam Cooke's SAR label) and was a brother to Bobby Womack who imparted a churchy underpinning to Mary's phrasing. "The Doctor" temporarily healed Mary's hit drought during the summer of '68, and she scored in '69 with "Never Give A Man The World" and an effervescent "Dig The Way I Feel" (all three penned and produced by the couple). After that, apart from a minor hit in '74 for Reprise and the disco anthem "Gigolo" for Epic in 1982, Wells' tenure as a hit maker was history.

Mary toured the oldies circuit incessantly until the 1990 onset of throat cancer progressively robbed her of her most precious commodity. An array of industry heavyweights contributed funds to offset her spiraling medical bills, but they couldn't restore her health.

Holloway had a chance to hang out with Wells not long before the end when both singers appeared at the same function. "She was like, 'Brenda, had I only known, we would (have done) things differently,'" said Holloway. "I loved her. She always had stress. She always had problems. She always was a part of her problems. But then in those latter days, she began to reflect and she began to see and she knew." Motown's first queen died too young at the age of 49 on July 26, 1992.

STEVIE WONDER

Recorded by LITTLE STEVIE WONDER on Tamla Records

FINGERTIPS PART 2

By HENRY COSBY and CLARENCE PAUL

60¢

06264

JOBETE MUSIC COMPANY

Little Stevie Wonder was already a legend in the making at age 13 when his 1963 release "Fingertips Part 2," which showed off the young star's harmonica mastery, hit the streets.

More than any superstar from Motown's golden age except Michael Jackson, Stevie Wonder endures as a **contemporary force** *of such magnitude that it seems impossible he's been recording for close to 40 years. He's unerringly steered his own creative course over the last three decades, introducing the Moog synthesizer to the masses and investing his music with an unswerving social conscience.*

Born May 13, 1950 in Saginaw, Michigan, Steveland Judkins was not born blind, but apparently lost his sight as a result of receiving too much oxygen in the hospital incubator.[19] When he was 3, his mother, Lula Mae Hardaway, moved her brood to Detroit, where the radio offered the rambunctious child an instant rhythm and blues education. Harmonica and piano came naturally to him, and word of his amazing gift spread as he duetted with guitar-toting pal John Glover. It was only a matter of time until someone from Motown caught wind of his talent. That fellow was the Miracles' Ronnie White.

Stevie Wonder headlined a star-studded holiday show in 1967 (photo courtesy of Hank Thompson).

"My brother talked to me about this guy," said White in 1993. "He talked to me, and I had put him off. And I don't know how much time had passed, maybe a year even. But he caught me and trapped me one time, and he said, 'Look, the guy's over here. Why don't you come on over right now?' So I said, 'Okay, all right, all right.' So I went over, and this little blind kid had his drums set up in my mother's living room. And he was playing drums—bongos, rather—and blowing harmonica and singing. And it just blew my mind.

"So I took him over to the studio and introduced him to Berry, and to Brian and Eddie Holland and Lamont Dozier. They signed him and put him to work with Clarence Paul, who was one of the persons who was very influential in Stevie's development." Paul would serve as an invaluable mentor to Little Stevie Wonder (Berry's sister Esther referred to the lad as a wonder one day in the studio, and the handle stuck) in the years to come.

Once Stevie was officially signed, sealed, and delivered to Tamla, it remained to be discerned how to present the lad's talents in a commercially viable manner. "I Call It Pretty Music, But The Old People Call It The Blues," his two-part debut single in the summer of '62, was a studio jam showcasing Wonder's awesome chromatic harp-blowing ability. His pre-pubescent vocal, limited to delivering the title line on the turnaround of every stanza, betrayed a shaky vocal command. His encore, "Little Water Boy," was a swinging vocal duet with Clarence (its Paul-penned flip, "La La La La La," is more closely associated with the Blendells, an East L.A. rock band that covered it in 1964). Even Stevie's hand-clapper "Contract On Love," issued around Christmas of '62, failed to click on the charts despite a strident vocal from the lad and the bopping harmonies of an uncredited doo-wop group.

"At that time, we were just writing something, and it ended up with Stevie," said Janie Bradford, who wrote "Contract On Love" with producers Lamont Dozier and Brian Holland. If failing to nail a hit with his first releases brought him down, Stevie never let on. He made himself available as a session musician whenever needed, his boundless energy and affinity for playing pranks on everyone (he was a world-class mimic, leading to all sorts of phony inter-office phone calls) still bringing a chuckle to the unsuspecting Hitsville denizens he victimized.

"When Stevie Wonder came there, being a little boy running up and down the stairs, bumping into folks—he was doing it on purpose, I think, 'cause he loved to play blind, and he could really find his way around," said Mable John, whose farewell Tamla single in 1963 was produced by the precocious youth. "But he just loved getting your goat."

"He got around better than I did. I remember he came in my office one day, and I had a jar of pennies. I would take all my pennies and save them for my son. Stevie came in, and he took my pennies and ran! Ran out of the building, he was outside in the yard before I could catch him. And then when I took the pennies, he said, 'You gonna take a poor little blind boy's pennies?'" laughed Janie. "So he was always full of the devil."

"He was like our little sweetheart, being younger. He had lots of energy. He would run around the studio," said the Velvelettes' Bertha Barbee McNeal (Stevie blew harp on their '63 debut "There He Goes"). "Being the baby of all of us, he was just pampered. I mean, we loved him to death. He knew everybody, and he'd come up to you and feel your whole face. That's how he knew, even before you said anything, who you were."

The 12 Year Old Genius was a live album from 1963 that featured the child prodigy's "Fingertips Part 1" and "Part 2."

Though the title of Wonder's album *Tribute to Uncle Ray* was about as subtle as a Mack truck in hammering home the pair's sightless bond (he's referred to as "Tamla's 11-year-old musical genius" in the liner notes, further encroaching on Brother Ray's turf), Paul coaxed some marvelous remakes from the young man. They didn't tackle the easy stuff: "Don't You Know," "Come Back Baby," and "Drown In My Own Tears" rate with the most emotionally gripping pieces in the Charles canon, and Stevie did all three proud. Not everything on the '62 LP came from Ray's corner. A rocking "Frankie & Johnny" contrasted with a jazz guitar-dominated interpretation of the chestnut "The Masquerade Is Over." Gordy contributed a mid-tempo "My Baby's Gone," and Clarence and Stevie brainstormed the minor-key blues "Sunset."

Virtually simultaneously, Tamla emphasized its new discovery's versatility by releasing a second LP. *The Jazz Soul of Little Stevie* was an all-instrumental

Paul production (Motown's assistant A&R director co-wrote eight of its selections) that let Stevie loose.

"They were trying to get a record on Stevie," said saxist Hank Cosby, who co-wrote four tracks with Paul. "Clarence Paul, he had the closest contact with Stevie's mother. That's how he got into Stevie. And Clarence and I were pretty good friends." Stevie's percussive attack sounded a lot like Preston Epps on "Soul Bongo," and he throttled his portable traps on another theme that would propel him to stardom in the not-too-distant future.

"I was playing a song that he liked," said Cosby. "The song ended up being called 'Fingertips.' In fact, Clarence named the song. Stevie was playing a lot of bongos in those days, and so Clarence was watching his fingers. And he said, 'Let's call it "Fingertips!"' Good idea! So that's how that song came in. We had nothing but the music. I wrote the music, and Stevie, he didn't know what to do. He ended up just ad libbing." Thomas "Beans" Bowles' flute dominated this "Fingertips." Switching between piano, organ, drums, bongos, and harp, Stevie made a credible jazz-rooted LP even as Gordy's Workshop Jazz label was proving that selling such highbrow product was no walk in the park. Then again, Wonder could assimilate anything.

"As a kid, he used to go in the movie theater, and he'd come back and play almost the whole movie! I would listen to him and say, 'This is impossible!' And you could not play nothing around him that he didn't pick up. Anything he heard, he could play, and keep it. And a lot of the producers became aware of it, and they were scared to play anything around him!" laughed Cosby.

Little Stevie was as precocious as he was talented. Even as a youngster, he wasn't above giving harmonica tips to Motown star Marvin Gaye (Photo courtesy of David Alston's Mahogany Archives).

Just because he hadn't yet crashed the hit parade was no reason to exclude crowd-pleasing Little Stevie from the Motortown Revues. At one engagement at Chicago's Regal Theater, he performed a retooled "Fingertips" sporting scattered new vocal segments.

"Clarence had a big-band arrangement made," said Cosby. "Johnny Allen, one of our arrangers, did the big band. I did the small band, he did the big band. And Berry heard the big-band arrangement in Chicago. They were playing a show. And he called in a remote and had it recorded. Everything was an accident. (Stevie) would say, 'Everybody say yeah!' and it caught on. The audience said 'Yeah!' Next thing I know, Stevie was blowin' his harmonica and tearing the place down." Edited into a two-sided single, "Fingertips—Part 2" became one of 1963's unlikelier No. 1 pop hits (okay, Kyu Sakamoto's "Sukiyaki" and the Singing Nun's "Dominique" beat it hands down).

The live 45 unfolded in "you are there" form, opening cold with Stevie's echoing "Everybody say yeah!' exhortations in front of the rabid Regal horde before he blew his harp, supported by a roaring bank of horns. Wonder closed with a nursery rhyme riff, then the big band broke into a torrid swing as the emcee incited a last round of applause. But Stevie wasn't done, despite various band members shuttling on and offstage in preparation for the next act. Marvelettes bassist Joe Swift (some sources peg the perpetrator as Larry Moses) copped a taste of unintentional infamy by audibly yelling "What key? What key?" amidst the general chaos. After a last infectious chorus, the song fades out. Its immediacy—and that of the rest of the pop chart-topping album it hailed from, *Recorded Live–The 12 Year Old Genius*—hit home with record buyers during the summer of 1963 in a way his studio sides had yet to do.

Two of Motown's heaviest hitters—Stevie Wonder and Martha Reeves—at the ballpark in 1968 (Photo courtesy of David Alston's Mahogany Archives).

Little Stevie was now a legit star, though settling on a hit follow-up proved elusive. Back at Hitsville, Paul deposited him in the midst of a gospel choir for the frantic "Workout Stevie, Workout"; Wonder's chromatic harmonica darted to and fro like a mouse on speed as the track hurtled atop a torrid sanctified rhythm that brought out the best in his youthful vocal delivery.

Dispatching Wonder to L.A. reaped rewards on both wax and celluloid. He gave the Frankie Avalon/Annette Funicello celluloid romps *Muscle Beach Party* and *Bikini Beach* a much-needed taste of soul, bouncing around as though he'd ingested way too much sugar just before the cameras rolled. Back in the recording studio, Stevie worked with producers Hal Davis and Marc Gordon on a sublime "Castles In The Sand." Seagull cries introduced the teen beat ballad, Wonder's plaintive vocal surrounded by soaring violins and spiced by his trademark bongos. Backed by the Detroit-cut "Thank You (For Loving Me All The Way)" (a Paul/Eddie Holland/Mickey Stevenson collaboration), "Castles" was a mid-level pop hit in early '64.

The rollicking "Hey Harmonica Man," a Davis/Gordon production released that summer, emanated from outside sources (co-writer Lou Josie had cut some rockabilly for Argo) but fit Stevie like a silk glove. He animatedly answered its insistent vocal group with a dynamic vocal and a barrage of jabbing harp riffs laid over a percussion-laden groove. Tamla celebrated Stevie's 14 years on earth by excising the "Little" from his name on the pop hit (its Detroit-cut flip "This Little Girl," produced by Hank and Norman Whitfield, rocked just as hard).

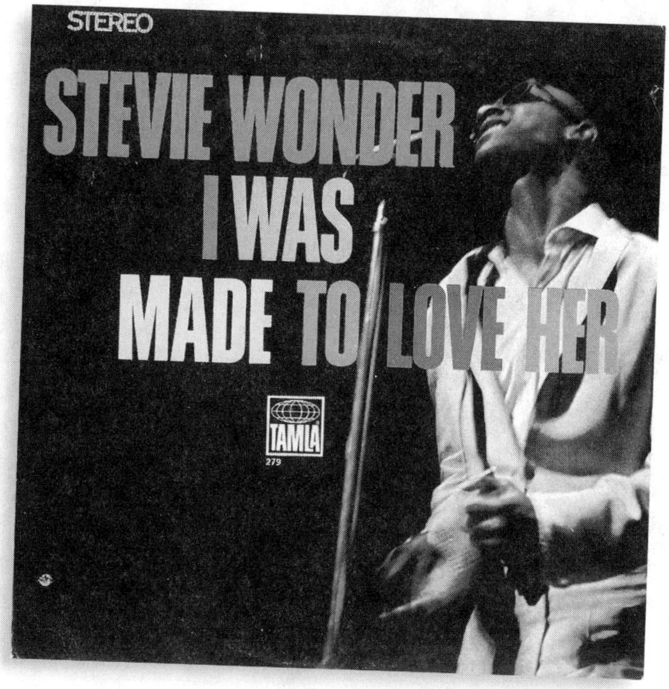

The title track to 1967's *I Was Made To Love Her* was a catchy tune that foreshadowed the disco stylings that were to dominate the 1970s.

Wildly disparate albums by Stevie were arriving at frequent intervals. *With a Song in My Heart*, issued in December of '63, presented the youngster crooning ancient pop standards using florid Ernie Wilkins arrangements better suited to Doris Day (producers Stevenson and Paul didn't let him blow a note on harp). *Stevie at the Beach*, out in the summer of '64, was aimed squarely at the teenage demographic—almost. Largely produced by Davis and Gordon in L.A., it sported the instrumentals "Ebb Tide" and "Red Sails In The Sunset," spotlighting Wonder's exquisite harmonica. But its highlights were the irrepressible vocals "Happy Street" (from one of those beach movies) and Frank Wilson's Bo Diddley-beat "The Party At The Beach House."

"He was just an incredible package of creative genius–just wired, excited, trying to discover even himself creatively. So it was just a lot of fun," said Wilson. "We were actually trying to do a sound that was more conversant with the motion picture industry at that time, and the whole beach and movie scene." Unfortunately, Stevie's next two singles, "Happy Street" and "Kiss Me Baby," stiffed.

Stevie co-starred on Hitsville's first full-scale overseas invasion in late March and early April of 1965. His next single, a live cover of Tommy Tucker's Checker label smash "High Heel Sneakers," was excerpted from the LP *Motortown Revue* in Paris. The big band on "Fingertips" had been replaced by a succinct horn section and prominent organ, Wonder's deepening pipes pounding the bluesy shuffle home. Though it came out only a year-and-a-half after Tucker's, Stevie's remake gave him his first hit in 15 months.

Once "Uptight (Everything's Alright)" hit the streets in late '65, Stevie never had to worry about chart prospects again. Written by Wonder, co-producer Cosby and Sylvia Moy (a Detroiter who had been singing locally prior to bringing her portfolio to Hitsville), its thunderous Benny Benjamin-stoked drumrolls and trumpet-heavy punch signaled the kickoff of stage two of Stevie's career. "We were talking about 'uptight, uptight, uptight,'" said Cosby. "Once again, I did the music, and I used about four or five horns. The track was cut when Stevie heard it. And all we had was 'Uptight.' That's all we could sing. In fact, it would have been a different meaning. But Sylvia, we gave it to her, and in a couple of weeks, it came back. Bit by bit, the song just grew. That's the way she would write."

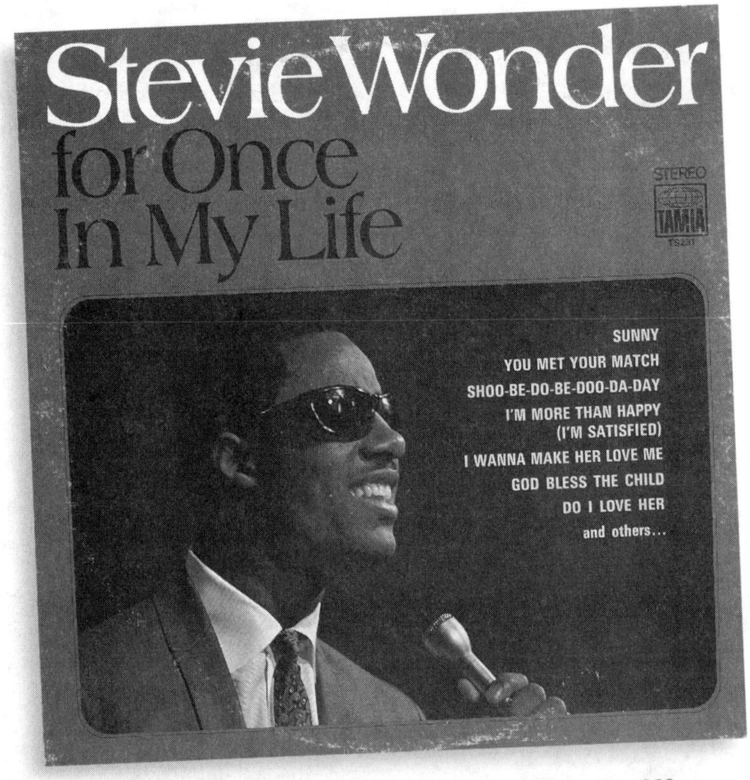

Stevie Wonder put his own stamp on "For Once in My Life" in 1968, and belted out a hit single and album in the process.

A sudden maturity graced "Uptight" that was absent from Stevie's bouncy beach numbers: He no longer sounded like a hyperkinetic kid. "Uptight" breezed to the top of the R&B charts in January of '66 and peaked at No. 3 on *Billboard's* pop listings. From there on, apart from "Someday At Christmas" at year's end, Wonder's Tamla singles would invariably muscle their way into the upper reaches of the hit parade.

Stevie, Hank, and Sylvia developed into one of Hitsville's most prolific songwriting trios. "We kind of clicked," Cosby said. "Sometimes we'd come up with the idea. And then sometimes we'd come up with the music first, 'cause Stevie's full of tunes. Oh man, he's got tunes—the stuff he would throw away, another producer would go crazy to get. I'm serious! Him and Sylvia and I, we would talk. We'd talk about the song, and she would go and write the lyrics. We would come up with the music, and that was it." Moy took her time crafting lyrics. "Sometimes she'd be very slow writing a song," said Cosby. "She'd be a month. And Stevie would be very impatient. Everybody would be all upset with her, and we'd get her in the studio, and the song would be half finished. We'd have to finish writing it in the studio."

Wonder was growing up, learning the ways of the world on the road and in the company of musicians far more seasoned than he. "Stevie was funny, man," said McDougal. "He lived life to the hilt. Even though somebody had to be with him most of the time—which was Clarence Paul—he just had a great time. He was a womanizer, meaning that he would do stuff like, 'Hey, man, how's that girl look? How's she look?' Then he would feel a girl's face to see how she really looked. And he's like any other man—he wanted the most beautiful girl he could find.

"But he was always playing music. Always."

Wonder stayed in the same bag for his next major hits. "Nothing's Too Good For My Baby," a Moy/Cosby/Stevenson collaboration produced by the latter pair in much the same aggressive mode of "Uptight," was a significant hit that spring. "We were trying to copy off the other one that was such a big hit," admitted Cosby. Its flip, the tender "With A Child's Heart," nipped at its heels on the R&B lists a couple of months later. Paul made an unbilled bow as Stevie's duet partner on a moving revival of Bob Dylan's "Blowin' In The Wind" that cracked the pop Top Ten and vaulted all the way up to No. 1 on the R&B charts late that summer, its relaxed groove clearly inspired by Sam Cooke's similar version. The Paul/Moy/Wonder rouser "Ain't That Asking For Trouble" merited hit status but languished as the 'B' side.

Up-Tight Everything's Alright, Stevie's spring '66 long-player, was his strongest yet, fully establishing him as a legit soul singer. Alongside his last four smashes were the subtle charmer "Hold Me" (co-penned by Stevie, Morris Broadnax, and producer Paul), a delicious "I Want My Baby Back" from Norman Whitfield and the Tempts' Eddie Kendricks and Cornelius Grant; a doo-woppish "Pretty Little Angel" that had been canceled as a single in late '64, and a playful Motownized duet reading of the oldie "Teach Me Tonight" with an uncredited Levi Stubbs (backing harmonies ostensibly courtesy of the Four Tops).

By 1965, at age 15, Wonder already had five Motown LPs to his credit and a spectacular future ahead of him (Photo courtesy of David Alston's Mahogany Archives).

Ron Miller had a knack for writing new songs that felt like old standards, and he gave Stevie quite a few of his best ones. "A Place In The Sun," a loping Paul-produced smash for Stevie at the end of '66 that Miller wrote with Bryan Wells, required the 16-year-old to project a world-weariness that couldn't have come naturally for such an upbeat young man, but Wonder pulled it off flawlessly. The holidays brought two welcome gifts from Stevie: the Yuletide single "Someday At Christmas" and another strong LP, *Down to Earth*. Cosby and Paul split production, loading the set with the quality originals "Thank You Love," "Be Cool, Be Calm (Keep Yourself Together)" (both by Stevie, Moy, and Cosby), and "Angel Baby (Don't You Ever Leave Me)," along with the title cut. Miller and Wells came back with "Travlin' Man," which made respectable chart inroads for Wonder during the spring of 1967. But its flip was just as hot: "Hey Love," a breezy, uplifting Wonder/Paul/Broadnax etching, broke into the R&B Top Ten.

No such problems with split airplay interrupted the rapid rise of Wonder's next single to No. 2 pop status and the top R&B slot that summer. Constructed over an unusual repeating chord progression (Stevie, Hank, Sylvia, and Stevie's mom share credit for writing it, though the latter's actual hands-on involvement with songwriting was reportedly minimal), "I Was Made To Love Her" opened with a snatch of melodic Wonder harp before relating a time-tested tale of love between a rich girl and a poor boy ending happily for a change.

"It was a funny thing how I came to record that," said Cosby. "All I had was the four bars. I said to myself, 'What can I do with four bars? That's not a song.' So what happened—and believe me, this was the beginning of disco—we played those four bars over and over and over and over. That's what the whole song is about: Those four bars." Stevie added some funky keyboard to the track. "That was the first time I think anybody had recorded a clavinet," said Hank. "In fact, the company ended up giving him one."

Another hit, another album: *I Was Made to Love Her* held a handful of splendid originals led by the Wonder/Moy confection "I'd Cry," a driving "Everybody Needs Somebody (I Need You)" from Stevie, Cosby and Broadnax, and "Every Time I See You I Go Wild," a pounder penned by Wonder, Cosby and Moy. The other eight numbers were all tried-and-true R&B classics culled from the Jobete songbook and elsewhere. Stevie was knocking out splendid material at such a fevered pace that "Until You Come Back To Me (That's What I'm Gonna Do)," co-written with Broadnax and producer Paul, was somehow relegated to the shelf (Aretha Franklin was no doubt grateful: She went gold with it in 1973).

That autumn, Wonder knocked out another Top Five R&B hit, the relentless "I'm Wondering." James Jamerson's slinky bass gave the Wonder/Cosby/Moy copyright a surging undertow, and Stevie's concise harp solo added to its appeal. "That's another one that we had the music, we had to put something to it. In fact, Stevie did some of the lyrics on that," said Cosby. The year's Yuletide feast was more bountiful. The album *Someday at Christmas* had a centerpiece, "What Christmas Means To Me," that drove just as hard as any non-seasonal Motown offering.

Stevie, Moy and Cosby were responsible for his first smash of 1968, "Shoo-Be-Doo-Be-Doo Da-Day," which blasted to the top of the R&B charts utilizing a sleek and sensuous rhythm powered by prominent keyboard backing. Producer/co-writer Don Hunter entered into the equation for the massive mid-'68 hit "You Met Your Match." In the midst of an unbroken series of smashes Stevie freely experimented, cutting a 1968 album heavy on harmonica instrumentals under Cosby's watch that emerged on Gordy rather than Tamla. Furthering the intrigue: the LP and its single, a plush arrangement of the Burt Bacharach/Hal David ballad "Alfie," both came out under the reversed moniker of Eivets Rednow.

Virtually every major Motown act (and a great many lounge lizards worldwide) took their best shot at Miller and Orlando Murden's exhilarating "For Once In My Life," but it was Wonder that propelled it to No. 2 on *Billboard's* pop and R&B lists in late '68. Stevie was initially none too thrilled with joining their ranks. "I don't think he liked Ron Miller," said Cosby. "A lot of times these guys would let personalities get involved with business. I loved the song. I always thought the song was a great song. So Stevie, he didn't want to do it. In fact, Stevie didn't want to do nobody's stuff but his. He's always been that way, but more so with Ron.

Stevie Wonder continued to put out hugely successful albums for Motown in the 1970s, including *Innervisions* in 1973.

"After I recorded the music, Ron was runnin' around: 'You done messed up my song, man! What did you do to my song?' That's the attitude he had taken. And Stevie didn't want to do it anyway. But I talked him into it. Finally got him into it. And it was great. I always felt like the song was great, and I felt like his performance was great." Instead of drowning it in the syrup sweetening so many readings, Stevie invested it with a zesty tone, slipping in a delicious harmonica break that served to underscore his originality. Stevie, Cosby, and Moy collaborated on the luxuriant flip, "Angie Girl," and they brainstormed more first-class material for *For Once in My Life*, issued in late '68 with the enchanting "I'd Be A Fool Right Now," "I Wanna Make Her Love Me," and the Moy/Wonder-penned "Do I Love Her."

Both sides of Stevie's initial '69 single made a huge impact. "I Don't Know Why," a collaboration by Stevie, his mom, Hunter, and Riser surfaced first, its steady-building arrangement helping push it to hit status that spring before deejays flipped it three months later and embraced the lovely "My Cherie Amour," a Wonder/Cosby/Moy theme that climbed to No. 4 on the pop and R&B lists. It was Miller and Wells' turn next. They handed Stevie the country-tinged "Yester-Me, Yester-You, Yesterday," a Riser-arranged smash near year's end. "That was given to us by Mr. Gordy as an assignment," said Johnny Bristol, who co-produced it with partner Harvey Fuqua. "Harvey and I were fortunate to get that break to do 'Yester-Me,' 'cause Ron Miller wrote that song. I always liked that song."

As was usually the case with the prolific Miller, "Yester-Me" was no mere exercise in boilerplate R&B. "I think he was a writer who wrote extremely classical standard songs that just went across the board," said Bristol. "They were standard material. They weren't necessarily R&B or pop. I just don't think he could write funky groove songs." Bassist James Jamerson did everything in his power to remedy that situation, laying down an elastic bass line. "Yester-Me" appeared on the late '69 LP *My Cherie Amour*, an intimate affair dotted with romantic pop standards. Richard Morris' "Pearl," "Somebody Knows, Somebody Cares," and the Moy/Wonder copyright "I've Got You" upheld the "sound of young america" quotient.

Stevie's approach was undergoing continuous reshaping. "Never Had A Dream Come True," his first hit of 1970, sported an infectious singalong intro, a relaxed mid-tempo drive, and an exhilarating lyric (it was another Moy/Cosby/Wonder copyright). As he neared legal manhood, Stevie produced his own R&B chart-topper "Signed, Sealed, Delivered I'm Yours," which nearly followed suit on the pop side that summer. Built around a repeating riff highlighted by Riser's punchy horn chart and featuring one of Stevie's most searing vocal efforts, it came from a new combination of writers: Stevie and his mother were joined by Lee Garrett (a blind performer from Philly that McDougal had produced some sides on) and ex-Motown secretary Syreeta Wright, who had cut "I Can't Give Back The Love I Feel For You" in 1968 for Gordy as Rita Wright. The pair linked romantically and married on September 14, 1970, only to divorce a year-and-a-half later.

Its flip "I'm More Than Happy (I'm Satisfied)" saw Tempts' guitarist Cornelius Grant joining Moy, Stevie, and producer Cosby in its birth. "Hank and I had played in the same band before (Joe Williams & the Staccatos). He actually told me he needed a song for the 'B' side," said Grant. "He said, 'Tell me what you come up with.' And I sort of came up with the music, the track and everything, and Sylvia Moy basically came up with the lyrics and storyline."

"Heaven Help Us All" was the last hit Miller would give Stevie. It was a touching plea for peace that didn't come off as preachy thanks to Tom Baird's churchy arrangement and a thrilling reading from Wonder that landed it high on both charts late in the year. Perhaps just for kicks, he recast the Beatles' "We Can Work It Out" in a more soulful mode and nailed a major hit in early '71. It hailed from the superb *Signed Sealed and Delivered* LP, which housed four smashes bunched on side one followed by the could-have-beens "Sugar," "You Can't Judge A Book By The Cover," "Anything You Want Me To Do," and "I Can't Let My Heaven Walk Away."

Gordy allowed Stevie to produce the entirety of his next album, *Where I'm Coming From*. Issued in April of '71, it spawned the hit "If You Really Love Me," a Stevie/Syreeta gem that ebbed and flowed like the sea. But the real news was transpiring behind the scenes. Upon hitting his 21st birthday in May, Stevie's contract with Motown expired. Rather than sign anything right away, he cloistered himself away in New York with a Moog synthesizer—then a new contraption introduced to him by engineers Malcolm Cecil and Robert Margouleff. He reemerged with a brilliant new body of work that made it clear nobody would produce Stevie from here on but Stevie. Hardball negotiations secured complete artistic freedom for him at Motown.

The 1970s were a whirlwind of mammoth musical successes: *Music of My Mind* and *Talking Book* (1972), *Innervisions* (1973), *Fulfillingness' First Finale* (1974), and the two-LP 1976 masterpiece *Songs in the Key of Life* lifted Stevie to new levels of pop superstardom. With the unforgettable hits "Superstition," "You Are The Sunshine Of My Life," "Living For The City," "Don't You Worry 'Bout A Thing," "Boogie On Reggae Woman," and "Sir Duke" riding the airwaves, even a horrific 1973 auto accident that left him in a coma for a week couldn't slow Wonder down for very long. His unceasing creativity remains a true wonder.

[1]Sharon Davis, *Motown–The History* (Middlesex, U.K.: Guinness Pub. Ltd., 1988), p. 21.

[2]Much of the information on James Jamerson's early years life was culled from his essential biography: Dr. Licks, *Standing in the Shadows of Motown–The Life and Music of Legendary Bassist James Jamerson* (Wynnewood, PA: Dr. Licks Pub., 1989).

[3]The singer's biography was a primary source for information: David Ritz, *Divided Soul: The Life of Marvin Gaye* (New York: McGraw-Hill, 1985), p. 11-12.

[4]David Ritz, *Divided Soul–The Life of Marvin Gaye* (New York: McGraw-Hill, 1985), p. 118-119.

[5]The latter two titles laid unreleased until the compilation of Motown's 1995 boxed set. *The Jackson 5–Soulsation! 25th Anniversary Collection.*

[6]The singer's autobiography was a primary source for information: Martha Reeves and Mark Bego, *Dancing in the Street: Confessions of a Motown Diva* (New York: Hyperion, 1994).

[7]Ibid, p. 154-155.

[8]Ibid, p. 165.

[9]Smokey Robinson with David Ritz, *Smokey: Inside My Life* (New York: McGraw-Hill Book Pub., 1989), p. 113.

[10]Much of the information here on Smokey Robinson is culled from his autobiography: Smokey Robinson with David Ritz: *Smokey: Inside My Life* (New York: McGraw-Hill Book Co., 1989).

[11]Berry Gordy, *To Be Loved* (New York: Warner Books, Inc., 1994), p. 104.

[12]A 1999 Temptations CD reissue in Motown's Lost and Found series, *You've Got to Earn It,* unearthed their unreleased 1964 version. Every bit as torrid as the Miracles' better-known rendition, it features Eddie Kendricks' falsetto up front and an unstoppable James Jamerson bass line that's amazing even by his lofty standards.

[13]Much of the information in this section on the Supremes' early years was culled from Mary Wilson's autobiography: Mary Wilson with Patricia Romanowski and Ahrgus Juilliard, *Dreamgirl: My Life as a Supreme* (New York: St. Martin's Press, 1986).

[14]Much of the information in this section on the Temptations' early years was culled from the essential autobiography: Otis Williams with Patricia Romanowski, *Temptations* (New York: G.P. Putnam's Sons, 1988), p. 13.

[15]"Which Way To My Baby" finally saw light of day in 1996 on the Motown anthology *The Temptations—One By One.*

[16]Al Green with Davin Seay, *Take Me to the River* (New York: Harper Collins, 2000), p. 118.

[17]Berry Gordy, *To Be Loved* (New York: Warner Books Inc., 1994), p. 139-140.

[18]Charlie Gillett, *Making Tracks—Atlantic Records and the Growth of a Multi-Billion-Dollar Industry* (New York: E.P. Dutton & Co., 1974), p. 39-40.

[19]Leonard Pitts, Jr., liner notes, *Stevie Wonder—At the Close of a Century*, Motown 012 153 992-2, 1999.

YAMAHA

MORE MOTOWN GREATS FROM A-W

ABDULLAH

The late 1960s were a racially divisive era in America. The black militancy movement was hurtling ahead full throttle, and Abdullah was as radical a figure as roamed the halls of Hitsville. The Brooklyn emigre's daily fashion statement consisted of "a head rag, Bedouin clothing, and a scimitar in his waistband."[1] His "I Comma Zimba Zio (Here I Stand The Mighty One)" on the flip of "Why Them, Why Me" was heavy stuff, but Soul released it in the fall of '68. Abdullah's association with Motown was brief. A heated dispute with creative division head Ralph Seltzer precipitated his instant dismissal.[2] "He came in with all this 'whitey' stuff. I mean, he was all uptight about everything," said McDougal. "He went off, and they put him out."

ARTHUR ADAMS

L.A.-based guitarist Arthur Adams hooked up with Motown-distributed Chisa Records in 1969, waxing three 45s over the next couple of years that deftly blurred the boundaries of soul and blues. The 1996 CD anthology *Motown's Blue Evolution* made use of two soulful unreleased tracks Adams cut for Chisa, "Cold Cold Heart" and "Let Me Love You Tonight."

Adams traveled a circuitous route to the Chisa roster. Born Arthur Lee Reeves on Christmas Day of 1940 in Medon, Tenn., his aggressive guitar style was influenced by Howard Carroll of the legendary gospel-singing Dixie Hummingbirds as well as blues immortals B.B. King and slide master Elmore James. "B.B. was my main influence," said Adams in 1998. "I always liked B.B.'s voice, too. He just had a tremendous voice."

Dynamic blues guitarist Arthur Adams boasts a lengthy resume that includes a brief stint as a Chisa artist and studio session player (Photo courtesy of Arthur Adams).

Adams broke into the Nashville blues circuit during the late '50s. While touring Texas with singer Gene Allison in February of 1959, he ended up stranded in Dallas. Making the best of it, Arthur made Dallas his home for five years, honing his chops with his Mighty Men behind Lightnin' Hopkins, Lowell Fulson, James, and Buddy Guy, whose extra-long guitar cord inspired Adams' penchant for charging through the audience in mid-solo like an enraged Brahma bull. He cut 45s for Jamie, Valdot, and Duchess (the latter operated by future Motown sales department mainstay Al Klein) as Arthur K. Adams, co-writing and playing on Lattimore Brown's 1960 Excello 45 "Somebody's Gonna Miss Me" (covered the next year by Sam Cooke).

A 1964 deal with Vee-Jay Records brought Adams to Los Angeles, but the financially strapped label never released his promising "I Feel Alright." So the versatile guitarist made quick inroads into the city's studio scene, doing sessions for ex-Motown A&R boss Mickey Stevenson's Venture Records as well as waxing a tough '67 blues outing, "She Drives Me Out Of My Mind," for the Bihari brothers' Modern Records.

Chisa was the province of South African jazz trumpeter Hugh Masekela and Stewart Levine, and Jazz Crusaders trombonist Wayne Henderson was also involved with the fledgling L.A. concern. "What we did, we remodeled that office over on Western Avenue—7406 Western," said Adams. "We built a little studio there where we could rehearse, and we put together all that stuff with Chisa." The downbeat original "It's Private Tonight" (backed with "Let's Make Some Love") was Arthur's first Chisa 45 in the autumn of '69. Despite everyone's best efforts, it failed to hit. "I was so hurt behind that song," he said. "We got so much reaction. You don't come up with a song that everybody says has it that doesn't make it. But that's part of the business."

Two follow-ups—"My Baby's Love" with "Loving You" in 1970 and "Can't Wait To See You Again" the next year—similarly failed to do the trick. Between his session duties for everyone from Quincy Jones and the Jazz Crusaders to Sonny Bono and Jerry Garcia and his own progressively slicker albums for Blue Thumb, Fantasy, and A&M, Arthur veered away from the blues. He reverted to his roots during the mid-'80s and now reigns as one of L.A.'s most dynamic bluesmen. After a 1999 album on the Blind Pig logo, a set at the 2000 Chicago Blues Festival, and several European tours, there's no doubt that Arthur is, to quote the title of one of his CDs, back on track.

LUTHER ALLISON

The last musical commodity anyone expected Motown to covet in 1972 was a fiery young Chicago blues guitarist. Nevertheless, the label pacted Luther Allison and released three of his albums; 1974's *Luther's Blues* ranks with the hottest blues sets of the decade.

The 14th of 15 children, Allison was born in Widener, Ark., on August 17, 1939. He got acclimated to stinging the strings at age 10 by twanging a diddley bow (a wire attached to the wall that was fretted with a bottle), approximating the keening cry of a slide guitar. His family moved to Chicago in 1951, and soon he was smitten by the sound of his older brother's band. "Ollie, he had a group called the Rolling Stones, I believe from 1952 or '53 through 1957," said Allison in 1994. "By the time I got home from school, they were into their practice. It sounded good to me. One day, I said, 'Hey, please show me how to play boogie-woogie on this guitar.' He said, 'Sit down on my lap, and let's go.' Two years later, I said, 'Hey, this is what I want to do.'"

Forming an outfit known as the Four Jivers, Allison established himself as a fierce competitor on the city's

West Side circuit during the late '50s and early '60s. "People like me, Freddy King, Magic Sam, Buddy Guy, we kinda had what the new generation is creating today," he said. Armed with boundless energy, Allison assumed leadership of King's local band when Freddy hit nationally. Luther cut his first session for Delmark in 1967 and a full-length debut LP for the Chicago firm two years later. By then, he was entrenched on the blues-rock circuit. Poised to make his big move, Luther signed with Motown and commenced work on 1972's *Bad News Is Coming* at Hitsville (the Tempts were tracking "Papa Was A Rollin' Stone" at the same time).

Recorded with a Motown rhythm section of bassist Bob Babbitt and drummer Andrew Smith, *Bad News Is Coming* was dominated by covers, goosed by Luther's take-no-prisoners lead axe and histrionic vocals. *Luther's Blues* was a contemporary blues masterpiece in 1974, again laid down in the Motor City. The blistering "Let's Have A Little Talk," a funky "Now You Got It," and the pummeling slow blues title item were joined by a pair of welcome relics from the Jobete catalog: Singing Sammy Ward's searing "Part Time Love" and "Someday Pretty Baby." His 1976 Motown farewell, the overly slick *Night Life*, was a disappointment.

Despite triumphant stands at two subsequent editions of the Ann Arbor Blues Festival (his '73 set was captured for posterity by Motown), the hookup between Luther and the label never resulted in the anticipated breakthrough. "I was very happy with the Motown trip," said Allison. "But let's face it: Motown didn't know what they had. The blues weren't in. I think it was a miracle for them to choose me.

Blues guitar legend Luther Allison marched to his own powerful beat during his stint with Motown in the early 1970s.

"We were everybody's voices."

When they moved from Detroit to Los Angeles, I just got lost in the shuffle."

Allison migrated to Europe and made an overseas name for himself during the '80s. He finally left Paris in 1994 to come back stateside, ready to reassert his claim as the heir to the contemporary blues throne. Three ferocious albums for the Alligator label and concerts that routinely lasted more than three hours announced his return. But Allison was felled by lung cancer on the verge of his ascendancy, passing away on August 13, 1997.

THE ANDANTES

andante: Music adj. & adv. Moderately slow.

That's how *Funk & Wagnalls Standard Encyclopedic Dictionary* defines the ancient Italian musical term. Around Motown during the 1960s, however, the Andantes could best be described as omnipresent. First alto Jackie Hicks, second alto Marlene Barrow, and soprano Louvain Demps provided flawless but largely uncredited studio backing on countless Motown smashes, augmenting the Four Tops on all their H-D-H-produced hits and singing backgrounds for the Supremes, Marvelettes and Vandellas with no one outside Hitsville any the wiser.

The group acquired its distinctive name before they set foot into Hitsville and prior to Louvain's arrival. Hicks and Barrow were singing spirituals with a third girl, Emily Philips, at Hartford Baptist Church in Detroit when piano accompanist Mildred Dobey coined their musical moniker. "We used to do trios in church, and she always played for us," said Jackie, who was born November 4, 1939. "She said it meant soft and sweet. We kind of liked it, too." Those sanctified Andantes harmonies that graced so many Motown classics came straight from the source. "We probably started singing as a group in church at maybe around 12," said Jackie.

Louvain had been the first paying customer to set foot inside the Rayber Music Writing Company in 1959, set up by Berry and wife Raynoma to help young Detroit performers find an outlet for their songs prior to the advent of Motown. Born in New York on April 7, 1938 and raised in Detroit from age 5 (she attended Pershing High with future Motown composer Sylvia Moy; her grade school classmate Little Willie John was the first to recommend her for an audition), Demps brought along a song her friend Rhoda Collins Howard had written.

"She asked me to go and sing this for her, and make the record," said Demps. "So when I got over there, Marv Johnson played for me, Brian Holland played for me, and then they went and got Berry, and he played. I was going to make this record for my girlfriend, but I had to take an audition. I made up some jazzy something or another. 'Blue Moon,' that's what it was. They were excited about it. Then I saw Raynoma, and she agreed to do this record for my friend. But I had to have $100 to cut the record. They were offering people that could sing to cut, but you had to have $100. So we went down in this little basement and cut this little record."

Louvain's soaring soprano made an impression on Rayber's regulars. "They had told me to start coming around there, and maybe they could use me to sing on some of the other stuff. But they were really making fun of me, because I had this real high voice. Nobody had that type voice. But I did lower it for the audition." Along with Robert Bateman, Sonny Sanders, and Brian Holland, Demps sang with Raynoma Gordy's Rayber Voices, the vocal group that backed most of the solo artists Berry produced during the late '50s and early '60s.

Marlene and Jackie attended Northwestern High School with pianist Richard "Popcorn" Wylie, who brought the Andantes to Motown in 1960. "We were friends. Then he contacted us one day and said that he had landed a session with Motown, and he already had his band, and he was going to be singing lead and he wanted voices behind him," said Jackie. "So we learned the songs that he wanted, and we went and recorded with him. And after that, things didn't work out for him, so he left. We were trying to leave, too, and then they kept saying, 'Well, we need girls to hand clap and sing behind other artists, and we're just getting started here. We could definitely use you.' To be honest, we weren't really interested.

"Then the girl Emily that sang with us, she got married, and her husband didn't want to sing. That's how we ended up with Louvain, 'cause we were saying, 'Well, we don't have but two people, so we can't do it.' Not being interested, we were looking for any excuse to get out of it. They said, 'Well, we've got another girl here that happens to sing lead. What does Emily sing?' We said, 'She's the top voice.' They said, 'Oh well, see if you can blend with Louvain. She's looking for somebody to sing with.' So that's how we ended up with her."

"Since I was there and their girl was missing, they just kind of put us together," said Louvain. "That was really the start of it. We had no rehearsal together or anything. It was just nice. When their third voice was really not going to come back, they asked me to join them." Their early assignments included Eddie Holland's "Jamie" and Mary Wells' "Laughing Boy."

The Andantes had to be available at a moment's notice. "Twenty-four-hour call, really. We were everybody's voices. So what they did, they just asked us to be ready at any given time. I didn't have a car and didn't know how to drive, and after a while it got so busy that they just told me to get in a cab and just come on. So each time I came, I always came in a cab," said Demps. "There were weeks that I don't think we ever stopped singing. All day, and all night, too!" said Hicks. "Sometimes they'd wake you up in the middle of the night, almost: 'The Tops are on their way in town. We're picking 'em up from the airport. Can you be in the studio in an hour?' It might be 2, 3 in the morning."

Their vocals were often one of the last ingredients added to a production. "Sometimes we all did it together, in the beginning. Everybody was in there together. But then later, it was more that they put down a scratch vocal, or they already had down the vocal that they wanted, and then we came in and put the background behind it," said Louvain. "A lot of times, we did it before they did it. We were on a track first. It was just according to who was in town at the time," said Jackie. "A lot of times, the lead singer would just come in and do the lead, and everything else would be ready."

Crown jewel status at Motown came at the price of anonymity. "It's been kind of kept under wraps. The pride and joy that you had in doing them, you couldn't really tell anybody about it," said Louvain. "My friends would know, because I would tell them. But then again, you would say, 'Oh yeah, well, that's us.' 'Oh sure, yeah, uh-huh.'" Her friends may have been skeptical, but Gordy recognized the importance of their gospel-rooted backing vocals.

"We were very good, and very quick. Where we could get those harmonies together, they just couldn't—you know. I don't even know why ours came out like that. **It was just something made in heaven,** I think, because it just clicked, and it wasn't a lot of struggle," said Demps. "I would get real happy doing the sessions. Somehow or another, my voice would cut through real strange, and they'd say, 'What's wrong with you?' And when it's time to say something like on (Mary Wells') 'My Guy,' my voice goes up two octaves: 'What you sa-a-a-y?' I mean, they'd stand around looking at me!"

Louvain relished working with Holland-Dozier-Holland. "It was cream of the crop. It was really, really nice. When you got in there, you knew that you were going to sing something really good," she said. The Andantes combined with the Four Tops on their H-D-H-produced smashes, starting with "Baby I Need Your Loving" and "Ask The Lonely." Just as he didn't want to give the Funk Brothers a forum for having their own hits, Gordy allowed the Andantes to record under their own name only once. H-D-H came up with the pounding "(Like A) Nightmare" for them, and so few copies of the V.I.P. single trickled out in 1964 that it may as well have been unissued.

"I couldn't stand that," said Jackie, "because it sounded too much like something that the Vandellas should have been singing, to me. I don't know about the other two girls, but that's the way I felt about it." Even then, the three principals didn't sing lead. Future Marvelette Anne Bogan fronted the number (Louvain can't recall who led the flip, "If You Were Mine"). "They never even asked, 'Would you like to try to lead something?'" said Demps. "I did a couple of demo things. Mary Wells' *My Guy* album, with Mickey Stevenson, when they were trying to get her to learn the thing, I did the scratch vocal for her. It wasn't bad. It was pretty smooth."

The Andantes did plenty of work behind the scenes at Motown, but they also performed with the likes of Kim Weston (second from left). Shown here with Weston in 1965 are (from left) Jackie Hicks, Louvain Demps, and Marlene Barrow (Photo courtesy of Louvain Demps).

Live engagements were few. "That was not our preference," said Jackie. "You really had to travel, and we were like the house band that did not travel with the groups. It was better that way, because it was more productive for them." Still, the Andantes squeezed in a few shows. "We did live stuff with Kim Weston," noted Louvain. "Once a year they had that big Christmas show at the Fox Theater, and one time Marlene and myself, we recruited Duke Fakir to sing with us for that." There were also moonlighting studio sessions with Bobby "Blue" Bland and Little Carl Carlton in Detroit and Windy City trips to sing behind Vee-Jay stars Jerry Butler, Betty Everett, and the Dells. "We were in Chicago about every other weekend for a while," she noted. "On one of the things, we took Mary Wilson with us. We needed an extra voice."

Eventually Pat Lewis and future Dawn member Telma Hopkins joined their elite ranks as occasional replacements if an Andante was indisposed. "When we were backgrounding, there were times when we needed extra girls, and we started singing with them," said Jackie. "But they actually had their own groups. They were working at a studio called United Sound." Lewis had recorded with the Adorables for Golden World in addition to waxing her own "Can't Shake It Loose" for the firm in 1966; Hopkins would later join Tony Orlando & Dawn.

The Andantes were left high and dry when Motown vamoosed for the coast in 1972. Jackie and Marlene remained in the Motor City; Louvain headed for Atlanta in 1973 (she sings in church there every Sunday). She's ready to see the Andantes receive a little belated recognition.

"I mean, that's a whole lot of singing," said Demps. "It would be nice if one day we could walk across the stage and we could hear the applause. And they'll say, 'Jackie, Marlene, and Louvain—the Andantes!' I would just be a happy woman. Not so much just for me, but for them."

NICKOLAS ASHFORD & VALERIE SIMPSON

Arriving at Hitsville from New York, Nickolas Ashford and Valerie Simpson quickly made themselves indispensable as Jobete songwriters and then by producing some of Marvin Gaye and Tammi Terrell's top-selling duets.

Ashford, born May 4, 1942 in Fairfield, South Carolina and raised in Willow Run, Michigan, and Simpson, born August 26, 1946 in the Bronx, New York, both hailed from staunch gospel backgrounds. Nick arrived in New York with dreams of becoming a dancer. He met 17-year-old Valerie at Harlem's White Rock Baptist Church, where she sang in the choir and played piano, and he enlisted in the joyous flock. Just for kicks, they began writing pop songs. When a batch of their compositions resulted in a $64 windfall, they were on their way, soon joining Scepter/Wand Records as staff writers. The duo debuted as recording artists in 1964 under the billing of Valerie & Nick with "I'll Find You" for the New York-based Glover imprint. In collaboration with Joshie Jo Armstead, they wrote "Never Had It So Good" (a hit for Ronnie Milsap) and several duet vehicles for Chuck Jackson and Maxine Brown in 1965. Late that year, Ray Charles recorded the trio's "Let's Go Get Stoned," and it became a huge 1966 hit. Their "I Don't Need No Doctor" soon followed suit to a lesser degree for Brother Ray (Nick cut his own concurrent version for Verve). "Let's Go Get Stoned" caught the ear of Holland-Dozier-Holland, and they helped bring Nick and Val into Hitsville the same year.

Nick and Val had to prove themselves when they first arrived in the Motor City. "They felt like outsiders," said McDougal. But it didn't take long for the pair to impress the denizens of Studio A. **"Nick and Val were just beautiful people to work with,"** said Funk Brothers percussionist

Jack Ashford. "We respected 'em, because their music was always good. Challenging, too." Johnny Bristol was in a perfect position to judge their merits. Along with Harvey Fuqua, he produced the Ashford/Simpson-penned "Ain't No Mountain High Enough" and "Your Precious Love," the first two duet smashes by Marvin Gaye and Tammi Terrell in 1967. Nick and Valerie soon took over production duties as well for Gaye and Terrell's '68 R&B chart-toppers "Ain't Nothing Like The Real Thing" and "You're All I Need To Get By."

"They knocked me out when they came in as writers," said Bristol. "With their material, I thought they were incredible."

As the ravages of Terrell's brain tumor made it impossible for her to record, Simpson anonymously filled in for her on much of the last Marvin and Tammi album, *Easy*. Misleading though it may have been, Simpson reproduced Terrell's voice quality and intonation so skillfully that no one was the wiser on the hits "What You Gave Me" and a posthumous "The Onion Song."[3] Other Ashford & Simpson-penned Motown hits included the Marvelettes' "Destination: Anywhere" in '68, Smokey & the Miracles' "Who's Gonna Take The Blame" in 1970, and Martha & the Vandellas' '72 stormer "Tear It On Down."

Nickolas Ashford and Valerie Simpson hit the ground running as a songwriting team at Motown in 1966, penning a series of successful releases for many of the company's top acts.

"He wore his eyebrows arched, shaved his mustache to a point like the devil. He didn't look like the devil; he looked like a holy man," said Martha Reeves of Ashford. "And he looked like he was pure. And she was sweet as a button. She was married to a guy, and she looked like she was so innocent. They looked like little babies. And then the next thing you know, they had fallen in love."

Nick and Val worked with Diana Ross when they wrote and produced the Supremes' 1968 release "Some Things You Never Get Used To," and when Motown scheduled Diana's solo debut in 1970, they turned to the duo—who responded by penning and supervising the diva's first three Paul Riser-arranged hits: "Reach Out And Touch (Somebody's Hand)," a chart-topping revival of "Ain't No Mountain High Enough," and "Remember Me." Simpson contributed to the project in another crucial way.

"Nick and Valerie used to write all of these songs, so Valerie used to show Diana how to sing it. And Diana used her style of singing," said McDougal. "If you get Valerie Simpson's record and listen to it, you can hear Diana Ross. It wasn't Valerie copying off of Diana, it was Diana copying off of Valerie." Simpson's 1971 Tamla debut album *Exposed* came with Diana's glowing testimonial in longhand script on the rear cover photo. It was produced by Simpson and her hubby; they also wrote eight of its 10 songs. Exposed was one of the first Motown LPs to individually credit the Funk Brothers. Valerie rolled her own 88s, and Armstead augmented Nick and Val on background vocals.

"I Don't Need No Help," its solo opener, stood apart from typical Motown fare by being half a cappella and half accompanied only by Valerie pounding her own rock-ribbed piano. The orchestration was lush on the rest of the set, which included both sides of her first Tamla 45, "Back To Nowhere" and "Can't It Wait Until Tomorrow," and the funky "Sinner Man (Don't Let Him Catch You)." A righteous recasting of The Beatles' "We Can Work It Out" suggested Aretha's gospel-fired earthiness.

Janie Bradford at Mary Wilson's house with her husband (Weldon A. McDougal III photo).

Though sales were relatively slim on Simpson's first offering, Tamla tried again the next year with an eponymous encore album and another 45. Her tender "Silly Wasn't I" climbed to No. 24 on *Billboard's* R&B lists at the end of 1972, but Val wouldn't achieve stardom at Motown. "She was doing really good on some of her releases," said Weldon. "Then she said that she didn't want to record anymore unless Nick was on the record with her."

The coosome twosome defected to Warner Bros. in 1973 and began racking up hit duets, pausing long enough to tie the knot the next year. It was an amicable parting with Motown—they wrote and produced the Dynamic Superiors' '74 smash "Shoe Shoe Shine," and as the decade closed, Diana's "The Boss" and "It's My House." Nick and Val have thrived in recent years as radio hosts, record label bosses, and performers.

JANIE BRADFORD

Sitting at the front desk as a receptionist, working for the Jobete publishing company, writing hit songs—Janie Bradford made herself essential at Motown in overlapping roles from day one. The St. Louis native was one of the first people Gordy welcomed into his extended family, and she proved a loyal employee for two decades.

The two met through Jackie Wilson. "Jackie was a family friend, and my sister (Clea) is a singer. And they used to work a lot of the same local clubs," she said. "Now this is before he made it. So once he got his hit, the first hit, 'Reet Petite,' he came to our house and told her that she had to come down and meet his writer. You have to remember, Jackie was a family friend—'cause in my mind, he was not a celebrity. I was 14 at the time. But this writer—whoever wrote Jackie a hit—was a celebrity. So I had a fit. I wanted to meet the writer. And Jackie said, 'Well, you're not old enough to go to the club.' I said, 'Well, I'm tall enough, 'cause I'm 5-8 1/2.' I was 5-8 1/2 then, at 14. I said, 'I can dress up in some of my sister's clothes and look older.'

"After begging forever, he agreed to let me go. So he brought Mr. Gordy over and introduced him. I was so disappointed!" she laughed. "I don't know what I expected a celebrity to be, but he was just a human man. There was no halo. There were no wings. So I had kind of an attitude. Jackie said, 'This is my songwriter.' I said, 'Well, if he's a songwriter, I can write a song better than he can any day!' So he was looking for songs, which I had no knowledge of. I was just mad because he was just a plain old man! I guess he didn't forget. About two months later, he came by the house to listen to my songs.

"I had totally forgotten who he was. But there was another gentleman with him that I remembered, and I put two and two together, and I did a curse and walked them in, told them to have a seat. And I've always written poetry for the school paper. I didn't know nothing about songwriting at that point, and had no desire to write songs. So I knew there was a difference between poetry and songwriting, but I went and got my poetry and pretended I thought they were song lyrics. Which I probably didn't even know the word 'lyric' at the time. I just saw words. And I said, 'Okay—here are my words.'

"In about two months I had two songs in Jackie Wilson's *Lonely Teardrops* album. After that, he went in and showed me how to take the poetry out and put the song in with the hook, and keep bringing the title back, and all this kind of stuff," she said. "So then when he showed me how to write, I just kept writing, writing, writing." Janie attended high school in St. Louis and shuttled between the two cities as a teen. "I couldn't wait 'til whenever to get back to Detroit, especially after I met Mr. Gordy and started at Motown and all that," she said. After Berry purchased the Hitsville building in August of 1959, he installed Janie as its receptionist. "At the desk, I used to prepare the artists' contracts," she said. "I used to do the copyrights, which now is part of publishing. Whatever came across the desk to be done, I had to do that. It wasn't just answering the phones."

Her impromptu lyrical contributions as Gordy created Barrett Strong's "Money (That's What I Want)" helped the label nail its first national hit in 1960. Janie proceeded to write with a host of the label's songsmiths, including Smokey Robinson long before he was labeled a genius. "He was just Smokey!" she laughed. "I remember looking in the file cabinets eight or nine years ago, and I was reading these lyrics that were in the Jobete catalog. And I was saying, 'Golly, this sure is a dumb lyric! Who wrote this?' And I looked on the file. It said Janie Bradford and Smokey Robinson. I said, 'Well, if I didn't know better, *he* should have known better!'"

Unlike some of her fellow staffers, Bradford didn't balk at moving to L.A. when Motown picked up stakes in 1972. "I'd always come back and forth to California on vacation," she said. "When they said that they were moving here, I said, 'Thank you, Jesus!'" Upon leaving Motown, she launched the *Entertainment Connection*, a show-biz publication. Today, she spearheads an annual L.A. charity event, *Heroes and Legends*, which raises money to support children in the arts.

JOHNNY BRISTOL

Though he had to shelve his performing ambitions for the entire time he worked at Motown, Johnny Bristol still crafted a slew of hits at Hitsville as a prolific producer/songwriter.

Born February 3, 1939 in Morganton, North Carolina, Johnny went north as part of his Air Force hitch. "They sent me to Mount Clemens, Michigan, actually. I was about 18 years old," said Bristol. While serving his country, he met Duke Fakir's brother, who introduced him to Berry's sister Gwen. Bristol and 19-year-old fellow Air Force recruit Jackey Beavers formed a singing duo and signed with Anna Records, a Detroit firm owned by Gwen and Billy Davis. Johnny & Jackey debuted in 1959 with "Let's Go To A Movie Baby" and its flip "Lonely And Blue," encoring with "Hoy Hoy" and "No One Else But You."

Gwen and Harvey Fuqua formed Tri-Phi Records in '61, and Johnny & Jackey came along to cut four 45s over the next year-and-a-half. Three of those offerings later figured into Bristol's Motown legacy: Jr. Walker would wax "Carry Your Own Load" and "Do You See My Love For You Growing" in the early '70s, while Diana Ross & the Supremes benefited mightily from their Bristol-produced '69 revival of "Someday We'll Be Together" (Johnny & Jackey's original emerged in November of '61). "Baby Dont'cha Worry" with "Stop What You're Saying" was the pair's final Tri-Phi release. Beavers went on to record solo for Checker and Revilot.

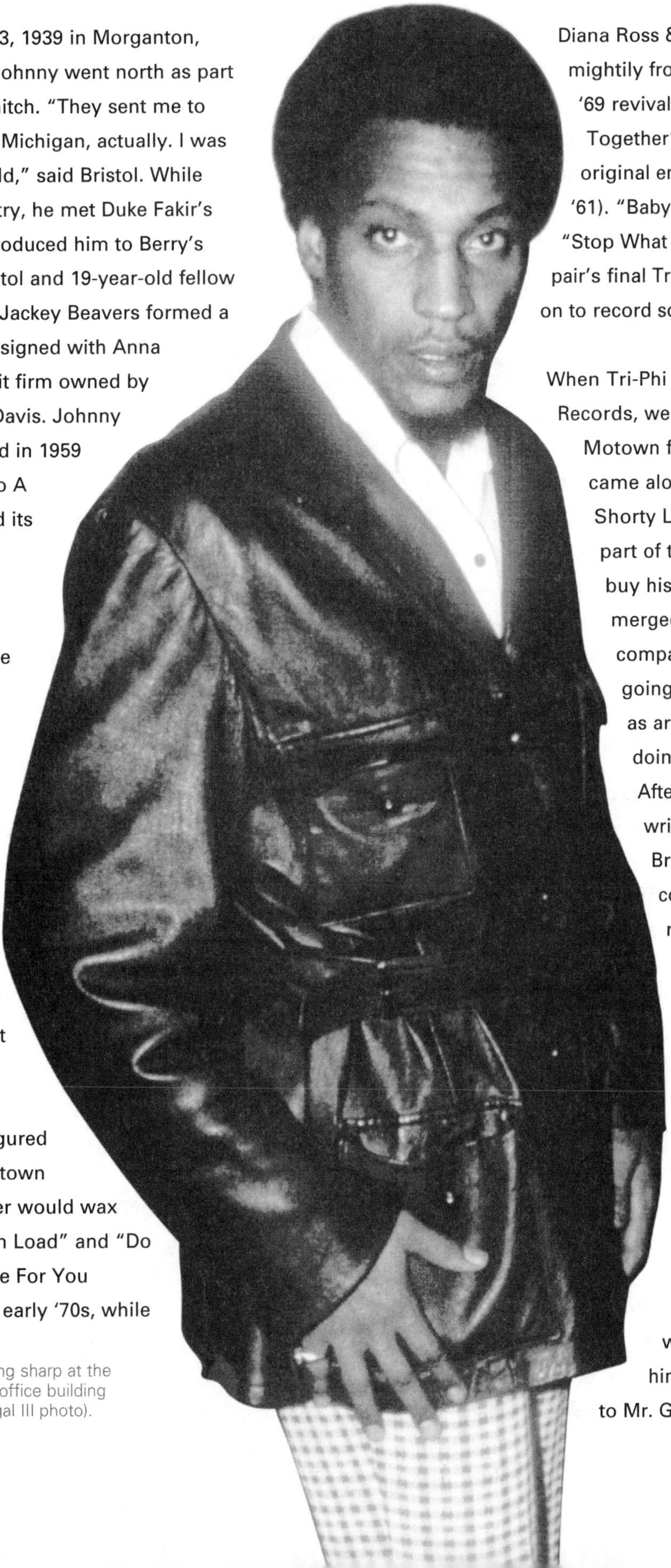

Johnny Bristol looking sharp at the Woodward Avenue office building (Weldon A. McDougal III photo).

When Tri-Phi and its sister label, Harvey Records, were absorbed into the Motown family in 1963, Bristol came along with Fuqua, Walker, Shorty Long, and the Spinners as part of the deal. "Berry decided to buy his sister's company. She merged everything over to his company. 'Cause we had been going back and forth anyway, as artists—working there, and doing what we were doing. After that, I just became a staff writer for Motown," said Bristol. Like so many of his co-workers, Bristol found romance there, too, marrying Berry's niece Iris.

Graduating to the elite producer ranks wasn't easy. "That took a while, because I had to go a different route to get into that. It wasn't so much the competition as it was getting someone to speak up for you," said Bristol. "I went to Harvey and asked him how he felt about talking to Mr. Gordy and having me as his partner as a producer. And I made (Harvey) an offer that whatever we did together, we'd split 50-50, even if I wrote something and he wasn't in town. He traveled a lot. So he agreed, but yet I had to ask him for about maybe another four or five months if he's done it, when's he gonna do it, and if he's gonna do it. So one day I bumped into Berry myself. And I said to him, "I had been talking to Harvey about the possibility of being his partner as a producer. Do you think that's a possibility?' And he said, 'Well, that's up to Harvey. I don't care.' So I went back to Harvey and told him I had spoken to Mr. Gordy, and what he had said. And all he had to do was send a memo so they could draw up a contract for me. And he did finally send the memo."

Bristol produced or co-produced Walker, the Four Tops, Smokey Robinson & the Miracles, Stevie Wonder, Gladys Knight & the Pips, and, of course, Ross and the Supremes' "Someday We'll Be Together." He and Fuqua supervised several smashes by the star-crossed duo of Marvin Gaye & Tammi Terrell.

"If I came up with a song, I could pretty much hear in my mind's ear who should do this song," he said. "I could hear Marvin Gaye singing it, or him and Tammi, or Gladys Knight. For whatever reason, I could hear that particular artist singing this particular song. So I would present it that way. When I became a producer, I could produce a song on anyone who was not exclusive, such as the Supremes were to Holland-Dozier, or the Temptations to Norman Whitfield.

"Once you got a hit record, you could pretty much keep that artist as long as you could produce the hits. If your record was better than everyone else's, you had the shot at the 'A' side." But sitting behind the glass wasn't the same as giving voice to those hits himself. "When I took Berry 'Someday We'll Be Together,' he said I was more valuable to him as a writer and a producer. That was complimentary, but it didn't do anything for my desire to sing," said Bristol, who left Motown in 1973. "My contract had expired, and we were in the process of negotiating. I guess we just agreed that we disagreed."

Gordy might have felt a pang of regret when Bristol went out as a singer and promptly scored his own Top Ten pop smash in '74 with "Hang On In There Baby" for MGM Records. "A great feeling," noted Johnny. "I can't even put it in words." Cut in L.A. with H.B. Barnum arranging, the song sailed all the way up to No. 2 on *Billboard's* R&B charts. Despite more hits for MGM in 1974-75 ("You And I," "Leave My World") and a Top Five R&B smash, "Do It To My Mind," on Atlantic in '76, Bristol struggled to mount a successful solo career. "The problem there was still the same as all artists complain about—promotion, or lack of it," he said.

After a minor 1981 R&B hit with "Love No Longer Has A Hold On Me," Bristol faded from active performing status. "I have been taking a wonderful sabbatical, pursuing my faith and getting knowledge about God and the things that have become meaningful to me," he reported. Though Johnny is creating new music again of an inspirational nature, his calling card will always be the brilliant body of work he made at Motown. **"I just feel so fortunate** that I had the experience of being there when it started, and seeing these people grow," he said, "and seeing their brilliance come out, and just being a part of that team."

DORSEY BURNETTE

If ever two young men epitomized the image of hell-raising rockabilly roughnecks, it was Memphis-born brothers Dorsey and Johnny Burnette. Their yelping, fire-breathing 1956 sides with lead guitarist Paul Burlison for Coral as the Rock & Roll Trio are among the ultimate recorded examples of the rockabilly idiom. Everyone mellows out sooner or later, though, and in 1964 a solo

Dorsey found himself on Motown's Mel-O-Dy imprint for three pop-slanted singles.

Born December 28, 1932 in Memphis, Dorsey and younger brother Johnny enjoyed using their fists (Dorsey was a Golden Gloves fighter) and partying hearty just as much as they dug knockdown rock and roll. "One of my strongest memories of going over to his house," said blues harp great Charlie Musselwhite, once their Memphis neighbor, "was that everybody always had bloodshot eyes."[4] Teaming with Burlison, the three went to New York in '56 and won *Ted Mack's Amateur Hour* three times in a row, convincing Coral Records to sign them up.

The Rock & Roll Trio's blistering "Tear It Up," "Oh Baby Babe," "The Train Kept A Rollin'" (Burlison's loose amp tube created a unique fuzztone effect), and "Rock Billy Boogie" vibrated with savage ferocity as Johnny screamed and Dorsey slapped his upright bass (Dorsey took over vocals for "Sweet Love On My Mind"). But the Trio's sides were too primal to sell. Piqued that his brother received favored billing, Dorsey quit a week before the Trio lip-synched "Lonesome Train (On A Lonesome Track)" in Alan Freed's 1957 film *Rock! Rock! Rock!*

The battling siblings patched up their differences and relocated to Hollywood, where they waylaid Ricky Nelson outside his home and pitched him some of the rockers—"Waitin' In School," "Believe What You Say," "It's Late"—that became late '50s smashes for Ricky on Imperial (where the Burnette Brothers waxed a vicious "Warm Love" in early '58). Dorsey scored two 1960 hits of his own for Era Records: "(There Was A) Tall Oak Tree" and "Hey Little One." After a few more Era 45s and a '61 cover of Slim Harpo's swamp blues "Rainin' In My Heart" for Dot, he landed at Mel-O-Dy.

Dorsey waxed three 45s for Mel-O-Dy in '64, but "Little Acorn," "Jimmy Brown," and "Ever Since The World Began" couldn't duplicate the success of his Era efforts ("Jimmy Brown" even gained British release). Johnny, a teen idol thanks to his 1960 hits "Dreamin'" and "You're Sixteen," drowned in a California boating accident August 1, 1964. While at Motown, Dorsey wrote and produced "Sad Boy" for Stevie Wonder, though the stately ballad failed to hit in the fall of '64. Burnette enjoyed '70s country success before dying of a heart attack on August 19, 1979 in Canoga Park, California.

G.C. CAMERON

When the rest of the Spinners split Hitsville in 1971 to join Philly soul producer Thom Bell and make mega-hits for Atlantic, G.C. Cameron stayed behind. He had come into the group in late 1967, well after they signed their original pact with Motown, and his contract had yet to expire. G.C. would carve out a successful solo career on Mowest and then Motown in L.A.

G.C. Cameron in Los Angeles outside the Continental Hyatt House on Sunset Boulevard (Weldon A. McDougal III photo).

Born in McCall's Creek, Mississippi on September 21, 1945, George Curtis Cameron began raising his voice in song as a lad in church choir. "Everybody from Mississippi sings!" he laughed. He and his family moved up to Michigan in 1955. "There were a lot of young people from here during that era that were from Mississippi that migrated north to Detroit," he noted.

After completing a Vietnam tour with the Marines in September of '67, G.C. joined the Spinners and fronted some of their finest Motown and V.I.P sides—"Bad, Bad Weather (Till You Come Home)," "Message From A Black Man," their Stevie Wonder-produced 1970 smash "It's A Shame," and its follow-up "We'll Have It Made"—before inaugurating his Mowest solo stint in 1971 with the Corporation-connected "Act Like A Shotgun." Cameron worked with the best: Smokey Robinson was behind his '73 offering "Don't Wanna Play Pajama Games," Norman Whitfield helmed "No Matter Where" the same year (his first 45 on Motown proper), and Van McCoy stepped in to supervise "Let Me Down Easy." Marvin Gaye and Willie Hutch provided vocal backgrounds for his 1975 release "Tippin'" (Gaye was G.C.'s brother-in-law, Cameron having married Gwen Gordy).

Freddie Perren of the Corporation emerged to produce G.C.'s 1975 hit, "It's So Hard To Say Goodbye To Yesterday," which benefited from prominent placement on the soundtrack to the motion picture *Cooley High*. "When American-International Films did the *Cooley High* movie, all of the songs that they had used in the movie were Motown songs that had been recorded and released before. They had a slot for one original new song, and that was 'It's So Hard To Say Goodbye To Yesterday,'" said Cameron. "(Gwen) worked it out so I would be the one to perform the song. Naturally, I got credits in the movie. The first name you see after the movie's off is mine, which was very, very exciting to me at that time." His last Motown hit came in 1977 on "You're What's Missing In My Life."

G.C. has been a double threat of late. In addition to steering his own solo course, he reunited with the Spinners in July of 2000. Music remains a passion. "It's still there, the desire to go conquer," he said.

CHOKER CAMPBELL

Veteran tenor saxist Walter "Choker" Campbell made his Motown mark during the '60s, though not as a house soloist. He led the mighty big band that hit the road with the early Motortown Revues as well as occasionally leading a similar outfit in the studio.

Born on March 21, 1916 in Shelby, Mississippi, Campbell debuted on wax as a bandleader in 1950 with the instrumentals "Spinnin' A Disc" and "Besame Mucho" for the Lucky 7 logo (his crew billed as the Bachelors of Rhythm). The saxman paused at Jack and Devora Brown's Detroit-based Fortune Records two years later to cut "Rocking And Jumping" (vocal by Honey Brown) and its flip "Frankie And Johnny"; next stop was higher-profile Atlantic, where Choker cut two singles in October of '53: "Last Call For Whiskey" (featuring singer Harold Young) preceded "Have You Seen My Baby." Another track from the date, "The Choker," was shelved.

That wouldn't be the last time Campbell entered a New York studio for Atlantic. He played with blues shouter Big Joe Turner on a May 1957 session that included "Love Roller Coaster" and "I Need A Girl," backing Turner as he mimed "Feelin' Happy" and "Lipstick, Powder And Paint" in the 1956 film *Shake, Rattle & Rock*. A tuxedoed Campbell enjoyed plenty of face time in the quickie flick, soloing on both tunes and reconstituting "The Choker" as incidental dance music. Campbell also cut with blues guitarist Lowell Fulson for Checker on a '57 date. After a 1958 45 of his own for Apt—"Walking On My Thin Sole Shoes," his first vocal effort, which was coupled with the instrumental "Walk Awhile"—Campbell gravitated to Motown.

During his lengthy tenure under Gordy's employ, the label gave Campbell his own 1964 album. *Hits of the Sixties!* actually concerned itself with *Motown* hits of the '60s, Choker and his 16-piece outfit tackling the Supremes' "Baby Love," Martha & the Vandellas' "Heat Wave" and "Dancing In The Street," the Miracles' "Mickey's Monkey," the Four Tops' "Baby I Need Your Loving," Marvin Gaye's "Hitch Hike," and Little Stevie Wonder's "Fingertips." Snappy arrangements of the Supremes' "Come See About Me" and Gaye's "Pride And Joy" were pulled for a 45.

In 1969, Campbell followed in Gordy's footsteps by inaugurating his own Tri-City label in Saginaw, Michigan. He died July 20, 1993 in Detroit.

BRUCE CHANNEL

Short-lived Mel-O-Dy Records' best bet for hitdom was probably Bruce Channel, only a couple of years past pacing the pop charts with "Hey! Baby" when he joined the Motown roster. Born on November 28, 1940 in Jacksonville, Texas, Channel auditioned "Hey! Baby" for Fort Worth producer Major Bill Smith in late 1961. Delbert McClinton, then leading the locally popular Straitjackets, provided the essential harmonica riffs. "Hey! Baby" kicked up enough local dust to interest Mercury Records in nationally distributing it on its Smash logo. By March, it was the nation's top record. McClinton stuck around to blow on Channel's "Number One Man" and "Come On Baby."

The law of diminishing returns being what it is, Smash eventually dropped Bruce, precipitating his signing with Mel-O-Dy. No sign of McClinton graced Channel's first 45 for the logo in the spring of '64. Horns and backing vocals pushed a rocking version of Porter Wagoner's country standard "Satisfied Mind" and its upbeat original flip, "That's What's Happenin'," which sported a snappy trumpet solo. The same approach was used for his follow-up "You Make Me Happy" that summer, but its 'B' side, "You Never Looked Better," was in a countrypolitan mode bearing distinct resemblance to Leroy Van Dyke's '61 smash "Walk On By."

Channel continued to record after Mel-o-dy folded. His Dale Hawkins-produced "Mr. Bus Driver" was a minor hit for Mala in late '67. He's prospered since then as a country songwriter.

Bruce Channel bounced to several different labels in the 1960s, recording "You Make Me Happy" with Mel-O-Dy in 1964, one year before the label folded (Photo courtesy of David Alston's Mahogany Archives).

CHRIS CLARK

On the recommendation of L.A.-based Motown prexy Hal Davis, statuesque California blonde Chris Clark strolled into Berry Gordy's office one day, performed an impromptu a cappella rendition of Etta James' "All I Could Do Was Cry" (an R&B classic co-written by B.G. himself) and walked out with a contract. The versatile Clark later joined Motown's front office and moved into the film business as an Oscar-nominated screenwriter on *Lady*

Sings the Blues. Along the way, she became romantically involved with the boss.[5]

That Clark happened to be of the Caucasian persuasion didn't dissuade Gordy from trying to make her a star. The gambit ultimately fell short, though she cut some nice sides in an R&B-slanted mode. After biding her time as a Motown receptionist beginning in 1963, Clark finally got her shot a couple of years later (in the interim, she cut Frank Wilson's Jobete-published "My Sugar Baby" for the tiny Joker logo in 1965 as Connie Clark).

Taking a first-hand interest in launching her, Gordy provided both sides of her late '65 V.I.P. debut: "Don't Be Too Long" and the slinky "Do Right Baby Do Right" were solid R&B-styled entries, Clark particularly effective on the latter (vocal harmonies were provided by her labelmates, the Lewis Sisters). The tough H-D-H opus "Love's Gone Bad," flipped with a cover of the Supremes' "Put Yourself In My Place," followed during the summer of '66. Chris kept the resident heavy-hitters in her corner for her third V.I.P. entry in early 1967: Berry wrote and produced "I Want To Go Back There Again," while Marvin Gaye took over on the attractive 'B' side, "I Love You."

Gordy moved Clark over to Motown in the summer of '67 for her debut LP, *Soul Sounds*.

Pictured in a tight-fitting black dress on its cover, her blonde mane teased in sweeping '60s splendor, the 6-footer looked more like Dusty Springfield than an archetypal Motown diva. But she hung tough on the Supremes' "Whisper You Love Me Boy" and the Four Tops' "Until You Love Someone" (both H-D-H copyrights), Berry's "Day By Day Or Never," Frank Wilson's "Sweeter As The Days Go By" and "Do I Love You (Indeed I Do)," and a percolating remake of the Miracles' "From Head To Toe" that served as her first 45 on Motown proper that September, coupled with Margaret Johnson's "The Beginning Of The End" (later covered by the Supremes).

Issuing "Whisper You Love Me Boy," introduced on Mary Wells' *My Guy* album in 1964, as a Motown 45 in early '68 didn't garner any more attention than the rest of her output. So Gordy moved her to a brand-new label in 1969. Weed Records' entire catalog consisted of her LP *CC Rides Again*, and it was a rocked-out mess, Chris clawing her way through Three Dog Night's "One," the Beatles' "Get Back," and Blood, Sweat & Tears' "Spinning Wheel" (even a remake of Brenda Holloway's "You've Made Me So Very Happy" was weak). The trippy promotional slogan "All your favorite stars are on Weed" likely smoked both album and label.

THE COMMODORES

The Commodores were big news around the recording world in the early 1970s (Photo courtesy of David Alston's Mahogany Archives).

Motown's most successful '70s act came roaring out of all-black Tuskegee Institute to **stir up a new strain of funk** upon signing with Mowest in 1971. The Commodores consisted of Florida-born guitarist Thomas McClary, drummer and fellow Floridian Walter "Clyde" Orange (the only non-Institute attendee), Tuskegee-born bassist Ronald LaPread, Mississippi-spawned keyboardist Milan Williams, trumpeter William King (another Alabamian), and young saxist Lionel Richie (born June 20, 1949 in Tuskegee).

McClary, Richie, and King were part of the Mystics, a seven-piece freshman campus combo. The Mystics merged with an upperclassman outfit known as the Jays and the first edition of the Commodores was born, their name a result of a blindfolded Williams dropping his finger on the word in the dictionary. LaPread and Orange solidified the lineup in the summer of '69.

After seeing them gain some hard-fought experience on the New York club circuit, Commodores manager Benny Ashburn introduced them to an enthusiastic Motown vice president Suzanne de Passe, who slotted the band as a cross-country warmup act for the Jackson 5—not a bad way to accrue a little arena experience. "The Zoo (The Human Zoo)," their Mowest debut in March of '72, sported a dissonant intro straight out of the Twilight Zone. Written and produced by Pam Sawyer and Gloria Jones, it settled into a brisk Latin funk groove featuring duet lead vocals by Orange and Richie (Orange was initially the main singer, but Richie was convinced to assume lead duties because he wasn't ensconced behind a drum kit).

"Don't You Be Worried," an irresistible stomper produced and arranged by Tom Baird, occupied the plug side of their Mowest encore in early '73 (Orange co-wrote it and sang lead). Richie took over for the mellow "Are You Happy" that summer, but after three releases the Commodores remained hitless. That changed fast when de Passe fired a synth-loaded instrumental by Williams at

The Commodores cracked the Top 20 with "Machine Gun," a title dreamed up by Barry Gordy in 1973.

Gordy's ears. Not only did the chairman love the funk workout, he dreamed up its title: "Machine Gun." This one wasn't firing blanks: It shot up the R&B Top Ten on Motown proper and just missed the pop Top 20. With the R&B chart-topping status of their explosive "Slippery When Wet," the Commodores took their place among Motown's elite.

THE CONTOURS

Most of Motown's top singing groups were meticulously groomed and impeccably synchronized. The Contours were uncouth and proud of it, bringing acrobatic energy to their act and splattering rough edges all over their early '60s sides for Motown and its Gordy subsidiary. Billy Gordon's sandpapery leads were integral to the group's 1962 smash "Do You Love Me (Now That I Can Dance)," as vicious a rocker as the label ever produced.

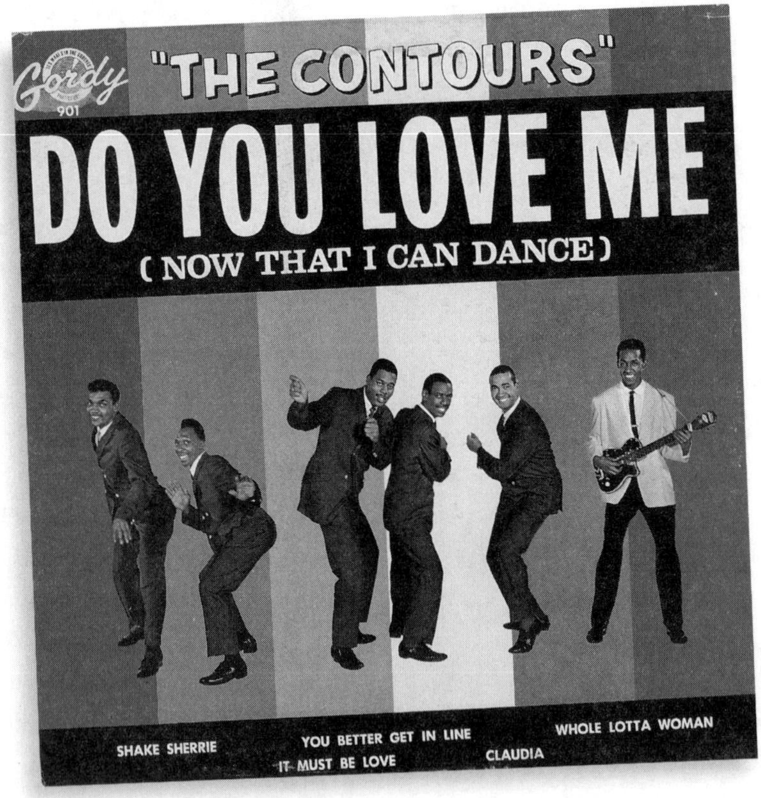

The Contours had two successful runs with their hit "Do You Love Me." The song was the group's breakthrough hit in 1962, and then gained new life in the late 80s thanks to the movie *Dirty Dancing*.

Gordon, Billy Hoggs, Joe Billingslea, Sylvester Potts, and Hubert Johnson came together as the Blenders in 1959. Born December 22, 1938, Potts was a product of Northeastern High, the same school that Mary Wilson, Bobby Rogers, and Martha Reeves attended. "Everybody at that time was singing in groups in school. You go into the bathroom, get that echo chamber," said Potts. The young crew was inspired by fellow Detroiter Hank Ballard's dance-crazy Midnighters. "I knew the Midnighters when they used to rehearse in my basement," said Sylvester. "My father and the one who originated the Midnighters, Alonzo Tucker, used to play together."

The group practiced its harmonies on the main drag. "We just hung around on 12th Street. That was the place to be," said Potts. "We wrote a song called '12th Street.' That was one of the other songs we auditioned with Berry. That was our 'hood. That's why Berry called us thugs! We sung in just about every club on 12th, and some on the North End."

Ironically, the quintet renamed itself after a company in direct competition with Motown.

"Before we went to Berry, we went to this Contour Recording," said Potts. "Wes Higgins owned that label at the time. Joe just happened to look up there and see that name, Contour Recording. He said, 'That'd be a good name for us.'" Gordy wasn't immediately impressed.

"Went to Berry Gordy and auditioned, and he told us to come back in a year," said Potts. "Hubert said, 'I

David Ruffin rocks the
20 Grand in Detroit.

Hitsville U
2648

Hitsville U.S.A. at 2648 W. Grand Blvd.–Motown's Detroit headquarters.

Eddie Kendricks by himself after breaking away from the Temptations.

Left to right: Eddie Kendricks, Brenda Mabra, G.C. Cameron, and Motown president Ewart Abner attend Jack "the Rapper" Gibson's annual convention in Atlanta.

Eddie Kendricks in his post-Temptations solo days.

Eddie Kendricks greets one of his legion of fans.

C.P. Spencer of the Originals, at the Uptown Theater in Philly.

The Originals at the Uptown Theater in Philadelphia. Left to right: Freddie Gorman, Walter Gaines, and Hank Dixon.

Gladys Knight
gets down.

Gladys Knight & the Pips with veteran comedian/emcee Timmie Rogers at the Latin Casino in Cherry Hill, N.J. Top row: Timmie, Gladys, Edward Patten. Bottom row: Bubba Knight, William Guest.

Gladys Knight at Valley Forge Theater, Valley Forge, Pa.

Gladys Knight & the Pips at the Latin Casino in Cherry Hill, N.J. Left to right: William Guest, Gladys, Edward Patten, and Merald "Bubba" Knight.

Jazz trumpeter Hugh Masekela at the Showboat Bar, one of Philadelphia's top jazz clubs.

Hugh Masekela (right) & the Union of South Africa behind the Philadelphia Art Museum and on stage (top).

The best seat in the house could be had for $4.50 at the Supremes' 1967 gig in Memphis (Photo courtesy of Hank Thompson).

The Isley Brothers and Weldon meet up backstage at the Apollo. Left to right: Ronnie Isley, Weldon, O'Kelly Isley, and Rudolph Isley

Sammy Davis, Jr., tearing it up at the Cocoanut Grove in L.A.

The Jackson 5 at home. Left to right: Jermaine, Michael, Marlon, Jackie, Tito.

The Jackson 5 and Weldon.

Michael Jackson and Suzee Ikeda.

Michael Jackson and his puppies. "Make sure you get a good picture of the dogs' face!," said the animal-loving lad.

Members of the Jackson 5 at home. Left to right: Randy, Jackie, and Tito.

The "Jackson 6": Marlon, Jackie, Rev. Jesse, Michael, Jermaine, Tito. The quintet was performing at the reverend's annual Operation PUSH concert in Chicago.

Sitting in his Houston hotel room, the pint-sized superstar informed Weldon, "Listen, man, I'm getting ready to do a face, and I want you to take a picture of it!'" As you can see, Weldon obliged.

Marvin Gaye says hello to top-rated New York deejay Frankie Crocker of WWRL backstage at Madison Square Garden prior to one of Marvin's concerts.

Marvin Gaye relexes before a show at Madison Square Garden.

Marvin was the big name on a Hollywood Bowl card (right) in the spring of 1963 (Photo courtesy of Hank Thompson).

He wasn't always keen on playing the role of a star, but Gaye certainly looked the part on Hy Lit's TV show.

Gaye got up close and personal with his fans during a *Soul Train* appearance, which was also attended by his second wife, Janis Hunter (foreground).

Mary Wilson of the Supremes with Willie Hutch on left and Roland Bonham, L.A.'s top R&B deejay, at a Los Angeles theater.

Pete Rivera (Hoorelbeke), drummer and lead singer for Rare Earth, looking angelic backstage at McCormick Place in Chicago.

Rare Earth ready to "Celebrate" at carvernous McCormick Place in Chicago.

Valerie Simpson doing a solo in San Antonio before performing a non-stop diet of duets with future husband Nicholas Ashford (top, with Val at a Hitsville session).

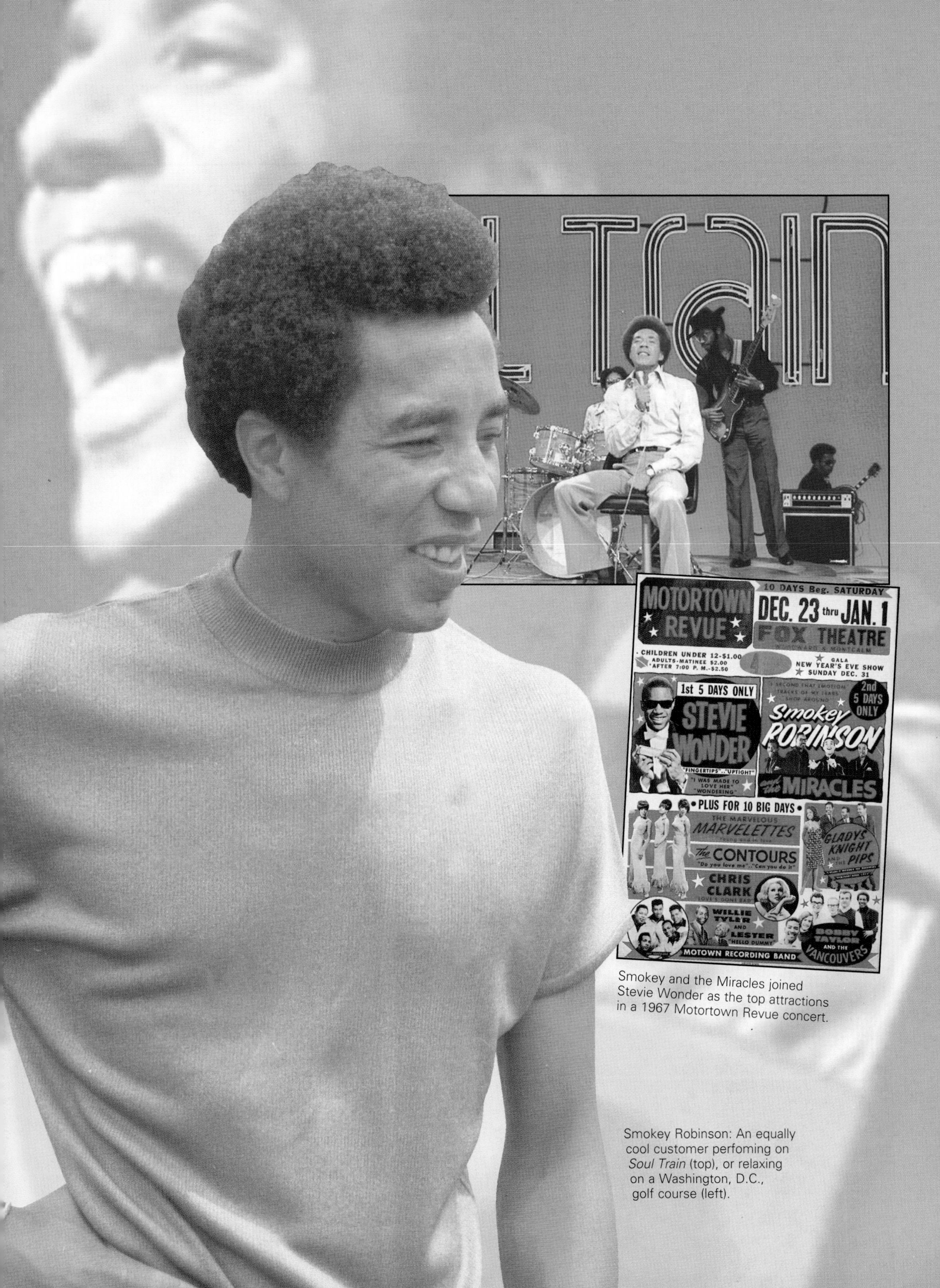

Smokey and the Miracles joined Stevie Wonder as the top attractions in a 1967 Motortown Revue concert.

Smokey Robinson: An equally cool customer perfoming on *Soul Train* (top), or relaxing on a Washington, D.C., golf course (left).

Bill Griffin, Smokey Robinson's replacement, leads the Miracles on stage.

Stevie Wonder was a budding prodigy during a mid-60s record hop in New Jersey (far right), and a full-blown star by the time he appeared on *Soul Train*.

William Guest of the Pips sitting pretty at Weldon's home in Philadelphia.

Smokey Robinson coaxes a grin from Berry Gordy at Berry's home for a "Save The Children" screening.

Stevie Wonder and Don Cornelius renew acquaintances on *Soul Train*.

The debonair Chuck Jackson at the Apollo Theater in New York.

Joe Jackson, proud papa of the Jackson 5, hangs out with Weldon A. McDougal IV during the group's final tour.

Weldon A. McDougal III looking sharp on the outskirts of Las Vegas.

The Supremes in Detroit: Jean Terrell (left), Mary Wilson and Linda Laurence.

The Temptations at the Latin Casino in Cherry Hill, N.J. From left: Dennis Edwards, Otis Williams, Melvin Franklin, Richard Street and Damon Harris.

The Temptations at the Apollo: Damon Harris takes lead, with Otis Williams, Richard Street and Melvin Franklin in immaculately harmonized support.

The Temptations at the Uptown Theater in Philadelphia.

The Four Tops at the Valley Forge Theater in Valley Forge, Pa. From left: Obie Benson, Levi Stubbs, Duke Fakir, and Lawrence Payton.

The Undisputed Truth in rare form on Philadelphia TV.

Joe Hinton shows off a more buttoned-down look.

The Tempts' Melvin Franklin and Otis Williams at the Uptown Theater in Philly.

The Temptations gathered around their mic stand at the Uptown Theater in Philly. From left: Melvin Franklin, Paul Williams, Otis Williams and Eddie Kendricks.

An all-star gathering at Berry Gordy's L.A. home: (from left) Billy Dee Williams, Berry, Myra Waters, Diana Ross, Diana's manager Shelly Berger, Anna Gordy Gaye, Smokey Robinson (the little girl is Billy Jean Brown's daughter).

Mary Wilson and her son at home in L.A.

Diana Ross and Gwen Gordy Fuqua (then Harvey Fuqua's wife) pal around before a *Save The Children* screening.

Different Shades of Brown. Left to right: Steven Warfield, Ronald Logan, Nate Newsome, Marvin Sutton.

Berry Gordy—a portrait of the chairman that hung in the lobby of the Woodward Ave. building.

Carolyn Crawford belts out a tune at the Sigma Sound Studio in Philadelphia in the mid-1970s.

know, let's go over to my cousin's house!'—who was Jackie Wilson. Until then, we didn't know Hubert was related to Jackie. We went over to Jackie and sang the same songs that we did for Berry at the audition. Jackie said, 'Have a seat,' and he went upstairs and called Berry. Berry called us back, we sung the same songs again, and he signed us to a contract.

"It's a matter of who you know," added Potts. The originals they worked up for both auditions included the rocking "Move Mr. Man," which ended up on their only Gordy album. Gordon and Hoggs collaborated with Smokey Robinson on their stomping debut "Whole Lotta Woman," a Gordy production released in February of '61 that started out very differently. "Actually, it was a ballad. It was called 'Gloria With The Pretty Eyes,'' said Potts. "We converted it and put a groove to it. It changed the whole concept of the song—for the better, I might add." Their encore that August, "Funny"—penned by producer Mickey Stevenson along with Gordon and Potts, who sang lead—was a marvelous doo-wop ballad. On the flip, "The Stretch" rocked hard. Producer Mickey wrote the workout with Berry's sister Loucye and her husband, saxist Ron Wakefield.

Gordy worked with the Contours extensively in the studio. "I discovered he had a great ear. On one particular song, we were flat, and I didn't think it was flat. And Berry said, 'No, you're flat.' Later on I listened, and he was right," said Sylvester. The group's stage gymnastics are the stuff of legend. "We used to do flips and splits," he laughed. When guitarist Huey Davis came aboard, the group expanded to a sextet, with Gordon and Hoggs handling most of the leads.

Berry didn't write the Contours' incendiary calling card with them in mind. "We were down in the studio rehearsing a song that I wrote called 'It Must Be Love,'" said Potts. "Berry was standing in the stairway listening to us, 'cause the stu
downstairs. He said, 'That's a nice son
I like it. I got a song for you guys. I was
to the Temptations, but they're not here
give it to you.'" Gordon screamed the ly
his life depended on it, and the fake fade
quarter mark (the idea of the Satintones' S
Mack) was a great gimmick, the bane of u
deejays nationwide.

Issued in June of '62 on the fledgling Gord
"Do You Love Me (Now That I Can Dance)" to
R&B charts and vaulted to No. 3 pop. The Con
were now stars, billed high on the southern
Motortown Revue swing that fall, where their o
escapades rated a word of warning from Berry t
female inhabitants of the bus. "He told 'em to st
away from the Contours: 'They'll ruin you. They'
bunch of hoodlums.' He was right! We were at th
time a rowdy bunch," laughed Potts. **"We wa
like the rebels of Motown."**

The Contours were the stars of the first Gordy labe
LP that fall. Named after their smash, it sported the frantic Billingslea/Potts-penned "It Must Be Love." "O
guitar player at the time, Huey Davis, he came up with the words, but I came up with the melody and the music," said Sylvester of the latter. "I was always pretty good with coming up with good tracks, but Huey was better with words than myself." Smokey's clever "The Old Miner" was a tall tale integrating different cigarette brands into its narrative, while "Claudia" was penned by producer Clarence Paul, Andre Williams, and pianist Joe Hunter. Its surging rhythm and husky harmonies again hinted the Contours were capable of more than dance fare. "Billy Hoggs was doing most of the lead on that," reported Potts.

The album also sported both sides of the Contours' next single. "Shake Sherry," another hellfire rocker from producer Gordy, managed respectable sales for

follow-up in early '63. "You Better Get In Line" on e flip was another uninhibited Gordy copyright uiting Gordon's larynx-shredding lead. The formula eld when Berry unleashed his "Don't Let Her Be our Baby" by the Contours that March. Rousing as it sounds now, the tune stiffed. "He wrote all the earlier things," said Potts. "Then he got tired and turned us over to other producers."

Berry entrusted the group to wife Raynoma for their next one, "You Get Ugly," a novelty she wrote with her brother, Mike Ossman. "I hated that song," chuckled Potts, noting its conceptual similarity to Jimmy Soul's "If You Wanna Be Happy." Brian Holland, Lamont Dozier, and Freddie Gorman collaborated on the 'B' side, "Pa, I Need A Car," its gliding groove hinting at a sleeker Motown sound even if Gordon's lead was as smooth as ground glass.

Berry's ex-wife Thelma, of all people, helped get the Contours back on track. She co-wrote "Can You Do It" with the Monitors' Richard Street, who produced the ebullient number with an intro referencing "Do You Love Me" before breaking into an up-to-date rhythm perfect for doing the Jerk. The result was a national hit in the spring of '64, coupled with the uptown soul-tinged Andre Williams production "I'll Stand By." Stevenson and Ivy Jo Hunter picked up on the dance that fall, writing and producing "Can You Jerk Like Me" for the Contours and ending up with a No. 15 R&B hit in early '65. Its mellow 'B' side, "That Day When She Needed Me," charted too.

The original Contours lineup was ripped asunder in mid-1964. "We broke away. We had a dispute with Berry about a few things," said Potts. "We was all supposed to leave. That was the original idea. We had a meeting. It was making a stand, really. And if we had all stuck together, we could have got what we wanted, I later found out. But Billy Gordon double-crossed us, and because he did that, we just broke away. I came back nine months later. They asked me to come back because they had an engagement at the Howard Theater." New Contours Council Gay and Jerry Green helped pick up the slack.

While Sylvester was on hiatus, Gordon sang lead on the amusingly cynical "First I Look At The Purse," co-written by Smokey and fellow Miracle Bobby Rogers. "He and I were in a station wagon coming from Richmond, Virginia, and he just looked at me and said, 'What does every man look at first?'" recalled Rogers, whose fey falsetto reading of that query opened the Contours' rendition, in 1993. "I said, 'Well, man'—I tell a lot of jokes—I said, 'Well, first I look at the purse.' That's how we wrote that song for the Contours." Gordon's gravelly lead and an unstoppable rhythmic thrust gave the group a No. 12 R&B hit in the summer of '65.

It was Gordon's farewell bow. He was replaced by Joe Stubbs, younger brother of the Four Tops' Levi. "We had to get rid of Billy, because he had a big drug problem," said Potts. "It just wasn't working. We knew Joe Stubbs. In fact, he substituted for Levi on one of those Motown Revues. Levi had throat problems, and Joe did some of the lead things with him. He approached us, and we gave it a try. But Joe had other aspirations. He really wanted to try to do some other things on his own." Stubbs signed on in time to torch "Just A Little Misunderstanding," the torrid work of Stevie Wonder, Morris Broadnax, and Clarence Paul, who co-produced it with Stevenson. It roared up to No. 18 R&B during the summer of '66. Ex-Falcons lead Stubbs didn't stick around long (he'd soon join 100 Proof Aged in Soul), but "Just A Little Misunderstanding" and its upbeat flip "Determination" ensured he'd be remembered fondly.

The Contours were a little rough around the edges, but what they lacked in polish they made up for in daring, energy and attitude (Photo courtesy of David Alston's Mahogany Archives).

"Clarence Paul said, 'I heard you guys are looking for another lead singer. There's a kid singing at a club down here called the Green & Gold. You ought to go check him out,'" said Potts. "It was Dennis Edwards. He was playing keyboards and singing, and I said, 'Hmmm! This guy can sing!' So we approached him about singing with us, and he was more than delighted. He even told everybody in the club, 'I'm singing with the Contours now!'"

Edwards, a Birmingham, Alabama, native who began singing in his father's church when he was only two, had been gigging around his adopted hometown of Detroit with his Firebirds. "I played the piano, keyboards. Self-contained little group," he recalled in 1984. "I think we were pretty good at that time. They were my very first group."

Continued Potts, "But we made a startling discovery—that Dennis couldn't dance! So we worked with him. I often told the Temptations, 'We broke Dennis in for you!' We stayed up all night with him. There wasn't too many songs. He had to do some songs in the background, because Jerry Green was doing most of the leads that Billy did."

Dennis unleashed his melismatic roar on the Contours' last Gordy single, the William Weatherspoon/James Dean-produced "It's So Hard Being A Loser," a song first intended for Jimmy Ruffin that didn't live up to its title by turning in respectable pop and R&B chart entries for the Contours in the spring of '67 (he also led "Your Love Grows More Precious Everyday," a splendid flip that was the work of Davis and Potts). Another Edwards-led stormer, "Baby Hit And Run," garnered a strong Northern Soul reputation after its belated 1974 U.K. release.

That was it for the Contours at Hitsville. "Motown moved to California," said Sylvester. "We would have had to go out there, and we didn't want to pick up roots and go out to L.A." Billingslea put the group back together with Potts during the mid-'70s for concerts. Sadly, ex-Contours bass singer Hubert Johnson committed suicide July 11, 1981. Then, out of the blue, "Do You Love Me" became the rage all over again in 1988 when it graced the soundtrack of the hit film *Dirty Dancing*. "That really just opened it wide open for us," said Sylvester. "On that *Dirty Dancing* tour, it lasted for seven months, and we went all over the world."

The current Contours, with Potts and Billingslea, are as busy as ever, though some of the acrobatics have sensibly been phased out. "We still do a lot of choreography," said Potts. "We're still on our feet, spinning and dancing. But none of that flipping and jumping out in the audience."

HANK COSBY

When Hitsville sought the services of an expert tenor saxist and arranger early in its existence, Hank Cosby answered the call. By the end of the '60s, he'd written and/or produced some of the label's greatest triumphs, and played on quite a few more.

Born in Detroit on May 12, 1928, many of Hank's musical influences hailed from the jazz spectrum. "Detroit was just loaded with musicians. They'd come from everywhere," he said. "I was liking Coltrane back in those days. And we had a lot of guys—Yusef Lateef was right here local. And we had Sonny Stitt staying in Saginaw. He was coming down on the weekends. We had some real monsters. They led the way for all of the musicians. We had a guy, Lefty Edwards. He was local. He could really play." Edwards ended up playing Motown sessions.

Pianist Joe Hunter, Motown's first house bandleader, brought Cosby aboard. "I think he knew

Berry, and Berry mentioned to him he needed some musicians. So Joe took us by there— Jamerson, myself, Benny Benjamin, the trombone player George Bohanon," said Cosby. "We were playing at a place called Phelps' Lounge." One of Hank's initial studio forays in 1961 found him in familiar company, though not in town. "The first record that we cut, that was the Motown guys, Jamerson and all of us. We had just left Jackie Wilson's band," he said. "Joe Hunter, he's one of those guys that's always into something. He'd hooked up with John Lee Hooker. John Lee Hooker needed to take a band to Chicago, and so he brought me these two songs.

"So I said, 'Well, where's the music?' He said, 'There ain't no music! You have to watch Johnny Lee Hooker's hands!' In other words, every time he moved his fingers to a different position, that was a different chord. So I sat there and watched him, and I wrote the chords out. This was the only way we could make it. Otherwise, we couldn't have made it. Jamerson's on bass, Benny Benjamin on drums, Joe Hunter on piano. Don't leave out Mike Terry—he's the baritone player." With a band like that, no wonder Hooker's "Boom Boom," a major 1962 hit on Chicago's Vee-Jay Records, is so together.

Cosby exhibited versatility during Motown's golden years, arranging a slew of classic tracks and blowing up a storm during his muscular tenor solos on the Temptations' "The Way You Do The Things You Do," "My Baby," and "I'll Be In Trouble," the Miracles' "Going To A Go-Go," and Gladys Knight & the Pips' "I Heard It Through The Grapevine." "I played a lot of solos. I really don't remember all of 'em," he said. "Guys would come to get me when they needed a solo, and I'd do the solo. Prior to that I was doing a lot of arranging. I loved to arrange."

Clearly, writing hits also ranked high on Hank's priority scale. Cosby, Stevie Wonder, and lyricist Sylvia Moy collaborated on a series of major sellers for the multi-talented teen, including "Uptight (Everything's Alright)," "Nothing's Too Good For My Baby," "I Was Made To Love Her," "I'm Wondering," and "My Cherie Amour." He also co-produced Martha & the Vandellas' "I Promise To Wait My Love" with Quality Control head Billie Jean Brown.

Like so many Hitsville stalwarts, Hank found romance on the job when he met his wife, Pat. "She was the switchboard operator when I first met her. We've been together ever since," he said. His responsibilities were immense. "Hank Cosby was the guy who was in charge of the studio," said McDougal. "He would give out studio time. He was the one who paid the musicians. He would say who was on the session and who wasn't. He was a very important guy."

Motown unceremoniously cut Cosby loose in 1972. "The real truth never came out, so I'll just leave it alone," said Cosby. "But it was time for me to go. There's always somebody trying to better themselves over somebody else. I had people knifing me a long time in the back, and finally somebody said something that got to Berry." He moved to New York and worked for CBS Records, then relocated to L.A. and a post with Fantasy before returning home.

"Once upon a time, man, I thought Detroit was the greatest place in the world. Couldn't nobody tell me no different," he said. "I went in the Army and I couldn't get back here fast enough. And then they had the '67 riot. It's been a different place ever since." He doesn't take his horn out of its case much anymore, but Hank relishes the days when he was first-call sax soloist at the era's most successful soul label.

"We were lucky," he said. "We came together, and we were young and foolish. But we did accomplish together. **We loved music."**

CAROLYN CRAWFORD

Winner of the 1963 Tip Top Bread talent contest (first prize was a Motown session), Carolyn Crawford outlasted the standard short-term commitment to such fresh-faced recruits. She was only 15 when she beat out a slew of other talented newcomers to win the annual WCHB radio-sponsored contest (entry was predicated on the submission of wrappers from loaves of Tip Top). Crawford arrived at Hitsville equipped for stardom, belting her own atmospheric mid-tempo workout "Forget About Me" like a seasoned pro. It comprised half her debut Motown single in late '63, paired with Berry's "Devil In His Heart."

Hal Davis (in hat), "Mr. Motown" in Los Angeles, hard at work at Mowest studios (Weldon A. McDougal III photo).

Carolyn's best-known Motown waxing, the Smokey Robinson/Janie Bradford/Mickey Stevenson composition "My Smile Is Just A Frown (Turned Upside Down)," became a national chart hit in early 1965, rising to No. 39 during a one-week run on *Billboard's* R&B list. Carolyn's youthful delivery was well suited to its yearning lyrics and mid-tempo lilt, a subtle vibes solo not the least of its charms. Its flip was a choppy, relentless Crawford original, "I'll Come Running."

Crawford bowed out of Motown at the close of '64 with "When Someone's Good To You," another slinky mid-tempo outing with a male vocal group trying its best to sound like the Impressions (its 'B' side was "My Heart"). She was the only Motown notable apart from McDougal to later join Kenny Gamble & Leon Huff's Philadelphia International operation. She was briefly with Chapter 8 in 1975 (replaced by Anita Baker), and nailed a minor hit for Mercury in 1979 with "Coming On Strong."

HAL DAVIS

Los Angeles was the only metropolis where Berry Gordy's name wasn't synonymous with Motown's during the mid-'60s. Hal Davis helmed the L.A. office and was its figurehead.

"When Berry first came to L.A., when he was making his early trips out to L.A. once the office was open, everybody in Los Angeles and Hollywood knew Hal Davis," said Frank Wilson. "They didn't know Berry Gordy. And they called Hal Davis 'Mr. Motown.' So whenever Berry would come around, and they would refer to Hal as **'Mr. Motown,'** that would crack Berry up!"

Davis hailed from Cincinnati and had taken ill as a child. "He had polio. His mother used to take him around, and didn't get his injections, and she'd take him around singing in churches," explained Brenda Holloway, Davis's top mid-'60s discovery. "I don't even know if the vaccine had been perfected then. But Hal caught polio, so he had a shoe that was really big."

Hal had made some platters of his own— the rocking "Read The Book Of Love" in '60 for Bob Keane's Del-Fi logo, "My Only Flower" with "You're The Girl" for Cincinnati-based Federal in 1961, and a 1963 duet 45 with Holloway for Minasa. He produced a variety of Motown artists during the mid-'60s, usually with Marc Gordon: Stevie Wonder, Marvin Gaye, pop crooner Tony Martin, and Holloway, whose "Every Little Bit Hurts" was an early '64 smash.

"Hal lived in the studio. Hal ate breakfast, dinner, lunch—they should have had a shower there for him," said Holloway. He also held down a day job in the early years. "Hal worked for the county of Los Angeles. He cooked for the county, and he worked at night in the studios." Romance eventually blossomed between the two. "I was actually Hal's girlfriend after I got out of high school," Holloway said. "At one point I was going to marry Hal, but he was just a little bit too old for me."

"Hal was the consummate record man," said Wilson. "I suppose the reason Berry liked him so much was because he was so dedicated to records and producing and finding new writers. He was constantly seeking out new talent. He was in the studio easily an average of 16 to 18 hours a day."

"He used to spend hours and hours in the studio with me, working on material, trying to get the right sound," said singer Blinky Williams, another of his proteges. "Hal Davis would stop and punch in a word or a lyric, just to hear the 't' or the 'p.' He would book sessions for me like at 2:30 in the morning after I'd gotten off work if I worked at a club or something. He would like that time of the morning because he still had lots of energy, and he was nocturnal and so was I."

Davis's influence on Motown's artistic direction was again strong after the label's base of power shifted west during the early '70s. He was in charge of the historic 1973 duet album by Diana Ross and Marvin Gaye and helmed some of the Jackson 5's biggest hits, including "I'll Be There" and "Never Can Say Goodbye." When Davis passed away a few years ago, Berry delivered the eulogy—a fitting farewell from one "Mr. Motown" to the other.

SAMMY DAVIS, JR.

Sammy Davis, Jr. could do everything except score a hit for Motown. The dynamic star of stage, screen, and the Vegas strip co-founded a Motown subsidiary, Ecology Records, with Berry in 1969, but it only released one 1971 single: Sammy's "In My Own Lifetime" paired with "I'll Begin Again."

Eddie Kendricks, Gladys Knight, and Sammy Davis, Jr. mellow out at the Cocoanut Grove in Los Angeles. Weldon took Gladys and Eddie over to see Sammy's dynamic show (Weldon A. McDougal III photo).

Born December 8, 1925 in Harlem, Davis was born into show biz. His dad was a vaudeville dancer, his mom a chorus girl. Tiny Sammy tap-danced in the 1933 film short *Rufus Jones for President*, and remained in Will Mastin's trio with his dad into the '50s. But Davis was destined for greater things, recording solo for Capitol in 1949 and a few years later for Decca, scoring pop hits with "Hey There" in 1954 and "Something's Gotta Give" and "That Old

Black Magic" in '55. Davis courageously battled back from the loss of his left eye in a 1954 car wreck.

Though he starred on Broadway and in Hollywood, today Sammy is most often associated as a prime conspirator of the Rat Pack, the infamous gang of boozy swingers that ruled late-night Vegas during the early '60s. Alongside Frank Sinatra, Dean Martin, and Peter Lawford, Davis personified an endless party lifestyle. He enjoyed pop hits with the dramatic "What Kind Of Fool Am I" (1962), "The Shelter Of Your Arms" (1963), and "I've Gotta Be Me" (1968) for Sinatra's Reprise imprint, also starring in the Rat Pack flicks *Ocean's Eleven* and *Robin and the Seven Hoods* and the acclaimed Broadway musical *Golden Boy* during this period.

Sammy's zany "Here Comes The Judge" routine on the NBC-TV comedy hour *Rowan & Martin's Laugh-In* led to Davis's Motown hookup. Shorty Long was about to cut a number patterned after Sammy's jive patter in the skit, and Davis was the natural choice to deliver the spoken intro. "They asked him to do Shorty Long's record," said McDougal. "He agreed, and right after that, they started negotiating."

Sammy Davis, Jr. entertaining as only he could at the Cocoanut Grove in Los Angeles (Weldon A. McDougal III photo).

Davis's Motown debut was the LP *Something for Everyone* in 1970. *Ecology* came and went the next year. Business aside, there was still plenty of party time for the man many hailed as America's greatest entertainer. "I used to go out on the road with him. The reason I went out on the road was to introduce him to the R&B disc jockeys," said McDougal. "He'd tell me at night, 'Listen, man, after the show, I'm having a party, and I want you to definitely come. In fact, I'm making a party just for you.' I said, 'Oh man, this is great!' So I go up there, and everything was goin' on beautiful. There's dancing, and all the showgirls were up there.

"But then Sammy came in—and everything was still going on—and he said, **'Man, enjoy yourself.** Everybody dance and everything.' And then all of a sudden, Sammy went to sleep. He was sitting at the table, right? And just as he went to sleep, everything stopped. Everybody just walked on out like it was nothing. So I found out that every night that Sammy used to have those parties, because it would take him time to come down after performing. I used to think that was very strange."

Sammy's stock shot up sky-high again when his saccharine "The Candy Man" for MGM Records went gold in 1972. Throat cancer ended his fabulous career, and life, on May 15, 1990.

DEBBIE DEAN

Her chipper vocal technique pitched somewhere midway between Connie Francis and Wanda Jackson, Debbie Dean started out at Motown by answering the Miracles' "Shop Around" with "Don't Let Him Shop Around" in early 1961 and encored that summer with "Itsy Bity Pity Love" (its 'B' side, "But I'm Afraid," was a captivating pop trifle). "Everybody's Talkin' About My Baby," out in March '62, was unexpurgated girl group rock and roll provided by Berry, Dean inserting a chirpy hiccup in her delivery (the 45 came complete with a picture sleeve). After a long absence, Debbie resurfaced in 1968 on V.I.P. with "Why Am I Lovin' You" and as Deke Richards' songwriting partner for Martha & the Vandellas' "I Can't Dance To That Music You're Playin'," the Temptations' "Why Did You Leave Me Darling," and Edwin Starr's "Backyard Lovin' Man."

KIKI DEE

Though basically an unknown quantity stateside when she signed with Tamla in late '69, Kiki Dee was a minor British pop star. Born Pauline Matthews in Bradford, England on March 6, 1947, Kiki signed with British Fontana in 1963 and found Northern Soul favor with "On A Magic Carpet Ride" prior to her Motown sojourn. Her first Tamla single paired the forceful "The Day Will Come Between Sunday and Monday" (written by Pam Sawyer and Joe Hinton, produced by Clay McMurray, and arranged by David Van de Pitte and Jerry Long) and a remake of David Ruffin's "My Whole World Ended (The Moment You Left Me)" in the spring of 1970. It was followed closely by her only Tamla LP, *Great Expectations*—apparently dashed when her early '71 Rare Earth follow-up, "Love Makes The World Go Round," stalled at No. 87 pop. Dee *was* destined for stardom—elsewhere. Her "I've Got The Music In Me" was a huge 1974 hit, and "Don't Go Breaking My Heart," a peppy duet with Elton John, went gold in '76.

DIFFERENT SHADES OF BROWN

It pays to have friends, especially when they have direct connections to booking agents at the Motor City's top R&B nightspot. That's a lesson the Different Shades of Brown learned when a chance encounter led to the sharp quartet from Springfield, Ohio, joining Motown.

By the time Tamla released the Shades' debut single, "Label Me Love," in 1972, their ranks also included Ronald Logan (born May 12, 1947), Marvin Sutton (born January 13, 1950), and bass-baritone Steven Warfield (born June 28, 1950). "Every last one of us started in the church," said tenor Nate Newsome (born November 1, 1944).

"When I came home from the service on leave—it was like November of '68—Ronald, Stevie, a guy named James Griffiths, and a guy named Trent Smith were singing, but they didn't have a name," said Newsome. "They had said that Trent was leaving, and they had decided that they were going to get me to be in the singing group without even asking me. Still, they didn't have no name. I got out in January of '69. I'll be honest with you, I was planning on going back to Germany to sing. But man, they sounded good! They sounded good, with no steps or nothing.

"We spent about four weeks, four Mondays, coming up with a name for the group. So we ended up saying

"The group was bad..."

the Different Shades of Black. But two things happened. One, we felt like the Different Shades of Black would work for that time—you know, black power and all that—but it would probably grow thin. So we said, 'Well, just change it to Brown!' Different Shades of Brown, the perfect name. Plus, we had all the shades—we had real, real dark, we had my complexion, then we had kind of light, and then we had real light.

"A couple of months after that, the guy named James Griffiths, which we called him Jimbo, he fell in love. Left the group. Marvin came. Now Marvin, Stevie, Ronald and myself, we're the four that signed with Motown," said Newsome. "It was incredible what he added to the group."

Different Shades of Brown: (from left) Nate Alexander, Steven Warfield, Nate Newsome (photo courtesy of Nate Newsome).

Practicing twice a day, the Shades honed their harmonies. Their second gig found them opening for the Dells, and in 1971, a friend caught their act. "I happened to go home one weekend," said Brenda Mabra. "They were in a garage singing. I went to visit my cousin, and I was walking, and I passed them. I knew who they were, and I stopped in. They were so good. I said, 'Wow! I could probably get them booked at the 20 Grand.' And I did. The guy even took my word that they were good. I had told Weldon about 'em, because they were looking to sign with somebody."[6]

"We ended up working a 10-day engagement with the Stylists. It was a Motown backup group," said Newsome (the Stylists' only V.I.P. single, "What Is Love" with "Where Did The Children Go," was issued in mid-'71). Producer Clay McMurray took an interest, and the Shades went to Hitsville for an audition. "We did 'California Dreamin'' with our guitarist, the way we did it, and next thing I know they sent somebody down to see if we were signed," said Nate.

The lead vocals were split on the Shades' debut, issued on Tamla in May of '72. The exhilarating "Label Me Love" featured Logan up front. "Stevie had a little bitty part on the end," said Nate. Its mid-tempo flip, "Life's A Ball (While It Lasts)," featured Marvin's high-flying lead. Soon after it was cut, the Shades made a personnel move. "Ronald found Christ and became a minister before we even did 'Label Me Love' publically," said Nate. A suitable replacement was located pronto. "Nate Alexander was from Dayton. We had heard about Nate down through the years, but we didn't ever think he'd be in our group, 'cause we were gonna be together forever."

The quartet's encore came out in July of '73 on Motown instead of Tamla, pairing two ballads, the Hitsville-cut "When The Hurt Is Put Back On You" and "Sending Good Vibrations," both spotlighting

Newsome's stratospheric front work, though the first also featured Alexander (born November 13, 1945) near its end. When Motown relocated to L.A., the Shades migrated west for almost a year, though the material they cut there with McMurray—"Then Again Maybe," "Out In The Country"—never saw light of day. Newsome believes their smooth "Hearts And Flowers" was released briefly, though it's not listed in the standard Motown discographies.

He isn't naming names, but Nate believes a much bigger Motown group played a major role in killing the Shades' career at the label. "We had run into problems with people going to Berry, really being jealous of us," he said. After McMurray gave them the full lowdown, the group requested its release. Newsome and Sutton later joined Ellsworth Senior and Mike Harris as the Lovemakers on Island Records. There they cut two mid-'70s 45s, "When You're Next To Me" and "Down And Out" ("My Girl Is Really Dynamite" backed both), McMurray again producing.

The Shades' Motown tenure may have been shortened by factors beyond their control, but Newsome isn't bitter. "A lot of people heard us. But if the company had done with us right, a lot more people would have heard of us," he said. Nate remains firmly convinced of one thing, though. "The group was *bad*. We worked hard at that."

THE EASYBEATS

Thanks to "Friday On My Mind," an engaging piece of British pop-rock produced by Shel Talmy, the Easybeats were hot in 1967. By the time Motown's Rare Earth subsidiary corralled them, they had cooled considerably. Nevertheless, their "St. Louis" nicked No. 100 on *Billboard's* pop chart for a week in late '69. The Easybeats formed in Australia in 1965 and relocated to England the next year. Guitarist George Young hailed from Scotland; guitarist Harry Vanda and bassist Dick Diamonde were Dutch, and vocalist Steven Wright and drummer Gordon Fleet were British. Young and Vanda wrote "Friday On My Mind," a huge British hit for the band during the fall of 1966 that leaped the pond in early '67 on United Artists. "St. Louis" (backed with "Can't Find Love") was their only Rare Earth 45; a scheduled 1970 album, *Easy Ridin'*, was canceled.

BILLY ECKSTINE

The incomparably debonair Mr. B prevailed as a swoon-inducing matinee idol—the African-American equivalent of handsome crooner Frank Sinatra—during the 1940s. By the time he hooked up with Motown in 1965, the 50-year-old Eckstine was a suave half-century old.

The Pittsburgh native, born William Clarence Eckstein on July 8, 1914, paid his dues on the northeastern club circuit before pianist Earl "Fatha" Hines hired him as his vocalist in 1939. Eckstine enjoyed considerable acclaim fronting Hines' band on the luxurious 1940 blues "Jelly, Jelly" (written by Hines and Eckstine) and "Stormy Monday Blues," a 1942 R&B chart-topper not to be confused with T-Bone Walker's similarly titled hit six years later.

He left Hines in 1943 and, along with saxist and fellow Hines alumni Budd Johnson, assembled his own bop-fueled big band in '44, spotlighting Dizzy Gillespie, Charlie Parker, Miles Davis, Gene Ammons, Dexter Gordon, Leo Parker, Art Blakey, and Sarah Vaughan. Eckstine employed his mile-wide vibrato to rack up hits for National with "Last Night & Now Tonite Again" and "A Cottage For Sale" in 1945 and "Prisoner Of Love" (revived in slightly grittier form by James Brown) and "You Call It Madness (I Call It Love)" the next year. Mr.

B broke up the band in 1947 to croon love ballads for MGM Records: "Everything I Have Is Yours" in '48, "Fools Rush In," "Bewildered," "Caravan," and "Temptation" in '49, "I Apologize" (1951), and "Kiss Of Fire" in '52. Eckstine wasn't immune to the rock and roll bug, awkwardly covering Bobby Helms' "The Tennessee Rock 'n' Roll" in 1956 for RCA Victor and belting "Like Wow" on Roulette in '59.

He was just coming off a long stint at Mercury when Motown beckoned in 1965. There was an existing connection: The Four Tops had toured with Eckstine.[7] His first 45 on the logo, "Down To Earth" with "Had You Been Around," came out that May, followed by an LP, *The Prime of My Life*. Motown persisted with "Slender Thread" and its flip "Wish You Were Here" and "A Warmer World" with "And There You Were" in '66; 1967's "I Wonder Why (Nobody Loves Me)" with "I've Been Blessed"; "Thank You Love" with "Is Anyone Here Going My Way" and "For Love Of Ivy" with "A Woman" in '68, and "My Cup Runneth Over" with "Ask The Lonely" in '69, along with two more LPs—1966's *My Way* and 1968's *For the Love of Ivy*. Eckstine moved to Stax's Enterprise logo in 1969. Isaac Hayes produced the first of his four albums for the Memphis firm. He died March 8, 1993 in Pittsburgh.

THE ELGINS/DOWNBEATS

This quartet was a hybrid of two Tamla acts. Vocalist Saundra Mallett (later Edwards) had cut "Camel Walk" with "It's Gonna Be Hard Times" in July of 1962, co-billed with the Vandellas, while Johnny Dawson and Robert Fleming were part of the Downbeats, whose only Tamla single "Your Baby's Back" and "Request Of A Fool" intrigued Berry Gordy enough to release it twice—in late '59 and again in early '62. Dawson and Fleming had been members of two other local outfits, the Sensations (not to be confused with the Philly group of "Let Me In" fame) and the Five Emeralds.

With the addition of Cleo "Duke" Miller, the quartet was off and running. "Darling Baby," their first V.I.P. offering on New Year's

Billy Eckstine was already a legend in the making when he arrived at Motown.

Eve of '65, was an easy-grooving doo-wop-tinged Holland-Dozier-Holland concoction that spotlighted Edwards' captivating pipes. The name change to the Elgins must have been a last-second decision. Early pressings of "Darling Baby" still listed them as the Downbeats. It blasted up to No. 4 on *Billboard's* R&B listings in early 1966, though pop sales were light. Its flip, "Put Yourself In My Place," was doomed to eternal also-ran status: It pulled identical duty on Chris Clark's V.I.P release "Love's Gone Bad" and the Supremes' "You Can't Hurry Love" later that year.

The Downbeats officially became The Elgins with the group's 1965 release "Darling Baby" on V.I.P.

"Heaven Must Have Sent You," another Brian Holland/Lamont Dozier production, made it back-to-back R&B smashes for the new group during the fall of 1966. This was state-of-the-art H-D-H, its infectious drive pushing Edwards into another exceptional lead turn. Once again, the Elgins had a Top Ten R&B hit on their hands, coupled with "Stay In My Lonely Arms," an H-D-H gem from the Four Tops' encore album the previous year.

Before 1966 ended, the Elgins cut their V.I.P. debut album, *Darling Baby.* Its five covers displayed a refreshing lack of attention to in-house publishing concerns: Marvin Gaye's "How Sweet It Is (To Be Loved By You)" was the lone Motown standby. "Good Lovin'" (originally by the Olympics but a Young Rascals smash) and Wilson Pickett's "In The Midnight Hour" proved excellent vehicles for Edwards, while another Pickett house rocker, "634-5789," and Percy Sledge's deep soul treatise "When A Man Loves A Woman" were entrusted to the Elgins' male contingent. Holland and Norman Whitfield collaborated on a relaxed "No Time For Tears," and the bluesy "It's Gonna Be Hard Times," Saundra's '62 single with the Vandellas, was recycled for LP consumption (the rest of the Elgins weren't even on it).

H-D-H handed Saundra "I Understand My Man," one of the LP's highlights and eventually the Elgins' third 45 in the summer of 1967 (flipped with Harvey Fuqua's "It's Been A Long Long Time"). When it flopped, the Elgins' tenure at V.I.P. came to a close—almost. In the fall of the '71, encouraged by the belated British hit campaign the Elgins' "Heaven Must Have Sent You" had waged a few months earlier ("Put Yourself In My Place" similarly garnered some overdue chart respect from the English soul crowd that fall), V.I.P. gave it another U.S. airing. Lightning didn't strike twice.

YVONNE FAIR

Virginia-born Yvonne Fair arrived at Motown in 1970. Her first 45 was issued that June on Soul, pairing "Stay A Little Longer" and "We Should Never Be Lonely My Love," but she was already experienced.

Born in 1942, Fair came into the Chantels as a road replacement for founding member Jackie Landry. James Brown shared a bill with the group at the Uptown Theater in Philly, liked Fair's attitude, and hired her as an opening act. The Hardest Working Man in Show Biz produced her debut for King Records, "I Found You" (a prototype for his own "I Got You [I Feel Good]") paired with "If I Knew" in early 1962, and she made several more for J.B.: "Tell Me Why" with "Say So Long" that summer, "It Hurts To Be In Love" with "You Can Make It If You Try" in the fall, and "Straighten Up" with "Say Yeah Yeah" for Henry Stone's Miami-based Dade imprint in '63.

Yvonne Fair had a productive ride at Motown beginning in 1966 (Weldon A. McDougal III photo).

Brown was still her boss in 1966 when she cut "Baby Baby Baby" and "Just As Sure (As You Play, You Must Pay)" for Smash, but Yvonne was touring with Chuck Jackson when the Motown connection was made. Though the firm was slow to release an encore following her Soul debut, there was a role for her in Gordy's 1972 Billie Holiday film bio *Lady Sings the Blues*. Yvonne scored her first Motown hit in 1974 with a revival of Norman Whitfield's "Funky Music Sho' Nuff Turns Me On," previously a solid seller for both Edwin Starr and the Temptations. She scored again later that year with "Walk Out The Door If You Wanna" (another Whitfield copyright, "It Should've Been Me," adorned the flip and sold big in Great Britain; it had been a '68 hit for Gladys Knight & the Pips). "Love Ain't No Toy" rounded out her Motown hit trilogy in 1975. Fair passed away June 3, 1994 in Las Vegas.

THE FANTASTIC FOUR

Considering that they'd been recording for Ed Wingate's Ric-Tic Records—Motown's chief local rival—with a cadre of the same musicians who were residents at Hitsville, it stood to reason that the Fantastic Four's elongated winning streak would continue after they moved over to Soul in 1968. But it was not to be.

Maybe they just didn't receive the same loving attention they did at Ric-Tic, whose close-knit family atmosphere resembled that of Motown earlier in the decade. Lead "Sweet" James Epps, Joseph and Ralph Pruitt, and William Hunter got off on the good foot at Ric-Tic with "Girl Have Pity" in '66, next issued the pleading "Can't Stop Looking For My Baby"—a mid-tempo glider reminiscent of the Tempts—and justifiably broke through huge with the dramatic "The Whole World Is A Stage," which vaulted to No. 6 R&B in the spring of '67.

Their next Ric-Tic offering, the inspiring "You Gave Me Something (And Everything's Alright)" (the handiwork of Al Hamilton, his brother Ronnie Savoy, Norma Toney, and William Garrett), nearly matched the chart showing of its predecessor, stopping at No. 12 R&B that summer. Both sides of the driving "As Long As I Live (I Live For You)" and "To Share Your Love"—actually a revival of Bobby Bland's '64 hit ballad "Share Your Love For Me"—made potent national noise that fall. Producer Hamilton, born in Detroit in 1937, was giving his charges a run for their chart money; his Ric-Tic single "You've Got To Pay The Price"—the instrumental flip of his "Where Do I Go From Here"—was a hit under his Al Kent alias.[8]

The gently pulsing "Goddess Of Love," penned by Kent and Toney, kept the Fantastic Four's string of Ric-Tic successes alive and thriving as 1968 dawned. After "Man In Love" missed the hit parade, the Dale Warren-arranged "I've Got To Have You" brought the group back to the winner's circle that spring. "I Love You Madly," their last typically immaculate Ric-Tic biscuit from the pens of Garrett and Mike Hanks, blasted up to No. 12 R&B in the fall of '68 and transferred over to Soul in mid-run.

Amazingly, it would prove their only chart entry at Soul. The label saluted the group's recent past in March of '69 by gathering their Ric-Tic triumphs on *Best of the Fantastic Four*, but it didn't help. "I Feel Like I'm Falling In Love Again" was issued right around the same time but stiffed (by then, Wallace Childs had replaced Hunter). Ditto "Just Another Lonely Night" that fall and "On The Brighter Side Of A Blue World," a Kent production arranged by Paul Riser, in March of 1970 (Clay McMurray took over to helm and co-write the flip, "I'm Gonna Carry On").

The Four joined Eastbound Records and got things going again in '74 with "I'm Falling In Love (I Feel Good All Over)." Switching over to the Westbound subsidiary, the Fantastic Four scored with "Alvin Stone (The Birth & Death Of A Gangster)" in '75, "Hideaway" the next year, and "I Got To Have Your Love" in '77.

KING FLOYD

New Orleans singer King Floyd was so hot on the strength of his 1971 million-selling R&B chart-topper "Groove Me" for Atlantic-distributed Chimneyville that when the opportunity arose to pick up an LP he'd cut in 1968 for the Mercury-affiliated Pulsar logo in Los Angeles, Motown jumped on it, reissuing *Heart of the Matter* in April of '71. It was produced by Crescent City expatriate Harold Battiste, with keyboard wizard Mac "Dr. John" Rebennack also looming prominent in its execution.

"I had known of Mac, but I had never met him before," said Floyd in a 1997 interview. "We were working with (guitarist Alvin) 'Shine' Robinson out there. Mac said, 'Hey, man, let's do an album on you. I like the way you write!' So we just went at it, you know.

"I did a promotional tour in Louisiana, but it wasn't a seller. I guess that was my first flop. But after 'Groove Me' was released and was a big record, Motown bought up the masters and put it out under the V.I.P. label." In addition to *Heart of the Matter* (the last LP to appear on V.I.P.), a single coupling a bubbly "Heartaches" and the smooth "Together We Can Do Anything" hit the shelves. Floyd wrote or co-wrote everything on the LP—notably a percolating "Take The Place Of A Dying Man" and "Love Ain't What It Used To Be"— with Rebennack assisting on a pair (the surging "Groov-A-Lin" hinted at imminent Floyd endeavors).

Born February 13, 1945 in New Orleans, Floyd began singing at 12. "I started working professionally on Bourbon Street at 16-and-a-half," he said. "Of course, I had somebody else's ID to get into the clubs. Mr. G (singer Joe 'Mr. Google Eyes' August) gave me my first gig. I was doing just about everybody's (material)—Ben E. King, Otis Redding, Sam Cooke, Jackie Wilson."

Moving to New York in 1963 after a military stint, Floyd fell in with composer/singer Don Covay. "He taught me how to write," said Floyd. Jimmy Tyrell, Floyd's manager at the time, got him a contract with James Brown's short-lived Try Me label, but the connection failed to produce anything tangible. "I didn't get recorded, because (Brown) was so busy, man. After a year—we had a one-year contract with options—I told my manager Jimmy, I said, 'Listen, I don't want to fool with this. I really just want to try something different.' So I moved to California, and I produced my first record on the Original Sound label. It was called 'Walkin' And Thinkin',' backed with 'Why Did She Leave Me.'" While at Original Sound, King wrote and arranged for well-endowed B movie queen Jayne Mansfield. "Walkin' And Thinkin'" also came out in '65 on Uptown, backed with "Love Makes The World Go Round," and he had a '66 Uptown follow-up, "Come On Home (Where You Belong)" with "I Don't Care (No More)."

Floyd had a previous quasi-Motown connection in L.A. as a composer for Mickey Stevenson's Venture Records before growing disenchanted in 1969 and returning home. That's where he met manager Elijah Walker, who resuscitated his career in '70. "Groove Me" was basically produced by trumpeter Wardell Quezergue at the same session at Jackson, Mississippi's Malaco Studio as Jean Knight's Stax R&B chart-topper "Mr. Big Stuff." "Groove Me" initially found no takers. "Stax refused me. They had an offer, and they turned it down," said Floyd.

Quezergue's syncopated, reggae-tinged arrangement and Floyd's sexy, high-pitched vocal were irresistible, though its flip, "What Our Love Needs," was originally the designated plug side before New Orleans deejay George Vinnett turned it over and started spinning "Groove Me." Floyd came back strong in '71 for Chimneyville with "Baby Let Me Kiss You" and the next year's "Woman Don't Go Astray," but the hits dried up during the disco era. He retired from music altogether in 1987 to manage a Los Angeles homeless shelter but began mounting a comeback in 1995, reuniting with Malaco in 2000 to cut a new album, *Old Skool Funk.*

Musical tastes changed during his absence, but King Floyd never lost his groove.

HARVEY FUQUA

An imposing figure who held down a wide range of crucial roles behind the scenes at Motown—producer, songwriter, early promotion man, and brother-in-law to the boss (he married Berry's sister Gwen)—Harvey Fuqua's greatest contribution was bringing Marvin Gaye to Detroit.

Harvey Fuqua was credited with bringing Marvin Gaye to Motown, but he also made great contributions as a writer and producer for such stars as Jr. Walker, Gladys Knight and the Pips, Shorty Long and The Spinners (Photo courtesy of David Alston's Mahogany Archives).

Born July 27, 1929 in Louisville, Kentucky, Harvey was a cousin of the Ink Spots' Charlie Fuqua; impeccable harmonies ran in the family. He first met his future co-lead singer in the Moonglows, Bobby Lester, in high school. Harvey moved to Cleveland in 1952, assembling a jazz group called the Crazy Sounds. Local deejay Alan Freed changed their name to the Moonglows and was responsible for their debut 78 on his own Champagne logo. By the time they signed with Chicago's Chance Records in 1953, Fuqua was joined by Lester (whose stratospheric pipes alternated out front with Harvey's), Prentiss Barnes, and Pete Graves. The Moonglows cut five fine Chance singles before moving to Chess, where their immortal "Sincerely"—a textbook example of the advanced "blow harmony" technique Fuqua espoused—blasted to the top of the R&B charts in 1955.

More classic ballads followed during the mid-'50s—"Most Of All," "In My Diary," "We Go Together," "Over And Over Again"—and the Moonglows appeared in the quickie flicks *Rock Rock Rock!* and *Mister Rock and Roll* (Fuqua turned up solo in 1959's *Go, Johnny, Go!*). After the dirge-like "Ten Commandments Of Love" proved a '58 smash, the original Moonglows lineup broke up. Fuqua recruited a young Washington, D.C. quartet, the Marquees, to take their place. The new lineup cut a few last sides for Chess before disbanding, but Harvey saw something special in one introspective tenor, so he brought Marvin Gaye with him to Detroit.

Harvey had a good reason to venture up to the Motor City: Autonomy. After producing for Anna Records, he formed a couple of new record labels, Harvey and Tri-Phi, in 1961 with Gwen (one of Anna's owners). The labels attracted the Spinners, Shorty Long, Jr. Walker & the All Stars, Johnny & Jackey, and bluesman Eddie Burns. In 1963, both labels and much of their roster were absorbed by Motown—bringing Harvey into the fold as a writer and producer. Often teamed with Johnny Bristol, Fuqua supervised Marvin and Tammi Terrell's "Ain't No Mountain High Enough" and "Your Precious Love," Gladys Knight & the Pips' "Just Walk In My Shoes," Tammi's solo "I Can't Believe You Love Me," and Walker's "Pucker Up Buttercup." Fuqua produced Gaye's last album for Columbia in 1982, *Midnight Love*, and he can still sing, forming a new contingent of Moonglows to perform on the recent PBS-TV show *Doo Wop 50.*

RAYNOMA GORDY SINGLETON & THE RAYBER VOICES

Until the 1990 publication of her tell-all autobiography *Berry, Me, and Motown*, the crucial role Raynoma Liles Gordy Singleton played in Motown's launch had been swept under the rug. Since then, Berry has acknowledged her crucial contribution in his own bio. Miss Ray, as Berry's second wife was known around Hitsville, led the Rayber Voices (a contraction of Raynoma and Berry), the vocal group that backed Marv Johnson, Barrett Strong, and other early stars on their first platters.

Born March 8, 1937 in Detroit, petite Raynoma Mayberry was a piano prodigy as a child, fluent in the classics as well as doo-wop and pop. She studied music theory at Cass Technical High School and tried to get a foothold in show business by recording her songs in the family basement. Still in her teens, she married and had a son, but the union was brief. At age 20, Ray refocused, winning an amateur show at the 20 Grand as a duet act with her sister Alice. Emcee Winehead Willie sent the pair over to see Berry Gordy, then just getting started himself.

Berry soon learned his next wife had perfect pitch and could write arrangements like a pro. "She was their right arm, because she was so musically intelligent. She wrote the first charts that I ever had to go on stage with for the band," said Mable John. "She sat on the floor at night on the back of her legs with just a pen and the manuscript paper, and wrote all of the charts, every part, for all of my music that I was going to perform at the Flame Show Bar. Not even with a piano, not with a tape, or anything. Just in her head."

"Ray was so nice," said the Andantes' Louvain Demps. "We'd go to United Sound, and she'd make sandwiches for everybody so nobody would be hungry. Before some of the guys got on their feet, she was doing that for them. She's just an incredible lady, but they don't talk about it too much. If it were not for her, a lot of the people would not be what they are today, because she actually taught music, and taught them how to read."

The Rayber Voices generally consisted of soprano Ray, tenors Brian Holland and Sonny Sanders, and bass Robert Bateman, though Louvain sometimes spelled Mrs. G, who married Berry in 1960. Ray also temporarily introduced an odd keyboard contraption called the Ondioline to the Motown soundscape. When she played it on the Tempts' "Dream Come True," it resembled a string section—sort of like a primitive synthesizer. Her contributions were vast.

"Ray was the one that was on the floor doing the directing at that time. 'Cause Berry—I mean, he'd come up with stuff, but he wasn't that musical. But it was Miss Ray. People don't say that, but that's true. She was the one that got the violins in there," said Louvain, noting Ray's violinist nephew Dale Warren Ossman often arranged for the label. "He had just came out of school." Under the alias of Little Iva and Her Band (this was a year before another Little Eva hit with "The Loco-Motion"), Ray had a Miracle single of her own in early 1961. "When I Need You" was a yearning ballad with definite teen pop overtones that she had written for Berry while recuperating from a miscarriage back in 1958. Raynoma exhibited a sweet, unaffected delivery on the heart-tugger, backed by the instrumental "Continental Strut."

Domestic difficulties forced Miss Ray's exile to New York in 1963 to open a Motown satellite office in the fabled Brill Building, with older brother Mike Ossman—a Jobete writer himself—assisting. The operation uncovered George Clinton, then fronting his Parliaments, and the Serenaders, whose George Kerr and Sidney Barnes wrote for Jobete prior to branching out. But the underfunded enterprise crashed when Raynoma bootlegged copies of Mary Wells' '64 smash "My Guy" to provide urgently needed capital.[9]

Busted and booted from Motown, the company that she had co-founded during happier times, she and new husband Ed Singleton relocated to Washington, D.C., and formed Shrine Records. Despite a batch of 45s during the mid-'60s, hits weren't forthcoming, and both went back to Motown in 1967. By decade's end, neither the marriage nor the Motown post would be in effect, though Ray's enduring ties to Berry resulted in a '70s Jobete stint in L.A.

HERMAN GRIFFIN

For a guy that never scored a hit at Motown or anywhere else, Herman Griffin's name pops up with some regularity whenever the history of Detroit R&B is recounted. His 1958 single "I Need You," cut for the obscure HOB logo (the acronym stood for House of Beauty; proprietor Carmen Murphy owned a Detroit hair salon), was the first Berry Gordy composition published by his own Jobete Music. It was also the first track of many to officially credit the Rayber Voices—a vocal backing group presided over by Berry's wife Raynoma.

Further, as Mary Wells' husband, Griffin reportedly masterminded her ill-fated decision to renounce her Motown contract and exit for greener pastures when she hit the age of 21 in 1964. Griffin's own pre-Motown discography included a '58 date for producer Robert West ("Dog Gone Shame" was a torrid rocker) and a

1960 single for Anna ("Hurry Up And Marry Me" paired with "Do You Want To See My Baby"). He hopped aboard Tamla in '60 for the mid-tempo churner "True Love" with "It's You" and switched to Motown in '62 for the dramatic uptown soul effort "Sleep (Little One)." He frequently conducted for Wells during her Motortown Revue segments, doing backflips while Mary sang ballads to the consternation of some Motown execs.[10]

Griffin didn't abandon his own singing career, popping up on Mercury in 1965 with the Van McCoy composition "Dream Girl" and its flip "Nothing Beats A Failure But A Try." The session resonated with Motown connections: Dale Warren, Raynoma Gordy's nephew, did the charts, and Andre Williams produced. Griffin passed away in the late '80s.

HEARTS OF STONE

Weldon McDougal wasn't Motown's only Philadelphia connection. Carl Cutler, who hailed from the City of Brotherly Love, fronted the Hearts of Stone, a vocal group that cut a 1970 album and two singles for V.I.P. John Myers, Floyd Lawson, and Lindsay Griffin rounded out the quartet.

"The other guys were from the South. I met them through my cousin. My cousin was on the road. They were singing in a carnival that traveled around the country," said Cutler, whose cousin danced with the same nomadic tent show. "They said that they needed another lead singer. And she said, 'Well, my cousin can sing! Y'all should come to Philly. When we get to Philly, I'll introduce you to him.' And I had a group at the time that I was singing with. They introduced me to 'em, and I said, 'No, I got a group.' We were singing at this old club, we were rehearsing for a show. And they came and they sang, the three of 'em came and sang, and they blew my mind. That's when I said, 'Okay, I'll sing with y'all! This is the kind of stuff I want to sing!'

"There was three of 'em at the time, and that made it the Four Pennies," said Cutler, born November 1, 1945. "I was the youngest. I was like the baby when I first got with 'em. They was like six to seven years older than me." The Four Pennies cut two 1966-67 singles for Brunswick, the first pairing "You Have No Time To Lose and "You're a Gas With Your Trash." "We did pretty good, but it didn't go too good. So then we went on the road for a little while. We went to Canada. We hooked up with another manager, Stephanie DeParis. We did a demo, and she sent it to various companies. Motown sent a telegram to us, and a matter of a couple of months later, we took a plane down to Detroit. They liked our music and the song we wrote, and recorded it. And we got a contract. They wanted to change the name, and we called ourselves the Hearts of Stone."

The Hearts of Stone's *Stop the World—We Wanna Get On*, from 1970.

Their new name wasn't inspired by Otis Williams & the Charms' 1954 smash of that title, but from the tough times the Four Pennies encountered while touring. "Going through things on the road, and sometimes not eating all you want to eat," said Cutler. "Sometimes I said, 'This here road gives me a heart of stone.' Then we said, 'Let's call ourselves the Hearts of Stone!'"

Hank Cosby produced the group for Motown. "He was the one who heard the demo. He said, 'Yeah, I want to work with these guys!'" said Cutler. Cosby shared writers' credit with Lawson and Myers on "It's A Lonesome Road," half the Hearts' V.I.P. debut single in September of '70. "Really, we wrote the song," said Cutler. "Back then in those days, you had to share one of them songs with the producer. You had to do it." Hank, his protege Joe Hinton, and Cosby's secretary Donna Sekulidis came up with the flip, "Yesterday's Love Is Over." The Hearts were involved in penning both sides of their V.I.P. encore, "If I Could Give You The World" and "You Gotta Sacrifice (We Gotta Sacrifice)," released in June of '71.

The group flew to Hitsville twice to record (a second LP went unissued). "It was really a pleasure and an experience for me," he said. "I was green. I was like the greenest one of 'em all. But it turned out that Hank gave me the most control. I was saying to myself, 'Why is he telling me?' Any other time my suggestions didn't work with the group, because I was the youngest, and I was the last one to come in the group. But when I got up there, it was turned around."

Their LP *Stop The World...We Wanna Get On* came out in October of 1970 and mixed originals with a wide array of covers encompassing Jobete copyrights (Jr. Walker's "What Does It Take [To Win Your Love]," Brenda Holloway's "You've Made Me So Very Happy") and outside hits by Brook Benton ("Rainy Night In Georgia"), Sly & the Family Stone ("Thank You [Falettin' Me Be Mice Elf Agin]"), and the Hollies' "He Ain't Heavy, He's My Brother."

"Hank had that track. He was doing that track for Chuck Jackson, and Chuck Jackson never got around to doing it. So he said, 'I've got a track that ain't doin' nothin',"' said Cutler of the latter. "I said, 'I want that song!' Because I used to try to get my group to sing it. They said, 'I don't want to sing that white-boy song!' I said, 'Man, do you hear them words?' I used to argue with 'em about trying to sing that song. When Hank said that, I jumped at it. I leaped in joy!" The other Hearts might have relented earlier had they known Dobie Gray cut an unissued version for White Whale before the Hollies discovered it. "I tried to do it twice," said Cutler. "I said, 'Hank, please let me do it one more time.' He said, 'Nope, nope. That's a cut! That's a cut!'"

The prospect of relocation helped break the Hearts. "They wanted us to move to Detroit, and I was down to move to Detroit. I said, 'Okay—that gets us closer, we've got more time, and we can get in with all the writers. They don't have to send for us, fly us down, when we're right there. We get the first pick.' They didn't want to leave. They didn't agree with me on that, so I lost on the vote," said Cutler. "I think I stayed with 'em about three years after that, and I started losing interest." There's a happy ending. Cutler now fronts a new edition of the Hearts of Stone, their polished harmonies delighting doo-wop and soul fans from Philly to Wildwood, N.J.

JOE HINTON

A Hank Cosby protege from Atlanta not to be confused with the veteran R&B vocalist who scored big in 1964 with a falsetto-soaked rendition of Willie Nelson's country ballad "Funny" for Don Robey's Houston-based Back Beat label, Motown's Joe Hinton vacillated between producing, writing, and singing during his stint at Hitsville. He cut a single for Soul, released in January of '71, that paired "Let's All Save The Children" with "You Are Blue." McDougal shepherded Joe and the Undisputed Truth onto Hy

Lit's popular Philly TV program one day to promote their respective singles. Hinton and the Andantes' Louvain Demps almost became a professional duo after both moved south following Motown's exodus from Detroit. "We kind of teamed up together, but the thing just didn't go. It just didn't work. I don't know what the formula was, but whatever it was, we didn't have it," said Demps.

HOLLAND-DOZIER-HOLLAND

Their names are so synonymous with Motown's golden years as monumentally successful writers and producer that their mere initials designate the ultimate in Hitsville excellence. When Holland-Dozier-Holland hit their stride in 1963-64, knocking out chart-topper after chart-topper for the Supremes and smashes for Martha & the Vandellas and the Four Tops, so did Motown. When the triumvirate exited in 1968 amidst legal unpleasantness, ultimately founding their Invictus and Hot Wax labels to challenge their ex-employers on their own turf, it sent Berry Gordy's empire into a momentary tailspin as fresh material grew scarce.

Detroit natives Brian Holland (born February 15, 1941), Lamont Dozier (born June 16, 1941), and Eddie Holland (born October 30, 1939) all started out as singers. Brian's 1958 debut "(Where's The Joy?) In Nature Boy" for the tiny Kudo logo (they billed him as "Briant") betrayed a shaky vocal command, but the bluesy rocker atoned with slinky guitar riffage and engaging enthusiasm. The intense Jackie Wilson-inspired blues ballad "Shock" on the 'B' side, written by Berry and his brother Robert, sported a stinging guitar solo and slightly off-key backing vocalists.

Lamont Dozier (left), Eddie Holland and Brian Holland teamed up to write many of Motown's biggest hits, including "Heat Wave," "Where Did Our Love Go," "Stop!, In the Name of Love," "Can I Get A Witness" and "How Sweet It Is (To Be Loved By You)." The Temptations and Supremes rose to stardom singing some of the trio's best material (Photo courtesy of BMI Archives Photo Collection).

Lamont's more extensive discography dated back to 1957, when his Romeos, whose ranks also included Ty Hunter, cut two singles for Fox: "Gone, Gone, Get Away" and "Fine, Fine Baby," the second picked up nationally by Atco. His 1960 solo debut for Anna as Lamont Anthony, "Popeye The Sailor Man," ran into flack from King Features which alleged unauthorized use of its cartoon legend's name,[11] so Dozier recut it as "Benny The Skinny Man" over the same rocking track. No such snafus marred his '61 Check-Mate 45 "Just To Be Loved."

Eddie was the only one to enjoy tangible success as a singer prior to their teaming up, his uncanny vocal resemblance to Jackie Wilson both a blessing and a curse. "That was his reason for being signed up. He was the first artist Mr. Gordy signed," said Janie Bradford. "Mr. Gordy wanted somebody, I guess, like Jackie, that he could build himself. And Eddie Holland had that voice. I think that's what hurt Eddie. Because he really has a great (voice). But I think at the time, Jackie was just kind of overshadowing him by being one step ahead of him already."

Lamont Dozier (left), Eddie Holland and Brian Holland were a hit-writing machine at Motown in the 1960s.

Gordy produced Eddie's '58 Mercury debut "You" before writing the ballad "Merry Go Round" for Eddie as Tamla's second release in 1959 (like Marv Johnson's "Come To Me," it was leased to United Artists). "It Moves Me," its Gordy/Billy Davis-penned 'B' side, was an upbeat entry with a socking backbeat and the Rayber Voices prominent. "Because I Love Her," his first UA follow-up, was a flute-encrusted ballad with little R&B input (the flip "Everybody's Going" was a rocking return to form). Berry wrote "Magic Mirror," a 1960 UA 45 spotlighting Eddie's tenor (like "Merry Go Round," Johnson would recut it for UA), and its violin-backed ballad flip "Will You Love Me." Holland closed out his hitless UA tenure with "The Last Laugh," yoked to Berry's lively "Why Do You Want To Let Me Go."

It didn't take long for Eddie to crack the hit parade upon returning to Motown. Written and first cut by Barrett Strong on the cusp of his temporary departure from Hitsville and Mickey Stevenson, "Jamie" opened with sumptuous strings, Holland offering an enthralling performance that vaulted to No. 6 on *Billboard's* R&B list in early 1962 and an impressive No. 30 pop.

"I wrote it for myself, but I left the company. The track was still there, so Eddie just overdubbed his vocal on it," said Strong. "He did a great job. By him singing it, it was my hit, too." "Take A Chance On Me," its Brian Holland/Freddie Gorman/Robert Bateman-penned flip, possessed similar appeal. "Jamie" would be Holland's top Motown seller as a singer. Brian and Mickey's "Last Night I Had A Vision" didn't chart, nor did an exotic "If Cleopatra Took A

Chance" in the spring of '62 ("What About Me," the forceful flip, was more effective).

That May, Motown issued Eddie's eponymous debut LP, mostly comprised of recent 45s but encompassing a driving "True Love Will Go A Mighty Long Way" (the work of both Hollands and Stevenson), the lovely "A Little Bit Of Lovin'," and the upbeat minor-key "Gotta Have Your Love." Both sides of Eddie's next single came from the LP: Holland's self-satisfied grunts intensified the Wilson parallels on "If It's Love (It's Alright)," a Brian Holland/Stevenson composition, while Mickey and George Fowler supplied the infectious 'B', "It's Not Too Late."

Sometime in 1962, Eddie's enthusiasm for performing began to fade. "I guess after his first hit record and album, he got out there and decided he didn't want to sing," said Gorman, who had been collaborating with Brian and Lamont. "He started to write. So then it became Holland-Dozier-Holland." Nevertheless, Eddie continued to record. Before year's end, his relaxed "Darling I Hum Our Song," one of the earliest H-D-H copyrights, elicited a splendid performance. Martha & the Vandellas got more mileage from it as the 'B' side of "Quicksand" the following year. Hand claps, a prominent vocal chorus, and plenty of horns powered "Baby Shake," a '63 outing modeled shamelessly on Wilson's "Baby Workout." Its 'B' side, "Brenda," struck much the same forlorn feel as "Darling I Hum Our Song," spiced by mournful trombone.

"What Goes Up–Must Go Down," credited to Holland-Dozier, was a strange piece of business. Lamont ostensibly supplied the comic monolog detailing the horrors of an unfaithful woman, the Andantes and Four Tops harmonizing behind him. Eddie's own "I Couldn't Cry If I Wanted To" reverted to the splendid ballad tradition that fall (the Tempts later weighed in with it as the flip to "[I Know] I'm Losing You"), with a torrid flip, "I'm On The Outside Looking In."

Eddie's recording fortunes went on the upswing in early '64. The scorching H-D-H-penned rocker "Leaving Here" was his first pop chart entry in two years, and a streamlined "Just Ain't Enough Love," another gem from the prolific triumvirate, followed suit that spring. The bubbly "Candy To Me" made it three minor hits in a row late that summer, and it also ended his Motown recording career: He had become too important as a wordsmith.

"He was the master," said Temptations guitarist Cornelius Grant. "Eddie Holland was probably the other person, other than Smokey, who was a master at putting together lyrics. I guess he just seemingly hasn't reached the prominence of Smokey because they finally had a parting of the ways with Motown. But the stuff with the Supremes will go on forever."

Lamont's confident "Dearest One," issued on Mel-O-Dy in the summer of 1962 (backed by "Fortune Teller Tell Me"), is generally credited as the first official H-D-H writing collaboration and must be one of a very few of their Motown copyrights not to hit. The trio embarked on an unparalleled string of smashes with Martha & the Vandellas, the Supremes, and the Four Tops cementing their reputation as the label's top production team.

Sometime in late '67 or early '68, H-D-H determined that they warranted a bigger piece of the corporate pie. They effectively went on strike, and soon lawsuits flew in both directions. When the legal smoke cleared, the trio inaugurated their own Invictus and Hot Wax labels, nailing a slew of hits with Freda Payne, the Chairmen of the Board, the Glass House, the Honey Cone, Laura Lee, and 100 Proof Aged in Soul, often employing the moonlighting Funk Brothers. They also reverted to being artists. Brian and Lamont teamed to score with "Don't Leave Me Starvin' For Your Love (Part 1)" in late '72 for Invictus, and Lamont's solo triumphs included "Why Can't We Be Lovers" in 1972 for Invictus and the 1973-74 hits "Tryin' To Hold On To My Woman," "Fish Ain't Bitin'," and "Let Me Start Tonite" on ABC. The prolific and still active triumvirate has long been based in L.A.

BRENDA HOLLOWAY

The way she stunningly filled a skintight gold pantsuit was what caught Berry Gordy's eye, but it was Brenda Holloway's seductive voice that made her Motown's first major Los Angeles discovery.

Born June 21, 1946, in Atascadero, California, and raised in Watts from age 2, Brenda and her younger sister (by two years) Patrice came up poor but immersed in music. "I grew up singing in church," she said. "I used to sing in the choirs and stuff, but I sang in school, too." She also studied violin in elementary and high school. "I just used to love the sound of a violin. The violins just take you away," she said. "I'd be outside in the backyard, and the dogs would be howling, and I would be playing my violin." The era's popular female singers were influential, too. "I listened to a lady by the name of Sarah Vaughan, and Dinah Washington, and Aretha Franklin, and Dionne Warwick, and Mary Wells," said Brenda. "Teresa Brewer, she was not a black artist, but she had a little cry in her voice. And my sister and I, we just developed that."

At the tender age of 12, Patrice made her first 45, a dance number called "Do The Del-Viking." "It was a local hit," said Brenda. "She was like 12 years old, and she liked to eat a lot of food. And she was real chubby. And she said, 'I'm gonna keep on eating 'cause I'm hungry, but you can dance, because Brenda, you have the figure! So you go ahead and do the dance, and I'm gonna go out and just sing.' So I said, "Okay.' So I went with her, and I was doing the dance and demonstrating the dance, and she was singing. And it went over very well."

Brenda, who sang with Whispers founders Walter and Wallace Scott in high school, didn't have to wait long to cut her solo debut. Record shop owner Kent Harris, who cut two hilarious 1956 singles for Crest as Boogaloo & His Gallant Crew (his "Clothes Line [Wrap It Up]" was the basis for the Coasters' "Shopping For Clothes"), helped bring Holloway to Del-Fi Records boss Bob Keane's attention. Keane cut Brenda's "Echo" for his Donna label in 1962, backed with "Hey Fool," and was so enraptured that he quixotically tried to break the ballad twice more, as "Echo-Echo-Echo" and then "More Echo."

She was also a member of the Wattesians, whose bouncy girl group confection "I'll Find Myself A Guy" came out on Donna the same year. Hal Davis, soon Motown's L.A. head, was instrumental in their formation. "Hal had put the group together with me, Priscilla Kennedy, Pat Hunt, and a girl named Barbara," said Brenda. As a prelude to their Motown collaborations, Davis and Holloway cut "It's You" with "Unless I Have You" as Hal & Brenda for Minasa in 1963. That same year, Brenda cut a solo "I Ain't Gonna Take You Back" for Catch.

Meeting Berry Gordy was Holloway's overriding goal when she and manager Davis attended a deejay convention at L.A.'s Cocoanut Grove. She decked herself out in a dazzling ensemble guaranteed to quicken pulses. "It was actually a gold lame pants set," she said. "(Hal) told me, 'I can get you an interview with Berry Gordy." I said, 'No you can't!' He said, 'Yes I can! I have a friend that's gonna be coming down. His name is Jack, and he's with Berry. I want you to come go with me on Saturday, and you can sing!' They had a lot of different suites and a lot of different people, and a lot of other disc jockeys.

"Then I started singing a song called 'My Guy,' 'cause I didn't have any songs of my own. I loved Mary Wells, and she was Miss Motown right from the beginning, so I kept going from room to room and meeting different people, and singing 'My Guy,'" said Brenda.[12] "We were there from about 10 o'clock in the morning. It was really early. I kept on singing until about 1 or 2 o'clock. I was like, 'Oh, Hal, this is ridiculous! I'm tired!' 'Cause I had on high heels, and I'm only 16 years old. I was trying to look grown and look cute and all that, but I was getting tired. In a minute this group of men had came in the room.

"I remember this little short man, he stood out in my mind. I didn't know who he was, but I told him, 'You know, I'm trying to meet Berry Gordy. Where is he? 'Cause I'm getting tired. I'm ready to go home, 'cause I've been here singing since early this morning.' So they went in the room, and he came back. He said, 'I am Berry Gordy!' I almost fell through the ground! I said, 'Huh?' He said, 'I am Berry Gordy. I really like the way you sing, and I want to sign you up. The only catch is that you're gonna have to graduate before I'll do anything with you.' I said, 'I can do that!' And he signed me up."

Holloway had a relatively brief but eventful stint as the darling of Motown, shining on ballads like "Every Little Bit Hurts."

Hal and partner Marc Gordon produced Brenda's first Tamla 45 in L.A., the stately masterpiece "Every Little Bit Hurts." "Frank Wilson was responsible. This guy named Ed Cobb wrote the song," said Brenda. "He did some songs for Ketty Lester, 'Love Letters.' And I really, really liked the song, but Frank Wilson's wife at the time, she did a demo. And I loved the way Barbara sang. I could never do this song justice, because they let Barbara do the demo, and you know I wasn't any competition for Barbara. I said, 'Let her do it!' They went, 'No, no! You can do it!' I said, 'No I can't!' So we were like feuding and fussing. Hal said, 'Well, I'm making the decision. You're gonna do it.' I'm like, 'Okay.' So at the session, he was fussing like he always did, and I was crying. Everybody said, 'How did you get that much feeling?' I said, 'Cause I was really crying. Hal made me mad!'"

"'Every Little Bit Hurts' was done at Armin Steiner's, which was his garage. Upstairs, he had converted it to a recording studio," said Wilson. The song bounded up to No. 13 on *Billboard's* pop charts in the spring of '64. But there was a tragic footnote: "Shortly after Barbara did the demo," said Brenda, "she died." Brenda wrote its flip, "Land Of A Thousand Boys," with Patrice. "Now you know why I wrote that one—I was looking for a perfect man!" she laughed.

Though Gordy generally harbored an aversion to anything set to a waltz time signature, the sumptuous "Every Little Bit Hurts" was too good to ignore. Dick Clark featured Brenda on *American Bandstand* and invited her to join his *Caravan of Stars* that summer. "It was fabulous," she said. "We did get tired, because we were traveling a lot on the bus. But Dick saw to it that even in the years when there was a lot of prejudice, if everybody couldn't eat at one place, then Dick would take us to the most fabulous restaurants. I don't eat steak now, because for 40 days I ate steak on the *Dick Clark Caravan of Stars!*"

Cobb, formerly of the Four Preps, penned another sublime ballad for Brenda's encore. Davis and Gordon again helmed "I'll Always Love You," which charted pop that summer on a smaller scale. Wilson wrote the spine-chilling flip, "Sad Song." Holloway's first and only Tamla album, *Every Little Bit Hurts*, was dominated by splendid ballads and found Holloway exploring the Jobete songbook as well as the chestnuts "Unchained Melody" and "Embraceable You," Wilson and Jeffrey Bowen's "Too Proud To Cry," Davis' "Can I," and her own "Suddenly."

Brenda inherited a few goodies left in the can when Wells defected on her 21st birthday. She also inherited Wells' producer, Smokey Robinson, who produced her sultry mid-tempo "When I'm Gone" in Detroit. "He let me hear Mary Wells' version," said Brenda, who was sorry to see one of her favorite singers exit. "I was sad, but I was happy that I got a chance to sing that song. 'Cause everybody wanted a song from William Robinson." Holloway and the Hitsville crew meshed seamlessly, and "When I'm Gone" became a solid hit in early '65.

Smokey delved into his cache of overlooked Wells gems again for "Operator," the flip of Mary's smash "Two Lovers" in 1962. It fit Brenda nicely, and she enjoyed a hit with it in mid-'65. Its jaunty 'B' side "I'll Be Available," was another of Smokey's metaphorically enriched gems that Wells had done just prior to leaving. "Smokey's a natural," Holloway said. "You just sing his song, you know it's going to be a hit, 'cause he's a poet. He's going to make it rhyme and reason and sound good and sexy and all that."

Brenda opened for the Beatles during their chaotic 1965 U.S. tour. "We couldn't even hear ourselves. We were in San Francisco, and the crowd got loose. Everybody said, 'Get out of there! Throw your wig away! Do whatever, just get out of there!' That wig came off. We went running! Because it was like a big herd of cattle, thousands and thousands of people, charging for the stage," said Brenda. "We were scared. Guitars and everything was going in the air!"

After that, her momentum sagged. Gordy's "You Can Cry On My Shoulder" never made it past "bubbling under" status in the fall, and Wilson's "Together 'Til The End Of Time," a ballad reuniting her with her boyfriend Davis and Gordon as producers, did no better in early '66. Mickey Stevenson and Hank Cosby took over for a dramatic "Hurt A Little Everyday" later that summer. "Where Were You," an up-tempo ditty from the Lewis Sisters, occupied the 'B' side. A second proposed album, *Hurtin' & Cryin'*, was canceled.

But Wilson reinvigorated his friend's chart fortunes in 1967 with the pounding "Just Look What You've Done For Me," a collaboration with R. Dean Taylor that just missed the R&B Top 20 that spring. "I wrote that for her before Berry asked me to move to Detroit. I didn't cut it until I got to Detroit," he said. It was paired with the Ashford & Simpson-penned rouser "Starting The Hurt All Over Again."

"I was so comfortable in his lyrics and his melodies. It was like a part of me. Frank's songs were a part of me. Smokey's songs I studied," she said. "But on Frank's I could be me, 'cause all the licks and all the curves and all the words and all the feelings, they were tailor-made, like Mary's songs were written by Smokey," she said.

Brenda co-wrote one of Jobete's most valuable copyrights, the exhilarating "You've Made Me So

Very Happy." "That's the song we wrote in Las Vegas," said Frank. "We were there for a business meeting for Motown, all of the staff and everybody was there. And I think one of our acts was playing Las Vegas as well. Brenda and Patrice were there, and she was working on a chorus, and so she had Berry listen to it. And Berry called me, and we got together and we wrote the song."

"Berry was giving me a few pointers on the tense of a song—like present tense. Your songs always have to come from the present tense," Holloway added. "Then my boyfriend quit me. I said, 'I'm so sad. You know what? I'm gonna write a song about being happy, 'cause this man is crazy! Leaving me?' I said, 'I'll show him,' like the new guy came into my life after this piece of trash left, and I was watching him leave!

"I said, 'Patrice, come here and help me. This is a hit!'" Soon Brenda and Patrice (who cut an unissued "For The Love Of Mike" for Motown) had the song worked out. "I got on the phone and said, 'Berry, I think I've got a hit! Berry, come on and listen to it!' He listened to it, I played it. He said, 'I think you got a hit. I'll be right over.'" Wilson handled the bridge. "That made the song!" she said. When Berry took her into the studio, Brenda was less than thrilled with the mellow tempo he wanted. "I was upset with Berry, because I didn't want to do the song like that," she said. "We were on the verge of the psychedelic, all that rock and funk and all of that. I'm like, 'Uh-uh, Berry, I want to do it different.' And then again, 'I'm Berry Gordy. You're Brenda Holloway. I'm putting up the money. We will do it the way I want it, thank you.'"

Seductive Brenda Holloway was Motown's first big West Coast artist. She got plenty of air play in the mid-60s with hits like "Operator," penned by Smokey Robinson.

Brenda's compelling rendition stalled after reaching the Top 40 in late '67, but Blood, Sweat & Tears' remake catapulted the rockers to gold record status a couple of years later. "I wanted to do it like Blood, Sweat & Tears," said Brenda. "Thank God for the other version!" laughed Wilson, who wrote the attractive 'B' side for Holloway, "I've Got To Find It."

It would be Hollway's last Motown release. She wrote a letter to Gordy confiding her suspicions that she was being discriminated against when it came to top material, grooming, TV opportunities, and management. The 21-year-old star bemoaned what she considered second-tier treatment because she hailed from the West Coast, though her postscript "I will always LOVE Motown and you!" suggested this was much less than an ultimatum.

"He took it as that. He had a lot of challenges, and he had a lot of artists besides me," she said. "Berry wanted me for Vegas, because I'm from L.A. And I wasn't interested in nothing but making some hits on the charts, Motown style. I don't want to wait for

Vegas. I'm only 19, 20 years old. Vegas is for old people. Vegas is for dancers. What am I doing? So Berry and I would constantly bicker about what he was trying to save me for. You know, you're so impatient when you're 19, 20. You don't know what you're doing. All you want to do is just do everything fast, and just stumble and fall over yourself. But anyway, we would conflict.

"For me to go to Motown and not get the immediate attention that I really needed to do my craft and my artistry, it just really, really staggered me. And I was just very, very unhappy. Because I was getting lost in the shuffle too many times. So I expressed that to Berry. He was getting ready to do something, but I just got so frustrated. So frustrated until—so you know I was crazy—I was in the middle of a session with Smokey, and left. I snuck out of the studio, got in a cab, and came back to Los Angeles.

"I was pulling a move that was not a stable one," she concluded. "I should have listened to the logic of Berry Gordy and just had patience and just waited. Because every promise that he made me, he fulfilled it." Brenda married Rev. Alfred Davis and disappeared from public life at the ripe old age of 22, though there was a 1972 single for H-D-H's Music Merchant label, "Let Love Grow" with "Some Quiet Place." Holloway officially reemerged in '95 to perform with Brenton Wood on the L.A. oldies circuit. In 1999, she was honored with a prestigious Pioneer Award by the Rhythm and Blues Foundation. That same year, Fantasy's Volt subsidiary released Brenda's first new domestic secular album in 35 years, *It's a Woman's World.*

Brenda's secular pursuits contrast with her sanctified activities as a member of Blinky Williams' Hollywood Choir. "I'm doing fine. I'm happy, I'm secure, I'm still singing," she reported. And she still looks great in gold.

THE HORNETS/ JOHNNY POWERS

The Beatles were busting out all over in early 1964, and the Hornets might have been Motown's homegrown response if they'd been willing to sacrifice their hair for the company. Strictly a studio creation, the Hornets' only V.I.P. release that February paired "Give Me A Kiss" and "She's My Baby," Clarence Paul sharing production duties with Andre Williams.

"We didn't do gigs like that," said Johnny Powers, half of the Hornets along with Mike Valvano of Mike & the Modifiers (who cut "I Found Myself A Brand New Baby" for Gordy in '62). "Mike was writing the songs. We just did it in the studio. They tried to come up with a name. I guess Berry came up with the Hornets." Johnny insists the Fab Four weren't their inspiration. "It was not a spinoff from the Beatles, it was just a fun thing we just screwed around in the studio and did," he said. "They wanted to put us out as the Hornets. The reason why we didn't go out was because Berry wanted us to shave our heads!" Johnny and Mike were good friends. "We met at Motown," noted Powers. "And then we produced together, hung together."

Undoubtedly the only artist to record for both Motown and Sun, Powers was the first white singer at Hitsville. The label never released any of his solo stuff, but Johnny filled a number of important support roles, adding foot stomps to several Supremes classics and banging tambourines with Valvano. "There was a lot of things done down there—slappin' two-by-fours, there was shakin' stuff. There was just all kind of effects we used down there," he said.

Born in East Detroit in 1938, John Pavlik grew up in Utica, Michigan, on a nourishing diet of country music. When Elvis got hot, Johnny eagerly volunteered for the rockabilly brigade, debuting on Fortune in 1957 with "Honey Let's Go (To A Rock And Roll Show)" and "Your Love." "I was young. Fortune was kind of the company around town that was really making a little noise," he said. "I think I went down on my own, and decided to cut a record. I paid 'em a hundred bucks." Fortune boss Devora Brown decreed Pavlik wasn't a proper stage moniker. "They said I had to change my name. I was eating a candy bar, and they asked what kind of candy bar I was eating. I said a Powerhouse. They said, 'That's your name—Johnny Powers!'"

Johnny cut another barnburner for the local Fox diskery ("Long Blond Hair, Red Rose Lips" backed with "Rock Rock") in '58. "That was George Braxton. He owned a real estate company. Just didn't have the knowledge of how to bring a record in. Didn't have enough money, I guess," said Powers. "'Long Blond Hair' started taking off, and then it just never did happen." One of his demos found its way onto Sam Phillips's desk, and Johnny went to Memphis in August of '59 to wax "With Your Love, With Your Kiss" and its flip "Be Mine All Mine," his only Sun biscuit.

"When I signed at Sun, that was kind of at the end of the Sun Records rope," he said. "Sam was slowly unwinding the company." Nevertheless, Phillips recruited a stellar house band for the date: Saxist Martin Willis, bassist Billy Lee Riley, and pianist Charlie Rich were on hand.

Motown signed the young rocker to a five-year pact in 1960. "I knew Berry from before, 'cause every time I was out there promoting records doing record hops, Berry would be there with Jackie Wilson or something. It was getting kind of funny, 'cause every time we'd turn around, we'd keep bumping into each other," he said. "The guy that was handling me at the time was working for Motown," said Powers. "He asked me if I would just consider going there. I said I didn't want to go there because it was just a local label. I said, 'Sun Records

Johnny Powers, who teamed with Mike Valvano to form The Hornets, was the first white singer at Motown (Photo courtesy of Johnny Powers).

to that? Seems like going backwards instead of going forward,' not knowing what was going on there. Anyway, the guy brought me there, and I said, 'Okay, I'll sign a deal.' It was a great experience for me."

During his last years at Hitsville, Johnny began moonlighting in production at another studio. When his Motown contract expired in 1965, he left to join them full-time. "We were all a family, and we all got along real good together and became very close friends. It was a good thing there, but it was not working for me as far as the type of music that was happening back then," said Powers. "They would have the sessions cut before I would even get there, and then try to put my voice on. It didn't work for me. I'm used to having the music wrapped around me, and not me around the music. Sometimes you'd get in the wrong key. It just wasn't working out, so I decided to start producing records."

Johnny reemerged as a rockabilly ambassador during the '80s, touring Europe frequently. He's still in demand overseas as well as around his Utica home base.

IVY JO HUNTER

"There was another guy over there during that time that brought the funk in Motown called Ivy Hunter," said the Pips' William Guest. "Ivy never did get the recognition. Isn't that amazing?" Agreed fellow Pip Bubba Knight, "Everybody recorded his songs, but he don't get the recognition."

Indeed, it is surprising that Ivy George Hunter's Motown legacy isn't more widely revered. Hunter distinguished himself during his long Hitsville tenure as a producer, songwriter, and singer. He made a 1970 album, *Ivy Jo Is In This Bag*, that was canceled prior to release, although V.I.P. did issue two 45s, "I Remember When (Dedicated To Beverly)" with "Sorry Is A Sorry Word" and a '71 encore, "I Still Love You" with "I Can Feel The Pain," credited to Ivy Jo.

"I was the one that brought Ivy Jo to Motown. I found him walking around in Lee's Sensation. That's where I met him," said Hank Cosby. "Ivy Jo had to do his own thing."

Hunter grew up in the Motor City, attending Cass Tech before joining the Army. He auditioned for Mickey Stevenson as a vocalist but was channeled into writing. His greatest victory came when he co-wrote Martha & the Vandellas' '64 smash "Dancing In The Street." Though he wrote or co-wrote a plethora of other Motown classics, often in cahoots with Stevenson—the Four Tops' "Ask The Lonely" and "Loving You Is Sweeter Than Ever" (the latter with Stevie Wonder), Marvin Gaye's "You," the Marvelettes' "I'll Keep Holding On," the Spinners' "I'll Always Love You," the Isley Brothers' "Behind A Painted Smile"—the dreadlocked Hunter never equaled the impact of that immortal Martha & The Vandellas anthem.

"He kind of rebelled against the system. Said he ain't gonna cut his hair until he got a hit. I was hoping he got a hit soon, 'cause his hair got a little out of hand there for a minute," said G.C. Cameron. "But a brilliant cat. He was a man who had a brain to think, and could orchestrate things." He kept writing and producing after Motown left town—and did eventually trim his locks.

WILLIE HUTCH

Long before he joined its roster, Willie Hutch was making Motown records. Or records that sounded like it, anyway. His late '60s productions for Mickey Stevenson's Venture Records were so skillfully modeled on the Hitsville formula that you'd swear they were tracked at Studio A. That made him a natural choice to join Motown's L.A. community during the '70s.

Born December 6, 1944, in the City of Angels, Willie McKinley Hutchison spent his high school years around Dallas, making it back to the Coast after a hitch in the Marines. He initially made his mark as an L.A. soul writer, co-penning the Marvellos' "Something's Burnin'" with producer Marc Gordon for Warner Brothers' Loma logo in 1966 and scribing "I'll Be Loving You Forever" and "Train Keep On Movin'" by the Versatiles for Johnny Rivers' Soul City imprint the same year (the group soon changed its name to the 5th Dimension). But Hutch had a voice, too, as evidenced by his '69 debut LP *Soul Portrait* for RCA.

Hal Davis woke Hutch up late one night in dire need of lyrics to go with a song title that he'd laid tracks for. Willie was up to the challenge, and even before "I'll Be There" became a mega-hit for the Jackson 5 in 1970, he was part of the West Coast Motown team. Hutch's first Motown hit as a performer in the spring of '73, "Brother's Gonna Work It Out," and its equally potent follow-up "Slick" were from his soundtrack for the blaxploitation film *The Mack* (he performed the same function for Pam Grier's *Foxy Brown*). The light-fingered guitarist scored two hits in '75, "Get Ready For The Get Down" and the Top Ten R&B hit "Love Power," and "Party Down" did very well for him the next year. After supplying Motown with highly engaging soul for most of the decade, Hutch moved over to Whitfield Records in 1978.

THE ISLEY BROTHERS

Like Gladys Knight & the Pips and Chuck Jackson, the Isley Brothers joined Motown in mid-career, after they had enjoyed sustained success on their own terms. "The Isley Brothers were producers," said McDougal. "Now, all of a sudden, they were being produced." Their holy-roller brand of gymnastic, fire-breathing excitement was perhaps too frenzied for the label's carefully crafted credo. Their 1965-1969 tenure resulted in five chart entries, "This Old Heart Of Mine (Is Weak For You)" the only genuine smash.

In their earliest secular years, the Cincinnati-based Isleys could have been mistaken for a gospel act, so sanctified was their incendiary presentation. Lead singer Ronald Isley (born May 21, 1941) and his older brothers O'Kelly (born December 25, 1937) and Rudolph (born April 1, 1939) developed their vocal attack at Cincy's First Baptist Church. There was a fourth brother in the group, but Vernon was hit and killed by a motorist while riding his bicycle in 1954. The devastated trio carried on, taking their doo-wopping ambitions to New York in 1956. Among their idols were the Dominoes, Drifters, and Diablos. They cut 45s for Teenage, Mark-X, Gone ("The Drag"), and Cindy without setting the world on fire.

That changed abruptly when RCA Victor brought the Isleys on board. Their second 45 for Nipper's master was the blazing two-parter "Shout," which conjured up the unbridled excitement of a Baptist revival meeting and gave them their first hit in 1959. It inaugurated a frustrating trend for the trio—their originals were invariably outdone on the charts by covers (Joey Dee & the Starliters' '62 revival of "Shout" far outsold the Isleys). Producer Bert Berns handed the Isleys "Twist And Shout," which had stiffed in a previous incarnation by the Top Notes on Atlantic, and their fiery screams, poured over a brassy Latin rhythm, gave the Isleys a smash for Wand Records in '62 (typically, the number is now more closely associated with the Beatles). Another Wand rocker, "Twistin' With Linda," kicked up some chart noise later that year, though the classic "Nobody But Me" would await hit status until the Human Beinz revived it in '67.

Seldom remaining with one label for long, the Isleys moved on to United Artists, where they waxed the first version of "Who's That Lady" in '64, and Atlantic, where some of their sides featured the wild licks of unknown young guitarist Jimi Hendrix. They also briefly established their own T-Neck Records (named after their adopted homebase in New Jersey) to unleash the two-part "Testify," but the time wasn't quite right for that enterprise to take off.

Looking for a way to maximize their profile in the pop market, the Isleys cast their lot with Tamla in late 1965. They got down to business under the supervision of Motown's hottest writing/production team, Holland-Dozier-Holland, and nailed a smash their first time out with a pile-driving "This Old Heart Of Mine (Is Weak For You)," a No. 6 R&B and No. 12 pop smash in early '66. Its mid-tempo flip, "There's No Love Left," showcased another exciting lead by Ronnie.

Robert Gordy must have dug the Isleys' pre-Motown output. Berry's younger brother co-wrote and produced the Isleys' Tamla encore "Take Some Time Out For Love" in a shrieking "Twist And Shout" motif that captured their unique call-and-response excitement better than anything else they did for Motown. The rocker only lightly dented the pop charts in the spring of 1966. H-D-H provided the lovely flip, "Who Could Ever Doubt My Love," tailor-made for Ronnie's shivering tenor. A month later they tried another H-D-H gem, "I Guess I'll Always Love You." Blessed with an unstoppable glide and a burbling baritone sax solo ostensibly by Mike Terry similar to the one on "This Old Heart Of Mine," it should have done better than the middle reaches of the pop and R&B hit lists that summer.

H-D-H saw no reason to waste precious originals on the Isleys' first Tamla album, 1966's *This Old Heart of Mine*. Nearly everything had been previously tackled by other Motown luminaries: "Nowhere To Run," "Stop! In The Name Of Love," "I Hear A Symphony," "Baby

O'Kelly, Rudolph and Ronald Isley had already hit it big with "Shout" before joining Tamla in 1965.

Don't You Do It." The Isleys beat the Supremes to "Put Yourself In My Place" by a couple of months, though it would associate itself more closely with Diana's girls as the flip of "You Can't Hurry Love" (the Isleys' was a sizable British hit in mid-'69). The blistering "Seek And You Shall Find" was enriched by Rudolph and Kelly's churchy harmonies and raucous horn blasts.

"This Old Heart of Mine (Is Weak for You)" was the biggest hit for the Isleys during their five-year Motown run.

Custody of the Isleys next went to Hunter, whose more aggressive approach characterized "Got To Have You Back," the Isleys' first single of '67 and a minor hit that spring. Norman Whitfield stepped in to helm their next offering: "That's The Way Love Is" received a torrid dance treatment with punching trumpets and a tough backbeat, 180 degrees removed from the throbbing treatment the producer fashioned for Marvin Gaye's '69 smash version. It somehow avoided the charts altogether that summer, paired with Ivy's pretty "One Too Many Heartaches."

*Soul on the Rock*s, released in the fall of '67, was an improvement from a standpoint of both original material and dynamic execution. Other than a faithful interpretation of "Whispers (Gettin' Louder)," Jackie Wilson's '66 Brunswick smash, and an unexpected assault on Paul Revere & the Raiders' garage rocker "Good Thing," the LP overflowed with fresh songs. Berry Gordy and Smokey Robinson collaborated on "It's Out Of The Question," while "Behind A Painted Smile" from Ivy Jo and Beatrice Verdi opened with a flowery "Love Is A Many-Splendored Thing" quote before breaking into a rambunctious gait. "Behind A Painted Smile" was a massive hit in England, nearly equaling "This Old Heart Of Mine." Hunter's "Why When Love Is Gone" sported a guitar-bass unison intro, "Save Me From This Misery" percolated over a mid-tempo groove, and "Catching Up On Time"—by Clarence Paul, Leon Ware, and Morris Broadnax—was a torrid rocker. Johnny Bristol and Harvey Fuqua were behind "Tell Me It's Just A Rumor Baby." "It never got a lot of excitement from the company," said Bristol of the latter.

If it worked for sultry Kim Weston—as it did so resoundingly in 1965—why couldn't the relentless "Take Me In Your Arms (Rock Me A Little While)" do the same for the Isleys? With Brian Holland and Lamont Dozier behind the glass, their redo packed much the same punch yet proved only a moderate hit during the spring of '68. Frank Wilson wrote and produced "All Because I Love You," issued that fall.

Ready to regain complete artistic control, the Isleys left Motown to relaunch T-Neck, a move paying immediate dividends in 1969 when their funk-drenched "It's Your Thing" gave the group its first million-selling R&B chart-topper (it nearly did the same on the pop lists). Joined by younger brothers Ernie and Marvin, the

Isleys would reign as one of the first families of funky soul throughout the '70s, their track record substantiating they really did know best how to create their own singular sound. Motown tried to capitalize on their increased visibility in '69 by throwing together a third album shamelessly titled *Doin' Their Thing.*

Kelly Isley died in his sleep of a heart attack on March 31, 1986, at age 48, a tragedy that spurred Rudolph to retire from secular music in favor of preaching the gospel. Ronald remains eminently capable of torching any house with his melismatic pipes.

CHUCK JACKSON

Signing urbane uptown soul singer Chuck Jackson in 1967 should have been a coup for Motown, in view of his track record as a proven hit maker. Perplexingly, the partnership never really took flight.

Born in Winston-Salem, North Carolina, on July 22, 1937, Chuck was raised in Latta, South Carolina, and started out as a young gospel singer. "When I was like 8 or 9 years old, I had a radio show every Sunday morning," he said in a 1996 interview. "I would play the piano and sing." At 13, he moved to Pittsburgh. A college scholarship wooed him back to South Carolina for a time, but the Steel City eventually won out.

"When I got there, there was a girl I had written a song about. Her name was Willette. I took it to this guy—somebody told me about a guy that owned a record store, and he sold records. But he managed groups. I went down, and at that time, he had the Dell-Vikings. And I auditioned for him, and he recorded me on 'Willette.'" Jackson joined the Dell-Vikings not long after they scored with "Come Go With Me" and "Whispering Bells" in 1957. The group thrived for a time despite a tangled web of personnel and label changes. He led the Dell-Vikings on "Willette" for Joe Averbach's Fee Bee label, and fronted their rocking "Cold Feet." Averbach recognized Jackson's solo potential, cutting a few sides that were endlessly reissued once he broke through.

It was Jackie Wilson that handed Jackson his big break, offering the promising young singer a slot as his opening act when the Dell-Vikings shared a 1960 bill with Mr. Excitement at the Howard Theater in Washington, D.C. "I joined him at the Apollo Theatre maybe a month later. Scepter Records saw me there. It was the first date that I played with him. Scepter Records saw me and asked me if I would sign. I said yes. That was Luther Dixon and Florence Greenberg," said Jackson. "Luther Dixon was a very charming man. And he said to me, 'We don't have the money to promote you like those other companies that we know have been back here to see you. But we will go 100 yards for you, and we will form a label for you.' They sounded so sincere, man, and they were so small. I figured, if these guys make it, I make it."

It was the right move. The swirling, strings-enhanced uptown soul sound was the rage in New York, and Jackson's awesome baritone was tailor-made for such a sophisticated setting. With Dixon at the helm, "I Don't Want To Cry," Jackson's first offering for Scepter's Wand subsidiary in early '61, catapulted to the R&B Top Five and notched sizable pop sales. Arranged by Carole King and written by Jackson and Dixon, it touched on Chuck's real-life romance woes.

"I was in Philadelphia, and I was seeing this lady. And she was seeing one of the Flamingos. She was much older than I was, and so was the Flamingo. So I came to her apartment one day. I had a key. I was on my way upstairs, and I heard somebody shoot down the other stairs," he laughed. "I knew that she had been seeing him, but they was supposed to have broken up. Anyway, I found out later that it was him. So I left.

"Luther, after the show was over at the Apollo, a few weeks later we were in the house and he was saying, 'Just tell me—I want you to tell me the worst thing that ever happened to you, and that's what we're gonna write about.' So I said, 'There was this woman in Philadelphia, and I went to her house, and this guy ran down the back stairs, and I was so hurt, but I didn't want to cry.' He said, 'That's it! I don't want to cry!' He had a guitar, and we started writing."

Composer Burt Bacharach came to revere Jackson, handing him the major hits "I Wake Up Crying" (1961, co-written by Hal David) and Chuck's top seller, the resplendent "Any Day Now (My Wild Beautiful Bird)," co-penned with Bob Hilliard, in the spring of '62. "(Bacharach and Hilliard) came over and told Florence they would pull the track from them and wouldn't release the song if they put anybody on it other than me," said Jackson. "That's how I got it."

Jackson's string of hits for Wand extended to the dramatic "Tell Him I'm Not Home" in '63, a teasing "Beg Me" the next year, and a 1965 duet remake of Chris Kenner's "Something You Got" with Maxine Brown that pierced the R&B Top Ten. But with Dixon moving to greener pastures (ex-Motown singer Herman Griffin briefly produced Chuck) and the hits growing less bountiful, Jackson closed out his Wand tenure and in September of 1967 signed with Motown.

Chuck Jackson was a big-time performer when he arrived at Motown in 1967, but the likeable South Carolina native never hit on the right formula with writers and company brass and ultimately found more success elsewhere.

By the following February, his first single for the firm, a sparkling remake of the Miracles' "(You Can't Let The Boy Overpower) The Man In You," hit the shelves. "Smokey knew how to cut me," said Jackson. "When I first went to Motown, he was the first one to cut me. Because he was the reason I went. I mean, Smokey had been on me for years to go to Motown. When I got there, he had that ready for me. So we went right in and recorded that the first week I was there." James Jamerson's bass line rumbled and wriggled as Chuck sang the hell out of Robinson's macho advisory, yet the superb track barely scratched the pop charts. With Al Cleveland his partner, Smokey also supplied the 'B' side, "Girls, Girls, Girls." Chuck hit high notes worthy of an opera singer, his diction impeccable.

Chuck Jackson Arrives! was the singer's first Motown LP (we must assume they meant "arrives" in the Motor City, since he'd arrived as a star seven years previous).

Chuck Sings Jobete might have been more accurate: Ivy Jo Hunter and Stevie Wonder had previously laid "What Am I Gonna Do Without You" on Martha & The Vandellas, the H-D-H-penned "I Like Everything About You" had surfaced on the Four Tops' second album, and "Your Wonderful Love," "Ain't No Sun Since You've Been Gone," and "Lonely, Lonely Man Am I" were associated with the Tempts.

Jackson waited more than 13 months for the label to try again for a hit. The odds of breaking Bert Berns' incendiary "Are You Lonely For Me Baby" so soon after Freddie Scott's shattering original R&B chart-topper in 1966 were remote, yet Jackson's bang-up remake proved a sizable seller in the spring of '69. Jimmy Webb's "Honey Come Back" cracked the R&B hit lists for Jackson that fall, though Glen Campbell picked up the pop spins.

The oddly titled '69 LP *Goin' Back to Chuck Jackson* contained more recycled gems: The Four Tops' "Loving You Is Sweeter Than Ever" and "You Keep Running Away," the Tempts' "No More Water In The Well," and two recent hits from outside the Jobete catalog, Tyrone Davis' pleading "Can I Change My Mind" and Joe Simon's "The Chokin' Kind." "I like that album a lot," said Jackson. "I had a few things at Motown that was really good. But you have to go and look for it. I loved the Tyrone Davis thing I covered, and 'The Chokin' Kind.'" "Rosalind," "Can You Feel It Baby," and Ashford and Simpson's "Cry Like A Baby" worked pretty well, too.

Jackson was a victim of highway robbery when his late '69 outing "The Day My World Stood Still"—the handiwork of Smokey, Cleveland, and ex-Flamingo Terry Johnson—avoided the charts. Chuck sounded at the end of his rope, emoting over strings and insistent guitar. Its flip, "Baby, I'll Get It," was every bit as expressive in a cheerier mode. It came out on V.I.P. rather than Motown, as did his last two 45s for the company, the brass-leavened "Two Feet From Happiness" with "Let Somebody Love Me" in early '70 and "Pet Names" with "Is There Anything Love Can't Do" at the dawn of 1971.

The uptown soul approach came back into play on Jackson's '70 V.I.P. album *Teardrops Keep Fallin' on My Heart*. "I'll Fight ('Til I Win Your Love)," "Just A Little Love (Before My Life Is Gone)," and "I Can't Let My Heaven Walk Away" were right in Jackson's wheelhouse, as were Smokey's "Have You Heard About The Fool" and Brook Benton's Tony Joe White-penned hit "Rainy Night In Georgia." Even B.B. King's minor-key blues "The Thrill Is Gone" clicked.

Jackson left Gordy's empire soon thereafter, scattering hits on ABC, All Platinum, and EMI American. He remains a spellbinding performer, still capable of rattling any venue's rafters. "It was a bad move to go to Motown," he said. "Motown was not a Chuck Jackson record company. They didn't know the New York sound. I'm not talking about the studios now, I'm talking about the singer. They didn't know how to cut me. I'm sure that was a lot of it.

"They always cut their singers octaves higher than they actually sang. That's why a lot of people there, when you would see 'em in person, when they'd bring 'em down to where they were supposed to be, it was a different sound in their voices. Because they would always cut you out of your range. And when they tried to cut me out of my range, I started to really scream. It just didn't work."

JAY & THE TECHNIQUES

"Robot Man," Jay & the Techniques' only Gordy release from late 1972 (backed with "I'll Be Here"), doesn't rate high in lead singer Jay Proctor's book of musical memories.

"I don't know how that Motown thing came about. We only did one record, and actually, I didn't even lead that one," he said in 1995. "I think (producer) Jerry Ross called me sometime in the '70s. He said, 'Motown wants to sign you to do a couple of things.' And they had this song, 'Robot Man.' And I absolutely hated it. I wouldn't even sing it. One of the other guys sang it. And they put it on the Motown label. We just did that one record, and that was it."

"Robot Man" didn't feature many (if any) original members of the integrated group from Allentown, Pennsylvania, that hit huge in 1967 with Ross's cheery Philly soul productions "Apples, Peaches, Pumpkin Pie" and "Keep The Ball Rolling" for Mercury's Smash subsidiary. Born October 28, 1940, in Philadelphia, Proctor grew up immersed in doo-wop tradition. "I did start singing on the street corners when I was a little boy," he said. "Even with the bigger guys, because I sounded like a little girl when I was a kid. I was fortunate enough to be able to carry a tune at a young age, so they used to come get me to lead some songs for 'em.

"I was in a group called the Sinceres. It was a mixture of Allentown boys and some boys from Bethlehem. A boy named Billy Floyd wrote a song called 'You're Too Young.' We were all like doo-woppers. We used to practice at his house all the time. There was a guy who owned a paint company, and he decided he would like to see what he could do with us. He took us underfoot for a little bit, and he paid for having a record recorded and stuff. I think it sold about 100 copies, and I know my mom got at least 99 of 'em." Backed with "Forbidden Love," it was issued on the Jordan logo in 1960. "That was the name of the paint company, Jordan Paint."

Jay & the Techniques came together informally a few years later. "A friend of mine, Lucky Lloyd, who was the other lead singer at the time with me, he and I used to walk around the streets singing a lot in Allentown," said Proctor. "Another friend of ours walked up to us one day and asked us if we'd like to be in his group. We said sure. So we went over there, and there was a whole houseful of people, man. I mean, lots of singers and musicians and the whole bit. That's pretty much how it all started, actually. A lot of people try to give me credit for starting the group, but that's not the case. I really joined someone else's group. And what happened was, even the guy whose group it was, he eventually dropped out. And we just whittled it down until we got the six guys, seven guys that became known as Jay & the Techniques."

A girl named Barbara Carter gave the integrated outfit its name. "The guy that asked us to join the group, that was his cousin. We were sitting around trying to figure out a name, and she was looking in a magazine. And it said something about techniques in it. She said, 'Oh, how about the Techniques?' She was laughing and joking about it. I said, 'That sounds pretty good.' Everybody said, 'Yeah, that ain't bad! The Techniques!'"

An Allentown deejay set the group up with a demo session at Philly's Cameo-Parkway Records. "Jerry Ross was there. That's how we met Jerry, at Cameo-Parkway. As luck would have it, he really liked the group. In particular, he liked my singing. He said, 'I'm on my way to Mercury Records, and I'm going to take you guys with me.' That's how we got on Mercury," said Jay. "He gave us 'Apples, Peaches, Pumpkin Pie.'" Proctor didn't dig the bubbly ditty initially. "No, not at all. It wasn't soulful enough for me. I didn't care for it that much. But I wanted to make records, and I figured this man must know. He had Spanky & Our Gang and Keith and he had all those people, so I said, 'Hey, I'll do it.'" The number broke into the pop Top Ten in mid-'67 and got the group on Ed Sullivan's show.

Before year's end, they had another smash with "Keep The Ball Rollin'." "The gentlemen that wrote it, Sandy Linzer and Denny Randell, they came in and played it right at the session. I was doing another session, and they came in and they wanted Jerry to hear it, and they got on the piano. Of course, I didn't like that one, either," said Proctor. "Then when Jerry got hold of it, and the arrangers got hold of it, and I went in and did the actual recording, I couldn't believe it was the same song. I grew to really like it a lot." Jay & the Techniques scored two lesser hits for Smash in 1968, "Strawberry Shortcake" and "Baby Make Your Own Sweet Music," stayed at Smash until decade's end before moving to Motown. Today Jay is a perennial draw on the Carolina beach music circuit.

JAZZ CRUSADERS

Mixing Gulf Coast R&B and blues into their bebop jazz excursions made the Jazz Crusaders a force to be reckoned with during the 1960s, though it didn't please the jazz critics.

Pianist Joe Sample, drummer Nesbert "Stix" Hooper, tenor saxist Wilton Felder, and trombonist Wayne Henderson—the core Crusaders—were Houston natives and grew up grooving to both genres. When they came together as a unit, their approach reflected that cooking hybrid. Moving to L.A. in 1958 (when they gigged as the Modern Jazz Sextet), they found the going rough before signing with Richard Bock's Pacific Jazz Records. They released their first album, *Freedom Sound*, as the Jazz Crusaders in 1961. Several more—*Lookin' Around* and *The Thing* in '62, *Stretchin' Out* in '64, 1966's *Powerhouse*—followed at regular intervals.

They joined the Chisa roster in 1970, releasing the album *Old Socks New Shoes, New Socks Old Shoes* and a single, "Way Back Home," that illustrated their R&B leanings (it would be made into a hit by Motown saxman Jr. Walker the following year). A 1971 Chisa encore set, *Pass the Plate*, harbored a potential hit in its title track, coupled on 45 with "Greasy Spoon." Their name was an obstacle when McDougal tried to promote "Pass The Plate" as a crossover item. "It was an R&B record. So I would go to all the stations—mainly in Texas. So I went to Houston, and I said, 'I've got a record by the Jazz Crusaders.' He said, 'But we don't play jazz on this station.' I said, 'Man, this record is not jazz! It's just their name.' He said, 'Man, I'm sorry. I can't play it!' So he played the record. He said, 'Man, the record ain't bad, but their name, Jazz Crusaders—I just can't play it.' So then I had a meeting with them in L.A. and I told 'em, 'Man, I'm having trouble getting the record played because your name is the Jazz Crusaders. Why don't you just call it Crusaders?' Next thing I knew, it was Crusaders." When Mowest issued "Spanish Harlem" with "Papa Hooper's Barrelhouse Groove" in late '72, the Crusaders it was (by then, they had exited the company).

Whether Weldon's advice had any bearing on the name alteration or not, the Crusaders racked up the R&B hits "Put It Where You Want It" in 1972 and "Don't Let It Get You Down" the next year, even garnering pop spins. Unfortunately, they were no longer on Chisa, having jumped to Blue Thumb. All four core members also logged countless hours as top L.A. session musicians during the '70s and beyond. And once they no longer labeled themselves as such, even the stuffy jazz cognoscenti figured them out.

MABLE JOHN

Who was Motown's first solo chanteuse? If you guessed Mary Wells, try again. Diminutive dynamo Mable John's 1960 debut "Who Wouldn't Love A Man Like That" shipped a few months before Wells set the airwaves ablaze with her gritty "Bye Bye Baby."

Born November 3, 1930, in Bastrop, Louisiana, Mable was the oldest of 10 kids in a highly musical family. The Johns relocated to Cullendale, Arkansas, when Mable was 3 months old, then moved again to Detroit when she was 12. Along with her talented siblings, she initially performed gospel music in local houses of worship. "We sang in churches, and for all kinds of musical programs," said John in 1999, noting they sang material by "the Dixie Hummingbirds, the Soul Stirrers, the Blind Boys—everybody that was singing and that was out there at that time."

Mable first crossed paths with the matriarch of the Gordy clan while working for her Friendship Mutual Insurance Company after school, yet it wasn't Mrs. Gordy who introduced Mable to her son. Once the two did join musical forces, the struggling songwriter and the young singer hit it off beautifully, Gordy taking a personal interest in shaping and sharpening John's act. "I really got started with grooming in '56," she said. "And then I was groomed for a whole year before I did anything anywhere. Because that was Berry's motto—to make you an act and not a gimmick. He wanted you to be an artist, not someone that had to have a record to be recognized or to perform to get a job.

"He was so good with me until I became crippled. I absolutely could not perform unless Berry was on stage playing piano for me, until one night with Billie Holiday. He decided to just stay away for the first show and not show up. And I had to go on without him being at the piano. And from then on, he never played piano for me again. He said that if I could only sing with him playing, that means that I wasn't ready for the business."

Those two weeks opening for Holiday at the fabled Flame Show Bar were important to building Mable's confidence. "That was the biggest thing in Detroit, the

Mable John was the first female star at Motown during the company's early days (Bruce D. Bramoweth Collection).

Flame. When you got there, you had made it," she noted. By then, Mable's astonishingly gifted younger brother (by seven years), singer Little Willie John, was a national sensation. At age 17 in 1955, he crashed the charts with a jumping "All Around The World" for Syd Nathan's Cincinnati-based King Records. The following year, the ill-fated youth topped the R&B charts with "Fever" (their brother Mertis penned Willie's heartrending '56 hit "Need Your Love So Bad"). Mable and Willie performed together in 1960 at Harlem's Apollo Theatre.

Gordy recruited Flame bandleader Maurice King—later a mainstay of the label's Artist Development Department—to groom John. "Berry put me with him, for him to work with me on my singing and staging, before he even had a company," said John. So it was only natural that Mable would begin her recording career nestled securely under Gordy's wing. "He was managing the Miracles, and somehow I talked him into managing me," said John. "When he was shopping for deals, he didn't find a deal for me anywhere else. Smokey Robinson and I told him in New York at a BMI Awards dinner, 'If you will start your own record company, we'll record for you.' And I said to him, 'If you do, I will stay with you forever.' He said, 'Don't ever promise anyone that. If I can't give you what you're really looking for and someone else can, it would be wrong for you to stay with me, knowing I can't give it to you. We'll always be friends. That'll be forever. But you might not be with the company forever.' And he didn't even have a company at the time. Well, he started the company, and he signed me to Tamla."

After debuting with "Who Wouldn't Love A Man Like That," John encored in the spring of '61 with the wistful Gordy composition "No Love." "That was a great song," said Mable. "We did one version with strings. I think we did the strings in New York, and the regular instrumentation in Detroit." It was coupled with Gordy's easy-swinging "Looking For A Man." Before year's end, Mable tried again with "Action Speaks Louder Than Words," a downbeat lament provided by the boss man benefiting from forceful horns (it was also cut by David Ruffin for Check-Mate that same year). A male vocal group and thin organ provided haunting support for the blues-soaked flip "Take Me," a Mickey Stevenson tune produced by staffer Fay Hale.

Tamla released "Who Wouldn't Love A Man Like That" again in June of '63, but this was no reissue of an aging master tape: The precocious Little Stevie Wonder, then only 13 years old, decided he wanted to take a crack at producing Mable. "He listened to what Berry had done on me, and him being a very natural-born creative young man, said to Berry Gordy, 'I'd like to produce that song over again on her,'" she said. "I might have been the first person he produced at the company. And to tell you the truth, as much as I love Berry and the song, I do like the way Stevie produced it on me. Because it had a young, poppish sound, more than a soulful sound." "Say You'll Never Let Me Go" adorned the 'B' side.

After that promising remake failed to sell appreciably, Mable made a painful decision to break away from her mentor. "When I called Berry from Chicago and told him that I wanted a release, I just cried when I said it to him," remembered John. "He said, 'Why?' I said, 'The direction that the company is going into, I don't think I can measure up, because I'm not a pop singer. I'm a blues singer. And I really need to be in a company that's that kind of label, because I'm gonna get lost in the shuffle.' He said, 'Well, if that's what you want, we'll always be friends.'" They remain so to this day.

Mable made the correct decision. She signed with Memphis-based Stax Records, collaborating with producers Isaac Hayes and David Porter and scoring a national R&B smash in the summer of 1966 with her simmering "Your Good Thing (Is About To End)." The blues-soaked follow-ups "You're Taking Up Another Man's Place" and "Able Mable" failed to follow suit, so in 1969 Mable joined the ranks of Ray Charles' backing vocalists, the Raeletts, for a dozen-year run. She fronted the alluring group on their 1970 hits "I Want To (Do Everything For You)" and "Bad Water" for Brother Ray's Tangerine label.

Today, Dr. Mable John heads her own ministry in Los Angeles. Her Joy Community Outreach to End Homelessness program feeds and clothes the poor, and she conducts Sunday services for her parishioners. But Mable still squeezes in a musical performance here and there, reuniting with the Genius at the 1998 Chicago Blues Festival and glowing behind the mic just as incandescently as she did back when Berry Gordy hammered out her piano accompaniment.

MARV JOHNSON

Though he was the focal point of the first Tamla 45 in January of 1959, Marv Johnson's Gordy-produced hits enriched the coffers of United Artists Records instead of fledgling Motown (Berry wisely retained publishing for Jobete). Johnson's initial waxings were blueprints for the emerging Motown sound, stressing bouncy rhythms, a tambourine-accentuated backbeat, chunky piano and guitar contrasted by a burbling baritone sax or fluttery flute, and the Rayber Voices chanting in the background.

Detroit-born Marv made his debut on October 15, 1938, his childhood musical exposure encompassing spirituals, jumping R&B, and a whiff of raw-boned blues. After graduating from Cass Technical, Johnson paid road dues with a neighborhood vocal group, the Junior Serenaders, before Sonny Woods, an ex-Midnighter then mentoring the Downbeats (the same outfit soon to sign with Tamla), took an interest in the teen's Clyde McPhatter-derived vocal style. Cut in January of '58 with Beans Bowles' band, Marv's doo-wop-soaked debut 45 for the tiny Kudo logo coupled "Once Upon A Time" with "My Baby-O." But Berry noticed Marv's talents during a rehearsal with the Downbeats at Specialty Studio, setting the wheels in motion.

Berry was suitably impressed with Marv's "Come To Me," cutting it in late '58 at United Sound and selecting it to launch his brand-new Tamla imprint. Bateman's forceful bottom deftly counterpointed Marv's high-flying tenor, Beans Bowles' airy flute solo giving the Gordy production unusual potency. Marv played piano on the haunting flip "Whisper," another of his originals. United Artists discovered it had acquired a hot item when "Come To Me" shot up to No. 6 on *Billboard's* R&B charts in early '59 and No 30 pop.

Johnson encored with producer Gordy's "I'm Coming Home," another national hit capturing the same happy-go-lucky vibe. Later that year, Marv registered his biggest smash yet, the irrepressible "You Got What It Takes," which found an enraptured Johnson describing his homely girlfriend. "You Got What It Takes" stopped one slot short of pacing the R&B hit parade in late '59, cracking the pop Top Ten and making Marv a star. The tune was credited to Gordy, his sister Gwen, and writing partner Roquel "Billy" Davis, yet blues guitarist Bobby Parker had cut a virtually identical song by the same title back in 1957 for Chicago's Vee-Jay Records and was credited as sole composer.

Parker sounded perplexed when asked about the change in writer's credit. "I have no idea. It was strictly a cover deal," he said in 1993. "I was a little fish swimming around in a big pond. It was hard to fight. 'You Got What It Takes' is still wrapped up with Motown." No such anomalies marked the flip to Johnson's hit, the impassioned ballad "Don't Leave Me." Gordy, Brian Holland, Bateman (the two listed as Brianbert), and Smokey all pitched in on it.

The good times continued as Marv's first 45 rpm offering of 1960, the effervescent "I Love The Way You Love," matched its predecessor's lofty R&B chart showing and actually bettered it by a spot on the pop listings. Bowles' flute and the Rayber Voices provided an enticing backdrop for Johnson. This one was the work of Gordy and three associates collectively billed as "Mikaljon" (another of Berry's odd contractions): His wife Raynoma's brother Stanley "Mike" Ossman, Motown promotion man Al Abrams, and Berry's well-muscled driver, John O'Den. Johnson went to New York to take advantage of Teddy Randazzo's violin-enriched arrangement for its Gordy-penned flip, "Let Me Love You."

Both zesty Detroit-cut sides of Marv's Gordy/Johnson-penned single "Ain't Gonna Be That Way" with the Gordy/Holland/Janie Bradford collaboration "All The Love I've Got" saw minor pop chart action that summer. The recriminatory rocker "(You've Got To) Move Two Mountains," written by Berry but waxed in New York, pierced the pop Top 20 that fall. "Happy Days," co-written by Gordy and Toni McKnight, gave Marv his final R&B Top Ten trip as 1960 ended (Marv's own up-tempo "Baby, Baby" provided a delightful flip).

The singer's UA debut album in March of '60, *Marvelous Marv Johnson*, surrounded the singer's handful of hits with seven Tin Pan Alley standards that must have confounded his fans. More Marv Johnson, issued three months later, consisted of nothing but embryonic Motor City soul: Johnson's own "This Heart Of Mine (Will Surely Sing)," the Marv/Berry/Smokey collaboration "Clap Your Hands," and Gordy and Bradford's "When You've Lost Your Love" (a prominent "Produced by Berry Gordy, Jr." banner adorned its cover). The scarcity of his third LP from late '61, *I Believe—Marv Johnson Sings Golden Spirituals*, indicates its lack of sales.

Despite his myriad duties at fledgling Hitsville, Gordy found time for Marv: "Merry-Go-Round," another strings-enhanced New York effort that UA was surely familiar with (the firm had licensed Eddie Holland's '59 rendition, the second Tamla single after Marv's "Come To Me"), was a sizable pop and R&B hit in March of '61. Johnson's mainstream appeal was underscored by his appearance in the quickie rock-and-roll flick *Teenage Millionaire* that same year, as he lip-synched both sides of his August UA release, "Show Me" and "Oh Mary" (the latter penned by Gordy and Mickey Stevenson).

"Marv was a wonderful person, in my mind. I don't know if he was as wonderful to himself. He seemed lonely," said Janie Bradford. "He'd like to come in and

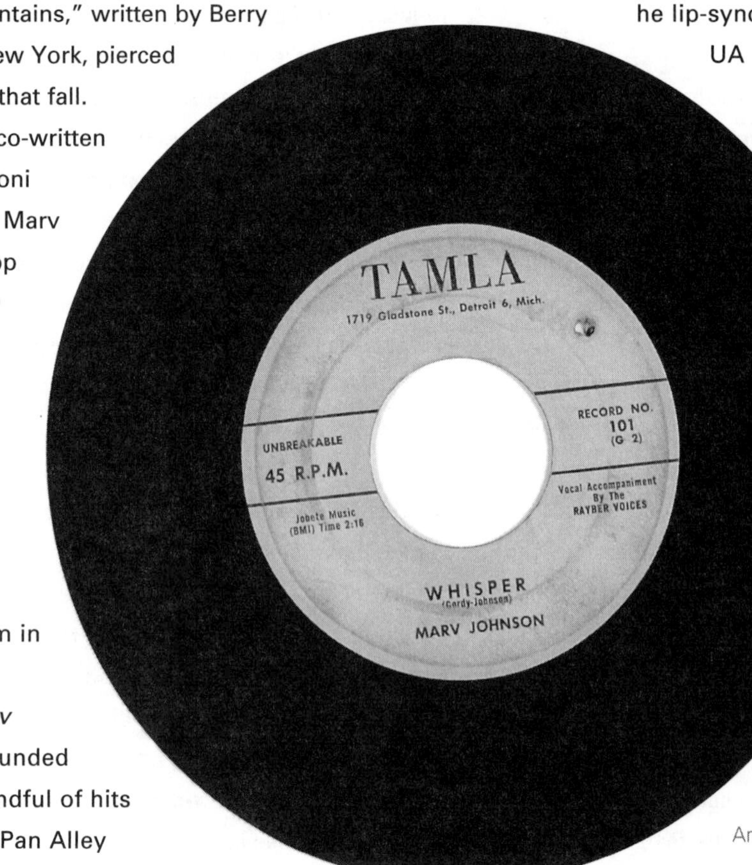

Marv Johnson's "Whisper" was the maiden release on the Tamla label (Photo courtesy of David Alston's Mahogany Archives).

impress whoever was there. I worked as a receptionist. I was in the lobby. So whoever was sitting around the lobby, he wanted to impress. That's the reason I say he was wonderful to me, 'cause I got the benefit of that. He'd come in after a tour and say, 'Here, Janie! Here's $50!' I loved it!'"

"I loved the guy," said the Andantes' Louvain Demps. "A lot of people thought that he might have been stuck up or something, but I really liked him very, very much. He was the first guy that walked me to the bus stop when we got through recording, or we got through practicing. He would always walk me to the bus stop, and just always was nice."

Johnson's fortunes cooled over the course of 1961, whether he recorded in the Motor City (he covered "I've Got A Notion" only a few months after new Motown recruit Henry Lumpkin introduced it) or New York (Smokey's sturdy "Easier Said Than Done"closed out the year; another Eddie Holland UA retread, "Magic Mirror," opened '62). With Gordy mostly out of the picture as a source for material, New York's heaviest producers and writers lined up to work with Marv—Jerry Leiber and Mike Stoller, Burt Bacharach and Hal David, and Bert Berns.

After Johnson's own "The Man Who Don't Believe In Love" failed to hit in early '64, UA dropped him. It was time to go home. Pacted to Gordy, his melismatic tenor rode herd on the brassy mid-tempo "I'm Not A Plaything," which he wrote with Bradford. Paired with Berry's groover "Why Do You Want To Let Me Go" in mid-'65, neither grabbed the public's attention.

"I Miss You Baby (How I Miss You)," the work of Clarence Paul and Morris Broadnax, was another story; its pounding excitement translated into Marv's first national hit in five long years during the spring of '66 (the singer supplied the less frantic flip, "Just The Way You Are"). Marv had to wait two-and-a-half years for his third and final danceable Gordy release, "I'll Pick A Rose For My Rose" (he wrote it with James Dean and William Weatherspoon).

Sharp-eared English soul aficionados embraced "I'll Pick A Rose," sending it into the British Top Ten in early '69 and granting "I Miss You Baby" retroactive hit status that fall. The result was a British tour, and Tamla-Motown slapped together a splendid LP containing several songs unissued in the U.S.: A lighthearted "So Glad You Chose Me," the majestic "I Wish I Liked You (As Much As I Love You)," and Marv's renditions of three Jobete oldies—Herman Griffin's "Sleep (Little One)" and the Miracles' "Everybody's Gotta Pay Some Dues" and "Bad Girl."

Marv's stock had fallen drastically back home. "When I first went to Motown, he would sweep up. He was the janitor," said McDougal. "I said, 'Hey Marv, you'd be a good promotion man.' And he said, 'You think so? I don't know if I could do it.' I said, 'Listen, people know you. You're Marv Johnson. The disc jockeys will listen to you, whatever you want to say!'

"I talked to Berry Gordy. I said, "Mr. Gordy, I'd like to talk to you about Marv Johnson.' He said, 'What about him?' I said, 'Why don't you let him be a promotion man? I think he would do well.' He said, 'That sounds like a good idea. Well, work it out, work it out.' So then I told Barney Ales. And Barney said, 'Oh, you think you can make Marv a promotion man?' I said, 'Yeah!' I took him to Birmingham, Alabama, the first place, and the guys knew him, and everything worked just like I knew it would."

After a long layoff, Johnson rejuvenated his singing career during the late '80s. Tragically, he collapsed and died onstage in Columbia, South Carolina, on May 16, 1993. Without Johnson's UA hits generating much-needed cash flow, Motown's road to success might have been considerably bumpier.

TERRY JOHNSON

Chicago's Flamingos were one of the greatest R&B vocal groups of the 1950s. Their breathtaking ballads "I'll Be Home," "A Kiss From Your Lips," and "The Vow" for Checker Records had made them stars by the time Terry "Buzzy" Johnson joined their ranks in 1958, just in time to participate in their dreamy classics "Lovers Never Say Goodbye" and "I Only Have Eyes For You" for George Goldner's End logo. But as R&B tastes shifted during the '60s, the Flamingos were less of a draw.

"He was the first tenor with the Flamingos. We worked with the Flamingos quite a bit back in those days, and we knew each other real well," said the Miracles' Pete Moore. "Terry always wanted to get into songwriting and producing, and he saw us and Motown as an opportunity for him to do so. So when he came to Detroit, he started working with Smokey and myself. We did a few things together for a while." Terry was a co-writer and co-producer of Smokey and the Miracles' "Baby, Baby Don't Cry" and "Here I Go Again" and Bobby Taylor & the Vancouvers' "Malinda" in 1968. The next year, he cut his own Gordy 45—"My Springtime" with "Suzie"—that was canceled and rescheduled with the big ballad "What 'Cha Gonna Do," penned by Terry and Smokey, as the 'A' side.

Gloria Jones, here shopping for furs in Cherry Hill, N.J., was a versatile singer, writer and producer (Weldon A. McDougal III photo).

GLORIA JONES

Along with her frequent partner, British songwriter Pam Sawyer, Cincinnati-born Gloria Jones brought a female perspective to the Motown's producers ranks during the early '70s. After singing in her minister father's choir and studying classical piano as a child, she joined the Cogics, an L.A. gospel group that included Frank Wilson, Blinky Williams, and Billy Preston. She went secular to work with L.A. stalwarts Barry White and Gene Page and sang briefly with Brenda and Patrice Holloway. Jones met writer/producer Ed Cobb in 1965 and cut the two-part "Heartbeat" and a revival of the Dell-Vikings' "Come Go With Me" for Uptown and "Tainted Love" for Vee-Jay-distributed Champion.

Jones cut her own Motown single, "Why Can't You Be Mine" and its flip "Baby Don'tcha Know (I'm Bleeding For You)," in May of '73, followed by the Paul Riser-arranged album *Share My Love* four months later. She was more active as a writer and producer, sometimes composing under the alias of Laverne Ware. She and Sawyer wrote Gladys Knight & the Pips' 1970 smash "If I Were Your Woman" (with Clay McMurray), "It's Bad For Me To See You" for Yvonne Fair, "I Ain't Going Nowhere" for Jr. Walker, and "The Zoo (The Human Zoo)" for the Commodores. Gloria didn't focus her energies solely on Motown. She became involved with Marc Bolan, leader of British rockers T. Rex, and thrived on that country's Northern Soul scene.

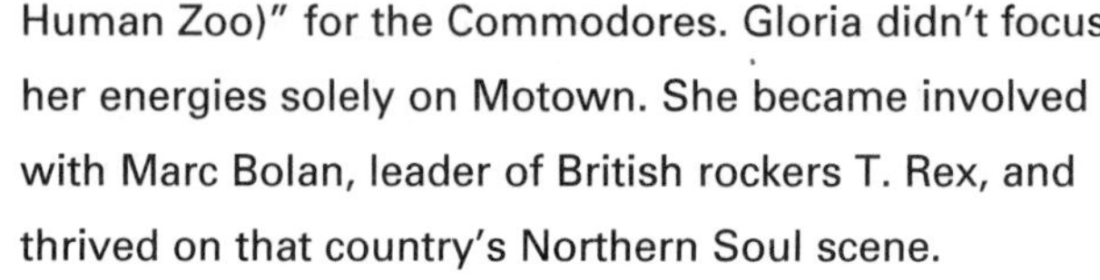

BOB KAYLI

This odd sobriquet masked the singing identity of Berry Gordy's younger brother Robert, who came out of left field to nail a minor pop hit with his rocking novelty "Everyone Was There," produced by Berry in late 1958 and issued on New York-based Carlton Records. He continued to record under the Kayli alias during Motown's early years, but proved more valuable as the head of Jobete Music from 1965 to 1985 following his sister Loucye's untimely death.

Born July 15, 1931, in the Motor City, Robert Gordy had written "Everyone Was There" in hopes that an artist from his brother's fledgling stable would record it, but there were no takers during a session at United Sound. So Robert sang it himself, his hiccupped lyrics paying clever tribute to fictional rock and roll queens Peggy Sue, Skinny Minnie, and Bony Moronie. Carlton picked up the master ("Everybody Was There" and its rhumba-tinged flip "I Took A Dare" credited the "Barry [sic] Gordy Orchestra"), and Kayli performed it on Dick Clark's Saturday evening ABC-TV program. But the maiden voyage stalled at No. 96 on *Billboard's* pop charts.

Kayli landed at Gwen Gordy and Billy Davis' Anna logo in 1959 to wax the mild pop rocker "Peppermint (You Know What To Do)." He tried again for Tamla in late '61, Berry producing his little brother's "Small Sad Sam," which came from outside the Jobete catalog and parodied Jimmy Dean's countrified pop smash "Big Bad John." Its flip, "Tie Me Tight," was a self-penned R&B number that proved Bob was capable of more than lightweight novelties. A year later, he bounced over to Gordy for another 45, "Hold On Pearl" with "Toodle Loo," to complete his Motown discography. Multi-faceted Robert was named a Motown vice president in 1969 and portrayed a dope dealer alongside Diana Ross in *Lady Sings the Blues*.

EDDIE KENDRICKS

Eddie Kendricks exited the Temptations in March of 1971 in the wake of perhaps his greatest triumph as their lead singer—the pristine "Just My Imagination." Though he would remain on Motown as a solo artist, topping that last masterpiece without the luxury of the Tempts' sumptuous harmonies would be a considerable challenge for the rail-thin high tenor.

The company did not encourage Eddie's solo aspirations. "They were having so much trouble with that group, first with David," said Frank Wilson, who would produce most of Kendricks' solo triumphs. "Then along comes Eddie, and they were about sick of it already.

"They thought it would destroy the group. And Eddie was such an integral part of the Temptations sound, and Eddie was such a moody person—I'm sure they thought that 'If this boy gets a hit, then we can kiss the Temptations good-bye.'"

When Eddie (born December 17, 1939, in Birmingham, Alabama) exited the Tempts, it left him in a funk. "Ewart Abner told me to take Eddie Kendricks out of town, because he was creating a lot of problems," said McDougal. "He was so distraught, you know. I didn't know what was going on. Eddie and I were friends, so I just said, 'Okay, Eddie, we'll go on a promotion tour. We'll go to New York.' We were in L.A. at the time. 'And Chicago—we'll get you in *Jet*.'

"So he said, 'Man, people don't like me, man.' I said, 'Are you crazy?' He said, 'Man, I'm tellin' you—I can't make it by myself.' I said, 'I'm gonna prove to you that they like you.' I already knew that the disc jockeys would always ask me, could I bring the Temptations to do interviews. They were really too busy, and they were too big to go to a station. At that time, the Temptations, you could start a havoc. So anyway, when Eddie left the

Temptations, 'Just My Imagination' was No. 1. And that was Eddie singing lead. So we go to the radio stations, and I tell 'em I've got Eddie Kendricks, 'Oh, man!' I knew I'd have no trouble getting an interview. And the people like in Philadelphia, the phones would light up, man, everybody wanting to talk to Eddie."

He no doubt acquired more confidence when his first Tamla solo offering, the surging Wilson production "It's So Hard For Me To Say Good-Bye," became an R&B hit in the spring of '71. The gossamer-streaked "Can I" followed suit at year's end (both appeared on his first solo LP, *All By Myself*), and "Eddie's Love" did decent business during the summer of '72. Then he started picking up steam: "If You Let Me" in late '72 and "Girl You Need A Change Of Mind (Part 1)" in early '73 broke into the R&B Top 20, and "Darling Come Back Home" just missed.

Rail-thin Eddie Kendricks had talent and style, both with the Temptations and as a '70s solo star.

A new strain of dance music was brewing, and Kendricks got in on the ground floor. "The first disco record they had was 'Girl You Need A Change Of Mind,' which was No. 1 at Studio 54 in New York for a long time; which was what really clued Motown into disco," noted co-producer Wilson. Eddie pioneered the movement during the latter half of '73, when his pulsating "Keep On Truckin' (Part 1)" topped both the pop and R&B charts, followed closely by "Boogie Down" which also paced the R&B hit parade and stopped at No. 2 pop. Along with co-producer (and ex-member of the Radiants, a Chicago soul group that hit for Chess in '65 with "Voice Your Choice") Leonard Caston, Jr., Wilson was responsible for conceiving both smashes. "Me and Leonard Caston, we did a lot of songwriting together, so first it would have been in the living room," he said. "And Anita Poree came up with the lyrical germ 'Keep On Truckin'."

Eddie nailed another seven Top Ten R&B smashes during the mid-'70s, including the chart-topping "Shoeshine Boy" (the only one to go Top 20 pop). He remained with Tamla into 1978 before jumping ship to go with Arista. After returning for the Tempts' acclaimed 1982 *Reunion*, Ruffin and Kendricks toured and recorded as a duo. Lung cancer silenced Eddie's golden falsetto for good on October 5, 1992.

EARL KING

A series of Motown recording sessions during the late summer of 1963 has assumed the stature of legend, not due to its spectacular success but because circumstances beyond the participants' control forced their burial in the company's vaults for decades.

To this day, only three songs have surfaced from the time a cadre of New Orleans R&B luminaries piloted a station wagon north to Hitsville in search of fresh recording opportunities. The all-star crew consisted of guitarist Earl King, singers Johnny Adams (who would proceed to hit in 1969 with a stunning "Reconsider Me") and Chris Kenner (already a star, thanks to 1961's "I Like It Like That"), singer/entrepreneur Joe Jones (who notched a national smash in 1960 with "You Talk Too Much"), piano-pounding Esquerita (a pal of Little Richard's who whooped it up on a series of rafter-rattling late '50s rockers for Capitol), and a funk-dripping Big Easy band.

King packed plenty of recording experience and considerable success as a composer for the trip. Born Earl Silas Johnson in the Crescent City on February 7, 1934, he teamed with Huey "Piano" Smith when both were still in their teens. "Huey Smith gave me my first gig," said King in a 1995 interview. "He had a little trio, and I used to go there and sing with him 'til they got tired of that, and they wanted to hear some guitar playing, and I didn't play guitar. Huey, he told the guy that owned the place, said, 'Well, we ain't got too much problems. Earl got a good ear. I'll show him how to work with the guitar some, 'cause he knows a little bit about guitar.' So every day, he and I would practice and play and practice. I got the nerve enough to go on a gig one night with the guitar. Of course, I had to use a capo then to change keys."

Earl's main guitar influence was dazzling showman Eddie "Guitar Slim" Jones, whose Specialty label smash "Things That I Used To Do" was one of 1954's biggest sellers. "He was incredible. He had some kind of charismatic thing about him that he drew people before he even started making recordings. He'd just go somewhere and perform, and the next time he'd go back there, there'd be a mob!" said King. "You go up to his room, he's got these big old pieces of paper on the wall, man, with thumb tacks in 'em. He writes his songs on there with eyebrow pencil. He'd curse you out, he'd say, 'I'm gonna play these songs for you. Anybody that touches one of these songs, lightning's gonna strike you!' Eight o'clock in the morning with the amp cranked up, man, you could hear him two blocks away."

Though he waxed his first platter for Savoy in 1953 with Huey under his real name, a label mix-up on "A Mother's Love," his first Specialty single the next year, left him with the alias of Earl King (it was supposed to read King Earl). Signing with Johnny Vincent's Ace logo in '55, King scored his first Top Ten R&B hit with the two-chord south Louisiana blues "Those Lonely Lonely Nights." He cut a slew of great Crescent City R&B sides for Ace ("My Love Is Strong," "It Must Have Been Love," "Everybody's Carried Away") over the rest of the decade.

In 1960, Earl switched to Imperial Records, and under Dave Bartholomew's direction cut the two-part "Come On" (later covered by Jimi Hendrix) and "Trick Bag" two years later. Nineteen sixty-two brought his only other R&B chart entry, "Always A First Time," for Imperial. King was scoring as a songwriter, laying material on Fats Domino and Lee Dorsey ("Do-Re-Mi").

"It was told to us by Joe Jones, who was the coordinator of that little tour up to Motown, that we was going up there to record," said King. "It didn't happen that way when we got there. It was like, we had to audition. The drummer that was with us was Smokey Johnson. They came down there and heard us playing, and one of the producers there heard Smokey playing, and he called for B.G. himself, Berry Gordy.

"B.G. came over. He didn't say nothing to nobody, he just stood up and listened and nodded his head to Clarence Paul, letting him know, that's it. He walked up to us and said, 'Look, y'all be in the studio to start recording tomorrow morning. Seven o'clock.' Just like that.

"So I did about 12 sides on me up there, and a couple of sides on Esquerita, a couple of sides on Joe Jones, and somebody on their staff, some group they had up there. I left some tapes up there for the Contours, and some chick named Hattie Littles. I never met her, but the guy told me to bring some songs down and she would do them.

"When we got back to New Orleans, somebody said Joe had threatened Berry Gordy about if he didn't give him 10,000 bucks, they wouldn't be able to put the stuff out. So they got frightened and canned the stuff. They didn't want to go through no litigation. It was really crazy."

Three of those long-lost King masters finally surfaced on the 1996 anthology *Motown's Blue Evolution*. It's easy to see why Gordy got so excited. "Three Knocks On My Door," "A Man And A Book," and "Hunger Pains"—the latter riding a driving "Come On" groove—are typically luminous King compositions, trumpeter Wardell Quezergue's brassy arrangements splendidly framing Earl's bluesy vocals and consistently inventive lyrics. The New Orleans contingent stuck around the Motor City for at least three weeks: "Three Knocks On My Door" was waxed on August 18, the other pair on September 8. The temporary setback didn't hurt King's career. The guitarist cut three superb albums for Black Top Records during the '80s and '90s.

LIZ LANDS

This lady was a class act, boasting a four-octave range and mostly confining her Motown pursuits to the gospel field. Born February 11, 1939, in the Georgian Islands, Liz moved to New York City at the age of 5 with her missionary foster parents and was enrolled at the Chatham Square Academy of Music studying classical singing when she was 7. While still young, she shared the prestigious Carnegie Hall stage with the great Mahalia Jackson. Dr. Martin Luther King introduced her to Gordy at a Southern Christian Leadership Conference meeting in Detroit.

Lands appeared on Motown's Divinity gospel subsidiary in 1963 with a rousing "We Shall Overcome" and "Trouble In This Land." "We Shall Overcome," arranged by Clarence Paul and Divinity head George Fowler with the Voices of Salvation, also adorned the other side of Dr. Martin Luther King's "I Have A Dream" speech on a Gordy 45. Another Lands coupling arose on Gordy before year's end: "May What He Lived For Live" (a tribute to assassinated President John F. Kennedy by Berry, his sister Esther, and actor W.A. Bisson, better known as Stepin Fetchit) and "He's Got The Whole World In His Hands," with vocal backing by the Voices of Love. Two-thousand copies of "May What He Lived For Live" were distributed to delegates at the 1964 Democratic National Convention—the brainchild of young administrative assistant Joseph Lieberman, who would make headline news at another Democratic convention 36 years later.

After two gospel-oriented singles, Liz went secular in early '64 with "Midnight Johnny" and "Keep Me." Both sides of the Gordy 45 credited the Temptations as backing vocalists, though a female group is prominent on the uptown soul-slanted Gordy production "Midnight Johnny," written by Berry, ex-wife Thelma, and the Monitors' Richard Street. That wasn't the only time Lands slipped into a pop mode at Motown. In August of '63, Lands focused her operatic range on the Sinatra torch number "In The Wee Small Hours Of The Morning" in front of an after-hours trio (the track laid unissued until the 1998 comp *Motown Celebrates Sinatra*).

Since she was the sister-in-law of Windy City soul singer Johnny Sayles and often played area clubs, it's no surprise that the chanteuse popped up on Chicago's One-derful! logo in 1967 with "One Man's Poison" and its flip "Don't Shut Me Out." The shocking part is how sassy and bluesy Lands sounds on the strutting 'A' side—a far cry from the straight-laced way she tackled Sinatra's chestnut. Both tracks emanated from saxist Eddie Silvers, the latter incorporating Ashford & Simpson collaborator Jo Armstead into the mix. Lands surfaced in 1980 on an LP by ex-Stevie Wonder bandleader Hamilton Bohannon, singing the Originals' "Baby, I'm For Real."

LEE & THE LEOPARDS

Only one single for Gordy in 1962–in fact, the second release overall on the purple label, following the Tempts' "Dream Come True"–but an exceptional one. "Come Into My Palace" has a hint of Sam Cooke to its mellifluous lilt, though a raw Motor City edge informs its chunky rhythm. Since Mickey Stevenson and Brian Holland were joined in its creation by one Lee Henry Moore, it's safe to assume that he's the front-billed Lee. The group also waxed "Don't Press Your Luck" for Fortune Records right around the same time; a cruder affair vaguely reminiscent of the Falcons' "I Found A Love," its clumsy arrangement blunts its impact, though the group's sanctified harmonies save the day. Strangely, "Come Into My Palace" and its flip "Trying To Make It" reappeared on New York-based Laurie Records a year or so after their Gordy debut.

THE LEWIS SISTERS/ LITTLE LISA

Helen and Kay Lewis were valuable to Motown's mid-'60s West Coast operation as writers (they penned "Just Walk In My Shoes" for Gladys Knight & the Pips), performers (they waxed two 45s of their own for V.I.P.), background singers (for label mate Chris Clark's "Do Right Baby Do Right"), and according to one published account, as vocal stand-ins when Hal Davis and Frank Wilson laid down backing tracks later used by other Motown artists.[13]

"The Lewis Sisters were two of Hal's writers," said Wilson. "Hal worked tirelessly with them. They supplied him with a lot of songs. They were in the studio a lot as artists with Hal, so he produced them as well as recorded a lot of their songs." The Motown connection wasn't their first studio experience. Helen and Kay had cut *Way Out...Far!*, an album of pop standards, for Liberty in 1959. The sibs debuted on V.I.P. in the spring of '65 with "He's An Oddball" and "By Some Chance" and encored in the fall with "You Need Me" and "Moonlight On The Beach," the pair cited on the latter as "The Singing School-Teachers." They had bit parts in the '72 film *Lady Sings the Blues*, produced by Berry Gordy and starring Diana Ross.

Only 9 years old and sweet as she could be, Little Lisa was Kay Lewis's daughter. "Hang On Bill" and its flip "Puppet On A String," her lone V.I.P. single, received a rave review in the September 11, 1965, issue of *Billboard*, but the glowing prediction didn't pan out. She later cut an album for Canterbury under her full name of Lisa Miller.

HATTIE LITTLES

Like Mable John and Sammy Ward, Hattie Littles was too resolutely bluesy to fit Berry Gordy's pop-accessible Sound of Young America formula. Her only single, "Your Love Is Wonderful" and "Here You Come," was released on Gordy in the fall of 1962, with Berry writing both sides and the Fayettes earning vocal credit behind her on the 'B' side. An earlier single, "Back In My Arms Again" (we may never know if there was any connection to the Supremes' mega-hit) and the flip "Is It Love," had been canceled from the Gordy production schedule a few months earlier.

The Shelby, Mississippi, native was discovered while working as a waitress at Lee's Sensation in Detroit. Three victories in the popular nightspot's weekly talent contest were enough to prompt Motown to offer the 27-

year-old belter a four-year contract. "Clarence Paul had brought her there as an artist," said Janie Bradford. "She had a big, strong voice." Though she sang in church, belting the blues was Hattie's principal strength. "She was a blues singer, I'll tell you what she was," said Hank Cosby. "She was very exceptional."

Along with the Spinners, Littles hit the road for six months as an opening act with Marvin Gaye's revue in April of 1963. She reportedly refused to perform her new release onstage because she wasn't overly fond of it, preferring to sing the material of Bobby Bland, B.B. King, and Ruth Brown (actually, the mid-tempo "Here You Come" was well-suited to Littles' pipes). Perhaps that reluctance factored into Hattie being a one-off Gordy artist. In any event, she weathered rough times after leaving the label before resurfacing as one of the many acts in Ian Levine's retro-Motown stable during the late 1980s.

Hattie eventually set her sights toward singing gospel. "She would call me, and when I'd come into Detroit, I never missed a time when I would go to one of the churches wherever she was, and I would sing," said the Andantes' Louvain Demps. "She would tear down the house with this gospel stuff." Littles died of a heart attack in June of 2000, forgotten by all but the most dedicated Motown aficionados. "I felt that she had never had the press that she should have had," said Frances Nero, another chanteuse whose entire Motown output similarly consisted of one single. "Hattie, she had a beautiful voice."

THE LOLLIPOPS

The Lollipops' "Cheating Is Telling On You" and flip "Need Your Love" was first scheduled for release on Gordy, then shuttled to V.I.P. and issued in the fall of 1969, revealing a talented female vocal group that never had much of a chance to shine at Hitsville. A recently unearthed "Look What You Done Boy," produced by Duke Browner (its co-writer with Arnetia Walker), demonstrates the group's allure. Prior to arriving at Motown, the Lollipops recorded "Step Aside Baby" with "Lovin' Good Feelin'" in 1967 for Impact, the same label that the Shades of Blue cut their hit version of Edwin Starr's "Oh How Happy" for the year before. Browner's "Crying Over You" was the logo's next release. After their Motown dalliance, the Lollipops defected to RCA.

SHORTY LONG

Diminutive in stature but treetop tall when it came to talent, Frederick "Shorty" Long was an ebullient singer whose best waxings for Soul had a happy, infectious, party vibe.

Born Frederick Earl Long on May 20, 1940, in Birmingham, Alabama, the multi-instrumentalist got his nickname for obvious reasons: He stood an inch over 5 feet tall. Influenced by Little Willie John and Johnny Ace as well as his Baptist upbringing, Shorty played piano in local clubs before heading north to Detroit in 1959. He recorded for Harvey Fuqua and Gwen Gordy's Tri-Phi label in 1962, the company releasing three 45s. "I'll Be There" graced two of them; it was initially coupled with "Bad Willie" and then "Too Smart" a few months later. His final Tri-Phi platter, "Going Away" and it's flip, the rocker "What's The Matter" (where Shorty cuts loose with a couple of bloodcurdling screams), came out the next year before the logo and its sister label Harvey were acquired by Motown. Shorty came along as part of the deal.

"That was my man!" said McDougal, who often accompanied Long on the road in a promotional capacity. "A real fun guy. Very talented. He was always singing and playing. When we went into the hotel, I'll never forget it, he would ask 'em, do they have a piano anywhere around. And if they did, if I ever wanted to see him anymore, he would be up there playing and writing and doing songs."

A hint of back-alley blues permeated Long's first offering on Soul in March of '64. "Devil With The Blue Dress," penned by Mickey Stevenson and Long (who enjoyed the rare privilege of writing quite a bit of his own material at Motown) settled into a greasy, lowdown groove from the get-go, Shorty endorsing his Chanel No. 5-wearing temptress as a male vocal group and biting lead guitar egged him on. The 45 inexplicably avoided the charts, but fellow Motor City denizen Mitch Ryder was listening. A couple of years later, the young rocker and his Detroit Wheels shifted the number's tempo into overdrive, segued it with Little Richard's "Good Golly Miss Molly," and enjoyed a Top Five pop hit.

Undaunted, Shorty tried again that summer with the self-penned rocker "Out To Get You," its hellfire piano boogie-driven rhythm and spirited vocal group interplay sounding nothing like any other 1964 Motown production (co-writer Stevenson was in charge). Long ostensibly handled the harmonica solos himself on "Out To Get You" and its bluesy "Blue Dress"-influenced flip, "It's A Crying Shame (The Way You Treat A Good Man Like Me)."

Here Comes the Judge: Shorty Long hands Weldon his sentence shortly before performing on Hy Lit's TV program (Weldon A. McDougal III photo).

After a long gap between releases, the wee singer resurfaced in the fall of '66 with "Function At The Junction," a good-time anthem written by Shorty and Eddie Holland in the same tradition as Willie Dixon's name-dropping "Wang Dang Doodle"—a hit for Chicago blues chanteuse Koko Taylor the same year. Shorty invites everyone from Ling Ting Tong and Mohair Sam to James Bond and the cast of *I Spy* to drop by as James Jamerson's insistent bass, prominent piano, and the Originals keep things lively. "Function At The Junction" propelled Long onto the pop and R&B charts for the first time, backed by a moving reading of the H-D-H ballad "Call On Me" (it did similar duty as the 'B' of the Four Tops' "Baby I Need Your Loving").

Shorty's apparent love for rock and roll from the previous decade may have sparked his early '67 remake of the Big Bopper's '58 smash "Chantilly Lace," an odd choice for a single that went nowhere commercially (backed by Long's treatment of the Four Tops' H-D-H-penned '65 'B' side "Your Love Is Amazing"). He did much better on "Night Fo' Last," something of a sequel to "Function At The Junction" brainstormed by Long and Clarence Paul that occupied both sides of a hit 45 in early '68. Shorty played organ on the instrumental flip.

The first voice heard on Long's biggest hit isn't his own. "Here Comes The Judge," the collective brainstorm of Shorty and Quality Control queen Billie Jean Brown with an assist from Suzanne de Passe, was a humorous novelty based on a zany routine on NBC-

TV's free-wheeling comedy hour *Rowan & Martin's Laugh-In* that cast Sammy Davis, Jr. as a jive-talking barrister. So it was entirely fitting that Davis contributed the "Hear ye, hear ye" clarion call to Long's platter (the unbilled gig led to Sammy's brief Motown stint). Shorty wasn't the only one trying to cash in on the "Here Comes The Judge" phenomenon.

"When I went to get the record played, I had a hard time because Pigmeat Markham had the record out at the same time," said McDougal (the veteran chitlin' circuit comic's Chess release wasn't precisely the same song, but it was very similar). "They were playing Pigmeat Markham's all the time. And there was a strange thing—the disc jockeys would say, 'Hey, man, we're playing Pigmeat Markham because he's a black artist.' I said, 'What the hell is Shorty Long, man?'" The two releases battled to a draw, peaking at the No. 4 slot on *Billboard's* R&B charts in the summer of 1968, though Shorty had a clear-cut edge when it came to pop spins. "Sing What You Wanna," a Long concoction sporting a carefree groove belying its heartbroken lyrics, adorned the other side.

Shorty Long's hit "Here Comes The Judge" in 1968 was inspired by a skit starring Sammy Davis Jr. on *Rowan and Martin's Laugh-In.*

Here Comes The Judge, Long's impressive debut album, emerged in late '68 with a cover photo of Shorty decked out in judge's robes and a white wig, toting a hefty tome titled "Time" (for jail time to be served). As many versions of Titus Turner's "People Sure Act Funny" as were floating around—Turner's own and Arthur Conley's Atco reading high among them—the number never rocked harder than in Long's hands, Jamerson cooking like crazy under punchy horns. "Here Comes Fat Albert," immortalizing Bill Cosby's obese comedy character, an infectious "Don't Mess With My Weekend" written by Shorty and Sylvia Moy, and a rollicking revival of the Cadets' '56 hit "Stranded In The Jungle" were guaranteed to elicit a smile, though Shorty delivered his own moving ballad "Another Hurt Like This" just as convincingly.

In early 1969, Shorty suddenly got serious. He and Moy came up with "I Had A Dream," a noble plea for worldwide brotherhood with a dense Paul Riser arrangement that was likely too different from his previous happy-go-lucky hits to follow suit. His last Soul single, a slick cover of Procol Harum's surreal "Whiter Shade Of Pale" closed out by a lengthy trumpet solo, came out in June and was equally at odds with Shorty's party hearty image.

There would be no more chances for 29-year-old Shorty. He drowned in a June 29, 1969, boat mishap while fishing on the Detroit River. "It was on a Sunday in Detroit. He had a small boat, like a rowboat. And they had these big tankers that come down the river in Detroit. One of them, it wasn't that close to him, but it must have been close enough to him that it made a wave, and it turned the boat over. That's how he drowned," said McDougal. "The thing that's so ironic, I was supposed to be with him. And I always said, if I was there, I don't think he would have drowned."

Soul raided the archives that fall for a posthumous LP, *The Prime Of Shorty Long*, its production credited to Shorty himself (a rare honor for a Motown artist). Long again displayed a '50s allegiance, updating Fats Domino's "Blue Monday" and "I'm Walkin'," reworking Dean Martin's "Memories Are Made Of This" into funky soul, and crooning his idol Ace's '53 hit ballad "Cross My Heart" (mistitled "I Cross My Heart" on the LP and miscredited to Ivy Hunter). The pounding "Baby Come Home To Me," arranged by guitarist Robert White, the Long/Moy creation "Lillie Of The Valley," and a lovely "I Wish You Were Here" written by Shorty and Mickey were granted full Hitsville elegance by arranger Paul Riser. The doo-woppish ballad "When You Are Available" found Shorty collaborating with Mr. and Mrs. Marvin Gaye, while "The Deacon Work" reverted to the tough dance stance that made him a star.

"Here Comes the Judge" was Shorty Long's biggest hit and the title song on a 1968 LP.

Shorty Long was indeed in his prime when he died. There's no telling what he might have accomplished in the years ahead.

LOVE SCULPTURE

If it'd only known what it had, maybe Motown would have retained the services of Love Sculpture past one LP on Rare Earth Records. *Blues Helping*, first out in the U.K., did little to launch the band, but once leader Dave Edmunds stepped out on his own (or Dale Edmunds, as Rare Earth's press release renamed him), stardom enveloped the rock guitarist. Edmunds doubled on keys for the project, backed by bassist John Williams and drummer Bob "Congo" Jones.

Born April 15, 1944, in Cardiff, Wales, Edmunds championed American rockers Chuck Berry, the Everly Brothers, and Ricky Nelson in his teens. He formed Love Sculpture in 1967, the name emanating from Jones' predecessor, Tommy Riley. Though "River To Another Day," their first single for EMI-affiliated Parlophone, bordered on psychedelia, the band switched over to blues when the EMI suits suggested it do so. Released in August of '69, *Blues Helping* was the end result, its lack of hit singles potential underscored by the fact that Rare Earth didn't bother to issue one. In late '70, Edmunds scored his first solo hit for MAM with a slide-soaked reprise of Smiley Lewis's "I Hear You Knocking" and never looked back.

HENRY LUMPKIN

The late Henry Lumpkin passed through Hitsville during the early '60s without scoring a hit, but he left a positive impression in his considerable wake. "He was a big, tall, kind of heavy-set guy. He could sing, too," said Hank Cosby. "I liked Henry Lumpkin."

Love Sculpture, shown here in 1969, was one act Motown probably let get away too quickly. Dave Edmunds (right) went on to solo stardom after the group's brief Motown stop.

"I've Got A Notion," his Motown debut in January of '61 (backed with "We Really Love Each Other"), was a forceful mid-tempo outing sparked by reverb-laced guitar tweaking his big voice. Written by George Fowler, Robert Bateman, and Brian Holland, the tune was redone by Marv Johnson for release on United Artists a few months later. His Motown encore in January of '62 coupled "What Is A Man (Without A Woman)" with "Don't Leave Me," pushing the latter mid-paced outing with gutsy, gospel-fueled intensity in front of a smooth male vocal group.

"He was a young fellow, full of energy. I used to call him 'Punkin,'" said Gino Parks, whose "Blibber Blabber," slated for Miracle issue that same year but canceled, was an uncredited duet with Henry. "He sort of resembled Chubby Checker. Same heftiness and everything. We were a little older than he. He was just out of high school. He was still a teenager at that time."

Lumpkin had the honor of waxing the original "Mo Jo Hanna," which came out in July of '62, flipped with "Break Down And Sing," as his Motown farewell. Marvin Gaye and the Underdogs would revive the blues-soaked voodoo rocker within the Motown family, chanteuses Esther Phillips and Tami Lynn covered it from outside—yet the Clarence Paul/Andre Williams-penned number never hit for anyone. Lumpkin surfaced on Buddah in 1967 with a flute-laced "Soul Is Taken Over" (backed with "If I Could Make Magic") co-written and co-produced by ex-Motown cohort Robert Bateman. He encored with "Honey Hush" and "Your Sweet Lovin'" the next year for the same firm.

TONY MARTIN

Star of film, TV and radio, pop crooner Tony Martin was a Hollywood legend. In a futile attempt to crash the MOR field, Motown signed Martin along with Connie Haines and Bobby Breen and issued "Our Rhapsody" and its flip "Talkin' To Your Picture" (both written by L.A.-based Billy Page, the scribe behind Dobie Gray's "The 'In' Crowd") in late 1964.

Born Alvin Morris, Jr. on Christmas Day of 1912 in Oakland, California, Martin changed his name upon arriving in Hollywood. Choosing "Tony" after reading about a gambler by that name and "Martin" in tribute to bandleader Freddy Martin, he starred in a slew of movies. "To Each His Own," "There's No Tomorrow," and "Begin The Beguine" were among his recorded hits. Martin resumed his career after World War II, cavorting onstage in an act with his wife, dancer Cyd Charisse. It had been seven years since Martin scored a decent pop hit with "Walk Hand In Hand" for RCA when Motown scooped him up. Most of his singles were cut in L.A. by Hal Davis and Marc Gordon: "The Bigger Your Heart Is" and flip "The Two Of Us," his Motown encore, was issued in the summer of '65. "Ask Any Man" with the Davis/Frank Wilson-penned "Spanish Rose," his third and final Motown single, came out at the start of '66. There was also a 1966 LP, *Live At the Americana*.

HUGH MASEKELA

South African jazz trumpeter Hugh Masekela traveled a treacherous road to international stardom due to his country's apartheid policies prior to founding Motown-distributed Chisa Records with business partner Stewart Levine in 1969.

Born April 4, 1939, in Witbank, South Africa, Masekela was given his first horn by Archbishop Trevor Huddleston. He grew up influenced by a vast array of American jazz luminaries, including Louis Armstrong, Dizzy Gillespie, and Miles Davis. After playing in several young bands, he emigrated to England in 1959 to escape the brutality surrounding the apartheid that divided his native land. Settling in New York in 1960, Masekela was aided by Miriam Makeba (his wife during the mid-'60s) and Harry Belafonte in getting established. With Levine as his producer, he scored a No. 1 pop smash in 1968 with his highly infectious instrumental "Grazing In The Grass" for Uni Records, setting the stage for Chisa's inauguration the next year. Hugh cut two LPs for the company—1970's *Reconstruction* and the next year's *Hugh Masekela and the Union of South Africa*—and a pair of singles, notably a '70 reprise of the H-D-H standby "You Keep Me Hangin' On." Three decades later, he remains a jazz stalwart.

Hugh Masekela (right) & the Union of South Africa behind the Philadelphia Art Museum (Weldon A. McDougal III photo).

BARBARA McNAIR

A sultry actress with a flair for drama and an accomplished singer who breathed a touch of soul into the loungiest of standards, lovely Barbara McNair was ubiquitous on TV and in the movies during the late '60s and early '70s. Less remembered is the fact that she recorded for Motown—except by Great Britain's Northern Soul contingent, who swear by several of her non-hits (her unissued Motown master "Baby A Go-Go" swept the Northern Soul circuit in 1999).

"She would work in clubs where Frank Sinatra worked," said McDougal. "Or she'd work in Vegas, Atlantic City."

Born March 4, 1934, in Chicago (some sources say 1939) and raised in Racine, Wisconsin, young Barbara was dazzled by silver screen stars Rita Hayworth and Ethel Waters at her local movie palace's Saturday matinees. Studies at the Racine Conservatory of Music and Chicago's American Conservatory of Music led to a year at UCLA, but New York had the action. Top clubs like the Village Vanguard and the Purple Onion booked the gorgeous newcomer, and she was a winner on *Arthur Godfrey's Talent Scouts* in 1955. Sarah Vaughan, Peggy Lee, and June Christy were her vocal influences, and by late '57 McNair was recording for Coral, debuting with "Bobby" ("Flipped

Over You," half of the second of her five Coral 45s, sounded promising).

Broadway welcomed her in the musical *The Body Beautiful*, and Barbara toured with Nat King Cole during the early '60s in *I'm With You* and *The Merry World of Nat King Cole*. All that theatrical polish put McNair in a position to help Motown crack the MOR field. Yet there was a sultry R&B ambiance to "You're Gonna Love My Baby," her debut for the label in late '65. She wrote it with Ron Miller and another scribe, and Berry produced it with an eye toward Phil Spector (it was flipped with "The Touch Of Time"). She encored the next fall with an elegant cover of the Supremes' James Dean/Eddie Holland-penned "Everything Is Good About You" (backed by "What A Day") and introduced Smokey Robinson's bewitching "Here I Am Baby" in early '67, paired with a cover of the Supremes' "My World Is Empty Without You."

Her tasty "Steal Away Tonight" was slated for Motown release during the summer of '67, but canceled. The label tried again with the Frank Wilson/Deke Richards-helmed "Where Would I Be Without You" in early '68, sliding a reprise of "For Once In My Life" on the flip. Barbara's "You Could Never Love Him (Like I Love Him)" and "Fancy Passes" comprised her final Motown 45 that fall. There were two LPs: *Here I Am* in '66 and 1969's *The Real Barbara McNair*. Despite her mainstream TV and movie fame—she played a nun opposite Elvis Presley and Mary Tyler Moore in the 1969 film *Change of Habit* and hosted her own 1969-71 TV variety program—McNair wasn't above the outrageous. She was surely the only Motown act to be photographed for a *Playboy* pictorial (in the October 1968 issue, for those so inclined). Barbara still trods the musical theater boards, specializing in Duke Ellington and big-band material.

Barbara McNair eventually gravitated to Broadway and the big-band sound, but she made an impression at Motown with some nice tracks, including "What a Day," the flip to "Everything is Good About You" (Photo courtesy of David Alston's Mahogany Archives).

Barbara McNair was better known as a glamorous star of stage and screen than she was a Motown hit maker.

THE MESSENGERS

They may have had a limited discography, but the history of the Messengers, a Milwaukee rock band, is a tangled web indeed. Bassist Greg Jeresek (born July 3, 1947) was the unifying thread, forming the first group of Messengers in 1963 in Winona, Minnesota, and naming them after a CB radio known as the Viking Messenger. They cut a single for Amos Heilicher's Soma label in early '65, pairing the originals "My Baby" and "I've Seen You Around," before splitting up that summer. Jeresek ventured forth to attend the University of Wisconsin in Milwaukee and assembled another crew of Messengers (guitarist Peter Barans, born June 23, 1946, in Chicago, drummer Augie Jurishica, born in Milwaukee on May 2, 1947, and vocalist Jeff Taylor, born March 10, 1947, in Detroit), who waxed a revved-up garage band treatment of Wilson Pickett's "In The Midnight Hour." Local deejay Paul Christy placed it with Chicago's USA Records, and it became a regional hit in 1967.

Opening for the Dave Clark Five inside Chicago's cavernous McCormick Place, the Messengers were spotted by Motown's Jeffrey Bowen. He approached the band right after the show, and off to Hitsville they soon flew (organist Jesse Roe wouldn't sign a contract, precipitating his dismissal).[14] They cut "Window Shopping" and its flip "California Soul" (a '68 hit for the 5th Dimension), which came out on Soul in mid-'67—no small feat, considering the subsidiary seldom showcased Caucasians. Meanwhile, USA recruited another band from the Boston area, renamed them Michael & the Messengers, and had them recut the Reflections' "(Just Like) Romeo & Juliet" to another round of regional acclaim.

The original Messengers surfaced again in 1969 with an eponymous album for the new Rare Earth logo, with organist Michael Morgan doing the vocal honors. After another long gap, their "That's The Way A Woman Is" became a pop hit on Rare Earth in the fall of '71, rising to No. 62 in *Billboard.* No more Messengers releases turned up on any Motown imprint after that. "That night when we had the opening party for the Rare Earth label, I'd say if they had about 10 groups, only two of 'em really made it," said McDougal. "It was Rare Earth and the Messengers."

MIKE & THE MODIFIERS

You couldn't go wrong in the summer of 1962 with four-chord rock and roll laid over a doo-wop base. Mike & the Modifiers chimed in with a sturdy example of the genre on their "I Found Myself A Brand New Baby" for Gordy Records. A long, dramatic intro prior to the band's entrance led to tasty two-part harmonies on the chorus equidistant between Dion and the Everlys.

Detroiter Mike Valvano joined the fledgling Motown operation in 1960 when he was 17. His Modifiers included Roy Gasperada and three others that formed a self-contained musical unit. Though they only cut one 45 ("It's Too Bad" occupied the 'B'), Valvano made himself useful around Hitsville for much of the decade as a songwriter, acetate cutter, chauffeur, foot-stomper, and recording artist. With Johnny Powers, he was half of the Hornets, whose "Give Me A Kiss" and flip "She's My Baby" came out on V.I.P. in February of '64. He later produced Rare Earth acts Stoney & Meat Loaf and Xit, a Native American band from New Mexico.

AMOS MILBURN

Postwar R&B pioneer Amos Milburn was undeniably on the downhill slide when he made Motown one of his last significant label affiliations in 1962. But the boogie piano master still had plenty left in his tank.

A product of the fertile Houston blues scene where he was born April 1, 1927, Milburn was entranced by the blues from a young age, listening to boogie masters Meade Lux Lewis, Albert Ammons, and Pete Johnson and jump blues pioneer Louis Jordan. Apprenticing locally after serving in the Navy during World War II, he was spotted by talent scout Lola Anne Cullum, who got him signed to Eddie and Leo Mesner's L.A.-based Aladdin label in 1946.

His Aladdin debut, "After Midnight," sold respectably on the West Coast, and a rocking "Down The Road Apiece" became an early calling card. The hits began to flow like cheap wine for Amos in 1948 with his signature R&B chart-topper "Chicken Shack Boogie" and "Roomin' House Boogie" (1949), "Sax Shack Boogie" and "Bad, Bad Whiskey" (1950), "Let's Rock A While" (1951), and the booze odes "Let Me Go Home Whiskey" and "One Scotch, One Bourbon, One Beer" in 1953. Milburn could croon a blues ballad with the best of 'em—witness his R&B chart-topper "Bewildered" in late '48.

Despite his herculean efforts in the invention of rock and roll, Milburn was unable to make the leap to teen fandom (and if his scalding New Orleans-cut '56 reprise of "Chicken Shack Boogie" couldn't do the trick, nothing would). After Aladdin cut him loose in 1957, he paused at Ace (with close friend Charles Brown) and King before settling in at Motown in the fall of 1962. There he stayed for a year-and-a-half, though the logo only issued two 45s. Released in early '63, "I'll Make It Up To You Somehow" was credited to producer Clarence Paul, Lamont Dozier (who played drums on the date), and Johnny Powers. "My wife and I wrote that song, one hundred percent," said Powers. "Clarence Paul was my producer. He knew I wrote the song. I was going to record the song, and then he put it out on Amos." Milburn and Paul penned the flip "My Baby Gave Me Another Chance," another admirable variation on the style that made Amos famous. A few months later, the label tried again with a moving "My Daily Prayer."

Motown issued a splendid LP, *Return of the Blues Boss*, in the spring of '63, combining remakes of past triumphs with fresh material in an attempt to jump-start Amos's career. He revisited his Aladdin classics "In The Middle Of The Night," "Darling How Long," "Bewildered," and "Baby You Thrill Me," affably delivering "One Scotch, One Bourbon, One Beer" and "Bad, Bad Whiskey" with a confidence unfazed by time. Saxist Hank Cosby honked with abandon on the driving "Hold Me Baby."

Unissued performances unearthed for Motown's 1996 Milburn compilation *The Motown Sessions 1962-1964* included the wonderful throwback "I'm In My Wine" (perhaps Milburn's lyrics were a little too adult for Motown's youthful image), the gospel-charged duet "I Wanna Go Home" with an uncredited female (Brown and Milburn previously cut it for Ace), the jumping "I'm Gonna Tell My Mama," and a swinging "Chicken Shack Boogie" that afforded solo space to Little Stevie Wonder's harmonica. Along with various permutations of the Funk Brothers, Milburn's studio compatriots included Texas blues guitarist Curley Mays and the Andantes.

At one of Milburn's final Motown sessions, Andre Williams wrote and produced a catchy "Mama's Boy" that vaguely resembled Fats Domino's rolling output (the Fat Man often cites Amos as a prime early influence). The same March 12, 1964, date also elicited the sanctified rouser "I'll Leave You In His Care"—perhaps an attempt to atone for all those joyous salutes to inebriation that Milburn had fearlessly delivered over the years.

A pair of strokes laid Amos low in 1968, and he died on January 3, 1980.

THE MONITORS

Fear of being involuntarily hauled off to Vietnam for an open-ended stint in a rice paddy had made the Valadiers' '61 hit "Greetings (This Is Uncle Sam)" more timely than ever by the spring of 1966, when the Monitors redid it and enjoyed their biggest hit for V.I.P.

Lead singer Richard Street, Sandra Fagin, John "Maurice" Fagin, and Warren Harris all hailed from the Motor City. Street fronted the Distants on their regional '59 hit "Come On" for producer Johnnie Mae Matthews prior to the Otis Williams-led outfit morphing into the Temptations without him. He also worked behind the Hitsville scenes producing and co-writing "Can You Do It" for the Contours in 1964 and toiled as a Quality Control analyst.

"Say You," the quartet's first V.I.P. offering (written by Robert Dobyne, Charles Jones, and Robert Staunton), made some R&B chart noise in the early weeks of '66 on the strength of its gliding mid-tempo groove and alluring harmonies behind Street's lead ("All For Someone" gave the group a swaying, strings-enhanced ballad showcase on the flip).

"Greetings (This Is Uncle Sam)," their V.I.P. encore, hadn't changed since the Valadiers waxed it a half a decade earlier—the doo-wop ballad framework survived intact, Street's lead was just as strong as Stuart Avig's on the original, and the drill sergeant barking orders sounded every bit as obnoxious. Producers Mickey Stevenson, Hank Cosby, and Ronnie Dunbar (the latter and house engineer Lawrence Horn were added as co-writers) brought nothing new to the tune, but its timeliness was inescapable. "Greetings" climbed to No. 21 R&B that spring. "Number One In Your Heart," a torrid rocker by Clyde Wilson and Wilburt Jackson supervised by Harvey Fuqua and Johnny Bristol, was wasted as the 'B' side.

That was it for the Monitors as hit makers, but they made three more V.I.P. singles that should have been. Fuqua and Bristol helmed "Since I Lost You Girl," an ear-catcher with a driving beat that Street and Harris contributed to as writers; Harvey and Johnny wrote the equally insistent "Don't Put Off 'Til Tomorrow What You Can Do Today" on the flip, out in late '66. Street was on fire on "Bring Back The Love," another pounder by James Dean, William Weatherspoon, Eddie Holland, and Jack Goga in the spring of 1968. Its flip was a reprise of the Tempts' '63 spine-tingler "The Further You Look, The Less You See". Both sides of their last 45, the brotherhood plea "Step By Step (Hand In Hand)" and "Time Is Passin' By," were sizzlers supervised by Dean and Weatherspoon issued in mid-'68 on Soul.

As if to neatly tie up all the loose ends of their career at the label before bidding them adieu, Soul issued an album, *Greetings! We're The Monitors*, in late '68 that held nearly all their singles plus a few tunes unavailable elsewhere. "Share A Little Love With Me" boasted a guitar/bass unison line strong enough to hang a Ford Mustang on, a snaky baritone sax solo, and a hair-raising lead from Street; "Serve Yourself Another Cup Of Happiness" was another Dean/Weatherspoon-generated rocker; the delicious "You Share The Blame" came from Smokey and fellow Miracle Ronnie White, and there was a cover of Jay & the Techniques' strident '68 hit for Smash, "Baby Make Your Own Sweet Music."

Street wouldn't be idle after leaving the Monitors. He replaced an ailing Paul Williams with the Tempts in 1971 and stuck around more than two decades.

FRANCES NERO

An annual talent contest sponsored by WCHB radio and Tip Top Bread uncovered some fine young talent for Motown. Frances Nero won the gala 1965 event at the Fox Theater in downtown Detroit, her prize

"That place used to really, really cook."

a Motown recording contract. Nero's rendition of the Shirelles' "Everybody Loves A Lover" was good enough to beat runner-up Ronnie McNeir. "It was judged by Berry Gordy," said Nero. "Actually, I was the first contestant to win that contest without the bread wrappers. They had a thing where you had to turn in so many bread wrappers, but this time it was based solely on performance and talent."

Born March 13, 1943, in Asheville, North Carolina, Frances made her public singing debut as a seventh-grader over radio station WNIC, belting a rendition of the Orioles' "Crying In The Chapel." "I could play a few songs on the piano, and that was the one that I could play and sing," said Nero, who moved to Detroit in February of 1960. "During the time I was going to high school, all my friends either wanted to go to Los Angeles, California or New York. But something about the name Detroit intrigued me, and I always wanted to come to Detroit." Nero sang in a few jazz clubs prior to signing with Motown but did precious little performing while under contract, though she slipped in one gig with the Funk Brothers as her rhythm section.

"I did a thing with them at a place called Chappie's Lounge. That place used to really, really cook," she said. "I was the opening act for Kim Weston."

Producer Mickey Stevenson wrote "Keep On Lovin' Me" with James Dean and William Weatherspoon, utilizing the Originals as backing vocalists. "The song they gave me, it was actually written for the Marvelettes," she said. "It was a track for the Marvelettes, and I understand they turned it down. So some lyrics were written for me, I guess like the day before. I went in the next day, and they told me to sing it. It was recorded right quick, both songs." The same writers were responsible for the attractive mid-tempo outing "Fight Fire With Fire," issued on Soul in March of 1966.

Unfortunately, that was Frances' lone Soul release. "From what I understand, it sold 10,000 copies," she said. "But they didn't pursue it. I guess they were just trying to keep up with their commitment, letting whoever won that first prize record," she said. "Back in those days, I was kind of like part of the wallpaper. I was just kind of checkin' everything and everybody out, 'cause I was married," she said. "I was 22 years old, and I had two children."

Frances opted out of her Motown pact after cooling her heels for what seemed an eternity. "I won the contest for a year, and then they had the option to take up other years if they wanted to. I stayed there for actually two years, and after the second year I asked for a release. He didn't want to give it to me," she said. "But I'm not one to wait around on someone else. I have dreams of my own. So he said if he hadn't done anything with me in six months' time, to come back and he would give me the release. And he hadn't done anything, so of course I got the release."

Later in the decade she hooked up with Raynoma Gordy Singleton and her husband Ed Singleton at Shrine Records. "I did a song called 'Lady In Waiting.' I can't even remember the other song. Then I did a couple of tunes with Gino Parks for them. I never heard anything of 'em until I went to England in '89 and someone brought this record to show to me. It was on the Shrine label, and there was my name: Frances Nero."

It took two more decades, but Frances proved she could cut a hit. Motown revivalist Ian Levine produced Nero's "Footsteps Following Me" for his Motor City logo, and it developed into a surprise British chart entry that earned Frances an appearance on the prestigious *Top of the Pops* TV show.

Her Motor City output was later compiled stateside by Hot Records. More recently she cut an EP for her own AJA imprint. Writing for a local paper and operating a tour service currently takes up Nero's time. "I haven't been doing anything," she said. "I just don't want to be out there anymore."

THE ORIGINALS/FREDDIE GORMAN

For the latter half of the 1960s, the Originals filled a parallel role to the Andantes at Motown, supplying backing vocals on hits by Jimmy Ruffin, Shorty Long, Marvin Gaye, and Stevie Wonder. But when Marvin gave them the shimmering "Baby I'm For Real" in 1969, the versatile quartet departed the ranks of anonymous session singers for good.

First tenor C.P. (short for Crathman Plato) Spencer, tenor Hank Dixon, and baritone Walter Gaines had been in the Five Stars, whose 1957 Mark-X single "Ooh, Shucks" was Berry's first production. C.P. and Walter were also formerly with the Voice Masters, who cut the first two 45s for Gwen Gordy and Billy Davis' Anna label in 1958: "Hope And Pray" with "Oops I'm Sorry" and "Needed" with "Needed (For Lovers Only)."

Bass singer Freddie Gorman first surfaced beside future Satintone William "Sonny" Sanders in the Quailtones, who cut "Tears Of Love" with the Gorman-penned "Roxanna" for Josie in 1955. "I must have been maybe 15 years old at the time," he said. "The oldest guy might have been about 18. But three of us were in high school. We recorded the record with Sax Kari. He was a saxophone player. And he owned a record shop. We somehow got down there and auditioned for him." Freddie first crossed paths with Gordy as a member of a subsequent doo-wop aggregation that cut for the fledgling producer prior to Motown's advent. "I was with a group called the Fidelitones," he said. "It was me, Sonny Sanders, Brian Holland, and a fellow named Bosco. Bosco lived over on the other side of town. I never got Bosco's real name." The Fidelitones' "Pretty Girl" and "Game Of Love," both written by Freddie, never saw light of day.

The Originals with Ty Hunter (Weldon A. McDougal III photo).

Berry was always on the lookout for new songwriters and Freddie fit the bill, co-penning the Supremes' debut "I Want A Guy" and the Marvelettes' 1961 mega-hit "Please Mr. Postman." Gorman was indeed a mail carrier, though Hitsville wasn't on his route. "I was over there so often in my uniform, you might have thought so," he laughed. "I was a postman, I guess probably the youngest one in Detroit. It was Brian Holland and myself who were partners writing, and then we brought Lamont Dozier into the network of writers, so there were three of us."

Gorman unfurled his deep pipes on a solo Miracle single in 1961. "The Day Will Come" and "Just For You" confidently echoed the uptown soul movement. "That's 'Popcorn' Wylie you hear on the organ," said Freddie. "It sold well in Detroit, but that was as far as it got, because there was no all-out promotional push on it. If you listen to it, the vocal that I did was different from what was happening at the time. I really don't think they knew what to do with the record."

Other labels were proliferating, offering Gorman a chance to pursue his dream of stardom. "Things started to happen over at the company, but it wasn't enough happening for me to quit my job. At least I didn't think so," he said. "I was still working at the time at the post office, and my partners had started to do songs and complete them before I could get over there. I'd get over there and they'd say, 'Man, we're finished! We've written two songs today!'

"Writing was not my main objective. It was as a singer. That's what I aspired to be. That's where I came from. That's how I started. When no one was producing on me—at that time, you had to have a producer's contract to produce, so I couldn't produce myself. So I left. I asked for a release, without anyone being angry or falling out or anything. And I obtained it. At the same time, Bob Hamilton had come to the company, and I didn't really meet him and get to know him that well. But he had been there as a producer, and I don't think the company was happy with what he was doing, and they let him go. He went to Golden World. We both wound up over there."

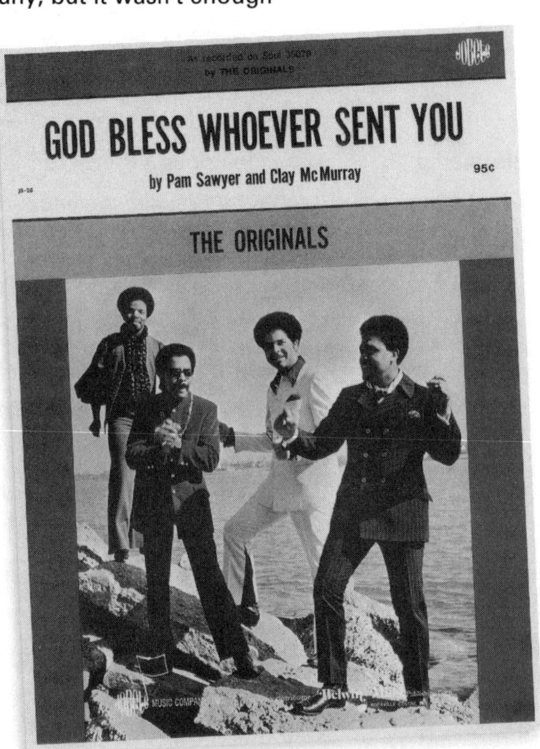

The Originals made waves with Top 20 songs such as "God Bless Whoever Sent You" in 1971 after serving for years as background singers, studio men and writers at Motown.

While at Golden World, Motown's local rival, the pair wrote the Reflections' 1964 pop smash "(Just Like) Romeo & Juliet." "Bob had for years tinkered around with it. The owner of Golden World, Mr. Ed Wingate, he had the group the Reflections, and he wanted to record 'em. That song, we thought it was tailor-made, because it had a pop feel, as opposed to the R&B thing that we were doing," said Freddie. There was also time for Gorman to cut two excellent 1965 45s for Golden World's Ric-Tic subsidiary: The strings-enriched "In A Bad Way" with "There Can Be Too Much" and "Can't Get It Off My Mind" with the hard-driving flip "Take Me Back."

Dozier was the catalyst for the formation of the Originals. "Walter Gaines got out of the service. He was a good friend of Lamont's. And they got together, and Walter expressed that he wanted to sing again. So they decided to try to get a group together," said Freddie. "So they got C.P. Spencer, they got Ty Hunter. And then Lamont and I were good friends, we were still hanging out together. So he suggested me. So I came over, and we got together with the guys. I had seen Walter and C.P. around, and I knew Ty. We used to do record hops together. And we started to harmonize together, and I was swept by the sound. I thought our sound was really great, our harmony. So I went back to Golden World and asked them to give me my contract back."

The plan hit a snag. "Ty couldn't go with us. He was on Chess. They wouldn't give him a release," said Gorman. "So at that time, Hank Dixon, who was in the service also, he had decided to give it a career, and then after eight years or so, he changed his mind and he got out—he came around and got in the group. We got Hank Dixon just before we put a girl in the group."

Their talents were put to superb use from 1965 to 1969 as backing vocalists for Jimmy Ruffin's "What Becomes Of The Brokenhearted" and "Gonna Give Her All The Love I've Got," Marvin Gaye's "Chained," Shorty Long's "Function At The Junction," Stevie Wonder's "For Once In My Life," and David Ruffin's "My Whole World Ended (The Moment You Left Me)." "Sometimes the leads would be on when we'd do the vocals, or sometimes we'd do the vocals before," noted Freddie. "Most of the time, they used the four of us and the three Andantes."

In early '67, the Originals finally scored a single of their own on Soul, transforming Lead Belly's "Goodnight Irene" into pounding Motor City R&B under Clarence Paul's direction and reprising "Need Your Lovin' (Want You Back)," a rocker penned by Gaye and Paul that had served similar duty on Marvin's "Take This Heart of Mine" a few months earlier. For this outing only, former Falcon/Contour Joe Stubbs—Four Tops lead Levi's brother—sang lead.

"Eddie Holland was the A&R director. They had started having big hits on the Four Tops," said Freddie. "I guess they didn't want to deal with Joe as a single artist, so they decided to put him with a group. They said, 'Let's put him in the Originals.' Joe was with us about six months, and that's when we recorded those songs." The group suffered a setback when their three benefactors acrimoniously exited the label.

"We went to Motown with Holland-Dozier-Holland to produce us. Then they left," said Gorman. "So there we were at Motown without a producer. It was kind of an awkward position." A few songs had been laid down before H-D-H bailed, and Soul finally got around to releasing "We've Got A Way Out Love" in early '69. "That one was the one we had done just before they left. The company released it, but it wasn't finished. It was supposed to have some strings and horns and things of that sort on it," said Gorman. "It was just the rhythm track and the vocals." Its flip, "You're The One," was a lush ballad mobilizing Ivy Jo Hunter as producer, though Marvin and Anna Gaye were in on its composition. A stirring "Green Grow The Lilacs" was issued three months later. "Ron Miller and Tom Baird, they put that together for us," said Freddie. "Tom Baird was such a master of harmonies."

Gaye would prove the group's savior. "Marvin and I used to do record hops," said Gorman. "Walter knew him earlier from Anna Records. Walter and C.P. and Lamont all went back to Anna Records, which was before Motown. So Walter knew him when he came to town from Washington. He had listened to our harmonies, especially when we were doing the background thing for him. He knew everybody, and just like myself, he was swept by the harmony. Because he was a group man himself, coming out of the Moonglows.

"So he got us together and said he had a song for us. We went over to his house and it was 'Baby, I'm For Real.' We started working on it. Everybody just knew right off. He had the idea of switching parts. You had four different leads on 'Baby, I'm For Real,'" said Gorman. "A lot of people when we first got out there were so shocked—they thought it was one person leading, maybe two—but definitely not four. I did the first verse, Hank does the second verse, Walter does the bridge, and then C.P. comes in." "Baby, I'm For Real," the work of Mr. and Mrs. Gaye, floated over breath-taking doo-wop harmonies and Paul Riser's airy backdrop, recalling a more innocent past and signaling Marvin's imminent future. It soared to the top slot on the R&B charts in late 1969 and climbed to No. 14 pop. "It's just one of those kind of songs that, it just stays. It touches people," noted Gorman. The Originals composed the ballad flip, "Moment Of Truth."

The group's debut album *Green Grow The Lilacs* had come out a few months earlier, but it was hastily retitled *Baby, I'm For Real* in honor of the smash.

Though the LP was dominated by lavish ballads ("I've Never Begged Before," "Love Is A Wonder"); there was a romping treatment of the hoary "Red Sails In The Sunset" and Ivy Jo's "Why When Love Is Gone."

Gaye also helmed the Originals' follow-up hit. "The Bells" was another ethereal doo-wop-derived ballad enriched by David Van de Pitte's multi-layered arrangement and lovely vocal interplay. "Marvin Gaye once said that we sounded like we were all brothers, same family. The diction and everything was so close," said Freddie. "The Bells" was a No. 12 pop and No. 4 R&B hit in early 1970. Marvin, a perfectionist in the studio, supplied the mellow flip, "I'll Wait For You."

"You'd do it over and over until he heard it. You were thinking it was okay, but there was something he was listening for, and that's what he wanted to hear," said Gorman. "But we didn't mind working with him, because we were all group people, and we loved the harmonies. He was a harmony man and a group man, and we all understood each other." Ballads took precedence on the group's mid-'70 encore LP *Portrait of the Originals*, though "Don't Stop Now" took an effervescent up-tempo route.

"We Can Make It Baby," in the same mode as his previous pair, was Marvin's last gift to the Originals. The mid-1970 hit was a two-sider: Frank Wilson supervised "I Like Your Style," written by all four Originals and Pam Sawyer in a more traditional Motown mode. "They flipped it, and we started getting airplay for that," said Gorman. Marvin had created another gem for the group, but "Just To Keep You Satisfied" was buried. "He had recorded it on us, and they wouldn't release it, Quality Control. Going out, he had the background say, 'I want your body,'" said Freddie. "Someone was appalled that we would say that. And they canned it, and it made him totally angry. What he did later on is he kept the same track and the same vocals, but he redid the melody and the lyric and released it on his *Let's Get It On* album."

The quartet was making up for lost time: *Naturally Together* made it three albums in less than a year-and-a-half. Chuck Jackson's "I Wake Up Crying" and Brook Benton's "Rainy Night In Georgia" were tasty cover choices, and the Supremes' dashing "My World Is Empty Without You" received an unusual ballad treatment. Producer Clay McMurray and Sawyer co-penned "If You Gonna Leave (Just Leave)" and a passionate "You Were My Everything," and Vincent DiMirco's "Once I Have You (I Will Never Let Go)" recalled Gaye's fragile beauty.

McMurray retained the reins for "God Bless Whoever Sent You," a sublime ballad that was a No. 14 R&B hit at the beginning of 1971. "That was Walter doing the primary lead," noted Gorman. After that, the group had several producers: Joe Hinton helmed the Berry Gordy original "Keep Me," while Johnny Bristol supervised "I'm Someone Who Cares" in early '72.

Spencer went solo in 1972, replaced, ironically by ex-Voice Master Ty Hunter. Born in 1943, Hunter had started out in the Romeos with Dozier and made singles of his own for Anna ("Everything About You" was a national hit in 1960), Check-Mate (ditto 1962's "Lonely Baby"), and Chess ("Bad Loser," "Darling, Darling, Darling") before a stint with the Glass House on H-D-H-owned Invictus Records in 1969.

Stevie Wonder employed unusual pedal steel guitar flourishes when he produced their "Game Called Love" in 1974 (the same year the Originals headed for L.A.). "That was Stevie's thing, and at that time he was trying to give us a little country feel," said Gorman. Dozier returned to produce the *California Sunset* LP, spawning their first R&B chart appearance in four-and-a-half years, "Good Lovin' Is Just A Dime

Away" (issued on Motown). "We worked hard on that album. That was like working with Marvin again," said Gorman. Frank Wilson helmed their last Soul hit, "Down To Love Town," in a disco bag, and it nicked the charts in late 1976.

Spencer returned during the late '70s, briefly making the Originals a quintet (Hunter died of cancer February 24, 1981). Freddie, Walter, and Hank still dish up heavenly harmonies as the Originals in L.A., their ranks now incorporating Hank's daughter, Terrie.

"We're just having a good time singing the old stuff again," said Freddie.

GENO PARKS

Motown's early years were loaded with wonderful platters by singers who weren't around Hitsville long enough to relish the worldwide acclaim. Few deserved it more than Geno Parks.

Born Gene Purifoy in the Fairfield section of Birmingham, Alabama—the same Ensley-Tuxedo Junction area that spawned the Tempts' Paul Williams and Eddie Kendricks as well as Dennis Edwards—on June 26, 1933, his melismatic delivery underscores his gospel roots. "I sang with the Harmony Four. That was in high school. And I also sang with the Five Spirituals," said Geno (though it was spelled Gino on his records, this is his preferred spelling). "When I was going to college, I sang with a group called the Evangelistic Gospel Singers. We were the first blacks on TV in Birmingham, Alabama." He relocated to the Motor City in 1954. "I went to see my mother one Christmas, and I never came back. I was attending Miles College in Birmingham, and my mother asked me to come visit her. And I went to visit her, and I just stayed."

Geno started singing locally in the summer of 1956. "I was going to school in Detroit," he said. "I was singing in

Geno Parks had a short but sweet tenure at Motown, waxing a handful of modestly successful releases. (Photo courtesy of Geno Parks).

a neighborhood bar. I started singing along with the band, just impromptu. So the fellow said, 'Well, come on up and do the gig.' So I did the gig. They paid me, so I started doin' the gig. But the guitar player was affiliated with Fortune Records. And they asked me if I wanted to sing in a group, which is my thing. My thing is groups, singing background. That's what I like to do. I said, 'What the heck, I ain't got nothin' else to do. I'll try it out.'"

Jack and Devora Brown's mom-and-pop Fortune operation boasted a dazzling doo-wop stable despite its diminutive size, including the Diablos and Andre Williams, who had cut some sides with the Five Dollars but was looking for another group. Out of that search came the Don Juans with Geno installed as first tenor, as well as the anonymous "New Group" (with Steve Gaston, Bobby Calhoun, and James "J" Johnson) that backed Andre on his 1957 national smash "Bacon Fat." "He went out as a single, he went on the road," said Parks. "When he came back, we hooked up."

"I knew I needed something else in the back of me, because I wasn't clicking by myself," said Williams in 1996. "So I sent for Geno, just to do a duo with me. And it clicked, and I just went on and took Geno. We just started goin' on the road together."

"We were booked out of Universal in New York," said Parks. "We did a little of the East Coast, but mainly we were in the South. We did one-nighters in the South with the Tab Smith Orchestra." Though he'd been billed under his surname of Purifoy on a Fortune duet or two with Andre (he contributed outrageous dialects and twisted harmonies to Williams' immortal "The Greasy Chicken"), Geno found a less exotic moniker might behoove him when promoting his solo Fortune single "Last Night I Cried" (paired with the upbeat "Just Go") at a televised record hop in Flint, Michigan.

"When I got to the TV studio, they didn't believe I was who I was because of the name Geno, and Purifoy," he explained. "It sounded funny for a black man. So I had a problem getting into the studio. There was a guy, he was working as a publicist, a p.r. person for Jack and Devora Brown at Fortune. And his name was Leo G. Parks. So I just assumed it. What the heck—it was simple, spelled easy, can't mess it up. So I just took his name Parks, and just kept Geno.

"We performed together up until 1960, Andre and I, as a duo. We split in '60 because I got married. The marriage didn't last that long, but that was the reason for our parting ways. It was because I assumed the responsibilities of a husband. The frivolity had to leave, because I had obligations that I had to fulfill being married. So I went as a single, and Andre went as a single," continued Parks, who had plenty of gigging opportunities on the Motor City circuit.

"I played 'em as a single and a duo. Denny's Show Bar. Oh, yes! That was in Detroit on the corner of Linwood and Euclid. Oh, man—that was one of our main spots! The 20 Grand and Denny's, Lee's Sensation, and Phelps'—down the street from Lee's Sensation, walking distance," he said. "Wilson Pickett would be playing Phelps'. I would be playing Lee's Sensation. During intermission, we'd swap up—I'd go down there and gig with him, he'd come up there and gig with me. Everything was love during that time."

Gordy brought Parks into Hitsville in 1960. "Nothing was happening at Fortune, so I left," he said. "The contract expired, and I signed with Motown." "Blibber Blabber," his rocking duet with an uncredited Henry Lumpkin, was slated for issue on fledgling Miracle in 1961 but never saw light of day. "That was another head arrangement thing, something that just popped up in Berry's mind," he said. "He was trying to do something that sounded like 'Yakety Yak.'" Its projected flip, "Don't Say Bye Bye," had been cut before as the 'B' side of Ron & Bill's otherworldly "It" in 1959 for Tamla.

Instead, a Mickey Stevenson-produced solo single emerged on Tamla in June of '61. "Everybody used to stay in the studio. It was like an all-day thing, sometimes an all-night thing," said Parks. "There was a session set up for Mary Wells. She was late. We were all ready to go. She was late. Hadn't called or anything, so the band is there. The Funk Brothers are there, right? So Mickey and I decided since Berry wasn't there and nobody else was there, we'd try to get something in. We were out in the hallway. There was a piano in the hallway, and he played some chords and I made up some words.

"We did 'That's No Lie' and 'Same Thing' at the same time. Same session. Waiting for Mary Wells to make it." Both were 24-karat gems: "That's No Lie" was a supercharged blues ballad, Parks laying down a passionate vocal reminiscent of James Brown at his pleadingest.[15] "Same Thing" rocked with a vengeance over choppy seventh chords, Geno summoning up a taste of Jackie Wilson-inspired swagger and Hank Cosby blowing up a storm during his honking sax solo. He came back in June of '62 with the exquisite "For This I Thank You," a standout produced by Clarence Paul that kicks off with a dramatic vocal curlicue before breaking into an easy minor-key swing buttressed by the Love-Tones' harmonies. Andre Williams was largely responsible for "Fire," Parks again contributing to the lyrics without receiving official credit.

That was the extent of Geno's Motown discography. "After awhile, things just wasn't happening for me. So I got a job at Chrysler, and I had bought a house, and all that sort of stuff. I had bills and things. I couldn't hang out like I used to, just for the sake of hanging out," he said. "While I worked for Chrysler, my contract expired, and I went with Golden World." "Talkin' About My Baby" and its 'B' side "My Sophisticated Lady" were released in early '66 by Golden World; a complement of moonlighting Funk Brothers provided the grooves, and Andre was its producer. Berry's ex-wife Raynoma and husband Eddie Singleton supervised Parks's "Nerves Of Steel" in Detroit for the Crazy Horse imprint in a year or so later before the security of a day gig removed Geno from musical action.

"I went to work for an insurance company in 1968. I worked as an agent in Detroit from '68 to '69. I didn't like that so well. My major in college was accounting, so I became a field auditor, and I traveled around the country auditing books. I got transferred to the home office, which was here in Atlanta. I've been here ever since," he reported. With recent retirement from Atlanta Life Insurance Company comes more time to enjoy the tranquility of domesticity with wife Mary and daughters Gena and LaTreasie along with the possibility of a musical comeback. "I'll pursue it if it's made feasible," he said.

CLARENCE PAUL

His greatest role at Motown was as mentor to Little Stevie Wonder, but Clarence Paul wore many hats at Hitsville as writer, producer, and on one Wonder hit, uncredited duet partner.

Born March 19, 1927, Paul hailed from sturdy gospel stock. Along with older brothers Curtis and Lowman Pauling, he grew up singing spirituals around their homebase of Winston-Salem, North Carolina, billed as the Royal Sons Quintet. Lowman would proceed to make his secular mark as lead guitarist and primary songwriter for the "5" Royales, one of the top vocal groups of the '50s with the 1953 R&B chart-topper "Baby Don't Do It" for Apollo and "Think" and "Dedicated To The One I Love" in 1957 for King.

Clarence attempted to mount a recording career as a singer with 45s on Roulette in 1959 ("Falling In Love" and flip "May Heaven Bless You") and Hanover (a catchy "I Need Your Lovin'" paired with "I'll Be By Your Side") the next year. Roy Hamilton made "I Need Your Lovin'" a hit on Epic during the spring of 1959 with a nearly identical treatment. Paul and his ex-vocal partner Mickey Stevenson split supervision on a single by Cornell Blakely for the Rich logo, Clarence producing and co-writing the uplifting "I've Got That Feeling" while Stevenson took care of a rocking "I Want My Share" himself (both published by fledgling Jobete).

Mickey brought Clarence into Motown as assistant A&R director. "They were friends from a long way back," said Kim Weston, Stevenson's ex-wife. "Clarence was a pro when he came to Motown. He had been in the business for years," noted Hank Cosby. Paul co-wrote Marvin Gaye's second hit "Hitch Hike" in '63 and hooked up with Hank Cosby for Little Stevie's '63 breakthrough "Fingertips." Paul produced "A Place In The Sun," "Hey Love," and "Travlin' Man" for Wonder, and sang a couple of duets with the lad: 1962's chaotic but fun "Little Water Boy," on which he was co-billed, and uncredited on Stevie's moving remake of Bob Dylan's "Blowin' In The Wind," which paced the R&B charts in 1966 and went Top Ten pop.

Paul left Motown in 1968 after a heated disagreement with creative division head Ralph Seltzer.[16] Rejoining Stevenson at Venture Records, he produced Calvin Arnold and Madlyn Quebec and co-wrote Vernon Garrett's "Hop, Skip & Jump," giving Stevie's "Angel Doll" new life on the flip. He died May 6, 1995, in Los Angeles.

PAUL PETERSEN

Quite a contrast, portraying Donna Reed's adorable teenage son on her squeaky-clean half-hour TV sitcom from 1958 to 1966 and recording under the mighty Motown banner. But Paul Petersen was 21 when he signed with the firm's West Coast branch in 1967, old enough to cut something meatier than "My Dad," his cloying '62 smash.

Born September 23, 1945, in Glendale, California, Petersen broke in as a Mouseketeer, then co-starred in the 1957 Cary Grant/Sophia Loren film *Houseboat* before joining Carl Betz, Shelley "Johnny Angel" Fabares, and the ill-fated Bob Crane in Reed's ensemble cast. Teen TV stardom sparked a successful recording career, Paul notching 1962 hits with the novelty "She Can't Find Her Keys," the Gerry Goffin/Carole King-penned "Keep Your Love Locked (Deep In Your Heart)," and "My Dad" for Colpix.

Frank Wilson supervised Petersen's first Motown platter, writing "Don't Let It Happen To Us" and its flip "Chained." The R&B-tinged 45 came out in the spring of 1967; Marvin Gaye would have more luck with "Chained" the next year. Petersen waited more than a year to encore: R. Dean Taylor's "A Little Bit For Sandy" had a hint of bubblegum pop in its catchy chorus and better fit Petersen's lighthearted delivery. Wilson and two cohorts supplied another R&B number for the flip, "Your Love's Got Me Burning Alive." After his Motown dalliance, Petersen continued to act and write and is now an advocate for ex-child stars in the film and TV industry.

THE PRETTY THINGS

The Pretty Things were cut from the same unkempt British Invasion blues-rock cloth as the Rolling Stones. In fact, lead guitarist Dick Taylor played with Mick Jagger and Keith Richards prior to forming the group. The band had already undergone retooling by the time their psychedelic concept album *S.F. Sorrow* turned up in Rare Earth's initial batch of 1969 releases (it had already been issued in the U.K. on Columbia). Only Taylor (born January 28, 1943, in Dartford, Kent,

The Pretty Things, 1969.

England) and singer Phil May (born November 9, 1944, in the same locale) remained from the original lineup, though Taylor would depart prior to the release of their 1970 Rare Earth encore *Parachute*. Organist John Povey, bassist Wally Allen, and drummer Twink had all come on board by the time *S.F. Sorrow* was recorded.

The band formed in 1963 in Kent, naming itself after a 1955 Bo Diddley rocker. With Brian Pendleton on rhythm guitar, John Stax on bass and harp, and drummer Viv Prince, the group scored its first British hit the following year with "Rosalyn" for Fontana. Its biggest single, "Don't Bring Me Down," came out that fall and pierced the British Top Ten. More U.K. hits followed—"Honey I Need" and "Cry To Me" in '65, "Midnight To Six Man" and "Come See Me" the next year. Despite their ballsy blues-rock attack, the Pretty Things never charted in the U.S. *S.F. Sorrow* is reputed to have been the first rock opera, and their "Private Sorrow" with "Ballroom Burning" was the first single release on Rare Earth in July of '69.

BARBARA RANDOLPH

The Four Tops' early H-D-H-produced albums were so stuffed with potential hits that some deserving numbers got lost in the shuffle. The overlooked "I Got A Feeling" led off the *Four Tops On Top* LP in 1966, and it possessed the same rousing drive when Soul issued Barbara Randolph's alluring remake in August of 1967—even though hers was produced by Hal Davis in L.A. Barbara gained valuable early experience in her teens when she briefly replaced Zola Taylor as the lone distaff member of the Platters prior to ex-Chantel Sandra Dawn's stint with the group. Her solo potential was at least temporarily realized at Motown: Randolph's sexy vocal on "I Got A Feeling" should have resulted in a hit but didn't.

Soul tried again a year later with another H-D-H revival, this time Marvin Gaye's "Can I Get A Witness" (both of her 45s shared the same pop-slanted flip, "You Got Me Hurtin' All Over," co-written by producer Davis). A scheduled album was canceled and Randolph's Motown tenure ended uneventfully, though she filled in for Tammi Terrell on occasion as Marvin's duet partner when Tammi's failing health prevented her from making live appearances.

RARE EARTH

Motown had undertaken a few half-hearted attempts to crack the rock market prior to 1969, but none ignited nationally like Rare Earth—group *and* label. The Detroit sextet's thundering remake of the Tempts' "Get

Ready" was a massive pop hit that year, ensuring that the new Motown subsidiary named after them would endure for a while.

The group started out as a blue-eyed soul outfit called the Sunliners, constructed around the stirring lead vocals of drummer Pete Hoorelbeke (who adopted the stage surname of Rivera) and saxist/flutist Gil Bridges. Rounded out by future Motown engineer Russ Terrana on guitar, Ralph Terrana on keys, bassist John Persh, and saxist Steve Fischer, the Sunliners recorded "The Swingin' Kind" with "All Alone" for Ed Wingate's Golden World label in 1965. But their main claim to fame from 1964 to '69 was as one of the Motor City's premier live Top 40 bands.

Rare Earth.

Changing their moniker to Rare Earth in 1968, the group made a spacy debut album, *Dreams/Answers*, for Verve (co-producer Dennis Coffey was in the midst of rewriting the rules for Motown lead guitarists with his distorted rock licks). Margaret Gordy brought Rare Earth into Hitsville, convincing vice president Barney Ales of their potential. Over the course of five all-night Studio A sessions during the fall of '69, Rare Earth committed its club set to tape.

Short of material, the band stretched its treatment of Smokey's "Get Ready" to 21 1/2 minutes in length. That marathon performance blanketed the entire second side of *Get Ready*, released in August of '69 as the third album on the Rare Earth logo. Though it took four months to crack the pop album lists, *Get Ready* eventually skated up to No. 12 on *Billboard's* charts, lingering for more than a year. A severely edited single version of the title track appeared in February of '70, but it blasted up to No. 4 pop and surprisingly managed Top 20 R&B status.

With Pete rattling the rafters vocally from behind his drum kit, Rare Earth was a knockout live act. "Man, they would tear the place up," said McDougal. *Ecology*, Rare Earth's encore album, emerged that summer to similarly lofty sales figures and contained another hit Tempts remake produced by Norman Whitfield. "(I Know) I'm Losing You" again pierced the pop Top Ten and R&B Top 20. "Born To Wander," supervised by writer Tom Baird, was pulled from Ecology and hit as well. *One World*, their solid-selling '71 LP, harbored the resonant rock anthem "I Just Want To Celebrate," Rare Earth's last Top Ten pop entry that fall.

The paranoid rocker "Hey Big Brother" was a Top 20 pop seller at the end of the year, but after the double-LP *Rare Earth In Concert* scored in early '72, things began to unravel. Insisting on writing their own material for the *Willie Remembers* LP was a mistake, and Whitfield couldn't halt the tailspin by helming 1973's funky *Ma*. Frank Wilson supervised their revival of "Chained" in '74; Stewart Levine helmed "It Makes You Happy (But It Ain't Gonna Last Too Long)."

Personnel changes were always on the horizon. Rod Richards, Rare Earth's 1969-70 guitarist, was spelled by Ray Monette from '71 to '76. Bassist Persh, who doubled on trombone, exited in '72 in favor of Michael Urso, and Kenny James, the band's keyboardist in '69-'70, gave way to Mark Olson from '71 to '74. Percussionist Edward Guzman joined the ranks in 1970. Only Hoorelbeke and Bridges were constant presences, and they ended up wrangling in a court of law over who owned the band's name after it fell apart. Any bruised feelings didn't stop the band from reforming to record for the fledgling Prodigal imprint in 1977, but that album and two followups failed to regenerate their momentum.

For their first few years, though, Rare Earth made Motown a legitimate rock force.

DAVID RUFFIN

It's not as if David Ruffin hadn't been on his own before. Prior to joining the Tempts in 1963, the bespectacled, ultra-thin dynamo had cut a spectacular '61 single for Billy Davis and Gwen Gordy at Anna ("I'm In Love") and two more gems for the couple 's Chess-affiliated Check-Mate: "Action Speaks Louder Than Words" and "Mr. Bus Driver–Hurry."

Born January 18, 1941, in Whynot, Mississippi, David had a heart condition as a child, but it didn't stop him. He moved to Detroit in his early teens, singing with the Dixie Nightingales before going secular. Older brother Jimmy, already on Motown, had tried in vain to procure a solo contract for David prior to his joining the Temptations. "I was trying to get him at Motown, and they wouldn't sign him," said Jimmy. "I kept after people, 'Why don't you sign my brother?' And one time somebody told me, 'We've got the Ruffin we want.' People could not see David's voice, really. They just didn't like his hoarse, raspy sound. Motown wasn't into that."

David Ruffin was booted from The Temptations in 1968 and had to go it alone, both on the stage and off, until his death from a drug overdose at age 50 in 1991 (Photo courtesy of David Alston's Mahogany Archives).

After the furor of his being voted out of the Tempts in June of 1968 died down, David relaunched his solo career at Motown with "My Whole World Ended (The Moment You Left Me)," a No. 2 R&B and No. 9 pop smash in early 1969. With the Originals ladling out buttery harmonies in the midst of an epic tale of heartbreak, "My Whole World Ended" (penned by co-producers Johnny Bristol and Harvey Fuqua along with Pam Sawyer and Jimmy Roach) kicked off a new phase of Ruffin's life.

David Ruffin had success as a solo artist in the late 1960s and 1970s, including his '69 release "My Whole World Ended."

"I just happened to have that song. We were assigned to do David Ruffin right when they had the split. I came up with that and a couple more," said Bristol. "It was perfect timing. It was amazing. He did a great job." The mood was nearly as bleak on the 'B' side, "I've Got To Find Myself A Brand New Baby," its propulsive rhythm track again offering stark contrast. Bristol was also responsible for David's follow-up "I've Lost Everything I've Ever Loved," another exquisite plunge into the depths of depression softened somewhat by a majestic mid-tempo arrangement. Once again, Ruffin attacked the song with a vengeance—you really believe he's on the edge of ending it all—and he enjoyed a hit that summer that just missed the R&B Top Ten.

Much of *My Whole World Ended*, Ruffin's first solo album, retained the same gloomy tone, Ruffin's spiraling falsetto shrieks punctuating George Gordy and Allen "Bo" Story's anguished "The Double Cross," the Hank Cosby/Pam Sawyer/Joe Hinton copyright "Somebody Stole My Dream," Bristol and Sawyer's "Pieces Of A Man," and the devastating "World Of Darkness," the ultimate antidote to the sunny optimism Ruffin espoused on the Tempts' "My Girl." A cover of Joe Simon's 1968 hit "Message From Maria" extended the grim ambiance, though Robert Knight's "Everlasting Love" and another Gordy/Story number, "We'll Have A Good Thing Going On," were lighter.

Berry Gordy took over the reins for Ruffin's last hit of 1969, imparting a concentrated shot of gospel feeling to "I'm So Glad I Fell For You" with the help of the Hal Davis Singers (indicating the number was laid down in L.A.). The firebreathing flip "I Pray Everyday You Won't Regret Loving Me" reverted to the Detroit sound on a stormer penned by Bristol and Gladys and Bubba Knight. Both graced David's encore LP *Feelin' Good*, alongside Nick Ashford and Valerie Simpson's "What You Gave Me," Clay McMurray's "I Don't Know Why I Love You," and "The Letter"—not the Box Tops' then-recent hit, but a collaboration by Smokey Robinson, Al Cleveland, and Terry Johnson. A cover of Johnnie Taylor's '69 Stax hit "I Could Never Be President" predictably drew more sparks than Dave Mason's "Feeling Alright."

Teaming David with older sib Jimmy for the 1970 Soul album *I Am My Brother's Keeper* was an inspired idea, even if the set only spawned one hit: A Frank Wilson-produced revival of Ben E. King's '61 classic "Stand By Me." David wouldn't find his way back on the charts for nearly three years, despite the quality releases "Don't Stop Loving Me" and "You Can Come Right Back To Me" in '71 and "A Little More Trust" the next year. Finally, "Common Man," produced by Philly-based Bobby Miller, restored Ruffin to prominence in the summer of '73. His eponymous album that year also featured the Kenny Gamble and Leon Huff-penned "I Miss You," again helmed by Miller—an important cog in the Philly International hit-making machine. Harold Melvin & the Blue Notes had torched the original the year before in Philly.

After a couple more Ruffin singles bombed, he came back bigger than ever in late 1975. Van McCoy had recently produced the original RCA version of "Walk Away With Love" by the Washington, D.C.-based Choice Four to little response. When Ruffin dug into the number, he took it all the way to the top of the R&B listings and went Top Ten pop, regenerating his star power. McCoy supervised "Heavy Love" and "Everything's Coming Up Love" for David, both garnering Top Ten R&B status in 1976. "On And Off," another McCoy creation, closed out '76 for Ruffin in solid style, and the partnership extended into 1977 for "Just Let Me Hold You For A Night" and "You're My Peace Of Mind" the next year.

A 1979 move to Warner Brothers resulted in the R&B smash "Break My Heart," but David returned to the Tempts for the 1982 Reunion tour and scored a couple of duet hits with Eddie Kendrick (who had dropped the 's' by then) during the late '80s. The older Ruffin got, the more destructive his inner demons grew. On June 1, 1991, a cocaine overdose removed him from our midst at age 50.

"The David Ruffin that he showed to the public was not really David. It was a David that he concocted and manufactured for public consumption," said Jimmy Ruffin. "They never really knew the guy. He'd just show people what he wanted them to see. But he never did want people to see the real him. Because he didn't feel comfortable. I guess that's why he's dead. Those people who can't be themselves and have to play these roles, the business will kill them."

JIMMY RUFFIN

Motown never placed much promotional muscle behind Jimmy Ruffin. That David's older brother still scored two Top Ten R&B smashes in 1966 for its Soul subsidiary testifies to the strength of his vocal appeal.

"I think that they just didn't like me personally. I'm outspoken," said Ruffin. "I wasn't a part of the clique."

Born May 7, 1939, in Collinsville, Mississippi, Jimmy and his younger brother David were raised in a relatively well-to-do environment, their early musical pursuits permeated in southern gospel tradition. "Choirs, solo, glee club—all kinds of stuff," said Jimmy. "We sang in a family group, which was essentially my group, really. The group was called the Spiritual Trying Four. We were these kick-ass Jackson 5-type gospel guys, David and I." He accrued more vocal experience in the service. "I sang in the military, in doo-wop groups. Traveling shows in the military, entertaining troops," said Ruffin. "Finally left the military and went back to Mississippi for about eight to 10 months, and then went to Detroit."

David was already there. "He convinced me to come up to Detroit, and I finally went, because I had family there," said Jimmy, who made a local name for himself after debuting at the Ebony Club in Muskegon. "My brother kept insisting that I audition. So after I auditioned for the record companies and everybody wanted to sign me, finally I ended up going down to Motown after some encouragement from certain people like Mary Wells and Marv Johnson."

Ruffin inaugurated Berry's short-lived Miracle imprint with the self-penned rocker "Don't Feel Sorry For Me" in January of 1961. "I heard that record and cringed when I first heard it. When I heard it, to me, I heard Jackie Wilson," he said. "I was copying Jackie Wilson without knowing I was doing it. Motown liked it, but I felt a little bit embarrassed. I didn't want to sound like anybody." Two-and-a-half-years separated Ruffin's first two singles. "I recorded bits and pieces of stuff, but I didn't have any releases," he said. "I was working for Ford Motor Company, and playing in Detroit on weekends. At one period of that time, I was playing guitar with my brother, before the Temptations. I was like his musical director." The two were versatile. "One night David and I were doing a gig, and we were playing for John Lee Hooker, because his band didn't show up—with David on drums and me on guitar."

Finally, Ruffin landed on Soul and had the second release on the purple-hued label in mid-'64, the easy-grooving Norman Whitfield production "Since I've Lost You." "We wrote that, actually. I didn't get credited for it," said Ruffin. "The song originally was called 'They Call Me Mr. Blue.' I'm the one that changed (the line) to, 'My life is so blue.' It wasn't like a big record, but it let me know I had a commercial sound." Eddie Holland and producer Whitfield wrote the flip "I Want Her Love." Smokey Robinson handed Jimmy the mid-tempo "As Long As There Is L-O-V-E Love" as his first Soul follow-up in 1965. "I just said, 'Hey, man, why don't you write me a song?'" said Ruffin. "I kept bugging him, and he finally brought that song in."

Despite Jimmy Ruffin's reservations about the opening of "I've Passed This Way Before," the song cracked the Top 20 in 1967.

All the years of struggle paid off in the summer of '66 when the anguished "What Becomes Of The Brokenhearted"—the brainchild of James Dean and William Weatherspoon, and Paul Riser—made Jimmy a star. "The producers had planned to record it on the Spinners. They had the track, and I just happened to hear it, and told the producer, 'Hey, this song is not for the Spinners,'" said Ruffin. "I didn't even hear the lyrics, just the melody. He just said, 'Well, sing it.' Gave me the lyrics—they hadn't finished the lyrics, but just a verse and a chorus—and I started singing it to the track. He said, 'You're right.'" With Weatherspoon and Mickey Stevenson behind the glass and the Originals providing backing vocals (as they would on several of his subsequent hits), Ruffin poured his heart and soul into the sweeping stunner.

"After we recorded it, they sat on it forever. And the spiel that I did on the beginning of it, which was on Diana Ross's version, they took that off. That's why there's such a long introduction. There was this talking part. They didn't think a black guy could sell this," he said. "It was so different. If you look back at the records that were out at the time, that was definitely a different record." Mickey wrote the 'B' side "Baby I've Got It" with Dean and Sylvia Moy, handling the production himself. Ruffin credits two deejays on Chicago's WVON radio, E. Rodney Jones and Pervis Spann, with launching the record. "These are the guys that are responsible for my success," he said. "They broke the record in Chicago. Then after the record broke in Chicago, it broke everywhere else, and then Motown started sending me out to promote it." Meanwhile, McDougal worked the record hard around Philly, exposing it to the East Coast. No more toiling at the Ford plant for Jimmy: "I quit the job after 'Brokenhearted' was a hit," he said.

Dean (a first cousin to Brian and Eddie Holland) and Weatherspoon were also responsible for Ruffin's second smash before year's close, "I've Passed This Way Before." "Dean and Spoon were ex-soldiers," said Ruffin. "We'd all been in the military together, so we got along fine." This time, the pair left Jimmy's introductory monolog intact. "I'll never feel comfortable with that, 'cause I did it like I don't believe in it. Because they took the talking part off 'What Becomes Of The Brokenhearted.' Now with 'I've Passed This Way Before,' I thought, 'What am I doing this for? They're going to take it off.' So I did it with no conviction." "I've Passed This Way Before" nevertheless vaulted into the R&B Top Ten and pop Top 20.

The Miracles' Bobby Rogers named the '67 debut LP *Jimmy Ruffin Sings Top Ten.* "When I went Top Ten with 'Brokenhearted,' he came in there," said Jimmy. "He was going, 'Damn, Jimmy Ruffin's in the Top Ten! Wow!'" The action shot on the cover wasn't Ruffin's cup of tea. "There's a picture of me taken live of me at the 20 Grand," he said. "With a big record like 'Brokenhearted,' why wouldn't they do a proper photo session?"

The set contained three intriguing covers: "Halfway To Paradise" and "Bless You" had been 1961 pop hits for young crooner Tony Orlando on Epic, while "Black Is Black" was borrowed from the momentarily hot European rock band Los Bravos. "I do a lot of pop stuff," he said. "I grew up on MGM musicals and Frankie Laine, all kinds of stuff. Mario Lanza. These are people that I used to be into growing up—Mahalia Jackson, gospel, doo-wop, blues."

The album featured both sides of Ruffin's next single: James Jamerson's pulsing bass introduced the urgent "Gonna Give Her All The Love I've Got," a Whitfield/Strong copyright in the same mid-tempo mold as his two prior hits that rose to No. 14 R&B in the spring of '67. Producer Whitfield would later recycle it on Marvin Gaye. "Norman was one of my best friends," noted Ruffin. Dean and Weatherspoon's storming "World So Wide, Nowhere To Hide (From Your Heart)," easily one of Jimmy's hardest-driving waxings, deserved better than 'B' side status.

"Don't You Miss Me A Little Bit Baby," another fine outing by Whitfield, Strong, and Roger Penzabene that percolated over a simmering rhythm, was a national hit for Jimmy in the summer of '67. "Roger was a Jewish guy that everybody thought was black," said Ruffin. "I didn't, but most people around Motown did—until he died. Killed himself, committed suicide."

Then the hits stopped. Dean and Weatherspoon's "I'll Say Forever My Love" should have extended his streak in early '68, and Norman and Barrett's "Don't Let Him Take Your Love From Me" was right in Ruffin's mid-tempo wheelhouse but also missed that summer. Jimmy's treatment of the Whitfield/Strong in-house favorite "Gonna Keep On Tryin' Till I Win Your Love" didn't crack the hit parade either. The saucy "Sad And Lonesome Feeling" on the 'B' side might have been a better bet. The Dean/Weatherspoon-generated "Farewell Is A Lonely Sound" avoided the U.S. charts in '69 but became a Top Ten British hit in 1970 (Frank Wilson's flip "If You Will Let Me, I Know I Can" fared better when Eddie Kendricks revived it in 1972).

Jimmy's second Soul LP, *Ruff'n Ready*, came out in 1969. Mostly comprised of recent 45s and extraordinarily strong, the set featured a Brian Holland/Lamont Dozier-produced treatment of ? & the Mysterians' garage rock anthem "96 Tears" that retained the prominent organ from the original but beefed up the surging groove with tight horns. Jimmy had fun updating Marv Johnson's "You Got What It Takes" with producer Richard Morris, while "Love Gives, Love Takes" emanated from Dean and Weatherspoon. "I'll Say Forever My Love" and "It's Wonderful (To Be Loved By You)" were huge 1970 sellers for Jimmy in Great Britain. "These were Top Ten hits in England, but they weren't in America, because they weren't promoted," he said.

A year-and-a-half later, Soul released *The Groove Governor*, the source of Ruffin's last two Soul singles. The bravura "Maria (You Were The Only One)," issued in late 1970, slipped Latin overtones into a standout by Lawrence Brown, Allen "Bo" Story (who had cut for Anna and Check-Mate a decade earlier), and George Gordy. "That song should have been a bigger record," said Ruffin. "No promotion." The loping 'B' side "Living In A World I Created For Myself" from the same team was scarcely less potent. Gordy, Story, and Brown also came up with Jimmy's Soul farewell, "Our Favorite Melody," while Johnny Bristol and Harvey Fuqua were behind the uplifting flip, "You Gave Me Love." *The Groove Governor*—a title that baffles Jimmy to this day—incorporated another "Maria" ode in the form of R.B. Greaves' smash "Take A Letter Maria" alongside Dean and Weatherspoon's "Let's Say Goodbye, Tomorrow," "On The Way Out (On The Way In)," and "Just Before Love Ends."

Jimmy and David teamed for an invigorating duo album, *I Am My Brother's Keeper*, in the autumn of 1970 for Soul. "Just something I wanted to do as an ode to my family," he said. "That's why there's a picture of my mother and my father on the back. I got those pictures together. David, that's the time when he was into the cocaine, and I had to twist his arm to get him to do that. I had to first convince the company to do it, and then try to convince him."

Their dynamic remake of Ben E. King's '61 smash "Stand By Me," produced by Frank Wilson with an eye toward pseudo-live ambiance, gave Jimmy his first chart entry in three years. "I had to do most of the singing on the end of it, 'cause he never showed up for the session," said Ruffin. "He wasn't that crazy about doing it. He didn't show up for the session, and Frank had me doing all the singing at the end that David was supposed to be doing."

The pair mellowed out on the flip by Pam Sawyer and Gloria Jones, "Your Love Was Worth Waiting For." The LP saw the sibs bouncing off one another in incendiary fashion on "True Love Can Be Beautiful," "Set 'Em Up (Move In For The Thrill)," and Duke Browner's "The Things We Have To Do." Tyrone Davis' "Turn Back The Hands Of Time," the Delfonics' "Didn't I (Blow Your Mind This Time)," and the Hollies' "He Ain't Heavy, He's My Brother" rated cover treatment. Both halves of their second Soul 45, Sawyer and Jones' "When My Love Hand Comes Down" and "Steppin' On A Dream" (by Joe Hinton, Dean, and Hank Cosby) were aboard.

Over the years, Jimmy built a sizable fan base over in Great Britain. "I just came to England because there was work," he said. Fed up with the lack of promotion, Jimmy split in 1970. "That's why I left America. Somebody at Motown who I won't name—one of the Motown hierarchy—helped me to pull the wool over the eyes of the Motown company to get me out of there, because they wouldn't let me go," he said.

Ruffin kept recording in the U.S. Through LeBaron Taylor, he did a 1973 single for Atco, "Tears Of Joy" with "Goin' Home," and made a minor R&B chart impact in '74 with a self-penned "Tell Me What You Want" for Chess (New Yorker Jimmy Roach, who had worked in a similar capacity for Motown, arranged its 'B' side, "Do You Know Me"). "I did it for Polydor in England," Ruffin said. "They heard it on import and tracked me down to get me to sign it with Chess." The British connection paid off in 1980, when Robin Gibb of the Bee Gees wrote and produced his "Hold On To My Love," a Top Ten pop hit on Robert Stigwood's RSO logo.

After many years of English residence, Jimmy was weighing a move back to the states when interviewed for this book.

SAN REMO GOLDEN STRINGS

Sounds like stiff competition for the 101 Strings, doesn't it? Guess again. The San Remo Golden Strings—apparently named after an Italian town—was a high-falutin' alias for familiar Motor City moonlighters trafficking in comparatively sedate violin-dominated fare.

"That was Gil Askey as arranger and the producer," said Hank Cosby. "I don't know who he used as the rhythm section. He probably used Motown players." Berry inherited the franchise from Ed Wingate's Ric-Tic operation when he acquired his chief local competitor, for whom the Golden Strings instrumentals "Hungry For Love" and "I'm Satisfied" had dented the pop charts in 1965. Gordy Records reissued "Festival Time," out the year before on Ric-Tic, in the spring of '67 (backed with "Joy Road"). Blessed by an uncredited vocal by Laura Lee, "Festival Time" remains a hot item on the British Northern Soul scene. *Hungry For Love*, the Strings' Ric-Tic LP, was restored to print in the Gordy catalog, and the imprint issued a second LP, *Swing*, in '68.

THE SATINTONES/ CHICO LEVERETT

Berry Gordy was picky about vocal groups during Motown's earliest days, so when he signed the Satintones in 1959, you know they had something special.

The original lineup consisted of lead and second tenor James Ellis, first tenor William "Sonny" Sanders (born August 6, 1939, in Chicago Heights, Illinois), lead/baritone Charles "Chico" Leverett, and bass Robert Bateman. Ellis had previously sung with the Five Sounds, Sanders had harmonized with Freddie Gorman in the Quailtones and Fidelitones, and Bateman was a charter member of the Rayber Voices, who backed Marv Johnson, Barrett Strong, and Mary Wells on their early Gordy productions. Leverett had pulled a solo on Tamla's first release in the 54000 series, the firm issuing his "Solid Sender" with "I'll Never Love Again" for local consumption in June of 1959 (the Raybers handled his harmonies, too). Four months later, the Satintones debuted on Tamla with two rockers, "Motor City" and "Going To The Hop." Both sides were penned by Gordy and Leverett, with Ellis doing the lead honors on the vastly preferable 'A' side.

The Satintones inaugurated Motown's 1000 series in February of '60 with a doo-wopping "My Beloved" with the slinky "Sugar Daddy," a Gordy/Sanders/Leverett creation. Strings were added to one pressing of the Ellis-led 'A' side (written by Berry, Chico, and Brian Holland) to impart an uptown soul feel. The quartet got into hot water with their Motown encore in early 1961: Smokey's "A Love That Can Never Be" passed muster, but "Tomorrow & Always"—an answer to the Shirelles' late '60 smash "Will You Love Me Tomorrow"—was withdrawn from the marketplace over copyright infringement issues.[17] "Tomorrow & Always" existed in two completely different versions. A few weeks later, "A Love That Can Never Be" reemerged on a third variation of Motown 1006, this time paired with the lovely Ellis-led ballad "Angel."

Tenor Vernon Williams came in to front the stately "I Know How It Feels" and its flip "My Kind Of Love," issued that summer. Sammy Mack also became a Satintone around this time; Leverett was out, and Ellis split before the group disbanded. A rocking adaptation of the ancient artifact "Zing Went The Strings Of My Heart" owing little to the Coasters' '58 version and "Faded Letter" closed out their Motown discography that autumn.

Two Satintones went on to greater things following the group's demise. The deep-voiced Bateman distinguished himself as a Motown recording engineer and producer (he co-helmed the Marvelettes' "Please Mr. Postman") before leaving to work with Wilson Pickett, Mary Wells (at 20th Century Fox), and Lou Courtney. Sanders got started as an arranger on Eddie Holland's '62 Motown hit "Jamie" before defecting to Golden World to clef the Reflections' '64 smash "(Just Like) Romeo & Juliet" and Edwin Starr's "Agent Double-O-Soul" and "Stop Her On Sight (S.O.S.)" for Ric-Tic. Sonny became involved with Carl Davis's Brunswick/Dakar operation in Chicago as the decade progressed, arranging Jackie Wilson's "(Your Love Keeps Lifting Me) Higher And Higher," Barbara Acklin's "Love Makes A Woman," and Young-Holt Unlimited's "Soulful Strut" (not a Young-Holt waxing at all, but that's another story). And Leverett surfaced in 1963 on King's Bethlehem logo with the coupling "Baby (Don't Leave)" with "Work Work."

THE SERENADERS

In 1963, Raynoma Gordy established Motown's New York outpost in the fabled Brill Building. The venture folded not long thereafter, but it did net the Serenaders, who cut a fine single for V.I.P. Three Serenaders went on to enjoy lasting success in the music business: George Kerr wrote and produced for Motown and All Platinum (he had his own 1970 hit for the latter, "3 Minutes 2—Hey Girl"); his writing partner Sidney Barnes cut the suave "New York City" for producer Herb Abramson before joining psychedelic soul-rockers Rotary Connection late in the decade, and Timothy Wilson (born November 17, 1943, in Salisbury, Maryland) scored a '67 hit for Buddah with "Baby, Baby Please." Bass Howard Curry rounded out the quartet.

Saying Wilson got started young is a profound understatement. Adopting Frankie Lymon and Little Anthony as his prime role models, he joined Tiny Tim & the Hits at the tender age of 13. "The group was originally called Five Hits and a Miss, and the Miss was a girl," he said. "She decided to leave the group, and that left the boy as a lead singer. I used to always come around and sing around. Never really took anything real seriously. So one of the other members of the group was more aware of my talent than I was, really. So he asked me to join the group.

"In 1958, Bobby Freeman came to town. He came to one of the ballrooms in Salisbury. We were on the show," he said. "When Bobby came in, his manager took a liking to us. His name was Walt Summers. So Walt says to us, 'Hey guys, do you guys have any original material?' So we said, 'Yeah, we got some original material.' He said, 'Well, can I hear some?' We said, 'Yes, you can hear it.' He says, 'Where can we go to audition?' Well, the guy who was managing us at the time, he owned a cab stand across the street. So he says, 'Well, we'll go over to the cab stand, and we'll let you hear some of this stuff.'" Four days later, they made demos, and the following week the group recorded the Lymonesque "Wedding Bells" and "Doll Baby" at New York's Bell Sound for Roulette. "I just missed Frankie Lymon by hours," Wilson lamented. "Frankie had just left out of the studio when we came in."

When the group broke up, the rest formed the Diplomats and scored a 1964 hit for Arock, "Here's A Heart." Wilson went in a different direction. "After Tiny Tim & the Hits disbanded, the other members moved to Long Island. I remained in New Jersey," said Wilson. "George Kerr had previously heard the group Tiny Tim & the Hits. After he had found out that we had split, then he became interested in me as a lead singer for the Serenaders. He was the originator of the Serenaders." The quartet made a '63 Wilson-led single for Riverside, "Adios, My Love."

"In 1963, we found out that Motown was opening an office in New York," said Timothy. "We made it out there just to be one of the first groups to audition for Motown. We compiled a bunch of original material of different types—ballad, up-tempo, different meters—so we had a variety of songs going in. We auditioned for Ray Gordy, who was married to Berry at the time. We auditioned for her, and she liked the group. And the next time we auditioned, we auditioned for Ray and Berry himself.

"We didn't even know that Berry was in the room when we were auditioning for the second time. After we finished our audition, Ray says, 'Well, guys, I want you to meet Mr. Gordy.' We didn't know who he was. He was just sittin' there. We thought maybe he might have been a producer for Motown, somebody like that. In a way, I guess that was good that we didn't know who he was," he continued. "Berry was impressed with what he heard. He says, 'Well, would you guys be interested in going down to Motown to record?' Our answer, of course, was yes. And he realized the songwriting ability of George Kerr and Sidney Barnes, based on the material that we presented to him. Later on, they became songwriters for Jobete Music."

Though the auditions took place in the Brill Building, the Serenaders cut their session at Hitsville under the stewardship of Berry and Miss Ray. "We recorded three or four songs for them, and Berry released 'If Your Heart Says Yes' and 'I'll Cry Tomorrow.' There's probably still a couple of other songs in the archives someplace that we did. I sang lead on the 'A' side," said Wilson, "and George sang lead on 'I'll Cry Tomorrow.' While we were there, George got a little hoarse, and Eddie Kendricks helped us out on a song called 'Say, Say Baby.' Different acts used to hang around the studio, especially when somebody new was coming in to record. We came in, pretty sharp guys from New York with the hairdos and so forth, so it created some excitement for the newcomers down there.

"Once George and Sidney became songwriters, Ray suggested that I should pick up a couple of guys to go out on the road as the Serenaders. The record, believe it or not, took off," said Wilson. "It was destined to be a smash, but because of some political reasons that happened back in New York, Berry opted to stop the record. That's the reason the record didn't become a national hit. But it was well on its way."

Despite that setback (which closed out his Hitsville affiliation), Wilson found romance within the extended Motown family, marrying Ray's sister Alice in 1965. He made two solo 45s for United Artists' Veep logo ("Come On Home" and "He Will Break Your Heart") that same year, then waxed "Baby, Baby Please" for Buddah with Kerr at the helm. "He came to me one day with a song that he had recorded for a girl," said Timothy. "He said, 'Tim, I think you can do this song. This girl that we put on the track, I don't really like the way she's coming off. I think you can bail me out on this thing, 'cause I got a deal for it if it comes off.' So I went to his house on a Sunday. We rehearsed 'Baby, Baby Please,' and recorded it that Monday night. I did one take on it. That was it. He wouldn't let me do anymore. He said, 'We got it. That's it!'"

Wilson's mile-high tenor shimmered on the tender ballad, a No. 45 R&B hit at the end of '67. It spawned three more Buddah releases ("Pig Tails," "Loving You," and "My Queen Of Hearts") the next year. Timothy's live band during this period was the young but already funky Kool & the Gang. Two fine Wilson 45s for Mercury's Blue Rock imprint—a Van McCoy-penned "I Wanna Know Right Now (Do You Love Me)" and "Are You Really Happy"—came out in '69.

In addition to maintaining his own career, Timothy recently discovered a surefire path to the fountain of youth—he joined the reformed Teenagers, eliciting memories of his childhood idol Lymon. They recently starred on PBS-TV's *Doo Wop 51* special.

THE SISTERS LOVE

After lifting their heavenly voices behind Ray Charles for years as his indispensable Raeletts, the Sisters Love stepped out to make their own sweet music. By the time they joined Mowest for the March 1972 single "Mr. Fix-It Man" with "You've Got To Make The Choice," there had been a personnel change or two, the lineup solidifying as ex-Raeletts Lillie Fort and Gwendolyn Berry, lead singer Vermettya Boyster from Jacksonville, Florida, and Jeannie Long.

Sisters Love gather at Motown's L.A. office. Jeannie Long is second from the left, and lead singer Vermettya Boyster is on far right (Weldon A. McDougal III photo).

"They told me that when they were Raeletts, Ray would call them 'Sister Gwen,' 'Sister Lillie,' and Merry Clayton, they called her 'Baby Sister,'" explained Long, a native of Waukegan, Illinois. "So when they left Ray, they just took on the name Sisters Love." Clayton was an early Sister, but Long was aboard when the quartet signed with L.A.-based A&M, best known for co-owner Herb Alpert's hits with the Tijuana Brass.

"We were the first black group that signed onto A&M," said Long, who had only sung in church prior to joining the Sisters Love (she had been working for actress Gail Fisher when J.W. Alexander's wife mentioned the group was seeking fresh blood). "They weren't really ready for a black group. Hosea Wilson was the promotion director." Wilson and Chicago soul singer Gene Chandler were steering the Sisters Love's career; the group cut six A&M 45s, beginning with 1969's "Eye To Eye (Let's Get Together)" with "Forget It, I've Got It." They encored with a cover of the Beatles' "Blackbird," "The Bigger You Love" in 1970, and "Ha Ha Ha" in early '71.

In the summer of '71, the group had a No. 20 R&B hit with its fifth A&M offering, "Are You Lonely?" "That was produced by Gene Chandler," said Long. "Gene didn't like the lead, so he took Vermettya into Chicago, and she redid the lead vocal on that." "And This Is Love," flipped with "The Bigger You Love," closed out their A&M tenure later that year.

The Sisters Love did all their recording for Motown at the Mowest studios in Hollywood.

After "Mr. Fix-It Man" ("I think Gwen was the lead on that song," noted Jeannie), they issued the slightly suggestive "You've Got My Mind" with "Try It, You'll Like It" that October. In January of '73, the quartet tried again with the Gloria Jones/Janie Bradford-penned "(I Could Never Make) A Better Man Than You" and its flip, "Give Me Your Love."

The Original Spinners, the Spinners' breakthrough LP from 1967, included songs from Smokey Robinson, Barry and Robert Gordy, and Harvey Fuqua.

"It was Mettya that sang most of the lead," said Long. "She was something. She was a very strong lead person." The group circled the globe with the Jackson 5, opening for them on the Gary group's first British jaunt. "We toured Europe a lot. We were in Germany, we were in London. In fact, when they made their first performance for the queen, we were with them," noted Long. "That's when Michael was a little tyke. In fact, I remember him having to stand on a milk crate to reach the microphone."

A projected Sisters Love LP on Mowest was canceled, but their "My Love Is Yours (Till The End Of Time)" with "You've Got My Mind" came out on Motown in late '73. The promising "I'm Learning How To Trust My Man" only came out in England that fall. Boyster eventually returned to her gospel upbringing with the Clara Ward Singers. She was replaced, but "it wasn't the same." Berry passed away a few years ago, but the rest of the former Sisters Love keep their vocal cords in shape in church. Jeannie belongs to Blinky Williams's Hollywood Choir and ex-Motown arranger H.B. Barnum's Life choir.

THE SPINNERS

Sometimes even groups boasting exceptional talent couldn't break through to Motown's first tier. The best songs went to the biggest acts, and even classy vocal quintets like the Spinners had to scramble for worthy material. When they did get hold of some, they took no prisoners.

Tenors Bobbie Smith (born April 10, 1936), C.P. Spencer, and Billy Henderson (born August 9, 1939), baritone Henry Fambrough (born May 10, 1935; some sources cite 1938), and bass Pervis Jackson (born May 17, 1938) hailed from Ferndale, on the outskirts of Detroit, and came together in 1955. They harmonized in gin joints and on local talent contests as the Domingos prior to changing their name to the Spinners in tribute to Smith's shiny hubcaps. Spencer, who would go on to sing with the Five Stars, Voice Masters, and Originals, was replaced by George Dixon, and he was succeeded by Edgar "Chico" Edwards in 1962.

Harvey Fuqua heard something in their splendid vocal blend. He polished the Spinners to a high gloss and took them to Chicago in the spring of 1961 to wax a delightful doo-wop theme that he'd written with Berry Gordy's sister Gwen. The harmonies cushioning

"That's What Girls Are Made For" recalled the Moonglows at their finest, and when he and Gwen made it the debut release on their Tri-Phi logo, the dreamy ballad took off that summer—all the way to No. 5 R&B and No. 27 pop in *Billboard*. "Heebie Jeebies" on its flip showed the group could rock and roll.

That creamy-ballad-on-one-side/rocker-on-the-flip formula held fast for the rest of the Spinners' Tri-Phi tenure. "Love (I Am So Glad I Found You)," "What Did She Use," and "She Loves Me So" (with Harvey on lead) were sumptuous ballads, while "Sudbuster," "Itching For My Baby But I Don't Know Where To Scratch," and "I Got The Water Boiling Baby (I'm Gonna Cook Your Goose)" upheld the Motor City rock-and-roll tradition. "I've Been Hurt" was the only track to hint at more soul-oriented pursuits. "She Don't Love Me," the group's last Tri-Phi 45 in late '62, was a typically spine-chilling ballad; its flip "Too Young, Too Much, Too Soon" was a catchy upbeat number penned by Harvey and Gwen with tasty vocal ensemble parts.

When Motown absorbed Tri-Phi and its sister Harvey label in 1963, the Spinners came over as part of the deal. It took a while, but Motown released fresh product on the quintet in late 1964. "Sweet Thing," a Mickey Stevenson composition, was an infectious upbeat outing, Smith's lilting tenor flying over propulsive horns and chunky piano. "How Can I," its Harvey-and-Gwen-penned 'B' side, had more of a pop slant to its tempo-shifting arrangement.

The pumping encore "I'll Always Love You" was the Spinners' first Motown hit. Under the supervision of Mickey and Ivy Jo Hunter, Smith held sway over a relentless rhythm, and "I'll Always Love You" sailed into the R&B Top Ten and pop Top 40 pop during the summer of '65 (it was released as by the Detroit Spinners in England to avoid confusion with a British group of the same name). The quintet's doo-wop roots surfaced anew on the other side, Harvey's mellow "Tomorrow May Never Come." Stevenson and Hunter's upbeat "Truly Yours" went to No. 16 R&B for the Spinners during the spring of '66, with a bittersweet "Where Is That Girl" penned by Harvey and Johnny Bristol on the flip.

"For All We Know," issued in the spring of '67, had a gentle nostalgic tone but brought the group's hit streak to a halt. Hunter's "I Cross My Heart" on the other side was similarly offbeat; a jagged drumbeat threatened to kick off a groove but never did. *The Original Spinners*, their strong debut LP, came out that summer with Fuqua's "I Just Can't Help But Feel The Pain," Smokey Robinson and Pete Moore's hand-clapper "Like A Good Man Should," and Berry and Robert Gordy's "It Hurts To Be In Love" the only unfamiliar entries. Though they toured with Marvin Gaye's early revue and perfected their choreography with Cholly Atkins, the Spinners couldn't pay the bills by performing alone, so they moonlighted as chaperones, drivers, and road managers.

"They chauffeured the Tempts around so much, they thought they were the Tempts' drivers," said G.C. Cameron. "They paid some serious dues." McCall's Creek, Mississippi, native Cameron, who had arrived in the Motor City in 1955, took over for Edwards after completing a grueling tour of Vietnam duty with the Marines in September of '67 and contributed most of the leads on their remaining Motown releases. The Contours' Dennis Edwards was his conduit to the Spinners. "Dennis and I, we went way back, years and years ago in Detroit, when we grew up. He was working at a little place," said Cameron, "I think it was on Joy Road in Detroit.

The Spinners may have been one of the more under-appreciated groups at Motown. The group continued to prove its worth after departing the company in 1972, producing a series of hits with Atlantic. The re-assembled Spinners are still touring in the new millennium.

"Dennis and I used to go by all the time and sing there. So Dennis told my brother Dave that the Spinners were looking for someone," he continued. "Dennis told them that he knew someone. He asked me if I was interested, and I said, 'Of course!' 'Cause I was home from Vietnam, and there was really nothing I was doing but trying to find what to do. I went in and auditioned, and I was the only one that auditioned that day, and I was the only one they needed.

"I got with the group, I think it was in October, and opened up for Marvin in November at the Apollo. I think it was for Thanksgiving that we opened up for Marvin. So it was that quick and that big of an abrupt change from Vietnam, from the rice paddies to the stage."

Even with a few thunderclaps overdubbed to darken its atmosphere, the insistent "Bad, Bad Weather (Till You Come Home)" couldn't get going on the charts in late '68. "George Gordy and Allen 'Bo' Story and Larry Brown wrote and produced that song," noted Cameron, who sang stirring lead. "It's just a great and interesting song. We all talk about it in the dressing room. Bobbie always talks about 'Bad Weather.' He loved the song." There was also a revival of the Moonglows' '55 classic "In My Diary" in late '69, their first V.I.P. release. "That

was one of Harvey Fuqua's favorites," said G.C. "Harvey produced that on us. He had been taking care of the group as management for so long."

Norman Whitfield produced a funk-soaked "Message From A Black Man" in early 1970; the Whitfield/Barrett Strong composition graced the Tempts' *Puzzle People* LP the year before. "That one was done in a falsetto voice," said lead Cameron. "That was interesting because I was trying to get the feel of it, coming back from Vietnam at that time and how the country was developing. Everything going down as it was made me reflect on the message itself."

It took a rapidly maturing Stevie Wonder to restore the Spinners to the charts. He wrote (along with wife Syreeta and Lee Garrett), produced, and played several instruments on the stunning "It's A Shame," which roared up to No. 14 pop and No. 4 R&B in mid-1970. "Stevie and I became very tight, so we were like inseparable for a period of time," said Cameron. "One night we went out to a club and came back, and he had been working on this song for us called 'It's A Shame.' I went down in the basement at his house when I brought him back home that night and listened to it, and that was it. I think the next day we went in and recorded it. It took it a year to get out. We had to fight to get it released." Cameron's bravura lead shifted between melismatic tenor and startling falsetto, and the groove was incendiary. Its flip "Together We Can Make Such Sweet Music" anticipated future Philly endeavors with its violin-enhanced mid-tempo strut.

V.I.P. issued the group's aptly titled encore LP *2nd Time Around* that fall, comprised of recent singles, a few unfamiliar titles ("Pay Them No Mind," "My Lady Love"), and covers of the Five Stairsteps' "O-o-h Child," David Ruffin's "I've Got To Find Myself A Brand New Baby," and the Dells' "I Can Sing A Rainbow/Love Is Blue."

The Spinners could more than hold their own in the singing and choreography departments when they broke through with Motown in the 1960s (Photo courtesy of David Alston's Mahogany Archives).

Stevie and Syreeta collaborated on the Spinners' next V.I.P. release, "We'll Have It Made," which similarly benefited from Wonder's wondrous production skills. It went Top 20 R&B in early 1971, backed with a revival of Ruffin's heartbroken "My Whole World Ended (The Moment You Left Me)." "That was during the time I was phasing out with the group," said Cameron, who left the Spinners in 1971. "What a lot of people didn't realize, one of the reasons I had to stay at Motown was because my contract was not up, and theirs were. We signed individual contracts, and I came in much later in the game," he said. "I had no choice but to remain behind when they went over to Atlantic."

G.C. put in a good word for his pal Philip Walker to serve as his replacement. Billing himself as Phillippe´ Wynne, the gospel-imbued tenor would share lead duties with Bobbie Smith during the group's '70s heyday on Atlantic. While Cameron inaugurated a solo career at Motown, the Spinners hooked up with Philly producer Thom Bell, and any stray thoughts of having toiled in the Hitsville shipping department receded into history. Utilizing the sleek Philly sound for a backdrop, the Spinners perched at the peak of the R&B charts in '72 with "I'll Be Around" and "Could I Be Falling In Love," in '73 with "One Of A Kind (Love Affair)," and in 1974 they paced the R&B hit parade with "Mighty Love–Pt. 1," scoring another gold record duetting with Dionne Warwick on "Then Came You."

Their fancy onstage footwork every bit as flawless as their rich harmonies, the Spinners reigned as soul superstars throughout the rest of the decade on Atlantic. Cincinnati native Wynne left in 1977 (he died

July 14, 1984) and was replaced by John Edwards, who'd had his own Top Ten R&B hit in '74 with "Careful Man." Membership remained constant until mid-2000, when Edwards fell ill. Guess who got the call to fill in? None other than G.C.

"It's very exciting right now for us, being back together after a 30-year hiatus," said Cameron, who had just completed a solo CD when the call came. "Fitting in right where we left off is just amazing." The reunion worked out so well that, upon Edwards' return, the plan was to make the Spinners a permanent six-man operation.

EDWIN STARR

Great as the talent was parading through Hitsville, nobody was going to outsing Edwin Starr. Windows rattled and the heavens shook when this gent opened his mouth—especially when he passionately protested a futile "War" tearing the nation apart in 1970.

Born Charles Edwin Hatcher on January 21, 1942, in Nashville, the singer grew up in Cleveland and joined his first vocal aggregation, the Future Tones, in his early teens. "We never recorded, but that was my own individual group that I had in Cleveland," said Starr. "That was from 1955 to 1960." In 1962, he joined the Bill Doggett Combo as vocalist. "His manager, a guy by the name of Don Briggs, saw me performing with the Future Tones," said Edwin. "And he liked very much what I was doing, and he asked me, would I be interested in joining the Bill Doggett organization. And I said to him, 'Yes I would, definitely,' even though it was less money than I was actually making. But it was a lot more experience. So I got a chance to get my road experience by traveling with Bill for two-and-a-half years."

While playing New York City, Edwin had a cinematic epiphany. "We had like three or four days off in New York," he recalled. "I went to the movie while I was there, and the movie just happened to be 'Agent 007,' you know, the James Bond movie. And James Bond, that whole ideology behind the James Bond films, happened to be the flavor of the month. So I watched the movie like three times, and then I went back to my hotel room, and was sitting there contemplating on the idea of what the movie was all about, and trying to figure out how to incorporate that into a song. And I came up with 'Agent Double-O-Soul.'

Edwin Starr on Ed Hurst's show on the Steel Pier in Atlantic City (Weldon A. McDougal III photo).

"So I went to Bill, and I said to him, 'I'd like to record this.' And he said to me, 'Well, maybe in a year's time, we might be ready for you to record.' And I said to him, 'I can't wait a year. This is a current topic now, and if I do wait, by the time I get a chance to actually go in and record it, it'll be old hat.'" Convinced his secret agent salute was a surefire hit, Edwin quit, and the right opportunity swiftly presented itself. "It was during the same time in the same week that I had left Bill Doggett," said Starr. "I had given my notice, looking for some avenue to record the song." Detroit deejay LeBaron Taylor was the conduit. "He introduced me to Ed Wingate, and from there they signed me to Golden World, and created the label Ric-Tic."

Edwin Starr had a big voice to match big songs such as "War" (Weldon A. McDougal III photo).

The brassy pumper "Agent Double-O-Soul," produced by Richard Parker and arranged by Edwin and ex-Satintone Sonny Sanders, broke into the R&B Top Ten and barely missed the pop Top 20 in mid-'65 on Ric-Tic. "Back Street," another hard-charging Starr original, celebrated partying on the other side of the tracks and hit in early '66. "That was pretty much a musical anthology of my life, the way I lived and how I lived and everything," he said. "And that I always tried to stay true to the music. Although you live in one environment, you favor another."

The dynamic dancer made it three hits in a row before winter was over. "When I wrote the next song, the initial thought of the song was, 'S.O.S.—sending out soul,'" he said. "But then when I realized what I had written, I had written a prelude of 'Agent Double-O-Soul.' So I changed it. I got with a guy named Richard Morris, and Richard and I changed it to 'Stop Her On Sight' to make it like a girl/guy song. But the whole idea of the song came from the television program *20,000 Leagues Under the Sea*, 'cause I was laying watching that, and they did the Morse code thing on the TV show. And that's where I got the intro for the record." "Stop Her On Sight (S.O.S.)"; powered by Starr's fire-and-brimstone vocal, cracked the R&B Top Ten.

"Headline News," Starr's fourth Ric-Tic offering, made some pop chart noise in the spring of '66, arranged by Mike Terry (likely the baritone saxman soloing midway through), but "Girls Are Getting Prettier" and "You're My Mellow" missed. Edwin did figure into another major seller in 1966, though few knew he was fronting the Holidays' Golden World release "I'll Love You Forever," a Don Davis composition that vaulted to No. 7 R&B in the spring of 1966.

"There was no such group as the Holidays," said Starr. "What happened was that Don Davis asked me to do a demo recording. And he, unbeknownst to me, put the record out using my voice on the lead, and calling it the Holidays. Which everybody knew that it was me, and that there was no such group as the Holidays. But the record got so big that they had to create a group to perform." Detroit soulsters J.J. Barnes and Steve Mancha reportedly sang backgrounds on "I'll Love You Forever." "I don't know who was in the background," Starr said. "I just walked in the studio. He said to me, 'Do me a demo of this song.' Handed me the lyrics, and that was it. What you hear on the record is that demo that I did that night."

Starr also experienced major success as a composer that year with the mellifluous "Oh How Happy" by the white soul quartet Shades of Blue. "I wrote the song as a dare," he said. "I took the Shades of Blue to the record company, and I was told that they didn't record white groups. Which kind of like was a fallacy to me, because the Reflections were a white group. So I couldn't understand what they were saying. So anyway, I took the group to Harry Balk, who was a friend of mine who had Impact Records." Balk must have been pleased when "Oh How Happy" sailed up to No. 12 pop that summer.

When Gordy acquired Wingate's operation and several of his main acts, Starr was among the last to hear the headline news. "I didn't know it at all," he said. "It was a done deal by the time I got back to the United States. I was in England performing at that time, and I went back to the United States to go to the Apollo Theatre to co-star with the Temptations. And one of the Temptations told me that I was a Motown artist. It was a shock to the system, to say the least—and then it took two years before they actually recorded me, 'cause they didn't know what to do with me as an artist."

The scorching "I Want My Baby Back" was Gordy's first attempt to harness Edwin's prodigious lungpower in late '67, written by Norman Whitfield, Tempts guitarist Cornelius Grant, and Eddie Kendricks. It was backed by a superior treatment of the house favorite "Gonna Keep On Tryin' Till I Win Your Love," Starr unleashing spine-tingling gymnastics on the Whitfield/Barrett Strong tune as violins soared and percussion rumbled.

"I liked it very much," said Starr of the latter. "But that was one of the reasons why most of the artists left the company, too—because we were all doing the same songs, over and over and over again. So consequently, as writers, we were losing out 100 percent all the way around, 'cause we couldn't get a chance to get our foot in the door as a writer. Because they were using only a handful of writers at the company, they were using their material."

He strutted back in the spring of '68 with the James Dean/William Weatherspoon-generated "I Am The Man For You Baby" (his first R&B chart entry for Gordy), paired with "My Weakness Is You" (its writers included Whitfield and Grant). Edwin lit into the Miracles' "Way Over There" that fall, and Dean and Weatherspoon's "If My Heart Could Tell The Story" on the 'B' was no shrinking violet, either. *Soul Master*, Starr's first LP in the fall of '68, featured Richard Morris's title cut, Dean and Weatherspoon's relatively sedate "Time Is Passin' By," and a cover of Bobby Taylor & the Vancouvers' Ashford & Simpson-penned "I Am Your Man," along with the most alluring "Oh How Happy" ever committed to tape.

Finally, at the beginning of 1969, Edwin marched up to the No. 6 slot on both the pop and R&B listings with "25 Miles." "I wrote that five years before it was ever recorded," he said. "A friend of mine by the name of Mickey Shapiro had a nightclub called Mickey's Hideaway in Lansing, Michigan," he said. "And I used to do his nightclub. It was like a college student-type club. And I didn't have a closing number. So I wrote '25 Miles' as a closing number, 'cause I knew how powerful it was, and it just got bigger and bigger and bigger every time we did it in the club. Then finally, on one occasion, I was doing a television show called *20 Grand Live*, and I did the song on the TV show.

"The next day, the telephone was ringing off the hook. People was wanting to know who was (singing) this song, where this song was at, how could they get it. And Barney Ales said to me, 'Go in the studio and record it.' I said, 'Well, I tried to record it once before, and I was told that it was just a good rock-and-roll song. There was nothing special about it.' He said, 'Well, I'm telling you to go in and record it.' So I went in and recorded it, and it became one of the biggest hits that they had."

Who provided the pounding foot stomps pushing "25 Miles"? "Me, Harvey, a couple of the Spinners, if I remember correctly," said Johnny Bristol, its co-producer with Harvey Fuqua. "Harvey and I liked it very much, and we sat down and we worked out some stuff with Edwin. Then we worked some things out that we wanted on it. We came up with the idea of putting the 'Come on feet, don't fail me now!'—all that stuff wasn't in there when he came to us." Edwin wrote the pounding flip, "Love Is My Destination," with Hank Cosby. Bristol and Doris McNeil provided an edgy "I'm Still A Struggling Man" as a follow-up; it sold respectably that summer.

25 Miles, Starr's second Gordy long-player that spring, was another blazing collection that found him working with producers Whitfield ("He Who Picks A Rose"), Smokey Robinson (remakes of Mary Wells' "You Beat Me To The Punch" and the Miracles' "Mighty Good Lovin'"), Morris ("Soul City [Open Your Arms To Me]"), Deke Richards ("Backyard Lovin' Man"), and Dean and Weatherspoon ("Who Cares If You're Happy Or Not [I Do]"). Edwin was granted the rare honor of writing and producing the roaring "24 Hours To Find My Baby."

Motown teamed Starr with Los Angeles-based Sondra "Blinky" Williams to form a new duo in the summer of '69. "What they were trying to do was, they had a policy of piggybacking different artists together to try to focus more attention on the lesser of the two artists. But in our particular instance, we both were on a par with each other. Neither one of us was more popular than the other," noted Starr. The duo enjoyed a mild pop hit with a radically rearranged "Oh How Happy" and made an LP for Gordy, *Just We Two*. Edwin's own status was rising at Hitsville: He co-wrote his funky early 1970 hit "Time" with Richard "Popcorn" Wylie and helmed it himself.

Whitfield had already cut what would become Edwin's only No. 1 pop hit on the Tempts for their *Psychedelic Shack* album a few months earlier, but Starr would wrench it away, investing the angry protest with shattering strength. "He brought it to me, him and Barrett Strong," said Edwin. "It had originally been recorded by the Temptations, but it was a much watered-down version in regards to what the song actually represented. So he said to me he would beef up the track, and I said to him, 'Well, as long as you let me do the vocals the way I feel the vocals, then we've got a deal.' So I did the vocals the way I felt the interpretation of it. And what you hear is the first take, and that was it."

The rock-tinged "War" became a rallying cry, heading straight for the top in August of 1970. "Someone needed to speak out, and that's the way we spoke out," said Strong. "We spoke out in music and song." But there was a downside to its political ramifications. "I got a little heat from it," Edwin said. "While the song was No. 1, I never did any work at all. I mean, there was very few places where you could go and sing, 'War—what is it good for?' in the political atmosphere of the United States."

Starr produced a third of his *War & Peace* album that summer, notably the stirring "Running Back And Forth" (he co-wrote it with Wylie) and the Ashford & Simpson-penned theme "California Soul." Edwin and Bristol split authorship of "I Just Wanted To Cry," and Johnny produced revivals of Marvin Gaye's "At Last (I Found A Love)" and a Little Milton-style "All Around The World." Ivy Jo Hunter brought "I Can't Escape Your Memory;" Cosby was responsible for "Adios Senorita," and Fuqua contributed "I Can't Replace My Old Love."

Whitfield and Strong came right back at year's end with another seething protest ode for Edwin, "Stop The War Now," which broke into the R&B Top Five despite Edwin's misgivings. "I always felt that the statement 'War—what is it good for?' was strong enough," he said. "There was no need to say 'Stop the war,' because it was inevitable that it was going to be stopped." Norman and Barrett must have written

"Funky Music Sho Nuff Turns Me On" from personal experience. It gave Edwin a No. 6 R&B smash in the spring of '71. "Stop The War Now" and "Funky Music" turned up on Starr's album *Involved.*

1972 wasn't Starr's year. Neither "Take Me Clear From Here" nor "Who Is The Leader Of The People" were hits. After just missing the R&B Top Ten with his self-produced "There You Go" in mid-'73 and a lesser chart entry on "You've Got My Soul On Fire," Edwin did the soundtrack for the 1974 film *Hell Up in Harlem* with Freddie Perren and Fonce Mizell. He exited Motown the next year to sign with Granite Records before switching to 20th Century and nailing sizable hits in '79 with "Contact" and "H.A.P.P.Y. Radio." For the last 17 years, Edwin has resided in England, where he remains a Northern Soul star of the brightest magnitude.

MICKEY STEVENSON

Only Berry Gordy himself wielded more power over Motown's creative output than William "Mickey" Stevenson. He came to Hitsville in search of a recording contract as a singer, but Berry instead played a hunch and hired the streetwise Stevenson as his first A&R (artist and repertoire) director, even before the job had been properly defined. From there on, Mickey's familiar imprimatur appeared on a plethora of Motown smashes as writer, producer, or both.

Stevenson hailed from a show business background. His mother, Kitty Stevenson, was a Detroit R&B chanteuse who recorded with pianist Todd Rhodes' orchestra for Sensation and King during the late '40s and early '50s. Her son followed in her footsteps as a doo-wop singer and fledgling record producer. Once officially installed as A&R head, Mickey quickly made himself invaluable, building the house band, choosing and providing material, collaborating with the label's creative geniuses, and solving a myriad of problems so Berry—an expert at delegating authority—didn't have to. With Clarence Paul serving as his assistant, Stevenson was a powerful presence around the halls of Hitsville. Among his recruits were Martha Reeves (who worked as his secretary while awaiting entree to the Motown talent roster) and the Velvelettes.

"Mickey was exposed to the business at an early age," said Hank Cosby. "He had good ears. See, some people have natural gifts. On these natural gifts, he would emphasize everything. Like a chord—he could hear chords, he could hear the notes, he could hear the parts that should be sung. And if you're singing a bad note on one of his songs, he'd tell you right away. 'Wait a minute, you're flat! Go up a half a step.' He'd tell 'em that. He had those kind of ears."

Often but by no means exclusively collaborating with Ivy Jo Hunter, Mickey was in on the creation of "Dancing In The Street" and "My Baby Loves Me" for Martha & the Vandellas, "Stubborn Kind Of Fellow" and "Pride And Joy" for Marvin Gaye, "Beechwood 4-5789" and "I'll Keep Holding On" for the Marvelettes, "Needle In A Haystack" for the Velvelettes, "Ask The Lonely" for the Four Tops, "Devil With Blue Dress On" for Shorty Long, and "It Takes Two" for Marvin and Mickey's wife Kim Weston (they became romantically involved while Kim was on the label and married in 1964).

In January of 1967, Mickey left Motown after MGM Records tendered a lucrative offer to have him head its West Coast record division. Bringing Weston with him, he accepted the prestigious post, but soon discovered manufacturing hits wasn't quite so easy outside Hitsville. Nevertheless, many fine late '60s sides were cut for MGM's Venture subsidiary under Mickey's watch, more than a few produced by Clarence Paul and many sounding noticeably Motownish.

STONEY & MEATLOAF

Both halves of this duo, which made one eponymous album and two singles for Rare Earth in 1971, have gone on to greater achievements since leaving Motown. Their first Rare Earth offering, "What You See Is What You Get" (backed by "She's A Lady") was a minor hit in the spring of '71; "It Takes All Kinds Of People" (flipped with a remake of the Tempts' "The Way You Do The Things You Do") wasn't. Shaun "Stoney" Murphy is from Michigan; Marvin Lee Aday—Mr. Loaf—originally hailed from Dallas but got his start as a rock screamer in L.A. They were cast members in a traveling production of *Hair* when they piqued Motown's interest.

After splitting, their careers took off. Stoney cut a 1973 Motown single of her own, "Let Me Come Down Easy" with "It's Always Me," joining Bob Seger as a backup vocalist the same year. In 1995, she took on the added role of fronting Little Feat. Loaf's 1977 platinum album *Bat Out of Hell* established the hefty screamer as an imposing rocker with a theatrical bent. He's appeared in the films *The Rocky Horror Picture Show* and *Roadie*. McDougal first encountered Loaf during the Rare Earth label's gala kickoff party at the Roostertail. "I think when I saw him he was just as cantankerous as he is now," he chuckled.

BARRETT STRONG

Tamla celebrated its first national hit in early 1960 when Barrett Strong's rocking "Money (That's What I Want)" put Berry's little company on the map. After leaving for a few years when his encores failed to catch fire, Strong returned to Hitsville in the mid-'60s to collaborate with producer Norman Whitfield. Together, they created monumental sellers for the Tempts, Marvin Gaye, Edwin Starr, Gladys Knight & the Pips, and the Undisputed Truth.

Born February 5, 1941, in West Point, Mississippi, Barrett's family moved to the Motor City when he was five. Contrary to persistent reports, Diablos lead singer Nolan Strong was not his cousin. "He was just a guy that had the same last name I had," said Barrett, who played piano with his older sisters as a teen. "We had a singing group, a gospel group together." Ray Charles was a primary influence on Barrett as he grew up on the northwest side of the Motor City, and Marv Johnson was one of his neighborhood buddies.

Jackie Wilson had attended school with one of the Strong sisters, and it was Mr. Excitement that brought Barrett and Berry together in 1957. "(Jackie) was over to my house, and he heard me sing and play the piano. He liked what I was doing, so he told me that he had a friend that was in the music business. He wanted me to meet him, so he brought him over to my house." Strong's 1959 Tamla debut single, "Let's Rock" and flip "Do The Very Best You Can," sold so little locally that it doesn't even appear in most Motown discographies.[18]

Janie Bradford was part of the Hitsville clique. One day in 1959, a lightning bolt of inspiration struck. "Most of us—Brian Holland, myself, and there were two or three more that were still in our teens, were going to school," Janie said. "And we wouldn't come 'til afternoon. So consequently sometimes we would stay late after working hours. This was after working hours, and we were hanging around. Mr. Gordy was playing piano, and he had this riff going. And he said, 'Come on! Think of something everybody wants!' I said, 'Well, money! **That's what I want!'**

"We stood there and just kept writing and throwing out lyrics and improving on the melody, and the whole thing. It just came together," she said. "I'm not a spontaneous writer, but 'Money' was a spontaneous-type thing. It was a moment-type thing. Barrett Strong was there. He plays piano a little better than Mr.

Gordy. So he said, 'Well, let me play it for you, Mr. Gordy.' Naturally, by him singing it—he just kept singing it as we were writing it—so it went on him. He became the artist."

"We were just playing around on the piano in the studio, and came up with a groove. Berry and his secretary went out and wrote the lyric, and that's how it came about," said Strong. Things were so casual that when a white guitarist and bassist dropped in out of the blue that day, they were put to work on what turned out to be a landmark Motown recording. "Just walked up and asked if they could be on the session," said Barrett. "We said yes, and they played on the session. Never saw them again in life. Two young kids on their way home from high school."

That unknown axeman's crunchy low-end riffs, Barrett's Brother Ray-styled 88s, and Benny Benjamin's throbbing tom-toms (abetted by Brian Holland's tambourine) congealed into a thick, grinding rhythm spiced by the Rayber Voices' churchy chants. Strong screamed its cynical fiscal message with the urgency of a man down to his last two nickels. "Money" was one of the first things Gordy produced in his own studio, and its immediacy also informed the hypnotic flip "Oh I Apologize," a collaboration by Berry and Smokey emphasizing Strong's sanctified roots.

When Gordy issued the single on Tamla, an avalanche of orders made it clear that his fledgling operation was unable to handle the demand. Up stepped big sister Gwen with a solution: "Money" was licensed to her better-distributed Anna label for national consumption. It vaulted all the way up to No. 2 on *Billboard's* R&B listings in early 1960 and achieved an impressive No. 23 pop placement—Berry Gordy's first major triumph as a label boss, even if Anna did reap a piece of the monetary reward.

"When that came out, they had a party, and Pops Gordy made a stage, and we all got on there and we took pictures," recalled Louvain Demps, one of the Rayber Voices. "They called me in for the session. I was so glad." Strong hit the road to earn some of that "Money," and everyone from Jerry Lee Lewis to the Beatles eventually weighed in with contrasting versions.

Released in the summer of '60, Strong's next Gordy-produced single was the unabridged rocker "Yes, No, Maybe So," the work of Gordy and Smokey. "It's sort of a strange song," said Barrett. "But I thought it was nice." It was flipped with a bluesier "You Knows What To Do" penned by Berry and Brian Holland and was marketed the same twin-pronged way: Tamla handled the local action while Anna took it national. Strong's piano solos and earthy vocals were delightful, but lightning didn't strike twice. By the time his Charles-styled rocker "Whirlwind" (Janie and Barrett penned it and the Raybers did a convincing Raelettes imitation) and its 'B' side, Berry and Smokey's insistent "I'm Gonna Cry (If You Quit Me)," came out that fall, Tamla was equipped to handle its own national distribution. Yet nothing substantial happened sales-wise.

Returning to the subject matter of his breakthrough on "Money And Me" before year's end failed to produce another fiscal windfall. "That was supposed to have been the follow-up to that," said Barrett, who covered his buddy Marv Johnson's smash "You Got What It Takes" for a 'B' side. When "Misery" with "Two Wrongs Don't Make A Right" didn't do the trick during the summer of '61, Strong split. "Just looking for something different," he said.

Strong hightailed it to New York before the end of '61 to work with legendary writers and producers Doc Pomus and Mort Shuman on a nice Atco single pairing the rocking "Seven Sins" and the hushed soul ballad "What Went Wrong." "I was in New York, hanging around the Brill Building all the time. I would see Elvis Presley and all the guys coming in and out of there. And I ran into Doc Pomus there. I met him there, and then he introduced me to Mort Shuman," said Strong. "They decided to be my managers. They signed me to Atlantic."

Young, footloose, and fancy-free, Strong moved next to South Philadelphia. "Hung around there for awhile, then I came back to Detroit, then I went to Chicago and hooked up with Vee-Jay Records," he said. Record Row on South Michigan Avenue rolled out the welcome mat. Barrett cut a 45 for Vee-Jay's Tollie subsidiary in '64 coupling the brassy driver "Make Up Your Mind" with a Latin-tempoed "I Better Run," both produced by his co-writer, Richard Parker. He split authorship of the Dells' 1965 hit ballad "Stay In My Corner" with Wade Flemons and Bobby Miller. "I was with Vee-Jay for a while, then I moved over to OKeh Records," he said.

But Motown's pull proved irresistible and Strong returned to Hitsville in 1966. "They were doing my style of music then," he said. "They were doing something a little different when I left, but they were doing the more soulful, R&B-style stuff, so I thought I had a place there. So I had an idea I thought I could take back and see if they could do something with it. I had 'Grapevine.' I took it back, and they did something with it."

Teaming with Norman Whitfield, Barrett allowed his performing aspirations to lapse in favor of being half of one of Motown's top songwriting duos. "We used to hang around together, parties and things during the school days," he said. "When I came back over to the company, he was there, so we just hooked up." Together they crafted "I Heard It Through The Grapevine," "Friendship Train," "The End Of Our Road," "War," "Smiling Faces Sometimes," and the funk-soaked treatises "Cloud Nine," "I Can't Get Next To You," "Psychedelic Shack," and "Papa Was A Rollin' Stone" for the Tempts.

Strong left Motown for good in 1973. "I wanted to try something different," he said. Strong paused at Epic long enough to make a little noise as a singer with "Stand Up And Cheer For The Preacher" that summer before scoring his last hit to date in '75 for Capitol with "Is It True." "I did a couple of albums for Capitol, and they were okay, but nothing fabulous," he said. Today Strong operates his own label, Blaritt Records, in Southfield, Michigan. He has high hopes for his rap, gospel, and R&B stable, just as Berry once championed Barrett. And he's working on some new material of his own that just may put Strong back in the limelight.

BOBBY TAYLOR & THE VANCOUVERS

Barriers naturally seemed to tumble around Bobby Taylor & the Vancouvers. They were the first interracial act to achieve stardom at Motown, and their self-generated 1968 smash "Does Your Mama Know About Me" sensitively tackled the inflammable issue (in those days, anyway) of interracial dating. Fated to be primarily remembered for bringing the Jackson 5 to Motown, Taylor and the Vancouvers nevertheless made their own significant musical contribution.

Taylor got his musical start in his native Washington, D.C. Enamored of Nat King Cole and Ray Charles, he headed west to pursue a master's degree in music at the University of California at Berkeley. The pre-Taylor Vancouvers came together in 1958 at the opposite end of the continent: Vancouver, British Columbia. "The very first group was called the Shades," explained guitarist Tommy Chong in 1994. "Then we became Little Daddy and the Bashers. We met Bobby in 1966 in San Francisco. We were down there starving, trying to make it. Then we hooked up, and he came up to Vancouver as a drummer. He was a great drummer. We sounded so good, we started attracting all the good musicians. So we just hooked up in Vancouver and formed this supergroup called Bobby Taylor & the Vancouvers."

Along with Taylor and Chong, the Vancouvers consisted of guitarist Eddie Patterson, bassist Wes Henderson, organist Robbie King, and drummer Ted Lewis. The band played a soul/jazz mix for a hip crowd at a late-night Vancouver club, the Elegant Parlor. "Our club started at 11 and went through to 6 in the morning," Chong said. "I played with James Brown's band, I played with Ike Turner's people. They all used to come down to the club, and we'd jam."

Bobby Taylor, songwriter Al Cleveland, and the Four Tops' Lawrence Payton listen to one of Bobby's songs in the Woodward Ave. building (Weldon A. McDougal III photo).

Their big break came when the Supremes dropped by the Parlor. "First the band came down. Then they got Mary and Florence to come down. And then they told Diana to come down, and Diana came down ... Then they phoned Berry, and Berry came down. Berry flew from Detroit." Soon the Vancouvers were on their way to Hitsville.

The group made quite a splash with "Does Your Mama Know About Me," their Gordy debut single in early '68. "It was a poem, actually," said co-writer Chong. "I'm a poet more than a songwriter. It was a poem, and Tom Baird—he's not in the group, he was a producer. He was a musical genius. He used to play with us once in a while. He came out, he wanted us to do some of his songs. And he was looking through my writing, and he saw the 'Does Your Mama Know About Me' poem. And he says, 'Let me take that home.' And he took it home, and when he came back, man—I'm a songwriter! Beautiful song." The public agreed, propelling it to Top Five R&B status and racking up sizable pop sales that spring.

Three of Baird's compositions graced the self-contained group's eponymous debut album that August. The lilting, jazzy "So This Is Love," a subtly grooving "One Girl," and the driving "If You Love Her" (co-penned with Taylor) didn't feel much like Motown productions despite Gordy's production. Taylor glistened on a variety of covers, most of them from Jobete: An Otis Redding-style treatment of "Try A Little Tenderness," a frantic revival of the Tempts' '65 hit "It's Growing" and the metaphorically flush "Fading Away," both Smokey Robinson masterworks; the enchanting "You Gave Me Something (And Everything's Alright)," and a raveup "I Heard It Through The Grapevine" modeled on Gladys Knight & the Pips' then-recent hit.

"We made the wrong choice there," said Chong. "We never heard Marvin's version. We heard Gladys's, and so then we did our version. Then we switched right over to Marvin's when we heard his." The album contained two additional hits: The Ashford and Simpson-penned "I Am Your Man," a Frank Wilson production that dented the charts that autumn ("That was one that Bobby went off and did on his own," said Chong) and "Malinda," their last hit near year's end, written and produced by Smokey, Al Cleveland, and Terry Johnson. The Supremes covered "Does Your Mama Know" on their *Love Child* album a few months later.

Judging from the photo adorning the front of their Gordy LP, the shades-wearing Taylor and his rugged-looking Vancouvers didn't resemble your typically immaculately coiffed and attired Motown act—precipitating the occasional hassle on the road. "We got yelled at a few places," said Chong. "We got yelled at—where were we? I think in Chicago. After our hit, we came back and we played some ballroom. A big ballroom where the Tempts used to play. It was in the black area. And they said, 'The Vancouvers!,' and (the audience) looked up: 'Get those white boys off the stage!' But we used to play, man, blow everybody away."

That outsider image may have led to their Motown downfall. "They were trying to bury us from day one, because we were sort of outlaw-type guys. We were on the Diana Ross tour for a while, and we used to do all this radical shit on the road, singing about white girls and everything. Diana didn't appreciate it," he claimed. "We were okay as long as we were in Vancouver, and in Canada. The minute we got down in the states, they sort of divided and conquered us. They got us in the studio, and Smokey took Bobby. And then we found the Jackson 5, then Bobby went off to produce their records." Bassist Henderson cut a 1969 single of his own for the brand-new Rare Earth subsidiary, coupling "In Bed" and "Reality."

Taylor had his own fish to fry. In addition to producing the Jackson 5's first Motown masters (most of them shelved), he became a solo act as the Vancouvers split up. "None of us liked the recording life," said Chong. Taylor's own '69 Gordy album *Taylor Made Soul* was more in tune with the label's standard formula. Two singles were culled: A splendid "It Should Have Been Me Loving Her" was paired with a revival of the Miracles' "My Girl Has Gone," followed by the uplifting "Oh, I've Been Bless'd" (shifted to V.I.P. for a January 1970 release).

The LP's highlights included a bluesy "How Long Has That Evening Train Been Gone" (payback time—the Supremes had featured it on the same *Love Child* LP that sported "Does Your Mama Know"); a stirring "I Just Can't Carry On" demonstrating Taylor's falsetto range, "Out In The Country," and Smokey's "Little Miss Sweetness." Jerry Butler's mellow "Need To Belong" suited Taylor more snugly than an overblown treatment of The Beatles' "Eleanor Rigby."

Canadian-born R. Dean Taylor enjoyed modest success as both a composer and performer at Motown in the early 1970s.

After being shuttled to the new Mowest imprint for a last single in late '71 ("Hey Lordy" b/w "Just A Little Bit Closer"), Taylor left. He surfaced in 1975 with a minor hit on Playboy, "Why Play Games," and remains musically active. Chong maintained a higher profile (pun fully intended) as half the enormously popular stoner comedy duo of Cheech & Chong.

R. DEAN TAYLOR

Though R. Dean Taylor's 1970 smash "Indiana Wants Me" was a Motown release, you'd never suspect it from its laidback countryish feel. Of course, it did appear on the Rare Earth subsidiary, where Motown placed its rock acts. But the Canadian-born Taylor had worked for years as a Hitsville composer prior to his performing breakthrough, collaborating with Holland-Dozier-Holland and helping to write "Love Child" for the Supremes and "All I Need" for the Temptations with other songsmiths.

He was born Richard Dean Taylor in Toronto in 1939 and was a country enthusiast during his formative years. His "I'll Remember" gained U.S. release in 1962 on Mala. Brian Holland brought Taylor into Motown, and he reportedly had an uncredited hand in composing the H-D-H classics "Standing In The Shadows Of Love" and "7 Rooms Of Gloom" and the Supremes' "Love Is Here And Now You're Gone."[19] Taylor's own early singles for V.I.P. plugged him into more of a standard Motown formula sound—"Let's Go Somewhere" (backed by "Poor Girl") was a Canadian hit in early '66, and "There's A Ghost In My House," issued in the spring of '67 (flipped with "Don't Fool Around") was a belated British Northern Soul sensation. He officially shared writing credit with H-D-H this time, Brian producing the 'A' side with Lamont Dozier.

After "Gotta See Jane" with "Don't Fool Around" emerged on V.I.P. in 1968, Taylor moved over to Rare Earth and came up with the biggest hit of his career as a singer his first time out on the logo. "Indiana Wants Me," a dramatic tale of a fugitive on the lam, was a pop smash during the fall of 1970, catapulting Taylor from the relative anonymity of being a songwriter into the performing arena. *I Think Therefore I Am*, his debut LP, was released before year's end, and his next two Rare Earth singles, "Ain't It A Sad Thing" and "Gotta See Jane," were minor hits during the first few months of 1971. But Taylor's stint in the national spotlight was short-lived. "Taos New Mexico," his last Rare Earth single, barely scraped the charts in the spring of '72. He inaugurated his own label, Jane Records, the next year.

Tammi Terrell was a shooting star at Motown before her life and career were tragically cut short by a brain tumor at age 24.

TAMMI TERRELL

The duet magic that Tammi Terrell brewed up with Marvin Gaye during the late '60s has become so indelibly ingrained in the Motown success story that her solo recordings usually receive comparatively short shrift. That's a pity; as unforgettable as that series of hit duets was, lovely Tammi didn't require anyone's help to turn heads during her tragically truncated life.

Born Thomasina Montgomery on April 29, 1945, in Philadelphia, Tammi sang in church as a wee lass. By the time she was 11, she was competing in area talent contests. Producer Luther Dixon, riding high at Scepter/Wand Records thanks to Chuck Jackson and the Shirelles, inked her to a pact with Scepter, and in late '61, the 16-year-old songbird debuted as Tammy Montgomery with "If You See Bill" and "It's Mine." She encored in the spring of '62 on Wand with "Voice Of Experience" with "I Wancha To Be Sure," but stardom was still a ways down the road. Gene "Daddy G" Barge, then blowing his lusty tenor sax beside Gary U.S. Bonds, crossed paths with her in Wildwood, New Jersey, when she was singing with Steve Gibson & the Red Caps, a vocal group long past its 1940s heyday (Damita Jo previously held down the same post).

James Brown recognized Tammi's budding talent and brought her aboard his revue, producing a single for her in 1963 on his Try Me imprint (she was personally involved with the Godfather of Soul as well).[20] Still doing business as Tammy Montgomery, her "I Cried" squeaked onto *Billboard's* Hot 100 in August of '63, backed with "If You Don't Think." After a 1964 single on Checker, "If I Would Marry You" (co-written by Tammi and noted New York producer Bert Berns), Montgomery put her show biz ambitions on the hold to attend the University of Pennsylvania. Contrary to some reports, she wasn't married to boxer Ernie Terrell, whose sister Jean would replace Diana Ross in the Supremes.

Tammi Terrell and Marvin Gaye rode a string of hits in the late 1960s, including "Good Lovin' Ain't Easy To Come By" in 1969.

Reports vary as to how Tammi joined the Motown roster. One account has it Berry caught her act when she was singing duets at the 20 Grand with Windy City soul crooner Jerry "Iceman" Butler. A similar featured spot with Chuck Jackson's troupe may have also played a role. Once she joined the talent stable, Tammi was assigned to producers Harvey Fuqua and Johnny Bristol, who co-wrote her vibrant Motown debut "I Can't Believe You Love Me." Issued in late '65, it became her first substantial national hit early the next year, its strings-enhanced arrangement recalling her previous uptown soul leanings. Harvey's delicious "Hold Me Oh My Darling" adorned its flip, a male vocal group audibly including Fuqua surrounding her sexy delivery.

"Tammi was very good," said Bristol. "I enjoyed her commercial sound in her voice, and her personality in the studio was just incredible. She was just fun." "Come On And See Me," a muscular mid-tempo Fuqua/Bristol creation, made it two hits in a row for Tammi during the summer of '66, backed with "Baby Dont'cha Worry." Tammi sounded mesmerized by her "man-of-steel's" big, strong hands on the Smokey Robinson/Al Cleveland-penned charmer "What A Good Man He Is." The late '67 single was the only one of her four Motown solo singles not to chart (some accounts claim it never hit the streets at all).

By then, the company's promotional efforts were primarily focused on her duet smashes with Marvin anyway. Once "Ain't No Mountain High Enough" blazed forth during the summer of '67—followed in short order by "Your Precious Love," "If I Could Build My Whole World Around You" and its flip "If This World Were Mine," "Ain't Nothing Like The Real Thing," and "You're All I Need To Get By," all in a little over a year—their priorities were clear. With their cooing love songs, their legion of fans swore they were romantically entwined. But Tammi was actually involved with the Temptations' David Ruffin.

Tragically, Terrell wouldn't live long enough to savor her stardom. She collapsed in Gaye's arms during a concert at Virginia's Hampden-Sydney College in the summer of 1967 and was diagnosed with a brain tumor. Several operations were performed that took a drastic toll on Terrell's health and performing capabilities, but she valiantly tried to resume her career. When she couldn't make an engagement, labelmates Barbara Randolph and Brenda Holloway filled in.

Motown released the aptly titled *Irresistible*, Tammi's only solo LP, in January of '68. It contained Smokey's "He's The One I Love," a pounding "Can't Stop Now (Love Is Calling)," the Fuqua/Bristol/Sylvia Moy collaborations "Tears At The End Of A Love Affair" and "I Can't Go On Without You," a gender-switched treatment of the Spinners' Tri-Phi debut "That's What Girls Are Made For" with Fuqua's voice again recognizable in the background, and a reading of the Isley Brothers' 1966 smash "This Old Heart Of Mine (Is Weak For You)" that became her last solo hit in early '69 (backed with the prophetically titled "Just Too Much To Hope For").

Tammi's health slipped steadily away. "She was from Philly. I knew her before she went to Motown," said McDougal. "When she passed away, I was the in-between, more or less, for her and Motown. She was sick, and they were waiting for her to recover. Everybody was so busy at Motown doing what they were doing, they didn't know that Tammi was as sick as she was." She passed away on March 16, 1970, a month-and-a-half shy of her 25th birthday. Gaye was devastated, sequestering himself away from the public for an extended period.

SAMMY TURNER

Nearly five years after he enjoyed a taste of pop stardom with his updated treatment of the ancient English folk theme "Lavender Blue," Sammy Turner paused at Motown in early 1964 to cut a single. He was signed through Raynoma Gordy's short-lived Jobete office in New York.

Born in Paterson, New Jersey, on June 2, 1932, Turner was paying the bills as an accounting clerk at a Jersey factory when agent Herb Lutz caught the Air Force vet moonlighting at a local nightspot. Lutz steered his new protege to the attention of Big Top Records, which initially co-billed him as lead singer of a vocal group, the Twisters, on a revival of the hoary "Sweet Annie Laurie" that inched onto the pop charts in early '59.

Turner went solo with the vacuous but lovely "Lavender Blue," receiving the full strings-and-choir treatment under the supervision of Jerry Leiber and Mike Stoller. The delicate ballad rose to rarified heights on the pop and R&B hit parades in the summer of 1959. Turner rolled through one ancient Tin Pan Alley artifact after another, notably the Leiber/Stoller-produced follow-ups "Always" (the lively swinger was a bigger R&B seller than pop in late '59, just missing the top slot) and its equally polished flip "Symphony" (a minor hit itself) as well as "Paradise" in early '60. Seven additional Turner 45s on Big Top bombed.

Turner's one Motown single appeared in early '64. He was still trafficking in much the same sound: Bristling violins, rumbling percussion, and a choir set a dramatic uptown soul stage for "Right Now," Turner turning in a splendid performance on a song co-written by Ray's brother Mike Ossman and Harry Bass. A heavily orchestrated revival of the Platters' '55 R&B chart-topper "Only You" graced the flip, Turner displaying a vocal similarity to ex-Platters lead tenor Tony Williams. While working with the label, Turner did some writing with George Kerr and Sidney Barnes. He surfaced on Verve in '66 with "Our Love Will Grow And Grow," backed with a less-than-scrumptious-sounding "Pink Sugar And Purple Salt."

THE TWISTIN' KINGS

The second album bearing the Motown logo following Mary Wells' debut was *Twistin' the World Around*, an instrumental-dominated 1961 collection by the Twistin' Kings. Apparently they were the Hitsville house band, augmented by a vocal group on "Old Folks Twist" and "Mexican Twist" (the latter sporting spoken interjections in an ersatz Jose Jimenez accent).

It would have been tough to utilize "Twist Ala B.G." and "Flying Circle Twist" for what they were intended. The former, named after writer Berry Gordy, sounded more like a Halloween theme than something Chubby Checker might endorse. Sales department head Barney Ales joined producer Gordy in co-writing everything on the LP, including a Latin-tempo "Twisting Ales Style" and the jazzy "Congo Twist," a drums-and-piano workout that provided both sides of the band's second 45—"White House Twist" and the singalong "Christmas Twist" preceded it.

THE UNDERDOGS

Cracking the rock market didn't come easy for Motown. Rare Earth finally did the trick, but there were scattered attempts before that. Few of them sported a tougher edge than the Underdogs' "Love's Gone Bad"; released on the V.I.P. subsidiary in January of 1967. It had all the hallmarks of classic garage rock, though written by an unlikely source: Holland-Dozier-Holland. Clarence Paul exhibited his versatility by supervising the track; the group's treatment of "Mo Jo Hanna," the R&B grinder he'd penned with Andre Williams for singer Henry Lumpkin in '62, graced its 'B' side. Two releases and a few months earlier, V.I.P. had issued a more conventional treatment of "Love's Gone Bad" by Chris Clark. Neither sold appreciably.

Hailing from the well-to-do Detroit suburb of Grosse Pointe, the Underdogs (vocalist/bassist Dave Whitehouse, lead guitarist Tony Roumell, rhythm guitarist Chris Lena, and drummer Michael Morgan, the latter trio sharing the vocal load) had previously recorded for the local Hideout logo, leading to their first two 45s being picked up nationally by Frank Sinatra's Reprise Records: "Man In The Glass" with "Friday At The Hideout" in 1965 and the following year's "Little Girl" with "Don't Pretend." A third, "Surprise Surprise" with "Get Down On Your Knees," was limited to Hideout availability.

True to their name, the Underdogs didn't get much of a chance at Motown. "Love's Gone Bad" was their only V.I.P. release, though they did serve as a warmup act on a Motortown Revue at Detroit's Fox Theater, sharing the stage with Stevie Wonder, the Tempts, Martha & the Vandellas, Tammi Terrell, Jimmy Ruffin, Gladys Knight & the Pips, and J.J. Barnes.

THE UNDISPUTED TRUTH

Norman Whitfield's **funk revolution** was on a real roll at the dawn of the 1970s. As if cranking out monster hits by the Temptations didn't offer enough creative pressure, the producer assembled a one-man, two-woman vocal trio, The Undisputed Truth, to handle his overload.

"I think that was one of his brainchilds," said his songwriting partner Barrett Strong.

What's more, Norman tried to appeal to a psychedelic sensibility by outfitting his proteges in headbands and hippie threads that eventually gave way to white afro wigs and metallic-painted faces. Sometimes the output of the two groups seemed interchangeable. The Tempts had cut "Smiling Faces Sometimes" as an album track prior to the Undisputed Truth's 1971 smash; the Truth nailed a mid-level R&B hit on "Papa Was A Rollin' Stone" in mid-1972, a few months prior to the issue of the Tempts' Grammy winner.

The Undisputed Truth outside WDAS in Philadelphia. Left to right: Brenda Joyce Evans, Billie Rae Calvin, Joe Harris. (Weldon A. McDougal III photo).

As often happened around Hitsville, Whitfield combined two separate entities to form one outstanding group. Joe Harris had been a member of a Detroit vocal trio, the Fabulous Peps, with Tommy "Storm" Hestor and Ronald Abner that recorded the clever "Detroit, Michigan" (they name-checked everyone from Mary Wells and the Supremes to Soupy Sales and Hitsville itself) for Mike Hanks's D-Town label (also home to singer Lee Rogers, who hit with "I Want You To Have Everything" in '65) and its sister Wheelsville logo ("With These Eyes") before calling it quits in 1967. Billie Rae Calvin and Brenda Joyce Evans had been two-thirds of the Delicates, an L.A. group brought to Motown by Bobby Taylor. Brenda and Billie sang backgrounds in 1970 on Diana Ross' "Ain't No Mountain High Enough," Edwin Starr's gut-wrenching "War," and the Four Tops' *Still Waters Run Deep* LP.

Typically, both sides of the Truth's Gordy debut single in early '71 were recycled from Whitfield's past. "Save My Love For A Rainy Day" had graced the Tempts' '67 album *With a Lot O' Soul*; "Since I've Lost You" had been Jimmy Ruffin's first Soul single in 1964 (the Tempts cut it too). "Save My Love For A Rainy Day" proved a decent-sized R&B seller for the new trio, though it paled in comparison to what came next.

"Smiling Faces Sometimes," another Whitfield/Strong masterpiece, had just come out on the Tempts' *Sky's The Limit* album in marathon 12-and-a-half minute form when the Truth's rendition was issued on a Gordy 45. Backstabbing wasn't unheard of in the music business or in life, and slathered in funk by arranger Jerry Long, the tune came soaked in deep-seated paranoia.

"You see that all the time," said Strong. "Especially

when you're doing somewhat nice, you'll see a lot of that. Everybody wants to be your friend." Great as the Tempts were, the Truth outdid 'em by a mile. Harris brought an intimacy to his lead vocal that made it seem he was sharing a secret, Billie and Brenda commiserating one minute and piping up in their own behalf the next in front of a stealthy rhythmic bed. During the summer of '71, "Smiling Faces Sometimes" catapulted the Truth to stardom, sailing to No. 3 pop status and No. 2 R&B. Its flip, the driving "You Got The Love I Need," found Harris proficiently trading off with his female cohorts. An eponymous debut LP followed in its wake, the trio resuscitating "I Heard It Through The Grapevine" with a groove midway between Gladys and Marvin.

The Undisputed Truth performs for the cameras. Left to right: Joe Harris, Brenda Joyce Evans, Billie Rae Calvin (Weldon A. McDougal III photo)

Whitfield took a personal interest in breaking his new group. "The first time I ever met 'em was in Norman Whitfield's office. And he said, 'Listen, man, these are some young guys,' and he introduced me to 'em," said McDougal. "He said, 'What I want you to do, Weldon—I think they're gonna be big, so I want you to promote 'em.'

"They saved *Soul Train. Soul Train* used to be in Chicago, with Don Cornelius, and Sears was their sponsor. So I saw Don Cornelius, and he said, 'Listen, man, can you bring a big group over here or somebody? 'Cause Sears said if I don't get no big acts, they're not gonna sponsor us anymore.' So I was coming in town with the Undisputed Truth. And when I got to Chicago, the record 'Smiling Faces' was No. 1. I said, 'Hey, man, I've got the Undisputed Truth.' He said, 'For real? You can bring 'em over?' I said, 'Yeah!' And we went over, and they did the show," said Weldon. "At that time, James Brown called him, and said he'd do the show. And it was because the Undisputed Truth, who had the No. 1 record, made the rest of the artists feel like this show was worthwhile. And Sears sponsored 'em again."

True to form, both sides of the Truth's next single had already been tackled by the Tempts. "You Make Your Own Heaven And Hell Right Here On Earth," another socially supercharged Whitfield/Strong opus, had appeared in 1970 on their *Psychedelic Shack* LP, but given a thickly layered arrangement by Paul Riser, the Truth's remake nevertheless made its own splash at year's end. The group greeted the new year with its encore album, *Face To Face With The Truth,* which spawned the resolutely funky "What It Is," a decent-sized hit in the spring of '72.

The Truth's original "Papa Was A Rollin' Stone" was no less funky than the Tempts' universally embraced reading and good enough to rate plenty of spins midway through the year (this time, Norman raided his own catalog for Gladys & the Pips' '69 smash "Friendship Train" as a 'B'). After that, the Truth stopped shadowing the Tempts. Harris sounded remarkably like

Jerry Butler on "Girl You're Alright," a Pam Sawyer/Clay McMurray ballad that Whitfield co-produced with Clay, while "Mama I Got A Brand New Thing (Don't Say No)" and "Law Of The Land"—the title track of their third Gordy album in mid-'73—throbbed with intensity.

Though Harris remained a constant, personnel changes were otherwise common. Brenda left, replaced by Diane Evans, then both ladies split when the Truth expanded to a quintet (Calvin Stephenson, Tyrone Douglas, Tyrone Barkley, and Virginia McDonald were the new recruits). The group scored its last Top 20 R&B seller in the spring of '74 with "Help Yourself," a mid-tempo Whitfield copyright from their fourth LP, *Down To Earth*. The times had changed: On "Big John Is My Name," a stomper from the same album, Whitfield didn't bother to mask its drug references in the first stanza. "I'm A Fool For You," the group's last '74 hit, hailed from the same LP.

Joe Harris, Billie Rae Calvin and Brenda Joyce Evans joined forces in 1971 and rose to prominence on the funk scene as The Undisputed Truth behind the writing talents of Norman Whitfield.

With Whitfield at the controls, the group headed for outer space in 1975, with the minor hit "UFO's" and an album entitled *Cosmic Truth*. "Higher Than High," the Truth's last Gordy hit, was closer to P-Funk than the Motown sound. When Norman launched his own label, he took the Undisputed Truth along, scoring a couple of 1976 hits with "You + Me = Love" and "Let's Go Down To The Disco." By then, Chaka Khan's sister, Taka Boom, had joined its ranks.

THE VALADIERS

The first white vocal group on Motown sounded anything but. The Valadiers polished their doo-wop harmonies to a glistening edge prior to arriving at Hitsville, the teens convincing many fans of their three singles for Miracle and Gordy (and a few unsuspecting show promoters) that they were of African-American extraction—at least until they encountered them in person.

Lead singer Stuart Avig—the last member to come aboard—Jerry Light, Jerry Bernstein, Art Glasser, and Marty Coleman passed their audition for Berry Gordy, who had turned down an a previous integrated edition of the group (their Latin name translated to "brave soldiers"). The Valadiers came together in school; the two Jerrys attended Mumford High, the rest of the group hailed from Oak Park High. Entering Hitsville for the first time in February of '61, the quintet cut the smoothly harmonized ballad "Take A Chance" and two other numbers, but Frankel's father refused to sign a contract in behalf of his underage son, forcing him from the group.

Avig and Light dreamed up the musical playlet "Greetings (This Is Uncle Sam)" in a flash after happening upon a newspaper headline in the studio a few months later outlining President Kennedy's plan to expand his armed forces.[21] Traditionally, songs dealing with military service tended to be ultra-patriotic drivel, but "Greetings" presented a more realistic and amusing scenario. Light's growling drill sergeant barked orders at reluctant recruit Avig, whose creamy lead carried the first half of the ballad. Flipped with "Take A Chance" from the previous session, "Greetings" was issued on the short-lived Miracle logo in late 1961 and became a hit, topping out at No. 89 on *Billboard's* pop charts that November. Its storyline assumed new relevance by 1966, when the Monitors scored a solid R&B seller with it at the height of the Vietnam conflict.

The boys provided something of a sequel to "Greetings" with "While I'm Away," another soulful ballad reeking of rich doo-wop harmonies that came out as Gordy's third single in the spring of '62, backed by an up-tempo "Because I Love You," which sported a rhumba-spiced beat. "I Found A Girl," their last Gordy offering in early '63, was a peppy upbeat effort with snappy background harmonies. The attractive mid-tempo "You'll Be Sorry Someday" adorned its flip.

Avig and a reformed edition of the Valadiers with no other original members recorded a half-dozen sides for Ian Levine's Motor City imprint during the late '80s.

CONNIE VAN DYKE

Young Detroit model Connie Van Dyke was just coming off being named Miss Teen of the U.S. when she waxed her only Motown single. "Oh Freddie," released in early 1963, was a Smokey Robinson theme that could have suited Mary Wells—slightly demure, with a Latin tinge. On the flip, Van Dyke took on "It Hurt Me Too," introduced by Marvin Gaye as the 'B' side of "Stubborn Kind Of Fellow" the previous year, belting it hard enough to blow out the walls of Studio A. Working the local club circuit, she later joined the Wheelsville imprint, ripping into the up-tempo "Don't Do Nothin' I Wouldn't Do" under William Garrett's supervision.

Conny (the way she spells her name on her Web site) moved to Los Angeles toward the end of the decade with acting ambitions and appeared in the biker film *Hell's Angels '69* and on various TV cop shows. Country music became her specialty during the '70s, with an album for Andy Williams' Barnaby logo and a featured role in Burt Reynolds' *W.W. and the Dixie Dance Kings*. She's recently returned to show business after taking time out to raise her son.

THE VELVELETTES

The Velvelettes' five-part harmonies always lived up to their name, whether they were delivering winsome ballads or the sassy chants "Needle In A Haystack" and "He Was Really Sayin' Somethin'" for producer Norman Whitfield during the mid-'60s on V.I.P. Records. Cousins Bertha Barbee-McNeal and Norma Barbee-Fairhurst were born in Shannon, Mississippi, and raised in Flint, Michigan; lead singer Caldin (Carolyn) Gill-Street and her older sister Mildred Gill-Arbor lived in Kalamazoo, Michigan. Betty Kelley was Cal's best friend.

(From Left) Cal Gill, Bertha Barbee and Norma Barbee recorded just one LP as the Velvelettes, but they scored several individual hits, including "Needle In A Haystack" in 1964.

Bertha and Norma had already been on record as background singers for their uncle, Simon Barbee. "He asked Norma and myself and another cousin by marriage, Joyce, to do background work," said Bertha. "We formed a group and called ourselves the Barbees, which was my maiden name and Norma's maiden name. So we sung around for several years, and we got to the point where we started buying little outfits, matching outfits. And it culminated into a record. My uncle very excitedly one day told us, 'Hey, we've got this producer coming from Detroit named Mickey Stevenson. He's just a young producer, and he's gonna help us make a record.' 'Yay-y-y!' My uncle had written a song called 'The Wind,' and the other song was going to be called 'Que Pasa.'" The Barbees' only single came out on the tiny Stepp label in 1957.

The group broke up, and Bertha enrolled as a music major at Western Michigan University in Kalamazoo. "When I went to Western, I went and saw this baby grand piano that was in what we called a student center. A bunch of us girls—my roommate and myself, and a bunch of us went over there to just kind of lollygag around," she said. "I had been taking piano lessons since I was 9. I had learned by ear, after taking classical, how to play early rock chords with my uncle. So boy, I flew to that piano and started playing some of our Barbees songs.

"So a lot of kids gathered around, a lot of girls, and they said, 'Why don't we start up a singing group?' Believe it or not, there was probably at the beginning about 12 girls in this singing group. We hadn't named ourselves at all. But Mildred, who now sings in the Velvelettes, she was one of those girls. So we sung around campus at sock hops, etcetera, for a couple of months. And then finally there was this fraternity Alpha Phi Alpha. They were going to have a talent show, and first place was going to be $25. Now $25 then was like $100. So me and Mildred were like, 'Girl, we're just going to have to dismiss some of the other girls.'

"I told her, 'I have a cousin in Flint who can really sing.' And she said she had a sister who also had a best friend who could sing. So the other girls were dismissed—and very tenderly—and that was really how the Velvelettes were formed at that time, all five of us. My cousin would come up, and we'd practice in their music hall, where everybody else was practicing on classical stuff, and here we were on this little rock stuff in these little practice rooms. It was really weird. But we did win first place and got the $25."

The quintet then answered to a more exotic handle. "Cal was in the end of middle school, and she was taking French," said Bertha. "We were trying to come up with a name, and she said, 'Why don't we call ourselves the Beautiful Women, or the Beautiful Girls?' And that was where the Les Jolie Femmes came in. We dismissed that after a while because nobody could pronounce it except Cal.

"We were harmonizing one night in the car," she said. "Four-part harmony, and I think every now and then one of us would go up to a fifth chord. It was beautiful! Me being a music major, I'm like, 'Wow!' So we would just amaze ourselves with harmonizing. Somebody said, 'Boy, the harmony sounds very smooth!' It was very smooth, the way we would modulate from one chord to another. Then somebody said, 'Yeah, smooth like velvet!' Then when somebody said velvet, I don't know who, they thought of the Marvelettes or something, evidently. And somebody said, 'Velvet—Velvelettes!' That's where our name was born, right in a car!"

There was never any question about who would sing lead. "When Mildred said that she had a younger sister that could sing, which was Cal, and Cal's friend Betty Kelley came to my dorm, and my cousin, where we all got together, we knew we had to decide who was gonna lead. So it was the kind of a thing when we heard Cal, we all looked at each other and said, 'Hey, that's it! Cal is it!'" said Bertha. "It was just a unanimous decision right from the beginning. And she was the youngest, too.

"Norma, my first cousin, the girl could go up so high it was unreal. Beautiful voice. So Norma was always the highest. And then below her was Betty Kelley. Of course, Cal's the lead. And me and Mildred, when we first started, I was higher than Mildred. I was like a high alto or something. And Mildred was the lowest."

Fellow Western Michigan student Robert Bullock had connections with a certain record company in Detroit. "He was in the audience when we won the talent show. After that, he came up and introduced himself and said, 'I'm Berry Gordy's nephew,' and he mentioned his mother, Esther Gordy, who we naturally didn't know at the time. And he said, 'They just started a recording studio called Motown. You know, you girls should come on and try to audition.'"

They were also encouraged by Cal's minister father. "One day he took us in a snowstorm, threw us in the car, and we went to audition for Motown. It was on a Saturday. It was very bad weather," said Bertha. "I think it took us like four hours, three-and-a-half, to get there." When they finally arrived, a haughty secretary was less than cordial. "We said, 'We're here to audition for Motown.' And she said, 'Well, where are you from?' We said, 'Kalamazoo.' And she looked at us real funny, 'cause Kalamazoo isn't like Detroit or Chicago or Flint. She goes, 'Kalama-who?'" said Bertha. "She was saying, 'No, we don't have auditions on Saturday.'

"A few of us had tears in our eyes. We had worked ourselves up to this, and to have driven all that way, we were very disappointed. You can imagine, being teenagers. We were on our way out the door, and at that moment, the recording studio door opened. Who should walk out but Mickey Stevenson.

"If he had came out five minutes later—it's weird. He recognized me and my cousin. He goes, 'Norma! Bertha! What are you girls doing here? Are you still singing?' We said, 'Yeah, we formed another group. We came here to audition. She won't let us in!' So he looked at her and said, 'Oh, I've been knowing these girls way back. Come on in!' You should have seen us look at that girl, sort of like 'Hey, forget you! We're goin' in.' So he did audition us. We were in.

"He said, 'You've got five in your group! Why do you have so many?' That's when I said, 'Oh, I'm the piano player, Mickey!' So when we got ready to audition, which I did play the piano, he just said, "You're in, but as far as you playing that piano, Bertha, we have our own music and musicians. So you just get right on up. I guess you guys are just gonna have to have five in the group.'"

"Our folks told Berry that we would have to stay in school. That was the only way that they would sign the contracts for those of us that were under 21, that education was more important. So he agreed to that," said Norma. "The fact that we were all in school—we were in college in the later years—that was pretty unique for the Motown artists at that time."

Norma had dreamed up what would be the 'A' side of their first single, "There He Goes," some time before. "I was a little teenager, and I had broken up with a little kid, what we called a boyfriend, at the time. I was feeling really sad and lonely, and I sat down at my piano and a lyric came to mind," she said. "Then I went over to visit Bertha—this is before we started the group the Velvelettes—and she started playing a few chords."

Both the plaintive "There She Goes" (writer's credit assigned to Stevenson) and its rocking flip "That's The Reason Why" (Robert Hamilton was listed as writer and co-producer with Mickey) featured Little Stevie Wonder's harmonica. Instead of appearing under the Motown banner, their debut 45 mysteriously came out in 1963 on the IPG (Independent Producers Group) label (its meager catalog included Jay Wiggins' "Sad

Girl" and *Car 54 Where Are You* sitcom cutup Joe E. Ross's immortal "Ooh Ooh"). "I really never understood that myself," said Bertha.

Before long, there were only four Velvelettes. "Betty left shortly after we made 'There He Goes.' She was on that one. One of the Vandellas quit the group, for whatever reason. We had so many in our group, and Betty Kelley actually favored this gal a lot. So that's when Berry Gordy came to our group and asked her, would she be willing to take this girl's place. Betty checked with us, she thought about it, she pondered it. It wasn't one of those nasty breakoff things," said Bertha. "We had so many in the group, so in a way it was a blessing in disguise. Although that did hamper our five-part harmony thing and we loved her."

Norman Whitfield took over for the Velvelettes' first release on V.I.P., writing and co-producing (with Stevenson) the stomping girl group classic "Needle In A Haystack," which climbed to No. 45 on *Billboard's* pop charts during the fall of '64. "This was Norman's baby," said Bertha. "He really worked with us, probably more than any of the other girl groups.

"Norman, when he gave us a song, he would sing the lead, and he'd say, 'You girls just make up a background.' He might have one line that he wanted as a background. So we would get in the room—which we loved to sing—so we would do that and just make up a background," she continued. "You remember a group called the Chiffons? 'He's So Fine'?" asked Bertha. "I ain't gonna say stole, but we picked the 'doo-da-langs.'" The same pair wrote the elegant flip, "Should I Tell Them," though Mickey took over the producer's chair.

Though they went on one Dick Clark tour that also included the Supremes, not all their gigs were so glamorous. "(Berry) had drivers every weekend take us to what they called sock hops. Because Detroit is so big, these teenagers had parties all over. So his driver had all these sock hops that we were supposed to stop by and pantomime, lip-synch our record. That was very exciting. We would stop by, and the kids would go 'Oooooh!'" she said. "I remember one time we went out on a sock hop, and our record stuck!"

Norman, Mickey, and Eddie Holland combined to brainstorm the Velvelettes' irresistible rocker "He Was Really Sayin' Somethin'," which went to No. 21 R&B and No. 64 pop in early '65, Cal's lead dripping streetwise sass. "That was the majority of ours' favorite. To be honest, 'Needle In A Haystack,' it was alright. We were like, 'Ahhh, okay.' But when 'He Was Really Sayin' Somethin'' came out, all of us loved that," said Bertha. Not the least of its charms was the immortal backing refrain, "Bop-bop-sookie-doo-wa-da." "We probably made up half if not three-fourths of the backgrounds," noted Bertha. "Throw A Farewell Kiss," the lovely 'B' side, was another Whitfield production written with Eddie Holland.

Both sides of the Velvelettes' third V.I.P. single that May, the attractive "Lonely Lonely Girl Am I" (the handiwork of producer Whitfield, Holland, and Tempts' lead Eddie Kendricks) and Norman's spine-tingling "I'm The Exception To The Rule," would later be reworked by the Tempts. Whifield also helmed "A Bird In The Hand (Is Worth Two In The Bush)," which drove relentlessly, and its Holland/Marv Johnson-written flip, "Since You've Been Loving Me."

"While we were doing all this, I was trying to graduate from college," said Bertha. "That did slow me up a little. It was kind of a sacrifice, trying to write papers and go to the studio and be in there on the weekends, and then trying to do my work. So it was kind of rough and tough there for a while. The other girls were in high school, and my cousin Norma was going to Flint Junior College. I think Mildred was trying to go to nursing school, and Mildred at the same time had her baby first. So we were all going through some changes."

Domesticity won out. "We made 'A Bird In The Hand,' and shortly after that was when all of us quit the group to get married and have kids, except for Cal," said Bertha. "They were gonna do an album on us. We didn't know that at the time. I definitely would not have quit Motown had I known that they were gonna do an album." Said Norma, "In the '60s, if you weren't married by 21, you were considered an old maid. So marrying and having a family was extremely important in the '60s. And that's what we did."

Cal located her own replacement Velvelettes, Philadelphian Sandra Tilley and Annette McMillan. She continued to record and tour, though the storming Harvey Fuqua/Johnny Bristol-helmed "These Things Will Keep Me Loving You,"was the group's last V.I.P. single. It made a No. 43 R&B showing in late 1966 and became the Velvelettes' only British chart hit.[22]

In 1969, Cal married Monitors lead singer Richard Street. With no new releases on the horizon, Sandra joining the Vandellas, and Annette ready to retire from the road, the Velvelettes were done. Until 1984, that is, when a pageant for the Black Concerned Women of Kalamazoo brought all the original members back together except for Kelley.

"We got two standing ovations, I think. They just wouldn't stop clapping. We were almost drawn to tears," said Bertha. "We just said, 'Hey, this is it! We gotta do this! This makes us feel good, and it makes other people feel good.'" They've performed together ever since.

SINGING SAMMY WARD

Berry Gordy was fixated on the lucrative concept of reaching the widest possible audience, leaving blues singer Sammy Ward at a distinct disadvantage.

Hailing from the densely populated Ensley section of Birmingham, Alabama, Ward came from a sanctified brood. "Sammy's brother sang with the same group for a while that Paul Williams' father sang with, the Ensley Jubilees," reported labelmate Gino Parks. Any sanctified ambitions Sammy may have harbored had been jettisoned by the time he established himself in the Motor City. "He used to work a lot with us around the clubs in Detroit also—mainly Lee's Sensation and Denny's," said Parks, who recalls Ward's showstoppers to have been Brook Benton's mellow "It's Just A Matter Of Time" and Lloyd Price's houserocker "Stagger Lee."

Ward's only release on Motown proper was his 1960 duet with Sherri Taylor, coupling the hot local seller "Lover" with "That's Why I Love You So Much." Sherri's mother Clara operated C&T Records, a tiny area label that had a publishing connection with Robert West's LuPine label, and Sherri co-wrote "Too Young To Love" for a C&T girl group, the Taylor Tones. Other than that, all of Ward's 45s would appear on Tamla.

Berry and Smokey Robinson wrote Singing Sammy's first Tamla single, the rocking "That Child Is Really Wild," a fine example of the primordial Motown sound with rock-ribbed piano, a choppy rhythm, and Ward's aggressive vocal. It came out with two alternate flips: "What Makes You Love Him," the work of Berry, brother George, and Roquel "Billy" Davis, was Ray Charles-inspired blues with a long intro that Ward scorched with his testifying, while Smokey's "Who's The Fool" had an easy-going groove contrasting with Sammy's forceful accusations of cheating (a slashing guitar solo wasn't the least of its charms). The tinkering paid dividends: "Who's The Fool" became a No. 23 hit on *Billboard's* R&B charts in the summer of '61.

Tamla released a different, more polished but less

intense "What Makes You Love Him" in late '61, backed by Mickey Stevenson and William Weatherspoon's "Don't Take It Away," and tried again with "Big Joe Moe"(written by Stevenson and Brian Holland) with "Everybody Knew It" in early '62. The diminutive Ward never came up with a stronger Tamla two-sider than in late '62 with the upbeat blues "Someday Pretty Baby," a sparkling Gordy/Ward collaboration with an extended opening coda that gave Sammy room to engage in a little secular preaching (Little Stevie Wonder's harp was conspicuous), and its stunning minor-key blues flip "Part Time Love," submitted by Motown staffer Janie Bradford and keyboardist Richard "Popcorn" Wylie.

"Popcorn would come over and play and leave me the track, so I'd just write and sing to them," said Bradford, whose composition certainly brought out the best in Ward. Sammy's final single for the label was one of the initial outings on Soul in the summer of 1964, teaming the guitar-laden "Bread Winner," a sumptuous slow blues credited to staffer Fay Hale, with Mickey's "You've Got To Change."

Somehow, Ward's gutsy delivery only resulted in one hit during his stay at the label. "It might have been timing with he and I, so far as Motown is concerned," noted Mable John. "And then some things are just for the beginning, and not the long haul." He left behind a wealth of unissued material in the Motown archives and adapted to the Motor City soul sound after leaving on a stirring single for Groove City, "Stone Broke," with fellow ex-Motowners Wylie (who wrote it) and Robert Bateman contributing background vocals. "Sister Lee" occupied its flip.

When Motown excavated its vaults to compile the *Switched On Blues* anthology in 1970, it exhumed "What Makes You Love Him," "Bread Winner," "Part Time Love," and nearly six glorious minutes of "Someday Pretty Baby" without offering any info about the man singing them. Perhaps that fueled Ward's latter-day dissatisfaction toward the firm.

"Sammy Ward was very bitter," said Parks. "I couldn't get him out from being so bitter. I said, 'Being bitter's not gonna help you any.'" He managed to perform on occasion in his later years while holding down a day job, journeying to England with Frances Nero on one occasion to sing at a weekender. But the Motown hierarchy had forgotten him by the time of his passing a few years ago. "When Sammy died, Hattie Littles and I were the only Motown artists there," said Nero. "I gave the eulogy. Sammy was a good guy."

KIM WESTON

Singers with the class and sophistication of Kim Weston weren't easy to come by, even at Motown. What's more, for much of her Hitsville tenure, Kim was married to A&R boss Mickey Stevenson, which should have multiplied her chances at major stardom. But that romantic liaison seems to have been a mixed blessing: She was never honored with an LP of her own.

"I don't know why I never had an album," Weston said. "But that was one of the reasons that I left. I was there for six years almost, and never had an album. I felt I wasn't treated right."

Born Agatha Natalie Weston in Detroit on December 20, 1939, Kim's roots lie in sanctified soil. She grew up singing in choirs, and at 17 joined the Wright Specials, a group aligned with Rev. James Cleveland. "James tutored the group," she recalled. "Our manager, Mr. Thomas Wright, he was an outgoing person. The group had worked with people like James, the Caravans, Shirley Caesar, the Davis Sisters. So he went to Motown."

George Fowler was in charge of Hitsville's fledgling gospel imprint, Divinity Records, and the Wright Specials were the stars of its first two 45s, "That's What He Is To

Me" and flip "Pilgrim Of Sorrow" in July of '62 and "Ninety-Nine And A Half Won't Do" with "I Won't Go Back." The group had an in with Fowler. "I guess that had a lot to do with it, because his brother was our pianist," noted Kim. "His name was Ernest Fowler."

The jump to performing R&B came not long thereafter. "I was in church one Sunday, and a friend of mine came by. We were having a concert. And he came by and asked me if I would do some demos for a friend of his. And that friend happened to be the cousin of Brian and Eddie Holland," she said. "I was just doing the demo to get the money. I wasn't thinking about becoming a professional." Eddie didn't dig his cousin Johnny Thornton's material but loved the singer—leading to Kim's secular switch. "It took me a lot of thought for me to do that," she said.

Weston made her debut on Tamla in 1963 with a passionate "It Should Have Been Me," a "triangle" song written by Mickey and producer Norman Whitfield in the soapy tradition of Etta James' "All I Could Do Was Cry." "That was Norman's very first release too, at that time," said Weston. "He was quiet—not quiet, but he was much different from what he turned out to be." As it turned out, it was the other side of Kim's debut, the pleader "Love Me All The Way" (credited to producer Stevenson and sales head Barney Ales), that climbed to No. 24 on *Billboard's* R&B charts that summer. "The jocks in the South turned it over," she noted. Gladys Knight & the Pips had the hit with "It Should Have Been Me" in 1968, again under Whitfield's supervision.

Producer Stevenson and arranger Johnny Allen were listed as co-writers of Kim's smoldering "Just Loving You" later that year, its arrangement shimmering with class and Weston's delivery stunning in its crystal clarity. "That's my all-time favorite of all my records," Weston said. "Mickey and I wrote that together. My name's not on it, but we wrote it together. That's the one (that everybody) really said sounded like Dinah Washington. She definitely had an influence on me and my sound." Mickey shared writing and production credits with the Miracles' Ronnie White on the flip, the more R&B-oriented "Another Train Coming."

Kim Weston and Marvin Gaye teamed up for the memorable "It Takes Two" in 1967.

The indefatigable Smokey Robinson assumed the reins for both sides of Weston's next single, writing the delicious "Looking For The Right Guy" with White and penning "Feel Alright Tonight" himself. "Smokey's a great producer," noted Kim. Tamla issued it during the summer of 1964, the same year Kim married Mickey. "I met him before I went to Motown, but we got close at Motown," she said. That same year, Weston teamed for the first time on wax with Marvin Gaye, though the pair had already toured together.

"After my first release, the lady that was over at the talent management company, Mrs. Ardena Johnston, handled Marvin and me. So she put us together," Weston said. "She made a package of the two of us." No wonder the duo sounds so comfortable on "What Good Am I Without You," produced and co-written by her hubby. The song breaks into an easy swing over tinkling 88s, punchy brass, and brisk handclaps and was a pop success in late '64. "Marvin and I got along real well," said Weston. "As a matter of fact, we adopted each other as sister and brother."

Smokey and Mickey supplied the lilting 'B' "I Want You 'Round."

A grand uptown soul arrangement framed Kim's stirring delivery on "A Little More Love," written by Mickey and Hitsville newcomer Sylvia Moy and released by Tamla in late '64 (producer Stevenson teamed with Ivy Jo Hunter to write another stately ballad for the 'B' side, "Go Ahead And Laugh"). Bafflingly, neither "A Little More Love" nor its early '65 follow-up "I'm Still Loving You"—a densely orchestrated collaboration by Stevenson, Moy, and Hunter—dented the hit parade.

"Usually, when an artist had a hit, they would have a record," Weston mused. "Before the hit died down, they would release another record. That never happened with me. I don't know what the problem was. Maybe because I was real quiet back then. People just didn't know how to take me." The same fate befell "A Thrill A Moment," a bongo-spiced spine-chiller by Kim, Ales, and co-producers Stevenson and Hunter from the spring of '65. "That's one of my favorites too, that I co-wrote with Mickey," she said. Weston brought heartbreaking sadness to its 'B' side "I'll Never See My Love Again," which she penned with producers Stevenson and Hunter. Kim's unreleased-at-the-time "Do Like I Do" apparently utilized the same backing track, though the Andantes' chants were different. "He's an excellent writer," said Kim of Ivy Jo.

Kim Weston's Motown career had plenty of highlights, despite the fact she never cut a solo album.

Sometimes being married to Motown's A&R boss was clearly a disadvantage. Take the case of Martha & the Vandellas' 1966 hit "My Baby Loves Me," first earmarked for Kim. "Mickey took it from me and gave it to Martha, because he got mad at me," she said. "To spite me, he took it and gave it to her. And then he did the same thing with 'Dancing In The Street,' 'cause that was written for me." The jazzy "My Baby Loves Me" would have certainly suited Weston. "Actually, I did a lot of jazz at Motown. They just never released it," she said. "I did 'The Man That Got Away' on the Motown Revue."

As soon as the prolific Holland-Dozier-Holland became involved in Weston's career, hits began to flow. Instead of retaining the sublime uptown soul aura, H-D-H created the storming up-tempo "Take Me In Your Arms (Rock Me A Little While)" and gave Weston her biggest solo hit at No. 4 R&B in late 1965 (backed by another less torrid H-D-H confection, "Don't Compare Me With Her"). "Take Me In Your Arms" earned her a spectacular appearance on NBC-TV's weekly music series *Hullabaloo,* Kim belting the number while perched atop a towering pedestal as the show's dancers writhed below her as though worshiping a tribal goddess.

H-D-H handed Weston another surefire smash, "Helpless," which maintained the same irresistible up-tempo feel and just fell short of the R&B Top Ten in the spring of '66. The cooker had graced the Four Tops' second LP the year before. "They needed a record for me, and the Tops already had their album," reasoned Weston. Recycling their catalog as Norman Whitfield would later, the trio had Kim redo "A Love Like Yours (Don't Come Knocking Every Day)" for the 'B' side (it did identical duty on Martha & the Vandellas' "Heat

Wave"). "'Helpless' was a good song. I don't know what was happening then," she said. "Something was happening, 'cause it stayed in the charts for the longest time, but it didn't go anywhere."

Weston was regularly featured in the local clubs, including an extended stay at Chappie's Lounge with pianist Joe Hunter and guitarist Eddie Willis. "I went out to Chappie's to do a weekend gig, and it turned into two years," noted Weston. "I did a lot of work. I worked on the Motown Revues, but I did a lot of work by myself." She ventured overseas with a complement of Funk Brothers before most of her labelmates did.

"The first time we went over, we went over with Kim Weston," said percussionist Jack Ashford. "It was Uriel Jones, Earl Van Dyke, Robert White, and myself. We went over and did that thing as a feel-out thing, trying to feel that market out. So when the report came back so good, that's when Berry and a whole slew of everybody went."

Weston reunited with Gaye in 1966 for one of the transcendent duets in Motown history. "It Takes Two" crackled with palpable electricity, strings and horns swirling behind a grittier-than-usual Marvin and an alluring Kim. It jumped to the No. 4 R&B slot and a No. 14 pop showing in early '67.

"Sylvia Moy wrote that," said Weston. "She collaborated with Mickey Stevenson. After Mary Wells left, they put somebody else with Marvin, and it didn't work. My husband was the A&R director. I think he wanted me to do it at first, but being the A&R director, he didn't push me as he should have." Hank Cosby split production duties with Mickey on "It Takes Two," while its flip, "It's Got To Be A Miracle (This Thing Called Love)," had a tremendously uplifting radiance. An album of duets, Take Two, actually beat the 45 to the shelves by a few months, blessed with the presence of "Baby Say Yes" (written by Mickey and Kim), "Heaven Sent You I Know," and "I Love You, Yes I Do."

It would prove Weston's last Motown triumph. In January of '67, Mickey left to join the front office of MGM Records, and Kim exited, too. "I didn't feel I was treated right," she said. "If they didn't treat me right and he was there, I didn't think that I'd be treated fair after he left." Stevenson knew how to make Motownish records even though he was no longer in Gordy's employ, and Kim's first MGM single, "I Got What You Need," squeaked onto the pop charts for a week in the spring of '67. But "That's Groovy" didn't, nor did the punchy "You're Just The Kind Of Guy" (the work of future Motowner Willie Hutch) or its classy ballad flip "Nobody."

Weston took an entirely different tack on her aptly titled MGM album *For the First Time*, cut with a crew that swung in a different manner than the Funk Brothers. "I worked with Count Basie in New York, and then we went in the studio with the band," said Kim. Her second MGM long-player the following year, *This is America*, contained the inspirational "Lift Ev'ry Voice And Sing," a clarion call to her people. "I was asked to sing 'The Star-Spangled Banner.' And I said, 'Well, I prefer singing the black national anthem,'" Weston said.

After Kim left MGM, there was a 1969 duet project with Johnny Nash, a remake of the Marvelettes' "Danger, Heartbreak Ahead" for People, and *Kim Kim Kim*, a stirring 1971 album for Memphis-based Volt (she appeared at the historic *Wattstax* concert at the L.A. Coliseum in 1972). She divorced Stevenson during the '70s, sang jazz and appeared in theatrical productions, and gave back to her community by working with youth in the arts for 17 years. More recently, Weston took a breather in Israel before returning stateside to resume her singing career. She was still recuperating from being hit by a car as the new millennium arrived, but was ready to hit the stage again and hoping to work with more talented kids.

"A lot of people are trying to get me to go back into it. I guess when I get my health back together," she said. "I'm hoping that maybe I can go back in that direction. It was such a beautiful program."

Norman Whitfield bided his time before finally getting his chance to shine as a writer and producer at Motown. When he finally took over as the company's top producer, he blazed a trail of hits that included some of the most memorable songs of the late 1960s and early 70s (Photo courtesy of BMI).

NORMAN WHITFIELD

No producer was more important to Motown's industry domination after the departure of H-D-H than Norman Whitfield. In addition to writing some of the company's most monumental hits—"I Heard It Through The Grapevine," "Cloud Nine," "War," "Smiling Faces Sometimes," "Papa Was A Rollin' Stone"—with partner Barrett Strong, his imaginative productions injected a heady blast of funk into Hitsville during the late '60s and early '70s.

"We were having fun. We took a different turn," said Strong. "We came and just really went real funk: Sly (Stone), then you have George Clinton—you have a lot of people. There are a lot of influences there—Ray Charles, and what have you." The two split the lyrical and musical contributions down the middle. "It was an equal thing, total collaboration."

Whitfield made an indelible impression on those he worked with. "Incredibly talented. Brilliant. Dominant, very powerful, strong, sure," raved the Spinners' G.C. Cameron about the gent who produced and co-wrote their "Message From A Black Man." "The way he cut strings on his songs, he cut high strings. It was two to three octaves higher than the normal. There's a difference in the sound."

Norman wasn't a Motor City native. "He was from Brooklyn, New York, and then he moved to Detroit," recalled Strong. As he matured, Norman became as cunningly adept with a pool cue as with the tambourine he wielded with Richard "Popcorn" Wylie & the Mohawks. Soon he was wedging his foot in the Hitsville door. "He would sit around listening and listening. Wouldn't say a word for almost a year. When he first came to Motown, he wouldn't say a word to nobody," said Hank Cosby.

"He was really, really young, and kind of more of a hang-arounder," remembered Janie Bradford. "And he refused for them to run him away. He kept hanging around until his first hit." For a time he was in charge of auditioning amateur hopefuls, but those tasks didn't stop him from helping to write Marvin Gaye's exultant "Pride And Joy." The Supremes' "He Means The World To Me" and the Velvelettes' "Needle In A Haystack" were among Whitfield's early production triumphs, and when he took over responsibility for the Temptations upon the giant success of "Ain't Too Proud To Beg," Whitfield's genius was recognized.

"In the beginning, I used to do all his arrangements," said Cosby. "And he was different from everybody. What he would do, he would bring me five records. And he could sit there and tell me what part he wanted of each record. He would say, 'Give me four bars of this, four bars of this, four bars of this, four bars of that.' And I put it all together, and he had a song. He could do all this in his head! I could never figure that out. That's the way he did on most of his stuff."

"He'd come up with ideas, but Whitfield didn't really play," said Tempts guitarist Cornelius Grant. "He tinkled around on piano a bit, but didn't play an instrument."

"He was the first one to come out with a 12- and 14-minute record. He was willing to take that chance, that shot at it. But something has to happen within that limit of time," said Funk Brother Jack Ashford. "He would give me the autonomy to do different things and experiment with things, like a press roll on the side of a cowbell with a stick. Little patterns that he would have me playing on the triangle. He just gave me that type of freedom, because he was certain of the fact that I would add something instead of just playing."

Once he wrote a winner, it wasn't unusual for Whitfield to have every act he produced cut the song ("Grapevines" abound), though he gave each a distinctive twist. After leaving Berry Gordy's employ, there was more success—he produced Rose Royce's platinum seller "Car Wash" for MCA in 1976—and a few disappointments (his self-named label didn't last long).

ANDRE WILLIAMS

Only a few years back, Andre "Mr. Rhythm" Williams refused interview requests. Now he's talking, and it was worth the wait. One of the mainstays of pre-Motown Detroit R&B and a prolific producer during the '60s who split his time between the Motor City and Chicago, the streetwise raconteur stored up a plethora of fascinating tales during his self-imposed silence.

Born in Bessemer, Alabama, on November 1, 1936, Williams mostly grew up on Chicago's South Side. Andre found his way into the doo-wop scene while in high school, singing with the Cavaliers, then the Five Thrills (he recorded with the latter for powerful deejay Al Benson's Parrot logo in 1953-54) and the Five Echoes (replacing Tommy Hunt, then in the military). Williams was more of a showman than a harmonizer. "I wasn't a hell of a singer. So I could make up for it by dancing and doing the splits," he noted in a 1996 interview.

Settling in Detroit on the advice of a Navy buddy, Andre joined another young doo-wop aggregation, renaming them the Five Dollars. They signed in 1955 with Jack and Devora Brown's Fortune label, known primarily around the Motor City for the waxings of Nolan Strong and the Diablos. "It was so small that the storeroom was a studio," said Andre of Fortune's shoestring setup. "They were using the record boxes that the records came in, they were using that as sound acoustics." Williams sang lead on the Five Dollars' initial session, cutting the unusual wordless pieces "Harmony Of Love" and "So Strange."

Getting a little more outrageous with the double-sided "Going Down To Tiajuana" and "Pulling Time," Andre hooked up with another vocal aggregation, the Don Juans, with Gino Parks their first tenor. His only national hit found Andre backed by a crew simply billed as "His New Group," again with Parks aboard. "Bacon Fat" was in all likelihood the most laconic rock-and-roll dance number of the '50s. Supported by the Charlie Morris Orchestra (quite a stretch, considering the backing largely consisted of an oily sax riff and the hypnotic vocal refrain "Diddlee-diddlee, womp-womp"), Williams engaged in a laidback monolog so cool it was ice.

"We had been going back and forth to this particular club, the Flamingo, in Memphis," he said. "There was two-lane highways then. And you could see these cotton pickers all on the side of the road. We would stop and kid around with them, then go up to their house and drink lemonade and eat. And I was eatin' a bacon sandwich. I just tapped it out, and I was coming up with the words, and I had the bacon in my hand, and folks with sacks on their backs. That's how I came up with 'Bacon Fat.'" Parks played an uncredited role in its creation as well.

Leased to Epic when Fortune couldn't fulfill the demand, "Bacon Fat" sizzled on the R&B Top Ten in early '57. But "Jail Bait" (a musical morality playlet that cast Williams as a sobbing defendant confessing to a judge that he'd fooled around with underage girls), another culinary stepper called "The Greasy Chicken" (Parks babbled crazy ethnic dialects behind him), and the Coasters-styled rocker "Georgia May Is Movin'" (flipped with the oddly titled "[Mmm– Andre Williams Is] Movin'") didn't capture the national fancy despite their demented brilliance. Next stop: Fledgling Motown.

Andre Williams (left) was one of the coolest cats to prowl the halls of Motown. The streetwise wordsmith coined such song titles as "Bacon Fat," "Jail Bait" and "Greasy Chicken" (Photo courtesy of Andre Williams).

"Berry was in the barber shop. He was working in the factory. The guy who did my hair introduced me to Berry, and asked me to go and listen to some of Berry's material," said Andre. "He had some good stuff. So I gave him Art Talmadge's phone number in New York, at United Artists. I had met Art Talmadge when I was in New York at the Apollo. As a matter of fact, he was courtin' me a little bit to see if I would come to UA once I left Fortune. Berry called Art Talmadge, and Art Talmadge gave him a meeting. And that's how (Art) got Marv Johnson.

"So Berry almost owed me something. I never called in the markers on it, but that was Berry's first productions, really big productions," he continued. "So then things started coolin' off. The jobs started getting farther in between. I ran into Berry. By then, Berry was kinda clickin'. Berry said, 'Well, why don't you come on over and work for me?' I said okay."

Andre produced Sammy Ward for Tamla and the Temptations' debut for Miracle (the latter in cahoots with Mickey Stevenson under the conjoined handle of Dre-Mic). He also wrote "Mo Jo Hanna" with Clarence Paul: Introduced by Henry Lumpkin in the summer of 1962, it was covered by Marvin Gaye on his '63 live LP for Tamla and a white rock group, the Underdogs, for V.I.P. in early '67. He also cut some vocals himself; "Rosa Lee" with flip "Shoo Ooo," was slated for 1961 release on Miracle but was never pressed. As befit two mavericks, Williams' relationship with Gordy was stormy.

"I was hired and fired out of Motown more than anybody," said free-wheeling Andre. "I was hired and fired out of there about six or seven times, because I just could never conform to his way. He had a dictatorship. **His way or no way."** Andre cites a broken romantic relationship with a front office worker as another reason for his fading status at Motown. "That kind of pissed Berry and all of 'em off," he said. "So he took all of my shit and put glue on it. Glued it to the shelf in the can, and none of it ever came out." Williams moved to Chicago, got married, and landed an A&R post at George Leaner's One-derful! and Mar-V-Lus Records. There he co-wrote and co-produced the Five Du-Tones' 1963 barnburner "Shake A Tail Feather" and Alvin Cash &

the Crawlers' grinding '65 smash "Twine Time." But his Motown escapades weren't over.

"Every time I'd get a hit at One-derful!, Berry would send for me," said Andre. "He was that type. He wanted to keep everybody under his roof. He didn't want to release nothing on me, but when I would leave and catch a hit, he would send for me. I would go back. I would mess up. He'd fire me. I'd go back (to Chicago) and get a hit, and he'd send for me again." Williams' later Motown accomplishments included producing Mary Wells' "Oh Little Boy (What Did You Do To Me)" and the Contours' "I'll Stand By" in 1964. According to Andre, the latter marked the first time a tuba ever graced a Motown platter. Just how transient was Williams? When shown a Gordy pressing of "I'll Stand By," he swore he didn't know it had been released!

Launching Mercury's Blue Rock subsidiary was Andre's next major project. During his mid-'60s A&R stint, the label released Sir Mack Rice's original "Mustang Sally" ("I cut it too slow," Andre moaned). Detroit beckoned anew when Ed Wingate—boss of Motown's prime local competition, Golden World and Ric-Tic Records—hired Andre and issued his "Sweet Little Pussycat" on Wingate and "You Got It And I Want It" on Golden World. From there, Williams formed Sport Records with a partner.

"Instead of coming back to Chicago, I said, 'I'm going to open my own label and knock this cat out the box!'" said Williams. "There's room enough in Detroit for two Berry Gordys!'" Despite scoring hits in 1967 with the Dramatics' "All Because Of You" and Williams' own "Pearl Time," Sport didn't last long. Andre landed back in Chicago at Chess, where he championed protege Jo Ann Garrett and nailed his last hit as a singer in '68 with the snarling "Cadillac Jack."

Andre was less active in the industry as the '70s progressed, and things got meager the following decade. By the early '90s, he bottomed out. "I had gotten depressed, frustrated, got heavy into drugs," he reported. But he eventually straightened up, coming back with a 1995 album reflecting past R&B glories and a subsequent series of wildly disparate contemporary releases—expletive-filled rap, crunchy rock, twangy alt-country—all dipped in old school cool.

Sondra "Blinky" Williams radiated soul (Weldon A. McDougal III photo).

BLINKY WILLIAMS

Sondra "Blinky" Williams deserved better from Motown than she got. Almost as many of her records were canceled as actually released, and the diminutive charmer who went by the single moniker of Blinky never scored a solo hit, though her duet rendition of "Oh How Happy" with Edwin Starr did crease the pop charts in 1969.

Born May 21, 1944, in Oakland, California, Blinky grew up in sunny southern California. "Father was a preacher, pastor of one of the larger churches in Los Angeles. I started singing when I was 6, started directing choirs when I was 9," she said. Her nickname was coined in her teens. "A guy named Anthony Lorick—he ended up playing for the Baltimore Colts—we were in high school together. I used to always blink," she explained. "He wanted to meet me. And he said, 'What's her name, Blinky?' So it's been that ever since."

L.A. harbored some prime young gospel talent, and Blinky was in the thick of it. "Billy Preston, Gloria Jones, Edna Wright (later lead singer for the Honey Cone), Sandra and Andrae Crouch, and Frankie Springs—we were in a group together as teenagers called the Cogics," she said. "We were called the teenage gospel wonders of the world. One by one, record companies sought us out. That's how we broke up—everybody ended up recording a single." Blinky's first 45, the Richard Simpson-produced "Heartaches" and flip "God Bless The Children," was cut in New York and came out on Atlantic in 1967 as by Sondra Williams.

"There was a place in L.A. called Maverick's Flat. This was a disco that Jim Brown, Lee Marvin, Liza Minnelli, and all of the Motown acts would frequent. It was a very classy disco in L.A. on Crenshaw. The Tempts were there one night. They just came out to hang out. And they'd heard about me through Hal Davis," she said. "So they came, and that's how I went to Motown. It was Paul Williams and Eddie Kendricks. They brought me to Motown and introduced me to Hal Davis and Shelly Berger, who ended up being my manager."

Blinky debuted on Motown in late '68 with the stunning "I Wouldn't Change The Man He Is," a Nickolas Ashford and Valerie Simpson-penned gem that would be recycled on Diana Ross' first solo LP in 1970 (Blinky's original was flipped with "I'll Always Love You"). "They heard my voice and went to Shelly, and Shelly listened to the material and he approved it, he and Berry," said Blinky, who enjoyed working with Nick and Val. "They'd sing the song for you, basically. They recorded about 12, 13 tunes on me in about three days," she said. "They were just really easy to work with. My raspiness didn't bother them. They liked it very much."

Her first performance as a member of Berry's stable was just as memorable. "I made my debut with Motown at the Forum the same night that Dennis Edwards made his," she said. "In fact, we did it together. Then they moved me partially to Detroit, which I hated. I lived in a hotel, the St. Regis Hotel, for about five months. They had me a suite at the Regis, seemed like forever. I was so spoiled and homesick, they sent me home—like just about every other week!"

Another show biz legend took an interest in Blinky's talents. "I was in the studio recording, and for some reason, my session was being fed through Sammy Davis's earphones. We were at RCA Studios. And he came in the studio barefoot, shirt all hangin' out, mad, and wanted to know, who was that singing? And he stayed there and talked to Shelly Berger. He said, 'I want her to be my opening act!' So I ended up being his act after I was with the Tempts for two years," said Blinky. "I was blessed, because I never had to work the chitlin' circuit." Recording late at night never bothered her. "A lot of my sessions were after 12 o'clock at night," she noted.

Blinky had the ignominious distinction of having one single canceled twice. "How You Gonna Keep It (After You Get It)" (another Ashford & Simpson creation) with its flip "This Time Last Summer" was slated for Motown issue in 1970 and scratched, then rescheduled on Soul the next year and bagged again. Further, all three of her projected solo albums—*Sunny And Warm* in 1970, *Softly* in '73, and an untitled Mowest LP in '72—were consigned to the vaults. Why?

"Your guess is as good as mine," said Blinky. "Just as I was getting hot, Diana was about to leave the Supremes. David had left the Tempts. There were a lot of breakups. Gladys needed a hit. Diana needed a hit. I sort of got tossed to the side.

"And then I was working with Sammy a lot, so there was some jealousy. Diana was the queen of Motown, and she needed a hit. So they cut her on 'I Wouldn't Change The Man He Is,' and then *Lady Sings the Blues* came into fruition. I did that theme, and again she needed a hit, so Blinky got tossed aside."

That's why she's best remembered for "Oh How Happy," her engaging duet with Edwin Starr, which sat on the pop charts for a couple of weeks in August of 1969 (backed by a revival of the Miracles' "Ooh Baby Baby") and spawned an album, *Just We Two*. Pairing Edwin and Blinky was the brainchild of Quality Control head Billie Jean Brown. "She asked Frank Wilson to produce it with her," said Blinky. "It was right after (Edwin) made '25 Miles,' and I was hot at Motown. I was in demand to work with all the acts. So that's what we did. They thought they would team us together and make us hot." "Oh How Happy" had been written by Starr under his legal handle of Charles Hatcher and had been a 1966 hit for the blue-eyed Detroit soul group Shades of Blue on Impact Records. Starr cut his own breathtaking version for his first Gordy LP, *Soul Master*, in 1968. Its chord structure was radically reworked for the duet.

Just We Two generated some sparks with remakes of Brenda Holloway's "You've Made Me So Very Happy," the Soul Children's "I'll Understand," and the Jerry Butler/Betty Everett evergreen "Let It Be Me." On the Jobete copyrights "I'm So Thankful" (penned by Wilson and Marc Gordon), "I'm Glad You Belong To Me" (by Richard Morris, Roger Penzabene, and Cornelius Grant), and Helen and Kay Lewis's "I See A Rainbow," Blinky proved she could keep up with Edwin's intimidating lungpower.

"He could always outdance me," she said. "Everything I did had to be choreographed, so he would be dancing all around me, so I did most of the singing. He always upstaged me because he danced so great." Blinky models one of the largest Afros in soul music history in the photo adorning the front of their LP. "My glasses were crooked. I hated that picture," she said.

After a long hiatus, Blinky resurfaced on Mowest in 1972 with revivals of Barrett Strong's 1960 Tamla smash "Money (That's What I Want)" and Butler and the Impressions' '58 hit "For Your Precious Love." Blinky also revived a pair of Billie Holiday chestnuts: "T'ain't Nobody's Bizness If I Do," from the soundtrack of *Lady Sings the Blues*, came out as a Mowest single in early '73, and two years earlier she caressed "God Bless The Child" on a gospel anthology. "I was definitely a Billie Holiday fan," she said. "Sammy had me do a nine-minute Billie Holiday medley when I performed with him." Blinky had another lusty legend in mind when she sang the theme to *Lady Sings the Blues*: "I was emulating Bessie Smith."

Her Motown farewell, the serene Clay McMurray production "You Get A Tangle In Your Lifeline," was cut in L.A. and came out in March of 1973. "He was one producer that I used to love to work with. I mean, so easy—he was calm, he kept me calm and relaxed. I could stay with Clay in the studio forever." She left Motown to work with Mickey Stevenson at Reprise.

"I was working with Sammy all the time, and (Motown) just didn't seem that interested in putting out material," said Williams. "They would record a lot, but nothing would get put out. So Quincy Jones really wanted me to leave. I started doing a lot of dates with Quincy. At the time, Sammy was co-managing me with Shelly Berger. I was Sammy's protege. Quincy wanted to cut me. Mickey Stevenson thought he could do better." Blinky later moved into the choir robe business, gradually receding from the road until she retired in '86.

Since late 1999, Blinky Williams has led the 55-member Hollywood Choir, which includes Holloway and the Sisters Love's Jeannie Long. In addition to raising their voices in praise of the Lord, they've backed country superstar Garth Brooks in live performance.

FRANK WILSON

Los Angeles seldom receives its due as a source for Motown hits during the label's golden years. Frank Wilson joined the label's L.A. office in 1964 as a writer/producer, and was so good at crafting hits that he was invited to move to Detroit to work at the home base.

Born in Houston on December 5, 1940, he left the Lone Star state in his teens and attended college in Louisiana. "Stayed in college about a year-and-a-half, and left there at 18 and came to Los Angeles," said Wilson. "When I came to L.A., I had getting out of Louisiana in mind." He sang in a gospel group, the Angelaires, before finding the inspiration in Brenda Holloway's singing to go secular.

Frank Wilson found success as a songwriter for Motown, both in Detroit and after the company's move to Los Angeles (Photo courtesy of David Alston's Mahogany Archives).

"Brenda's voice is what inspired me to start writing pop music," he said. "Up until then, I had been writing all contemporary gospel for a group that I had. But when I heard Brenda Holloway singing, I think it was 'There's Something On Your Mind' that Hal was doing on her, I was really inspired, and decided that I would like to write a song for Brenda."

When Motown opened its L.A. office under Hal Davis and Marc Gordon's stewardship in 1964, Wilson got in on the ground floor. "It was at that time that Berry Gordy had just paid a visit to Los Angeles for what was then called a disc jockey convention. Hal and Marc, I think they sold him a master on Brenda Holloway. A song called 'There's Something On Your Mind.' It was a remake. During that same trip, he mentioned to them that he wanted to open up a West Coast Motown office, and asked them if they'd be interested in running the office for Motown. This was after several meetings with them. I guess the very next day after the offer was made, they contacted me and told me about it, and asked if I would become a part of their team.

"So I agreed to come into the office, which was at 6290 Sunset Boulevard, right on the corner of Sunset and Vine. I agreed to do it," said Wilson, who wrote and produced prolifically even after the L.A. outpost was shut down a couple of years later. "At that time, (Motown) asked if I would stay on. They were going to let some of the people go—all of the people go, actually. He wanted to know if I'd stay on and work out of my house, and they would raise my salary, and etc. So I agreed to do that, and it must have been about six months later, the legal team came back out and mentioned that Berry Gordy wanted to know if I'd be interested in moving to Detroit. And I agreed to do that. That was in '66. So I actually went to Detroit in '66. Prior to that, the stuff we were producing was the type—I guess we were doing a lot of cover stuff. We had introduced Stevie to the Hollywood scene with *Muscle Beach Party*."

Along with his behind-the-scenes skills, Wilson was a talented singer. Davis did a little moonlighting in his off hours, producing sides for labels now forgotten. "He did two or three songs on me under different names," said Frank. "One was called 'Come Back Sandy,'" which I think was under the name Sonny Day." Wilson did some notable outside work, writing Ike & Tina Turner's "Somebody (Somewhere) Needs You" for Loma in '65.

For a brief period, he was poised to emerge as a Motown artist when his pounding "Do I Love You (Indeed I Do)" and the easy-grooving "Sweeter As The Days Go By," both cut in L.A., were slated for issue on Soul in late '65. At the last second, the 45 was canceled.

"We did both of those records, and Berry Gordy was excited about them. He was about to release them. I went to Detroit, and we were standing backstage at the Fox Theater. I hadn't been in town more than a week. They were having a Motown Revue at the Fox Theater. Berry Gordy, while we were standing in the wings together, he said, 'Frank, now you know I'm getting ready to release this record on you. We're excited about it. But I want to ask you a question. Do you really want to be an artist, or do you want to be a writer and a producer?' And it was right then and there I told him I wanted to be a writer and a producer. And it was decided that he would not release that record on me." "Do I Love You" is now worshiped as the most valuable Northern Soul 45 of all; two promo copies pressed up prior to that fateful backstage decision now change hands in England for as much as an astronomical 15,000 pounds.[23] "Wish I had one!" laughed Wilson. In November of 1979, Wilson's single was belatedly issued in England.

Once settled in at Hitsville, Wilson penned and produced hits for nearly every major act on the roster. He was intimately involved with the Tempts' "All I Need," the Supremes' "Love Child," the Four Tops' "Still Water (Love)," Marvin Gaye's "Chained," the Tempts/Supremes summit smash "I'm Gonna Make You Love Me," Holloway's "You've Made Me So Very Happy," and plenty more. But he wasn't sorry when Motown headed for the Coast in 1972.

"It was great for me, because I sold my house about six months after they moved out here, and I moved back to L.A.," said Frank. "It was wonderful to be back at home." "Keep On Truckin'" and "Boogie Down," his smash 1973 productions on Eddie Kendricks, threw gasoline on the disco explosion. But by 1975, he'd had enough of the industry. "I think the last thing I did was with the Originals, 'Down To Love Town.' I gave my heart to the Lord, and just decided that I was going to stop producing and just pursue my relationship with him. I told Motown that I was leaving, so I sort of stopped producing and writing. My contract was up in '76."

After a year-and-a-half, Wilson met a young group called Lakeside at a Bible study in his home, and he came out of his self-imposed hiatus to produce them. Other projects with Marilyn McCoo & Billy Davis, Lenny Williams, and the Mighty Clouds of Joy followed, but after three years he retired again. Since then, Wilson has taken on several overlapping roles—he's a minister, an author of books on improving relationships (*Unmasking the Lone Ranger*), and along with wife Bunny travels the country speaking to couples and singles from a Christian viewpoint.

SYREETA WRIGHT

There was something of a tradition of Motown secretaries becoming stars. Martha Reeves worked as Mickey Stevenson's secretary while awaiting her big break, and Syreeta Wright followed in her footsteps. Born in Pittsburgh, she and her family moved to Detroit when she was 11. After attending school in South Carolina as a teen, she abandoned her plan to be a ballet dancer and concentrated on singing. Brian Holland brought her into Hitsville, and after a couple of years behind the scenes, Holland hooked her up with Nick Ashford and Valerie Simpson, who had just the song for her Gordy debut single.

Released as by Rita Wright, their dramatic "I Can't Give Back The Love I Feel For You," produced by Holland (who shared writers' credit) and Lamont Dozier, was originally intended for Diana Ross but suited Syreeta's smoldering delivery, though it didn't chart in early 1968 (Suzee Ikeda would revive it for Mowest in '72). Wright collaborated with Stevie Wonder on his 1970 smash "Signed, Sealed,

Delivered I'm Yours," and her name also appeared beside his on "If You Really Love Me" and the Spinners' smash "It's A Shame." The union turned romantic, Wright marrying Wonder in September of 1970 but divorcing him a year-and-a-half later.

Syreeta Wright and Billie Jean Brown at the screening of Save the Children at Berry's Los Angeles home (Weldon A. McDougal III photo).

Stevie produced Syreeta's eponymous 1972 Mowest debut album, the Rita Wright alias permanently jettisoned. Mostly written by the pair apart from covers of Mary Wells' "What Love Has Joined Together" and the Beatles' "She's Leaving Home" (Wonder also played extensively on it), it spawned her first Mowest 45, "I Love Every Little Thing About You." Another Syreeta single from the same timeframe, "To Know You Is To Love You," ended up a 1973 hit for B.B. King. Wonder played keys on the blues great's version. It would be 1975 before Syreeta had a Motown hit of her own, "Harbour Love." She enjoyed her biggest success for the company in 1979 paired with another keyboard wizard, Billy Preston, on the No. 4 pop smash "With You I'm Born Again."

RICHARD "POPCORN" WYLIE/POPCORN & THE MOHAWKS

In addition to rolling the ivories on some of Motown's first productions and leading bands for some early regional Motown revues, Richard "Popcorn" Wylie made three singles of his own for the label with his band, the Mohawks. Popcorn didn't hang too long at Hitsville, but his musical associates certainly did—James Jamerson was the bassist for Wylie's Mohawks, and the Andantes were his backing vocalists.

"He's an excellent musician," said Jackie Hicks, noting the bandleader preached self-sufficiency. "He believed in having everything together. When he recorded, he said he wasn't gonna need anybody to play, and he wasn't gonna need anybody to sing. He was gonna take the whole group with him."

Born June 6, 1939, Wylie learned the 88s from his mother, a classical pianist. While playing football at Detroit's Northwestern High, a teammate told him he popped up everywhere like popcorn—hatching his nickname for life. Forming his own combo, Popcorn & the Mohawks, he debuted with "Pretty Baby" on Johnnie Mae Matthews' Northern logo before signing with Motown. The Mohawks included Jamerson, baritone saxist Mike Terry, drummer Lamont Dozier (Robert Finch was also a Mohawks timekeeper), and tambourinist Norman Whitfield.

Popcorn & the Mohawks cut "Custer's Last Man" (co-written by Wylie, Berry, and Smokey Robinson) and flip "Shimmy Gully" as their mid-1960 Motown debut, encored in the spring of '61 with "I'll Still Be Around" billed as Richard Wylie, and reverted to the Popcorn & the Mohawks tag for "Real Good Lovin'" and flip "Have I The Right" in late '61. Wylie landed at Epic for four 1962-64 singles before going the indie route. He wrote and produced for a myriad of Motor City labels—Correctone, Ed Wingate's Golden World/Ric-Tic operation, Ollie McLaughlin's Karen and Carla logos (Wylie's '68 Karen platter "Rosemary What Happened" garnered Northern Soul interest in England), and his own Soul Hawk and Pameline imprints.

Bridges had clearly not been burned between Popcorn and Motown, for in the autumn of 1971 he turned up on Soul with a scorching dance workout, "Funky Rubber Band." McLaughlin was the producer and Terry scribed the arrangement on the Wylie original, a slice of stripped-down funk featuring Popcorn's roaring vocal. An instrumental version of same graced the flip.

[1]Raynoma Gordy Singleton with Bryan Brown and Mim Eichler, *Berry, Me and Motown* (Chicago: Contemporary Books, Inc., 1990), p. 180-182.

[2]Ibid.

[3]David Ritz, *Divided Soul: The Life of Marvin Gaye*, New York: McGraw-Hill, 1985, p. 118-119.

[4]Charlie Musselwhite interview, 1988.

[5]Berry Gordy, *To Be Loved* (New York: Warner Books, Inc., 1994), p. 241-243.

[6]Brenda Mabra interview, 2001.

[7]A previously unreleased 1965 performance of "I'm Falling For You" by Eckstine and the Tops, cut live at the Apollo, is on the Tops' *Breaking Through*, a 1999 reissue in Motown's Lost and Found series.

[8]Hamilton, whose brothers Bob Hamilton (an ex-Motown producer) and Ronnie (Savoy) Hamilton were also Detroit R&B vets, cut a bluesy '57 version of "That's Why I Love You So" for Berry Gordy as Al Kent that predated Jackie Wilson's '59 hit. At that same auspicious Checker date, he cut an unissued rendition of "Lonely Teardrops"!

[9]Raynoma Gordy Singleton with Bryan Brown and Mim Eichler, *Berry, Me, and Motown—The Untold Story* (Chicago: Contemporary Books, Inc., 1990), p. 151-156.

[10]Susan Whitall, *Women of Motown* (New York: Avon Books, 1998), p. 37.

[11]David Bianco, *Heat Wave—The Motown Fact Book* (Ann Arbor, MI: Pierian Press, 1988), p. 21.

[12]Wells's "My Guy" was released shortly after Holloway's "Every Little Bit Hurts," so either Davis had obtained an advance copy or she sang one of Mary's earlier smashes instead.

[13]Tony Scherman, *Backbeat: Earl Palmer's Story* (Washington, D.C.: Smithsonian Institution, 1999)

[14]Gary E. Myers, *Do You Hear That Beat—Wisconsin Pop/Rock in the 50's and 60's* (Downey, CA: Hummingbird Pub., 1994), p. 28-37.

[15]Be forewarned: when Motown reissued "That's No Lie" on its *Switched On Blues* LP in 1970, they overdubbed some horrid rock guitar onto the track.

[16]David Ritz, *Divided Soul: The Life of Marvin Gaye* (New York: McGraw-Hill, 1985), p. 128.

[17]Steve Towne, "Motown Doo-Wop—The Satintones," *Goldmine*, No. 71, April 1982 and Robert Pruter, "Sonny Sanders Tells of his Years in the Quailtones, the Satintones, and as an Arranger in Detroit and Chicago," *Goldmine*, No. 48, May 1980.

[18]E-mail correspondence with Peter Gibbon of Ace Records in Great Britain confirmed its existence.

[19]Sharon Davis, *Motown—The History* (Middlesex, U.K.: Guinness Pub. Ltd., 1988), p. 69.

[20]Ibid, p. 59.

[21]Kevin Keegan, "The Valadiers—Something Old...Something New." *Goldmine*, Nov. 16, 1990.

[22]Motown's 1999 CD reissue *The Very Best of the Velvelettes* features a previously unissued 1967 recording with the second group, "I'm So Glad It's Twilight Time."

[23]Kev Roberts, *The Northern Soul Top 500* (Todmorden, UK: Goldmine/Soul Supply Ltd., 2000), p. 15.

BIBLIOGRAPHY

Allan, Marc D. "From Bob Seger to Little Feat, Singer Barely Has Time to Catch Her Breath." *Indianapolis Star and News*, June 28, 1996.

Benjaminson, Peter. *The Story of Motown.* New York: Grove Press, Inc., 1979.

Bianco, David. *Heat Wave—The Motown Fact Book.* Ann Arbor, MI: Pierian Press, 1988.

Bowman, Rob. Liner notes, *The Last Soul Company*. Malaco MCD 0030, 1999.

Bronson, Fred. Liner notes, *The Marvelettes—Deliver: The Singles 1961-1971.* Motown

37463-6259-2, 1993.

----------, Liner notes, *Martha Reeves & the Vandellas—Live Wire!: The Singles 1962-1972.* Motown 37463-6313-2, 1993.

Brown, James, with Tucker, Bruce. *James Brown, The Godfather of Soul.* New York: Macmillan Pub. Co., 1986.

Browne, Kimasi L. "Brenda Holloway: Los Angeles's Contribution to Motown." *California Soul: Music of African Americans in the West.* Edited by DjeDje, Jacqueline Cogdell, and Meadows, Eddie S. Berkeley, CA and Los Angeles: University of California Press, 1998.

Chin, Brian, and Nathan, David. Liner notes, *The Supremes*, Motown 012 159 075-2, 2000.

Clee, Ken. *The Directory of American 45 R.P.M. Records.* Philadelphia, PA: Stak-O-Wax, 1997.

Clemente, John. *Girl Groups—Fabulous Females That Rocked the World.* Iola, WI: Krause Pubs., 2000.

Cohodas, Nadine. *Spinning Blues Into Gold: The Chess Brothers and the Legendary Chess Records.* New York: St. Martin's Press, 2000.

Croasdell, Ady. Liner notes, *Rare Collectable and Soulful, Vol. 2,* Kent CDKEND 156, 1997.

Davis, Sharon. *Motown—The History.* Middlesex, UK: Guinness Pub. Ltd., 1988.

Edmonds, Ben. Liner notes, *Jr. Walker & the All Stars—Nothin' But Soul: The Singles 1962-1983,* Motown 37463-62702, 1994.

Erlewine, Michael, editor (et al). *All Music Guide to the Blues.* San Francisco: Miller Freeman Books, 1999.

Escott, Colin. Liner notes, *The Johnny Burnette Trio,* Bear Family BCD 15474, 1989.

Feather, Leonard. *The Encyclopedia of Jazz.* New York: Horizon Press, 1960.

Flynn, John. "Motown Loses Its Beat: Friends Mourn Percussionist Eddie (Bongo) Brown." *Detroit Free Press,* January 9, 1985.

Gallert, Jim. "The Famous Flame Show Bar." *Detroit Blues,* Spring 1997.

Galloway, A. Scott. Liner notes, *The Best of the Undisputed Truth,* Motown 31453-0570-2, 1995.

----------. Liner notes, *The Best of the Commodores,* Motown 31453-0358-2, 1995.

----------. Liner notes, *Motown Year By Year—The Sound of Young America 1969,* Motown 31453-0525-2, 1995.

Gari, Brian. Liner notes, *The Best of Paul Petersen,* AVI 5014, 1996.

Gaul, Emily. "Something About the Four Tops." *Goldmine,* March 3, 1995.

George, Nelson. *Where Did Our Love Go? The Rise & Fall of the Motown Sound.* New York: St. Martin's Press, 1985.

Gillett, Charlie. *Making Tracks—Atlantic Records and the Growth of a Multi-Billion-Dollar Industry.* New York: E.P. Dutton & Co., 1974.

Gordy, Berry. *To Be Loved.* New York: Warner Books Inc., 1994.

Gordy Singleton, Raynoma, with Brown, Bryan and Eichler, Mim. *Berry, Me, and Motown.* Chicago: Contemporary Books, Inc., 1990.

Green, Al, with Seay, Davin. *Take Me to the River.* New York: Harper Collins, 2000.

Gribin, Dr. Anthony J. and Schiff, Dr. Matthew M. *The Complete Book of Doo-Wop.* Iola, WI: Krause Pubs., 2000.

Hershey, Gerri. *Nowhere to Run: The Story of Soul Music.* New York: Da Capo Press, 1994.

Huston, Bruce. "Tammi Terrell Remembered." *Soul Survivor,* Vol. 2, No. 4, Winter 1985-1986.

Hutch, Willie, and Galloway, A. Scott. Liner notes, *The Very Best of Willie Hutch*, Motown 314530943-2, 1998.

Ingrassia, Thomas. "Motor City Records–Where the Sound of Young America Lives On." *Goldmine*, November 16, 1990.

Keegan, Kevin. "The Valadiers—Something Old...Something New." *Goldmine*, Nov. 16, 1990.

Koppel, Martin. Liner notes, *Popcorn's Detroit Soul Party, Goldmine/Soul Supply* GSCD59.

Laredo, Joseph F. Liner notes, *The Best of Marv Johnson—You Got What It Takes*, EMI 0777-7-98895-2, 1992.

----------. Liner notes, *The Complete Aladdin Recordings of Amos Milburn*, Mosaic MD7-155, 1994.

Leadbitter, Mike, and Slaven, Neil. *Blues Records 1943-70: A Selective Discography, Vol. 1, A-K.* London, Record Information Services, 1987.

Leadbitter, Mike; Fancourt, Leslie; and Pelletier, Paul. *Blues Records 1943-1970, Volume Two L to Z.* London: Record Information Services, 1994.

Levy, Arthur; Friedwald, Will; and Early, Gerald. Liner notes, *Yes I Can! The Sammy Davis Jr. Story.* Warner Archives/Rhino R275972, 1999.

Licks, Dr. *Standing in the Shadows of Motown—The Life and Music of Legendary Bassist James Jamerson.* Wynnewood, PA: Dr. Licks Pub., 1989.

McGarvey, Seamus. "The Five Royales Part 1." *Juke Blues* No. 31, Summer 1994.

Mills, David; Alexander, Larry; Stanley, Thomas; and Wilson, Aris. *George Clinton and P-Funk–An Oral History.* New York: Avon Books, 1998.

Moore, Clarence. "Songwriting and Singing for 20 Years." *Detroit Free Press,* July 19, 1985.

Mullins, Darrel E. "The Pretty Things: The Almost Brothers—25 Years of Bubbling Under With Phil May and Dick Taylor." *Goldmine*, Oct. 6, 1989.

Myers, Gary E. *Do You Hear That Beat--Wisconsin Pop/Rock in the 50's/60's.* Downey, CA: Hummingbird Pub., 1994.

Nathan, David. Liner notes, *The Very Best of Brenda Holloway*, Motown, 1999.

Oldsberg, Jim. Liner notes, *The Big Hits of Mid-America–The Soma Records Story 1963-1967*, Plum 14132, 1998.

Pack, Richard. "Kim Weston." *Soul Survivor* No. 10, Spring 1989.

----------. "Johnnie Mae Matthews—The Godmother of Detroit Soul." *Soul Survivor* No. 9, Summer 1988.

Paulus, George. "Andre 'Mr. Rhythm' Williams Comes Clean About Jail Bait, Bacon Fat, Pullin' Time & Greasy Chickens." *Blues & Rhythm* No. 108, April 1996.

Pitts, Leonard Jr. Liner notes, *Stevie Wonder—At the Close of a Century*, Motown 012 153 992-2, 1999.

Propes, Steve. Liner notes, *Del-Fi Brand Doo Wop Vol. 3—Honey For Sale*, Del-Fi DFCD 71258, 1998.

Pruter, Robert. *Doowop: The Chicago Scene.* Urbana, IL and Chicago: University of Illinois Press, 1996.

----------. *Chicago Soul.* Urbana, IL and Chicago: University of Illinois Press, 1991.

----------. "Sonny Sanders Tells of his Years in the Quailtones, the Satintones, and as an Arranger in Detroit and Chicago." *Goldmine*, No. 48, May 1980.

----------. Liner notes, *Windy City Soul*, Charly CDNEW 134, 1998.

Quaglieri, Al. Liner notes, *Rare Earth Anthology*, Motown 31453-0486-2, 1995.

Reeves, Martha, and Bego, Mark. *Dancing in the Street: Confessions of a Motown Diva.* New York: Hyperion, 1994.

Rice, Tim; Rice, Jo; Gambaccini, Paul, and Read, Mike. *Guinness British Hit Singles.* Middlesex, U.K.: Guinness Superlatives, Ltd., 1985.

Ritz, David. *Divided Soul: The Life of Marvin Gaye.* New York: McGraw-Hill, 1985.

----------. Liner notes, *The Jackson 5—Soulsation! 25th Anniversary Collection*, Motown 31453-0489-2, 1995.

----------. Liner notes, *Marvin Gaye—The Norman Whitfield Sessions*, Motown 31453-0355-2, 1994.

----------. Liner notes, *David Ruffin—The Ultimate Collection*, Motown 314530959-2, 1998.

Ritz, David, and Weinger, Harry. Liner notes, *Smokey Robinson and the Miracles—The 35th Anniversary Collection*, Motown 37463-6334-2, 1994.

Roberts, Kev. *The Northern Soul Top 500.* Todmorden, UK: *Goldmine/Soul Supply Ltd.*, 2000.

Robinson, Smokey, with Ritz, David. *Smokey: Inside My Life.* New York: McGraw-Hill Book Pub., 1989.

Roeser, Steve. "The Isley Brothers—Rock 'N' Soul Survivors." *Goldmine*, Nov. 29, 1991.

Sacks, Leo. Liner notes, *The Spinners—Their Early Years*, Atlantic 82332-2, 1991.

Scherman, Tony. *Backbeat: Earl Palmer's Story.* Washington, D.C.: Smithsonian Institution, 1999.

Smallwood, Sue. "Dave Edmunds–Repeat When Necessary." *Goldmine*, May 13, 1994.

Stax, Mike. Liner notes, *Nuggets—Original Artyfacts From the First Psychedelic Era* 1965-1968, Rhino R2 75466, 1998.

Taraborrelli, J. Randy. *Motown—Hot Wax, City Cool & Solid Gold.* Garden City, NY: Doubleday & Co. Inc., 1986.

Taylor, Marc. *A Touch of Classic Soul: Soul Singers of the Early 1970s.* Jamaica, NY: Aloiv Pub. Co., 1996.

Towne, Steve. "Motown Doo-Wop—The Satintones." *Goldmine*, No. 71, April 1982.

Underwood, Lee. "Knights Without Jazz." *Down Beat*, June 17, 1976.

Vick, Karl. "Horn Convicted for Three Murders." *Washington Post*, May 4, 1996.

Waller, Don. *The Motown Story.* New York: Charles Scribner's Sons, 1985.

----------. "Earth to Cloud Nine—Barrett Strong on 'Money,' Motown and the Muse." *LA Weekly*, Jan. 15-21, 1999.

Weinger, Harry. Liner notes. *The Temptations—Emperors of Soul*, Motown 31453-0338-2, 1994.

----------. Liner notes. *The Platters—The Magic Touch: An Anthology*, Mercury 314 510 314-2, 1991.

Weldon, Michael. *The Psychotronic Encyclopedia of Film.* New York: Ballantine Books, 1983.

Whitburn, Joel. *Joel Whitburn's Top R&B Singles 1942-1988.* Menomonee Falls, WI: Record Research, Inc., 1988.

----------. *Joel Whitburn's Top Pop Singles 1955-1990.* Menomonee Falls, WI: Record Research, Inc., 1991.

----------. *Joel Whitburn's Top Pop Albums 1955-1985* Menomonee Falls, WI: Record Research, Inc., 1985.

----------, (All *Billboard* chart positions courtesy of Whitburn's Record Research, Inc., publications)

Whitall, Susan. *Women of Motown.* New York: Avon Books, 1998.

White, Adam. Liner notes, *Hitsville U.S.A.*, Motown 374636312-2, 1992.

White, Adam, and Weinger, Harry. Liner notes *The Ultimate Rarities Collection 1: Motown Sings Motown Treasures*, Motown 314530960-2, 1998.

Williams, Otis, with Romanowski, Patricia. *Temptations.* New York: G.P. Putnam's Sons, 1988.

Wilson, Mary, with Romanowski, Patricia, and Juilliard, Ahrgus. *Dreamgirl: My Life as a Supreme.* New York: St. Martin's Press, 1986.

(All *Billboard* chart positions courtesy of Whitburn's Record Research publications)

WEB SITES

Brochu, Jim, "McNair Brings Musicals' Magic To Alex," <www.geocities.com/ Broadway/1183/barbara.html>.

Dennis, Robert, "Our Motown Recording Heritage (Part 2)," <www.recordingeq.com/motown2.html>.

Hamilton, Andrew; Ivy Jo Hunter, Hattie Littles, Frances Nero and Mike Valvano bios,

All Music Guide Web site, <www.allmusic.com>.

LeBlanc, Eric, eRIC's Blues Dates Web site, <http://www.bluesworld.com/0321.html>.

Payne, Barbara, "Not a Battle But a Blessing: The Damon Harris Story," Damon Harris Web site: <http://www.damonharris.com/story.htm>.

Ancestry.com Social Security Death Index Web site, <http://www.ancestry.com/search/rectype/ vital/ssdi/main.htm>.

Ashford & Simpson Web site, <www.ashfordandsimpson.com>.

AtoZ Birthdays Web site, <http://davytany.tripod.com/indexa2z.htm>.

Barrett Strong Web site, <http://www.barrettstrong.com>.

Both Sides Now Web site, <http://www.bsnpubs.com/motownstory.html>.

Blinky Williams Web site, <http://hollywoodchoir.net/>.

Bobby Breen Web site, <http://www.bobbybreen.com/pages/bobbybio.html>.

Conny Van Dyke Web site, <www.connyvandyke.com/bio.htm>.

Detroit Free Press Web site, <http://www.freep.com/motownat40/archives>.

Easybeats Web site, <http://www.algonet.se/~jonwar/easybeats.html>.

Find-A-Grave Web site, <http://www.findagrave.com/claimtofame/8.html>.

Frank Wilson Web site, <http://www.frankandbunny.com/frank.htm>.

Harvey Fuqua Web site, <http://harveyfuqua.com>.

Holland-Dozier-Holland Web site, <www.hollanddozierholland.com>.

Hugh Masekela Web site, <www.griot.de/biomasekela.html>.

James Jamerson Web site, <http://underfire.freeyellow.com/page1.htmhttp://srd.yahoo.com/
goo/Funk+Brothers/7/*http://www.bass101.com/jamerson/index.shtml>.

Jim & Nikki's Harmonious Page, <http://members.aol.com/wawawaooh/main.htm>.

Lewis Sisters/Lisa Miller Web site,<www.geocities.com/lonelytree519/Discographies.html>.

Mickey Stevenson Web site, <http://www.sangsistasang.com/mickey.html>.

Motown Alumni Web site, <http://motownalumni.com>.

Motown Musicians and Friends Web site, <http://underfire.freeyellow.com/page1.htm>.

Motown Web sites: <www.localdial.com/users/jsyedu133/Soulreview/motown3.htm>.

Ritchie's Cellar of Soul: Motown's Unsung Heroes Web site: <http://www.ritchie-hardin.com/ soul/mobackvo.html>.

Siege Home Page, <http://underfire.freeyellow.com/>.

Society of Singers Web site, <www.singers.org/tonymartin/tonymartin.html>.

Susaye Greene Web site, <http://supremextreme.com/susaye.htm>.

Wah Wah Watson Web site, <www.wahwah.com>.

Yvonne Fair Web site, <http://www.soulwalking.co.uk/Yvonne%20Fair.html>.

(Weldon A. McDougal III photo)